KU-742-932

HOLD THE HEIGHTS

ALSO BY WALT UNSWORTH

The English Outcrops
North Face
The High Fells of Lakeland
Peaks, Passes and Glaciers
Everest
This Climbing Game
Classic Walks of the World
Savage Snows
Encyclopaedia of Mountaineering

Fiction

The Devil's Mill
Whistling Clough
Grimsdyke

WALT UNSWORTH

HOLD THE HEIGHTS

THE FOUNDATIONS OF MOUNTAINEERING

I dream my feet upon the starry ways;
My heart rests in the hill.
I may not grudge the little left undone;
I hold the heights, I keep the dreams I won.

Geoffrey Winthrop Young

Hodder & Stoughton

LONDON SYDNEY AUCKLAND

British Library Cataloguing in Publication Data

Unsworth, Walt
Hold the Heights: Foundations of
Mountaineering
I. Title
796.509

ISBN 0-340-33913-6

Copyright © Walt Unsworth 1993

First published in Great Britain 1993

All rights reserved. No part of this publication may be reproduced or transmitted in any
form or by any means, electronic or mechanical, including photocopying, recording, or
any information storage and retrieval system, without either prior permission in writing
from the publisher or a licence permitting restricted copying. In the United Kingdom
such licences are issued by the Copyright Licensing Agency, 90 Tottenham Court Road,
London WIP 9HE. The right of Walt Unsworth to be identified as the author of this
work has been asserted by him in accordance with the Copyright, Designs and Patents
Act 1988.

Published by Hodder and Stoughton,
a division of Hodder Headline PLC
338 Euston Road, London NW1 3BH

Designed by Gerald Cinamon
Maps and drawings by Martin Collins

Photoset by Rowland Phototypesetting Ltd,
Bury St Edmunds, Suffolk

Printed and bound in Great Britain by
Mackays of Chatham PLC, Chatham, Kent

Contents

Preface 7

1 When Men and Mountains Meet 19
2 The Geneva School 25
3 The Opening of the Alps 37
4 The Coming of the English 53
5 Masters and Men 66
6 Where Angels Fear to Tread 89
7 'They Have Picked Out the Plums
   and Left Us the Stones' 102
8 'Too Venturesome to be Imitated' 117
9 Beyond the Alps 141
10 'Fine Opportunities for Breaking One's Neck' 152
11 Spreading the Gospel 170
12 The Americas 191
13 'Pikes Peak or Bust' 210
14 The Abode of Snow 229
15 No Fun at All 256
16 A Star in the East 270
17 Nordwand 281
18 To Shoot a Fox 304
19 Blanks on the Map 318
20 Reap the Wild Wind 333
21 The Last Blue Mountains 357

Notes 373
Selected Bibliography 403
Index 411

Acknowledgements

My thanks are due to the many writers, past and present, whose works I have consulted in the preparation of this book. I would also like to thank many mountaineering friends who have offered advice or loaned pictures, in particular Bill Birkett, Kenneth Henderson, Robin Hodgkin, Charles Houston, Chris McCooey, Terris and Katrina Moore, André Roch, John Town, Ivan Waller, Charles Warren and Bradford Washburn.

Walt Unsworth
Milnthorpe, 1993

Photographic credits

The author and publisher are grateful for the use of the following photographs. All other pictures come from the Walt Unsworth Collection.

Plate 6   main picture: French Government Tourist Office
Plate 7   main picture: André Roch; inset: Emile Gos
Plate 8   both mountain pictures: John Cleare/Mountain Camera
Plate 9   all pictures: André Roch
Plate 10   both pictures: John Cleare/Mountain Camera
Plate 11   Denali: Bradford Washburn; Mount St Elias: Fred Beckey
Plate 12   both pictures: Royal Geographical Society
Plate 13   both pictures: Bill Birkett Collection
Plate 14   Waller and Macphee: Ivan Waller; Wright: Ken Wilson
Plate 15   both pictures: Kenneth A. Henderson
Plate 16   both pictures: Terris Moore
Plate 18   both pictures: André Roch
Plate 19   all pictures: Kenneth A. Henderson
Plate 20   main picture: A. A. Solovyev; inset: R. A. Hodgkin
Plate 21   all pictures: R. A. Hodgkin
Plate 22   K2: John Cleare/Mountain Camera; House's Chimney and Houston: Charles Houston; Petzoldt: Kenneth A. Henderson
Plate 24   Houston party: Betsy Cowles; Hillary and Tenzing; Royal Geographical Society

Preface

This book tells the story of man's love affair with mountains. It is a story which has its beginnings in the mists of time when ancient peoples like the Chinese and the Aztecs worshipped their mountains, and sometimes feared the dragons that dwelt there. The eighteenth-century Romantics saw them as things of natural beauty to be viewed through a Claude glass, whilst those of a more scientific bent thought of them as outdoor laboratories for the measurement of air pressure. Energetic Victorians saw them as objects of conquest. It was the British who took elements of all these, wrapped them together, and called it a sport.

But it is a sport with a difference, one in which the only rule is that there are no rules. There is nothing to say what you may or may not do. When one generation attempts to lay down the law the next comes along to prove it wrong. 'Whatever number is right for a climbing party,' declared a Victorian expert, 'two is wrong.' Today it is the favourite number on a rope. Other maxims have gone the same way, for the fact is that the mountains make the rules, not the climbers. Instead of rules, climbing is governed by vague ethical considerations, subtle and shifting. It is also a deadly serious game, where even minor mistakes can exact the maximum penalty. It attracts strong characters and provides more than its fair share of drama.

Some observers might say that mountaineering can hardly be a sport at all. It is so wide-ranging as to be almost beyond definition. What does the man who climbs Everest, gasping for breath at every step, have in common with the athlete in shorts and T-shirt performing acrobatic moves on the boulders of Fontainebleau? Nothing – except that they may be one and the same person.

In writing this book, I did not want simply to catalogue the highlights: I have tried to seek cause and effect, draw conclusions, give explanations, discern a pattern or a thread. Without these the book becomes little more than a collection of twice-told tales. Despite the shifting nature of the subject, I felt sure that in the mass of material the true foundations of mountaineering could be discovered.

It was plain from the start that a totally comprehensive coverage, even of the major personalities and events, would need several volumes, so I have adopted instead a concentric plan similar to the effect obtained by dropping a pebble in a pond. The tightest ripples are those rings nearest the centre, then as they spread out they get wider but less well defined. The first real climb, the ascent of Mont Aiguille, is given in some detail, and there is a fair amount of detail about the Alpine pioneers, but as the nineteenth century advances and spills into the twentieth, the circle widens and becomes much more selective.

From the thousands of first ascents I have chosen those which seem in some way important to the growth of the sport. In some cases the words are the climber's own, written shortly after the event, but mostly I have described and interpreted it in my own words. Issues which are incidental to the main pursuit, such as the scientific aspects which so concerned climbers in the early days, are just mentioned in passing. I am more concerned with how the de Lucs climbed the Buet than with the air pressure they measured on top!

The canvas I have used is world-wide, for many nationalities have contributed to the development of the sport. Sometimes techniques were exported from the Alps and grew in foreign soil; sometimes a completely indigenous mountaineering culture arose. The interesting thing is the way all these various national strands have gradually come together, accelerated by international travel and by international journals of high quality. Not much happens these days without the entire climbing world knowing about it within weeks.

It is the universality of the modern sport which led me to bring this book to a conclusion with the ascent of Mount Everest in 1953. The ascent of the highest mountain in the world saw the foundations of mountaineering truly laid. This is not to say that nothing has happened in climbing since then. Of course it has, and I have offered some pointers towards this at the end of the book. But that is a different tale entirely and, to be told in full, would require another volume to itself.

For those readers who like to know the source of quotations, or who want more detail about some of the people and places, there are notes and references at the end of the book. I know that many readers appreciate these, but it must be emphasised that they are not essential to the book's enjoyment. Each chapter tells a perfectly clear story without reference to anything. The notes should be regarded as baroque curlicues, not pit-props!

When I embarked on this project some years ago, most of my climbing friends thought I was quite mad. The sheer scale of the thing was too big. One of them summed it up succinctly. 'That's one mountain you won't climb,' he said. And there have been many occasions since when I thought he was right. However, to him and to many other climbing friends I offer my thanks for all the help and advice I have received along the way. Without it the task would have been harder still.

Walt Unsworth
Cumbria, 1993

Maps

10 Mont Blanc Region
10 Pennine Alps
11 Bernese Alps
11 Eastern Alps
12 The Himalaya
13 The Karakoram
14 The Dolomites
15 Canada and North America

80 The Matterhorn
143 The Pyrenees
172 Mount Kenya
173 Kilimanjaro
173 Ruwenzori
177 New Zealand Alps
184 Caucasus
193 Andes
295 The Eiger
315 Yosemite Valley
327 The Nanda Devi Region
335 The Kangchenjunga Region
341 The Nanga Parbat Region
361 Everest

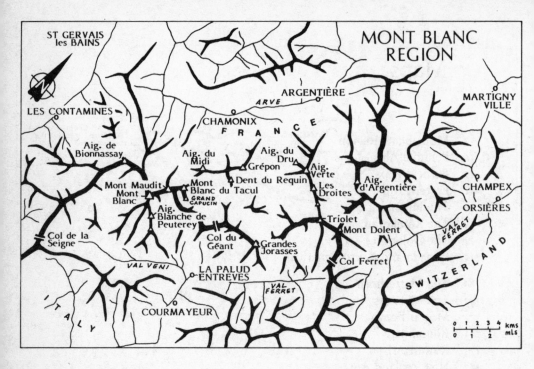

MONT BLANC REGION

ST GERVAIS les BAINS

LES CONTAINES

ARGENTIÈRE

ARVE

CHAMONIX

F R A N C E

MARTIGNY VILLE

Aig. de Bionnassay

Aig. du Midi

Aig. du Dru

Grépon

Aig. Verte

Aig. d'Argentière

CHAMPEX

Mont Maudit
Mont Blanc

Mont Blanc du Tacul

Dent du Requin

Les Droites

ORSIÈRES

GRAND CAPUCIN

Aig.
Blanche de
Peuterey

Triolet

Mont Dolent

VAL FERRET

Col de la Seigne

Col du Géant

Grandes Jorasses

Col Ferret

SWITZERLAND

VAL VENI

LA PALUD
ENTRÈVES

VAL FERRET

ITALY

COURMAYEUR

| 0 | 1 | 2 | 3 | 4 | kms |
| 0 | | 1 | | 2 | mls |

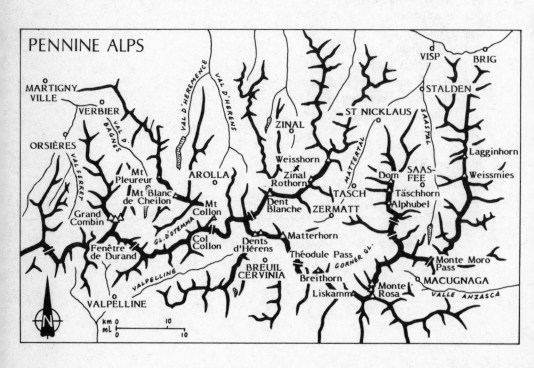

PENNINE ALPS

MARTIGNY VILLE

VERBIER

VISP

BRIG

STALDEN

ORSIÈRES

VAL D. BAGNES

VAL FERRET

VAL D'HÉRÉMENCE

VAL D'HÉRENS

ZINAL

ST NICKLAUS

SAASTAL

Lagginhorn

Mt Pleureur

AROLLA

Weisshorn

Zinal
Rothorn

MATTERTAL

Dom

SAAS-FEE

Weissmies

Mt Blanc de Cheilon

Mt Collon

TÄSCH

Täschhorn

Grand Combin

GL. D'OTEMMA

Col Collon

Dent Blanche

ZERMATT

Alphubel

Fenêtre de Durand

Dents d'Hérens

Matterhorn

VALPELLINE

Théodule Pass

GORNER GL.

Monte Moro Pass

VALPELLINE

BREUIL CERVINIA

Breithorn

MACUGNAGA

Liskamm

Monte Rosa

VALLE ANZASCA

| km 0 | | 10 |
| ml 0 | | 10 |

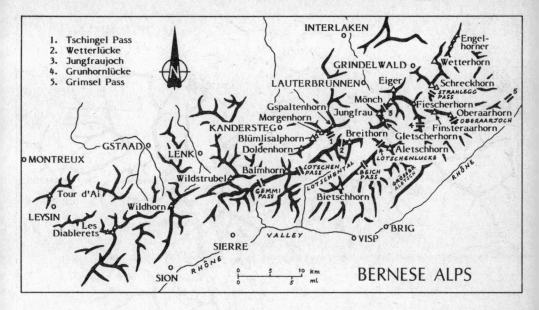

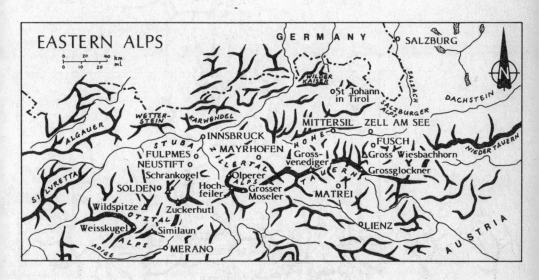

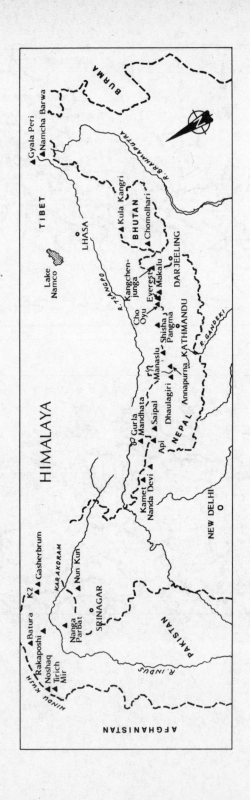

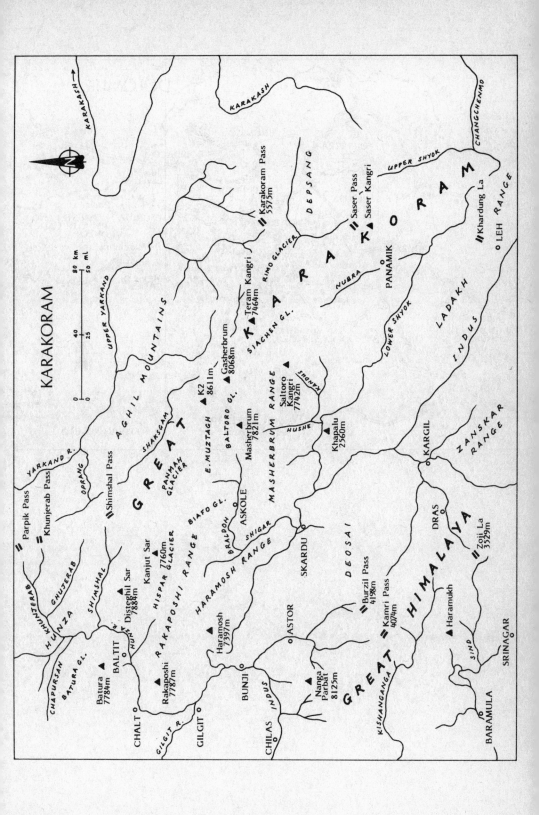

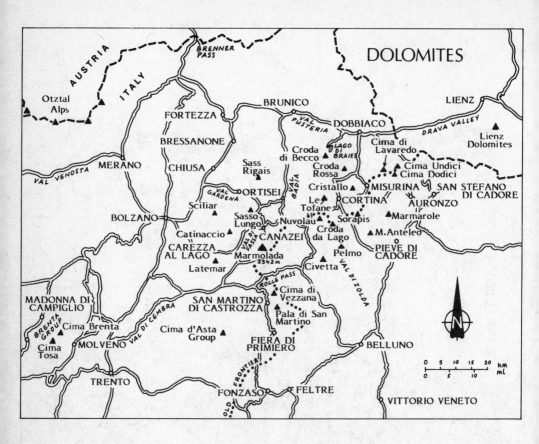

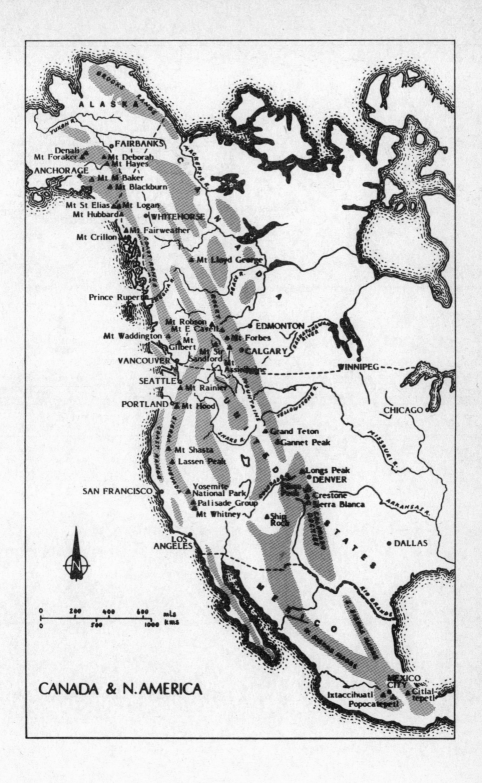

CANADA & N. AMERICA

HOLD THE HEIGHTS

When Men and Mountains Meet

On the 28th day of June, 1492, Antoine de Ville, Lord of Dompjulien and Beaupré, Captain of Montélimar and Saou, Chamberlain and Counsellor to Charles VIII of France, sat down to write a letter to the President of Grenoble.[1]

> Monsieur le Président, *he wrote,*
> I send you my hearty greetings. When I left the King he charged me to cause an attempt to be made to see whether it was possible to climb the mountain which was said to be inaccessible; which mountain I, by subtle means and engines, have found the means of climbing, thanks be to God; and now I have been here three days; and more than ten companions are with me – both Church men and other respectable people, and also one of the King's ladder-men; and I do not mean to leave here until I have received your answer, in order that, if you wish to send a few people to see us here, you may be able to do so; though I warn you that you will find few men who, when they see us up above, and see all the passage that I have caused to be made, will dare to come here; for it is the most horrible and frightful passage that I or any of my company have ever seen. I inform you of this in order that, having made sure of it at your pleasure, you may be so good as to write to the King by my lackey, the bearer of this; and I assure you that you will be causing him great pleasure, and me also, and you may be sure that if I can do anything for you, I will do so according to the pleasure of our master, so that he may give you that which you most desire . . . To describe the mountain to you – it is about a French league in circumference, a quarter of a league in length, and a cross-bow shot in width, and is covered with a beautiful meadow; and we have found a beautiful herd of chamois, which will never be able to get away, and some little ones of this year with them, one of which was killed, in spite of our intentions when we entered, for, until the King gives other orders I do not wish to have any of them taken. You have to ascend half a league by ladder, and a league by other ways, and it is the most beautiful place that I have ever visited.

> Wholly yours,
> Dompjulien

Antoine de Ville had good cause for some self-satisfaction and he was justified in asking that the authorities should verify his astonishing feat, because the Mount Inaccessible he had just climbed is one of the most impregnable-looking rock towers in the Vercors, just south of Grenoble: white limestone walls rising sheer for a thousand feet above the lush valley. The rock was called one of the 'Seven Wonders of Dauphiné' – though nobody seems to know what the other six were.

Antoine de Ville's name for the Inaccessible Mountain, Mont Aiguille in modern spelling, remains to this day. It was not climbed again until 1834 when a local man, Jean Liotard, made a remarkable solo ascent: 'Nailed shoes making the ascent perilous, Jean Liotard alone, with remarkable strength and hardiness, took off his shoes and scrambled across the rocks in a slanting direction and on the south face, now descending, now ascending and following a track which only his presence of mind discovered for him.'[2]

On reaching the top he shouted and hurled down rocks to announce his success to the amazed populace of the neighbouring communes before exploring the summit plateau and finding what might have been vestigial traces of prehistoric habitation.

His hour-and-a-half descent was accomplished 'with an astonishing sang-froid and an agility equal to that of the chamois', and with only the loss of his waistcoat, 'which he had lost among the rocks by trying to use it to help him grip hold of the sharp edges of the stones'.

Liotard's daring ascent probably follows the line used by today's *voie normale*, at the north-west corner near the place where a low col joins Mont Aiguille to some adjacent peaks. In 1878 the French Alpine Club fixed cables to make the climb easier. Modern climbers regard the route as having little technical difficulty, though very exposed, and on rock which is not always above suspicion. Jean Liotard was a courageous man. Whether Liotard's route was also the way in which Antoine de Ville first climbed the mountain five hundred years ago is not known. Mont Aiguille is not the most stable of mountains and there have been many rockfalls over the centuries.

Accounts survive of mountains being climbed, and dragons encountered on their summits, from the century before de Ville. But the ascent of Mont Aiguille in 1492 is the first recorded climb of any technicality, and curiously enough it had aspects which were to feature throughout the history of mountaineering: it used artificial aids, it was sponsored (the King was paying) and it saw the creation of the first mountain refuge. Moreover, though Charles may have ordered de Ville to make the attempt, there does not seem to have been any reluctance on his part – in fact, one gets the impression that great fun was had by all. The world would see nothing quite like it for the next four hundred years.

Four months after Antoine de Ville climbed Mont Aiguille, Christopher Columbus discovered America.

For thousands of years mountains have had a special meaning for man. Mountains were holy. The god Zeus was brought up on Mount Ida in Crete, whilst the basic laws which govern the western world were received on Mount Sinai by the prophet Moses. Across the ocean, on high Andean volcanoes, the Incas raised altars to their gods, whilst Japanese priests climbed Mount Fuji. In the Himalaya, mountains abound which are holy to Buddhists: Kailas, Kangchenjunga – even Everest itself, Chomolungma, the 'Goddess Mother of the World'. Where no natural mountains existed man built his own, such as the pyramids of Egypt or the temples of the Mayas.

Probably the earliest record of man's acknowledgement that mountains are holy comes from China, where there are nine recognised Sacred Mountains.[3] One of these is the Taoist shrine of Hua Shan in Shensi Province, near the great bend of the Yellow River. It is a rocky spur of the T'ung-kuan massif, rising in sharp peaks some 2000 metres high. The difficulties faced by the Taoist monks must have been similar to those of Antoine de Ville, yet they managed to build a series of shrines, linked by dizzy walkways, ladders and fixed ropes which would do justice to a modern Dolomite spire. Exactly when Hua Shan was constructed is not known – it probably grew over the centuries – but the legendary Emperor Shun is said to have made offerings there in 2250 BC and T'ang the Victorious, founder of the Second Dynasty, is recorded as doing likewise in 1766 BC, by which time the shrine was well established.

It is interesting that the Chinese ideograph for *immortality* is made by combining the ideograph for *people* with that for *mountain*. Gods and demons, princesses and dragons – the good and evil in all man's philosophies have their homes in the mountains. So ancient and widespread are these beliefs that they have become woven into the unconscious memory of the genus *Homo sapiens* and the severest agnostic can no more rid himself of them than can the most devout Buddhist.

On a more mundane and practical level, mountains have always been barriers to travel from one valley to the next, and one country to another. This was not necessarily a bad thing, for though traders and travellers might be inconvenienced, there was security in having a high wall between yourself and the outside world. Tibet exploited this right into the present century – until the Chinese invasion of 1950.[4]

Of course, mountains were always difficult for armies on the march, which is why Hannibal's dramatic crossing of the Alps in 218 BC, during the Second Punic War, is remembered to this day. Mountains are great levellers of unequal forces, as the British found to their cost for over a century on the Indian North-West Frontier and the Russians more recently discovered in Afghanistan.

The key to overcoming these mountain barriers, whether for trade or war, was exploration: probing the ice walls to find their weak spots, trekking the hidden valleys to see where they led. During the nineteenth century in particular remote ranges were penetrated by surveyors and adventurers of all sorts looking for commercial or military advantage. In the Karakoram and Hindu Kush, where Britain and Russia eyed one another suspiciously throughout the century, it became the Great Game, immortalised by Kipling's *Kim*. It was from the ranks of these explorers that the first high-altitude mountaineers came. But they, in turn, needed the senses of local people, accustomed to moving on mountain terrain, and employing many of the techniques and much of the equipment later formalised and refined by climbers.

As early as 1574 Josias Simler, a professor from Zurich, wrote a history of the Alps in which he included a chapter called 'Concerning the Difficulties of Alpine Travel and the Means by which they may be Overcome'. With little alteration the following extracts from Simler could be used in a modern climbing textbook:

> To counteract the slipperiness of the ice, they firmly attach to their feet shoes resembling the shoes of horses, with three sharp spikes in them, so that they may be able to stand firmly. In some places they use sticks tipped with iron, by leaning upon which they can climb steep slopes; these are called Alpine sticks, and are principally in use among the shepherds.
>
> Besides this, the old ice which sometimes has to be traversed has crevices in it, three or four feet wide – and sometimes even wider – into which, if a man fall, he must indubitably perish. It may happen, however, that these crevices are masked by fresh snow, or by snow accumulated by the wind, so that travellers in the Alps hire guides who know the neighbourhood to go before them. These men tie ropes round their waists, to which those who follow them are attached, and the leader sounds the path with a long pole, and carefully looks out for the crevices in the snow. But if an imprudent man falls into one of them, he is held up and pulled out by his friends who are fastened to the same rope. Where there is no snow covering the chasms the danger is less, though, where there are no bridges, it is necessary to jump across them. Only, when they are driving beasts of burden over such places – a thing which is done sometimes, though not often – they carry planks with them, and make little bridges for the beasts to cross upon.
>
> Against these calamities various precautions are taken. The eyes

should be protected by some dark material, or by what they call glass spectacles, and the rest of the body should be well fortified against the cold by skins and thick garments. The chest is best guarded against cold winds by paper or parchment, and if the feet have got numbed, the boots are taken off and they are plunged into cold water, to which warm water is gradually added. For by this means they are believed to get all right again.[5]

The crampon is one piece of climbing equipment which can be traced back as far as 500 BC to the Celtic community at Hallstatt in the Salzkammergut, though the modern version has nine more points than the three Simler describes. The Gauls had them in Roman times and their use seems to have been widespread from quite early on.

Despite the exploits of Antoine de Ville on Mont Aiguille, nothing specific has come down to us about the techniques of early rock climbing, though both miners and hunters must have done considerable scrambling. Travellers in steep places occasionally mention the use of a hand hook, presumably some sort of grappling iron like that advocated by Edward Whymper many years later, and miners and crystal-hunters would certainly have used a primitive form of piton to overcome difficult places, because something similar was already in use underground. (The old English miners called them *stemples*.)

Though rope was used for protection on glaciers it is doubtful whether it was used extensively on the crags, but there is the astonishing example of the men of St Kilda, that storm-tossed island beyond the Outer Hebrides, where climbing was done on the steep sea-cliffs to catch sea-birds and eggs for food. Sir Robert Moray described the climbing techniques used on the formidable Stac-na-Biorrach in 1678:

> After they landed, a man having room but for one of his feet, he must climb up twelve or sixteen fathoms high. Then he comes to a place where, having but room for his left foot and left hand, he must leap from thence to another place before him, which if he hit right the rest of the ascent is easie, and with a small cord which he carries with him he hales up a rope whereby all the rest come up. But if he misseth that footstep (as often times they do) he falls into the sea and the company takes him in by the small cord and he sits until he is a little refreshed and then he tries it again; for everyone there is not able for that sport.[6]

Another writer noted in 1764: 'A rope is the most valuable implement that a man of substance can be possessed of in St Kilda. In his will he makes it the very first article in favour of his eldest son.' The St Kilda men made their ropes of cowhide or horsehair, though sometimes they would use a hempen rope sheathed in cowhide to protect it from abrasion.

So though the Victorian era may have seen the birth of climbing as we know it, we can see there was a long, pre-natal period during which, I suspect, our forefathers accomplished climbs which would astonish us, if only we knew the truth.

Thirty years after the ascent of Mont Aiguille we hear of Cortez ordering his soldiers to climb the volcano of Popocatepetl (5452 m) during his conquest of Mexico, to bring back sulphur from the crater for the manufacture of gunpowder. It can't have been a great success for, in his report to the King, Cortez said that in future it would be more convenient to have the gunpowder shipped out from Spain.

At least two centuries before Paccard and Balmat climbed Mont Blanc in 1786, the Incas had been climbing mountains like Llullaillaco which is almost two thousand metres higher and they may even have climbed Aconcagua, the highest peak in the Western Hemisphere.[7]

But if we turn more often to Europe than other continents when we look at early examples of mountain endeavours it is not because more ascents were made there, but because such as were made were better recorded. Later on, other factors, social and economic, were destined to make Europe, and particularly the Alps, the crucible of mountaineering throughout the world.

Before 1750 there had only been seven Alpine ascents of any consequence, but by the end of the century that figure had risen to twenty-two and included Mont Blanc, the highest summit in Western Europe. It was an era which saw the beginnings of man's love affair with mountains, fuelled first by the Romantic movement, then increasingly by the growth of scientific enquiry.

People not only looked at mountains but began to investigate them scientifically. Glaciers were an obvious puzzle which had to be solved – where did they come from, how did they move? Quite a few mountaineers began their climbing careers because they were scientists. Even more used science as a veil of respectability for going climbing, though few could match a certain M. Plantade who made repeated ascents of the Pic du Midi in the Pyrenees for the avowed purpose of making scientific observations and died on its slopes in 1741, an old man, clutching his sextant and proclaiming the beauty of the mountains with his dying breath.

CHAPTER TWO

The Geneva School

It is fitting that Geneva, cradle of the Reformation and home of Rousseau, should see the birth of mountaineering. One need not look far for the reasons when, from the heights of the Salève above the city, are seen the great snows of Les Glacières, as the Mont Blanc range was then known. The enquiring scientific minds of Geneva had a natural laboratory on their doorstep.

Yet it was not Les Glacières which first gained their attention but a mountain called Le Buet (3099 m) in the Chablais Alps, twelve and a half miles north of Mont Blanc, near the little town of Sixt. As Sixt is only thirty-five miles from Geneva, through gentle valleys, it was much more accessible than Chamonix and the mountain itself certainly looks more accessible than the rugged peaks of Les Glacières.

The ascent was attempted in August 1765 by the brothers Jean André de Luc and Guillaume Antoine de Luc, sons of a Geneva watchmaker who was a friend of Rousseau.[1] Unfortunately, the hunter who was their guide misunderstood their intentions and led them instead to the rocks of Le Grenier de Commune, a subsidiary peak. It was high enough to observe Mont Blanc 'with admiration as well as horror', but as they had broken their thermometer – a not infrequent mishap in these pioneering ascents – they returned to Geneva.

Five years later it took two more attempts before they made it to the summit, where they stayed for three-quarters of an hour (mostly on a dangerous cornice which they chose to ignore) and performed experiments to determine the boiling point of water at altitude. What surprised the brothers most was the way they readily adapted to altitude. 'They were forced by the absence of any disagreeable sensation to remark what a wonderful adaptive machine is the human body, whose equilibrium remains undisturbed within whilst the atmosphere without is so changed in density.'

The view from the Buet reminded the Genevese scientists that the greatest challenge of the Alps was only a few leagues from their city. It was not a challenge that could go unregarded. Somebody had to climb Mont Blanc.

Mont Blanc (4807 m) is the highest summit of a fairly compact group of great peaks, which form part of the main Alpine chain between the Val Montjoie in the west and the Swiss Val Ferret in the east. On the southern flank of the group is a deep trench formed by the Val Veni and the Italian

Val Ferret, whilst to the north it is limited by the long valley of the Arve, wherein lies Chamonix. Today the principal summits form part of the frontier between France and Italy, but until 1860 the whole region was part of the independent Duchy of Savoy.[2]

The region was known as Les Glacières for obvious reasons, and Mont Blanc itself was referred to as Mont Maudit (a title since transferred to a nearby peak), except by the Chamoniards who seem always to have called it Mont Blanc.[3]

A priory was founded in the Arve valley in the eleventh century and the hamlet which grew up round it assumed the name Chamonix in 1330. It was visited by various Bishops of Geneva from time to time and even some tourists, including a Prince of Sulzbach in 1727, but it was the visit of two Englishmen, Windham and Pococke, in 1741 which began its rise to fame.

William Windham was an athletic young man, known in fashionable London circles as Boxing Windham because of his pugilistic ability. Disputes with his father caused him to live much of the time on the Continent where he met up with Richard Pococke, already a noted traveller in the Middle East and Egypt. Together with six companions and five servants, 'all of us well armed', they left Geneva on June 19 and arrived at Chamonix three days later after a very rough journey in which their horses several times lost their shoes. Next day at noon they set off to climb Montenvers, taking some locals as guides, and reached this belvedere after four and a half hours to gaze in wonder at the Aiguilles, 'the tops of which being naked and craggy rocks, shoot up immensely high; something resembling old Gothic buildings or ruins'. Not content with this, they scrambled down onto the Mer de Glace, where they toasted Admiral Vernon and success to British arms. They were back in Chamonix by sunset, much to the surprise of the natives, who thought the whole enterprise quite mad.

Windham's account of their journey[4] was published in 1744 and immediately attracted attention. Others came to Chamonix and by 1779 Dr John Moore[5] was complaining: 'One could hardly mention anything curious or singular, without being told by some of those travellers, with an air of cool contempt – "Dear sir, that is pretty well; but, take my word for it, it is nothing to the glaciers of Savoy."'

One of Moore's companions, the Duke of Hamilton, set off to climb the Dru, thinking it would make a better viewpoint. He was stopped in this startling enterprise by 'a part of the rock which was perfectly impracticable'. A century was to pass before the Dru was climbed.

Windham made no mention of Mont Blanc itself in his narrative but this is not altogether surprising because, though it may be the highest of the mountains, it is also the tamest when seen from Chamonix. Lesser peaks are much more impressive. Only on the Italian side does the old monarch impress. There great ridges sweep down in a chaos of rock and ice which lends substance to the idea that this is not only one of the great mountains of the Alps, but one of the great mountains of the world.

The scientists who observed Mont Blanc from the Buet and from Chamonix were not interested in its form. They were interested solely in the fact that it was the highest mountain in the Alps and to attain its top would advance scientific exploration. Height is what mattered – and height has remained a significant aspect of mountain climbing to this day, though the motives which led ultimately to the ascent of Everest in 1953 are very different from those which motivated the Genevese of the late eighteenth century. Nevertheless, in the early attempts on Mont Blanc were present all the bravery, doggedness, competitiveness, skill, jealousy, deceit, and publicity that have accompanied the sport of mountaineering, exposing all that is best and worst in human nature.

Four men played prime roles in the first ascent of Mont Blanc. Horace Bénédict de Saussure was Professor of Natural Philosophy at Geneva, a post to which he was appointed at the age of twenty-two. He had a European reputation as a scientist and between 1779 and 1796 wrote four authoritative volumes of *Voyages dans les Alpes*. Marc Théodore Bourrit began life as a miniature painter, a profession he abandoned to devote his life to the mountains. He was appointed Precentor of Geneva Cathedral, a sinecure which enabled him to climb all summer and write about it all winter. 'The indefatigable Bourrit', as someone once called him, wrote six great books which earned him the sobriquet of the Historian of the Alps. Unfortunately his climbing ability never quite matched his enthusiasm, and he knew it.

In contrast with these two distinguished men from the city were two from Chamonix. Michel-Gabriel Paccard was born in Chamonix in 1757 and became in due course the village doctor, having studied in Turin and Paris. He had some scientific attainments, being a corresponding member of the Turin Academy, and he had a continuing interest in Mont Blanc, making notes of all ascents and attempts down to 1825 – with one vital omission, as we shall see. And last, but not least, the fourth member of this strange quartet was Jacques Balmat, an ambitious crystal-hunter, brave as a lion but hungry for fame and fortune. Considering this group as a whole, they represented every motive from pure science to pure greed.

Seen from a viewpoint like the Brévent, across the Arve valley, the features of Mont Blanc can be readily identified. The skyline is an undulating white crest. On the extreme right is a pointed peak, the Aiguille du Goûter (3863 m) followed almost immediately by a rounded, aptly named Dôme du Goûter (4304 m). A dip, the Col du Dôme, follows and then the ridge rises gradually over two distinct humps (Les Bosses) to the summit (4807 m). Beyond the summit it drops again to the Col de la Brenva before continuing into further peaks which need not concern us.

Below the ridge just described a sheet of snow and ice descends towards the valley. At the bottom it is divided by a distinct large spur of rock, wooded in parts, known as the Montagne de la Côte. On the left of this spur is the longest stretch of glacier, reaching almost to the valley floor, the Glacier des Bossons, whilst on the right is the shorter Glacier du Taconnaz. Where these two glaciers meet, above the rock spur, is a crevassed region known as La Jonction. Higher up a band of rocks sticks out of the ice, continuing the line of the Montagne de la Côte; these are the Grands Mulets rocks. The way up lies to the right of these rocks; first to the Petit Plateau, overshadowed by the sérac-strewn slopes of the Dôme du Goûter, then steeply and over a big crevasse to the Grand Plateau, a huge snow bowl. Mont Blanc rises ahead. On its left side are two sloping bands of rock, the lower and upper Rochers Rouges, with a snowy ramp lying between them. It seems a possible way to the summit. Another alternative canvassed at the time was out of sight of Chamonix. Behind the wooded ridge which separates the Arve from the Montjoie valley lies the long Glacier de Bionnassay which is the western counterpart to the Bossons. In its upper reaches this glacier gives access to a stony plateau, the Désert de Pierre Ronde, and to a vantage point, the Tête Rousse, above which rises the rocky face of the Aiguille du Goûter. This too seemed a possible way to climb the mountain, although it did mean climbing the Aiguille du Goûter and Dôme du Goûter as well, en route.

De Saussure first visited Chamonix in 1760 and he returned the following year. So struck was he with the idea that Mont Blanc should be climbed that he offered a substantial reward to anyone who could do it. He even offered to pay the expenses of anyone who tried but failed. At first the only person to exhibit any interest in de Saussure's financial sponsorship was one of his guides, Pierre Simond, who in 1762 made a couple of desultory attempts, first by the Bossons Glacier and then, rather hopefully, round the back of the mountain by the Mer de Glace and Géant Glacier, where the savagely steep aspect must have been profoundly discouraging.

Four years later Bourrit paid his first visit to Chamonix. He heard about the reward and, though he was not interested in it for himself, the idea appealed to his entrepreneurial nature and fired his enthusiasm for Mont Blanc. He set about an unprecedented publicity campaign, writing and lecturing about the mountain.

Even so, it was not until 1775 that four local men from Chamonix decided to make an attempt. On July 13 of that year, Michel and François Paccard, Victor Tissay and 'the young Couteran' slept at the foot of the Montagne de la Côte and next day scrambled up the rocks and onto the ice at La Jonction, pushing on up the glacier to the start of the Petit Plateau. Tissay and Couteran[6] even investigated the rocks of the Grands Mulets before the mists came down and the party hastened to retreat to the valley.

Two months later there stepped onto the scene one of those fascinating characters who are such a feature of mountain exploration, though not mountaineers in themselves. Thomas Blaikie was a Scottish landscape gardener and botanist who had been sent to the Alps by two wealthy patrons to collect plant specimens. In Geneva he met Henri-Albert Gosse, a young naturalist and mountain lover who introduced him to de Saussure. From his meetings with the scientific society of Geneva, Blaikie obtained an introduction to Joseph Paccard, Royal Notary of the district and a man of influence in Chamonix. In his diary he wrote:

> After refreshing at a publick house at Chamouni went with my letter I had for Mr. Paccard, found him at home; he seems to be a man of respect in this place, he has three sons very genteel young men after some descourss there was two of them proposed to go allong with me in purpose to conduct me and at the same time to learn plants; the oldest is learning surgery the second is a Priest and the youngest about 20 is studying at the uneversity of Turin to be a Doctor.

The one studying to be a doctor was Michel-Gabriel Paccard.

Blaikie crossed the Mer de Glace with two of the Paccard sons and then, with Michel-Gabriel, embarked on a remarkable journey. They climbed up to the Lac du Plan de l'Aiguille, which lies on a shelf below the Chamonix Aiguilles, then crossed the small but steep Blaitière and Nantillons Glaciers (where they were nearly caught by an avalanche) before sleeping for the night at a high chalet known as Blaitière-dessus.

Next day they traversed below the Aiguilles to the Bossons Glacier and crossed this to the head of the Montagne de la Côte:

> Here we passed the Ice to gaine on the other side what they call the Montan de la Cote from the top of this you are opposite the Midle of Mont Blanc; from hence the eyes is fatigued with the vew of this plain and the Montain which apears only a mass of snow as there is few rocks betwxt you and the mountain but this desert mass of eternall snow. From hence we tooke our way higher up westward to what they call Aiguille de Gouté which is exceeding high perpendicular rocks which towards the mountain supports this bed of snow and Ice which forms Mont Blanc and these Glacieres; here we are above every mark of vegetation; this pic is 1980 toisses high or 12311 English feet which is only 29 feet lower than the top of the fameous pic of Teneriff. Here I wanted to go higher but My companion almost tired out would go no further and as there was no plants to be got we agreed to return down to Chamouni; here is an exceeding good way to descend the Ice by means of a Stick with an Iron pick at the end which you place behind and leans

upon and so slids down the Steepest ice; arrived in the evening at Chamouni.[7]

The next day they climbed the Brévent, already climbed by de Saussure, Bourrit and others, and two days later visited the wild Jardin de Talèfre in the very heart of the Mont Blanc massif. It was a place known only to crystal-hunters – even de Saussure had not been there. This concentrated little campaign by Blaikie[8] and Paccard was certainly the most serious mountain exploration of the Mont Blanc group to be carried out to date. In attacking the Aiguille du Goûter was Paccard looking for a way up Mont Blanc? It seems possible. Equally important, in view of later events, was the spirit of the whole enterprise.

In 1779 an unknown Frenchman made a meagre attempt at climbing Mont Blanc, but it was not until 1783 that the next serious sortie was made. Three local men took part: Jean Marie Couttet, Joseph Carrier and Lombard Meunier (nicknamed Grand Joras [sic]). They slept at the top of the Montagne de la Côte and on July 12 ascended as far as the Petit Plateau. Here Couttet was overcome by lassitude, which might have been incipient heat stroke or wine induced. The others refused to leave him, so they all came down. They had got little further than their predecessors but Meunier proffered advice for those that would follow: 'It is of no use to take any provisions for the journey; all that is wanted is an umbrella and a scent bottle.'

Marc Théodore Bourrit now entered the scene in earnest. He had worked himself up to such a pitch over Mont Blanc that he saw himself not as a mere recorder, but as actual conqueror of the highest mountain in the Alps. Two practical difficulties stood in his way: first, he was not a scientist, did not possess any scientific instruments (de Saussure refused to lend him his) and without a scientific *raison d'être* the expedition would lose much of its impact; second, he hated the cold and discomfort involved in mountain climbing and was even afraid of mountains, except in the abstract.

The second of these disadvantages he put to the back of his mind. The first was more immediately pressing. He had to have a scientist in his party, but who? He didn't want de Saussure because de Saussure's name was too famous and any credit would go to him, which was definitely not part of Bourrit's plan; Gosse refused to go, and there was no point in asking Guillaume de Luc, who hated him. In the end he thought of the young doctor he had met in Paris and Chamonix, Michel-Gabriel Paccard.

But the young Paccard of student days, impressed by the famous literary lion of Geneva, was not the Paccard of 1783. No longer impressionable, he was a tough egg and a good mountaineer: 'Paccard was full of energy and courage; he was touchy and did not suffer fools gladly; he was cultured, and a gentleman at heart. Bourrit had none of those qualities, except touchiness.'[9]

Nevertheless, the two men teamed up and with two other locals, Jean Claude Couttet and 'the miller Marie', made an attempt via the Montagne de la Côte in September 1783. They slept at the top of the rocks but the weather was bad next day and 'M. Bourrit did not dare to go on the ice,' Paccard recorded in his diary in disgust. As they retreated to Chamonix he decided to have nothing more to do with Bourrit. Did his disgust show? He was not a man given to hiding his feelings, and if this was so, he laid the seeds of much future distress.

The following year Paccard seems to have made an investigation of the Géant Glacier approach to Mont Blanc and like his predecessor, Simond, realised quickly how hopeless it was. Instead he turned his attention to the west where the great Bionnassay Glacier curled up from the Val Montjoie to the Aiguille du Goûter. With a few companions he climbed up to the Tête Rousse and saw the broken rock ridges of the Aiguille rising above. He noted the stonefall on the face of the Aiguille du Goûter (still a notorious hazard) and he went no further. The party retreated to Chamonix, Paccard having broken two barometers during the course of the expedition.

Paccard wrote to de Saussure telling him of this new route. Bourrit also got to hear of it and on September 16 – a week after Paccard's attempt – he set off with five guides to climb it. They all reached the Tête Rousse next morning but Bourrit fell ill and after making a sketch of the vale of Chamonix, retreated to the Désert de Pierre Ronde with three of his guides and gradually back to the chalets at the foot of the glacier, where he went to sleep.

Meanwhile the two remaining guides, Marie Couttet and François Cuidet, were doing some exploration of their own. They had left the others at the Tête Rousse and climbed the steep broken arête in the centre of the Aiguille du Goûter to reach the summit of the mountain. Then they continued over the Dôme du Goûter and reached the rocks beyond the col where the Vallot Hut now stands. Ahead of them lay the Bosses ridge and, tantalisingly close, the summit of Mont Blanc. But the day was by now well advanced, so the two men retreated to join Bourrit and tell him of their adventures. Couttet and Cuidet had gone higher on the mountain than any of their predecessors. It seemed that the way to the summit had been discovered.

The following summer, 1785, was cold and stormy so no attempt was made on Mont Blanc until September. On the 4th of that month, Couttet and Meunier repeated the previous year's climb but got no higher, being driven back by storms.

Bourrit had told de Saussure about his party's success on the Bionnassay route, which confirmed what the scientist had already heard from Paccard. He determined that the time had come to take a hand in the affair himself and, though he may have preferred to make the attempt solely in the company of his guides, he felt obliged to invite Bourrit along. Bourrit responded by bringing along his son Isaac, a bumptious youth of twenty-one.

It had been de Saussure's intention to use tents and camp as high as possible on the mountain before making a summit assault. Bourrit, however, forestalled this by having a hut built at the Tête Rousse which could serve as base.[10] Comfort was the order of the day: palliasses, sheets, blankets, pillows, wood and provisions were carried up to the hut, along with all de Saussure's scientific equipment. Fourteen guides and porters were needed for all this, some of whom returned at once to the valley, leaving de Saussure, the two Bourrits and nine guides to continue the ascent next day.

They ascended the arête until, at 11 a.m., de Saussure asked Pierre Balmat and Cuidet to go ahead and reconnoitre. They were absent for about an hour and a half and returned with the disconcerting news that there was much fresh snow on top, which would make the going laborious and possibly dangerous. Dr Paccard's diary takes up the story:

> M. de Saussure, who has always shown a dislike for snowy tracks – though he was a good walker on rocky ground – decided to make experiments where he was. All were glad of it except young Bourrit, who so far had only taken a little brandy and water, and wished to go on higher . . .
>
> M. de Saussure was tied like a prisoner in coming down, with a rope under the arms, to which François Folliguet was attached in front and Pierre Balmat behind. Couttet was in front to mark the steps. M. Bourrit was held by the collar of his coat by Tournier, and was leaning on the shoulder of Gervais. In the difficult places a barrier was made by a baton, on which M. de Saussure was able to lean, both going up and descending.[11] Young M. Bourrit, almost ill, ascended by holding to Cuidet's coat.

The Bourrits descended to Bionnassay but de Saussure spent another night at the hut making observations.

Both the Bourrits sent letters of criticism to de Saussure afterwards regarding his mode of descent. The younger Bourrit wrote: 'Sir, do you not envy me my twenty-one years? Who will wonder if a youth of this age, who has nothing to lose, is bolder than a father of a family, a man of forty-six?' It seemed the young man lacked none of his father's unendearing qualities.

De Saussure replied tartly: 'A moderate amount of boastfulness is no great crime at your age . . . You say you descended agilely. It is true, you descended agilely enough on the easy places, but in the difficult places you were, like your father, leaning on the shoulder of the guide in front and held up behind by another . . . In no language in the world can that style of progress be termed agile climbing.'

The events of 1784 and 1785 convinced de Saussure that if Mont Blanc was to be climbed it would only be from the Bionnassay side, at which the

Chamonix men took alarm. To reach Bionnassay from Chamonix meant a tedious walk over the Col de Voza and tourists would soon discover that St Gervais was a more convenient base, to the obvious disadvantage of Chamonix. In 1786, therefore, they decided to try Mont Blanc again, only this time making simultaneous ascents from Bionnassay and Chamonix.

On June 7 Pierre Balmat and Marie Couttet slept at the Pierre Ronde, whilst Joseph Carrier, Jean Michel Tournier and François Paccard slept at the top of the Montagne de la Côte. They were all to meet next day on the Dôme du Goûter, the idea being to see who got there first, thereby demonstrating, one way or another, the most convenient way up. As Carrier and his companions settled down for the night on the Montagne de la Côte, they were joined by the crystal-hunter, Jacques Balmat. Balmat was twenty-four, reputed for his cunning and generally disliked. The Chamonix men agreed that he could join them, provided he looked after himself.

Early next morning, aided by hard crisp snow, the Chamonix party reached the Dôme du Goûter an hour and a half before the others, thus demonstrating to their immense satisfaction the superiority of their village as a starting point. They pushed on across the col towards the Bosses Ridge but the sharpness of this appalled them; steep snow slopes fell away on either hand to dizzying depths and they were too afraid to proceed. They turned for home, convinced that this ridge was not the way to climb Mont Blanc.

On the descent the snow, so firm in the morning, had become softened by the sun. The guides ploughed down manfully, but Jacques Balmat, who had gone crystal-hunting at the Vallot rocks, fell further and further behind. When night fell he was still on the snow, the others having abandoned him. Eventually, tired out, he came to a crevasse which the others had obviously jumped but for which he no longer had sufficient energy. Balmat lay down in the snow and went into a cold and troubled sleep from which he awoke next morning with his clothes covered in hoar frost. No doubt he was surprised to find himself still alive, for it was firmly believed that to sleep out at altitude in the snow was certain death. Without more ado he made his way down to Chamonix, where he consulted the village doctor about his sun-blistered face.

How near the men of Chamonix came that day to climbing Mont Blanc! Today, the route up the Aiguille du Goûter and along the Bosses Ridge is by far the most popular way of climbing the mountain, attempted by hundreds every season. Yet such was the belief in the old pioneers' judgement that the route was not climbed for three-quarters of a century after their failure on it – and then only by one of the strongest parties of the day.

Events were now moving towards their bizarre climax. Paccard had been studying the mountain for three years through his telescope; he had talked with all the men who had been on the different attempts and he had decided that a more or less frontal assault might be best after all.

'I determined to make another attempt. My own guide was away and so when Jacques Balmat offered his services I accepted his offer and engaged him as a porter,' he wrote. The inference is clear: Paccard chose Balmat because the latter had shown his ability to survive a night out at altitude, and might have to do so again.

Many years later, Balmat gave a different version: 'I went to Paccard and said, "Well, Doctor, are you determined? Are you afraid of the cold or the snow or the precipices? Speak out like a man." "With you I fear nothing," was his reply.'[12]

On the evening of August 7, they bivouacked at some rocks near the top of the Montagne de la Côte at a place now known as the Gîte à Balmat, and began to ascend the glacier at four next morning. Route-finding was difficult because the hot summer had removed much of the snow cover and many of the crevasses were gaping. They weaved in and out endlessly: it took eight hours to pass the rocks of the Grand Mulets: 'Four times the snow bridges, by which we tried to cross the crevasses, gave way beneath our feet, and we saw the abyss below us. But we escaped a catastrophe by throwing ourselves flat on our batons laid horizontally on the snow, and then, placing our two batons side by side, we slid along them until we were across the crevasse,' Paccard later wrote.

Higher up they came across deep fresh snow which was extremely fatiguing. The glare from the sun hurt their eyes. Balmat was for turning back: his wife had recently given birth to a daughter and the child was sickly; now he felt he should return to help. Paccard would have none of it, realising it for the excuse it was. Instead, he took part of Balmat's load and they shared the task of trail breaking.[13]

The afternoon was wearing on as they laboured up the slopes from the Grand Plateau, taking the gangway between the upper and lower Rochers Rouges. The wind rose and whipped away Paccard's hat, though it was tied on by strings, and it became fearfully cold. Paccard thought they would have to suffer the high bivouac he had suspected at the outset, but there was simply no place to rest.

They struggled on, halting to catch their breath every few paces, though the bitter cold prevented them resting for long. Once above the rocks Paccard made straight for the top, but Balmat (who had a heavier load) took an easier slope and had to put on a spurt to catch up with his companion. They reached the top together, watched by two crows. It was 6.23 p.m., August 8, 1786.

They tied a kerchief to one of their batons and stuck it in the snow. Most of Chamonix was watching through spy-glasses and saw the signal quite clearly.

The doctor made a few observations with his instruments, then, at 6.58 p.m. – ten minutes before sunset on that day – they began their descent. They plunged down the upper slopes but night overtook them as they reached the Grand Plateau. Fortunately it was a night of clear sky and bright moon so they were able to continue their journey until they reached the Montagne de la Côte a little before midnight. Here they bivouacked until dawn, their hands frostbitten, partially snowblind, utterly exhausted. In the pale morning light they returned to Chamonix, Balmat leading the almost blind doctor down the Montagne de la Côte to the village.

The ascent took about fourteen and a half hours from their bivouac and the descent about five hours. A remarkable tour de force by both men, especially as the descent from the Grand Plateau, across the heavily crevassed Jonction, was by moonlight. One wonders whether the sight of Balmat leading the blind doctor into Chamonix was taken by many people as proof of Balmat's story that it was he, not Paccard, who was the hero of the hour.

It had been a notable victory. Almost at once, it began to turn sour.

Two friends of de Saussure were in Chamonix at the time of the ascent and, like the rest of the village, had watched events unfold. Once success was assured they hurried back to Geneva to tell the scientist the news. Balmat also hurried to Geneva, to collect his reward[14] and to talk with de Saussure – and Bourrit.

De Saussure came to Chamonix to try and repeat the climb but he was frustrated by the weather. Instead, he had a long and detailed conversation with Paccard, which he later committed to his diary and in a letter to a friend. For his own part, Paccard, who had kept meticulous notes about earlier attempts on Mont Blanc, wrote down only the briefest outline of his ascent with Balmat because he intended to write a full account for publication. De Saussure assured him that such a story would be widely received and he helped the young doctor by spreading word about the climb and even sending out a prospectus for Paccard's forthcoming book.

This was too much for Bourrit. Consumed by jealousy at Paccard's success (and perhaps remembering how the young doctor had once ridiculed him) he wrote and published *Letter on the first journey to the summit of Mont Blanc*, in which he made Balmat the hero of the climb and Paccard a craven fool who had to be dragged up most of the way. De Saussure saw the letter in draft before it was published and protested strongly, so that Bourrit was forced to tone it down somewhat – but not enough; the letter was widely received because of Bourrit's popularity with the reading public and Balmat's name blazoned across Europe.

Meanwhile, Paccard's manuscript was being quietly suppressed. He had entrusted its publication to the publisher J.P. Béranger in Geneva, who was a close friend of Bourrit. Béranger demanded constant revisions and corrections, until finally Paccard lost heart. In the following summer the great de Saussure himself climbed Mont Blanc and that finally killed any interest there might have been in Paccard's account. The book never appeared and the manuscript was lost.[15]

Chamonix was divided into pro-Paccard and pro-Balmat factions and there was even a fight between the two men in the village inn. Certainly Balmat came to believe that he and only he was the true conqueror of Mont Blanc; that he had discovered the route by the Rochers Rouges, that he had initiated the climb, that his strength and skill had clinched the victory. Forty-six years after the event Balmat gave an interview to Alexandre Dumas in which he repeated and embellished the story of how he had conquered Mont Blanc. No doubt Dumas embroidered it even more until it had the same historical truth as the tales of Alfred and the Cakes or James Watt and the boiling kettle. They erected a statue to Balmat in Chamonix. They forgot all about Dr Paccard.[16]

Not until the end of the nineteenth century did more careful research (instigated by Edward Whymper) begin to reveal more about the true role of Paccard in the first ascent of Mont Blanc. A search was made for the 'Lost Narrative', though without success, but during the search more and more supplementary material was discovered in long-forgotten archives which gradually but surely established Dr Paccard as the true originator and leader of the first ascent of Mont Blanc.

What became of the four chief actors in the drama? Paccard continued to climb and is even said to have been up Mont Blanc again. He became Mayor of Chamonix in 1794 and married two years later – a Marie Balmat! He died in Chamonix in 1827. Balmat became a local celebrity and built himself a new house at Les Pèlerins. He climbed Mont Blanc five more times, including the ascent with de Saussure in 1787 and Maria Paradis in 1809, but eventually he gave up climbing and became a gold prospector, dying in mysterious circumstances – possibly murdered – whilst looking for gold in the peaks above Sixt in 1834, aged seventy-two. De Saussure died, full of honours, in 1799, whilst Bourrit, who never did manage to climb Mont Blanc, died in 1819.[17]

CHAPTER THREE

The Opening of the Alps

It is hard for us to imagine today how difficult travel was at the time of de Saussure and the early alpinists. Such roads as existed were abominable, not only in the mountains but throughout Europe. To reach the Alps from England, for instance, involved a roundabout and prolonged journey: six days by diligence from Boulogne to Paris, two days from Paris to Chalon-sur-Saône, an overnight boat along the River Saône to Lyons, then a further four days in a diligence from Lyons to Geneva. Most people were accustomed to walking prodigious distances by modern standards – a useful attribute for mountain exploration – but it was not until the coming of the railways that Alpine climbing became more than a series of isolated adventures.

Despite its scientific eminence, Geneva was still a medieval walled city where the drawbridges were pulled up of an evening. The Captain of the Guard questioned each visitor closely as to who he was and where he was going and only when he was satisfied did he issue the visitor with a permit. Without a permit, no innkeeper would offer a visitor lodgings. It was forbidden to walk the streets on Sunday during church services, for Geneva was an island of Calvinism surrounded by a sea of Catholicism.

Beyond the city there was nothing to admire but the scenery. The villages were for the most part poor, with few inns and none at all in the more isolated places like Zermatt. In some parts of the Alps such as the Dauphiné, the poverty was extreme. Individual acts of kindness to visitors were not unknown, but suspicion and surliness, allied to a grasping nature, was the general way of things. Most communes had been closed for years; that is, only those families living there at the time of the closure could own land or share the common land.

The explorations of men like de Saussure were as real as the exploration of the Himalaya was to a much later generation, and *Voyages dans les Alpes* had the same impact on the public imagination as did the works of Shipton and Tilman one hundred and fifty years later. Of course, the reading public was much smaller and those who could afford to emulate de Saussure were fewer still.

Amongst the latter were the parish priests. These were men of some education, isolated spirits surrounded by ignorance, with little wealth but plenty of time to study and explore. One of the most notable of these early ascents was made by the Abbé L.J. Murith, a forceful character who was at the time priest at Liddes and later Prior of the St Bernard monastery. In

1779 he set off with two local chamois-hunters to climb a mountain called Vélan (3734 m) near his parish at the western end of the Pennine Alps.

Vélan is no mere walker's peak. It is heavily glaciated and there are many crevasses. The two hunters soon wanted to turn back but the priest would have none of it. He drove them on and they hacked steps in a steep ice wall to reach the summit. 'I believe I have ascended one of the first great peaks ever climbed in Europe,' he wrote to a friend. Indeed he had, and it was a notable feat.

Murith felt no compulsion to continue climbing. He told de Saussure that the ascent of Vélan had been 'too much trouble' – but he continued to explore the Alpine valleys, mainly in the interests of botany. Today's usual route up the Vélan by the Valsorey Glacier was discovered by monks from the St Bernard monastery some half a century later, perhaps inspired by their illustrious predecessor.

A little bit further north than Vélan, across the Rhône, rises the curiously isolated though attractive massif of the Dents du Midi. Below the peaks runs the long Val d'Illiez, now famous for the ski centre of Champéry but in the late eighteenth century a very remote place indeed. It was hardly the sort of place to inspire a cultivated man like the Abbé Clément, whose library boasted a thousand volumes on medicine and natural history. Clément hated the valley and the people he was condemned to serve, and the feeling was mutual. Perhaps it was sheer frustration which drove him to climb the Midi in 1788, when he was already fifty-four years old, but whatever the cause, Clément, like Murith, climbed nothing else.[1]

Of all the priest-climbers the one with the greatest dedication to the mountains (and the least to his calling) was Placidus à Spescha, a monk at the Benedictine monastery of Disentis, a village on the Vorderrhein in the east of Switzerland at the foot of the Oberalp and Lukmanier Passes. He was born of yeoman stock in 1752 just a few miles down the valley from the monastery and had a good education for a boy of his background in a remote part of Switzerland, though he spoke Romansch and never did fully master German, the 'official' language. With some other monks he was sent to Einsiedeln to further his studies and he acquired a passion for botany and geology. On his return to Disentis he became librarian and bursar and had, in fact, virtual control over the running of the monastery. He was not an easy man, being querulous and argumentative, and resented by the other monks who set about destroying his character by pointing to the heretical nature of his scientific leanings. Spescha maintained that his study of Nature had given him a better understanding of God.

From Disentis he explored the Tödi Alps, which rise north of the valley, and the Adula Alps to the south. His first ascent seems to have been Piz Aul (3027 m), almost immediately above the monastery, which he did alone at some time before 1770 and which he repeated twice later on with companions. Between then and 1799 his ascents were numerous and included such peaks as Piz Cristallina (3128 m), Stockgron (3418 m) and Piz Urlaun (3374 m). His two most famous ascents, however, were the Rheinwaldhorn (3402 m) in 1789 and the Oberalpstock (3328 m) in 1792.

His ascent of the Rheinwaldhorn, the highest of the Adula Alps, was made in the company of three doctors and a shepherd:

> On the following day the weather was unusually clear and pleasant. Provided with a guide we set off on the way to see the source of the Rhine and what lay beyond. On my own account I took a guide from the Zaport Alp, a shepherd named Antonio.
>
> The Rhine bursts as a river from an ice-vault and rushes over the stones past the Alp. We crossed the long Rheinwald glacier without difficulty or danger, and in three hours reached the hollow which lies between the Cuver (Guferhorn) and Piz Valrhein. Our guide, when he saw the precipices of the Lentathal with its and the other glaciers, and took account of the way up the Valrhein, refused to go a step further with us. No persuasion could bring him to it.
>
> However, the courageous shepherd took the lead, I came next, and the doctors followed. Soon my next follower clutched my robe, and each of the others the coat of his fore-goer. After a time I found it a little too much to hold up and draw after me all the three doctors, who allowed themselves very perceptible backslidings. I therefore in turn grasped for security's sake the tail of the shepherd's coat. In this way we wandered in a line over the narrow snow-ridges. Care was needful to avoid slips and false steps, for a fall on our right would in some places have been certainly fatal.
>
> From the depth of the hollow already spoken of up to the peak the ridge of the mountain is covered with snow and trends towards S. or S.W. For the first half it is steep, then becomes gentle for a short space, and is then again steeper than at first. Nothing rises above, nor is it broken by any ice or snow pinnacles. Only very long snow slopes stretch down from it into the depths of the valleys. The view on to the Lenta glacier is awful and almost perpendicular. We followed always the ridge of the mountain, but at last it became so steep that we were not able to find footing on it, and we had no implement with us fit for cutting steps. We were obliged therefore to cross a somewhat less steep snowslope, so as to be able to climb the peak from the W. side. Rengger, who was next behind me, slipped. I sprang to him, clutched him, and placed him on his feet again. Nothing serious could have happened to him; he might have damaged his skin or his clothes, but some level snow just under us

would have stopped him. Yet this accident made such an impression on the gentlemen that they would not go on with the expedition, so we made them seats and footholes in the snow. They had before them a wide view to the N. and W., and with that they contented themselves.

We had scarcely gained the W. side, when the shepherd let fall his stick, which slid downwards and was lost to view in a crevasse. What my feelings were at this unlooked-for ill-luck may easily be imagined, since the worst bit of the ascent lay before us, where, unprovided with crampons, we must make our way over the hard ice, which was bare of fresh snow. Luckily, however, I was able to persuade the good man to search for his stick. He approached the crevasse with slow steps, at each he cried out *Jesu, Maria*, finally he knelt down and grasped the stick. The hazardous corner was crossed and we breathed freely. Now, however, a fresh dilemma met me. When I tried to encourage the guide to complete the ascent of the summit he replied *Mi no*, 'Not I,' and as often as I made appeal to him he kept answering me quite composedly with his *Mi no*. So I had to climb the last peak alone, and I found no difficulty in doing so, as it was all snow.

When one stands on the summit itself, one is on a cornice of snow that overhangs to the N.E. I only found this out on the descent, otherwise I should have thought twice before going on to the very crest. Perhaps the fear that it might give way was the shepherd's reason for not following me.

From the top I saw near at hand nothing but bare mountains, wild pasturages, ice and snow; further off little but the hollows of the valleys, but countless peaks. The only instrument I had with me was a compass; I had not even a telescope. At that time my long sight supplied the place of the latter, at least for a general view, and for a close examination I had no time.[2]

On the Oberalpstock ascent, which he made with a servant of the monastery, Joseph Sennoner, they were nearly swept away by an avalanche. Spescha leapt onto a patch of old, firmer snow, rammed his alpenstock home and hung on grimly as the snow poured round him. Sennoner, who was behind, missed the brunt of the avalanche but was so unnerved by the experience that he refused to proceed until Father Placidus had heard his confession. It was a day to remember for young Sennoner, because on the way down he fell into a crevasse and had to be hauled out by his master.

In 1799 Masséna's French army swept into eastern Switzerland. They imposed a heavy fine on the Disentis monastery and took some monks as hostage, but Spescha succeeded in having the sum reduced and the hostages freed. Later, however, during Spescha's absence, Disentis and its monastery were burned to the ground by the French as reprisal for Swiss guerrilla activity in the area. Spescha, who had sold much of his valuable mineral collection to raise the fine, now found that his library and papers were burned and the rest of his collections looted or destroyed.

Spescha's faith must have been sorely tried at this time. The French were replaced by the Austrians, to whom Spescha was betrayed by the very monks he had helped rescue a few weeks earlier. He was accused of Jacobin sympathies and of being a republican, since he had recently, and rather unwisely, preached a sermon on the text 'Put not your trust in princes.' The Austrians took this as being directed against their own Emperor Francis II and so in September 1799 they sent Spescha as a hostage to Innsbruck where he remained until February 1801.

Curiously enough, this was one of the happiest periods of the monk's troubled life. He was able to study at the Academy, he wrote a book on the techniques of mountain climbing and he climbed the neighbouring peaks of Patscherkofel and Rosskopf. He even contemplated remaining in Innsbruck after his release but, inevitably perhaps, he returned to his own valley and his old ways.

Still persecuted by bigots, Spescha moved around the district from parish to parish as a local priest, never staying long at any one place. His unorthodoxy allied to an irascible temperament alienated him from many. Eventually he returned to his birthplace, Truns, where he died on August 14, 1833, aged eighty-one years.

The period after his return from Innsbruck was almost as fruitful in mountain exploration as had been the earlier days. In particular he took up again the challenge of the Tödi (3620 m), the biggest peak in the region. He attempted it no fewer than six times – a single-minded dedication to an objective reminiscent of the later exploits of Whymper or Dent. His last attempt was on September 1, 1824, when he was seventy-one years old. He reached a gap now known as the Porta da Spescha, just 263 metres lower than the summit, but he had the satisfaction of seeing two of his companions go on to reach the final goal.[3]

The vindictiveness of his fellow monks followed the old climber even beyond the grave, for they burned the manuscripts he left behind. No doubt much was lost, but Spescha had lived a long time and learned a lot about the ways of his fellow men – he had begun the habit of writing everything in duplicate and the copies survived.

In the opinion of the great Alpine historian, W.A.B. Coolidge, Spescha ranks with de Saussure as the founder of alpinism. It was the monk's misfortune to live in a remote part of Switzerland where the peaks have never been popular and to suffer interminable persecution.

*   *   *

At the turn of the century the enlightenment begun by de Saussure had spread to the furthest corners of the Alps and beyond. In 1794 Orazio Delfico climbed Monte Corno (2912 m), the highest summit of the Gran' Sasso d'Italia group in the Italian Appenines and there took scientific measurements 'according to the methods of M. de Luc'. Stanislas Staszic, a Polish priest, began his exploration of the Tatra Mountains and in 1805 climbed Lomnica (2634 m), thought to be the highest summit.[4] A few years later another Pole, the romantic poet Antoni Malczewski, made the first ascent of the North Summit of the Aiguille du Midi, above Chamonix, in 1818. During the year 1813 the Norwegian botanist Christen Smith made a journey into the as yet unnamed Jotunheimen and so discovered the highest European mountains north of the Alps. He climbed the small peak of Bitihorn where, in true tradition, he managed to break his barometer. In the meantime, Ramond de Carbonnières had begun his exploration of the Pyrenees as early as 1787, culminating in the ascent of Monte Perdido in 1802.

The career of Ramond de Carbonnières has curious parallels with that of Placidus à Spescha, though at a higher social level. He served Cardinal Rohan and the notorious Cagliostro and became involved in the Affair of the Diamond Necklace,[5] a scandal which Napoleon considered to have contributed to the outbreak of the French Revolution. Like Spescha and other liberals of the period, de Carbonnières was in favour of the Revolution and he even served in the first parliament, but the growing excesses of the Mob sickened him and put his own life in danger when he escaped to the Pyrenees. He was arrested, however, and imprisoned in Tarbes, only escaping the guillotine because his enemies forgot him.[6]

Like Spescha, he seems to have been a natural survivor. He was rehabilitated under Napoleon, who made him Prefect of Puy de Dôme, and after Waterloo he served Louis XVIII as the minister responsible for paying off war debts.[7] He died in 1827 at the age of seventy-two.

De Carbonnières was the first to explore the Pyrenees thoroughly and to give an account of them in his books *Observations faites dans les Pyrénées* (1789) and *Voyages au Mont Perdu* (1802). In the latter he described his struggles with Mont Perdu (Monte Perdido) in a style which was fifty years ahead of its time, reminiscent of Victorian climbing in its heyday.

'It was like ascending a ladder of ice,' he wrote, describing a couloir which led up the mountain. 'There was no possibility of zig-zagging, and so mitigating the steepness of the gradient. The angle of inclination continually increased, and the precipice continually grew more profound.'

The ascent continued:

> We proceeded thus for more than a couple of hours, and then we had only accomplished the least difficult portion of our task. We were approaching a hillock which rose in the midst of the glacier;

we did not know how to take it, and were at the end of our expedients. The guide Rondo proposed to turn it by climbing along the edge of the glacier, which we had hitherto so carefully avoided – an *arête*, sharp as the blade of a knife, and separated from the rocks by a wide space that opened before us like a funnel. This proposal, which we should have voted ridiculous an hour before, now afforded the only means of bringing our perilous adventure to an honourable termination. A dozen steps carved in the ice took us on to this *arête*; but we had to knock away the cornices, and test the ice with heavy blows from our sticks, to assure ourselves that it would bear our weight. In this way we succeeded in advancing thirteen steps in twenty minutes, balancing ourselves on the slippery track, with precipices to right and to left and behind us . . .

At every instant this ridge exposed us to fresh perils. Twice we were stopped by projections of rock which barred our path. We could neither go up nor down, but had to worm our way round them, at the risk of losing our balance and falling. Presently we found that we could follow the *arête* no further, and had no place of refuge except the rocks which we had at first supposed to be inaccessible. They are, it is true, carved into steps by the stratification; but, to realise the situation, you must first imagine a staircase in which the height of the steps is almost always greater than their width, and the ascent steeper by one-third than it should be, and then you must picture to yourself all the irregularities of the rocks, and our own uncertainty of what the rocks would be like when we got higher. Then, at last, you will understand with what eyes we looked upon this last resource that remained to us.

Here, however, we had to hoist ourselves up from step to step. The first man was pushed up by the man beneath him. Once safely anchored, he, in his turn, gave the other a hand. The risks, in the two cases, were at least equal, even if the disadvantages did not rest with the latter. For those who were ahead could not make a false step without endangering the rest of the company, or loosen a bit of stone without sending it flying over the heads of the others. For my own part, I was hurt rather badly by one of these falling stones, as I could only stiffen myself and let it hit me, my position not allowing me to get out of the way. This final scramble lasted more than an hour.

That attempt failed, but de Carbonnières returned in 1802. Now forty-seven years old he decided to conserve his energy by having his guides, Laurens and Rondau, reconnoitre a route preliminary to his own attempt. The two guides set out and met with a shepherd on the way who decided to accompany them. Together, the three peasants reached the summit of Monte Perdido on August 7. Three days later de Carbonnières made his own ascent led by Laurens and his brother, Palu.

Meanwhile, matters were stirring in the Eastern Alps where the huge bulk of the Gross Glockner, on the borders of Tyrol and Carinthia, was attracting local attention as early as 1779. There was some doubt as to its height compared with other great peaks in Tyrol such as the Gross Wiesbachhorn and the Ortler (Cima Ortles) but it needed the stimulus of de Saussure's ascent of Mont Blanc to provoke action.

Once again the chief protagonist was a churchman – but a churchman of a very different calibre to Spescha or Murith, for Count Franz Xaver von Salm-Reifferscheid was Prince-Bishop of Gurk and destined to become a Cardinal. He was rich and powerful and though he had scientific interests after the fashion of the time, he had no ambitions to undergo the rigours of mountain climbing. He could direct others to do that for him.

On June 16, 1799, acting on the instructions of Von Salm, two carpenters from the village of Heiligenblut, just south of the mountain, made the first attempt. Martin Klotz and his brother were the first members of what was destined to become a famous family of guides, but on this occasion they met with no success. Storms drove them back before they reached the first summit of the twin-peaked Glockner, the so-called Klein Glockner. They tried again on the 23rd and managed to fix a 140-metre rope on the steep upper slopes (presumably to assist the '*Herren*' when the time came) but once again storms drove them down.[8]

Contemplating these reverses the Prince-Bishop concluded that climbing the Gross Glockner might turn out to be a protracted affair, so he had Klotz and others build a cabin in the Leiter valley below the peak, as a permanent base. On August 24 the Klotz brothers and two other carpenters again failed to reach the Klein Glockner but their efforts were observed by telescope from the village and brought the official party scurrying up to the hut. Next day in fine weather the brothers were at last able to lead a party to the top of the Klein Glockner.

But did the Klotz brothers continue across the sharp ridge to the second summit? Did they in fact climb the Gross Glockner as well as the Klein Glockner? The evidence is contradictory. Von Salm had a medal struck in commemoration which bears the inscription GLOCKNER IN CARINTHIA PRIMUS CONSCENDIT D. 25 Aug. 1799, which seems pretty conclusive but makes a nonsense of what followed.

The events of 1799 were described in an anonymous diary[9] in which the writer asserted that there seemed to be no difference in height between the two summits of the Glockner. But it seems that Von Salm believed the second summit had not been reached and the task therefore not fully accomplished. He arranged for another, much grander expedition to take place the following year, 1800. He had the cabin extended and another hut, a sort of advance base, constructed higher up the mountain. Invitations were sent to distinguished savants to join the enterprise and no fewer than sixty-two persons assembled at the Leiter hut on July 28, 1800.[10]

The party set out next day for their momentous ascent, though few went further than the higher hut, including Von Salm. The Klotz brothers, their two carpenter comrades from the previous year, a botanist named Hoppe, Sigmund von Hohenwart (later to become Bishop of Linz) and two local priests all gained the Klein Glockner. The four carpenters and one of the priests – Father Horasch of Döllach – then crossed the knife-edged gap to the summit of Gross Glockner (3797 m).

On their return to the upper hut there was great rejoicing, not to say merriment – the Prince-Bishop being drawn down the Leiter Glacier on a sledge.

The Gross Glockner had undoubtedly been climbed and Father Horasch was the first 'tourist' to reach the summit, but in Von Hohenwart's diary of the event he says, 'The peasants placed the same long tree which *they used in the preceding year* instead of a ladder *for the ascent of the second peak.*' This seems to reinforce the inscription on the medal that Gross Glockner was climbed by Klotz and his companions in 1799. But if this was the case why did the Prince-Bishop organise the expedition of 1800?

On the day following the first ascent, Klotz and the other workmen climbed the peak again and erected an iron cross and, next to it, the log which they had hauled up the previous year to help them cross the gap. In this they were aided by an enthusiastic young botanist named Valentin Stanig who scrambled to the top of the pole in order, he said, 'to be higher than the Glockner or anyone else who had climbed it'. It is possible that Stanig had already climbed the imposing rocky peak of Watzmann (2713 m) near Berchtesgaden in the previous year and eight years later he was to make the first ascent of Triglav (2863 m), the highest mountain in what used to be Yugoslavia, now in Slovenia. 'His notes of his climbs display the greatest enthusiasm, and Stanig is deservedly reckoned as the earliest amateur mountaineer in the Eastern Alps.'[11]

Von Salm and Stanig were not the only persons in the Eastern Alps to be influenced by de Saussure. Archduke John of Austria, who knew Von Salm well, felt that since Mont Blanc had been climbed so too should the Ortler (3899 m), then the highest mountain in the Austro-Hungarian empire. In 1804 he sent his physician, Dr M. Gebhard, to attempt the peak, but Gebhard was unsuccessful and it was left to the chamois-hunter Josef Pichler with two companions, J. Leitner and J. Klausner, to reach the summit on September 28 in a howling gale.

Once again there was some dispute as to whether the summit had been reached and the whole thing was repeated the following year, this time with Dr Gebhard in tow.

The Archduke himself took no active part in the ascent of Ortler but he was in fact an active mountaineer, climbing amongst other peaks the Hochgolling and Ankogel. He would have made the first ascent of the difficult North-West Face of the Gross Venediger (in 1828) had not his guide met with an accident, thus curtailing the expedition.[12]

Between Murith's Vélan, or Clément's Dents du Midi, in the west of Switzerland and Spescha's Adula Alps in the east, there are two groups of importance, containing the highest of the peaks, and separated by the long trench of the Rhône valley. To the north of the river rise the Bernese Alps – the Oberland, with its long glaciers and heart of ice, whilst to the south lie the Pennine Alps, coxcombs of peaks, divided ridge by ridge by deep valleys which give the canton its name, Valais.

The great Alpine passes such as the Grimsel, the Gemmi or the Monte Moro were well known and over the centuries, too, it seems likely that some of the easier glacier cols were crossed, if not by hunters and crystal-seekers then by soldiers, refugees, prelates or surveyors. One of the latter, Samuel Bodmer of Berne, certainly crossed the Tschingel Pass between the Lauterbrunnen valley and the Gasterntal in 1710.

The exploration of the Oberland began in earnest with the exploits of the remarkable Meyer family and their associates. Johann Rudolf Meyer founded a prosperous silk mill in Aarau, the profits from which enabled him to visit the mountains and to sponsor the work of two notable surveyors, J.H. Weiss and J.E. Muller.[13] All three climbed Titlis together in 1787 but the two surveyors ranged more widely than this and Weiss is known to have climbed the Hangendgletscherhorn (3291 m) in 1798.

It was Meyer's two sons, Johann Rudolf II and Hieronymus and his two grandsons, Johann Rudolf III and Gottlieb who contributed most spectacularly to the Oberland story. Even by the standards of the day they were incredibly hardy: together or individually one reads of them doing long tough walks, enduring bivouacs under blizzard conditions and even bathing amongst the floating ice of glacier lakes. And the two older men were in their forties at the time!

On August 1, 1811, Johann Rudolf II and his brother Hieronymus set out from the head of the Lötschental to climb the Jungfrau (4158 m). They had with them three servants and three guides, a great black linen sheet meant to act as a tent, ropes, alpenstocks, a ladder, dark veils – but no scientific instruments because they said such things were a hindrance to venturesome climbers. This was almost heresy, of course, and was destined to rebound on them later.

At the first glacier pass, the Lötschenlücke, they sent the servants back.

The five others continued into an amazing world of ice, a central point in the Oberland where several great snowfields and glaciers unite and around the rim of which great peaks arise. It is now known as Koncordiaplatz, and here they camped.

On the next day they tried to find a way up the Jungfrau by way of the Kranzbergfirn, but in this they were not successful so they retreated and tried another tack, this time too far east. Eventually they worked out the lie of the glaciers and climbed up the Jungfraufirn to camp for their second night below a peak called the Trugberg.

On the morning of August 3 the two Meyers and two of the guides set out to climb the Jungfrau whilst the third guide returned to the valley for more provisions:

> . . . the first rays of the sun just reddened the rocks of the Jungfrau, rising close before us. We now proceeded up the masses of ice and snow which descend from the Jungfrau. We hoped, as the mountain was now quite close, to gain the summit by following this same snow-slope. But what we took for a continuous snowfield was an optical delusion, for, suddenly, in front of us, there appeared a *Tiefe* [descent] of 40 to 50 feet, to which one could only descend with difficulty; left and right slopes fell away steeply and deep. The way down to the foot of the summit of the Jungfrau lay along a sharp glacier-ridge or saddle. We attached, where this ridge commenced, a rope to an alpenstock driven deep into the snow, and sat ourselves astraddle on the sharp snow-saddle; thus we slid, one by one, safely down and came to the foot of the summit, to which we approached quite close, passing in and out between rocky points projecting from the ice.

They reached the summit at 2 p.m., where they hoisted their black tent as a flag, pulling their ladder to bits to make the pole. Half an hour later they were on their way down, delicately, gingerly, across the exposed ridges. One of the guides collapsed from fatigue and snow blindness and had to be led on the rope for the rest of the descent. Fortunately, they managed to reach their bivouac before dark, where their companion was awaiting them.

News of this ascent spread rapidly in the Alpine countries and excited great enthusiasm at first, then scepticism and disbelief. Where were the scientific results? Where, indeed, was the black flag? When the Meyers explained that they had made no scientific experiments they were given an old-fashioned look, but more to the point, the flag they had so laboriously hoisted on the summit had disappeared, possibly in a storm.

In the following year, 1812, the two Meyer brothers together with the sons of Johann II, Johann Rudolf III and Gottlieb, and a teacher from Aarau, Dr Thilo, conducted a vigorous six-week campaign in the Oberland.

Despite some atrocious weather they ranged back and forth amongst the glaciers. During this period Johann Rudolf III made the first known crossing of the Strahlegg Pass and Gottlieb repeated the ascent of Jungfrau, but the most significant climb was that of the Finsteraarhorn (4274 m), the highest peak in the Oberland.

The Finsteraarhorn is in the very heart of the Oberland glacier system. It is a long ridge of mountain, running north-west–south-east, with the summit roughly in the middle and two lesser peaks at either end of the ridge. Near the south-east end is an easy pass called the Gemslücke and it was from a bivouac here that J.R. Meyer III, with the guides Volker, Bortes, Abbühl and Huber, set out on August 15, 1812 to climb the mountain.

They turned north into an easy glacier bay called the Studerfirn and then attacked the steep slopes of the great South-East Ridge. They found themselves on a wall of ice flanked on the right by a huge tottering ice cliff. The steepness was such that they took to the rocks whenever possible, but it was six hours before they could reach the crest of the ridge. Meyer was exhausted and he halted at a forepeak (Meyer's Peak) with Huber, whilst the three other guides continued the ascent. It wasn't easy and the crux came at the end:

> None would take the lead in the assault on this last summit. Ice lay on the naked rocks, and nothing broke the view through the gap until the eye rested on the Finsteraar Glacier. At last Arnold von Melchthal, attached to a rope held by the others, clambered over the overhanging icecap (hohle Eishaube), and dragged the others after him. Now the highest point was conquered. It was four o'clock. Three hours had been spent in getting over a distance for which a quarter of an hour had seemed enough. The peak is sharp as a houseroof, and entirely plastered with ice, which hangs for several feet out over the precipices, so that the Finsteraar Glacier is seen through a hole in it.

The leader (erroneously referred to in the *Alpine Journal* as von Melchthal) was actually Arnold Abbühl and it was a fine piece of climbing – even today it is graded III and has a fixed rope to help climbers.

After fixing the necessary flag and taking a rest the three guides returned to their companions and then the whole party, fearful of attempting to descend the steep ice wall they had climbed that morning, descended instead the opposite side of the ridge to the Fiescher Glacier and climbed the Gemslücke to their bivouac after an exciting, exhausting day.

The ascent of the Finsteraarhorn was a truly astonishing feat. Not only had they traversed the peak but the climb was far and away the most difficult that had been made to date – fifty years ahead of its time. Small wonder that later Alpine historians found it hard to believe and long detailed arguments have been put forward to argue the case both ways. Astonishing, yes – but not impossible and we know now that many of these early hard men *were* capable of astonishing feats.[14]

Monte Rosa (4634 m) in the Valais is the second highest of all the Alpine peaks after Mont Blanc. It straddles part of the Swiss–Italian border like a white colossus; a huge, undulating snow plateau, culminating in a horseshoe of separate tops, or summits, each of which has its own name. Thus Monte Rosa is a generic name only – the actual highest top being known as Dufourspitze.

On the Swiss side it looks down on the Gorner Glacier and the Zermatt valley; on the Italian it heads the valleys of Gressoney, Sesia and Anzasca. De Saussure travelled up the Valle Anzasca and observed Monte Rosa from Macugnaga but was not impressed, which is surprising, for of all the aspects of the great mountain this is the most dramatic.

The earliest attempts on Monte Rosa were from the Italian valleys, because at the turn of the eighteenth century Zermatt was hardly known and the way to it was difficult and perilous, whereas the Italian valleys were readily accessible and Monte Rosa, floating like a distant white cloud, could be seen from Milan or Turin.

Local men were responsible for the early attempts – the Vincents and Zumsteins of Gressoney; Pietro Giordani, the doctor of Alagna; Giovanni Gnifetti, the priest of Alagna. The only two exceptions were the German explorer Dr Parrot[15] who made an attempt in 1813 and the Austrian army officer Baron Ludwig von Welden who in 1822 reached the peak now named after him, the Ludwigshöhe. Monte Rosa is unique in the Alps for the number of summits named after the early pioneers, for in addition to the Ludwigshöhe there is the Punta Giordani, Pyramide Vincent, Parrotspitze, Punta Gnifetti, Zumstein Spitze and Dufourspitze itself.[16]

The first attempt on the mountain was made by Niklaus Vincent and six men of Gressoney (including a Zumstein) in 1778 when they reached a rocky island near the Lysjoch, the col between Monte Rosa and the peak called Lyskamm. They called it Discovery Rock (Entdeckungs Fels) and visited it again on the succeeding two years.

In 1801 Pietro Giordani, the village doctor of Alagna, climbed the top now named after him, probably by the south-east arête, but the Punta Giordani is little more than a shoulder of the mountain and the first real attempt came in 1817[17] when Dr Parrot and Joseph Zumstein tried to climb the Pyramide Vincent but were driven back by thick fog. It was left to Joseph Niklaus Vincent, son of the first explorer and friend and companion of Zumstein, finally in 1819 to climb the summit which bears his name.

After Vincent's encouraging success the time had arrived for the men of Gressoney to make a concerted attack on the mountain. The Academy of

Sciences in Turin was anxious for the peak to be climbed so that it could obtain trigonometrical observations and was prepared to supply all the necessary instruments and an engineer, Molinatti, to conduct the survey. Consequently in July 1820 a large party led by Joseph Zumstein with J.N. Vincent (and including at least one other Vincent and Zumstein) set out for the top.

Poor Molinatti seems to have had a dreadful time what with sheer exhaustion and looking after the scientific instruments and he was forever dropping behind. So too were some of the porters and eventually the party was forced to bivouac in a deep crevasse. Zumstein later described the experience:

> Night approached, and still no signs of our porters. A large portion of our effects, including the tent and firewood, were still behind. We became alarmed, and the increasing cold added to our perplexity. It was 6 p.m., and the thermometer stood at $-7°$ [no doubt Réaumur $= 16.25°$ Fahr.]. So rapid a change in the temperature, amounting to $15°$ [$33.75°$ Fahr.] in so short a time, produced such an effect on me that I was already in a state of complete prostration. I had besides committed the imprudence of clothing myself too lightly, because on my former expedition I had suffered from the heat. Already the cold so penetrated me that my companions perceived I was growing pale. I lost all energy, and an irresistible drowsiness stole over me. The experienced chasseur, Joseph Beck, feeling anxious about me, began to shake me to warm my blood and restore defective circulation, by which means he soon set me to rights again. Meanwhile the cold continued to increase, and our perplexity was extreme ... Only one acquainted with the upper ice-world can appreciate the danger to which we were exposed. We had already determined towards nightfall to beat a retreat, although there was no moon to light us, when at length the long-wished-for porters arrived, dragging their heavy burdens – tents, coverings, and wood. Imagine our joy! Light of heart, we collected everything together, and hastened to the crevasse selected for our night-quarters.
>
> From the N. edge of the chasm a snow-slope, descending at an angle of about $25°$, led down into its depths. Joseph Beck, the old chasseur, the boldest of the party, was the first to effect the descent, by means of about forty steps which he cut in the surface. After a careful examination he assured us of the solidity of the bottom, which indeed consisted of snow heaped up by the wind, and so the rest of us followed him. We were all penetrated by the most fearful cold, I half numbed, quite unable to observe the instruments, and not even capable of assisting in the erection of the tent, which

the dauntless chasseur, Joseph Zumstein, raised with marvellous rapidity in the bitterest cold, whilst Marty set about preparing a cheerful fire in which he succeeded after much difficulty.

Some capital soup was cooked, and served out all round, but eaten with little relish. We were eleven in party under the tent, and lay on our right sides, covered with blankets and skins, and packed close together in a row, to prevent being frozen during the night.

It was at that time the highest bivouac ever undertaken, so it is hardly surprising that they were a little apprehensive as to the outcome.

Next morning they continued their ascent, making towards a pyramidal summit which seemed the highest point.

Herr Molinatti, exhausted by the rarity of the atmosphere, rested a little from time to time. The two Vincents, on the contrary, carried away by the utmost enthusiasm, hastened forwards to be the first to reach the top. I followed, panting, about fifty steps behind them. At length we stood at the foot of the snowy arête leading to the pyramidal summit. A snow saddle falling away sharply, stretched, as it appeared to us, in a SE. and NW. direction. The climb began, and the active chasseur Castel went ahead to cut steps with his axe in the ice to prevent us from slipping. The younger Herr Vincent followed him step by step. His brother and I soon overtook them, as the labour of step-cutting delayed their progress. Farther up, as we climbed the narrow ridge overhanging the Macugnaga Thal, the hard snow disappeared, and was succeeded by a coating of ice, which it required the utmost caution to traverse. Had we slipped, we should have fallen 8,000 feet sheer. It was fortunate, however, that neither of us was seized with giddiness. About ten paces below the summit we came upon rock much weathered, its cavities filled with ice, and, climbing over this with greater facility, we at length gained the summit. The younger Vincent was the first to set foot on it. He shouted, 'Long live our King! Long live all patrons of science!' We took up the words, so descriptive of our feelings, and proceeded to plant a banner in the ice. It was just past 10 a.m. Two barometers were at once set up for the sake of comparison, and after a quarter of an hour read off by me with the utmost care. At length we saw Herr Molinatti approaching with some of the guides, and I sent back the chasseur Castel to assist him. As a precaution, a rope was fastened round his middle. Castel went first, having the rope wound round his arm, and the brave Marty, holding him by the left hand, cleared out the steps for him. Thus, more dragged than walking, he at length reached us in safety.[18]

They had reached the summit now known as the Zumstein Spitze (4563 m) and they could see immediately that it was not the highest point. Beyond a gap lay a rocky crest, the top of which was some hundred metres higher.

Zumstein made several more attempts on Monte Rosa but he never succeeded in reaching the ultimate summit. That had to await the coming of the English.

CHAPTER FOUR

The Coming of the English

At the turn of the century the pace of Alpine exploration quickened dramatically. In the fifty years up to 1800 there had been some fifteen ascents of new peaks; the next half-century was to see ninety-seven. That only fifteen of these were climbed before 1820 is hardly surprising when one considers the turmoil in which Europe found itself in the aftermath of the French Revolution and the subsequent Napoleonic wars. For quite apart from the natural hazards of mountain travel, Europe was awash with the riff-raff of contending armies and Alpine valleys made convenient hiding places for bands of renegades and deserters.

Another influence, too, was steadily coming to bear on every aspect of European life and culture – the Industrial Revolution, creating a new, wealthy middle class, which in turn produced a greater number of professional people: one of the twin bastions of nineteenth-century alpinism, (the other being the local guides). The spirit of scientific enquiry begun by de Saussure and others in the eighteenth century was enhanced by the Industrial Revolution and the men who now took up the challenge were often professional scientists rather than gifted amateurs. Professional or not, many found science taking second place to the thrill of climbing.

It was a period of exploration; a desire to see what lay beyond the last blue mountain motivated the alpinists of this time. Most of the leading figures came from the Continent. Gottlieb Studer (1804–90) of Berne was one such, ranging throughout the Alps in no fewer than 643 expeditions and recording the story of Alpine development in his monumental work *Uber Eis und Schnee*, which he published in four volumes between 1869 and 1883. Louis Agassiz, Edouard Desor and J.D. Forbes concerned themselves with the problems of glaciers – they climbed the Jungfrau together in 1841 and Desor went on to make a number of notable ascents in the Oberland: the Gross Lauteraarhorn in 1842, then the Rosenhorn in 1844. That same year his guides, Bannholzer and Jaun, climbed the Hasli Jungfrau, better known today simply as the Wetterhorn.[1]

In the Oberland too F.J. Hugi, a geologist from Soleure, tried to climb the Finsteraarhorn from the west in 1828, but bad weather stopped him at a col now called the Hugisattel. A year later he tried again and though he failed, two of his guides, Jakob Leuthold and Johannes Währen, reached the summit and, in the manner of the time, raised a flag. Hugi was also one of the earliest climbers to try the Alps in winter; he attempted to climb the Eiger in January.

In the Eastern Alps Professor Peter Carl Thurwieser repeated the climbs of his illustrious predecessors on the Watzmann, Glockner, Ortler and the like, then went on to climb the Gross Wiessbachhorn, Dachstein and Habicht and numerous peaks in the Stubai, Otztal and Zillertal areas, in over seventy expeditions altogether. Thurwieser, who taught Oriental Languages at Salzburg, carried the statutory barometer and botanical specimen box on his trips, but according to Coolidge, the Professor's motives had nothing to do with science. He climbed purely for the love of it, and Coolidge describes him as 'the first real mountaineer in the Tyrol'.[2]

Compared with their European contemporaries, relatively few British travellers turned their attention to the Alps in the early part of the century, though Frank Walker began his distinguished Alpine career in 1825 when he crossed the Théodule and the Oberaarjoch: but it was to be thirty-three years before he returned to the fray with his son and daughter. Two intrepid ladies, Mrs and Miss Campbell, crossed the Col du Géant in 1822 – 'the earliest English Lady climbers of whom the names have come down to us'.[3]

Such tardiness may seem strange in view of the rapid dominance which British climbers gained in the second half of the century but until the railways appeared travel remained difficult and there was no background of mountain climbing in Britain. Walking up such modest hills as Britain possesses was hardly on a par with climbing Mont Blanc.

But after about 1840 various factors combined to bring the British more into the centre of Alpine events. Travel became easier, and there was a growth in the prosperous middle classes whose sons were now attending the reformed public schools where sport was encouraged with the thought that a healthy mind needs a healthy body to sustain it. The growth of 'muscular Christianity' found a perfect expression in alpinism and it is hardly surprising that many of the early climbers were parsons.

The mood of the nation was expansionist. Imperialism and exploration went hand in hand and national self-confidence was such that nothing seemed impossible. All these factors contributed to the rapid growth of British involvement in the Alps.

The scientific element declined fairly rapidly. In 1833 a would-be climber wrote rather pompously: 'It is a positive act of egregious folly for one not moved by scientific motives to endure the pain and danger of an ascent greatly above the line of perpetual congelation.'[4] A few years later most climbers would have laughed openly at such sentiments, for the British, with their genius for turning almost any activity into a sport, had done just that with mountain climbing. The transformation did not come about overnight, nor was it entirely painless. Its roots were in the national developments just mentioned and in an upsurge of publicity brought about by some remarkable men and their books.

John Ruskin (1819–1900) first visited the Alps when he was fourteen and they became at once the dominating passion of his life. His rigorous intellectual upbringing taught him to analyse nature with a fresh eye and to express his views in a manner which caught the public's attention. He stripped away from the Alps the imagined beauty with which the Romantics had tended to imbue them and pointed instead to the beauty of form which stemmed from the geological foundations. He taught people to look at mountains properly and admire them for what they really were.[5]

His preference was for the middle viewpoint; a position sufficiently elevated to give the subject majesty but not so high as to rival it in any way. In 1844 he was probably the first tourist to climb Bel Alp, a rocky knoll above the Rhône with superb views of the Oberland. He also climbed the Buet and crossed the glaciers to the foot of the Aiguille d'Argentière. He later climbed the Riffelhorn and was, incidentally, the first person to photograph the Matterhorn (1849).

Ruskin always maintained, however, that *climbing* mountains did not lead to 'some true and increased apprehension of the nobleness of natural scenery' as some mountaineers claimed. 'True lovers of natural beauty,' he thundered, 'would as soon think of climbing the pillars of the choir at Beauvais for a gymnastic exercise, as of making a playground of Alpine snow.' This branded Ruskin as an anti-mountaineer and in *Sesame and Lilies* (1865) he wrote his most quoted condemnation:

> The Alps themselves, which your own poets used to love so reverently, you look upon as soaped poles in a beer-garden, which you set yourselves to climb and slide down again 'with shrieks of delight'. When you are past shrieking, having no human articulate voice to say you are glad with, you fill the quietude of their valleys with gunpowder blasts, and rush home, red with cutaneous eruption of conceit, and voluble with convulsive hiccough of self-satisfaction.

Ruskin was present in Chamonix when Albert Smith returned from his much publicised ascent of Mont Blanc in 1851. There was the usual firing of cannons and Smith, having achieved his greatest ambition and not being a man notable for reticence, probably whooped it up in the village that night. Ruskin would have seen this as a vulgarisation of the Alps and it was probably the incident foremost in his mind when the famous condemnation was written, fifteen years later.[6]

So Ruskin tilled the soil and fertilised it, but he did not plant the seed. The man who did was a tall, slightly built and rather handsome young Scot called James David Forbes. Born in 1809 of a well-to-do Edinburgh family, Forbes studied law at his home university but became increasingly interested in science. At the age of twenty-two he became a Fellow of the Royal Society and a year later, Professor of Natural Philosophy at Edinburgh. Under the old Scottish university system, teaching was concentrated into six months of the year, which gave the young professor adequate time to indulge his passion for Alpine travel.

In 1835 he visited the Pyrenees. Four years later he was in the Alps, making the first circuit of Monte Viso, crossing various high passes and visiting the then virtually unknown Dauphiné region. In 1841 he further explored the Dauphiné before travelling to the Oberland where he joined Agassiz for three weeks during which he climbed the Ewigschneehorn (3331 m) and the Jungfrau – the second and fourth ascents respectively of these peaks. He also began his important study on the behaviour and structure of glaciers.

Forbes spent much of the following summer on the Mer de Glace, above Chamonix, furthering his glaciological studies. His conclusions became known as the Viscous Theory and caused Ruskin to comment: 'Forbes solved the problem of glacier motion for ever – announcing to everyone's astonishment . . . that glaciers were not solid bodies at all, but semi-liquid ones, and ran down in their beds like so much treacle.'[7]

In August 1842, Forbes made a journey through the Pennine Alps with the guide Victor Tairraz of Chamonix and Professor Bernard Studer of Berne, a cousin of Gottlieb Studer. He was the first British visitor to Arolla and Evolène, later to become a popular climbing centre with British alpinists, but then so primitive that Studer declined to remain there and left Forbes to it. Forbes, guided by one of the Pralong family, and accompanied by Tairraz and Biona, another guide, made his way up the Ferpècle valley onto the ice below the awe-inspiring bulk of the Dent Blanche and crossed a high col to Zermatt. He called the pass 'Col d'Hérens', and it became one of the most frequented passes of the high Alps.

For Forbes it was not without adventure, which he later described in his book *Travels through the Alps*:

> We began cautiously to descend, for it was an absolute precipice: Pralong first, and I following, leaving the other guides to wait about the middle, until we should see whether or not a passage could be effected. The precipice was several hundred feet high. Some bad turns were passed, and I began to hope that no insurmountable difficulty would appear, when Pralong announced that the snow this year had melted so much more completely than on the former occasion, as to cut off all communication with the glacier, for there was a height of at least thirty vertical feet of rocky wall, which we could by no means circumvent. Thus, all was to do over again, and the cliff was reascended. We looked right and left for a more feasible

spot, but descried none. Having regained the snows above, we cautiously skirted the precipice, until we should find a place favourable to the attempt. At length, the rocks became mostly masked under steep snow slopes, and down one of these, Pralong, with no common courage, proposed to venture, and put himself at once in the place of danger. We were now separated by perhaps but 200 feet from the glacier beneath. The slope was chiefly of soft deep snow, lying at a high angle. There was no difficulty in securing our footing in it, but the danger was of producing an avalanche by our weight. This, it may be thought, was a small matter, if we were to alight on the glacier below; but such a surface of snow upon rock rarely connects with a glacier without a break, and we all knew very well that the formidable 'Bergschrund,' already mentioned, was open to receive the avalanche and its charge, if it should take place. We had no ladder, but a pretty long rope. Pralong was tied to it. We all held fast on the rope, having planted ourselves as well as we could on the slope of snow, and let him down by degrees, to ascertain the nature and breadth of the crevasse, of which the upper edge usually overhangs like the roof of a cave dropping icicles. Were that covering to fail, he might be plunged, and drag us, into a chasm beneath. He, however, effected the passage with a coolness which I have never seen surpassed, and shouted the intelligence that the chasm had been choked by previous *avalanches*, and that we might pass without danger. He then (having loosed himself from the rope) proceeded to explore the footing on the glacier, leaving me and the other two guides to extricate ourselves. I descended first by the rope then Biona, and lastly Tairraz, who, being unsupported, did not at all like the slide, the termination of which it was quite impossible to see from above. We then followed Pralong, and proceeded with great precaution to sound our way down the upper glacier of Zmutt, which is here sufficiently steep to be deeply fissured, and which is covered with perpetual snow, now soft with the heat of the morning sun. It was a dangerous passage, and required many wide circuits. But at length we reached in a slanting direction the second terrace or precipice of rock which separates the upper and lower glacier of Zmutt, and which terminates in the promontory called Stöckhi. When we were fairly on the debris we stopped to repose, and to congratulate ourselves on the success of this difficult passage.

Exciting passages like this, especially when illustrated by drawings such as the one he made of the Matterhorn (which Ruskin also used in *Modern Painters* Vol. IV), made the public sit up and take notice. The book first appeared in 1843 and some thirty years later Sir George Airy, the Astronomer Royal, writing to Mrs Forbes, said: 'I suppose it may be asserted that the present popularity of Zermatt, a place which before was scarcely known, is almost entirely due to Professor Forbes's picture of the Matterhorn.'[8]

In the winter of 1842 Forbes could contemplate the extent of his explorations: 'I have crossed the principal chain of the Alps 27 times, generally on foot, by 23 different passes.' The following summer his health broke down and he never fully recovered, though in 1846 he made a spirited attempt at the Moine and in 1851 visited Norway.

The work of Ruskin and Forbes excited discussion in the university, the salon and drawing room, but who was catering for the ordinary middle-class chap, who, as J.R. Green so unkindly put it when describing 'the Alpine Clubist' a few years later, was 'solid, practical and slightly stupid'? To catch the popular appeal, something quite different was needed. It was provided by Albert Richard Smith.

Albert Smith was the son of a surgeon at Chertsey, a profession in which he followed his father, studying in London and Paris. As a child he had read a slim volume entitled *The Peasants of Chamouni*, which gave details of the accident to Dr Hamel's party on Mont Blanc in 1820, and the subject of Mont Blanc had fascinated him ever since.[9] He read every account he could get hold of by the early pioneers and actually constructed a small moving panorama representing the ascent, which, with his own dramatic recitation of events, terrified his little sister. Whether he realised it at the time or not, he had hit upon a way to fame and fortune.

In the autumn of 1838, during a break in his studies in Paris, he was able to fulfil his cherished ambition of visiting Chamonix. He had little money and could not afford the guides necessary for an ascent of Mont Blanc, though he did rather hope he could attach himself to some other party as a porter. Unfortunately nobody was climbing the mountain and so after visiting the Mer de Glace he continued his journey to Italy.

He returned to Chertsey to practise medicine and to devise a show on a somewhat grander scale than the old one of his childhood on the ascent of Mont Blanc, with which to amuse local literary societies. In 1841 Smith moved to London, initially to practise surgery but a growing reputation for light literary pieces – he was an original contributor to *Punch* – induced him to give up medicine and earn his living by the pen. With ready facility he turned out sketches, novels, plays and pantomime, all with considerable success. He had a ready wit, knew exactly what the public wanted and provided it.

In 1849 Smith visited Constantinople (Istanbul) and Egypt. On his return he not only wrote a book about it but put on a public entertainment called *The Overland Mail*, written by himself and illustrated by William Beverley. It was a further development of the techniques he had used to amuse his sister and the local literary societies and it proved just as popular with the general public.[10] Meanwhile, he had not forgotten Mont Blanc. He had visited Chamonix several times over the years but when *The Overland Mail* closed in August 1851, Smith determined to climb Mont Blanc.

In Chamonix he met up with three Oxford undergraduates, The Hon. W.E. Sackville West, C.G. Floyd and F. Philips, who were also intent on making an ascent and these young gentlemen, sniffy at first, readily consented to join forces once they discovered that Smith was 'Mr Albert Smith, the well-known comic author'.

Preparations were made. The guides dictated that each climber should have four guides, making a party of twenty and each *person* should have a porter as far as the Grands Mulets, bringing the total to forty. The provisions were as ample as they were exotic and contrast strangely with the modern practice of climbing Mont Blanc on a couple of Mars bars:

60	bottles of	Vin Ordinare.	6	packets of	sugar.
6	"	"	Bordeaux.	4	"	"	prunes.
10	"	"	St George.	4	"	"	raisins.
15	"	"	St Jean.	2	"	"	salt.
3	"	"	Cognac.	4	wax candles.
1	"	"	syrup of	6	lemons.
			raspberries.	4	legs of mutton.
6	"	"	lemonade.	4	shoulders of mutton.
2	"	"	champagne.	6	pieces of veal.
20	loaves.			1	piece of beef.
10	small cheeses.			11	large fowls.
6	packets of chocolate.			35	small fowls.

It was probably the last and grandest of the big expeditions to attempt Mont Blanc, so well parodied by Mark Twain in his *A Tramp Abroad* some thirty years later. Even at the time Smith had a suspicion that things were too elaborate, that they were being conned by the guides, and of course, he was right.[11]

The caravan set out at 7.30 a.m. on August 12 and bivouacked for the night on the rocks of the Grands Mulets. Here they were joined by two other parties, 'an Irish gentleman' and his guide and G.N. Vansittert who seems to have had three guides.

They left at midnight and reached the Grand Plateau after three and a half hours. At the foot of the Mur de la Côte, Smith was stumbling and wanting to go to sleep. He was all for giving up but the guides kept him moving and they reached the summit about 9 a.m. – not bad going for a large party – before Smith was allowed a nap.

The descent was uneventful. It was the fortieth ascent of the mountain and really quite unremarkable, except for the quantity of provisions consumed. Had Albert Smith not taken part it would readily have been forgotten.

But Smith had other ideas. He hired the Egyptian Hall in Piccadilly, a building whose façade looked like a set left over from *Aida*, and mounted an entertainment called *The Ascent of Mont Blanc*. It had its first performance on March 15, 1852, and ran continuously for some seven years. Smith told the story of Mont Blanc, and his ascent, against a background of pictures painted by Beverley. These were on a rolling screen illuminated from behind. The story lost nothing in the telling, but just in case the audience's attention should falter, the show was interspersed by patter songs, humorous asides and anything topical that might suit. Great St Bernard dogs lay in front of the stalls and girls dressed in Alpine costume decorated the stage. As Edward Whymper later commented, had Smith not died at an early age the show might be running yet. It was a huge success, had three Royal Command Performances, and made Smith a very rich man.[12]

In 1853 Smith published *The Story of Mont Blanc*, which was also successful, but the show, the book and the man were universally condemned by drawing-room critics. Smith was too down-market for the Victorian literary scene. Thackeray hated him, Dickens disliked him and he seems to have been the butt of everyone's jokes – 'His initials are only two thirds of the truth,' quipped Jerrold. Yet really he was a kindly, genial man who hated to hurt anybody. What annoyed the Establishment, of course, was Smith's blatant use of sensationalism; he was the Barnum of the lecture hall, brash beyond Victorian belief. And he was very successful – that hurt too.

Alpinists who came on the scene a decade or two later often poked fun at Smith's hyperbole without realising that it was done on purpose to keep the customers happy. They poured scorn too on the ignominious way in which he stumbled to the top, momentarily falling asleep on the summit, pointing out that the considerable quantity of wine consumed en route might have had something to do with it. Well maybe, but the symptoms Smith describes, headaches, nausea, stumbling, and a desire for sleep, are classic symptoms of mountain sickness due to altitude.[13]

For all that, the fact remains that when Smith was invited to join the proposed Alpine Club as an Original Member in 1857 he was the first future member to have climbed Mont Blanc. Three years later he had died of bronchitis. Smith was not a scientist, yet he had so obviously enjoyed his ascent that people came away from the Egyptian Hall with the idea that there might be something in this mountain climbing for the ordinary chap.

Hard on the heels of Smith's book came the reissue of Forbes's book in a more popular form and then in 1856 came Volumes III and IV of Ruskin's magnum opus, *Modern Painters*. In the same year Charles Hudson and E.S. Kennedy issued a small book, *Where There's a Will There's a Way*, which described a somewhat circuitous ascent of Mont Blanc done without guides (the first guideless ascent of the mountain) and Alfred Wills published *Wanderings among the High Alps*.

Wills was a lawyer, later a distinguished judge, who visited the Alps fairly frequently in the years 1846–54, during which time he made a number of excursions across high passes but nothing outstanding until in 1854 he ascended the Wetterhorn from Grindelwald.

He left Grindelwald early on the afternoon of September 16 with his 'personal' guides from Chamonix, Auguste Balmat and Auguste Simond (nicknamed Sampson) and two local men, Ulrich Lauener and Peter Bohren. Lauener, who was in command of the expedition, carried a flag made out of an iron sheet attached to a 12-foot mast with which to decorate the summit. He had assured Wills that theirs would be a first ascent.[14]

That night they bivouacked on the mountain and the ascent was continued next day. Here is Wills's classic account of what happened:

> While we had been making our short halt at the edge of the plateau, we had been surprised to behold two other figures, creeping along the dangerous ridge of rocks we had just passed. They were at some little distance from us, but we saw that they were dressed in the guise of peasants, and when we first perceived them, Lauener (who was a great hunter himself) shouted excitedly, 'Gemsjäger!' but a moment's reflection convinced us that no chamois-hunter would seek his game in this direction; and immediately afterwards, we observed that one carried on his back a young fir tree, branches, leaves and all. We had turned aside a little to take our refreshment, and while we were so occupied, they passed us, and on our setting forth again, we saw them on the snow slopes, a good way ahead, making all the haste they could, and evidently determined to be the first at the summit. After all our trouble, expense and preparations, this excited the vehement indignation of my Chamouni guides – they declared that, at Chamouni, any one who should thus dog the heels of explorers and attempt to rob them of their well-earned honours would be scouted; nor were they at all satisfied with the much milder view which the Oberlanders took of the affair. The pacific Balmat was exceedingly wroth, and muttered something about 'coups de poing', and they at length roused our Swiss companions to an energetic expostulation. A great shouting now took place between the two parties, the result of which was, that the piratical adventurers promised to wait for us on the rocks above, whither we arrived very soon after them. They turned out to be two chamois-hunters, who had heard of our intended ascent, and resolved to be even with us, and plant their tree side by side with our 'Flagge'. They had started very early in the morning, had

crept up the precipices above the upper glacier of Grindelwald, before it was light, had seen us soon after daybreak, followed on our trail, and hunted us down. Balmat's anger was soon appeased, when he found they owned the reasonableness of his desire that they should not steal from us the distinction of being the *first* to scale that awful peak, and instead of administering the fisticuffs he had talked about, he declared they were 'bons enfants' after all, and presented them with a cake of chocolate; thus the pipe of peace was smoked, and tranquillity reigned between the rival forces.

Once established on the rocks, and released from the ropes, we began to consider our next operations. A glance upwards, showed that no easy task awaited us. In front rose a steep curtain of glacier, surmounted, about five or six hundred feet above us, by an over-hanging cornice of ice and frozen snow, edged with a fantastic fringe of pendants and enormous icicles. This formidable obstacle bounded our view, and stretched from end to end of the ridge. What lay beyond it, we could only conjecture; but we all thought that it must be crowned by a swelling dome, which would constitute the actual summit. We foresaw great difficulty in forcing this im-posing barrier; but after a short consultation, the plan of attack was agreed upon, and immediately carried into execution. Lauener and Sampson were sent forward to conduct our approaches which consisted of a series of short zig-zags, ascending directly from where we were resting to the foot of the cornice. The steep surface of the glacier was covered with snow; but it soon became evident that it was not deep enough to afford any material assistance. It was loose and uncompacted, and lay to the thickness of two or three inches only; so that every step had to be hewn, out of the solid ice. Lauener went first, and cut a hole just sufficient to afford him a foot-hold while he cut another. Sampson followed, and doubled the size of the step, so as to make a safe and firm resting-place. The line they took ascended, as I have said, directly above the rocks on which we were reclining, to the base of the overhanging fringe. Hence, the blocks of ice, as they were hewn out, rolled down upon us, and shooting past, fell over the brink of the arête by which we had been ascending, and were precipitated into a fathomless abyss beneath. We had to be on the *qui vive* to avoid these rapid missiles, which came accompanied by a very avalanche of dry and powdery snow. One, which I did not see in time, struck me a violent blow on the back of the head, which made me keep a better look out for its successors. I suggested, that they should mount by longer zig-zags, which would have the double advantage of sending the debris on one side, and of not filling up the footsteps already cut with the drifts of snow. Balmat's answer, delivered in a low, quiet tone, was conclusive. 'Mais où tomberaient-ils, monsieur, si, par un malheur, ils glissaient? A présent, il y aurait la chance que nous pourrions les aider; mais si on glissait à côté – voilà, monsieur!' pointing to a block of ice which passed, a little on one side, and bounded into the frightful gulf.

For nearly an hour, the men laboured intently at their difficult task, in which it was impossible to give them help; but, at length, they neared the cornice, and it was thought advisable that we should begin to follow them. Balmat went first, then I, then Bohren, and the two chamois-hunters, who now made common cause with us, brought up the rear. We were all tied together. We had to clear out all the foot-holes afresh, as they were filled with snow. A few paces after starting, when we were clear of the rocks, I ascertained the angle of the slope, by planting my alpenstock upright, and measuring the distance from a given point in it to the slope, in two directions, vertically and horizontally. I found the two measurements exactly equal; so that the inclination of the glacier was 45°; but at every step it became steeper; and when, at length, we reached the others, and stood, one below another, close to the base of the cornice, the angle of inclination was between 60° and 70°! I could not help being struck with the marvellous beauty of the barrier which lay, still to be overcome, between us and the attainment of our hopes. The cornice curled over towards us, like the crest of a wave, breaking at irregular intervals along the line into pendants and inverted pinnacles of ice, many of which hung down to the full length of a tall man's height. They cast a ragged shadow on the wall of ice behind, which was hard and glassy, not flecked with a spot of snow, and blue as the 'brave o'erhanging' of the cloudless firmament. They seemed the battlements of an enchanted fortress, framed to defy the curiosity of man, and to laugh to scorn his audacious efforts.

A brief parley ensued. Lauener had chosen his course well, and had worked up to the most accessible point along the whole line, where a break in the series of icicles allowed him to approach close to the icy parapet, and where the projecting crest was narrowest and weakest. It was resolved to cut boldly into the ice, and endeavour to hew deep enough to get a sloping passage on to the dome beyond. He stood close, not facing the parapet, but turned half round, and struck out as far away from himself as he could. A few strokes of his powerful arm brought down the projecting crest, which, after rolling a few feet, fell headlong over the brink of the arête, and was out of sight in an instant. We all looked on in breathless anxiety;

for it depended upon the success of the assault, whether that impregnable fortress was to be ours, or whether we were to return, slowly and sadly, foiled by its calm and massive strength.

Suddenly, a startling cry of surprise and triumph rang through the air. A great block of ice bounded from the top of the parapet, and before it had well lighted on the glacier, Lauener exclaimed, 'Ich schaue den blauen Himmel!' (I see blue sky!) A thrill of astonishment and delight ran through our frames. Our enterprise had succeeded! We were almost upon the actual summit. That wave above us, frozen, as it seemed, in the act of falling over, into a strange and motionless magnificence, was the very peak itself! Lauener's blows flew with redoubled energy. In a few minutes, a practicable breach was made, through which he disappeared; and in a moment more, the sound of his axe was heard behind the battlement under whose cover we stood. In his excitement, he had forgotten us, and very soon the whole mass would have come crashing down upon our heads. A loud shout of warning from Sampson, who now occupied the gap, was echoed by five other eager voices, and he turned his energies in a safer direction. It was not long before Lauener and Sampson together had widened the opening; and then, at length, we crept slowly on. As I took the last step, Balmat disappeared from my sight; my left shoulder grazed against the angle of the icy embrasure, while, on the right, the glacier fell abruptly away beneath me, towards an unknown and awful abyss; a hand from an invisible person grasped mine; I stepped across, and had passed the ridge of the Wetterhorn!

The instant before, I had been face to face with a blank wall of ice. One step, and the eye took in a boundless expanse of crag and glacier, peak and precipice, mountain and valley, lake and plain. The whole world seemed to lie at my feet. The next moment, I was almost appalled by the awfulness of our position. The side we had come up was steep; but it was a gentle slope, compared with that which now fell away from where I stood. A few yards of glittering ice at our feet, and then, nothing between us and the green slopes of Grindelwald, nine thousand feet beneath. I am not ashamed to own that I experienced, as this sublime and wonderful prospect burst upon my view, a profound and almost irrepressible emotion – an emotion which, if I may judge by the low ejaculations of surprise, followed by a long pause of breathless silence, as each in turn stepped into the opening, was felt by others as well as myself. Balmat told me repeatedly, afterwards, that it was the most awful and startling moment he had known in the course of his long mountain experience. We felt as in the more immediate presence of Him who had reared this tremendous pinnacle, and beneath the 'majestical roof' of whose deep blue Heaven we stood, poised, as it seemed, half way between the earth and sky.[15]

Pure adventure! A hint of mystery, a hint of a race, a hint of *sport*! It reinforced what Albert Smith had been saying, but in a broader context. It wasn't just Mont Blanc that could offer excitement, but the whole of the Alps.

> Wills was pre-eminently a founder, for his account of his ascent of the Wetterhorn gave, as it were, the signal for the commencement in this country of alpine climbing, for the outbreak, as the critics of the time put it, of the 'cacoëthes scandendi.' It is true something had been done before by Professor Forbes ... but if Forbes laid the train it was Wills who set the match to it.[16]

CHAPTER FIVE

Masters and Men

The 1850s saw the Golden Age of alpinism, when most of but not all the major Alpine summits were attained for the first time. It was, too, an age of heroes: Stephen, Ball, Tyndall, Moore, Whymper and many others who became the founding fathers of a new sport, made much more accessible by the rapid spread of railways.

Some of the earlier explorers were still active and for some years there was an admixture of science and adventure. Typical of these is Melchior Ulrich of Zurich who explored the glaciers of the Pennines and Engadine, initiating such well-known passes as the Adler, Ried and Allalin in the Mischabel group which lies between Saas and Zermatt. He was a companion of Gottlieb Studer, who was still active, and of the priest of Saas Fee, Joseph Imseng, who was himself perhaps the last and most active of those early priest-mountaineers.[1]

Accounts of many of these early ascents are full of a *joie de vivre* so often absent in later years when climbers took themselves and their sport much more seriously. On the Finsteraarhorn in 1857, J.F. Hardy describes how, shortly after setting out, they came in sight of the glacier, 'and away we all started, like so many school boys, racing against one another, leaping over masses of rock, and frequently alighting on ground of too juicy a character to be pleasant, (for the whole hill side was full of springs,) but all bent on accomplishing the descent in a rush.'[2]

Their antics baffled the more cautious traveller like the Rev. S.W. King who wrote of 'young Cantabs and Oxonians scampering over pass after pass, with often apparently no other object than trying who can venture in the most novel break-neck situations, or arrive at the greatest height and back, or accomplish the furthest distance in the shortest time'.[3] It was said that if you met an Englishman climbing in the Alps it was ten to one he was a university man, five to one he was a Cambridge man, and even odds he was a Fellow of his college.

The ascent of the Finsteraarhorn in 1857 was typical of its time. It was not a first ascent (though it was the first by British climbers). The party consisted of William Mathews, his cousin Benjamin St John Mathews, E.S. Kennedy, J.F. Hardy and J.C.W. Ellis, with the guides Auguste Simond, J.B. Croz, Johann Jaun and some local men. The climbers were all Cambridge men, though the two Mathews cousins were not known to the others until they met by chance in the Alps. Hardy wrote an evocative account of the climbing they encountered:

> For the next two hours we are climbing up a wall of rock which seems almost vertical: now hand over hand; now getting well into a corner, and bringing our backs into play after the fashion of chimney-sweeps; now coming to some awkward place, where the tallest man must go first, for his arms alone are long enough to feel the way, and choosing some safe ledge, must stretch down thence a helping hand to his shorter brethren, who occasionally, too, are thankful for a shove behind; now completely baffled by some monstrous crag, we are driven to take to the hard snow at the side, and ascend by sharp short zigzags, which without the confidence-inspiring rope are not altogether pleasant; then back again to the rocks, and holding on like grim death, or taking advantage of some small, *very small*, plateau for a moment's delay, while we wipe the streaming sweat from our faces; on again, with a cry to those below to look out, for the stones beneath our feet are giving way and crushing downwards; – till at last our advanced guard gives notice that we have reached the top of the rocks, and that a great slope of snow stretches upward before us as far as we can see. One by one we clamber on, glad enough at the prospect of a change of exercise, and though the slope looks somewhat severe, the rope is soon readjusted, and we are making long zigzags up the incline, with our alpenstocks ringing merrily in the snow, and the detached fragments skimming away from us with increasing velocity.

The long arête leading to the summit they tackled unroped for, as Simond pointed out, if one was to slip he would drag the others with him. 'No, monsieur,' he said. 'Here it is every man for himself.'

Occasionally they felt impelled to crawl along on all fours giving one another a helping hand whenever necessary. In places the arête was corniced: 'Several times I had the gratification of seeing my pole pass right through,' wrote Hardy, adding that he got an uninterrupted view of the glacier thousands of feet below.

They gained the top at 11.53 a.m., admired the view – '17,000 square miles' – and then descended the arête. This time the rope was in use and Hardy describes how they divided into three groups of three (and one extra man going solo) using a method which was to become standard practice in the years to come:

> Croz and Kennedy remained stationary while I descended, till I came to a spot where I could not only stand steadily, but bear a

strain on the rope if necessary; then, while Croz and I waited, Kennedy joined me, and thus set me at liberty to make a fresh start, till, when I stopped a second time, Croz joined Kennedy, who then descended to me. Thus there was never but one person moving at the same moment, and though this plan necessarily occupies a considerable time, it is the safest method of descending such an *arête* as this.

Hardy does not say whose idea it was, but it was obviously not common knowledge at the time or he would not have described it in such detail.

Hardy, Kennedy and Croz reached their hotel at the Eggishorn at 1 a.m. next morning after being on the go for almost twenty-four hours. The others decided to bivouac for the night at the rocks of the Faulberg, returning to the hotel in time for breakfast next day. The cost to each climber had been a mere fifty francs sixteen centimes, even allowing for the fact that, as was common in those early days, extra men and provisions had been virtually forced on them.

The Finsteraarhorn ascent was typical of the routes being tackled by strong parties of the day. In this particular instance, however, there was a special aftermath. On their way to the climb William Mathews had broached the subject of an Alpine Club to Kennedy, who seized on the idea at once. The idea had been born in a letter from Mathews to the Rev. F.J.A. Hort earlier in the year but 'the infant's cradle was rocked by Kennedy on the summit of the Finsteraarhorn.'[4]

The Alpine Club held its first meeting on December 22, 1857. There were twenty members of whom eleven turned up at the inaugural meeting at Ashley's Hotel in Covent Garden.[5] Kennedy was in the chair and one of the first things the members did was to throw out the proposed rule that membership should only be open to those who had ascended to the top of a peak of 13,000 feet or more. It was pointed out that to stroll up an easy mountain like the Cima di Jazzi, which is over 13,000 feet, was hardly as meritorious as a dour struggle with a tougher peak of lesser height. This important concession showed that members were intent on a *climbing* club; that height alone was not important. Similarly, the idea that it should be a cosy dining club ('The cost of the dinner, exclusive of wine, shall not exceed Half-a-guinea') was soon abandoned in favour of regular monthly meetings at which important papers were read, dealing with mountain exploration. Within two years membership rose to eighty and increased steadily thereafter.

In 1859 a collection of some of the papers read before the Club was published by Original Member and publisher William Longman under the title *Peaks, Passes and Glaciers* and was an immediate success. It rapidly went through four editions and sold 2500 copies. Three years later two further volumes were issued, but such was the pace of mountain exploration that it became obvious something on a more regular basis was required and so in March 1863 the *Alpine Journal* appeared for the first time. The journal was quarterly and so able to keep members relatively up to date on affairs. With considerable foresight the editors interpreted the journal's title to include the whole of world mountaineering.

Both Club and journal were the first of their kind. Partly because of this, partly through the expertise of the leading members and their excellent standing in the society from which they came, the Alpine Club became a dominant force in the early years of the sport, the arbiter of all that was good and pure in mountain matters. Members proudly took to signing themselves 'AC' in Alpine hotel registers and a murmur of approval would run round the dining room when the hero put in an appearance. In the eyes of the general public he became a *type*, easily recognisable when introduced into popular literature, as he soon was.

The public's view of the Club and the Club's view of itself were rather different. But they were undoubtedly the experts in a new and exciting pastime. It was a position they tried to hold on to for far too long for, when the rest of the world caught up with them, they looked rather pompous, a king without his clothes.

That situation lay more than half a century in the future, but the seeds were sown from the start. It was inconceivable that a club formed by Cambridge intellectuals, who could afford to spend several weeks of each year in the Alps, could be anything but reflective of a narrow stratum of society. The ordinary working man could not afford to travel to the Alps, and by the time he could the Club was too set in its ways.

The Austrian Alpine Club was formed in 1862 and other European countries followed suit during the next decade or so. They were very different in concept from the British original, being large organisations open to all, organised into local sections and owning mountain refuges where their members could stay for a nominal sum. By 1887 the Alpine Club had 475 members. The Austro-German club (they had combined in 1874) had 18,020 members, the French 5321, the Italians 3669 and the Swiss 2607. By that year too the Alpine Club had contributed the princely sum of £15 towards the Alpine huts which their members so freely used, whereas the European clubs had contributed £40,585.

It was not until after the Second World War that the Alpine Club began to shed its blinkers and enter the world of modern climbing. It never became a *national* club like its European counterparts, despite some recent attempts to force it in that direction; the most fundamental change was the admission of women to membership in 1974. The sense of awe in which the Alpine Club was once held has long since gone, to be replaced by one of affection.

But in the beginning it was a very powerful body indeed. Its members tamed the Alps and shaped the future of mountaineering.

In the ten years following on Alfred Wills's ascent of the Wetterhorn 140 Alpine peaks were climbed for the first time, almost half of them by British climbers, most of whom formed the new Alpine Club. In 1855 that long-standing problem, the highest point of Monte Rosa called Dufourspitze, and the second highest summit in the Alps, was climbed by two of the Smyth brothers, Christopher and James Grenville, together with Charles Hudson, John Birkbeck and E.J. Stevenson. The two Smyths, with a third brother, Edmund, had almost reached the highest point the previous year but stopped at the slightly lower Ostspitze. They did, however, climb the Strahlhorn (4190 m) which, apart from the Breithorn, was the first of the big Zermatt mountains to be ascended.[6]

In 1859 another long-standing problem was solved. Hudson with G.C. Joad, E. Headland and G.C. Hodgkinson climbed the Bosses ridge of Mont Blanc from the Dôme du Goûter to the summit, by what is now the ordinary route from Grands Mulets, whilst two years later Leslie Stephen and Francis Tuckett climbed the whole ridge from the Aiguille du Goûter onwards 'thus achieving the undertaking commenced by Saussure and his companions seventy-six years before'.

Stephen's route up Mont Blanc and the Smyths' route up Monte Rosa are today amongst the most popular ascents in the Alps, and snow climbs of no great difficulty. The first ascensionists found them easy too and wondered why the early pioneers had not triumphed. The answer is that between the two lay a quantum leap in attitude.

The greatest interest, however, lay in the new peaks ascended, most of which were of a higher order of difficulty. In 1861 John Tyndall conquered the formidable Weisshorn (4505 m) and the following year T.S. Kennedy and W. Wigram climbed the Dent Blanche (4357 m) whilst J.L. Davies and J.W. Hayward climbed that most difficult of Mischabel peaks, the Täschhorn (4491 m).

In 1863 F.C. Grove and party climbed the Dent d'Hérens (4171 m) and the following year he was with Stephen on the first ascent of the Zinal Rothorn (4221 m). These examples are all taken from the mountains around Zermatt, which were rapidly acquiring the same status as those of the Oberland in the eyes of the thrusting young, but the Oberland was not neglected either (the Eiger, 1858; Aletschhorn and Bietschhorn, 1859) nor were other areas to the west and east – Monte Viso, 1861; the Ecrins, 1864. The list goes on, but enough has been said to show that the pot was wide open and being plundered right, left and centre. No wonder it was called the Golden Age.

A few of the more adventurous spirits, like Hudson and E.S. Kennedy, occasionally climbed without guides but by and large the Golden Age came about through a symbiotic relationship between the Alpine Club and a small corpus of élite guides.

As early as the twelfth century there were men willing to conduct travellers over the snowbound passes of the winter alps, or if need be, rescue them. The *marones* or guides of the St Bernard monastery with their famous dogs were only the best known of several such. The first known example of guides taking a visitor to the top of a mountain, however, is in 1588 when the Seigneur de Villamont climbed Rochemelon. His two guides provided him with crampons, carried the provisions and physically helped him up the mountain. No doubt there were others in the years which followed: chamois-hunters, shepherds, crystal-seekers and smugglers who took time out to earn a few extra francs.

Because of Mont Blanc and the influence of the Geneva school Chamonix had enough active men by 1823 to form a Corporation des Guides. The Oberland followed in 1856, Pontresina in 1861 and others thereafter. These organisations laid down rules which varied from place to place but whose main function was to standardise tariffs for the various ascents.

They were in effect trade unions with closed shops, which led inevitably to an abuse of their power. Chamonix was particularly notorious: four guides had to be taken on Mont Blanc at 100 francs each (equivalent to rather more than a month's wages for an English farm labourer), guides had to be hired on a rota basis and guides imported from other centres were resented and often abused.

There can be little doubt that in the early days at least, climbers were rooked, and not only in Chamonix. Some guides were employees of hotels, where the manager made all the necessary arrangements for the climbers (including ample provisioning) and paid the guides what he thought fit. Hired individually a guide's wages was usually eight francs per day.

The ascent of the Finsteraarhorn in 1857, mentioned previously, gives an excellent example of the sort of pressures put on climbers. The five Englishmen thought they could manage very well with the three guides they had with them – three of the best available – but the manager of the hotel on the Eggishorn persuaded them to take two local men (in his employ) at fifty francs each, plus three porters. The provisions amounted to seventy-four francs but it transpired that this was just for the climbers; the guides said they required 'only a little bread and meat' – which promptly added another forty francs to the bill. The climbers noted wryly that some of the 'bread and meat' was carried in bottles.

We should not be surprised at all this. To the peasants of the Oberland or Valais, often living at subsistence level, the English travellers must have seemed incredibly rich, well able to afford a little extra. At first, almost any

Englishman was referred to as 'an English milord', which indicates how the locals attributed this difference in wealth.

Even so, very few guides became wealthy in Victorian times. A popular guide, always in demand, might be slightly better off than his neighbours – an extra cow or two, more home comforts, an extended chalet perhaps – but often they were burdened with debts and mortgages. Guides died, leaving their families in straitened circumstances, dependent (if they were lucky) on charity from former employers. Not until the 1880s was an insurance scheme introduced by the European clubs.

According to Coolidge about one in ten of the healthy boys in an Alpine village might expect to become guides, though it was easier for the sons of existing guides to follow the family tradition and indeed, the same family names can be seen in the guides' lists of present-day Chamonix or Zermatt as were present a century or more ago. At first no qualifications were expected beyond strength and a knowledge of the area but in the 1870s a simple written and practical examination was introduced which the would-be guide took when he reached twenty. He was then given a *Führerbuch* in which clients could write brief testimonials.[7]

The average standard of ability was abysmally low. Many guides would do no more than lead clients on valley walks or simple glacier crossings. Coolidge recalls how one of his earliest guides recoiled in horror at the suggestion that they should attempt to cross the Strahlegg, a simple glacier pass. 'I never undertake such dangerous expeditions!' the guide said.[8] Even at the end of the century C.E. Mathews claimed that of the three hundred guides then in Chamonix 'those who could be relied upon in a grave emergency could be counted almost on the fingers of one hand.'[9]

From amongst this press of mediocrity came a relatively small group of outstanding guides whose names figure prominently in the literature of the period. In 1887, C.D. Cunningham, wishing to perpetuate the achievements of the great guides, wrote to eight leading members of the Alpine Club enclosing a sort of ballot as to which guides deserved recognition in this manner. Twenty-two names of living guides were forthcoming, plus another thirteen names of guides who were deceased. Cunningham published short biographies of them all in *The Pioneers of the Alps*, together with splendid portraits photographed by Captain Abney. The list is flawed in so far as it only included men from the Valais, Oberland and Chamonix, and there were certainly a few outstanding guides in other areas, and of course, a few later names would need to be added, but on the whole it represents the cream of guiding during the Golden Age.[10]

Most famous of all the guides was Christian Almer of Grindelwald, the 'unsurpassed and unsurpassable' as Coolidge described him. He it was who had chased the Wills party on the Wetterhorn in 1854, carrying his personal totem of a fir tree, and uniting with them in mutual triumph. The account of that affair in Wills's book made Almer a celebrity and assured him of success as a guide. But the little shepherd – he was only 5 ft 2 ins and like many small men a bundle of talkative energy – had no intention of resting on such easy-won laurels. He was a genuine lover of climbing for its own sake and made first ascents of the Mönch, Eiger, Fiescherhorn, Les Ecrins, Aiguille Verte and many more first-rate peaks and passes in the company of some of the best climbers of the day. He was also one of the earliest advocates of winter climbing, making an ascent of the Wetterhorn and Jungfrau in 1873. In 1896 he and his wife celebrated their golden wedding anniversary by climbing the Wetterhorn – in tribute, no doubt, to the peak which had given him fame and fortune. Almer had five sons, all of whom became first-class guides.[11]

Almer's only rival in general acclaim was Melchior Anderegg – *le grand Melchior* – a genial giant from the Oberland, a woodcarver whose work was exhibited at a London gallery and one of nature's gentlemen. Unlike Almer, who was fifty-three years old before he even saw the sea (and then it was the Mediterranean seen from a peak in the Maritime Alps) Melchior visited England as a welcome guest in the houses of his rich patrons. Lucy Walker seems to have fallen hopelessly in love with him, though Melchior was a married man and Victorian proprieties were observed. Lucy never married.[12]

Melchior's first ascents were less numerous than those of Almer but perhaps more impressive, including the Dent d'Hérens and Monte Disgrazia. He led the first ascent of the Bosses Ridge of Mont Blanc in 1859 and the first ascent of the Brenva Spur in 1865.

Almer and Melchior were together on the difficult crossing of the Col de la Tour Noire with Adams Reilly and H.B. George in 1863 – an expedition made in mistake for the easy Col d'Argentière, and which lasted for thirty-one hours. H.B. George wrote: 'Rivals in reputation, they yet work together like brothers . . . either of them may be regarded as the very standard of excellence to which all other guides are to be compared.'[13]

Rivals they certainly were. Almer made sure of the *second* ascent of the Brenva Spur in 1870, and when Melchior heard that Almer intended to take Miss Brevoort up the Matterhorn in 1871, thus making the first ascent by a woman, he quickly took Lucy Walker and her father to the top. Lucy thus became the first woman to climb the mountain and her father, who was sixty-three, was probably the oldest person to have made the ascent at that time. Almer, not to be so easily outdone, promptly traversed the mountain with Miss Brevoort: the first woman's traverse of the peak and only the fourth overall.[14]

The leading guides rarely needed to tout for custom because they were booked up for season after season, often by the same climbers or their friends. In the fateful year of 1865, for example, Almer had to leave Edward Whymper on July 7 because of a previous engagement to another party.

The Matterhorn tragedy occurred a week later – it is tantalising to speculate on what the story might have been had the two men remained together.

In his own village, amongst his contemporaries, a guide acquired status according to the constancy and quality of his employer. Best of all was a regular engagement with a member of the Alpine Club, or at least an *Englander*, because they were generally regarded (not altogether accurately) as the wealthiest and best climbers. Failing that, a regular client of any nationality was desirable and a guide who had lost his *Herr* was regarded with pity – or worse. One can imagine how village tongues wagged in such cases.

There is no way of telling how many guides never made a name for themselves simply because they never had the chance, but there must have been some, for chance played a large part. It was pure chance, for instance, that Thomas Hinchcliff, at the start of his great Alpine career, should enquire for a guide at the Grimsel inn and be introduced to Melchior Anderegg, whom he later recommended to Leslie Stephen and so launched Melchior on his meteoric career. Every guide needed the stimulus of a first-rate *Herr* to provide the expeditions which would make him famous.

The climbers planned the strategy and the guides undertook the tactics. They selected the line to follow and did the hard work of step-cutting. Sometimes they would refuse to undertake a climb if they thought it too difficult or dangerous: 'It goes, Melchior,' said a climber, examining the unclimbed Zmutt Ridge of the Matterhorn through a spy-glass. 'Yes it goes,' said Melchior, 'but I'm not going.'[15]

On the mountain the guides determined the success or failure of the expedition, for no climber would go against the wishes of his guide. It was this attitude which probably cost Professor Tyndall the first ascent of the Matterhorn in 1862, when his guide J.J. Bennen decided to retreat for no apparent reason. It is best summed up by little Peter Bohren, the Glacier Wolf, who replied to a client who questioned his judgement: 'Herr, you are master in the valley: I am master here.'[16]

The Victorians built up their guides into a race of supermen and for many years it was confidently asserted that no amateur could ever expect to be as good a climber as a good guide. To some it was just a question of fitness – a businessman who went to the Alps for a mere six weeks each year could not expect to be as fit as a guide who spent his whole life there; others looked for special physical attributes – George Wherry tried to prove that guides had specially adapted feet.

Certainly a special relationship grew up between climbers and their regular guides that transcended the employer–employee relationship of the nineteenth century. Some became family friends: the Wills family and Auguste Balmat for example, the Walkers and Melchior Anderegg, or Coolidge and the Almer family. The reasons behind this would make an interesting sociological study. Did it arise through common dangers shared? Was it the respect of youth for the older man in an age when such respect was normal and guides were often ten years or so older than the amateur on his first outing? In the Victorian panoply of service only one other person gained the same sort of affection, and that was Nanny.

Many of the leading climbers did climb guideless from time to time, but it was generally frowned upon. Those who always climbed guideless were very few; most notably perhaps were the Parker brothers[17] from Liverpool who crossed a number of passes in 1860 and in 1865 climbed the Wildstrubel and Finsteraarhorn, and A.G. Girdlestone[18] who, as an undergraduate, climbed the Wetterhorn and a number of other difficult peaks of the day. Towards the end of the nineteenth century the move to guideless climbing accelerated but, even so, guided ascents were more common until the First World War.

Guideless climbing is the norm today, in the Alps as elsewhere. This is partly because of the expense but principally because making the climb, planning and executing it, is seen to be part of the fun. Zermatt guides claim they could get a cow up the Matterhorn – so who wants to be a cow? Nevertheless, every decent-sized Alpine village has its Bureau des Guides, where there are men willing to take clients up the neighbouring peaks or even accept long-term engagements. They are enormously better qualified than their predecessors, for nowadays being a guide involves passing rigorous practical and theoretical examinations. Their activities are more varied too: they often run climbing schools, lead treks to distant mountain ranges and in winter, act as ski instructors. In 1980 Martine Rolland, of Chamonix, became the first woman Alpine guide.

The Golden Age came to an end in 1865. Not only were more new peaks climbed that year than in any previously (or since, for that matter) but two events mark it out as something rather special.

Up to that date nobody had succeeded in climbing Mont Blanc from the Italian side, which is much steeper than the French. On this side the mountain presents a formidable spectacle: huge walls of rock and ice broken here and there by monumental ridges, armed with pinnacles like a shark's teeth, some of which are big enough to be accounted peaks in their own right. The only possible access into the heart of this icy wilderness seemed to be the Brenva Glacier which led up to the southern wall on the mountain, the Brenva Face, but even this was not easy.

In 1863 a large party which included A.W. Moore and three of the best guides of the day, Almer, Melchior and Perren, went to Courmayeur specifically to reconnoitre the Brenva Glacier, but when they saw it (presumably for the first time) Melchior and Perren condemned the plan as 'a wretched piece of folly' and even Almer was less than keen, so the enterprise was abandoned. But in the following year when Moore and Almer were on Mont Blanc they took the opportunity of looking down the face onto the Brenva Glacier. What Moore saw – gentle slopes – raised again his hopes of a route from the south, though because of foreshortening he could not see how to get from the lower glacier to the gentle upper névé. Nevertheless, working on the principle that what the eye doesn't see the heart doesn't grieve over, he concluded that a way must exist.

On July 13, 1865, a strong party gathered at Courmayeur to climb Mont Blanc by the Brenva Face, 'or the reason why it could not be done definitely ascertained'. The two Walkers were there, Frank and Horace, father and son members of a prominent Liverpool business family. Frank was fifty-seven years old, but a strong climber. His son Horace had taken part in the Dauphiné campaign conducted by Whymper and Moore the previous year and in the current season, before coming to the Brenva, had with Moore made first ascents of Piz Roseg, Pigne d'Arolla and Ober Gabelhorn. George Mathews, of the famous Birmingham climbing family, was also present, as were the two guides Melchior and Jakob Anderegg. And, of course, there was Moore; a senior official at the India Office, and one of the best climbers of the day.

On July 14 the party set off with two porters for the Brenva Glacier. They found the going surprisingly easy; the porters seemed to know the way and led them along a path below the great ridge which bounds the glacier on the east. In this way they were able to avoid the lower icefall, where avalanches were thundering down, and eventually gain a small rock platform in which they bivouacked for the night.

Ahead of them they could see that the glacier was divided into two by a long snowy spur which seemed to lead towards the Mur de la Côte between Mont Blanc and Mont Maudit. Melchior, who had gone ahead to reconnoitre as the others settled in for the evening, came back with reports that a difficult icefall lay between them and the Brenva Spur. 'Such an icefall as I have never before seen!' he declared. He suggested that next day they should descend about a thousand feet to try for another way round the obstacle, but the others decided that a direct approach should be tried first.

They knew their man. Melchior had a reputation for caution and he had not changed his opinion of the Brenva formed two years previously. He thought the whole affair a dangerous fiasco and had spent much time 'indulging in observations of a Cassandra-like character'. These had no effect on the party and especially not on his cousin Jakob Anderegg, who 'notwithstanding his almost idolatrous respect and admiration for his cousin, ventured to deride his fears and chaff him generally in a free, not to say irreverent manner'. Jakob was prepared to risk more than Melchior – a factor which had an important bearing on the morrow.

Nowadays, climbers have worked out an entirely different approach to the Brenva Spur, but the pioneers found that Melchior had scarcely exaggerated the scale of the icefall. Nevertheless it went fairly easily and by 5.30 a.m. the party reached the foot of the spur. Soon they had climbed the rocks and after a brief halt for breakfast, continued to the top of a sharp pointed peak. Here they received a nasty surprise:

> On reaching it, the apparent peak proved not to be a peak at all, but the extremity of the narrowest and most formidable ice arête I ever saw, which extended almost on a level for an uncomfortably long distance. Looking back by the light of our subsequent success, I have always considered it a providential circumstance that, at this moment, Jakob, and not Melchior, was leading the party. In saying this, I shall not for an instant be suspected of any imputation upon Melchior's courage. But in him that virtue is combined to perfection with the equally necessary one of prudence, while he shares the objection which nearly all guides have to taking upon themselves, without discussion, responsibility in positions of doubt. Had he been in front, I believe that, on seeing the nature of the work before us, we should have halted and discussed the propriety of proceeding; and I believe further that, as the result of that discussion, our expedition would have then and there come to an end. Now in Jakob, with courage as faultless as Melchior's, and physical powers even superior, the virtue of prudence is conspicuous chiefly from its absence; and, on coming to this ugly place, it never for an instant occurred to him that we might object to go on, or consider the object in view not worth the risk which must be inevitably run. He therefore went calmly on without so much as turning to see what we thought of it, while I do not suppose that it entered into the head of any one of us spontaneously to suggest a retreat.

They had the misfortune to come upon the ridge when it was ice and not snow as it often is. It was extraordinarily narrow and sheer for hundreds of feet on either side. There was no possible protection to be had from their ice axes, or anything else:

> The space for walking was, at first, about the breadth of the top of an ordinary wall, in which Jakob cut holes for the feet. Being last in the line I could see little of what was coming until I was close upon it, and was therefore considerably startled on seeing the men in front suddenly abandon the upright position, which, in spite of the insecurity of the steps and difficulty of preserving the balance, had been hitherto maintained, and sit down *à cheval*. The ridge had narrowed to a knife edge, and for a few yards it was utterly impossible to advance in any other way. The foremost men soon stood

up again, but when I was about to follow their example Melchior insisted emphatically on my not doing so, but remaining seated. Regular steps could no longer be cut, but Jakob, as he went along, simply sliced off the top of the ridge, making thus a slippery pathway, along which those behind crept, moving one foot carefully after the other. As for me, I worked myself along with my hands in an attitude safer, perhaps, but considerably more uncomfortable, and, as I went, could not help occasionally speculating, with an odd feeling of amusement, as to what would be the result if any of the party should chance to slip over on either side, – what the rest would do, – whether throw themselves over on the other side or not, – and if so, what would happen then. Fortunately the occasion for the solution of this curious problem did not arise, and at 9.30 we reached the end of the arête, where it merged in the long slopes of broken névé, over which our way was next to lie. As we looked back along our perilous path, it was hard to repress a shudder, and I think the dominant feeling of every man was one of wonder how the passage had been effected without accident. One good result, however, was to banish from Melchior's mind the last traces of doubt as to our ultimate success, his reply to our anxious enquiry whether he thought we should get up, being, 'We must, for we cannot go back.' In thus speaking he probably said rather more than he meant, but the fact will serve to show that I have not exaggerated the difficulty we had overcome.[19]

Beyond the ice arête they found themselves on a steep snow slope which occupied them for the next two hours and a half until the way was barred by a rock wall. They realised that the spur had taken them further left than they had envisaged – more towards the actual summit of Mont Blanc than the col between it and Mont Maudit. So they traversed right, but discovered that they could never reach the col direct because between it and the spur lay steep walls of rock and ice plunging down into the upper bay of the Brenva Glacier.

They had to go straight up, though that did not seem inviting either. A line of séracs, which seemed liable to fall at any moment and sweep them off the mountain like crumbs off a tablecloth, stretched menacingly across their path. It was a place to be avoided, yet could not be avoided. They *should* not go on by all the canons of safe mountaineering, yet they *could* not go back, neither could they go to right or left.

Melchior, now leading, attacked the séracs at the most likely place and, after a desperate struggle, succeeded in overcoming the ice wall. Nothing fell; the ice remained secure.

It was the last obstacle. Another ice wall towered above but they were able to avoid it. On the gentler upper slopes (the very ones that Moore had seen the previous summer) they were able at last to traverse to the right, to the foot of the Mur de la Côte. It was 1.20 p.m.

By 3.10 they were on the summit of Mont Blanc and by 10.30 p.m. back in Chamonix – a twenty-hour day.

Moore's party had won a magnificent victory. It lifted climbing out of the era of mere peak bagging. It was the first route on the Brenva Face and there wasn't to be another for sixty-two years.[20]

Moore's triumph on the Old Brenva was the crowning achievement of the Golden Age. It should have heralded a new, even brighter dawn, but the day before there had been an accident on the Matterhorn.

Edward Whymper's Alpine career had begun by chance in 1860, when he was commissioned to do a series of wood engravings for William Longman, the publisher, on Alpine subjects. Born in London, son of a wood engraver, he had considerable artistic skill allied to a keen intellect. In everyday affairs of business or conversation, he got on quite well with his contemporaries and yet he seems to have been incapable of close relationships or lasting friendships. Even as a boy he had no friends; he was always the eager outsider, hovering anxiously on the edge of a group. His defence was a rigid self-discipline – but when he did gain a friend, he felt that joy of heart that only the friendless can know. If such a friend eventually proved treacherous the result could be traumatic.

Whymper's boyhood diary reveals him already set in his ways. As his biographer, F.S. Smythe wrote: 'To read this diary of the boy of fifteen, then to turn the next minute to the diary of the man of sixty is to bridge no gap, except in time. This atrophy which set in so early was not an atrophy of intellect but of spirit.'

Yet he was stirred by ambition: 'I had ideas floating in my head that I should one day turn out some great person.' Fame was the spur – but to what? He was excited by the polar adventures of men like Ross and Franklin and had ideas of visiting the Arctic, and to this end he thought that Longman's Alpine commission might serve a purpose in familiarising him with snow and ice. Instead, it was to change his whole life and affect the course of mountaineering.

That first season of 1860 was one of exploration for Whymper. He did no real mountaineering, but he managed to visit the most important areas of the Western and Central Alps and he met a number of well-known climbers. In the following season he returned to make the first English ascent of Pelvoux in the Dauphiné Alps, and his first attempt on the Matterhorn.

The Matterhorn was chosen simply because it and the Weisshorn were the two highest unclimbed peaks left in the Alps at that date and Whymper was out for a *coup* of the first magnitude; a climb that would put him

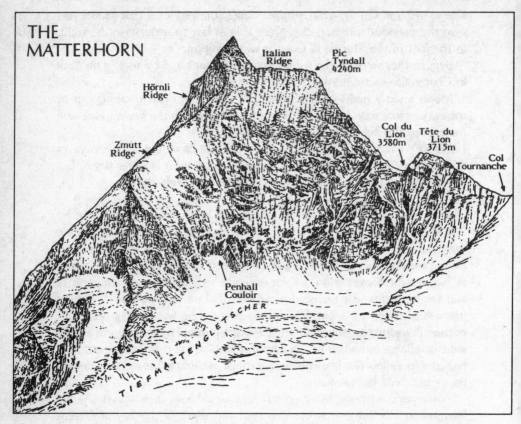

THE
MATTERHORN

Italian
Ridge

Pic
Tyndall
4240m

Hörnli
Ridge

Col du
Lion
3580m

Tête du
Lion
3715m

Zmutt
Ridge

Col
Tournanche

Penhall
Couloir

TIEFMATTENGLETSCHER

immediately in the front rank of alpinists. The fact that he was totally inexperienced never crossed his mind – nobody could ever accuse Whymper of humility. However, John Tyndall forestalled him on the Weisshorn, so Whymper turned to the Matterhorn, a mountain he had once described as 'a sugarloaf with its head knocked on one side'.

The Matterhorn (4478 m/14,690 ft) is a pointed obelisk of rock and ice standing astride the border between Switzerland and Italy in the Pennine Alps. It looks at its best from the village of Zermatt on the Swiss side: three sharp ridges climbing steeply to a point, seemingly impregnable. From Breuil on the Italian side the mountain has the appearance of a couchant lion, and looks far less steep. No other mountains crowd in on it. It gives the illusion of standing alone, majestic in its isolation.

When Whymper came to the Matterhorn in 1861 there had been few previous attempts on the mountain. Some locals had scrambled part-way up the Italian Ridge on several occasions in the previous few years; the Parkers had made their astonishing unguided attempts from Zermatt without success and in 1860 John Tyndall with Vaughan Hawkins had climbed up the Italian Ridge as far as a prominent feature known as the Great Tower.

Whymper, led by an inferior (and unknown) guide from the Oberland, failed utterly on the Italian Ridge.

Early in July of the following year Whymper made another attempt on the Italian Ridge, accompanied by R.J.S. Macdonald, the young clerk from the Colonial Office with whom he had climbed Pelvoux the previous year, and two good guides, Johann zum Taugwald and Johann Kronig. They camped on the ridge at about 12,000 feet but next day a storm prevented them going further, so they retired to Breuil. Here they met Jean-Antoine Carrel.

'Jean-Antoine Carrel, attracted by rumours, had come up to the inn during our absence,' wrote Whymper later. 'Carrel clearly considered the mountain a kind of *preserve*, and regarded our late attempt as an act of *poaching.*'

The seeds of the ultimate tragedy lie in that one sentence – and in the characters of the two men, Whymper and Carrel.

At thirty-three, Jean-Antoine Carrel was eleven years older than Whymper and a tall, lean man of soldierly bearing and stern features. He had fought in the war of independence against Austria and was, first and last, a patriot. He wanted the Matterhorn to be climbed by Italians for Italy, though this was something he kept to himself. He lived in Valtournanche, a village a little way down the valley from Breuil, and though at this time he was not a guide in the proper sense, he had tried to climb the Matterhorn on at least two occasions, with his uncle Jean-Jacques Carrel and other villagers. In this he was like the Oberlanders – Almer on the Wetterhorn, for instance – but with this difference: his passion was for Italy, rather than any financial gain. He cared little for money and the coming of the English, welcomed in other Alpine villages, brought only apprehension to the man whom Whymper described as 'the cock of Valtournanche'.

Whymper was fascinated by this rough soldier with his coarse barrack-room language. He trusted him implicitly and undoubtedly held him in special affection. It is doubtful whether Carrel saw their relationship in the same light, though one senses some sort of bond between them, perhaps, like that of the two strong men who stood face to face in Kipling's 'The Ballad of East and West'.

In 1862 and 1863 they made several unsuccessful attempts on the Matterhorn together, though in fact Whymper always did better when Carrel was not present. Was Carrel holding him back? Whymper certainly thought so later, at least momentarily. And there was the curious incident of John Tyndall's second attempt on the mountain in 1862 when, with the guides J.J. Bennen and Anton Walter, and with Carrel as one of the porters, they reached the foot of the final peak. The Matterhorn was within their grasp, but the last few feet looked formidable. 'Shall we go on?' Tyndall demanded of his guides – but Bennen was never a man to take a decision and Walter hesitated in deference to Bennen, so Tyndall put the question to Carrel. 'Ask your guides,' Carrel replied tartly. They retreated. Was this pique, because he was not put in command of an expedition to *his* mountain? Perhaps. Or perhaps it was more than that: perhaps it was the unhelpful response of a patriot.[21]

The next two seasons – 1864 and 1865 – saw Edward Whymper playing a major role in the climax of the Golden Age. With companions like Moore, Horace Walker and Adams Reilly and great guides like Almer and Croz he stormed through the Western Alps in a series of major first ascents, the like of which had not been seen before.[22] He even tried the Matterhorn by a new route on the East Face, with Almer, Croz and Franz Biener but they retreated in the face of heavy stonefall. 'Why don't you try to go up a mountain which *can* be ascended?' Almer demanded, reflecting the view of most guides that the Matterhorn was impossible.

But a bizarre series of events, moving with the inevitability of a Greek tragedy towards disaster, had already begun. In 1863 the Italian Alpine Club was founded in Turin, the brainchild of Quintino Sella, Minister of Finance, a man of immense power and influence. It was decided that the foundation should be marked by some outstanding mountaineering achievement – and what greater achievement could there be than the first ascent of the mighty Matterhorn? Sella sent for Jean-Antoine Carrel.

When Carrel heard Sella's plans he was overjoyed. At last his long ambition seemed about to be fulfilled; to lead an Italian party to the summit of the Matterhorn. The man chosen to lead the climb was a young friend of Sella's, Felice Giordano, who reconnoitred the mountain in 1864 and made more detailed plans with Carrel. An ascent was planned for 1865. In all these matters, Sella made Carrel swear to secrecy.

In July 1865 Whymper and Giordano arrived in Valtournanche within days of each other. Carrel at first promised to help Whymper, but then cried off.

> Jean-Antoine then said that he should not be able to serve me after Tuesday the 11th, as he was engaged to travel 'with a family of distinction' in the valley of Aosta. 'And Cæsar?' 'And Cæsar also.' 'Why did you not say this before?' 'Because,' said he, 'it was not settled. The engagement is of long standing, but *the day* was not fixed. When I got back to Val Tournanche on Friday night, after leaving you, I found a letter naming the day.' I could not object to the answer; but the prospect of being left guideless was provoking. They went up, and I down, the valley.
>
> The sick man declared that he was better, though the exertion of saying as much tumbled him over on to the floor in a fainting fit. He was badly in want of medicine, and I tramped down to

Chatillon to get it. It was late before I returned to Val Tournanche, for the weather was tempestuous, and rain fell in torrents. A figure passed me under the church porch. '*Qui vive?*' 'Jean-Antoine.' 'I thought you were in Breil.' 'No, sir: when the storms came on I knew we should not start to-night, and so came down to sleep here.' 'Ha, Carrel!' I said; 'this is a great bore. If to-morrow is not fine we shall not be able to do anything together. I have sent away my guides, relying on you; and now you are going to leave me to travel with the party of ladies. That work is not fit for *you* (he smiled, I supposed at the implied compliment); can't you send some one else instead?' 'No, monsieur. I am sorry, but my word is pledged. I should like to accompany you, but I can't break my engagement.' By this time we had arrived at the inn door. 'Well, it is no fault of yours. Come presently with Cæsar, and have some wine.' They came, and we sat up till midnight, recounting our old adventures, in the inn of Val Tournanche.

The weather continued bad upon the 10th, and I returned to Breil. The two Carrels were again hovering about the above mentioned chalet, and I bade them adieu. In the evening the sick man crawled up, a good deal better; but his was the only arrival. The Monday crowd did not cross the Théodule, on account of the continued storms. The inn was lonely. I went to bed early, and was awoke the next morning by the invalid inquiring if I had 'heard the news.' 'No; what news?' 'Why,' said he, 'a large party of guides went off this morning to try the Matterhorn, taking with them a mule laden with provisions.'

I went to the door, and with a telescope saw the party upon the lower slopes of the mountain. Favre, the landlord, stood by. 'What is all this about?' I inquired, 'who is the leader of this party?' 'Carrel.' 'What! Jean-Antoine?' 'Yes; Jean-Antoine.' 'Is Cæsar there too?' 'Yes, he is there.' Then I saw in a moment that I had been bamboozled and humbugged; and learned, bit by bit, that the affair had been arranged long beforehand. The start on the 6th had been for a preliminary reconnaissance; the mule, that I passed, was conveying stores for the attack; the 'family of distinction' was Signor F. Giordano, who had just despatched the party to facilitate the way to the summit, and who, when the facilitation was completed, was to be taken to the top along with Signor Sella![23]

Though these words were written some years after the event one can still sense the stab to the heart that Whymper felt at Carrel's 'treachery'. He had been let down by someone he trusted as a friend, and the pain of that hurt as much as the possible loss of the mountain. But the prime armour of the friendless is self-sufficiency and Whymper was not a man to take things lying down. He immediately made plans to climb the mountain without Carrel's aid.

Giordano had not gone on the mountain with the guides and he was obviously alarmed at Whymper's reaction. He wrote to Sella, 'I have tried to keep everything a secret, but that fellow, whose life seems to depend on the Matterhorn, is here, suspiciously prying into everything. I have taken all the competent men away from him and yet he is so enamoured of this mountain that he may go up with others and make a scene. He is here, in this hotel, and I try to avoid speaking to him.'[24]

Fate now began to move the pieces across the checker board with deadly play. On the morning of Carrel's defection a young Englishman arrived at Breuil across the Théodule Pass from Zermatt. Lord Francis Douglas was eighteen years old and starting to make a name for himself in climbing, having just made the second ascent of the difficult Ober Gabelhorn. With him as guide was Joseph Taugwalder of Zermatt, and in the course of conversation Taugwalder revealed that his father, Old Peter Taugwalder, had reconnoitred the Hörnli Ridge of the Matterhorn and thought it might be climbed. Here was the half-chance that Whymper had hoped for: he joined forces with Douglas and together they returned to Zermatt, where Old Peter agreed to lead an attempt on the Matterhorn.

No sooner had this been arranged than Whymper came across the great guide Michel Croz,[25] with whom he had climbed earlier in the season. Croz, it appeared, had been engaged by the Rev. Charles Hudson – for an attempt on the Matterhorn! Whymper must have been alarmed at this news, for Hudson was one of the best climbers of the day and Croz one of the best guides. It looked as though the mountain was slipping out of his grasp, what with Carrel on the Italian Ridge and the powerful Hudson–Croz combination on the Hörnli.

But a compromise was reached. Hudson agreed to join forces with Whymper and Douglas, provided he could bring along a young friend called Douglas Hadow. 'I consider he is a sufficiently good man to go with us,' he replied in answer to Whymper's questions as to Hadow's experience.

On July 13, 1865, at 5.30 on a brilliant and perfectly cloudless morning the following party set out from Zermatt: Edward Whymper, Charles Hudson, Lord Francis Douglas, Douglas Hadow, Michel Croz, Old Peter Taugwalder, Young Peter Taugwalder and Joseph Taugwalder. The two latter were Old Peter's sons acting as porters and Joseph was only to accompany them as far as the first bivouac.[26]

It was a large, unwieldy party to attempt a first ascent on a serious climb like the Matterhorn. Its mixture of experience and inexperience was horrifying for such a venture. Moreover, out of misplaced respect for each other's sensibilities as 'famous climbers' neither Whymper nor Hudson would assume overall command. The two chief guides, Croz and Taug-walder, spoke French and German respectively and could not communicate with each other. There was every ingredient for a recipe of disaster.

And what of the individuals in this strange group? Leaving out the two young Taugwalders there is a query against each of them except Croz and Lord Francis. Whymper was consumed with ambition, anger and frustration at what had happened. Old Peter (he was actually forty-five at the time) was a mediocre guide whose performance had been criticised on several occasions by experienced mountaineers. Douglas Hadow was a strong nine-teen-year-old, but in his first Alpine season. He had made a couple of minor ascents and a very rapid ascent of Mont Blanc, where according to one witness, he floundered about, falling into crevasses. Though one might get away with this on a snow plod like Mont Blanc, it will not do on the Matterhorn. He was the ultimate fatal flaw.

Perhaps Charles Hudson[27] saw in Hadow a younger version of himself, for he too was prodigiously strong. At thirty-seven Hudson, who was regarded by his contemporaries as one of the best climbers of the day, did seem irresponsible with youngsters in his charge. He had attempted the difficult Col de Miage with John Birkbeck Jnr in 1861 – and Birkbeck had slid 1800 feet, lucky to survive.

Despite its forbidding appearance the lower part of the Hörnli Ridge is little more than scrambling, so Whymper and his companions found the climb surprisingly easy. At noon they camped on the ridge. The guides went ahead to reconnoitre, returning with the news that there was no difficulty. 'We could have gone to the summit and returned today easily!' they cried.

On the morning of the 14th, the climb recommenced as soon as it was light. The route lay mostly on the left-hand side of the ridge, on the East Face, but they encountered no difficulty until they reached the Shoulder, that curious kink in the ridge, so well seen from Zermatt, and from where the final 'cocked hat' of the summit rears up. At this point the steepness of the rock forced them to the right, onto the North Face, for a traverse of 400 feet before they were able to climb up again and reach the final snow ridge leading to the summit.

As the angle eased Croz and Whymper detached themselves from the rope and sprinted for the summit. The race was a dead heat. The time was 1.40 p.m.[28]

The summit of the Matterhorn is composed of a more or less level ridge some 100 metres in length. The Hörnli Ridge, climbed by Whymper's party, leads to one end of the ridge, to a point called the Swiss Summit, at 4478 metres, whilst the Italian Ridge leads to the other end, the Italian Summit, some two metres lower. It was plain to Whymper that Carrel's party had not reached the Swiss Summit because the snow was unmarked – but had they reached the Italian Summit? He and Croz went over to investigate, and to their great joy that summit too was virgin.

Then they saw the Italians who were still 400 metres from the top. They shouted and threw down rocks to catch their attention. Carrel's party paused, then turned to retreat. Even at that distance Carrel knew who had beaten him, for he recognised Whymper's distinctive white trousers. For Whymper, victory was complete.

They erected a flag on the Swiss Summit (using Croz's blouse) and a cairn on the Italian Summit. Altogether they were on the top for an hour before starting the descent. Giordano saw Whymper's flag from Breuil and assumed it marked Carrel's victory. He sent a signal to Sella and Breuil was *en fête* – until next day.

Whymper and Hudson agreed on the order of descent. Croz was to go first then Hadow, Hudson, Douglas, Old Peter, Whymper and Young Peter. How such a bizarre order was arrived at is hard to fathom, for it was quite wrong. Anyone could have gone first – Young Peter for example – because in descent this is not a particularly crucial position, and to send Croz first was to waste his expertise and his great strength. Croz should have been immediately behind Hadow, the weakest member, watching and protecting him.

This was the first mistake. The second was to use a weak rope – and here again events are clouded in mystery. The first four members of the party were joined by a stout 200-foot rope, then, joining Douglas to the remainder, 200 feet of weaker rope – little more than sash line – was used. Why was this done when there was another stout rope available and in any case, the original 200 feet was really sufficient for the whole party?

Fate was now ready to play the checkmate move. Here is Whymper's graphic description of what happened:

> A sharp-eyed lad ran into the Monte Rosa hotel, to Seiler, saying that he had seen an avalanche fall from the summit of the Matterhorn on to the Matterhorngletscher. The boy was reproved for telling idle stories; he was right, nevertheless, and this was what he saw.
>
> Michel Croz had laid aside his axe, and in order to give Mr. Hadow greater security, was absolutely taking hold of his legs, and putting his feet, one by one, into their proper positions. As far as I know, no one was actually descending. I cannot speak with certainty, because the two leading men were partially hidden from my sight by an intervening mass of rock, but it is my belief, from the movements of their shoulders, that Croz, having done as I have said, was in the act of turning round to go down a step or two himself; at this moment Mr. Hadow slipped, fell against him, and

knocked him over. I heard one startled exclamation from Croz, then saw him and Mr. Hadow flying downwards; in another moment Hudson was dragged from his steps, and Lord F. Douglas immediately after him. All this was the work of a moment. Immediately we heard Croz's exclamation, old Peter and I planted ourselves as firmly as the rocks would permit: the rope was taut between us, and the jerk came on us both as on one man. We held; but the rope broke midway between Taugwalder and Lord Francis Douglas. For a few seconds we saw our unfortunate companions sliding downwards on their backs, and spreading out their hands, endeavouring to save themselves. They passed from our sight uninjured, disappeared one by one, and fell from precipice to precipice on to the Matterhorngletscher below, a distance of nearly 4000 feet in height. From the moment the rope broke it was impossible to help them.

So perished our comrades! For the space of half-an-hour we remained on the spot without moving a single step. The two men, paralysed by terror, cried like infants, and trembled in such a manner as to threaten us with the fate of the others. Old Peter rent the air with exclamations of 'Chamounix! Oh, what will Chamounix say?' He meant, Who would believe that Croz could fall? The young man did nothing but scream or sob, 'We are lost! we are lost!'

There is no need to dwell on the sad, almost demented descent of the survivors, on the recovery of the bodies and the subsequent judicial enquiry. All Britain was shocked at the disaster and *The Times* thundered 'Is it life? Is it duty? Is it common sense? Is it allowable? Is it not wrong?'[29]

The accident settled like a great grey cloud over mountaineering and suddenly, the Golden Age was gone.

As Whymper stood on the summit of the Matterhorn, watching the Italians retreat, he thought of Carrel:

Still, I would that the leader of that party could have stood with us at that moment, for our victorious shouts conveyed to him the disappointment of the ambition of a lifetime. He was *the* man, of all those who attempted the ascent of the Matterhorn, who most deserved to be the first upon its summit. He was the first to doubt its inaccessibility, and he was the only man who persisted in believing that its ascent would be accomplished. It was the aim of his life to make the ascent from the side of Italy, for the honour of his native valley. For a time he had the game in his hands: he played it as he thought best; but he made a false move, and he lost it.

After the accident, all passion spent, Whymper turned again to his old comrade. Three days after the first ascent Carrel had climbed the Italian Ridge at last, making the second ascent of the mountain. The Matterhorn no longer stood between them. Years later they explored the Andes together, but in 1874 they wrote their final chapter to the Matterhorn story when they stood, side by side, on the summit.[30]

CHAPTER SIX

Where Angels Fear to Tread

That great Victorian apostle of alpinism, W.A.B. Coolidge, vividly recalled the effect of the Matterhorn tragedy on mountaineering:

> Three days after the Matterhorn accident, and on the very day when that peak was first attained from the Italian side, the present writer made his first Alpine ascent ... He was thus one of the earliest recruits to mountaineering after *the* accident, and went on climbing for thirty-three years. Hence he can recollect vividly the sort of palsy that fell upon the good cause after that frightful catastrophe of July 14, 1865, particularly amongst English climbers. Few in numbers, all knowing each other personally, shunning the public gaze as far as possible (and in those days it *was* possible to do so), they went about under a sort of dark shade, looked on with scarcely disguised contempt by the world of ordinary travellers. They, so to speak, climbed on sufferance, enjoying themselves much, it is true, but keeping all expression of that joy to themselves in order not to excite derision.[1]

There had been relatively few accidents to climbers up to that time but what made the Matterhorn affair such a shock was that amongst the victims was a man rated as one of the best, if not the best, climber of his day, Hudson, and one of the finest guides, Croz. The death of a genuine 'milord', Douglas, didn't help matters either. But in addition to all this, six other climbers died in the Alps that year – a total of ten victims. This was as many as in the entire history of the sport to that date and it was a figure not matched for five years.[2] In 1882, when three Englishmen and four guides[3] were killed in Alpine accidents, Queen Victoria enquired of Gladstone whether she should speak out against the sport. He advised against it.[4] Gladstone realised that mountain climbing was by then too well established for any condemnation to be effective, and that the public, though they may disapprove of such a dangerous sport, would come to accept the inevitable death roll with a shrug. He was right, of course. When the next mountaineering fatality to affect Britain as a whole took place – the deaths of Mallory and Irvine on Everest in 1924 – the public saw it as heroic.[5]

In 1871 Whymper's great book *Scrambles Amongst the Alps* appeared. By then the Matterhorn had been climbed several times,[6] the public rage had abated altogether and only the drama remained to enthral generations of readers. In that year, too, Leslie Stephen published *The Playground of Europe*, an elegant portrayal of Alpine adventure which helped to woo public opinion further.

This is not to say that the general public *understood* either the motives or methods of mountaineers – a century was to pass before that began to happen – but at least there was no more active opposition.

With all the virgin summits of the Golden Age climbed there had to be a shift in emphasis which opened new horizons. Climbers began to realise that what they enjoyed was not so much the conquest of a summit, but the struggle to reach it. The *route* became the important thing and, perhaps to a lesser degree, so did the manner of doing it: whether it was done guideless, or in winter, or solo, for example. This realisation is the foundation of modern climbing.

Those who still hankered after high summits were forced to go further afield to the Caucasus, the Andes, the Rockies and ultimately the Himalaya. Whymper was one of these. To him mountaineering meant reaching unclimbed summits. On the other hand those who adopted the new creed had to sharpen up their skills to tackle the more difficult routes, and especially their skill on rock.

During the last three decades of the nineteenth century rock climbing progressed from 'scrambling' into a structured activity with its own equipment and techniques. It was a game which could be played near home, without expensive journeys to the Alps, although at first one was seen simply as training for the other.

Up to 1870 mountaineering could be likened to a rough diamond, crude but valuable; now it was cut into many facets, each of which, from time to time, sparkled with its own fire.

The principal protagonists in all this, whatever else they became – rock climbers on Scafell or explorers of the Canadian wildernesses – were first and foremost still alpinists. The Alps remained the heart of the matter. Despite the gloomy forecasts of the jeremiahs, the Alps still had a considerable number of virgin summits after 1865, many of them very fine mountains – to take just two examples, the Grandes Jorasses and Piz Palu, which were not climbed until 1868. In regions like the Dauphiné and the Eastern Alps there were many more. In addition, there were the previously neglected rock spires of the Chamonix Aiguilles and the Dolomites. The scope was still enormous and what with new routes on old peaks as well, it was easy for an active man or woman to stay at just one or two centres for the entire summer and never want for good climbing.

This in itself was a major change and one which did not go unchallenged by the traditionalists. Towards the end of the century Lord Conway wrote:

> The old-fashioned climber, the mountain hero of my boyhood, was a traveller and desired to be an explorer. When he went to the Alps he went to wander about and to rough it ... The change at first showed itself in a change of habit of the systematic climber, the man for whom Alpine climbing takes the place of fishing or shooting. Ceasing to be a traveller he acquired the habit of settling down for his holiday in a comfortably furnished centre, whence he makes a series of ascents of the high mountains within reach.[7]

Conway was stating the position of the *ex-centrist*, or climber who moved from valley to valley, against the *centrist*, who stayed in one place. Incredible though it may seem to us now, the two factions which built up around these viewpoints argued matters out as fiercely as they had done with the glacier theories of earlier days! But the shift in emphasis of climbing meant that the centrist had in fact won the battle before it was joined, besides which, with improved transport throughout the Alps, there was no longer any need for the kind of exploratory journeys made by the pioneers. One incidental result of this was that the high and icy cols, leading from one valley to the next, which figure so prominently in the adventures of the pioneers, gradually fell out of favour. Henceforth the emphasis was on peaks and new ways of reaching them.[8]

At the head of the Valle Anzasca, on the Italian side of the Pennine Alps, is the wide grassy bowl of Macugnaga, surrounded by steep mountain walls. None is steeper, more imposing, than the East Face of Monte Rosa, one of the highest mountain faces in the Alps. The great central part of the face is snow and ice which, lower down, is divided into three parts by two rock ridges, and the central part, squeezed between the ridges, is known now as the Marinelli Couloir. From time to time great avalanches roar down from the upper snows, sweeping the central rib and the Marinelli Couloir.

The challenge of such a face is obvious, but so are the dangers. In 1867 the great Christian Almer had declined to attempt it, as had other guides like the Laueners and Lochmatter. In the summer of 1872, however, an English party which had been climbing in the Tyrol turned up in Macugnaga en route for Zermatt and the Matterhorn. They had no intentions on Monte Rosa at all, but in Macugnaga they fell in with a most unusual character: a dapper, smooth-talking chamois-hunter who introduced himself as Ferdinand Imseng.

Ferdinand Imseng was born in the Saastal in 1845 but he had moved over the border into Italy because the hunting laws were less rigorous than they were in Switzerland. Out of season he worked in the local gold mine and for nine years had also taken work as a mountain porter. He was better educated than most of his contemporaries, a good talker, a bad loser, and a man of fiery temperament. His courage bordered on the reckless.

He persuaded the English party – much against their better judgement – into attempting the East Face of Monte Rosa. They consisted of the two Pendlebury brothers, Richard and William, the Rev. C. Taylor and their guide from Vent, Gabriel Spechtenhauser. Together with a porter, Giovanni Oberto, they all set out from Macugnaga on July 21, with Imseng promoted to chief guide for the ascent.

Like the ascent of the Brenva Face of Mont Blanc seven years before, the attempt on the East Face of Monte Rosa was a quite extraordinary leap into the unknown. The technical difficulties were of much the same order, but the Monte Rosa climb was intrinsically more dangerous. Curiously, too, the guiding situation was similar, for just as Melchior was opposed to the Brenva climb to the bitter end, so too was Gaber Spechtenhauser on Monte Rosa.

The party bivouacked for the night on the rocks of the Rücke Jägi (now called the Crestone Marinelli). The night was fairly warm, which did not bode well for the morrow, and it was a doubtful party which prepared for the climb. They crossed the Marinelli Couloir to reach the rocks on the far side, now known as the Imsengrücken, and climbed the snow and ice above the ridge in an attempt to reach the Grenzsattel. This took many hours; hours in which the snow grew softer and more dangerous, hours spent in avoiding and crossing crevasses of enormous size, hours threatened by séracs which were likely to fall at any moment. Twice they thought their end had come. On the first occasion there was a sharp crack above them and pieces of a sérac hurtled down onto the party, bruising several of them but doing no serious damage. On the second occasion, the snow around them began to slide but they managed to escape by seeking the shelter of a sérac, which acted as a buffer whilst the snow on either side slid down the face.

It became obvious that to make for the Grenzsattel was too dangerous so they turned towards a rib of rock coming down from the Grenzgipfel. The Rev. C. Taylor describes their progress:

> Whether the situation was really dangerous, we were unable to judge. But it was idle to speculate: the practical issue had to be tried: one stage more, and then the rocks – perhaps. Accordingly we passed under the sérac to the south, and scrambled up its side; a piece of work which under more favourable circumstances might have been thought difficult. We then made for the last sérac, which lay midway between us and the lowest point of the final ridge, and from which a small crevasse ran down obliquely to the right, so as to separate us from the slope by which we were to reach the rocks. The snow here seemed better than below, but, the incline being greater, it was deemed right to use every precaution before we fully committed ourselves. Imseng was sent to the front for the first trial, and went to the full extent of his own rope, now uncoiled for the

first time, while the main body of the party remained well placed below; Gaber next followed, changing places with R. Pendlebury; then, one by one, we stepped over the crevasse, till the last man had left his firm footing under the sérac, and the whole party was launched irrevocably upon the slope.

It was felt that the decisive moment was now at hand, and that in a brief space the fate of the expedition must be determined; but we gave our minds to the work before us, and wasted very little thought on possible consequences. The snow was not to be trifled with, but it bore the pressure put upon it, and showed no symptoms calculated to cause uneasiness; and, indeed, but for the recollection of what we had experienced below, it would scarcely have occurred to us at this point that there was any danger at all to be feared; but, as it was, we went with the utmost caution, fully resolved that up to the last step no chance should be thrown away. I have a sufficiently lively recollection of the scene, but there is little that I could say by way of description which would not be better left to the imagination of the reader. The simple fact was that six men, joined by some fifty yards of cord, were nearing the end of a short steep snow-slope. A few steps, and the head of the column was hopefully near the goal. A few more, with growing confidence but undiminished care, and the last film of doubt was scattered by a subdued *Jodel* from Imseng, which announced that the rocks of the 'Vorspitze' were reached, and the day was won.[9]

Imseng was actually a little premature with his jodel, for though they were out of danger, the rocks leading to the summit were more difficult than he had imagined and it was many hours before the party finally crossed the mountain and reached the Riffel Alp Hotel.

The climbing of the East Face of Monte Rosa led Imseng to fame and fortune as a guide – and tragically to his death. On August 8, 1881, he led Damiano Marinelli and a second guide, Battista Pedranzini, together with a porter, on what would have been the third ascent of the route. The day was hot and close. Instead of bivouacking on the initial rocks, as on the first ascent, Imseng took the party across the couloir and was ascending the second rocks when an enormous avalanche occurred. Marinelli and the two guides were swept away, but the porter miraculously escaped.[10]

In the same season that Imseng was leading the first ascent of the Marinelli Couloir, a much less publicised climb was taking place further east on the Cima Trafoi (3563 m) in the Ortler group. The young Maurice de Déchy, who was later to make a name for himself in the Caucasus, guided by the brothers A. and J. Pinggera, climbed the mountain for the first time by the South Face. This was not particularly difficult but in that same year T. Harpprecht and the guide Peter Dangl climbed the much more difficult North Face. The Trafoierwand is an uncompromising wall of ice set at sixty degrees and though only 400 metres – short by the standards of Mont Blanc or Monte Rosa – it is just as technically difficult. In some ways this climb was ahead of its time, a harbinger of the important role the short, sharp nordwands of the Eastern Alps were to play in the history of mountaineering.

It soon became evident to the climbing establishment that there were a number of Young Turks abroad who were not content simply to follow in the footsteps of the pioneers. New climbs were being done which were unjustifiable by older standards – a theme which was to recur with each generation in the years ahead – and there was a vague disquiet that the standards which had produced the epic ascents of the Golden Age were being disregarded. Matters came to a head in 1874 when Thomas Middlemore crossed the Col des Grandes Jorasses from Italy to Chamonix, led by Johann Jaun and with a somewhat terrified Joseph Rey as porter. Whilst Rey spent much time in praying for deliverance, Jaun climbed the steep rotten rocks of the gully which leads to the col, carefully avoiding the gully bed which was a natural chute for falling stones. Even so, stones did fall on them, and Middlemore confessed later to being black and blue with bruises. It was undoubtedly a dangerous climb. All the ice axes were lost, and the party had a difficult time making their way down to Montenvers on the other side.

The Establishment were furious. They thought that even if Middlemore was foolish enough to risk his own life on such a venture he should not risk the lives of his guides – ignoring the fact that the suggestion of the climb came from Jaun in the first place. Freshfield, Stephen, Moore and George castigated poor Middlemore, not only for the climb, but for what he had the temerity to say in a paper read to the Alpine Club:

> 'Shall fools step in where angels fear to tread?' The full justice of the latter clause I grant, but when the former is applied to such as are not content 'stare super vias antiquas,' I crave leave to plead my mild demurrer. The question is just this: nearly all the best things in the Alps have been done. What remains is stiff and possibly risky. How then shall we deal with this residuum? Some, with I am sorry to say, a certain flavour of official sanction, have counselled not simply caution, a thing which should always influence us, but have advised that the residual climbs, if involving possible danger, should be attempted neither by travellers nor guides. If this advice were followed, it would seem to me a cancelling of the indentures of the younger members who have apprenticed themselves to the noble pursuit to which this Club devotes its energies.[11]

D.W. Freshfield, editor of the *Alpine Journal* at the time, was still railing against the 'new' school at the end of the century, protesting, 'This is no mere Climbers' Club'. Martin Conway, like Freshfield very much a geographical climber, ignored the new climbs altogether and wanted to turn the Alpine Club into a sort of mountaineering section of the Royal Geographical Society.[12] Theirs was a view very different from that of the young men from Britain, France, Germany, Austria and Italy who were forcing the Alpine pace in the last years of the nineteenth century.

In 1876 Middlemore was joined by a young French climber, Henri Cordier, and Oakley Maund,[13] another young activist, together with the guides Jakob Anderegg, Johann Jaun and Andreas Maurer, in an attack on the Argentière Face of the Aiguille Verte. The mountains surrounding the Argentière Glacier form one of the most impressive cirques in the Alps. At the head is Mont Dolent and the Aiguille de Triolet, but the dominating feature is the ice-draped curtain which extends from the latter peak to the Verte, forming the south-western confines of the glacier and including such subsidiary summits as Les Courtes and Les Droites.

Middlemore had tried the climb the previous year with Lord Wentworth[14] (another member of the new breed) and Jaun, but had been defeated by the condition of the snow. The ascent, however, was Jaun's pet project, and so it was that a particularly strong party was assembled in 1876 to try again. The route chosen by Jaun was a narrow couloir to the right of the large rock buttress which is such a prominent feature of the Argentière Face of the Verte. Like the gully on the Col des Grandes Jorasses it was an obvious stonefall zone and, indeed, scarcely had they started the climb when a stone whizzed past Maurer's head and another struck Middlemore. Anderegg, who was leading at the time, quickly cut across the gully out of the firing line, finding a relatively safe ice slope of sixty degrees up which to cut steps.

The climbing was steep and difficult. 'In my experience of the Alps', wrote Maund later, 'I have seen nothing that will compare with the sustained splendour of this climb, either for sheer ice work or difficult rocks; and I feel convinced that without the combination of good weather, good guides, and good state of snow, it would be madness to attempt it.'

On three occasions they were forced to cross the deadly couloir from one side to the other and on one such crossing Maund was struck on the knee by a stone, 'cutting it and producing great pain for a few minutes'.

At 11.20 a.m. they at last escaped from the couloir in which they had been trapped for the past five hours. After a short rest they continued up the steep but perfect snow slopes above to reach the summit at 3 p.m. It had been a tremendous climb.

A few days later they returned to the Argentière Glacier and this time climbed the wall again, but to the summit of Les Courtes, which they found much easier than the Verte. It was the first ascent of the peak. Still not content with their achievements on this fantastic ridge, they determined to climb the remaining peak, Les Droites, but this time from the opposite side, the Talèfre Glacier. Anderegg, who was ill, remained in Chamonix.

They found the climb surprisingly difficult and again there was stonefall. However, they completed the first ascent, but on the descent, Jaun, hoping to save some time, led them down a couloir which almost proved their undoing:

> The snow proved deep and firm, and we had reached the lower part of the couloir where it narrows considerably, when we heard a roar far above and on looking up saw two enormous rocks coming with great bounds straight for us. We made a rush across the couloir as fast as we could go, as one touch from such blocks would have been instant annihilation. Cordier slipped and fell, dragging Middlemore down with him. I anchored and went flat on my face, as did Maurer, who was next in front of me. There was a rush of wind followed by a shower of snow, and the rocks were past! One mass, which must have weighed a ton, struck just above where Cordier slipped from, and passed close over his head. On looking round I saw Jaun lying spread-eagled on his back, while his hat was flying down the couloir. I thought he was killed, and Maurer told me afterwards that he had thought so too. But in a moment, to my great relief, he looked round, and picking himself up, cried to Maurer, 'Schnell zu den Felsen.' I need not tell you that very little time was lost in acting upon his advice, and in a few minutes we were safe on the rocks on the opposite (or right hand in looking up) side of the couloir. Once on them we had the greatest difficulty in getting off again, as they turned out very bad. We, however, succeeded at length in reaching the bergschrund at their base, which we crossed without difficulty, and were safe.[15]

All in all, a remarkable week's work!

One area of the high Alps still remained relatively unexplored at the end of the Golden Age. The Dauphiné Alps, to the east of Grenoble, had been the scene of the great tour of 1864 by Whymper, Moore and Walker, but since then little had been done there. It was off the beaten track, lacking in any sort of amenity and backward even by Alpine standards, as one visitor vividly described: 'It is hardly possible to conceive the squalid misery in which the people live; their dark dismal huts swarming with flies, fleas, and other vermin; the broom, the mop, and the scrubbing-brush are unknown luxuries; the bones and refuse of a meal are flung upon the floor to be gnawed by the dogs, and are left there to form an osseous breccia. The people in many parts are stunted, cowardly, and feeble, and appear to be stupid and almost *cretins*.'[16]

The first to realise the untapped potential of this obscure district was W.A.B. Coolidge and his aunt Miss Meta Brevoort. At the time of their first Dauphiné visit in 1870, Coolidge was twenty and his aunt forty-five and both had some five years' Alpine experience. There were a number of women climbers at this time, notably Lucy Walker, who was Meta Brevoort's great rival – a rivalry enhanced by the fact that Melchior was Lucy's guide and Almer was Meta's – but this combination of aunt and nephew was strange enough to cause comment wherever they went, especially as they always took along their noisy dog, Tschingel, which made them less than popular in Alpine hotels. Meta died in 1876, but Coolidge, though not of the same technical calibre as Middlemore or Dent, went on to amass a remarkable number of Alpine expeditions – some 1200 – before he retired from climbing in 1898. Meanwhile, he had also acquired a reputation as an outstanding Alpine historian – and a feud-maker of Sicilian intensity. He fell out with just about everybody. 'He could do anything with a hatchet but bury it,' observed Arnold Lunn, one of the many victims.

When Coolidge and his aunt visited the Dauphiné in 1870 they had as their guides Christian and Ulrich Almer who brought along Christian Gertsch as a porter from the Oberland, having been warned to expect little in the way of help from the locals. On June 28 they all made the first ascent of the Pic Central of the Meije, then Coolidge and the guides made the third ascent of the Ecrins, first ascent of Ailefroide and an ascent of Pelvoux. Miss Brevoort, to her chagrin, had to miss these climbs because she had injured her feet through wearing 'unbroken' boots on the Meije.

The Barre des Ecrins (4101 m), first climbed by Moore's party in 1864, is the highest summit in the Dauphiné, but the Meije is the second highest and since it was completely virgin had naturally attracted the party's first attention. It is a superb-looking mountain with three distinct summits: Grand Pic (3983 m), Pic Central (3974 m) and the Meije Orientale (3890 m). From below, the Coolidge party judged the central peak to be the highest and it was not until they reached the top, climbing rocks which Almer compared with those of the Italian Ridge of the Matterhorn, that they realised the West Peak (now called Grand Pic) was a few metres higher. They thought of attempting the traverse from one to the other, but Almer declared it impossible.[17]

The Dauphiné became Coolidge's favourite Alpine area throughout his long climbing career. He made a number of new ascents there and he and his aunt are commemorated by Pic Coolidge (3774 m), which he climbed in 1877, and Pointe Brevoort (3765 m), the South Summit of the Grande Ruine, which they both climbed in 1873.

The 1870s was the decade of the Dauphiné. Of the ninety-one most significant summits in the area, forty-eight were climbed for the first time between 1870 and 1879. It was like a miniature reprise of the Golden Age.

Yet there were differences. The Dauphiné peaks are spiky and curiously uniform in height – scarcely 300 metres separates the twenty highest peaks and another 200 metres the next fifty. Many summits are easy to reach, but anything worthwhile demands rock climbing skill, often on rock which is not of the soundest. It was the most natural link possible between the climbing style of the pioneers and that which was to follow on the Chamonix Aiguilles and the Dolomite towers.

The greatest prize was the highest point of the Meije. Most of the Young Turks had a go at it: Taylor and the Pendleburys of Monte Rosa fame, Oakley Maund, Eccles, Middlemore, Lord Wentworth, Cordier. The peak was tried from all sides and, of course, attempts were made to cross Almer's 'impossible' arête between the Pic Central and the Grand Pic, but all failed.

In 1875 two young Frenchmen met for the first time on the slopes of Mont Blanc. Henri Duhamel was twenty-one years old and so in love with the French Alps that he had recently persuaded his widowed mother to move the family home from Paris to a village near Grenoble. Henri Emmanuel Boileau de Castelnau was a scion of one of the oldest families in Languedoc and only seventeen, but already an experienced alpinist with the Matterhorn and a number of other peaks under his belt. Both men were attracted to the Dauphiné and especially the unclimbed Meije.

They went straight to the Meije from Mont Blanc, climbed the Pic Central and a new subsidiary summit, but failed to reach the Grand Pic. In the following year, 1876, Boileau de Castelnau for some reason did not attempt the Meije (although he was in the Dauphiné) but Duhamel did. He and his three guides climbed a couloir to the right of a great buttress on the South Face to reach a platform which became known as the Pyramide Duhamel from the cairn he built there. It was far short of the top, but it was a step in the right direction.

In 1877 Coolidge was back, making another attempt on the Meije with the Almers. His aunt had died the previous year after a short illness and he particularly wanted to climb the peak in her honour, but in this he was disappointed. Henri Boileau de Castelnau also tried again, with two local guides, the Pierre Gaspards, father and son, but they too failed. Coolidge returned home before the Frenchman made his attempt, but he did not fear their success. What could a youth of nineteen and two indifferent local men do where the great Almers had failed?

Boileau de Castelnau and the two Gaspards took plenty of provisions and 350 feet of rope in case they were forced to leave fixed rope in some places to secure a retreat. To help carry all this they took along a local man, J.-B. Rodier, whose lack of ability was such that they left him at the Glacier Carré to await their return.

The Glacier Carré is an icefield set high up on the mountain. To reach it the climbing had been severe, but now the three men cut steps across the ice with confidence and, finding the final peak easy, began to scent victory. Then, thirty feet from the top, they were stopped by an overhang.

> Gaspard *père* got up about twelve feet and found himself unable either to advance or return. He called for help which I was able to supply by standing on his son's shoulders, but only just in time as his strength was giving out. I then tried, but met with no greater success. Gaspard *fils* succeeded in getting a little higher, but he put us in such danger helping him down that I was ready to order the retreat. He was so exhausted by his efforts that on his return he could not move his limbs, and the nervous stress had been so great that he dissolved in tears. All three of us were pale and trembling and took a moment to rally ourselves. The biting cold paralysed our forces. The weather had been deteriorating for the last hour. We were enveloped in clouds whipped across by a violent wind which threatened to tumble us. We descended a little way, ready to retreat after having been within twenty feet of the summit, when Gaspard, furious at finding his efforts ineffective, proposed that we try to turn the obstacle on the N. face.[18]

This manoeuvre proved successful. At 3.30 p.m. they at last stood on the summit of the Grand Pic (3983 m).

When Coolidge heard the news he was furious. That the peak had been climbed at all was bad enough, but that it had been climbed 'by a young Frenchman who was a chamois hunter rather than a peak hunter' was too much. In the following summer he and the Almers returned to the Dauphiné and made the second ascent. It was, he later wrote, 'the longest continuously difficult climb in the Alps'.[19]

Sometimes the Meije is held up by romantics as the last great Alpine peak to be climbed, but this is nonsense. It wasn't even the highest unclimbed peak at that time. Even if we ignore marching pinnacles like the Aiguilles du Diable on Mont Blanc du Tacul, which are over 4000 metres, there were still peaks like the Géant (4013 m) and the Blanche de Peuterey (4107 m) which were not climbed until 1882 and 1885 respectively.

The idea of new climbs on old peaks led to the opening of some of the most majestic ridges in the Alps: the *grandes courses*, which were to be the staple diet of alpinism throughout the next century. The ridges were natural lines and a lot safer from stonefall than couloirs. They were, however, often technically quite difficult.

Amongst the best of these ridges might be mentioned the Biancograt on Piz Bernina done by Middlemore and his friends in 1876 and added to by Paul Güssfeldt two years later, and the self-explanatory Middlemoregrat of the neighbouring Piz Roseg, done a week after the Biancograt. In 1877

James Eccles and the Payots opened up the Peuterey Ridge on Mont Blanc and in 1879 Mummery and Burgener climbed the Zmutt Ridge of the Matterhorn. Examples from the 1880s include the Bumillergrat of Piz Palu, done by Hans Bumiller and three guides in 1887. In the same year Mummery and his wife did the Teufelsgrat on the Täschhorn. In 1895 Edward Broome did the Schalligrat on the Weisshorn.

The harder ridges tended to be mostly rock and some of them were not overcome until well into the present century, as for example the Rote Zähne Ridge of the Gspaltenhorn in the Oberland, done by Young and his companions in 1914; the North Ridge of Piz Badile, climbed by Zurcher in 1923; the Mittelegi Ridge of the Eiger done by Yuko Maki and three guides in 1921; the Hirondelles Ridge of the Grandes Jorasses which an Italian party climbed in 1927 and the North Ridge of the Dent Blanche climbed by Mr and Mrs Richards with Joseph and Antoine Georges in 1928.

But the great mixed ridges belonged properly to the nineteenth century and perhaps the East-North-East Ridge of the Dent Blanche might be taken as typical. It was done in 1882 by J. Stafford Anderson and G.P. Baker, with the guides Ulrich Almer and Aloys Pollinger. It was the latter who led the climb, a loping giant of a man, given to wearing broad-brimmed hats and speaking in a soft melodious voice which made him a favourite with the ladies.

They had crossed the Rothorn from Zermatt to Zinal and were intent on a new route on the Dent Blanche by the East-North-East Ridge, descending to Stockje and then traversing the Matterhorn back to Zermatt. It was, to say the least, an ambitious programme, especially as the weather was not properly settled.

Bad weather during the night seemed about to frustrate them over the Dent Blanche but eventually they decided to give the ridge a go. They had quite a job reaching it and once on it found the climbing difficult:

> For some time we stuck to the arête. At one place it narrowed to a knife-edge, with steep slopes on either side, down which the stones we discharged thundered and clattered in an unpleasantly suggestive manner, disappearing from sight after two or three mighty leaps. The ridge shortly becoming impassable, forced us again on to the north-west face of the mountain. It was much steeper and more difficult than before, and gave us considerable trouble. One bit I remember, composed of smooth slabs of rock at a steep angle with infinitesimal holds, and some of these rotten, which engaged Pollinger's attention a long time before he could reach secure footing, and give us the benefit of the rope. It was one of the nastiest bits of rockwork I have yet met with. In fact, from the moment we left the arête a second time to the moment when we reached the second

gendarme *en route*, the climbing was of a decidedly serious nature; sometimes we were working along narrow ledges, sometimes hanging on to the rocks with tenacious grip, whilst the leaders made themselves secure, at others clambering by the help of narrow clefts and gullies straight up the face, occasionally cheered by a bit of easy going, only to be thrown into despair again immediately by increasing difficulties, and at all times with the consciousness that a slip must *not* occur.[20]

The famous narrow crest of snow near the top of the climb which can sometimes be so thin that the wind blows holes through it, came as something of a shock to Anderson:

> The crest here narrowed to a knife-edge, descending steeply on either side, and rising up to a point some 30 feet away from us, afterwards falling where the rocks again appeared. The whole ridge was in a soft and nasty condition, and as Pollinger stepped on to it, he went up to the knees in the yielding snow. We must either turn back, or trust to it however, so we paid out the rope, as he cautiously worked along it just below the summit on its eastern side, his ice axe planted up to its head on the western slope. We all followed his example in silence, having first arranged that if the snow gave way under the leaders, those behind were to throw themselves on the opposite side; but it held, and just as Baker stepped on to the ridge, Pollinger recrossed it, and found once more a safer footing on the rocks.

They reached the summit at 3 p.m. and solemnly shook hands on finding themselves still alive. '*Wir sind vier esel*,' said Almer ('We are four asses') and unknowingly gave the ridge its name, Viereselgrat.

CHAPTER SEVEN

'They Have Picked Out the Plums and Left Us the Stones'

'The older members of the Club have left us, the youthful aspirants, but little to do in the Alps,' wrote Clinton Dent, tongue in cheek in 1876. 'We follow them meekly, either by walking up their mountains by new routes, or by climbing some despised outstanding spur of the peaks they first trod under foot. They have left us but these rock aiguilles. They have picked out the plums and left us the stones.'[1]

Dent was emphasising what Middlemore and others were saying – that the minor peaks were interesting in their own right and that rock was as important, if not more important than snow and ice. The reference to *walking* up the bigger mountains was not missed by his contemporaries. It delighted the Young Turks and angered the greybeards.

The minor peaks (some of which were actually over 4000 metres) were often very hard to climb by *any* route and the difficulty was in itself becoming a delicious part of the game. For a short time some misguided climbers (and Dent was one) took ladders to help overcome difficult pitches, just as the pioneers had once carried ladders to overcome crevasses on glaciers, but it was a laborious business and soon abandoned. Skills were developed to meet the situation and perhaps for the first time, mountaineering acquired true sporting characteristics.

Rock climbing skills were forced on the climbers because, without them, no progress could be made. This is not to say that these men and women were not all-round mountaineers as well. The greatest rock climber of them all, Mummery, also took part in two of the most daring ice climbs of the day, the crossing of the Col du Lion and the attempt on the North Face of the Plan. Nevertheless, the basis of mountaineering skill shifted from stamina to athleticism.

This was particularly the case in the Eastern Alps where the steep dolomite towers of the Tyrol and the limestone walls of the *Kalkalpen* demanded more than a simple grabbing technique. The Austrian Alpine Club was founded in 1862 and the German Alpine Club seven years later. When they combined in 1874 they had some 18,000 members, more than all the other clubs put together. Of course, many of these members were simply Alpine walkers but their subscriptions helped to build huts in the mountains where members could live cheaply. There are still far more huts in the Eastern

Alps than in the other parts of the range. Out of such a large membership, too, it was inevitable that many would be fine mountaineers.

Mountaineering in the Tyrol had from the first been largely a local affair. There had been the early enthusiasts such as von Salm and Stanig, but perhaps the first dedicated climber was Peter Carl Thurwieser, Professor of Oriental Languages at Salzburg, who between 1820 and 1847 made some seventy climbs, including the first ascent of the splendid Zillertal peak, Schrammacher (3411 m). But general interest was low. Lieutenant-Colonel Poltinger, with a surveying party, climbed the Glockturm (3355 m) in the Otztal range in 1853, but it was not climbed again for seventeen years, though it is by no means a difficult peak.

The mountains were not as high as those further west and therefore their 'conquest' not as attractive to the peak-baggers of the Golden Age, hot foot from London. It is true that J.H. Fox, D.W. Freshfield and F.F. Tuckett, with the guides F. Devouassoud and P. Michel, toured the area in 1865, climbing peaks like the Langtauferer Spitze (3529 m) in the Otztal and Grosser Moseler (3478 m) in the Zillertal, but by and large the mountains were left to Austro-German climbers such as Franz Senn, Paul Grohmann and Theodor Petersen. Senn was known as the *Gletscherpfarrer* – a latter-day Father Placidus, specialising in one area – in Senn's case the Otztal, as did Petersen. It was Senn who made the second ascent of Glockturm, with the great guide, Gaber Spechtenhauser. All three played a part in the founding of the German and Austrian clubs, but probably Grohmann had the greatest influence on his contemporaries. In 1865, Grohmann with the guides P. Fuchs and G. Samer climbed Hochfeiler (3510 m), the highest summit in the Zillertal range, and two years later with J. Huber and G. Samer made the first ascent of the splendid Olperer (3476 m). In 1869 he helped to open up the Dolomites with the first ascents of Sassolungo and Cima Grande.

There was also a number of notable guides in the Tyrol, though with the exception of Gaber Spechtenhauser and Hans Grass, few made their mark in the bigger peaks of the west.[2] Paul Güssfeldt, who made the first ascent of the Scerscen Eisnase in 1877, the complete Biancograt in the following year and the traverse of the Aiguille Blanche and Peuterey Ridge in 1893 (when he was fifty-three years old!) complained that the English stole all the best guides: 'The few good guides were in the hands of the Englishmen ... [they] were educated, well-informed people: but the merry German student saw nothing but their check suits and well filled purses.'[3]

The merry German student had no money for *any* guides, let alone the good ones, and Güssfeldt was overstating his case. A wealthy man and Privy Counsellor to Kaiser Wilhelm II, he could hardly complain on his own behalf. He was a member of the Alpine Club and his guides included Burgener, Rey and Klucker.

What is interesting is that the German students (using the word in its widest meaning) formed the only other considerable corpus of alpinism apart from the British middle classes, certainly to the 1870s and probably for some time after that. They were poor in the sense in which students are poor, which was different from the poverty of the lower working classes of the time, but being intelligent they found their own solutions to guideless climbing and, of course, were able to live cheaply in the hills, using the wide network of club huts. A distinctive philosophy arose which is traceable right through to Hermann Buhl in the 1950s: extraordinary self-reliance and self-assurance combined with a degree of fatalism.

Hermann von Barth was one of the earliest of this breed. A lawyer from Munich, he was an explorer of the limestone peaks of the Austro-German border, the *Kalkalpen* which, along with the Dolomites, were to be the breeding ground for rock climbers from those two countries. He was a considerable writer and influenced young German climbers at a time when the country was being welded into one nation, Wagner and Nietzsche were propounding their ideas and Siegfried was rising from his slumbers. 'Who climbs with me must be prepared to die!' Von Barth cried.

Such a philosophy encouraged solo climbing too, one leading exponent being Georg Winkler who in 1887, at the age of eighteen, soloed the Winkler Turme, a dramatic finger of rock in the Vajolet Dolomites. Winkler only stood four feet eleven inches and to help him overcome this disability when climbing he used an iron claw attached to a rope which he would throw up, hoping it would catch on a ledge. He would then pull himself up the rope hand over hand. Whymper had used a similar device on the Matterhorn and perhaps this is where Winkler got the idea from, but it is interesting to note that innovation in climbing equipment was a feature of the Eastern Alps – the karabiner, ice peg, modern crampons, all stem from these limestone hills, as indeed do fixed ropes. Winkler was killed the following year attempting to solo the West Face of the Weisshorn in the Pennine Alps. His body was recovered from the Weisshorn Glacier in 1955, sixty-seven years after his disappearance.

The purpose of soloing was not to demonstrate bravado but to follow a Nietzschean code of purity which dictated that as little as possible should come between the climber and his environment. Undoubtedly the leading exponent of this was Eugen Guido Lammer who, amongst many other climbs, made the popular Olperer–Fussstein traverse solo in 1884. Lammer believed there should be no permanent man-made structure above the tree line, including club huts, which he wanted done away with.[4] Today, when both ethics and conservation are very much in the forefront of discussion, Lammer's stance seems appealing, but he was more extreme than present climbers. With his fellow Austrian, August Lorria, he would deliberately climb at night, in bad weather, and on faces notorious for stonefall. An accident was inevitable. It took place on August 3, 1887, when the two men, guideless of course, were attempting to climb the Tiefenmatten Face of the Matterhorn by a route climbed only once before, by Penhall in 1879.

They had climbed to a point level with the teeth of the Zmutt Ridge when, finding the rocks coated in black ice, they decided to retreat. It was one o'clock and for the next four hours they managed to make a careful descent until they were forced to cross a gully known as the Penhall Couloir. Here a small avalanche swept them off their feet and they were carried 150–200 metres down the slopes. When at last they came to rest Lammer discovered he had a dislocated foot, but his companion, Lorria, was in a far worse condition. He had a bad head wound and a broken leg and had been half-strangled by the rope. He was unconscious and when he did regain his senses he thrashed about in wild delirium. Lammer tried to move him but found it impossible. His shouts for help were lost in the wastes of an empty glacier.

Realising they would both die unless something positive was done, Lammer removed his jacket and used it as extra protection for the injured man. He also shoved Lorria's hands into a pair of socks to keep them warm, then, having done all he could to protect the victim from the elements, Lammer dragged himself down the glacier to the hut which then existed on the Stockje rocks. Finding no one there he continued his painful journey down the long moraines of the Zmutt Glacier to the inn at Stafel Alp, where he arrived at dusk, utterly exhausted. A rescue party reached Lorria at eight next morning. He was again unconscious. During his delirium he had torn off all his clothes, yet had survived the night naked on the mountain. Both men were remarkably lucky.[5]

This seems to have been the end of Lorria's climbing career but Lammer continued his extreme ways, doing the Hinter Brochkogel North Ridge first ascent, solo, in 1898, for example, and died a very old man during the Second World War.

When the Nazi party came to power in Germany they deliberately twisted the philosophy of Nietzsche to their own purposes and this led some observers to believe that the extreme German climbing of the period was a product of National Socialism when in fact it was merely an extension of a philosophy Austro-German climbers had had from the beginning.

The Dolomites are different from any other Alpine region. The limestone here is not like other limestone, but contains magnesium as well as calcium and colouring matter which can shade the rocks from a deep grey to a rich red. The steep rock faces which are a feature of limestone country occur in wild profusion, linked by incredible ridges with pinnacles and towers everywhere. The only glacier of any note is on the Marmolata (3342 m), the highest of the mountains, and though there is a famous ice couloir on the Cima Tosa in the Brenta group, this is rock climbing country and, strangely enough in view of its rugged nature, walking country.[6]

The first climber to visit the area was John Ball, first President of the Alpine Club, who climbed Monte Pelmo in 1857 and, later, Marmolata di Rocca and Cima Tosa. He was followed by Paul Grohmann, Francis Fox Tuckett, Leslie Stephen and a number of other Alpine Club members who brought along their Chamonix or Oberland guides and with the somewhat dubious assistance of local men ascended various peaks. At first the only local guides of any consequence were Bonifacio Nicolussi, who specialised in his native Brenta, and Santo Siorpaes. It was only in the 1870s, as the enjoyment of rock climbing for its own sake began to be an accepted part of mountaineering, that the Dolomites came into their own.[7] During this period guides were not wanting who specialised in the steep dolomite rock and, just as had happened earlier in the Western Alps, a number of guiding families arose, including the famous Dimais and Innerkoflers.

Michael Innerkofler of Sexten, a powerfully built man of enormous strength, was perhaps the most famous of these early guides in the Dolomites. He climbed the Zwolferkogel in 1875, the adjacent Elferkogel three years later, the Grohmannspitze in 1880 (solo) and Cima Piccola di Lavaredo in 1881, some of the 'last great problems' of their day in the area. He died in 1888 at the age of forty in a silly accident on the Cristallo Glacier when a snow bridge collapsed, precipitating his two companions and himself into a crevasse. They fell fifteen to twenty metres and, though his companions were relatively uninjured, Innerkofler struck his head on some ice. Dimai and Siorpaes, who happened to be on the same route, were quickly on the scene, but Innerkofler was already dead.

One by one the towers and pinnacles, once considered inaccessible, were overcome. The central Vajolet Turme was climbed in 1892 by Dr Hans Helversen and the guide Hans Stabeler from Campitello and three years later Hermann Delago climbed the remaining tower. Not until the last year of the century was the traverse of the three towers completed, by Hans Barth and Eduard Pichl, via the Pichl Crack on the Delagoturme, a great S-shaped overhanging fissure which was one of the hardest things done at that date.[8]

Another peak which attracted much attention because of its apparent inaccessibility was the Fünffingerspitze (Cinque Dita), a mountain near the Sella Pass which, with a little imagination, can be seen to resemble the fingers of a hand pointing skywards. Between the first and middle 'fingers' there is a deep chimney which cuts right through the mountain and in June 1890 Ludwig Norman-Neruda, a climber who had made quite a name for himself in the Western Alps, tried to climb the south side of this fissure. Despite his considerable height and reach – he was six feet two inches tall – he was beaten by ice and indifferent guiding, but in August of that same year two young Austrians, Robert Hans Schmitt and Johann Santner, climbing guideless, managed to force their way to the summit, despite the water pouring down the chimney. On top they built two cairns and each man left a visiting card. The route became known as the Schmitt Kamin, and its ascent caused quite a stir in European climbing circles. 'The climb is by far the hardest I have ever accomplished,' wrote Schmitt, who was a very good climber usually given to understating difficulty. 'Who will bring down our cards?'[9]

The answer was provided the very next year by a woman climber, Jeanne Immink, led by Antonio Dimai and Giuseppe Zecchini, who repeated the route. At the same time Norman-Neruda climbed the south side of the chimney with his usual guide, the great Christian Klucker, and the two parties met on top. The Fünffingerspitze was one of Norman-Neruda's favourite peaks. He climbed it six times and it was whilst he was making his seventh ascent, in 1898, with his wife and a friend, via the Schmitt Kamin, that he died of a heart attack.[10]

But of all the Dolomite towers the most impressive was the Guglia di Brenta (Campanile Basso), a fantastic totem pole of limestone rising for some 200 metres from a gap in the Brenta Ridge. In 1897 a climber from Trento, Carlo Gabari, with a guide named Tavernaro and a porter, Pooli, began at the foot of the South Face and climbed upwards with surprising ease for about thirty metres when they were stopped by a steep yellow wall. They succeeded in overcoming this and christened it the Pooli Wall. They then followed a somewhat circuitous route round the pinnacle until they reached a ledge below the final wall, the Terrazo Gabari. Though scarcely 150 feet from the top they could not climb this last obstacle and were forced to retreat – no mean feat in itself.

Two years later the attack was resumed by two Innsbruck students, Otto Ampferer and Karl Berger who found that the key to the ascent from the Terrazo Gabari was to make an exposed traverse above the sheer North Wall, then climb a steep wall on small holds for about thirty metres to easier rocks which led to the top.[11]

Technical rock climbing was becoming increasingly necessary in the Western Alps, too, especially as climbers turned their attention to the rocky spires round Chamonix. Of these the boldest and most challenging were the Charmoz,[12] Noire de Peuterey, the Drus and Géant – all big, bold rock masses piercing the clouds, apparently inaccessibly. Not until the late 1870s were any of these seriously attempted.

The first to succumb was the Aiguille Noire de Peuterey (3772 m), climbed in 1877 by Lord Wentworth, guided by Emile Rey and J.B. Bich. Wentworth was a wealthy aristocrat, who had inherited all the adventurous flair of his grandfather, Lord Byron, and he was a keen rock climber who had spent several seasons in the Dolomites.[13] His chief guide, Rey, was one of the leading men of the new breed: a handsome, self-assured native of Courmayeur, who undertook guiding more as a paid adventure than from any need to earn a living. He had a successful woodworking business and was responsible for some of the new Alpine huts then appearing, including that on the Col du Géant.[14] He was an intelligent man, better educated than most guides, who taught himself German so that he could work better with the Oberlanders, especially Johann Jaun whom he greatly admired. A temperate drinker and non-smoker, he had a proper appreciation of his worth:

> Emile has always expressed decided views about the labourer being worthy of his hire; and he acts up to the opinions which many men hold regarding their own professions, although they are often loath to admit them when considering the claims of those who have risen to the top of the tree in humbler callings, but whose knowledge and experience they may, nevertheless, have availed themselves of. Rey never underrates his own power as a guide, and does not attempt to conceal that he is proud of the reputation he has won. He always draws a most distinct line between those of the higher and those of the lower grades in his craft. One morning, at the Montanvert, we were watching the arrival of the 'polyglots,' as an ingenious person once christened that crowd composed of nearly every nationality, who may daily be seen making their toilsome pilgrimage from Chamonix. Among them was an Englishman, who had first provided himself with green spectacles, a veil, and socks to go over his patent leather shoes, and who only wanted a guide to complete his preparations. Going up to Rey, and pointing first to the Mer de Glace, and then to the Chapeau, he inquired 'Combiang?' 'Voilà, Monsieur,' replied Rey, taking off his hat, and indicating with his left hand a group of rather poor specimens of the distinguished Société des Guides, 'Voilà les guides pour la Mer de Glace; *moi*, je suis pour "la Grande Montagne."'[15]

It was Wentworth who persuaded Rey to become a guide in 1876, and their excursion to the dramatic Aiguille Noire de Peuterey in the following year was the first of Rey's many associations with the Peuterey Ridge. The peak itself is the end of the long ridge. It towers over the Val Veni in a great triangle, with two long arms sweeping down to form an immense hollow known as the Fauteuil des Allemands.[16] Rey led them to the East Ridge of the mountain as the obvious way up, but he chose an inferior line – now called the Couloir Rey – which led to some difficulty before they reached the ridge proper. Once there, however, things went easily enough and they reached the summit at two in the afternoon. They had to bivouac on the way down, but reached Courmayeur without incident next day.[17]

Three years later Rey led G. Gruber to the Col de Peuterey by a route which became known as the Rochers Gruber, later a key escape route on this difficult section of Mont Blanc. Then in 1885 Rey made the first ascent of the Aiguille Blanche de Peuterey (4107 m), with Seymour King and A. Supersax as second guide. It was the last of the great Mont Blanc peaks to be climbed. It was not until 1893, however, that Rey completed the ascent of the Peuterey Ridge to the summit of Mont Blanc de Courmayeur with Paul Güssfeldt and two other first-class men, Christian Klucker and César Ollier. He never did manage to string the whole ridge together into a single expedition, something which was not accomplished until 1935.

Nor was Rey behindhand in repeating new routes done by others. He made the second ascent of both the Petit and Grand Drus, not using the pitons used on the former for the first ascent. He also made the third, fourth and fifth ascents of this peak, which he considered the hardest in the Alps.

In 1895 Rey fell to his death, possibly from a heart attack, whilst descending easy rocks unroped below the Aiguille du Géant.[18]

Alexander Burgener, 'The Bear of Eisten', was born in the same year as Rey, 1846, but took to guiding somewhat earlier than his Italian contemporary. His older brother, Franz, was already a guide and Alexander showed remarkable skill as a rock climber developed through chamois-hunting. The Saastal, in which he lived, has a number of small rocky peaks and hunting amongst these undoubtedly led to a natural ability on rock.

His career began in 1868 when he met a rich eighteen-year-old Englishman, Clinton Thomas Dent, who was about to embark on an illustrious Alpine career. Many years later Dent hinted that they got into a number of scrapes through their mutual daring: 'In those days we were not of an age ready to take good advice.'[19] But their daring paid off. In 1870, accompanied by Franz, they made the first ascent of the Lenzspitze (4294 m)[20] and a year later the first ascent of the classic Portjengrat (3654 m). Then in 1872 came the first ascent of the Zinal Rothorn from Zermatt; a much desired prize, which made the local guides so jealous of Burgener that they denied such a climb was possible. It was not without reason that Martin Conway wrote in Burgener's *Führerbuch*, 'Alexander is a thoroughly honest man.' All these climbs were basically rock climbs, and portents of the new order. These were the stones left after the plums had been gobbled up.

And the jealousy of the Zermatt guides stemmed from their complacency in regarding the traditional routes and the traditional ways as sacrosanct. Zermatt guiding was at a low ebb, whilst that of the neighbouring villages like Tasch, Randa, St Niklaus and the Saas hamlets was in the ascendancy. The men of Saas in particular were becoming highly regarded for their new outlook and daring, for besides Burgener there were Ferdinand Imseng, Benedict Venetz and Johann Petrus.

An even more obvious challenge than the Aiguille Noire de Peuterey was the Aiguille du Dru, a huge obelisk of rock towering over the Mer de Glace at Chamonix. It is the end of a ridge running down from the higher Aiguille Verte and as such was ignored by the earlier pioneers but, as Dent pointed out, the gap between the Verte and Dru was wide and deep enough to make the latter quite a separate mountain. In fact, two summits are recognised, the Grand Dru (3754 m) and Petit Dru (3733 m). In appearance it seemed too steep to be climbed, an immense arrowhead of granite. But Clinton Dent dismissed the notion. 'The mountain is too prominent to be inaccessible,' he declared.[21]

The long campaign against the Drus began in 1873 when a strong party consisting of T.S. Kennedy, Garth Marshall, the Rev. C. Taylor and the Pendlebury brothers, accompanied by five leading guides, made an attempt via the Charpoua Glacier, a steep little icefield on the right of the peak, which seemed the most likely way up. The idea was to reach the ridge between the Drus and the Verte, more or less at its lowest point, called the Col des Drus, then climb the ridge to the summit of the Grand Dru. In the event the rocks were iced and the guides, who scouted ahead, declined to take their patrons up.

Shortly after this Dent and Burgener, accompanied by a gymnastics instructor called George Passingham[22] and the elderly guide Franz Andermatten, made their first attempt, but fared no better and a second attempt three days later also failed. In the following year Dent and Burgener reached the Col des Drus. 'We looked down over the Glacier du Nant Blanc and did not like it. We looked upwards and liked it less,' wrote Dent.[23] Yet this ridge was to prove the way up eventually.

In 1875 they tried the Nant Blanc side – the opposite side of the ridge to the Charpoua – but soon retreated. Others made attempts, too, but very little was accomplished until in 1878, accompanied by J.W. Hartley and the two guides Burgener and Kasper Maurer, Dent finally succeeded in reaching the top on his nineteenth attempt. It was a magnificent obsession, matching that of Whymper for the Matterhorn a decade earlier.

It was also a considerable feat of rock climbing. Here is how Dent described the crux:

> What next? An eager look up, and part of the doubt was solved. There was a way – but such a way. A narrow flat couloir, its angle plastered with ice from top to bottom, invited, or forbade, further progress. Above, a pendulous mass of great icicles, black and long like a bunch of elephants' trunks, crowned the gully. We tucked ourselves away on one side, and the guides performed the best feat

of rock climbing I can imagine possible. Unroped they worked up, hacking out the ice, their backs and elbows against one sloping wall and their feet against the other. The masses of ice dashing down, harder and harder as they ascended, showed how they were working. Suddenly a slip above – a shout – a crash of falling ice. Then a brief pause, broken after a few minutes by a triumphant yell from above, and the end of a rope dangled down close to us. Using this latter aid considerably, we mounted and found the top of the couloir blocked up by a great overhanging boulder, dripping still where the icicles had just been broken off. 'Come on,' said voices from above. 'Up you go,' said a voice from below. I leaned as far back as I could, and felt for a hand-hold. There was none. Then right, then left – still none. So I smiled feebly, and said, 'Wait a minute.' Thereupon, of course, they pulled with a will, and struggling and kicking like a spider irritated with tobacco smoke, I topped the rock gracefully. How the first man did it, is, and always will be, a mystery to me. Then we learned that a great mass of ice had broken away under Maurer's feet while in the couloir, and that he must have fallen had not Alexander pinned him to the rock with one hand. From the number of times that this escape was described to me during the next day or two, I am inclined to think it was a near thing. 'The worst is over,' said Alexander. I was glad to hear it, but, looking upwards, had my doubts. The higher we went the bigger the rocks seemed to be. Still there was a way, and it was not so unlike what I had often pictured.

Another tough scramble, and we stood on a comparatively extensive ledge. Already we had climbed more than half of the only part of the mountain as to the nature of which we were uncertain. A few steps on, and Burgener grasped me suddenly by the arm. 'Do you see the great red rock up yonder?' he whispered, hoarse with excitement; 'in ten minutes we shall be there, and on the arête – and then –' I felt that nothing could stop us now; but a feverish anxiety to see what was beyond, to look on to the last slope, which we knew must be easy, impelled us on, and we worked harder than ever to overcome the last few obstacles. The ten minutes expanded into something like thirty before we really reached the rock. Of a sudden the mountain seemed to change its form. For hours we had been climbing the hard dry rocks. Now these appeared to vanish, and – blessed sight – snow lay thick, half hiding, half revealing the last slope of the arête. A glance showed that we had not misjudged. Even the cautious Maurer admitted that as far as we could see all was well; but he added, 'Up above there, possibly –' And now, with the prize almost within our grasp, a strange desire to halt and hang back came on. Alexander tapped the rock with his axe, and let out his pent-up excitement in a comprehensive anathema of Chamonix guides. Already we could anticipate the half-sad feeling with which we should touch the top itself. The feeling soon gave way. 'Forwards' we cried, and the axe crashed through the layers of snow into hard blue ice beneath. A dozen steps, and then a bit of rock scrambling; then more steps along the south side of the ridge – some more rock, and we topped the first eminence. Better and better it looked as we went on. 'See there!' cried Alexander, suddenly; 'the actual top.' There was no mistaking the two huge stones we had so often looked at from below. A few feet below them, and on our left, was one of those strange arches formed by a great transverse boulder, and through the hole we saw blue sky. Nothing could lie beyond, and, still better, nothing could be above. On again, while I could hardly stand still in the great steps the leader hacked out. A short troublesome bit of snow work followed, where the heaped-up cornice had fallen back from the final rock. Then Hartley courteously allowed me to unrope and pass him, and in a second I clutched at the last broken rocks, and hauled myself up on to the flat sloping summit. There for a moment I stood alone, gazing down on Chamonix. The dream of five years was accomplished. The Dru was climbed.[24]

Though Mummery was to extend Burgener further than Dent ever did, the guide always regarded the ascent of the Dru as a significant achievement. Once again the locals refused to believe that an offcomer like Burgener could be successful where their own men had declared the climb impossible. However, Chamonix was satisfied when in the following year the Petit Dru was climbed by three local guides, J.E. Charlet-Straton, P. Payot and F. Folliguet. It proved to be a much harder climb than its big brother.[25]

The Drus overlook the foot of the Mer de Glace, but at the other end of that long glacial valley, on the high ridge forming the Italian border, there rises an even more fantastic rock spire, unmatched in size and shape anywhere in the Western Alps. Only the Dolomites can offer anything to equal the looks of the Aiguille du Géant, but at 4013 metres the Géant is far higher than anything the Dolomites can offer. Seen from the Col du Géant it looks like a stone tower, slightly askew, with two little horns like something the Devil created; seen from the Tacul it has the more blade-like appearance of a granite scimitar.

As early as 1871 climbers were eyeing their chances on what many regarded as the highest unclimbed peak in the Alps.[26] In that year E.R. Whitwell with his guides Ulrich and Christian Lauener attempted to climb the 'north or north-west' side by means of a steep crack which Whitwell described as one of the hardest pieces of climbing he had ever experienced. They were forced to retreat by increasing difficulties when they were '100 to 150 feet from the top'. A year later T.S. Kennedy and his guides found Whitwell's cairn at the foot of the final tower though further progress was deemed impossible, '. . . the walls go up quite straight and I think one might as well try to climb up the outside of a bottle as to ascend this tower.'[27]

In 1876 the guide J.E. Charlet, the man who led the first ascent of the difficult Petit Dru three years later, made a solo attempt on the North Face of the Géant and left a stick on a shoulder high up which could be seen from Montenvers for a number of years. Charlet had hoped to use the stick to plant a flag on the summit, but the upper rocks were heavily verglassed so he retreated.[28]

The following year a very curious attempt took place. Lord Wentworth and a well-known Italian climber, G. de Filippi, tried to climb the Géant by firing rocket lines across the summit from a ledge on the south side to a similar ledge on the north side. 'A mechanism had been prepared for this purpose by Signor Bertinetti, of Turin.' At the third attempt they were successful in shooting a line across, but then the wind took hold of it and blew it back and in the end the experiment was abandoned. In reporting this incident, the *Alpine Journal* pursed its lips with uncharacteristic neutrality: 'Whether or not it is allowable to use such weapons against a peak, proved inaccessible by all ordinary means, is a nice question of mountaineering morals in which we do not feel called to express any opinion.'[29]

The Editor at the time was Douglas Freshfield, whom we have already met as a conservative guardian of tradition, but here he was voicing an ethical concern which was to affect climbing throughout its history. Following the lead of Freshfield and others the British took an uncompromising stance against any form of aid other than a rope and ice axe – even crampons were frowned on for many years. The Europeans took a freer view and in some cases went to the opposite extreme, fixing permanent pitons, permanent ropes and even excavating handholds in the rock.

In view of what was about to happen on the Géant, Freshfield's implied criticism was particularly prescient. Whitwell thought the Laueners would have climbed the Géant with the aid of pitons which he forbade (though he voiced this opinion with the benefit of forty years' hindsight) and when the great Mummery and Alexander Burgener looked at the problem of the Géant twice in 1880 and failed to solve it Mummery left a visiting card for anyone who might follow, on which he wrote, 'Absolutely inaccessible by fair means.' Two years later the card was retrieved by Alessandro Sella who was about to prove Mummery right.

The Sella family was immensely powerful in Italy. Quintino Sella had been responsible for the founding of the Italian Alpine Club and the Italian attempt on the Matterhorn which had precipitated the disaster of 1865. His nephew, Vittorio Sella, was destined to become one of the greatest of mountain photographers, and the rest of the family, too, seemed imbued with a mountain fever. But it was a fever fed on nationalism, understandable perhaps in the newly emerging country which Italy then was. The Géant stood on the Italian border, as did the Matterhorn and, like the latter two decades earlier, the Géant was 'a last great problem'. The first ascent of the Géant would make a splendid consolation prize for losing the Matterhorn.

In 1882 four members of the Sella family embarked on the project: the brothers Alessandro, Corradino and Alphonso (aged seventeen) with their cousin Gaudenzio. Their importance was only that of funding the venture and choosing the guides who were to make the route. Their choice fell on J.J. Maquignaz of Valtournanche, who was assisted by his son Battiste and nephew Daniel.

Maquignaz was fifty-three but had a formidable reputation as a rock climber. He had straightened out the route on the Italian Ridge of the Matterhorn, making it easier than Carrel's original way, and he had done the first traverse of the mountain with Professor Tyndall in 1868. Moreover he seemed (like Carrel) to be imbued with the same national fervour which motivated his employers. 'He had received many offers for the Géant,' wrote Alessandro Sella, 'but did not accept them because he would only have the Italian flag on the summit.'

The ascent was one of the most extraordinary in climbing history. At first the Sellas played no part in it, leaving the whole thing to their guides, who chose to attack the difficult South-West Face. For four days in July 1882 the guides prepared the route – chipping holds (but only where the rock was brittle, Sella ingenuously explained), hammering in large pitons and fixing ropes. Their leader carried a fir-pole of three metres and a half in length which he sometimes used as a ladder and which he subsequently left on the summit, but sometimes even this was not enough and several times the three guides formed a human ladder, with Joseph Maquignaz balanced on a narrow ledge while his son climbed onto his shoulders and then Daniel climbed onto *his* shoulders, in order to fix a rope.

Years later Daniel Maquignaz was asked why they had chosen the South-West Face, which required so much engineering, and he replied that: 'his uncle and he felt certain the N face would go, but the weather all the time they were at work was atrocious, and the face covered in ice. Moreover, the SW face was much quicker to get to, so that they determined to stick to that face until proved impossible, when with the earliest bettering of the weather they would transfer their energies to the N face.'[30]

In the event the guides stuck to the South-West Face and made their 'engineered' ascent a day before the official first ascent by the Sellas. With such precautions it is hardly surprising that the ascent by the Sellas went without incident. They left 100 metres of rope adorning the cliff. Three days later the climb was repeated by 'two Italian officials' and then by a Signor Trombetta, all guided by the Maquignaz, who fixed further ropes to the mountain.

Despite all this careful preparation the Italians made a big mistake – they failed to climb *both* summits of the Géant, and the one they missed out was the higher! Alessandro Sella was undeniably miffed about this, when he discovered his error. He lamely explained that a shortage of rope and time had prevented his accomplishing it and that the extra ropes left by the Maquignaz made subsequent ascents much quicker. In any case, he explained, the guides the day before had *almost* conquered it!

The news that the Géant had been climbed – and the way it had been climbed – spread through the Alpine centres. A young Englishman called W.W. Graham was staying at Zermatt: '. . . When the news arrived at Zermatt that the much-tried peak had been done, I determined to make use of M. Sella's staircase, as it was somewhat unkindly termed, the report being that he had festooned the peak with rope, not to mention iron stanchions and other aids to climbing.'[31]

A fortnight after the Sellas' ascent, Graham arrived in Chamonix and engaged two good guides, Alphonse Payot and Auguste Cupelin, for an attempt. After some delay due to the weather, they made their attempt on August 20:

> About half the ascent was accomplished without stopping and in silence only broken by a pant as one by one we raised ourselves up what may be best likened to a great staircase with very high narrow stairs; and I must say that it was the hardest climbing, from a muscular point of view, that I ever tried. Then, however, the character of the peak entirely changes. It becomes a surface almost as smooth as if it had been planed, whilst the rock, being a close quartz, offers no welcome cracks as hand or foot hold. This face has an inclination of 65° to 70° at least, and in most places more, and is only broken by two vertical clefts and a few very narrow ledges. We climbed three of these with the greatest difficulty, and reached the level of the rope we had seen, though we were still separated from it by the whole breadth of the face. We crossed very gingerly, the ledge being very narrow, and in most places there being absolutely no hand hold. Fortunately the face is not very wide, and we crossed in safety. Then we saw what we ought to have seen before, that the ropes stretched away below us for quite 300 feet, but, being laid in a cleft which was half full of frozen snow, they had been quite hidden. We now mounted merrily, the rope being a great assistance, and indeed in one place necessary, as there is a smooth slab quite fifteen feet high, and which could

only be climbed by a ladder or by nails driven in. The ascent of this cut our hands very badly, as the rope was a mass of ice. Then the way led round a large smooth slab on to the N.W. face; there the rope had become loosened at its upper end, and was hanging down useless. We hoisted Payot up and then he had to work along, hanging from the ledge by his hands till he reached the arête. We then passed him the rope and he fastened it more securely for the benefit of future climbers. We turned the corner, crept along a narrow ledge which overhung a magnificent precipice, and the difficulties were over. The rope was frozen to the rocks, but we were independent of it, as the slope decreased to about 40°, and we were able to go up, partly climbing, partly crawling. About 100 feet of this and we reached a rock step on which was cut the letter 'M', doubtless the point to which Maquignaz had ascended before bringing up M. Sella. With a jump we were up this and on the lower of the two little teeth on the summit ridge, the point which had been previously reached by the Italians, as was attested by a stone man and a tattered flag. Straight in front of us rose the other tooth, about twenty feet higher, but separated from us by an extremely awkward notch. The most obvious line of descent was blocked by a huge loose slab which vibrated, and we consequently had to let ourselves down a vertical drop of about fifteen to twenty feet, and then found ourselves on the little arête between the two teeth. This was of rock topped with ice and gradually narrowed from a foot to a few inches, with, on the right hand, an overhanging precipice of quite 1,200 to 1,500 feet, on the other, a slope of 70° falling almost to the Mer de Glace. Boots had been previously removed, but we were compelled to bestride the arête, which was fortunately short. The other tooth rose perfectly smooth for about ten feet, after which it appeared fairly easy. I as the tallest and lightest mounted on Payot's shoulders, he being astride the ledge. Fortunately there was a small vertical crack by which to steady myself, but as I gently raised myself on Payot I felt very like a man about to undergo the 'long drop'. Then with a pull I was up, and with the aid of the rope raised Payot, and in a minute or two more we were on the top. We promptly set to work to raise a stone man, and in doing so found a splendid crystal, of which I took possession. We hoisted our flag, having borrowed a portion of the Italian flagstaff and utilising my handkerchief.

The South-West Face is still the normal way up the Géant and it is still festooned with aids. Without them it would be much more difficult. The northern side of the mountain – the only one climbed without artificial aids – was not climbed until 1900.[32]

CHAPTER EIGHT

'Too Venturesome to be Imitated'

The second phase of alpinism – the so-called Silver Age – saved mountaineering from premature extinction. Without the outlook of people like Dent, the Pendleburys, the Pilkingtons and their European contemporaries, mountaineering can never have become much more than a sort of muscular geography. The idea that the route was as important as the summit meant that lesser peaks, unknown ridges and quite small rock faces could all be turned to advantage.

Rock climbing became all important. Dent described it thus: 'Rock-climbing and rock peaks are much more in favour now than formerly. The snow mountains no longer attract as they did of yore. Different terms are applied to them. People talk of one form of mountaineering as a rock-climb while they stigmatise the other as a snow grind.'[1]

But he went on to warn that over-specialisation was not good training, that a mountaineer needed all the basics of his craft. All climbers pass through a stone age, he said.

There was something much more sporting about the new kind of climbing, which is why there was an outcry against the use of artificial aids by the Sellas on the Géant. Twenty years earlier nobody had complained about Whymper using grappling irons. To say that there was a sense of revolution in the air is putting it too strongly perhaps; but liberation certainly.

It showed itself most clearly in the growth of guideless climbing, not only in the Eastern Alps but in the West too. Even as early as 1885 Dent could write: 'the relative merits of guides and amateurs have altered materially within the last few years . . . amateurs have improved very much more than guides. The alteration in relative efficiency is, I think, almost wholly due to the improvement of the amateur and not the deterioration of the guide.'[2] To some Victorian readers this was almost sacrilege, but Dent covered his back by confirming that the best amateurs could never expect to equal the best guides – in those days a basic canon of the true faith.

Unfortunately, there was also a steady increase in the number of accidents. This was attributed to rashness by amateurs overreaching themselves on guideless climbs, or to soloing, and certainly there were examples where this was true. Winkler was killed soloing the Weisshorn in 1888, and John Hopkinson with his son and two daughters were killed traversing the Petite Dent de Veisivi in 1898. But guided parties met with accidents, too. In 1899

O.G. Jones was killed on the Dent Blanche along with three guides, Furrer, Zurbriggen and Vuignier, and the accident was caused by Furrer falling. In the terrible year of 1882 that so disturbed Queen Victoria three well-known climbers were killed along with three famous guides.

Nevertheless, the Alpine Club felt it should make a stand and a respected former President, C.E. Mathews, wrote an article grimly titled 'The Alpine Obituary',[3] in which he defended the faith whilst admonishing the faithful. His advice was regarded as gospel by British climbers for years to come, including the oft-quoted 'Whatever number is right, two is unquestionably wrong.'

Even Dent thought some things had gone too far and he castigated solo climbing: 'Solitary expeditions on minor snow mountains are selfish, on more considerable peaks or passes unwise or worse, and on great rock or snow mountains unjustifiable. They may be magnificent but they are not mountaineering.'[4]

The growing number of accidents also provoked Dent into proposing an Alpine Distress Signal which would be immediately recognisable as such, and a sub-committee of the Alpine Club came up with the suggestion in 1894 that there should be: 'A regular series of short signs (which may be called "dots") continued during one minute at the rate of six dots per minute, and repeated in alternate minutes.'[5] It was adopted by the Club and shortly afterwards by the Austro-German and Swiss Alpine Clubs and is now recognised by the mountaineering world in general.

The hand of tradition was already beginning to rest heavily on British alpinism, but for a time at least there were some spirits able to ignore the sombre cautions. Some of these, like the Hopkinsons, Pendleburys, Pilkingtons, Slingsby, and Collie, had a new background of British rock climbing. Amongst the Europeans Guido Lammer was still climbing, sometimes with the British climber Oscar Eckenstein, an engineer credited with perfecting crampons. They were a well-matched pair, unorthodox, and neither likely to pay much attention to the Establishment. Then there were Pfannl and the Gugliermina brothers, Norman-Neruda and Leone Sinigaglia, and many more.

Women climbed alongside men, though not yet on their own. They usually climbed with husbands or brothers, like Mrs E.P. Jackson or Mrs Mummery, or they employed guides on their own account, like Isabella Straton or the Misses Pidgeon. The best of them were tough and determined. One such was Gertrude Bell, who later became a noted Arabist. '"If the women of the Angleez are like her, the men must be lions in strength and valour," cried a desert chief after some tough negotiations with Miss Bell. "We had better make peace with them."'[6]

Women had always been included in the Alpine fraternity (if not yet the Alpine Club – that took a century longer), but the progress they had made in establishing their credentials can be summarised by looking at Mont Blanc. The first woman had stood on the summit as early as 1808; Maria Paradis, a local girl whose sole aim was to publicise her refreshment stall. She was practically dragged up by the guides and though she became known as Maria of Mont Blanc, she never climbed that or any other mountain again. In 1838 Henriette d'Angeville, with a large retinue of guides and porters, as was then common, actually climbed to the top unaided – she wasn't dragged or carried and she continued climbing mountains until she was sixty-nine when, after ascending the Oldenhorn, she declared, 'It is wise at my age to drop the alpenstock before the alpenstock drops me.' In 1854 Mr and Mrs Hamilton climbed the mountain – the first ascent by a British woman, and incidentally the first recorded man and wife ascent anywhere. In 1876 Isabella Straton with Jean Charlet and two other guides made the first winter ascent of Mont Blanc – an important 'first' for a woman to snatch from all those male tigers!

Miss Straton shows how far women had come along the road of Alpine emancipation begun by climbers such as Lucy Walker and Meta Brevoort. Another outstanding lady was Miss Katherine Richardson, petite, fragile-looking and hard as nails. She made 116 major ascents, six of them first ascents and a further fourteen first woman ascents. Her endurance was phenomenal, on a par with that of Passingham. In 1888 she climbed the Meije in a day direct from La Bérarde, leaving the hotel at nine in the evening and returning in time for tea next day, at 5.30. It was the first woman's ascent of the peak. The *Morning Post* commented on another of that season's climbs: 'The honours of 1888 fall to a lady, Miss Richardson, who, with Emile Rey and J.B. Bich ascended the Aiguille de Bionnassay and traversed the E arête to the Dôme du Goûter, previously considered impossible.' Though its difficulty is no longer thought unreasonable, the Bionnassay–Goûter traverse is still described in the guidebook as one of the most beautiful climbs on Mont Blanc and one of the most impressive ridges in the Alps.[7]

Katy Richardson was not alone in her feminine toughness; Mrs Jackson descended the Ferpècle Arête of the Dent Blanche in 1884 with Dr Karl Schulz, a leading German climber, guided by A. Pollinger and J.J. Truffer. This was five years *before* its first ascent. In 1888 she made the first winter ascents of some great Oberland peaks – Gross Lauteraarhorn, Pfaffenstockli, Gross Viescherhorn and the Jungfrau, which she traversed. These were done in a space of twelve days and she suffered severe and permanent frostbite injury from the Jungfrau traverse.[8]

Mrs Le Blond was another distinguished mountaineer of the time and one of the founders of the Ladies' Alpine Club. According to Colonel Strutt, she had the best mountain judgement of any climber he had met, man or woman, amateur or professional. He also claimed she was the first to lead an all-female rope – one such being a traverse of Piz Palu with Lady Evelyn McDonnell.[9]

In an age reeking with prejudice these Victorian ladies really were quite incredible. Male climbers were thought of by the general public as rather eccentric or worse, but female climbers ... ! Dress was a handicap for women. Few dared to follow the advice of Mary Paillon, Miss Richardson's companion, and wear men's clothes. They either suffered in skirts or wore riding breeches under their skirts, removing the latter when they were at a decent distance from the hotel and putting them on again just before returning. There was also the impropriety of sleeping out alone with men who were not related to them and, worse still, sometimes just with guides. And there is no doubt some liaisons did develop this way. Lucy Walker carried a torch for Melchior Anderegg all her life, Isabella Straton married Jean Charlet, and Mrs Mummery put her foot down when it looked like her husband and Lily Bristow were getting too chummy.

Perhaps nothing symbolises these indomitable women so much as the career of the two Pidgeon sisters, Miss Anna and Miss Ellen, who did not begin their climbing until they had reached their mid-thirties when, in 1869, to the astonishment of the Alpine establishment, they mentioned that they had just crossed the Sesiajoch from Zermatt to Alagna. This high col, fairly simple on the Zermatt side, has a huge cliff on the other and it had never been descended. Indeed, the joch had been crossed only twice in the opposite direction, on both occasions by A.W. Moore, one of the leading climbers of the day. It is hardly surprising that there was some disbelief at the story told by those two unknown ladies – but the details of their account could not be denied, albeit they had crossed the col in mistake for the easier Lysjoch.

The two women took an unusually active part in the climb since the guide, Jean Martin, was not at all sure of his whereabouts and the porter was terrified. One of the women came down last which in descent is the position of leader. They were rightly critical of the guide for losing the way and of guiding in general. 'The powers of a mind sharpened by daily use in other matters will, we believe, be found to more than counterbalance the special knowledge of a Swiss peasant.' One suspects that poor Jean Martin came in for some sharp comments during the expedition and as for the porter, 'That such a poor creature should have been sent with travellers, and, above all, with ladies, on a glacier expedition, is a disgrace to Zermatt,' they wrote later.[10]

Whenever they were on their expeditions the sisters slept in whatever accommodation they could find, shepherd's huts, hay-lofts or, failing that, in the open. This experience was put to good use in 1873 when they made the first traverse by women of the Matterhorn from Breuil to Zermatt, guided by the great Jean-Antoine Carrel and two others. Storms trapped them in the hut on the Italian Ridge for three days and conditions were so bad that they were forced to bivouac on the Hörnli Ridge during their descent.[11]

Amongst the throng of good climbers beginning to crowd the last decades of the nineteenth century, two names stand out as pre-eminent. Ludwig Purtscheller was born in Innsbruck in 1849 and was six years older than A.F. Mummery, who came from Dover. In a general way they had little in common: Purtscheller was a handsome, athletic physical education instructor working for a meagre salary, whereas Mummery was a tall but pinched-looking hunchback with poor eyesight and the wealthy owner of a tannery. The Austrian was of retiring disposition, excessively modest and with a narrow circle of acquaintances; the Englishman was lively, full of good cheer and universally known as Fred. Each had the ability to draw others to him by exhibiting superlative skills. Men who were good climbers in their own rights were attracted by a charisma hard to define, but certainly there. It would be too pretentious to claim they each formed a 'school' of climbing – and they would certainly have laughed at the idea – but they did gather round them a clique of talented climbers. In the case of Purtscheller it was the Zsigmondy brothers, Schulz and Merzbacher; with Mummery it was Collie, Slingsby, Carr, Hastings and Lily Bristow, with others like the Pasteur family joining in from time to time.

Purtscheller began climbing when he was twenty-three and a teacher in Klagenfurt. He would visit the Carnic Alps or the Julians for a weekend, sometimes with companions, often alone. He became a great soloist and a man of attack, a firm believer that nothing was impossible until it was proved so and in this he established firmly the growing ethic of Eastern Alpine climbers which was to continue through Preuss, Welzenbach, Buhl and others for the next century.

The sheer number of his ascents was prodigious – some 1700 – rivalling Coolidge in this respect.[12] Eleven years elapsed before Purtscheller took his skills to the Western Alps. In the meantime he found plenty to do in his native Tyrol. An interesting expedition here was his ascent with Von Bohm and the Zsigmondy brothers of the South-West Face of Fussstein, a splendid rock peak next to the mighty Olperer in the Zillertal. This was in 1881, only a year after the mountain was first climbed by the Englishman Russell Starr. Curiously enough, for such a talented team, they failed to try the ridge connecting Fussstein with Olperer – Guido Lammer picked this up solo in 1884, one of the classic traverses of the Zillertal.

Even after 1883, when he first went to the Western Alps, Purtscheller continued to explore his own mountains. For example, 1887 saw him in the Otztal Alps with H. Hess, one of his earliest climbing friends, doing the first traverse of the Hochvernagtspitze, a mixed climb on rock and ice, and the Petersenspitze traverse to Wildspitze, a fine snow route to the second highest summit in Austria. In 1885, with Merzbacher and a local guide, he made the second ascent of the tremendous East Face of Watzmann, in the Berchtesgaden Alps. Gottfried Merzbacher was a noted Dolomite climber and he and Purtscheller later went to the Caucasus together.

But it was with other companions that the two notable years of 1884 and 1885 were spent. First there was Karl Schulz, lawyer and something of a stormy petrel, who fell out with Güssfeldt and was violently attacked by Lammer after the death of Emil Zsigmondy. Schulz made the second traverse of the Biancograt on Piz Bernina and the third ascent of the notorious Marinelli Couloir on Monte Rosa in 1883, with Alexander Burgener and Clemens Perren. This was the first ascent of the face after the disaster of 1881 in which Damiano Marinelli and his two guides lost their lives.

Schulz's abiding love was the Dolomites. Already in 1884, before he went to the Western Alps, he had made the first ascent of the difficult Crozzon di Brenta. Later that year he was, as we have seen, to make the first *descent* of the Ferpècle Arête on the Dent Blanche with Mrs Jackson, long before the ridge was climbed.

Purtscheller also had as companions two brothers of outstanding brilliance as climbers, Otto and Emil Zsigmondy.[13] Otto was twenty-four and his brother a year younger, but it was Emil who was the more daring and accomplished of the two: 'Too venturesome to be imitated,' said Dent drily. Julius Kugy knew both men well and climbed with them for a time. Of Otto he said he was 'the purest soul that I have ever met in my life ... Emil, the more famous of the two, was by comparison like a flame shooting towards heaven.' It was Emil's rash daring which made Kugy give up climbing with them. The pace was too hot for him: 'Otto was more to my taste, with his prudence and constant warning against excess. Purtscheller was more Emil's hot-headed type.'[14] When, shortly before his death, Emil published a book on Alpine dangers one critic wrote that the author was well qualified since he seemed to have suffered personally every possible type of mountain accident. In the book Emil stated that success in mountaineering is 'the triumph of man's will over the forces of nature'.[15]

The two brothers climbed the steep North Face of the Grosser Moseler in 1879 with their friends A. Bohm and E. Worafka. This face, known as Firndreieck, is still used as a test-piece for aspiring north-wall climbers. Also in the Zillertal that year the brothers climbed the Feldkopf, an exceedingly spiky rock peak which they regarded as the hardest rock climb in Tyrol at the time. The mountain later became the Zsigmondyspitze in their honour.

In the Eastern Alps these men, and especially Purtscheller, had often climbed solo and almost always without a guide. In 1884 they took their guideless tactics to the Western Alps and startled the Establishment with their feats. Not only did they knock off some important ordinary routes like the Weisshorn and Zinal Rothorn, but they made the first guideless ascent of the Marinelli Couloir on Monte Rosa, the first guideless traverse of the Matterhorn and a new, serious, route on the Bietschhorn in the Oberland. These climbs raised the status of guideless climbing to include the hardest routes of the day, and laid for ever the myth that amateurs could never equal guides.

But even these outstanding climbs were to be surpassed in the following year, 1885, when Purtscheller and the two Zsigmondys succeeded in traversing the Meije. The mountain had first been climbed eight years before but nobody had succeeded in crossing the ridge between the Pic Central and the Grand Pic, a savage affair with four huge gendarmes barring the way. Otto described the expedition:

> We reached the Pic Central by the ordinary route at 9.30. The weather being very fine at 9.55 we began the descent to the first gap in the arête separating the Pic Central from the first of the four rocky teeth in the ridge between that point and the Pic Occidental. This gap was attained very soon afterwards. The northern face of the two first teeth was covered with hard frozen snow. We crossed that face horizontally from one gap to the next; in the beginning, our crampons having just hold enough, we were not obliged to cut steps. The second gap was reached at 10.45. To get from this depression to the third was much more difficult; ice had taken the place of the snow, and the slopes had become extremely steep, rocks sticking out here and there. The third gap was reached at 11.15. The third and fourth of the teeth are square cut, rather 'low massive turrets of rock.' We had now to take to the ridge itself; having climbed an almost vertical wall of rocks we stood on the top of the third tooth, and at 11.45 in the fourth gap, from which we easily attained the crest of the fourth pinnacle. This forms a very thin wedge; its west face is a sheer precipice, some thirty or forty metres high. We proceeded as far as it was possible, and were then obliged to lower ourselves down by means of our rope, the rocks being overhanging. We fastened a large iron hook into a cleft of the rock, and, passing the rope over it, came safely down into the fifth depression at the foot of the Pic Occidental (2 p.m.). We had always heard that if this gap could be attained, the work would be done; but now the Grand Pic looked quite formidable from here, and we encountered great difficulties in climbing it. The first bit of the wall was comparatively easy, but then hand and foot hold became very scanty, and our leader Purtscheller, having left his knapsack and boots with us, had very hard work to overcome this *mauvais pas*. After having mounted about forty metres of very

smooth rock, we came to a point where all difficulties ceased, and a quarter of an hour later we stood on the summit of the Meije at 4.15 p.m.[16]

This was an astonishing *tour de force* by an unguided party. Today it is still regarded as one of the great classic ridges of the Alps (though now usually done the other way round) and the gap below the Grand Pic is called the Brèche Zsigmondy. Otto's account is interesting, too, in that it reveals the Austrians had no inhibitions about using crampons or even a modest piton.

But a few days later this triumph was to turn to ashes. Schulz had not taken part in the traverse because he had injured his hand and he had even failed on the ordinary route due to bad weather. The Zsigmondys promised they would not leave before taking him to the top. Otto thought they should just climb the ordinary route but Emil had plans on the dramatic South Face of the mountain, a majestic wall of rock towering above the Etançons Glacier. He was too forceful a character to be denied and so it was to the South Face that the party set out.

They gained the face below the Grand Pic about 6 a.m., where they were subjected to barrages of stones from the mountain and where, to make matters worse, a violent storm broke, trapping them on a ledge. But after a while the storm abated, and like a curtain being drawn aside, the clouds dispersed to reveal a bright blue sky and hot sun.

Their intention was to follow a prominent ledge on the face in order to reach a steep gully leading directly to the Brèche Zsigmondy. Though the ledge was covered with snow, there was a gap between the snow and the rock wall which allowed them to climb freely, though here and there the ledge was interrupted by steep rock pitches of ten metres or so which had to be climbed. In the end the terrace gave out onto a final patch of ice from which there was no escape except by climbing some forty-five metres up the steep rocks above. This landed them on a horizontal terrace and separated from their gully by a prominent pillar. Leaving Schulz behind the two brothers unroped[17] and investigated what lay beyond the pillar. Could they get into the gully? One glance was sufficient to dash their hopes – the gully was smooth and steep, its rocks glazed with verglas. They returned to the waiting Schulz.

Emil now tried a couloir in the rocks above but got nowhere. The time was 1.30 p.m. and Otto was for retreating. So was Schulz: 'Now, Emil, what do you think, haven't you yet given up all hope?' he said. To which the other replied: 'What would one have if one hadn't some hope?'

Suddenly, without warning, Emil tied onto a hemp rope and started climbing towards a ledge some thirty metres higher. The going was evidently very difficult and a little over half-way he called for more rope. Otto tied a silk rope to the other. When he was scarcely one metre from the ledge, all progress came to an end. He tried to hitch the rope over a projection above his head and come down with its aid, but the rope slipped off and he fell, slithering down the rocks, hitting a ledge and bouncing off in a wide arc above the heads of his two horrified companions. The silk rope snapped like cotton thread and he landed on the icefield at the end of the first ledge, slipped down this, and plunged 600 metres to the Etançons Glacier.[18]

The death of Emil Zsigmondy shocked and dismayed the climbing world. Just when it seemed that amateurs had proved their point, the forces of reaction were able to seize on the death of Zsigmondy as proof of the need for the cautious approach and for guides. Coolidge wrote what many thought:

> Every great peak in the Alps has now been conquered; but it does not follow that because a mountain has been climbed, every one of its faces or ridges can or ought to be done. If mountaineering is allowed to degenerate into a form of gambling in which the players stake their lives, it would cease to be what it is now, the noblest form of recreation known to man, it could no longer be defended ... The lesson, then, of the Meije accident is the need of exercising self-restraint and caution in climbing. As a rule these valuable safeguards are supplied by the guides of a party.[19]

Otto, broken-hearted at the loss of his brother, seldom climbed again. Schulz resumed his climbing exactly one week after the accident on the Meije and continued to climb for a number of years, mainly in the Eastern Alps.[20] And what of Purtscheller? He went on to climb in the Caucasus and to make the first ascent of Kilimanjaro, the highest mountain in Africa. The Aiguille Purtscheller, of which he made the first ascent, was named after him in the Mont Blanc group. In August 1899 Purtscheller and a friend were descending with a guide the steep snow slopes below the Dru when the guide's axe broke and he slipped, dragging his clients down the slope and twenty feet into a crevasse. Purtscheller's arm was broken and he spent six months in Swiss hospitals recuperating. Unfortunately, he caught influenza and in his weakened condition was unable to fight it off. He died in February 1900. The greatest guideless climber of his day had died after climbing with a guide.

Albert Frederick Mummery was born in 1855. He was what the Victorians called 'a sickly child', having a spinal deformity which made him somewhat hunchbacked, and increasingly myopic vision. He was a tall gangling youth who hated load carrying and was not a great walker, yet who seemed able to keep going on steep rock and ice ... Throughout his life he was a mass of paradoxes. Despite his appearance he was attractive to women and men found in him a natural leader. Despite his dislike of walking he visited the

Caucasus and the Himalaya, where strong walking is essential to success. He was one of the greatest rock climbers of his day, yet he had no time for the home-grown variety then beginning to flourish in the Lakes and elsewhere. And he had his enemies, amongst whom might be counted Davidson and Whymper.

There were two important phases to Mummery's climbing career: the ten guided years from 1879 when he climbed principally with Burgener, and the five unguided years from 1891. He made his first climb when he was sixteen (crossing the Théodule Pass) and by the time he was twenty-two he had a modest Alpine record, including Monte Rosa, the Matterhorn and Mont Blanc. There was nothing in this, however, to suggest the extraordinary ability and driving ambitions of the man. In fact, as far as we know, in 1877 and 1878 Mummery didn't visit the Alps at all.

August 1879 saw him crossing the Tiefenmattenjoch in the Pennine Alps, which gave him a close-up of the unclimbed Zmutt Arête of the Matterhorn and he was seized by ambition to be its conqueror. He knew that since the heady days of 1865, when Whymper and Carrel had battled for the first ascent, and the Hörnli and Italian (North and South) Ridges were climbed, nothing new had been done. Climbers had looked at the East and West Ridges – the Zmutt and the Furggen – and, echoing Melchior's immortal words, had turned away.

As luck would have it, when Mummery reached Zermatt he found Alexander Burgener free of engagements, and the guide, perhaps sensing something special about this Englishman, despite his appearance and despite his not being an Alpine Club member, agreed to attempt the Zmutt. After a few training climbs (one a pretty desperate affair not repeated for fifty-three years) they returned to Zermatt in time to learn that another party had set off for the Zmutt. The climber was William Penhall, pupil of George Passingham, a twenty-one-year-old firebrand whose meteoric climbing career had precipitated him into the Alpine Club at the age of eighteen. With him he had the great Ferdinand Imseng of Monte Rosa fame and Louis Zurbriggen.

Penhall's first attempt failed. As he retreated he met Mummery advancing and, though the weather did not look promising, Imseng became anxious. He did not want Burgener to snatch the Zmutt Ridge from under his nose, and scarcely had his party reached the village than Imseng suggested they should turn round and head back for the Matterhorn. Even the dynamic Penhall was taken aback. 'I should hardly have proposed it myself,' he later wrote. They had scarcely slept for forty-eight hours. But Imseng had a persuasive tongue, so they turned about and walked back for five and a half hours to the foot of the mountain.[21]

Had they but known it, this extraordinary forced march actually put them ahead of their rivals, who were still asleep. Imseng, however, thought that

Burgener would surely be on the ridge and so he led the party on a curious outflanking manoeuvre which took them across the dangerous couloir between the ridge and the West Face, now called the Penhall Couloir, and onto the great slabby West Face itself. Stones whistled down past them as they desperately sought a way up, sometimes on easy ground, sometimes on impossible slabs.

Mummery was not aware of his rivals until next morning when he was well established on the ridge and the others on the face, and they gave him a joyous yodel.

His party had been strengthened. Besides Burgener he had also acquired two other guides, Johann Petrus to scout out in front, and Augustin Gentinetta to bring up the rear. Only Burgener and Mummery were roped together. Petrus was a quick-tempered neighbour of Burgener from Eisten in Saastal and a very good rock climber. They found the most difficult part of the ridge was the great Zmutt Teeth where the ridge joins the main face of the mountain. But they overcame these, and the Tiefenmatten Slabs, to reach the Italian Summit of the Matterhorn at 1.45 p.m. About an hour and a quarter later, Penhall's party emerged victorious from the West Face, after a most hazardous climb that is seldom repeated even today. It was on this route that Lammer and Lorria came to grief attempting the second ascent eight years later.

Despite solving one of the outstanding Alpine problems of the day, Mummery was rejected by the Alpine Club in the following spring. The reasons for this are not clear but they seem to stem from the machinations of Davidson who, for whatever reason, had taken a dislike to Mummery. It was said Mummery was unsporting in 'stealing' the climb from Penhall, but this was ridiculous, for Penhall climbed with Mummery after the Zmutt affair and was one of his supporters. Whoever else took offence, it certainly was not Penhall. A rumour was started that Mummery's tannery was actually a shoe-shop in Dover and that the man was in *trade* – damning indeed in the Victorian hierarchy! But Mummery was never in trade and he took increasingly little interest in the tannery either, leaving it mostly to his brother who was his partner. He preferred to spend his time studying political economy and some years later he was co-author of a book on the subject with J.A. Hobson.[22] Perhaps his association with radical ideas upset Davidson, who was a snob.

His rejection by the Club upset Mummery greatly and he almost gave up climbing. Instead, he turned to the one man he could trust, Alexander Burgener. That summer they returned to the Matterhorn where they crossed the savage Col du Lion for the first time but failed in an attempt on the Furggen Ridge, the last unclimbed ridge of the mountain. In Chamonix they made an ascent of the Charmoz,[23] but failed on the Géant.

The season had seen the introduction of little Benedict Venetz into the team, a neighbour of Burgener in the Saastal and a fine rock climber. Whenever the climbing became particularly difficult, Venetz was pushed into the lead.

Mummery opened the season of 1881 by climbing the Charpoua Face of the Verte with Burgener, an outstanding problem which had almost been solved by James Eccles the year before; then he turned his attention to the Grépon, one of the great prizes which many had tried to grasp. Venetz, who had been ill, joined them and they first of all tried to climb the mountain from the Mer de Glace, but this proved too difficult so they switched their attention to the other side where the small but steep Nantillons Glacier fills the corrie between the Grépon and Blaitière. From here they climbed up a deep gully separating the Charmoz from the Grépon and came to a curious flake of rock forming a crack with the parent mountain which proved the key to access to the ridge. The crack became known as the Mummery Crack, though it was Venetz who first climbed it.

Soon they were on the summit, but that evening Mummery had second thoughts. He suspected that the real summit was further along the ridge. 'My dreams were troubled by visions of a great square tower ... at the other end of the summit ridge.' On a pinnacled ridge like the Grépon it would be easy to make a mistake. He decided to go back.

So once again the three men climbed along the ridge and this time they pushed towards the far end, helped by a curious ledge, 'suitable for carriages, bicycles, or other similar conveyances'. Then they came to the final tower:

> It was certainly one of the most forbidding rocks I have ever set eyes on. Unlike the rest of the peak, it was smooth to the touch, and its square-cut edges offered no hold or grip of any sort. True, the block was fractured from top to bottom, but the crack, four or five inches wide, had edges as smooth and true as a mason could have hewn them, and had not one of those irregular and convenient backs not infrequently possessed by such clefts. Even the dangerous help of a semi-loose stone, wedged with doubtful security, between the opposing walls, was lacking. Added to all this a great rock overhung the top, and would obviously require a powerful effort just when the climber was most exhausted.
>
> Under these circumstances, Burgener and I set to work to throw a rope over the top, whilst Venetz reposed in a graceful attitude rejoicing in a quiet pipe. After many efforts, in the course of which both Burgener and I nearly succeeded in throwing ourselves over on to the Mer de Glace, but dismally failed in landing the rope, we became virtuous, and decided that the rock must be climbed by the fair methods of honourable war. To this end we poked up Venetz with the ice-axe (he was by now enjoying a peaceful nap),

1 Mont Blanc (4807m) is the highest mountain in Western Europe. It inspired the scientist de Saussure (*below left*) to offer a prize for the first ascent – not claimed for many years until Dr M.G. Paccard (*below centre*) and J. Balmat (*below right*) climbed the peak in 1786. The following year de Saussure himself reached the summit.

2 EARLY ALPINISTS
Top left: Josias Simler (1530–76) was one of the first to describe snowcraft. *Top right*: Father Placidus à Spescha (1752–1833) devoted his life to exploring the Grisons and ranks with de Saussure as one of the founders of alpinism. *Centre left*: Albert Smith (1816–60) journalist and showman, responsible for popularising the Alps. *Centre right*: Henriette d'Angeville (1794–1871) made the second ascent of Mont Blanc by a woman in 1838. *Bottom left*: William Windham (1717–61) whose description of Chamonix made the village popular.

3 PIONEER ALPINE GUIDES
Top left: Johann Jaun, most daring of the younger guides. *Top right*: J-A
Carrell, Whymper's guide and rival on the Matterhorn. *Below left*: Emile
Rey, intelligent and popular. *Below centre*: Christian Almer, regarded as
the greatest of all early guides. *Below right*: Christian Klucker, the
Engadine schoolmaster with a formidable list of hard new routes.

4 Gustave Doré's dramatic impression of the Matterhorn accident of 1865 which brought the Golden Age of alpinism to an abrupt halt. *Inset*: the young Edward Whymper, whose obsession with the mountain led to the first tragic ascent.

5 NORWAY
Cecil Slingsby was largely responsible for the early development of climbing in Norway. His most famous ascent was Skagastolstind, a dramatic peak in the Jotenheim, in 1876. Here he is seen on a later ascent with Ole Berg, owner of the Turtegr Inn, and Thérèse Bertheau who made the first woman's ascent, 1894.
Inset: Slingsby (left) Howard Priestman, Thérèse Bertheau.

6 La Meije, one of the last great Alpine peaks to be climbed. The first ascent was by Henri Boileau de Castelnau (*inset left*) in 1877. The first traverse was in 1885 by Emil Zsigmondy (*inset right*) with his brother Otto and L. Purtscheller. Emil was killed attempting the South Face.

7 The South-West Face of the Täschhorn in the Pennine Alps – one of the most dangerous of faces, seldom repeated, but first climbed in 1906 by Young, Ryan, Lochmatter and Knubel. *Inset*: G.W. Young.

8 *Top*: Nanga Parbat, the Himalayan peak on which A.F. Mummery disappeared in 1895 and scene of the great German expedition tragedies of 1934 and 1937. *Above*: A.F. Mummery and his daughter. Mummery was the most influential climber of his generation; along with Welzenbach, the founder of modern alpinism. *Left*: Mount Assiniboine in Canada, first climbed in 1901 by James Outram, much to the chagrin of Norman Collie (*inset left*). Collie had been with Mummery on Nanga Parbat and many alpine climbs and had experience of climbing in many parts of the world, including six visits to the Canadian Rockies. In many ways he was the most complete mountaineer of his day.

and we then generally pulled ourselves together and made ready for the crucial struggle.

Our rope-throwing operations had been carried on from the top of a sort of narrow wall, about two feet wide, and perhaps six feet above the gap. Burgener, posted on this wall, stood ready to help Venetz with the ice-axe so soon as he should get within his reach, whilst my unworthy self, planted in the gap, was able to assist him in the first part of his journey. So soon as Venetz got beyond my reach, Burgener leant across the gap, and, jamming the point of the axe against the face of the rock, made a series of footholds of doubtful security whereon Venetz could rest and gain strength for each successive effort. At length he got above all these adventitious aids and had to depend exclusively on his splendid skill. Inch by inch he forced his way, gasping for breath, and his hand wandering over the smooth rock in those vague searches for non-existent hold which it is positively painful to witness. Burgener and I watched him with intense anxiety, and it was with no slight feeling of relief that we saw the fingers of one hand reach the firm hold offered by the square-cut top. A few moments' rest, and he made his way over the projecting rock, whilst Burgener and I yelled ourselves hoarse.[24]

The ascent of the Grépon terminated Mummery's first great Alpine period – and almost terminated his climbing altogether. He still found himself at odds with the Alpine Club, though he desperately wanted to be accepted by his peers. He did no climbing for four years and very little in the fifth. Not until 1887 did he return, to climb with his wife various standard peaks and to make the first ascent of the Teufelsgrat, a ridge on the Täschhorn. They were guided by Burgener and Franz Andermatten.

In 1888 he visited the Caucasus, and returned there in 1890. In the Alps he crossed the Schreckjoch for the first time, but otherwise did little until 1892, when his second important period began. Ironically it was during this quiet period, in 1888, that he was finally elected to the Alpine Club.

The three years 1892–4 were important not so much for the new climbs done or attempted, but for the spirit in which all three seasons were conducted. Mummery gathered about him a group of close friends: Ellis Carr, Norman Collie, Geoffrey Hastings, Cecil Slingsby and Lily Bristow, all of whom were good climbers and prepared to tackle the hardest climbs of the day without guides. Others joined in from time to time – C.H. Pasteur and his sisters, W.J. Petherick, Godfrey Solly – so that there was something of a jolly family atmosphere about the thing.

Most of these people had trained on Lakeland crags at home. In 1892, for instance, several of them had been involved in one or more of the hardest climbs of the year, Eagle's Nest Ridge on Great Gable, Moss Ghyll on Scafell and the Traverse of the Nose on Pillar Rock. Mummery himself did not like British rock climbing: 'Climbing as practised at Wasdale Head is both difficult and dangerous,' he said.[25]

That first year together Mummery, Slingsby and Carr attempted the North Face of the Aiguille du Plan; a great cascade of tumbling ice. They almost pulled it off, too – a climb which was not done until 1924 – but it beat them in the end and forced them into a hazardous retreat. The Charmoz was traversed with a large party including Miss Bristow and Miss Pasteur and the Grépon was traversed for the first time with Hastings, Collie and Pasteur. At the end of August Mummery teamed up with a guide again – the great Emile Rey – to make an unsuccessful attempt on the savage Hirondelles Ridge of the Grandes Jorasses, not climbed until 1927.

In 1893 with Slingsby, Hastings and Collie he made the first ascent of the Dent du Requin and the West Face of the Plan. He also took Lily Bristow across the Grépon, and up the Zinal Rothorn, the Dru and the Italian Ridge of the Matterhorn – a concentrated campaign of rock climbing probably unequalled by any other woman climber of the period. 'It has frequently been noted,' he later wrote, 'that all mountains appear doomed to pass through the three stages: An inaccessible peak – The most difficult ascent in the Alps – An easy day for a lady.'[26] Mummery allowed Lily Bristow to lead some of the pitches – almost unheard of then – but, despite her pleadings, he would not take her on a major new climb, although he had taken his wife on one, the Teufelsgrat, some years before. Lily Bristow never climbed with Mummery after the 1893 season, perhaps because Mrs Mummery grew jealous of the developing relationship between her husband and her schoolgirl chum.

In 1894 with Hastings and Collie, Mummery made the first guideless ascent of the Brenva Spur on Mont Blanc, A.W. Moore's great classic of 1865. Thirty years on and it still had an aura of inaccessibility, for there had only been five ascents and all by gifted climbers employing great guides. It was another ten years before a guideless party was again successful. There could be nothing more calculated to demonstrate to the Alpine world at large just how far ahead of the field were Fred Mummery and his mates.

The last climb of the year, and his last climb in the Alps, was the one which had brought him fame fifteen years before, the Zmutt Arête of the Matterhorn. In the following summer, 1895, Mummery, Hastings, Collie and a Gurkha officer called Bruce attempted to climb the Himalayan giant, Nanga Parbat. They failed and in their failure Fred Mummery and two Gurkhas disappeared, presumably overwhelmed by an avalanche.

Just before he left for India, Mummery's book of reminiscences was published, *My Climbs in the Alps and Caucasus*, perhaps the only book to rival Whymper's *Scrambles*. In it Mummery included his philosophy of mountaineering in a chapter called 'The Pleasures and Penalties of Mountaineering'.

It had a great influence, perhaps more on the Continent than in Britain, and in truth it does not differ materially from what climbers like Purtscheller, the Zsigmondys and Lammer were saying: 'There is an educative and purifying power in danger that is to be found in no other school.' Or 'High proficiency in the sport is only attainable when a natural aptitude is combined with long years of practice, and not without some, perhaps much, danger to life and limb.'

Above all, he defined climbing beyond any doubt: 'The essence of the sport lies, not in ascending a peak, but in struggling with and overcoming difficulties.'

In the few years remaining before the First World War alpinism expanded but did not noticeably advance. There were some very fine climbers active during these years and, surprisingly perhaps, most of them were guided. In fact most of them formed a team with their guide, or sometimes two guides – a shift in emphasis. One thinks of them together, permanently linked in memory: Fontaine and Ravanel, Mayer and Dibona, Ryan and Lochmatter, Young and Knubel. Women, too, were taking part in some hard first ascents: the Hungarians Rolanda and Ilona Eotvos were on the first ascent of the Tofana South Face with A. Dimai, G. Siorpes and A. Verzi in 1901 and the American Beatrice Tomasson climbed the classic route on the South Face of Marmolata with L. Bettega and B. Zagonel in the same year.

The Austro-German climbers, though still parochially attached to their limestone heartland, began to wander west in increasing numbers, bringing their philosophy of guideless climbing and ultimate freedom with them. One such was Karl Blodig, a dentist from Bregenz, who became the first person to collect all the 4000-metre peaks in the Alps, a feat he accomplished by 1911. When some of the sharp spires in the Mont Blanc range were elevated to the status of peaks, Blodig felt he had to climb those too and the saga continued until he was seventy-three years old, when he climbed the Grande Rocheuse and Aiguille du Jardin solo, causing the French expert Jacques Lagarde to comment that 'one can perform very great feats with very silly motives'.[27]

Heinrich Pfannl, a judge from Vienna, had brought a touch of eastern promise to the much maligned Aiguille du Géant in 1900, when, with his comrades Thomas Maischberger and F. Zimmer, he climbed the mountain by the North Ridge and North-West Face, the only free climb on this steep tower. The three Austrians had already done a series of very steep face climbs on their own limestone Alps, Zimmer the Dachstein South Face, one of the hardest climbs in the Eastern Alps at that time.[28]

The real star in the east, however, was Paul Preuss, a young scientist who is credited with 1200 climbs, including 150 first ascents and 300 solo ascents. He visited the Western Alps for the first time in 1912 where he had the shattering experience of witnessing the death of H.O. Jones and his wife on Mont Rouge de Peuterey, when their guide Truffer fell and pulled them from their holds. Preuss was soloing the route ahead of them, but abandoned it to hurry down to Courmayeur and raise the alarm. In the following year he was back to make the first traverse of the Aiguille Blanche de Peuterey from the Dames Anglaises Col to the Col de Peuterey with Carl Prochownick and Count Aldo Bonacossa, a serious route on a fine mountain and one which gave him an ambition to climb the entire Peuterey Ridge in one long expedition.

It was not to be. Later that year Preuss was killed attempting the North Ridge of the Mandlwand, a new route in the Gosaukamm. The Peuterey was not climbed entire until 1935.

The sheer audacity of many of Preuss's routes has tended to obscure his philosophy of climbing, yet without it he could be dismissed as a fearless 'necker', of the kind often seen in climbing. Perhaps also it was his misfortune to be overshadowed by the writings of people like Lammer, Purtscheller, Zsigmondy and Mummery. Yet Preuss took a stance which was both ethical and practical. From this stemmed his famous Six Theorems:

(1) One should not only be equal to any expedition which one undertakes, but more than equal to it.

(2) The standard of difficulty which a climber can conquer with safety when descending, and for which he can consider himself competent, with an easy conscience, should represent the limit of what he should attempt on his ascent.

(3) Hence the use of artificial aids only becomes justifiable in case of sudden threatening danger.

(4) The *Mauerhaken* (spike for driving in) is an emergency aid and not the basis of a system of mountaineering.

(5) The rope may be used for facilitating matters, but never as the sole means of making an expedition possible.

(6) The principle of safety is one of the highest principles. Not the spasmodic correction of one's own want of safety, obtained by the use of artificial aids, but that true primary safety which should result, with every climber, from a just estimate of what he is able, and what he desires, to do.[29]

This rigorous analysis was 'hurled like bombs into the self-satisfied and smug hypocrisy of sundry Alpine circles and led to animated debates for and against his assertions ... Whatever one's opinion may be, one thing is certain: Preuss asks for a purity of style, for an agreement between what a climber is able, and what he desires, to do, which makes it necessary to be a severe critic of himself. With this he has penetrated to the very spirit of mountaineering morality, the most secret recess of Alpine thought and feeling.'[30]

In other words, Preuss raised ethics to a higher conscious level than hitherto. But, sadly, his cry went largely unheard, and it wasn't until recent times, and the advent of Reinhold Messner, that such a powerful voice was again heard crying in the land.

The great ridges continued to fall, although they were by no means all conquered before the War. The Mittelegi on the Eiger held out until 1921 and the Hirondelles Ridge of Grandes Jorasses until 1927, for example.[31] One of those that did succumb just before the century turned was the Peuterey Ridge of Mont Blanc, not the entire ridge dreamed of by Preuss, but the final part, rising from the Col de Peuterey to the summit of Mont Blanc de Courmayeur, in itself a formidable challenge.

It was tackled in 1893 by Paul Güssfeldt, the German scientist who was Privy Counsellor to Kaiser Wilhelm II. Güssfeldt was a big solid man who did big solid climbs, long routes on high peaks, and usually with the best of guides. He was fifty-three when he attempted the Peuterey and already had several fine lines to this credit, particularly the Scerscen Eisnase (1877) and the famous Biancograt of Piz Bernina (1878). He made the fourth ascent of the Brenva Face in 1892 and, increasingly fascinated by Mont Blanc, was ready for the unclimbed Peuterey Ridge the following year.

He provided himself with two absolutely top-rank guides, Emile Rey and Christian Klucker and, as porter, César Ollier who later became a famous guide himself. So the party was immensely strong, though Klucker, the fiery guide from Engadine, nursed a permanent grudge. He didn't like Güssfeldt and thought he was a poor climber, though his opinion was no doubt influenced by the fact that Güssfeldt chose Rey as first guide.

They began the expedition by traversing the Aiguille Blanche de Peuterey by a somewhat dangerous route, later superseded by that of Preuss. The East Face was a death-trap. 'It began to get lively above our heads,' Güssfeldt later recalled. 'We decided to cross towards the left over two steep snow gullies, but before we had advanced a hundred steps we were driven back by falling stones.'[32] Nevertheless, they eventually reached the summit, descended to the Col de Peuterey and began the climb up the final ridge.

By three in the afternoon they had had enough for one day and bivouacked on a ledge at 4250 metres. The night was intensely cold and none of them could sleep; Rey sang to try and keep up their spirits. At dawn they partook of a meagre breakfast – Güssfeldt's was a raw egg which was so cold it had become granulated – and drank a bottle of champagne to dispel the numbing effects of the cold.

Hard ice and poor, verglassed rocks made for slow progress above, but they reached the top of Mont Blanc de Courmayeur at 12.55 p.m., and the summit of Mont Blanc an hour later.[33]

Of the other long classic ridges on this side of Mont Blanc the Brouillard was climbed by G.B. Gugliermina[34] with Joseph Brocherel in 1901, but the Innominata had to wait until just after the war in 1919, when it was climbed by Courtauld and Oliver with three guides.

Shorter, but infinitely sharper, was the Rote Zähne of the Gspaltenhorn (3437 m), a peak in the Oberland noted for its spiky ridges. The Rote Zähne is the South-West Ridge and lives up to its name. It rises dramatically from the col called the Gamchilucke, which separates it from the Morgenhorn, in a series of huge decaying teeth, including three major ones divided one from another by deep chasms.

In 1914, in the last season before the War, the ridge was tackled by Geoffrey Winthrop Young and Siegfried Herford with the guides Josef Knubel and Hans Brantschen. Both Young and Herford were fine rock climbers. The latter had recently done the Central Buttress on Scafell in the Lake District, for years regarded by many as the hardest climb in Britain. Young had put up one of the finest rock climbs in the Alps on the Grépon and both guides were at the top of their profession.

The season was not one of good weather and they climbed, as Young put it, in 'dangerous conditions, upon a rock of ill habit, under weather of ill omen'. In his classic book *On High Hills*, Young has described how the struggle with the savage gaps in the ridge was always problematical as to outcome. Even today the ridge is still graded TD inf., with pitches of V. It was Herford's last season. He was killed at Ypres in 1916 and Young, though he climbed again after the war, lost a leg in the conflict.

The old British dominance in the Alps was fading fast in the years before the Great War, but it did have one last flowering with Young and his great contemporary, Ryan, aided by three of the best guides in Josef Knubel and the Lochmatter brothers. Never again were British climbers to set the pace of Alpine development; perhaps because the financial climate was never as good as in pre-war days, perhaps because British eyes were turned to Everest on the one hand and our own homeland crags on the other.

Geoffrey Winthrop Young (1876–1958) was a son of Sir George Young who had made the first ascent of the Jungfrau from the Wengern Alp in 1865. In the following year, however, George's brother was killed climbing and thereafter all mention of mountaineering was forbidden in the Young household, though the family did go hill-walking in Wales. Young never lost his love of the Welsh hills and his Pen y Pass house-parties were virtually private club meets of climbing friends. He it was who persuaded George Mallory to join the first Everest expedition in 1921.

Young embraced the whole spectrum of British climbing: he persuaded J.M.A. Thomson to publish the first climbers' guidebooks (to Snowdonia),[35] and played a large part in 1944 in founding the British Mountaineering Council, the governing body of the sport in England and Wales. He even wrote a book on climbing the ancient stones of Trinity College![36] For many years his book *Mountain Craft* (1920) was regarded as the mountaineer's bible and his autobiographical books and poems were highly regarded. It is doubtful if even Slingsby (whose daughter he married) had a greater influence on the shape of British climbing.

He was, however, first and foremost a great alpinist, high technical competence, daring and prodigious stamina leading him to a series of great routes. On many, but not all, he was partnered by Josef Knubel of St Niklaus, one of a well-known guiding family who, though small of stature and a heavy smoker, seemed able to match Young step for step.

Their greatest season was in 1911. H.O. Jones was with them and from time to time they were joined by others as they attacked some of the outstanding problem climbs of the Alps. It was on their ascent of the Brouillard Ridge, where they were trying to improve on the Gugliermina route of ten years before, that Karl Blodig, who was with them, completed all the 4000-metre peaks when he reached the summit of Pointe Louis Amédée (Pic Luigi Amedeo, 4469 m). They failed on the Hirondelles Ridge of the Grandes Jorasses, though they did manage to descend it for the first time, but climbed the long West Ridge with its series of 4000-metre pinnacles. Another pinnacle, which fails by just four metres to reach the magic mark, is now called Point Young.[37]

But the highlight of the season was the first ascent of the East Face of the Grépon, that plum rock climb which had eluded the great Mummery himself. For this, Young, Jones and Knubel were joined by Ralph Todhunter and the guide Henri Brocherel. At forty-four, Todhunter was older than the others, but a superb climber with the strange affectation of climbing in white gloves.

They bivouacked below the face of the Grépon and on August 19, shortly after 3 a.m. climbed the modest Trélaporte Glacier which forms a skirt of ice below the rocks. There was some difficulty with the bergschrund, for the season was a dry one and the ice had contracted, widening the rift, but soon they were over it and heading for a prominent feature, the Tour Rouge. This was the previous limit of exploration but before long they had passed it, heading for the left-hand one of a pair of ridges which soared up to the mountain crest.

For a time Knubel, who was leading, lost his way in an area of blank slabs, but Young saved the day by discovering a traverse across a difficult gully which got them back on the right line. Soon they reached a triangular ledge which they christened the Niche des Amis, and which Knubel gloomily forecast would be their bivouac site when they were forced to retreat. But pitch followed pitch of rough granite, slabs and cracks, often with undercut holds. Todhunter, in the role of last man, casually strolled up after the others, coiling the rope as he went, 'in order to save time', as he remarked.

Afterwards, Jones, who was next on the rope, remembered that he seemed to be chased up the cliff by a pair of white gloves.

> The climbing was always difficult, [wrote Jones later] usually exceedingly difficult, twice verging on the impossible, but it was undoubtedly superb. Chimney, slab and crack, always steep, sometimes even overhanging, followed one another in rapid and bewildering succession; often the slabs provided only a crack-hold for the hands and the foothold had to be obtained by friction on vertical slabs of rough protogine.[38]

The first time it neared the impossible was at a deep chimney, interrupted by an overhang. Knubel had to stand on Brocherel's shoulders and hook his ice axe into nicks in the rock in a desperate method perfected by himself and his friend Franz Lochmatter which they called 'the axe cling'. Jones described it thus:

> It is impossible to convey any adequate impression of the next 30 feet. First there was the constricted part of the chimney slightly overhanging which gave out onto a slab provided with rudimentary holds; this in turn led to a hopeless overhang, which had to be turned by rounding a corner on the right, whence a steep slab, practically devoid of holds, led to a good stance and belay. Knubel's ascent of the last mentioned slab, relying solely on an axe, and its point inserted into a minute crack as hand-hold, and merely relying on friction for the rest, is one of the most remarkable climbing feats I know of. It was perhaps fortunate for the morale of the party that he was out of sight when doing it.

At last they reached the final pinnacle of the Grépon and the last and greatest pitch of the climb. They could have avoided it; the ordinary route to the summit lay only a few feet away, but they all felt that such a magnificent climb deserved a unique finish of its own. And there was one to hand. Above them reared a twenty-metre crack of intimidating aspect. Here is Young's account:

> Josef and Brocherel manoeuvred, exclaimed, and gritted off the spiny flake, and up into the splayed foot of the overhanging cleft. Brocherel, with his big head crushed skew-wise into his diaphragm by the rock, sprawled Promethean legs over invisible supports on the sloping floor of the gutter-shoot, and offered a pessimistic basis for Josef's acrobatics. The rest of us, clinging in a row underneath them, up the razor-edge of the flake – limpets of gargoyles above the profundity of red wall according to the point of view – followed their evolutions with cricked necks and tightening chests. The overhanging chimney was short. It looked to have something

of the character of a Gothic niche for a saint, surmounted by a canopy. The back of the niche was cracked, and the crack was prolonged upward and outward through the canopy-bulge.

From a crouching balance on Brocherel's shoulder Josef hooked his axe-pick into the crack, high up at the back of the niche. With this for hold he wrestled upward, with his feet using press-holds against the outward-sloping walls of the niche, to a more secure position under the pendentive. Bridged and straddled high above our heads, he tried again and again to reach out and up, and squeeze some part of one hand into the thin crack above the projecting bulge. Josef's reach is short: try as he might, writhe and grit furiously, he could not gain a secure hand-cling. Even the axe-pick refused to grip the fissure, since the rock, undercut below it, left the axe-shaft unsupported. The obstinate efforts were renewed time and again, until watching became intolerable . . .

A new sound from above recalled me. I looked up. Josef was in the throes of a last daring inspiration. He whipped his axe upward, balanced himself audaciously outward, and with lightning speed wedged the point of the axe-shaft into the crack above the bulge of the canopy, so that the axe-head projected horizontally and fraily into space, between our heads and the sky. Except for its sensational circumstance the next manoeuvre looked like a simple gymnasium trick. Using the wedged shaft as a horizontal bar, Josef dangled clear of the niche, and swung himself up on to it as adroitly as a Japanese juggler, until he was standing upon it – over us and nothingness. The rest of his climb looked to be a triumphal wedding-glide up a widening smile of appreciative chimney. But for minutes afterwards, while we shouted our admiration to all the echoes of the mountains, I could hear him fighting for breath, supine upon the flat summit overhead, as surely Josef never panted on a rock before! . . . As a manifestation of nerve, skill, and power, Josef's issue from the niche would have been remarkable on an 'hotel boulder' after an idle morning. Performed at the end of some ten hours of very exacting climbing and exploration, over a void that seemed to swallow the nerves into its yawn of hostile space, the feat seemed to us almost superhuman.[39]

The Knubel Crack, as it became called, was probably the hardest single pitch in the Western Alps when it was climbed and Young's ascent of the East Face of the Grépon was an elegant end to an elegant era. It brought to perfection the art taught by Mummery and uniting, unwittingly, the skills of the Eastern Alps and the Lakeland crags. The long Indian summer of Victorian mountaineering had outlasted the old Queen herself and her son Edward, too.

The world was about to be consumed by the horrors of war, after which nothing would ever be the same again, not even mountaineering. Yet even before Young brought Mummery's ideals to perfection on the Grépon he had taken part in a climb which perhaps symbolised the new age which was destined to dawn in the post-war Alps, for history is not a sequence of isolated events, but a series of overlapping waves. Even before the old order passed away the new order was upon us.

The climb in question was the first ascent of the South-West Face of the Täschhorn, one of the Mischabel peaks overlooking Zermatt, on August 11, 1906. The face is an ugly place, 900 metres high, made of rock which is impossible when it is snowed up and rotten when it isn't, and perpetually bombarded by stonefall. It is also technically difficult, and this combination of difficulty and danger still keeps most climbers away. There were only three more ascents in the next half-century. The Swiss guidebook describes it as '*une des plus difficiles et des plus dangereuses des Alpes*'.[40] It has never been an important route in itself, and yet it is the perfect harbinger of what the Munich School were to bring to the Alps after the war.

Along with Young and Knubel were V.J.E. Ryan and the two Lochmatters, Franz and Josef. Ryan was an Irishman, a moody character who flitted in and out of the Alpine scene round the first decade of the century like some dark familiar. He drove his guides relentlessly (though the Lochmatters seemed to take it in their considerable strides) and was by all accounts a thoroughly disagreeable person. It comes as no surprise to learn he was blackballed by the Alpine Club, who wouldn't have him at any price. Nevertheless, he was a brilliant climber.

His best season was in 1906 when he did three climbs destined to become popular classics in the years ahead: the Santa Caterina Ridge on Monte Rosa, the North-West Ridge of the Blaitière and the East Ridge of the Plan. The last of these is known as the Ryan–Lochmatter Route in honour of the first ascent.

1906 was the year of the Täschhorn. When the two climbers and their guides approached the great wall it was plastered with ice from recent bad weather, though this was not readily apparent at first because of the way the cliff lay back. A great gully cuts into the face, dividing higher up to form a diamond-shaped headwall, but there did not seem to be any reason to doubt success, and there was speculation about whether they would be on the summit by 9.30 a.m. or noon. The great couloir was too icy to attempt but they found a buttress which led them up without too much trouble to a snowy bracket overhanging space, which they reached at 7.30 a.m. They swallowed some food, little realising that this would be the last time they could stop and foregather until the end of the climb.

They set off as two ropes, with Josef Lochmatter leading Ryan and Franz, and Young leading Knubel. Almost at once they discovered the face was much more difficult than it appeared. Smooth walls alternated with ledges, except that the ledges were false ones, sloping out and coated in ice. Most of the walls were vertical or overhanging. There were no belays on which to hitch the rope – or rather, there turned out to be three in the entire climb – and Young soon felt he was climbing beyond his limit. 'Ryan was, however, as always, bent upon the immediate "forward"; and his imperious staccato sentences, as little modified as his own fearlessness by any hush of breathless circumstance, had their usual effect on his high mettled team.'[41]

It started to snow, though this scarcely seemed to affect the outcome, which was already highly questionable. A great chimney on which they had pinned some faith wouldn't go and so they traversed delicately to another one. They were now roped together in one human chain. For a while they followed the chimney up but that too gave out and left them facing a desperate situation: a vertical corner above which was a sloping roof.

Franz had taken the lead and he climbed it with great difficulty, almost coming off. Had he fallen they would surely all have perished, for he was on the end of 200 feet of rope and there was no way they could hold him. Young and Knubel, temporarily untied so that Franz might have enough rope, would probably have been swept from their holds.

But Franz conquered the pitch. 'Franz Lochmatter's mountaineering feat was the greatest I have witnessed,' wrote Young later, 'and after a number of years I can still say the greatest I can imagine ... I do not suppose that in its mastery of natural difficulty, in its resistance to the effects of cold and fatigue and to the infections of depression and fear, it has often been equalled on any field of adventure or conflict.'[42]

The others joined Franz, but not without a struggle. Ryan came off and swung over the abyss whilst Franz and Josef desperately pulled him up bodily. With Young it was more difficult, because he weighed more, and when he came off – as was inevitable on that pitch – he managed to help those above by springing away from the rock and therefore giving some slack to the rope, which could be more readily pulled in. Fortunately, he had had the wit to tie the rope into a body harness, which took the strain. With an ordinary tied waist loop he would have blacked out, as Ryan did, and all would have been lost.[43]

If retreat had seemed hazardous up to this point it now became imposs-ible. They were committed in a fashion which is reminiscent of the Nordwand climbers of thirty years later and Young's description of, say the crux pitch on the Täschhorn bears comparison with later descriptions of say, the Hinterstoisser Traverse on the Eigerwand. This was a different sort of climbing from that on the East Face of the Grépon, or the ridge of the Gspaltenhorn, which were classical, traditional. There was nothing classical or traditional about the face of the Täschhorn. The later climbs in this new mode were done without guides, yet despite Franz Lochmatter's genius, it is Ryan who saw the challenge. Curiously enough, in the previous season, 1905, he and the Lochmatters had strayed onto the upper part of Charmoz North Face, the very face which was to be Welzenbach's greatest climb and which was such a great milestone in the nordwand saga.

Ryan and his companions reached the summit of the Täschhorn at 6 p.m. and were back in the valley just before midnight. The climb was not repeated for thirty-seven years.

The Alpine scene was changing rapidly. The glaciers were retreating and the railways were advancing. The ice which used to tumble from the Bossons Glacier at Chamonix almost across the road was shrinking up the hill and throughout the region the long white tongues, cracked and blistered by the ages, were withdrawing to hang as withered pendants over acres of unsightly moraine. At the same time, the railways pushed on and up. They reached Zermatt in 1891 and Chamonix in 1901. Seven years later an incredible steam-driven cog railway climbed from Chamonix up to Montenvers.

More people came to the Alps and found different things to do there. Most importantly, they discovered the joys of skiing. Dr Michel Payot introduced skiing to Chamonix in 1896 and before long skiing had ousted mountaineering as the premier Alpine sport with an enormous effect on the region, both visually and economically.

Climbers' perceptions were changing too, not only amongst the top echelons of the sport, but amongst lesser lights. A Winchester schoolmaster, R.L.G. Irving, took a small group of his pupils to the Alps in 1904 and wrote an account of their adventures which provoked outrage amongst the die-hards of the Alpine Club who accused him of risking other people's sons. The expeditions were quite long and serious and one suspects that some of the critics were motivated by envy. One of the boys was called George Leigh Mallory.

CHAPTER NINE

Beyond the Alps

So far our story has concentrated on the Alps because that is where it all began and where it developed, struggling to find an identity which was eventually given to it by Purtscheller and Mummery. This brings us to the turn of the century (Mummery died in 1895 and Purtscheller in 1900), but for some years before this mountaineering was spreading beyond its Alpine birthplace to remote corners of the world.

In fact, throughout the nineteenth century mountaineering was inextricably mixed with travel and exploration. It was a century of discovery, the century of Livingstone and Burton, Stanley and Mungo Park. Burton, though not a mountaineer, made the first ascent of Cameroon Peak (4095 m) in 1861, the highest summit on the West African coast. The century saw the foundation of the Royal Geographical Society in London and watched it rise to a position of considerable influence. Today's geographers play with satellites and computers, but in those days it wasn't only Christianity that was muscular: geographers got to grips with the land. 'Most people would have no use for a geographer who was not an adventurer and explorer,' declared Halford Mackinder, setting out to climb Mount Kenya in 1899.[1]

Some saw this exploratory aspect as the proper way forward for climbing, pouring scorn on those who saw the activity in sporting terms: 'We want here to make mountaineers not acrobats,' fulminated Douglas Freshfield to the Alpine Club.

But though the exploratory element was bound to be important, even in the remotest ranges the sporting aspect was never entirely absent, and in the more accessible places like Norway or New Zealand, the Alpine ethic was there from the start. Now that a century has gone by we can see that in virtually every mountain range on earth climbing has followed more or less the Alpine pattern of development; though in some it took a long time.[2]

It is perhaps not too surprising that one of the first famous non-Alpine peaks climbed in the nineteenth century was Mount Ararat where, according to Genesis 8, Noah's Ark came to rest when the Flood subsided. Situated, as it is, on one of the main east–west trade routes on the border of Turkey and Russian Armenia, there has been no lack of reported ark sightings from the Middle Ages onwards.

Ararat rises as a great snow-capped volcanic cone to a height of 5165 metres and the first recorded ascent (Noah was only faced with a descent) was in 1829 by Dr Parrot, the man after whom the Parrotspitze on Monte

Rosa is named. Parrot had considerable climbing experience in the Caucasus as well as in the Alps, but as a subsequent ascent was claimed to have been achieved in Persian slippers, perhaps the climbing of Ararat is a borderline case when it comes to qualifying for the definition of mountaineering![3]

Parrot, however, was also active in the Pyrenees. In 1817 he walked across them from the Atlantic to the Mediterranean, in the course of which he climbed the Maladetta (3308 m), a peak upon which Ramond de Carbonnières had failed. The walk – surely the earliest of *Haute Routes*, so popular today – took Parrot fifty-three days, during which he ascended a number of peaks. In 1825 the French surveyors Peytier and Hossard climbed the difficult Balaïtous (3144 m) and two years later their colleagues, Coroboef and Testu, climbed the Estats (3143 m) and Montcalm (3077 m).

In 1838 Miss Anne Lister from Halifax made the first tourist ascent of the impressive Vignemale (3298 m) guided by two men from Gèdre near Gavarnie, Henri Cazaux and his brother-in-law Bernard Guillembet. These two had made the first ascent of the peak the previous year, and not without adventure. Climbing by way of the Ossoue Glacier they fell into a prominent feature called the Grande Crevasse, but, uninjured, they crawled out by a series of tunnels and corridors in the ice, and managed to ascend the final snow slopes to the summit. The ascent so unnerved them that they descended by another route, being forced to bivouac, but effectively traversing the mountain.

There was an interesting sequel to Miss Lister's ascent, illustrating again the sharp proprietorial attitudes climbers have always taken over their routes. A few days after her climb, the guide Cazaux conducted the Prince de la Moskowa to the top and was unwise enough to mislead the Prince into thinking he had made the first tourist ascent. He said that Miss Lister had been unwell during her climb (which was true) and that she had turned back before the summit (which was not true). Miss Lister was so angered by this that she refused to pay the guide until he had retracted, even threatening legal action. After some delay a document signed by Cazaux was secured, giving Miss Lister her rightful place in mountaineering history![4]

The highest point of all in these mountains, Pico de Aneto (3404 m), was climbed by Count Albert de Franqueville and a young Russian officer, Platon de Tchihatcheff, accompanied by four locals in 1842 and in 1856 the ascent of the second highest peak, Pico des Posets (3375 m) was accomplished by a Mr Halkett, guided by Redonnet and Barrau.

About this time, Charles Packe began his long association with the Pyrenees, during which he explored the range from end to end, and discovered (or rather rediscovered, because Ramond de Carbonnières had found it briefly some sixty years before) the famous Ordesa valley, the nearest equivalent in Europe to the great American canyons. Packe was a meticulous plodding man with a slight frame and unsuspected reserves of strength. He

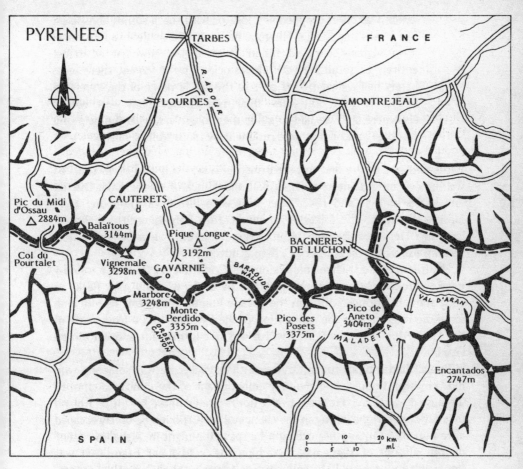

PYRENEES

TARBES

FRANCE

LOURDES

MONTREJEAU

R. ADOUR

N

Pic du Midi
d'Ossau
△ 2884m

CAUTERETS

Balaïtous
3144m

Pique Longue
△
3192m

BAGNERES
DE LUCHON

Col du
Pourtalet

Vignemale
3298m

GAVARNIE
o

BARROUDE
WALL

VAL D'ARAN

Marbore △
3248m

Monte
Perdido
3355m

ORDESA CANYON

Pico des
Posets
3375m

Pico de
Aneto
3404m

MALADETTA

Encantados
2747m

SPAIN

0   10   20 km
0   5   10   ml

was a great walker and, indeed, had little time for the more technical aspects of mountaineering, deploring in later years what he regarded as the acrobatic form of climbing.

In 1862 he produced a *Guide to the Pyrenees, specially intended for the use of mountaineers*, thus pre-dating Ball's *Alpine Guide* by one year.[5] In 1866 he explored and mapped, single-handed, 1000 square kilometres of the Monts Maudits and what with his botanising and geology he was, wrote his friend Russell, 'the Tyndall of the Pyrenees'.

Russell also describes just how primitive the climbing was:

> In those distant times, whatever may have been the case in the Alps, mountaineering was, in the Pyrenees, quite in its infancy, and climbing entailed all sorts of privations, hardships, and even risks, unknown to the present generations. Ice-axes had never been heard of, and when we crossed or scaled steep slopes of blue ice or frozen snow, we had to cut our steps either with a microscopic pocket-axe,

which was often dropped and lost, or with sharp stones and slates. Speed was impossible. The rope had only just made its appearance: it was scarcely ever used, and in crevassed glaciers we trusted almost entirely to sounding with alpenstocks. As for guides, there were barely half a dozen good ones in the whole range of the Pyrenees, and even those only knew their own district. They were useless elsewhere, and we had to guide them ourselves, with the help of a compass and of the most rudimentary maps, full of mistakes.[6]

Packe was one of the first to take British hills seriously and he introduced well-known mountaineers such as Ball and Hinchliff to the Lake District and Wales in 1858 and 1859. Later he was to introduce the young W.P. Haskett Smith to the Lakes, with momentous consequences for British climbing. He was quite prepared to bivouac and once slept out on Scafell, making use of the 'sleeping-bag', then a novelty.[7]

His friend and erstwhile companion was Count Henry Russell, a wealthy man of French nationality but half Irish by birth, who first met Packe in 1863 and who formed with him the Société Ramond two years later, a club for those interested in the exploration of the Pyrenees and a forerunner of the Club Alpin Français (CAF) which was not formed for another eleven years.

Russell had a more romantic nature than Packe; he was someone who did things on impulse and the very embodiment of the man who climbed 'because it was there'. He spent twelve hours pinned in the Brèche de Roland by a furious storm, exulting in the elemental fury, though he barely escaped alive next day. On another occasion he spent the night in 'a shallow grave' on the summit of Vignemale, watching the 'cold lunar beams'. 'It was impossible to catch cold,' he commented, 'for one was always cold – indeed, I was blue and frozen.'

For two decades Russell explored the Pyrenees, but from 1881 onwards he concentrated on Vignemale where he had a series of seven caves excavated in which he would sometimes arrange dinner parties in full evening dress. The parties were typical of Russell's sense of humour but the real purpose of the caves was to be a substitute for mountain huts, the erection of which he considered would be desecration. The seventh cave was only a few metres below the summit and was called Le Paradis. It was snug, dry and carpeted with straw. Here Russell celebrated his sixtieth birthday and ten years later spent seventeen days here in his final act of homage to the mountain.

There were during this period a number of professional guides, amongst whom the Passet cousins, Henri and Célestin, were much the best known. They were Gavarnie men, sons of the two brothers Laurent and Hippolyte Passet who had helped in the exploration of the Cirque de Gavarnie, where they had discovered the Col Passet and made a number of climbs.[8]

Henri was Packe's guide for many years, a trustworthy man with 'a round, good-natured, rather stolid, Basque face'. Like his cousin, he was a good ice man, and the ascent of the Couloir Swan, between the Grand and Petit Astazou, in 1885, with F.E.L. Swan was an outstanding climb of 600 metres which achieved a steepness of fifty-five degrees.

But Henri Passet was outshone by his cousin Célestin; perhaps the only Pyrenean guide of the period to match the top guides of the Alps. For many years he was Russell's guide, then he teamed up with Henri Brulle, a lawyer from Libourne, near Bordeaux. Brulle was the Mummery of the Pyrenees – innovative, thrusting, tackling routes far harder than any previously done in the region.

In 1884 he enjoyed, if that is the word, a solitary traverse of Vignemale:

> Another time I crossed the Vignemale alone, 'en col', under con-
> ditions which made this expedition the pleasantest of my 'sou-
> venirs'. A furious storm was raging. Enveloped in the morning in
> a dense fog, annoyed in the steep couloirs of the Cerbillonas by
> vultures which swept over me like avalanches, just grazing me with
> their long wings, assailed during three hours by hailstones of such
> size that they bruised and stunned me, deafened by thunder, and
> so electrified that I was hissing and crepitating, I notwithstanding
> reached the summit at half-past four in the evening, amidst incess-
> ant detonations. In descending the glacier I got lost in a labyrinth
> of crevasses, and while balancing myself on an ice wave I nearly
> dropped my ice axe. One of my legs, probably alarmed, began to
> shake; but a little severe scolding steadied it in the path of duty.
> As a climax night came on as black as ink, and I had to grope and
> feel my way down the endless valley of Ossoue. It was 11 o'clock
> at night when I reached Gavarnie, almost starved and quite exhaus-
> ted, but having lived the crowning day of my life.[9]

He also climbed with his friends, Count Roger de Monts and especially Jean Bazillac. As second guide they often took François Bernard Salles, a giant of a man whose strength was legendary.[10] In 1889 they climbed the Couloir de Gaube which rises from the Glacier des Oulettes as a narrow ribbon of ice between the Pique Longue and Piton Carré on Vignemale. It is 600 metres high, subject to stonefall and at an angle of sixty-five degrees at its steepest. The crux, a great jammed boulder, ice encrusted, comes almost at the top, when retreat is virtually impossible.

> We spent there two terrible hours, in an intense cold, and unable
> either to turn or to force the passage.
> At half-past three o'clock in the evening, as we had to come to
> a decision, Célestin determined to make a last effort, and this time

he won the day, thanks to a very light and well balanced ice axe from Grindelwald which he had luckily borrowed from me. I still remember with what anxiety we were watching his slow progress, whilst stoically receiving the pieces of ice-pavement flung about by the ice axe, which bespattered our heads and hands, at the imminent risk of hurling us down.[11]

A recent guidebook describes it thus: 'Legendary Pyrenean ice-climb ... the longest, most difficult, most severe of the range ... climbed in 1889 it was at that time an astonishing exploit.'[12]

Brulle made a number of the standard top Alpine climbs of his day and in later life grew attached to Mont Blanc. He made his fourth ascent at the age of eighty and three years later made a dramatic retreat from the Bosses Ridge, suffering from frostbite and incipient pneumonia. The strain proved too much and a month later he passed away quietly in Chamonix hospital.

The Norwegian coastline is over 1100 miles long, though if all the fjords and islands were counted it would be ten times that figure. Along most of this fractured coast there rise peaks whose magnificence in Western Europe is only rivalled by those of the Alps and Pyrenees. For the most part they are of superb rock – gabbro, syenite and granite – and though there is considerable glaciation in some areas, it is for rock peaks that the country is noted amongst climbers. Although the summits are not as high as the Alps, this is compensated for by the fact that many ascents start literally from sea level.

The Jotunheimen[13] was explored by the botanist Christen Smith in 1813, then by Christian Peter Bianco Boeck in 1818 and 1819. The latter was joined in the following year by Baltazar Mathias Keilau and, with the huntsman Ola Urden (the first known mountain guide in Norway), they made an ascent of Nordre Skagastölstind – though it had probably already been climbed by the local people who were evidently quite used to mountain travel. Pastor Ulrik Boyesen of Laerdal-Ardal reports that his parishioners used a rope when travelling over glaciers 'so that one man keeps walking ahead of another, keeping a certain distance, and if one falls into a crevasse, then the rest are not only warned, but are also able to pull him out.'[14]

Boeck and Keilau attempted without success to climb Skagastölstind, Galdhopiggen and Laudals Kaupe, but they did manage the shapely Falkenaebbe (Falketind). All their climbing was done in blissful ignorance: they floundered across glaciers commenting how they sometimes went into crevasses up to their necks, on Laudals Kaupe they were almost killed by an avalanche and one of them was saved because he was carrying a barometer which took the force of a falling rock which would otherwise have broken his spine.

In that same year, 1820, the Jotunheimen was visited by Gottfried Bohr, who made the first ascent of Nordre Dyrhaugstind and in 1821 and 1822, inspired by the writings of Keilau and Boyesen which had been published abroad, the first overseas visitor came to the mountains: a geologist from Dresden, C.F. Naumann, with a medical student named Schubert.

Naumann, used to dealing with Alpine peasants, was at first a bit put out by the independence of these Viking descendants who were technically inferior climbers to their Swiss counterparts but on average more intelligent and a lot better educated. 'They all understand thoroughly the use of a map and compass, articles regarding the use of which Swiss guides are frequently in the dark,' said one climber, describing his three guides in 1886.[15]

In 1827 two peasants from Romsdal, Christen Hoel and Hans Bjermeland, made an astonishing ascent of the Romsdalhorn (1555 m), a shapely peak which must surely have ranked as one of the most technically difficult rock climbs done anywhere at that time or, indeed, for some time after. They did it for a dare and built a cairn on the summit which is still there. It was not repeated until 1881 when Carl Christian Hall made the ascent on his seventh attempt.[16]

Glittertind was climbed by two Norwegian surveyors, H.N. Wergeland and H. Sletten in 1842 and the slightly higher Galdhopiggen (at 2468 metres Norway's highest mountain) received its official first ascent when Steinar Sulheim, a guide from Lom, led L. Arnesen and S. Flotten to the top eight years later – a surprisingly late date for a mountain which is fairly accessible and technically easy.

In 1868 Thomas J. Heftye founded Den Norske Touristforening (DNT), a tourist association created primarily for walking and climbing in the mountains. It built mountain huts and registered guides in much the same way as the European clubs of Austria, Switzerland and Italy which preceded it.[17] It also undertook the drawing of maps and the first reasonable map of the Jotunheimen appeared in 1870. The following year an English member, W.R. Thelwell, proposed that important paths should be marked by a special type of cairn. In 1880 it became the practice to paint a red T on each cairn and a network of such paths now exists throughout Norway, older but less publicised than the long-distance footpaths of Continental Europe.[18]

From the 1830s an increasing number of travellers visited the Norwegian mountains. Often they were British and usually they were out to shoot reindeer, though by all accounts they seemed singularly inept at this, and spent most of the time exploring with local guides such as the Vole clan, starting with Knut Vole in the 1870s, who made Glittertind their own. Guides like Jo Gjende, Knut Lykken, Johannes Vigdal and perhaps half a dozen more had a reputation amongst visiting mountaineers.

In 1872 William Cecil Slingsby visited Norway for the first time and began a love affair with the country and its mountains which was to last all his life. It was also the foundation for one of the most notable climbing careers of the late nineteenth century, for though Slingsby had done some scrambling in Britain he did not visit the Alps until 1878 and did not become one of the famous Mummery clique until 1892. He has been acclaimed as the Father of both British and Norwegian mountaineering. But it was his sheer enthusiasm, his ability to inspire others, which was his greatest legacy to the sport. A well-built man with a blond beard, Slingsby was not unlike a Viking – and he always claimed he had Norse blood in his veins.

In 1876 Slingsby joined the Bergen mountaineer Emanuel Mohn and the guide Knut Lykken in an attack on the splendid Store Skagastölstind (2404 m) in the Jotunheimen. They set out from Vormelid and in shifting mists which gave added drama to the already dramatic landscape of the Midtmaradalen, made their way up the Midtmaradalsbrae Glacier to a deep notch at the head of the valley, later named Mohn's Skar. Reaching this had been no easy matter, for the last few hundred feet was a steep slope of hard snow and the two Norwegians, unnerved at the prospect, begged a rest whilst Slingsby went on alone.

When he reached the skar he found the summit crags of Skagastölstind towering some 500 feet above, a fearsome-looking ridge of gabbro. Mohn and Lykken, who had rejoined him, thought it impossible so Slingsby took up the challenge alone:

> Suffice it to say that what under the most favourable conditions must be a tough piece of work, was made more so by the films of ice with which every little ledge was veneered. Three times I was all but beaten, but this was my especial and much-longed-for moun-tain, and I scraped away the ice and bit by bit got higher and higher. In sight of the others I reached what from the skar we had judged to be the top. I raised a cheer, which was renewed below, when I found that there was a ridge – a knife-edged affair – perhaps sixty yards long, and that the highest point was evidently at the further end. There are three peaklets and a notch in the ridge which latter again almost stopped me. For the first time I had to trust to an overhanging and rather a loose rocky ledge. I tried it well, then hauled myself up to terra firma, and in a few strides, a little above half an hour after leaving my friends, I gained the unsullied crown of the peerless Skagastölstind, a rock table four feet by three, ele-vated five or six feet above the southern end of the ridge.[19]

Slingsby's ascent roused some nationalistic ill-feeling in Norway. Mohn was criticised in the press for chickening out. The hapless Mohn defended him-self, saying that he doubted whether any Norwegian climber would have got to the top, whereupon a young artist called Harald Petersen rushed off to prove otherwise and, though he failed at his first attempt, he did succeed when he tried again in 1878. Like Slingsby he was forced to make a solo ascent because both of his guides – one of whom was Knut Lykken again – refused to go beyond Mohn's Skar. Depressed by criticism and perhaps by his own limitations, Mohn gave up climbing.

In 1879 Johannes Heftye, the son of the man who founded the DNT, with two guides from Ardal, Jens Klingenberg and Peder Melheim, found a new way to the top starting from the hotel at Turtegro on the opposite side of the mountain from Midtmaradal. It is a more accessible route than the original, done from the Bandet Col, and rather more elegant. It includes a fissure known as Heftye's Chimney and a very exposed ledge, and Slingsby, who did it some years later, compared it with the Grépon traverse.

Heftye rather soured his success by producing a pamphlet attacking Slingsby as a climber and claiming that his own ascent of a peak called Knutsholstind (done with Knut Lykken) was a much greater feat. This was too much even for the mild-mannered Slingsby. When he returned to Norway the following year he engaged the guide Johannes Vigdal and together they took a local girl, Oline Marie Sylfestdotter, 'a bright rosy-cheeked lassie', to the summit without any bother *and dressed in her Sunday best*. The rope wasn't used, Slingsby reported laconically, because that side of the mountain could be climbed anywhere. 'At 1.28 we reached the summit, raised a loud cheer, and put Marie on the top of the little cairn, and very bonny she looked in her picturesque costume.'[20] So much for the hardest ascent in Norway.

Slingsby's activities and enthusiastic reports in the *Alpine Journal* and elsewhere attracted a number of climbers to Norway throughout the rest of the century. It seemed particularly favoured by women climbers; apart from Miss Slingsby there was a Miss Green, mentioned in passing by Slingsby, Miss May Jeffrey who climbed Troltind in 1890 – the first ascent of a peak in the remote Lofoten Islands – and the indefatigable Mrs Main (Mrs Aubrey Le Blond) who visited the Lyngen Peninsula with Josef Imboden and his son in 1898 and 1899. It fell to a Norwegian woman, Therese Bertheau, to make the first female ascent of Store Skagastölstind on July 29, 1894. She was only just in time, for on the very next day another Norwegian, Fanny Paulsen, also climbed the peak and on the day after that Evelyn Spence Watson reached the top.[21]

The most systematic climber in Norway was a Dane, Carl Christian Hall, a Treasury official from Copenhagen. After a season in the Alps in 1878 he devoted himself wholly to Norwegian climbing; in twenty-one seasons he made numerous first ascents, including what was thought at the time to be the first ascent of the Romsdalhorn, which was in fact climbed in 1827.

In his seminal book *Norway, The Northern Playground* published just after the turn of the century, Slingsby regrets that the Norwegians themselves, with one or two exceptions, did not take up serious climbing. More surprising perhaps, is that after a short burst of popularity in the 1880s, Norwegian climbing fell out of favour altogether. Very little of importance was accomplished until well into the present century.

Spitsbergen did not become the Norwegian Svalbard until 1925, but this remote and barren group of islands had been visited by whalers and others from as early as 1773. The main island especially is extremely mountainous and the highest peak is generally agreed to be Newtontoppen (1712 m), though Perriertoppen, some forty kilometres north-west of it, is about the same height. Newtontoppen was climbed by A. Vassilev's party in 1900 and the other five years later by an Austrian group.

The first recorded climb in the islands seems to be by Scoresby who described how he climbed an unnamed peak of 1500 feet 'joined on the north side to another of about twice the elevation'.[22] The mountain was singularly rotten in texture and at one point he had to traverse a ridge sitting astride it, *à cheval*. In 1827 that enthusiastic Norwegian Keilau paid a visit and in 1896 and 1897 Sir Martin Conway led two expeditions during which a number of peaks were climbed. But the mountains of Spitsbergen have never been the prime target of expeditions: the islands' flora and fauna have been the chief interest.

Nor was Iceland of much interest to the Victorian mountaineers, though several went there. 'In Switzerland,' wrote James Bryce,[23] one of the most indefatigable mountain travellers of the period, 'the difficulty is to get to the top of your peak. In Iceland it is to get to its bottom.' Nor were the mountains much to write home about, though the huge mass of the Vatna-jokull excited wonder. This icecap (*jokull*) covers 8500 square kilometres and rises in great swelling white breasts from the southern shore; it may be the very thing that gave the land its name, for sailors would see it when still well out to sea.

It is fairly certain that in earlier times north islanders crossed the icecap on their way to the fishing station of Kambstun on the south coast, but the station was abandoned in 1573 after a disastrous storm in which fifty-three seamen lost their lives. The route across the glaciers then seems to have been forgotten. The first known crossing of recent times was made by a twenty-four-year-old Scottish lawyer, W.L. Watts, with five Icelanders, who crossed from Fljotshverfi in the south-west to a point near Kistufell at the northern edge of the ice between June 24 and July 7, 1875. The distance was about 100 kilometres.

The difficulty of travel in Iceland meant few visitors even approached the mountains, and the black ash *sandur* which guards the south coast did not help. E.T. Holland and C.W. Shepherd failed on the Vatnajokull in 1861. Interestingly, they were offered the use of crampons by the local people who clearly saw them as necessary for getting about on the icecap. It was not until thirty years later that F.W. Howell and two local men claimed the first ascent of Hvannadalshnuker, though according to one authority the peak had been climbed as long ago as 1813 by a Norwegian surveyor, H. Frisak.[24]

The mountains of Greenland are more attractive to the climber than those of Spitsbergen or Iceland, but the logistics of travel to such a remote land meant that exploration took precedence over mountaineering. Edward Whymper, whose original ambition it was to be a polar explorer, visited Greenland in 1872 but his achievements were quite small and it was perhaps the least successful of all his ventures.

In 1869 the German polar explorer Koldewey took a small steamer, the *Germania*, along the east coast of Greenland, overwintered, and the following summer discovered the Franz Josef Fjord. He edged the *Germania* for seventy miles amongst the icebergs in this huge arm of the sea. One of the party, Oberleutnant Julius Payer, made the first notable ascent in Greenland, of Payer Peak, but his over-enthusiastic estimate of the height of the mountains beyond was wide of the mark.

At the Royal Geographical Society meeting where this expedition was discussed, attention was drawn to the value of mountain ascents in exploration and members of the Alpine Club were exhorted to go and climb Greenland's icy mountains, though it was the 1930s before much more was achieved in this area.

Of the lesser mountain ranges of Europe perhaps the Tatra is most interesting. Lying on the border between former Czechoslovakia and Poland, in the nineteenth century it was at the north-eastern edge of the mighty Austro-Hungarian Empire. The peaks are spiky and rise to over 2500 metres, though the main range is scarcely more than fifteen kilometres long, a sort of miniature Alps in themselves.

The three highest peaks cluster round the Polski Hreben Pass at the eastern end of the range and are Gerlach (2663 m), Lomnica (2634 m) and Lodowy (2628 m). Lomnica was surprisingly climbed as long ago as 1793 by an English traveller called Robert Townsend and John Ball climbed Lodowy in 1843, but Gerlach had to wait until about 1855 before it was climbed by Z. Bosniachi and W. Grzegorzek. The Poles, who have always been excellent mountaineers, were soon developing hard, technical climbing on good granite.

Exploration continued in a more desultory fashion in other mountain areas such as Corsica and Spain. In only one other area of Europe outside the Alpine regions was mountaineering of any great significance, and it was out of all proportion to the scale of its mountains. That was in Britain.

CHAPTER TEN

'Fine Opportunities
for Breaking One's Neck'

The reasons why climbing developed so phenomenally in a country that can only boast very small mountains, most of which can be walked up by any reasonably fit person and where there is no permanent snow and ice, is bound up with the socio-economic climate of Britain in the nineteenth century, and, even, perhaps, with the national psyche. As the century progressed, Britain became the richest nation the world had ever known, with a large and prosperous middle class who had time to devote to leisure pursuits. But it went deeper than that; though the poor were very poor and the labouring classes had little time for leisure, neither were subservient – a European visitor remarked that the difference between Britain and the Continent was that Britain had no peasants. They had within them the seeds of adventure – a huge reservoir from which the middle classes were constantly replenished by the archetypal 'self-made man'.

Later in the century there was the Alpine precedent; alpinists turned to the British hills for out-of-season sport, to keep themselves in trim for the battles ahead, but there were people active in the hills long before the alpinists appeared in the record books. There were even climbing clubs, and because the mountains were so easy to climb it became natural to seek harder ways up, abandoning the path for the gully, the rib or the buttress. These in turn became ends in themselves: it was the problem which counted because the summit could be achieved easily by all and sundry. And since *mountains* were largely irrelevant in this respect, the roadside outcrops and even quarries could provide sport. The idea of rock climbing not as a means to an end but as an end in itself was uniquely British.[1]

Like Alpine climbing itself, British mountaineering had its origins in the Romantic Movement of the late eighteenth century and early nineteenth. The earliest tourists to the Lakes or Wales went to stand and stare, or perhaps make ascents of Skiddaw by pony, and they were aided by the numerous guidebooks which appeared – there were five popular guidebooks to the Lakes alone in the 1770s. There were professional guides like John Morten of Borrow's *Wild Wales* or Robin Partridge of the Salutation Hotel in Ambleside, but they were not guides in the Alpine sense, their purpose being to lead their client to the top of Helvellyn or Snowdon by the easiest path, sometimes at night in order to see the sunrise from the summit.

The first real fell-walker, in the sense of one striding across mountains irrespective of trodden ways, was probably Captain Joseph Budworth, late of the 72nd (Manchester) Regiment, a one-armed veteran of Gibraltar who, on a typical excursion, walked from Ambleside to Coniston and back, and threw in an ascent of Coniston Old Man for good measure – about twenty miles and a couple of thousand feet of ascent. On another occasion he and a friend tackled Helvellyn, together with Rydal Fell, Fairfield and Dolly-waggon Pike, with Robin Partridge as guide. They set off at 4 a.m., were on Fairfield at 7.15 a.m., on Helvellyn by 9.30 a.m. and down on the road at Wythburn before 11 a.m.!

Exaggerated though some of his prose may be to a generation completely familiar with the fells, Budworth still reads like a man who realised they had a physical challenge as well as a romantic beauty. Here is his attempt at a frozen grassy slope near Buttermere:

> I made many efforts to overcome the glassy hill; and although I had sharp nails in the balls of my shoes, and large stubbs to the heels, with a pike to my hazel stick, my efforts were useless; I tumbled twice, and slid bodily down the hill again . . . Although the surface was ice, the rough grass and water oozing through had made it both hollow and rotten. It soon got over my shoe-tops, and up to one knee, and then I felt myself conquered, gave up the pursuit, and determined to bear a great disappointment with due meekness.[2]

In Snowdonia, the first adventurous ramble was that of William Bingley, a Cambridge undergraduate who walked the Welsh mountains during the long vacation of 1798. His passion was botany but he was obviously imbued with the same spirit as Budworth, for he climbed Snowdon by seven different routes and then, accompanied by the Rev. Peter Williams, Rector of Llanberis, scrambled up the exposed sloping ledge known as the Eastern Terrace, on Clogwyn Du'r Arddu. This immense cliff was destined to play an important part in British climbing and it has been claimed that the ascent of Eastern Terrace by Bingley and Williams was the first real rock climb in Britain. One questions this: the scramble up Eastern Terrace is exposed but not difficult; how many shepherds had scrambled up Jack's Rake in the Lake District in search of lost sheep or, indeed, the Cuillin of Skye, which are equally difficult?

In 1802 the poet Samuel Taylor Coleridge, on a walking tour of the Lakeland fells, descended Broad Stand, a series of ledges leading from Scafell to the adjacent col called Mickledore. The ledges are distinctly awkward, but the tricky bit is hardly of sufficient substance to justify it being called a rock climb.

There was more substance to the Pillar Rock in nearby Ennerdale, and more of a challenge too, for here was the archetypal 'inaccessible pinnacle', untrodden by the foot of man. It was climbed in 1826 by an Ennerdale shepherd-cum-cooper called John Atkinson, probably by what is now known as the Old West Route, and many years later in 1861 the keeper of the lighthouse at St Bees and four friends made the first ascent of the eastern side.

None of these people had any connection with alpinism, but many of the early alpinists soon found the British hills to be a useful training ground, for fitness if not for technical skills. Some of the better Alpine guides knew them too, for guides were quite frequently invited back to England as house guests.[3]

Amongst the pioneer alpinists who visited British hills was Professor J.D. Forbes who in 1836 made the first ascent of Sgurr nan Gillean in Skye, with a local forester called Duncan Macintyre. 'I have never seen a rock so adapted for clambering,' said Forbes in describing his adventures. Charles Packe, famous for his Pyrenean exploits, walked the Lakeland fells botanising and introducing them to others, including Haskett Smith. Tyndall was there too and, as early as 1845, a seventeen-year-old schoolboy from York called Charles Hudson was averaging 27 miles a day across the fells; no doubt the foundation of his legendary walking ability.

But of all the early alpinists the one who came nearest to seeing the proper potential of the British mountains was a man of Swiss descent, C.A.O. Baumgartner,[4] a powerfully built, deep-chested man who was attracted to the more rocky places because of their challenge. In 1845 he made the first known traverse of the famous Crib Goch ridge leading to Snowdon and climbed both Pillar Rock and Broad Stand in 1850. Baumgartner realised that the challenge lay in the rock and that a summit wasn't really necessary.

There were other challenges – sea cliffs and abandoned quarries, for example, and there must have been scrambling done on both from the earliest times. John Stogdon, a pioneer of guideless climbing in the Oberland, wrote, 'The Hampshire chalk cliffs gave fine opportunities for breaking one's neck and the chalk cliffs of Swanage, Scratchell's Bay and Beachy Head, provided me with quite sensational risks.' These adventures were perhaps more important than Stogdon's celebrated traverse from Langdale to Wasdale via Bowfell gully in the snowy winter of 1869.[5] Fifty years later, just before his death, he still saw more clearly than most of his contemporaries the way things were going: 'I do not look on highly-developed modern rock-climbing as mere gymnastics, as some purists seem to do,' he wrote. 'The thin ledges and slight holds to which you cling when half way up a set of savage slabs, set at an angle of 70 or 80 degrees, where the void below seems to draw you down and the awful slope above hints at no mercy, have a tremendous fascination of their own. Whoever is able, let him enjoy this fierce delight.'[6]

Nevertheless, apart from a little winter gully work, few alpinists at first saw any connection between the British hills and the Alps, even when Alpine rock climbing had reached a fair degree of proficiency. Alpine rock was clean and sharp; British rock was covered in moss and slime. It is hardly surprising therefore that the first real pioneers were men who knew nothing better – home-trained climbers who had never been to the Alps, like F.H. Bowring and J.W. Robinson. Probably their climbing was what we call scrambling today, but their exploits encouraged a young undergraduate called W.P. Haskett Smith who in 1882 climbed Great Gully on Pavey Ark, a crag in the Lake District. In 1884 he climbed Needle Ridge on Great Gable, and two years later made his well-known ascent of the striking Napes Needle. These ascents, and most of the others he did at this time of lesser merit, were accomplished solo. They were almost certainly the first *sporting* rock climbs done in Britain; that is to say, they were accomplished for their own sake, for the challenge they offered, and were of such difficulty that even today they retain a climbing grade.[7]

Napes Needle is often wrongly quoted as the first rock climb in Britain because its striking shape makes it a memorable totem, much photographed in the early days of climbing. A photograph of the Needle exhibited in a shop window in the Strand influenced O.G. Jones[8] to take up climbing.

Jones described Haskett Smith's ascent of Napes Needle as 'one of the most daring things that have been done in the Lake District'. Yet within six years a far more difficult climb was done on the very next buttress to the Needle – Eagle's Nest Ridge – and this was entirely due to the influence of men trained in the Alps. If Haskett Smith showed the way, the next few years were dominated by men who had won their spurs in the Alps, such as the Pilkingtons, Walker, the Hopkinsons, Collie, Slingsby, Solly and many others. Amongst them they accounted for the first exploratory wave, at the same time bringing to British rock the alien mores of alpinism. One wonders how British rock climbing would have developed had an Alpine outlook not been grafted onto it.

By the end of the century the home-grown mountaineer and the alpinist were indistinguishable. A third strand had been added by this time: a Sheffield man, J.W. Puttrell, had begun climbing on the short but technically difficult Wharncliffe Rocks near his native city. These rocks were of a modified sandstone called millstone grit and Puttrell and his friends soon found their way onto other local 'edges' made of this superbly frictional rock, which climbers now call gritstone. The techniques developed on gritstone have played a considerable part in British rock climbing.

This was outcrop climbing and the pioneers did not restrict themselves to gritstone, but climbed limestone as well, not to mention sandstone, chalk or almost anything that came to hand! Their principal exploits were recorded by E. A. Baker in *Moors, Crags and Caves of the High Peak and the Neighbourhood* in 1903. Early gritstoners, transferring their techniques to other areas, were responsible for two of the hardest climbs around the turn of the century, Fred Botterill putting up Botterill's Slab on Scafell in 1903, whilst Baker, Puttrell and Oppenheimer in 1901 climbed the ferocious Ben Nuis Chimney on Arran. Both climbs are still rated Very Severe and the Nuis Chimney climb was not repeated for half a century.

The gritstoners were quickly absorbed into the Alpine ethic. Other forms of outcrop climbing such as limestone were discouraged until the resurgence in the years following the Second World War, when gritstone climbing in particular became the expression of the working-class climber.

Meanwhile, Owen Glynne Jones, who despite his Welsh name climbed almost exclusively in the Lakes, was probably the most accomplished of the British trained rock climbers in the last decade of the century, with routes like Walker's Gully on Pillar Rock, Jones's Direct on Scafell and Kern Knotts Crack, Great Gable. Of this last climb, done in 1897, it was said that 'it not only kept its reputation for a long time, but became one of the standards by which British rock climbing was judged.'[9]

In 1895 Jones met the two Keswick brothers, George and Ashley Abraham, who were making a name for themselves as mountain photographers.

Jones posed for the Abrahams on some of the most famous climbs of the day (they sold the pictures as postcards to tourists) and in return the Abrahams provided Jones with illustrations for his comprehensive *Rock Climbing in the English Lake District*. Between them they brought to the crags a degree of professionalism which some climbers considered undesirable. It was suggested that the Abrahams faked their pictures, by tilting the camera. But many of those who made the criticism had little or no experience of British rock climbing and the Abrahams were breaking new ground by actually showing climbers in action.

Jones's book ran to three editions and was the first popular guide to Lakeland crags, for though Haskett Smith had produced a pocket guide to British crags as a whole, somewhat similar in size to Conway's guides[10] to the Alps which had just begun to appear, these were such a hotch-potch of information as to be of little practical use. Jones mixed practical advice with reminiscence and good photographs. It is a pity he did not adopt the Conway format so that the book could be carried in the pocket – something the Abrahams corrected when they brought out their own *British Mountain Climbs* in 1909.

Jones's book was important for another reason too: it made the first attempt to codify climbs according to difficulty. Jones proposed four groups: *Easy, Moderate, Difficult, and Exceptionally Severe*. This adjectival system became the basis for British climbing grades, which have altered remarkably little in almost a century.[11]

Despite his pre-eminence on British rock, Jones's greatest desire was to be known as a first-rate alpinist. He was killed in 1899 on the Dent Blanche.

Five years before the death of Jones, J.M. Archer Thomson began climbing on the Welsh cliffs around Ogwen. He was thirty-one years old and, like Jones, a teacher. At that date – 1894 – only twelve climbs existed in the whole of Snowdonia, and most of those were gully scrambles of a standard far inferior to anything in the Lakes. Within two years Thomson added another fourteen routes and he continued to lead and dominate Welsh climbing until his death in 1914.

As early as 1870 C.E. Mathews and some of his Alpine Club friends had formed a Society of Welsh Rabbits, whose object was to meet at the little Pen y Gwryd inn in the heart of Snowdonia each Christmas and explore the Welsh hills. By 1897, with the advent of Thomson and technical climbing, the Pen y Gwryd habitués decided that a club was required and though at first it was meant to be Welsh orientated it was decided to make it open to all climbers and thus let in the Lakelanders. Mathews was the President and a third of the original members were already Alpine Club men. Thus the Climbers' Club, as the new body was called, fused together the various elements of English and Welsh climbing under an Alpine Club style of thinking.[12]

Not that all the Alpine Club members looked on the new sport of rock climbing favourably. As we have seen, D.W. Freshfield believed mountaineering should proceed along geographical lines and gently chided Mathews in verse:

> Why is it to the Alpine Club
> Our C.E.M. no longer keeps?
> Why should he found – himself as hub –
> A Climbers' Club for 'chimney sweeps'?[13]

The Scots held themselves aloof, as usual. They had formed their own club – the Scottish Mountaineering Club – in 1889, largely along Alpine Club lines. Gilbert Thomson, one of the founder members, wrote later: 'Almost every climb was a new one. We were in fact in much the same position as the pioneers of the Alps were some thirty years earlier. The mountains were there, but the mountaineers were not. The only proper route up any mountain was the easiest, and the only suitable time for an ascent was a fine summer day.'[14]

The club changed this outlook. Leading members J.H. Gibson, W.R. Lester, W.W. Naismith and W. Douglas climbed the Black Shoot of Stob Maol, a 300-foot gully of some severity, in May 1892. It was probably the first real rock climb in mainland Scotland and Lester in describing it felt that he ought to apologise for 'a pure piece of mountaineering gymnastics'. He assured his readers that there were easier ways up the mountain! Though the route is scarcely heard of today it was mentioned no less than twenty-one times in the first few issues of the club journal.

It is true to say, however, that the majority of Scots saw their own hills as places for walking and for winter sport, rather than rock climbing. In the year of the Black Shoot ascent, two English parties crossed the border and stole a march on the Scots. Horace Walker and Charles Pilkington climbed the Grey Castle, the huge West Buttress of Suilven. In the late summer a more important incursion was made by the Hopkinson brothers, a Manchester family well versed in English rock climbing and alpinism.[15] Three of the brothers, John, Edward and Charles, with John's son Bernard, descended Tower Ridge on Ben Nevis, climbed the North-East Buttress two days later and the 700-foot pinnacle, now called the Douglas Boulder, the day after that. All these climbs were quite outstanding for the time, but it was only a little later, when others claimed a first ascent, that Walker and the Hopkinsons revealed their adventures.

Two years later at Easter 1894 a strong party of English-based climbers, Norman Collie, Joseph Collier, G.A. Solly, and Geoffrey Hastings, made a number of climbs in Glencoe and on Ben Nevis, including the first ascent of Tower Ridge, descended by the Hopkinsons. It was in winter condition and Collie thought it compared with the Italian Ridge of the Matterhorn.

Norman Collie was also principally responsible for the exploration of the Cuillin Hills of Skye, the rockiest peaks in Britain, like miniature Chamonix aiguilles. He saw A.H. Stocker and A.G. Parker climbing there in 1886 and it was this which led to his own climbing career. During the following two years with a local man, John MacKenzie, as guide, Collie climbed all the summits with the exception of Sgurr Coire an Lochain – which he did not manage until 1896; it was the last mountain in Britain to be climbed.

The Skye climbs are the earliest in Scotland – the Pilkingtons had climbed the Inaccessible Pinnacle in 1880 and Stocker and Parker had climbed the shorter but more difficult side of the same needle in 1886 – grades Diff and V. Diff respectively today. Collie had crossed the notorious gap between Thearlaich and the Dubh Ridge in 1891 (V. Diff), the Pilkingtons had climbed the delectable Pinnacle Ridge (Diff) in 1880 to which Cecil Slingsby added a Severe variation in 1890. So Skye had its quota of climbs some years before the Scottish mainland and yet Skye is somehow different. Skye is scrambling, climbing, mountaineering all rolled into one, whether the climber wishes it or not. It has always been outside the mainstream and, despite all its advantages, it has never made a significant contribution to British climbing.

If Jones and Thomson were the technical leaders of their day, the man who welded the whole of British mountaineering together more than anyone else was the tall, lanky expatriate Scot, John Norman Collie,[16] eminent scientist, bachelor aesthete, connoisseur of wine and cigars and a good artist and writer. He was also a bit of a wag. In looks he was not unlike the popular conception of Sherlock Holmes and had the brain power to match.

Collie was devoted to Skye, but he also made important routes in the Lakes. Most famous of these was Moss Ghyll on Scafell which he climbed with Hastings and Robinson in 1892. It is a fearsome-looking gash and in its day was regarded as an outstanding problem. At the crux of the ascent they came to a great cave. Here is Collie's description of what followed:

> Over our head, the great roof stretched some distance over the ghyll. Our only chance was to traverse straight out along the side of the ghyll till one was no longer overshadowed by the roof above, and then, if possible, climb up the face of rock and traverse back again above the obstacle into the ghyll once more. This was easier to plan than to carry out; absolutely no handhold, and only one little projecting ledge jutting out about a quarter of an inch and about two inches long to stand on, and six or eight feet of the rock wall to be traversed. I was asked to try it. Accordingly, with great deliberation, I stretched out my foot and placed the edge of my toe on the ledge. Just as I was going to put my weight on it, off slipped my toe, and if Hastings had not quickly jerked me back I should instantly have been dangling on the end of the rope. But we were determined not to be beaten. Hastings' ice-axe was next brought into requisition, and what followed I have no doubt will be severely criticised by more orthodox mountaineers than ourselves. As it was my suggestion, I take the blame. *Peccavi! I hacked a step in the rock* – and it was very hard work. But I should not advise anyone to try to do the same thing with an ordinary axe. Hasting's axe is an extra-ordinary one, and was none the worse for the experiment. I then stepped across the *mauvais pas*, clambered up the rock till I had reached a spot where a capital hitch could be got over a jutting piece of rock, and the rest of the party followed.[17]

The Collie Step, as it is called, is a typical piece of Collie mischief, probably necessary at the time, but not without thought as to the shock effect it might have on traditionalists to whom any tampering with the natural rock was a sin. Similarly, the Grey Ghost of Ben Macdhui which he claimed to have seen and which caused quite a stir at the time was in all likelihood Collie having fun at the expense of a gullible public.

In the Alps Collie became one of the group that centred on A.F. Mummery and he was with Mummery on many of the latter's outstanding climbs. It was Collie who named and helped to climb the Dent du Requin, now one of the most popular peaks in the Chamonix area, and he was with Mummery on the first guideless ascent of the Brenva Spur in 1894.

Nor was the thrill of exploration neglected. Collie climbed in the Canadian

Rockies and the remote Lofoten Islands and he was with the ill-fated Mummery expedition to Nanga Parbat in 1895. He was indeed a paragon of mountaineering, the greatest all-rounder of his generation. 'Of all the whole-hearted mountaineers I have known,' wrote G.W. Young, 'Collie alone remained to the end wholly and passionately absorbed in the mountain world.'[18] Of the Alpine group of which Collie was a member Young wrote:

> Together they constituted a new prophetic brotherhood, representing a fresh approach to mountaineering and incorporating a body of novel doctrine in their writings. The two main elements of this teaching were, first, the enlargement of mountaineering idea to cover all distant ranges and the development of suitable climbing techniques; and secondly, the energetic implanting and promotion of climbing in our own islands, so as to provide for our mountaineering that local root and native nurture without which no British institution or interest can survive. There had been mountaineers before them in both these fields; but in their activities as a group, and in their writings, the two movements first came to a collective consciousness, and found effective expression.[19]

By the turn of the century the initial exploratory phase of British rock climbing was coming to an end. This so-called 'gully period' climaxed in two difficult gullies on Pillar Rock in the Lake District. In 1899, O.G. Jones with George Abraham and A.E. Field climbed Walker's Gully and in 1901 Claude and Guy Barton with L.F. Meryon climbed Savage Gully. From now on climbers had perforce to seek new routes up the more open ridges and buttresses.

Round about this time too there came a subtle change. More of the leaders were home grown. Most of them (but not all) still became alpinists, but whereas the pioneers had learned their craft in the Alps and practised their skills on British crags, now it was more often the other way round. There were still 'family' partnerships in the mould of the Pilkingtons and Hopkinsons, notably the Bartons, the Broadricks and the Abrahams, but there were other outstanding partnerships as well such as Steeple and Barlow, Thomson and Andrews.

Thomson continued to dominate Wales, turning his attention to Lliwedd. One of his partners was Oscar Eckenstein, an engineer who applied his science to the art of climbing, designing the first modern crampons and advocating the art of balance on steep rocks. This, of course, was a key to climbing steep slabs and walls, as distinct from the rock-hugging techniques often employed in gullies. It was particularly relevant on Lliwedd, a big, open cliff. Another partner was A.W. Andrews, who often climbed on the rocks of Cornwall. It may have been Andrews' traverses of the Cornish cliffs which gave Thomson the idea of a 'girdle traverse' across Lliwedd, in 1907 – the first such in climbing.

Probably Thomson's best-known achievement of the period was the ascent of Avalanche Route on Lliwedd, with the Red Wall continuation, which he did with E.S. Reynolds in 1907. It got its name from an incident on the first ascent when the leader was nearly swept off the cliff by a block of rock inadvertently kicked off the ridge above. For some years this was regarded as the most exposed climb in Britain, though technically it was far short of what was being done in the Lakes. Avalanche now rates a V. Diff grade, possibly Severe, whereas the two Pillar gullies – Walker's and Savage – rate Hard Severe and Very Severe respectively, even today.

Lliwedd has long since lost its aura of difficulty and it is not a popular crag today, even with beginners. However, it was about this time that a number of the most popular Welsh climbs were done. Mostly easy by present standards, they have throughout the years proved faithful stand-bys for the novice and unambitious. Tryfan was an obvious target, since it is the most cragbound peak south of the Scottish border, and in 1902 H.B. Buckle and G. Barlow put up Gashed Crag, whilst in 1911 E.W. Steeple, A.G. Woodhouse, G. Barlow, H.E. Brown and A.H. Doughty climbed the classic Grooved Arête, which ascends the East Face by a series of ribs and grooves until, high on the climb, at a ledge called the Haven, further direct progress seems very problematical. The pioneers avoided it by moving out onto an exposed slab on the right and then up – the famous Knight's Move, memorably named.

In 1915 E.H. Daniell, I.A. Richards, T. Roxburgh and R.B. Henderson attacked the unique Idwal Slabs in the hope of climbing the wall above them. They failed on the wall but the route up the Slabs – Hope – became one of the most popular in Britain. In the following year two similar climbs were added to the Slabs and could hardly be called anything else but Charity and Faith.[20] I.A. Richards took part in all these ascents and in the final conquest of the Original Route on Holly Tree Wall above the Slabs, in 1918. This last is VS today and the other climbs mentioned tend to be around V. Diff.

What Jones did for the Lakes, George Abraham did for North Wales with the publication in 1906 of *Rock-climbing in North Wales* and Ashley followed this two years later with *Rock-climbing in Skye*. Both books were in the large format which gave full expression to their photographs, and it wasn't until *British Mountain Climbs* (1909) and *Swiss Mountain Climbs* (1911) that they adopted a convenient size for the pocket. *British Mountain Climbs* was in print until 1948.[21] The Welsh (and Alpine) climbing establishment were of the opinion that publication constituted an ungentlemanly act that tainted climbing with commerce. (They conveniently ignored the fact that as a professional lecturer Whymper had been doing this ever since the Matterhorn disaster.)

But though the Abrahams were sometimes criticised they were never ostracised, partly because they were very good climbers and partly because they were so genial that everybody seemed to like them. There may well be another reason, too: the books they produced were very good and very useful, and I suspect that even their severest critics had a sneaking admiration for what the brothers had done in the way of publicising the sport.

> They rapidly coalesced into a formidable climbing team. Both were strong, vigorous and adventurous. George, though the elder, was much slighter in build; Ashley, already in his late teens approaching fifteen stone, made the perfect anchor man: 'They complemented each other completely, George more often leading, graceful, supple and balanced; Ashley, a moving column of strength and aggressive energy, in support.' In temperament as in physique, they were complementary; George was more excitable and volatile, Ashley always steady and equable. Yet they got on well together, enjoyed each other's company, and in over fifty years of climbing, mostly together, in all parts of Britain and the Alps, neither had a serious accident.[22]

Their books were based on a solid expertise. On a visit to Wales with Jones just a few weeks before his death they captured what were to become some of the most popular climbs in Snowdonia: Terrace Wall Variant, North Buttress and Milestone Ordinary on Tryfan, Hanging Garden Gully in Cwm Idwal and the adjacent Devil's Staircase. Here is how George described the last climb:

> The top pitch proved to be a veritable chimney, for a black hole leads upwards, apparently into the heart of the mountain; and we christened the place the Devil's Drainpipe ... the leader crawled up into its dark recesses, and the sounds of progress gradually faded into the distance, until I heard a call from the open air some fifty feet above my head. At the same moment there was an ominous rumble in the Drainpipe! It took a second to realize that a rock was descending its dark interior, and there seemed every probability that it would sweep me off the small ledge on which I stood. It was a helpless feeling, but the suspense was soon over for the rock whizzed out of the dark hole, and before the real danger could be appreciated, it had scratched some skin off my left ear, and gone crashing down the cliff to the bottom of the gully.[23]

In order to prepare for the Welsh book the brothers returned in 1905 and climbed Monolith Crack on the Gribin Facet; for long regarded as a Welsh

test-piece in much the same way as Kern Knotts Crack was in the Lakes –
though the latter was always the harder of the two.

To these exploits the brothers added popular routes like the New West
on Pillar Rock, Crowberry Ridge on Buachaille Etive Mor and Ashley, with
H. Harland, created the Cuillin classic, Cioch Direct. By modern standards,
of course, all these climbs are relatively easy but what is outstanding is
the high proportion of Abraham routes which remain firm favourites with
novices. On them and their companions, more than anybody else, rest the
foundations of British rock climbing.[24]

J.M.A. Thomson was prevailed upon by the Climbers' Club (against his
wishes) to produce pocket guides to Lliwedd (in 1909, with Andrews) and
the Ogwen District, 1910. He studiously avoided Jones's grading system,
and the Abrahams' pictures. They were the first club guides, now a regular
feature of British climbing.[25]

North Wales had another 'first' in 1912, when the Rucksack Club of
Manchester acquired a hut in the Carneddau mountains to use as a base.
This was the first of the many climbing huts (often small cottages) now to
be found in the British mountains.

In the Lake District climbers like Fred Botterill and L.J. Oppenheimer –
both trained on gritstone incidentally – were adding climbs of quality to an
area already well endowed. Oppenheimer's party added the ever popular
Bowfell Buttress (about V. Diff) in Langdale in 1902, whilst a year later
Botterill made his famous ascent of the slab which bears his name on Scafell.
Botterill's Slab is Very Severe and was a tremendous *tour de force* for 1903.
Botterill's description of this exposed lead is one of the most laid back in
climbing literature:

> Clearing away the moss from little cracks here and there I managed
> to climb slowly upwards for about 60 feet. The holds then dwindled
> down to little more than finger-end cracks. I looked about me and
> saw, some 12 feet higher, a little nest about a foot square covered
> with dried grass. Eight feet higher still was another nest and a
> traverse leading back to where the crack opened into a respectable
> chimney. If I could only reach hold of that first nest what remained
> would be comparatively easy. It seemed to be a more difficult thing
> than I had ever done but I was anxious to tackle it. Not wishing
> to part with the axe I seized it between my teeth and with my
> fingers in the best available cracks I advanced. I cannot tell with
> certainty how many holds there were; but I distinctly remember
> that when within two feet of the nest I had a good hold with my
> right hand on the face, and so ventured with my left to tear away
> the dried grass on the nest. However, the grass removed from the
> ledge, a nice little resting place was exposed – painfully small, but

level and quite safe. I scrambled on to it, but on account of the weight of the rope behind me, it was only with great care and some difficulty that I was able to turn round. At last I could sit down on the nest and look around me.

The view was glorious. I could see Scafell Pike and a party round the cairn. Far below was another group intent on watching our movements, a lady being amongst the party. I once read in a book on etiquette that a gentleman in whatever situation of life should never forget his manners towards the other sex, so I raised my hat, though I wonder if the author had ever dreamed of a situation like mine. I now discovered that our eighty feet of rope had quite run out and that my companions had already attached an additional 60 feet. Further, I began to wonder what had become of my axe, and concluded I must unthinkingly have placed it somewhere lower down. There it was, stuck in a little crack about five feet below me. Not knowing what was yet to come I felt I must recover it, so I lowered myself until I could reach it with my foot. I succeeded in balancing it on my boot, but in bringing it up it slipped and clattering on the rocks for a few feet took a final leap and stuck point downwards in the Rake's Progress. Standing up again I recommenced the ascent and climbed on to the second nest *à cheval*, from where, after a brief rest, I began to traverse back to the crack. This was sensational but perfectly safe. As usual I started with the wrong foot, and after taking two steps was obliged to go back. The next time I started with the left foot, then came the right, again the left, and lastly a long stride with the right, bought me into the chimney. The performance was what might have been called a *pas de quatre*. Complimentary sounds came from my companions below, but without stopping to acknowledge these I pulled myself up ten feet higher on to a good grass-covered ledge to the right of the crack, smaller but very similar to the Tennis Court Ledge of Moss Ghyll.[26]

There had been a number of mountain accidents in Britain by the turn of the century, usually to fell-walkers going where they shouldn't or not taking proper precautions in snow-filled gullies and the like. Professor Arthur Milnes Marshall was unluckily killed in 1893 trying to photograph Steep Ghyll on Scafell, which he had just climbed in the company of O.G. Jones and Joseph Collier – he fell barely a dozen feet – but the tragedy which brought a sobering douche to the climbing world was that of 1903, also on Scafell, when four acknowledged experts fell to their deaths. They were led by R.W. Broadrick of Windermere, who with his younger brother had made some outstanding climbs on Dow Crag. The four men were trying to reach a ledge 165 feet above Lord's Rake where sixteen years previously Edward

Hopkinson had built a cairn. The cairn acted as a magnet and there had been many attempts to reach it from below (Hopkinson had descended from the top of the crag to build it) but none was successful. The cairn's reputation for inaccessibility proved a fatal attraction. Exactly what happened is not known but it seems that Broadrick relinquished the lead and the new leader, Garrett, slipped, pulling the others to their death. They had persevered, says an anonymous writer, 'beyond where good anchorage (a place where the leader could be checked by the rope in case of a slip) was obtainable.'[27]

Harold Spender, distinguished Liberal journalist and member of the Alpine Club, fulminated in a letter to the *Manchester City News*: 'How long is this to go on, and how many more young lives are to be lost? There exists a Climbers' Club which is especially responsible for this new school of mountaineering. It stimulates but it never restrains. As far as I have observed, the club seems to possess no sense of the respect which in every sport should be paid to the high claims of human life. The peculiar danger of the Lake climbing lies in the natural rivalry that springs up among the climbing parties at Wastdale Head. No party likes to be beaten by another. Thus, every party, however raw and inexperienced, tries to achieve the most difficult climbs.'[28] It was the last feeble roar of the dinosaurs facing extinction.

And the extinction was coming not from the Joneses or the Thomsons, much less the Raeburns, but from the men who had assiduously trained on the dark gritstone edges of the Peak District. From Puttrell and Oppenheimer, Jeffcoat and Botterill and ultimately from a small curly-haired Welsh lad who began climbing on gritstone when he became a student at Manchester University in 1910. His name was Siegfried Wedgwood Herford and he soon began to make a name for himself on the rocks. Three years later, when J. Laycock wrote the first guide to gritstone called *Some Gritstone Climbs*, he dedicated it to Herford in appreciation of the young man's skill.

Later he revealed how fate had thrown them together in a chance meeting:

> One fine afternoon in 1910 I (tortuously) made my way up the North side of the Downfall ravine on Kinder Scout. Near Professor's Chimney I met a small climbing party, including a tall, strongly built young man with fair hair, blue eyes, and regular features. Herford's manner was then, as always, pleasing and unassuming. That afternoon we climbed, amongst other things, the Varsity Crack. Herford had then done little climbing, but he had always a deep and intense love for the hills, and it was not difficult to predict that he would become a climber of the first order. Thenceforward, we climbed together regularly.
>
> Herford was not one of those people – rare indeed, but occasionally met with – who do not know the meaning of the word difficulty,

or to whom any degree of exposure is negligible. Certainly his reasoning balanced mind and excellent physique were great assets. But his successes were the result of endeavour and resolution. He twice failed, for instance, to climb the Engineer's Chimney, Great Gable, before he succeeded. Yet no climb ever beat him in the end. Except perhaps on one occasion (the Central Buttress of Scafell), he always climbed well within his powers. He was brilliant, but brilliantly sane. He calmly measured himself against a climb; if in real difficulty he did not hesitate to descend. When he did advance, each foothold on the way seemed a new base, freshly won and firmly held. In descent, he climbed almost as smoothly and confidently as in ascent. From the beginning he climbed well, and steadily improving with experience he became, as it appears to be agreed, the best English rock climber of his day. He was a strong walker, and fast uphill. Once we meditated walking from Manchester to Windermere within twenty-four hours. By way of training Herford walked 63 miles into Wales in sixteen hours. He only gave up out of sheer boredom and slept beneath the haystack of a farmer who woke him in anger. The next day he climbed, alone, the Great Gully of Craig y Cae – a feat foolhardy for most, but not for him.[29]

He also introduced Herford to a new partner, almost his equal in skill, G.S. Sansom. In 1912 they paid several visits to Wasdale in connection with a proposed guidebook to Scafell and they made the second ascent of Jones's Direct Route from the Rake, the first girdle of the crag, and they finished off a route begun by the Hopkinsons years earlier and known as Hopkinson's Gully. But the highlight came on April 12 when Herford, in stockinged feet, ran out 130 feet of rope in a single pitch and became the first climber to reach the great prize of Hopkinson's Cairn.

That same season they began to examine the bold Central Buttress of Scafell and soon discovered the Great Flake – a huge leaf of rock stuck to the crag and separated from it by the Flake Crack. Below the Flake was a grass ledge known as the Oval and a plan began to form in their minds to climb Central Buttress from the Oval via the Flake Crack. It was obvious that such a climb would be extremely difficult, but during the succeeding two years various reconnaissances (in which Jeffcoat helped) showed that it might after all be done. In April 1914 Herford and Sansom were joined by C.F. Holland and H.B. Gibson in an attack on the Central Buttress. Here is Sansom's description of the events which followed:

> On April 19th of this year, Herford, Gibson, Holland and myself repaired to Scafell for the attempt. Herford and Gibson ascended Keswick Brothers' Climb and traversed out on to the Central Buttress, whilst Holland and I climbed direct from Rake's Progress

to the Oval. Gibson lowered me a rope down the crack and after removing my boots, I attempted the ascent. As far as the bulge, above mentioned, the climbing was comparatively simple but from this point to a large jammed stone 20ft higher it was extremely difficult, as the crack is practically holdless and just too wide to permit a secure arm wedge. Two fairly good footholds permit of a position of comparative comfort just below the jammed stone, and I noted, as Herford had suggested, that it was possible to thread a rope there. The stone itself afforded quite a good handhold, but the crack above overhung to such a shocking extent that the ascent of the remaining 12ft proved excessively difficult. My arms gave out long before the top was reached and a very considerable amount of pulling from Gibson was required before I joined him. Herford then tried the ascent on a rope and just succeeded in getting up without assistance. We thereupon decided to attempt the ascent in the orthodox manner, and preparatory to this we descended by Broad Stand and re-joined Holland on the Oval.

Our plan of attack was to climb up the crack and thread a loop behind the jammed stone, and I undertook to do this if Herford would lead the upper part which he was quite prepared to do. My first procedure was to soak two feet of the end of a rope in wet moss to render it stiff and to facilitate the threading. I then attempted the ascent but 6ft below the jammed stone I found my position too precarious to be pleasant and called to Herford for a shoulder. He came up without the least hesitation and standing on the bulge of the foot of the crack steadied my feet on small holds until I attained a safer position and was able to climb up to the chockstone. The stiff rope threaded very easily and making a double loop I ran my own rope through it for the descent which was, under those conditions, quite safe. After a brief rest, Herford tied on to the threaded rope and speedily reached the level of the chockstone. He made a splendid effort to climb the upper part but his strength gave out and he returned for a rest. A second equally fine effort was also unsuccessful and he climbed down to the Oval. I then made the attempt but soon abandoned it and we unanimously agreed to postpone the ascent until the morrow, leaving the threaded rope in situ. As Holland had already spent seven hours on the Oval, we decided to waste no more time and accordingly descended via the traverse into Moss Ghyll.

The next day, we climbed to the Oval direct from the Progress and one member ascended to the chockstone to renew the loop, which showed slight signs of wear from the previous day's use. We decided that combined tactics would be necessary and accordingly ran a second rope through the loop. Herford tied on one rope and I on the other whilst Gibson and Holland manipulated the respective ropes. I followed Herford closely up the crack and hung on to the loop whilst he used my shoulders as footholds. Directly he vacated them, I climbed 3ft higher and hung by my hands from the top of the chockstone whilst he again employed me as footholds which were most sorely needed at this point, for the crack is practically holdless and overhangs about 20°. A minute or two of severe struggling and he reached the top to the great joy of all members of the party. Herford thoughtfully hung a short loop over the tip of the flake to assist us in the ascent but even then we required much help from above and it was with a sense of great relief that we found ourselves on the crest of the flake. Murray who had been observing us from the recess, with some interest, was delighted with an invitation to join the party, so we lowered him a rope down the crack and induced him to remove the threaded loop on the way up. We were well satisfied with the day's work but not with the climb, in as much as it left 150ft of the Central Buttress still unclimbed.

Two days later, therefore, we set out – greatly regretting Gibson's absence from the party – to explore the upper part of the face. 50ft above the top of the Great Flake on the Central Buttress is an irregular 'V' shaped grass ledge, from the western end of which springs a wide chimney which is the lower section of the conspicuous Bayonet Shaped Crack running up to the very top of the crags. The upper section of this crack was, we knew, easy. The lower portion looked very unpleasant but we hoped to avoid it by climbing the steep face on the left with Holland and Slater belaying us. We climbed down steep rocks to the 'V' shaped ledge, 100ft below, and from there we were able to look down a remarkably smooth and almost vertical wall to the top of the Great Flake, 50ft lower. The wall was broken at one point by a right angled arête, which in spite of the fact that it overhung slightly, possessed sufficiently good holds to permit of a comfortable descent of 25ft. From its foot, a wonderfully exposed traverse across the almost vertical face on the left enabled us to pass behind a large detached pinnacle and to climb slightly downwards to the shattered ridge against the foot of which the Great Flake abuts.

Much elated at this discovery, we climbed back to Holland, and Slater and the three of us at once descended the easy rocks to the Cannon. Belayed from this point, I led across the traverse and up to the 'V' ledge. Herford then took the lead, Holland going second. Now the way by which we had descended necessitated an extremely difficult hand traverse on bad holds in an exposed situation and we therefore cast about for a better route. Herford first tried the Bayonet Shaped Crack but it looked repulsively difficult and he abandoned it in favour of a most exhilarating traverse across its foot on to the vertical wall beyond and upwards across the latter for 30ft to a steep slab which he followed for another 25ft to a good belay at the top of the lower section of the crack. We soon joined him here and climbed easily up the left wall of the upper portion of the Bayonet Shaped Crack, to the top of the crags.[30]

The Central Buttress of Scafell immediately became the hardest climb in Britain and twelve years later it had only been repeated twice: 'the difficulties met with are so great that the expedition ranks among the world's hardest.'[31] Known by its nickname of 'CB' it retained its aura of great difficulty for almost fifty years, and even today ranks as Hard Very Severe.

Central Buttress was the greatest of milestones in British climbing: 'Undoubtedly it stamped climbing with yet a new hallmark, and the inspiration due to it is not yet exhausted: all the great modern climbs in the British Isles are its lineal descendants. These men, too, gave evidence of the new spirit that had entered into the sport – the feeling that rock-climbing was an art in itself and could be pursued for its own sake and enjoyment. Unlike Jones and others of his day, they hadn't one foot on Scafell and the other on the Matterhorn. There was, indeed, something like an inversion of values; men began to measure the routes in the Alps against their own climbs.'[32] There was more of Puttrell than Haskett Smith about CB – a trend which was to continue ever after. Sadly the First World War removed many of these young men from the scene, including Oppenheimer, Jeffcoat and the great Herford himself.

CHAPTER ELEVEN

Spreading the Gospel

During the second half of the nineteenth century the steady improvement in communications began to open up the more remote areas of the world. New mountains were revealed, including the Ruwenzori, the fabled Mountains of the Moon. In the Himalaya in 1852, Peak XV was computed from survey measurements to be 29,002 feet and therefore the highest mountain in the world.[1] It was called after the first Surveyor General of India, Sir George Everest.

The Europeans who exported mountaineering to distant parts of the globe were of three sorts: first, the man (or woman) who in the course of travelling for business or pleasure, took the opportunity to do a bit of climbing. Two examples will serve. The first is James Bryce – diplomat and politician who travelled extensively and climbed whenever he could, from Iceland to the Hawaian Islands, where he climbed Hekla and Mauna Loa respectively. He made the ninth ascent of Ararat.

No less of an enthusiast, but a very different character, was Samuel Turner (1869–1929), who not only made the first ascent of the spectacular Ilam Rock in the Peak District (albeit with some aid from the rope) but also climbed in New Zealand and the remote Altai of Siberia.

The second sort of mountaineering enthusiast abroad was the European who established himself in an alien culture and converted the local people to climbing. Undoubtedly the prince of these was the Rev. Walter Weston (1861–1940) who, along with Usui Kojima, founded the Japanese Alpine Club in 1906 and became its first Honorary Member. Weston spent three periods as a missionary in Japan, spoke the language and made fifteen first ascents in the Japanese Alps.[2] In view of the impact the Japanese were later to have on mountaineering, Weston's enthusiasm bore incredible fruit.

The third and for mountaineering the most significant way climbing travelled further afield was more a case of showing the flag than spreading the gospel. This was by way of the specific *mountaineering* expedition, intent on climbing a peak or a series of peaks. We have already seen how some members of the Alpine Club saw this as the only true road for mountaineering to follow and in earlier chapters I have called them the geographical climbers, though in most cases the geographical motives were dubious – conquest was the real goal. Nevertheless there were always some who wanted to see beyond the last blue mountain.

Expeditions were at first quite small affairs – one or two climbers and perhaps a couple of Alpine guides, but towards the turn of the century Martin Conway and the Duke of the Abruzzi set a fashion for large-scale expeditions which included 'official' scientists, artists and photographers. The large expedition was sometimes as much a matter of national prestige as anything else and though it dominated the Himalayan and Andean climbing of the present century, the concept of the small party proved in the end to be the more enduring. What has certainly been proved over the years is that the size of the expedition is less important than the fact that the members should get on well together.

The Himalaya and the Andes deserve separate treatment, but perhaps a few examples from other parts of the world will suffice to show that mountain climbing was universal by the late nineteenth century. Interestingly enough these scattered ascents, though they may have added something to geographical knowledge, added nothing to the art of mountaineering.

The highest mountain in Africa is Kilimanjaro (19,340 ft), on the borders of what are now Kenya and Tanzania. The mountain is a vast massif of high land with two distinct peaks about seven miles apart, separated by an undulating plateau. To the west rises the great volcanic cone of Kibo, snow covered and with several fine glaciers, and to the east, in complete contrast, rises the rocky pinnacled Mawenzi (16,890 ft). The base of the mountain is surrounded by thick forest which gives way as altitude is gained to heathland, veldt and then volcanic ash.

In 1885 the territory was made a Protectorate by Germany and annexed as a colony five years later. During this period the mountain was visited by Dr Hans Meyer in 1887 with Leutnant von Eberstein as his companion. Even to reach the mountain they had to run the dangers of Arab slavers and the fearsome Masai, though the WaChagga, who have their shambas at the southern foot of the mountain, proved friendly and provided bearers. The two men climbed to the plateau then began the awful grinding ascent of the great cinder-cone of Kibo. It was bitterly cold and very exhausting and before long von Eberstein gave up. Meyer pressed on through gathering mist up a snowfield until he saw what he believed to be an ice wall about 120 feet above. It must have been a trick of the mist, but it was enough to make Meyer turn back. He was probably very near the summit rim – for the top of Kilimanjaro is a vast caldera, a mile across.

In the following year he tried again but was frustrated by a brush with Arab slavers and it wasn't until 1889 that he was able to return, this time accompanied by one of Germany's greatest mountaineers, Ludwig Purtscheller.

On October 2 they pitched camp on the barren plateau below Kibo and started their ascent by lantern light at 2.30 a.m. next day. By 7 a.m. they reached the first snow and by 9.50 the lower edge of the icecap – probably the place which had stopped Meyer two years earlier. Purtscheller cut steps

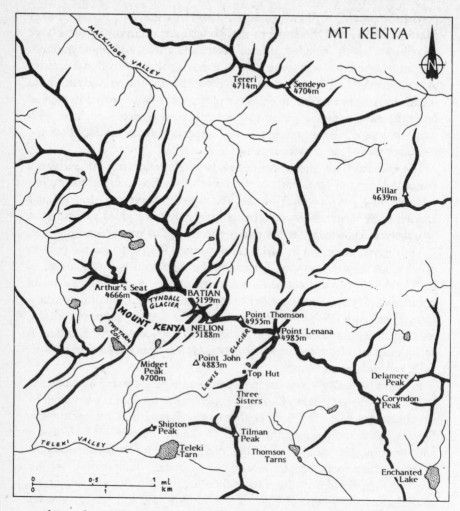

up this – the angle was thirty-five degrees – and though they came across a few crevasses there was no difficulty in reaching the crater rim at 1.45 p.m.

They descended to their camp but two days later were back again and this time went round the rim to the highest point where they raised the German flag and christened it Kaiser Wilhelm Spitze.[3]

The following week they turned their attention to the much more difficult Mawenzi peak and, though they reached a couple of the pinnacles on the mountain's shattered crest, they did not reach the highest point.[4]

Ten years later Meyer returned to Kilimanjaro and made a circuit of the mountain. He found the approach dramatically changed – the Germans had built a railway and good roads in their colonisation process. The mountain too had changed. The ice had shrunk considerably in the ten years, so that the snow line was 500 feet higher and there was no glacier lip on the

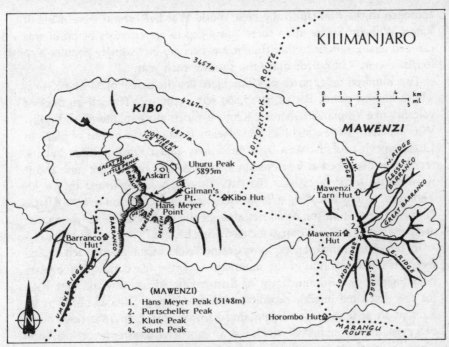

KILIMANJARO

3657m

KIBO

4267m

4877m

NORTHERN ICE FIELD

GREAT PENCK
LITTLE PENCK

Askari

Uhuru Peak
5895m

Gilman's
Pt.

Hans Meyer
Point

HEIM

KERSTEN

DECKEN

BARRANCO

UMBWE RIDGE

Barranco
Hut

N

MAWENZI

N.W.
RIDGE

N. RIDGE

LESSER BARRANCO

GREAT BARRANCO

Mawenzi
Tarn Hut

Kibo Hut

1 2
3
4

Mawenzi
Hut

LONGIK RIDGE

LOITOKITOK ROUTE

S. RIDGE

E. RIDGE

km
ml
0 1 2 3 4
0 1 2 3

(MAWENZI)
1. Hans Meyer Peak (5148m)
2. Purtscheller Peak
3. Klute Peak
4. South Peak

Horombo Hut

MARANGU ROUTE

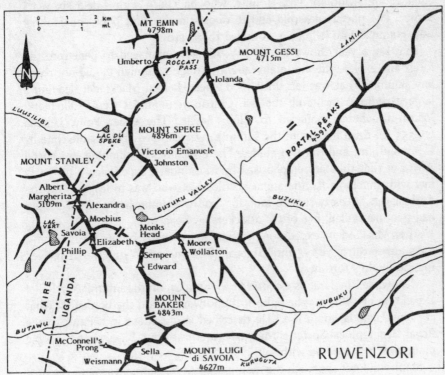

km
ml
0 1 2
0 1

N

MT EMIN
4798m

Umberto

ROCCATI
PASS

Iolanda

MOUNT GESSI
4715m

LAMIA

LUUSILIBI

LAC DU
SPEKE

MOUNT SPEKE
4896m

Victorio Emanuele

Johnston

PORTAL PEAKS
4391m

MOUNT STANLEY

Albert
Margherita
5109m

Alexandra

Moebius

Savoia

Phillip

Elizabeth

LAC
VERT

Monks
Head

BUJUKU VALLEY

BUJUKU

Moore
Wollaston

Semper

Edward

ZAIRE

UGANDA

BUTAWU

McConnell's
Prong

Weismann

Sella

MOUNT
BAKER
4843m

MOUNT LUIGI
di SAVOIA
4627m

KURUGUTA

MUBUKU

RUWENZORI

approach to the rim. Up to the First World War five ascents were made of Kaiser Wilhelm Spitze, then there was a gap of eleven years before it was climbed again, but since that time it has become increasingly popular as a tourist ascent – hundreds make the summit each year.

Two hundred miles north of Kilimanjaro lies the massif of Mount Kenya, whose highest point, Batian, is 17,060 feet (5199 m). Though an ancient volcano, like Kilimanjaro, Mount Kenya is much more splintered and spiky. With its sharp ridges, aiguilles and glaciers it would not be out of place in Chamonix. It was first seen by a missionary called Krapf in 1843 but his report was dismissed as nonsense by British geographers of the time and it wasn't until forty years later that its existence was confirmed by Joseph Thomson, who was leading a Royal Geographical Expedition to East Africa. Unfortunately Thomson could not attempt the peak because he was chased away by the Masai and barely escaped with his life.

In 1886 the Hungarian explorer Count Teleki managed to reach 13,800 feet, but his description of the mountain was very inaccurate. Three years later Piggott, the Administrator of British East Africa, saw the East Face for the first time but an expedition led by Captain Dundas failed in its attempt to penetrate the surrounding bamboo forest. In 1892 there were two expeditions, the first of which was an expensive disaster involving Astor Chanler and Leutnant von Hohnel, who had been with Teleki six years earlier. The porters deserted and to quote one account poor von Hohnel was 'pounded into jelly by a wounded rhinoceros.'[5]

That same year, however, Dr J.W. Gregory managed to penetrate the forest and explore the mountain fairly thoroughly, though he did not reach any summit. That was left until 1899 when Halford Mackinder, leading a large expedition including the two Courmayeur guides César Ollier and Joseph Brocherel, managed to climb Batian. The easier Point Lenana (16,355 ft), third highest of the summits, was climbed at the same time by C.B. Hausburg and the two guides. The difficulties of climbing in Central Africa at that time are emphasised by Mackinder's experience – his party met with smallpox, famine and a hostile chief who was in league with the Arab slavers. A party sent to look for food was ambushed and Mackinder had two men killed; five of the attackers lay dead too.

After Mackinder's expedition, nothing more was done on Mount Kenya for another thirty years, until Shipton, Tilman and Wynn Harris revived the mountain's fortunes.

Meanwhile, the famous explorer H.M. Stanley, on the Emin Pasha Relief Expedition of 1888, caught sight of the Ruwenzori, on the borders of what are now Uganda and Zaire.[6] He described the incident in a letter to the Royal Geographical Society: 'My gun-bearer cried out, "See, sir, what a big mountain; it is covered with salt!"'

Stanley did not approach the mountains but in the years around the turn of the century a number of missionaries and other travellers claimed to have reached considerable heights on the peaks.[7] The first visit by experienced climbers was in 1905 when Freshfield and Mumm of the Alpine Club, with the guide Moritz Inderbinnen, visited the range. Unfortunately they were badly advised and chose November, one of the worst months, due to heavy rain. Mumm and the guide reached 14,500 feet. Hard on their heels came a small expedition led by Dr A.F.R. Wollaston which managed to climb a peak in the Baker Group now known as Mount Wollaston.[8]

By now the extent of the mountains was becoming well known: a group of shapely glacier peaks about six miles wide and ten long, set in a wide belt of foothills, difficult of access because they are surrounded by deep glutinous bog and usually shrouded in mist and rain. Indeed, it was the weather which had prevented their earlier discovery; they simply weren't seen, despite the fact that ten of the peaks are over 16,000 feet high.

In 1906, a few months after Wollaston, the Duke of the Abruzzi arrived with a team of ten scientists and climbers, including guides.[9] The Duke, third son of the ex-King of Spain, was an Italian naval officer with plenty of money and a penchant for adventure. He had already climbed Mount St Elias in Alaska, where others had failed, and his expedition to the North Pole had succeeded in reaching the furthest north attained at that time, though not without cost. Three years later he was to make a significant contribution to the exploration of the Karakoram.

Abruzzi planned well and surrounded himself with the best of men and materials. Base camp was established on June 7 at the head of the Mobuku Valley and in little more than a month fourteen summits, all exceeding 15,000 feet, had been climbed, including the two highest in the range which Abruzzi called Queen Margherita (16,763 ft) and Queen Alexandra (16,703 ft) after the Queens of Italy and England respectively. Meanwhile, Sella made a photographic survey and others made geological, botanical and other scientific studies. All in all a very thorough job: 'In fifty days' work the problem of Ruwenzori was satisfactorily solved in all its aspects.'[10]

Like Caesar, the Duke came, he saw and he conquered. On both Mount St Elias and the Ruwenzori, Abruzzi succeeded where others had failed. Small wonder that men began to look on his expeditions as models of their kind and to copy them. Along with his contemporary, W.M. Conway, and to a certain extent, Whymper, he can be regarded as the founder of the 'large' expedition.

None of the problems which confronted mountaineers in Africa were to be found in New Zealand in the last quarter of the nineteenth century. The Maori wars ended in 1871 and the various provinces united into a national government in 1876. Settlement had proceeded apace and there was scarcely any unknown country, one of the last great discoveries being a route through the Fiordland Mountains of South Island to Milford Sound, made by Quintin Mackinnon in 1888, crossing the pass which bears his name and which is now part of the popular walk called the Milford Track.

The whole of the western side of South Island is occupied by a complex range of mountains collectively known as the Southern Alps, a name given them by Captain Cook, who saw their gleaming white summits from out at sea. The highest peak is named after him, Mount Cook (12,349 ft) although the Maori name is Ao-Rangi. Though the peaks are not as high as the real Alps, because of the heavy precipitation, the level of permanent snow is some 3000 feet lower – 5000 feet above sea level compared with the Alps' 8000 feet. On the west coast the mountains descend steeply towards the sea in difficult country, full of thick scrub, but on the eastern side wide plains run right up to the ranges without any interruption from foothills – Dr Haast, who explored much of the area, reckoned he could drive a buggy from Christchurch to the foot of the Tasman Glacier.[11]

The first explorer to set foot on the glaciers was Sir James Hector, who crossed from Matukituki to the Arawhata valley below Mount Aspiring, negotiating in the process the lower Bonar Glacier where he was 'the first man to use an ice-axe and rope in crevassed terrain'.[12] This was in 1863 but a year later three gold prospectors led by A.J. Barrington traversed many passes, ridges and glaciers in a winter expedition on the perimeter of the Olivine Ice Plateau. 'They nearly died from semi-starvation, exposure and frostbite. Even after a hundred years their expedition has not been equalled for boldness and endurance.'[13]

In 1882 the Rev. W.S. Green with the Oberland guides Ulrich Kaufmann and Emil Boss visited New Zealand with the express purpose of making the first ascent of Mount Cook. Green was an Irish parson and a member of the Alpine Club, though his climbing qualifications were somewhat vague. His only previous recorded ascent was with the guide Peter Knubel on Monte Rosa twelve years earlier, but he seems to have climbed in Norway and the Lofoten Islands in the interim. He had, however, all the vigour of his times.[14]

He arrived in New Zealand on February 5 and a week later was camped near the foot of the Tasman Glacier with his guides. In the next few days he suffered bad weather but was able to appreciate the marvellous world of snow and ice he had entered. The huge glacier ran up towards the Cook range where there were arrayed peak upon icy peak. 'This view I consider quite equal, if not superior, to anything in Switzerland, and the glacier beneath our feet had an area half again as great as that of the great Aletsch, the largest glacier of the European Alps,' he wrote.

They established a higher camp, at the foot of their goal. The mountain seemed precipitous on all sides. It formed one arm of a great cirque of peaks, the approach to which was barred by the chaotic and huge icefall

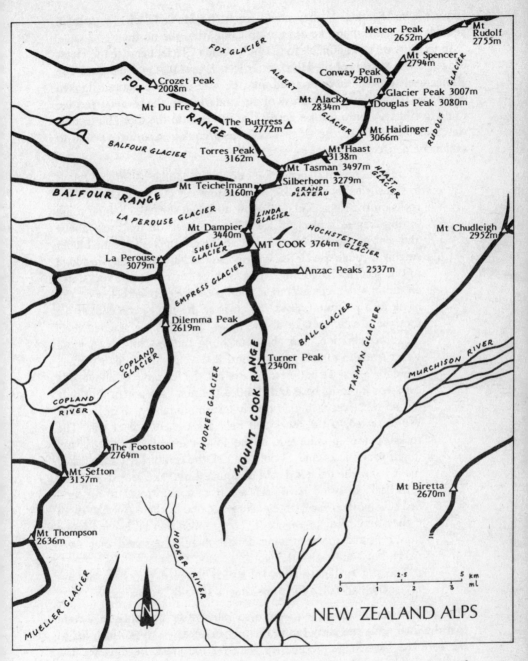

NEW ZEALAND ALPS

of the Hochstetter Glacier. Green and his men first tried the south arête of Mount Cook, then the east arête, but were beaten back on both. Fortunately the weather was good and they were able to see that above the Hochstetter icefall was a plateau of ice which they christened the Linda Glacier after

Green's wife, Belinda. If they could reach the Linda Glacier, it seemed possible that there might be a route up Cook from the north.

In fact it wasn't too difficult to reach the Linda Glacier because the Haast Ridge, on the far side of the Hochstetter Icefall, gave reasonable access. The glacier itself proved very crevassed and the way up the mountain looked hazardous. From the upper plateau of the Linda Glacier the best way seemed to be to climb up onto Cook's East Ridge and thus to the top. The trouble was that the route to the ridge was a steep couloir seemingly prone to avalanche dangers.

> More than one avalanche swept down the couloir as we worked up to the shelter of the rocks; we therefore cut our steps close to the rocks on the right, and every now and then sheltered behind some jutting crag as a block of ice splintered itself on the rocks above and sent its pieces whizzing past and over our heads, some blocks singing through the air like a cannon-shot. Now and then we added to our security by getting a grip with one hand on the rocks, not an unimportant consideration, as the ice-slope ended below on the brink of a profound abyss. When near the top of the couloir we thought it safer to take to the rocks, but soon we reached their upper termination, and above us hung the ice-cliffs, with loose séracs ready to tumble at any moment. To cross the couloir seemed too dangerous; we preferred to attempt the ice rampart above. We cut steps up to its base and climbed the first escarpment, but only to find ourselves facing an utterly insurmountable wall of blue ice. We retreated to the rocks and held a short council of war. The rocks on the opposite side of the couloir extended upwards, and might prove accessible. Should we risk the couloir? My men asked me if I saw the danger. I said of course I did, and feared we must turn back. It would have been a sore disappointment to me, and as I saw by their faces an equally great one to them. I asked them if they were ready to chance it. They replied that on leaving home they expected to meet some danger; here it was and they were ready, but I must give the word.
>
> The sun had now gone in, which lessened our risk, and no avalanche had fallen for some time; so I said, 'Forwards.'[15]

The last few feet of the couloir were desperately steep but once they were past the final rocks the party found themselves on easy slopes which led to the corniced East Ridge. Soon they were on the crest, heading for the summit, battling against a strong wind. The top was theirs for the taking, yet at this very moment of victory, some two hundred feet from their goal, they chose to turn back.

It was at the guides' suggestion, though Green at once agreed. It was

6.20 p.m. and the daylight was fading. The guides wanted to use what little daylight was left to secure their retreat which they knew would be difficult, but in fact there was never any chance that they could beat the onset of darkness and going to the summit would have made little difference, one feels. As it was, the descent became an epic of endurance:

On returning to the point where we first struck the arête we had to turn with our faces to the ice and descend backwards, so as to keep a good grip with our axes. Soon we reached the highest ridge of rocks, composed of highly indurated yellow sandstone, where we loosened a few fragments and deposited beneath them my handkerchief and Kaufmann's tin match-box. These rocks afforded no shelter whatever from the *Heiterwind*, which was steadily increasing in violence. The golden tint of parting day gleamed through the storm-clouds, giving a warm blush to the snow. My men urged me to go quicker and quicker, but to find the ice-steps backwards and look out for a firm grip was no easy job. The lower termination of this ice-slope was the worst bit of the whole descent. The ice thinned off over a ridge of rocks with a vertical fall of about 6 feet, and bad holding ground below. We could cut no steps and had kicked away all the grips coming up; there was nothing to which we could attach our spare rope. The thought of this spot bore heavily on my mind so long as we were above it, and there was only dim twilight when we reached its brink. Kaufmann and I placed ourselves as firmly as we could, while Boss slipped over the edge, and though he used his axe with great dexterity I felt an unpleasant strain on my hips before he could check his descent. Then came my turn. Kaufmann held the rope tight, slacking me down slowly, and then I got my feet on Boss's axe. Kaufmann had no one to slack him down, so Boss stood up to him, as close as he could with security, and let him down gently, while I jammed myself into the only crevice available. To cross the couloir was the work of a few minutes, and as we gained the rocks on the opposite side night closed in. Still we had no shelter. The wind was now blowing in fierce squalls, accompanied by showers of sleet and drenching rain. We could not find the rock-grips in the dark, so we groped our way once more in the ice-steps, but climbing in this manner became so dangerous that I called a halt on a little ledge at the side of the couloir. We stood for a few minutes, and thinking that we could stay there for the night, we took off our boots, wrung the water out of our socks, and put them on again. Not only did the wind and rain beat down upon us fiercely, but bits of falling ice struck our ledge, telling us plainly that it would not do for a lengthened stay. By this time the full moon had risen, and though we could not see it through the clouds it gave us some faint light. Once more, we took to the ice-slope, descended slowly to the lowest part of the rock-ridge, and turning to the left beneath its shelter succeeded in finding standing room on a little ledge from which we scraped the snow. It was less than two feet wide and sloped outwards, so that we had to hold on with our hands; and, as we were still about 10,000 feet above the sea-level, it was not all that might be wished for a night's lodging. There was no choice, however, as for thousands of feet below there was nothing but steep and crevassed ice-slopes. I served out a meat lozenge all round, and twice during the night repeated the dose; it was the only thing in the way of food or drink we possessed. The nine hours of darkness went slowly by. We stamped one foot at a time to keep life in it, then slapped our legs and shoulders with one hand, holding on all the while with the other. Sitting down, or even shifting six inches from the position we first occupied, was out of the question. The rain streamed down the rock and prevented the water with which our clothes were soaked from getting warm; and now and then a squall would swirl round the crags, bringing a deluge of rain with it. At last midnight came. We were getting drowsy. It seemed impossible to keep awake; to give way to sleep for an instant would be to fall from the ledge, and our whole time was occupied in watching so as to keep each other awake.

With the onset of daylight Green and his companions managed to retreat safely but tired to their camp.

But did they make the first ascent of Mount Cook?[16] They certainly thought so (Green thought he was only 30 feet from the top when they turned back). The purist would disagree. If the matter seems simple, how then do we regard those first ascenters – such as on Kangchenjunga, for example – where the actual summit was not trodden out of respect for the religious susceptibilities of the local people? Most would agree that where *difficulties* force a party to abandon a climb when the top is near, then an ascent has not been made. But what about if the retreat is voluntary – can we afford to take *motive* into account? It may well be that there can be no ruling on this and each case should be judged on its merits. Climbers often claim the game has no rules anyway. It does have 'ethics', however, which are just rules in academic disguise.

In 1885 two surveyors climbed Mount Ionia above the Arawhata valley, one of them using a miner's pick as an ice axe, and it seems that Green's exploits stimulated a local interest in the Southern Alps. In the years 1886–90 G.E. Mannering made five attempts on Mount Cook, usually with

M.J. Dixon who was with him on the final occasion when they reached a point about 200 feet from the top. In 1891 Mannering, A.P. Harper and others formed the New Zealand Alpine Club.[17]

There could hardly be a better example of the way mountaineering spread from Europe to the far corners of the world. Wherever the seed was implanted unclimbed peaks within the country concerned became immediate objects of national attention, the classic case being the Italians and the Matterhorn. This was also the case in New Zealand and when it was learned in 1894 that the English climber E.A. FitzGerald, accompanied by the famous guide Mattias Zurbriggen, was coming to New Zealand expressly to climb Mount Cook, three young local climbers decided to forestall them.

At twenty-four, Tom Fyfe was the leader of the group and he had just made, solo, the first ascent of Malte Brun, a peak across the Tasman Glacier from Mount Cook. They were all professional guides but Fyfe's companions were very young: Jack Clarke was just nineteen and George Graham about the same. They decided to attempt the peak from the opposite side to Green's route, which they rightly judged too avalanche-prone. Their route followed the Hooker Glacier then climbed via Green's Saddle and the North Ridge to the summit; the climb proved difficult and so dangerous on account of the bad rock that it was not repeated for sixty-one years! Nevertheless they got to the top and so made the first undisputed ascent of Mount Cook. It was Christmas Day.

FitzGerald was somewhat miffed by this colonial enterprise and promptly refused to attempt Mount Cook: 'I did not try the peak myself,' he wrote loftily, 'as my desire was to do virgin peaks only.'[18] He was a rich young man seeking a useful purpose in life and he thought that mountain exploration might be it, but the trouble with FitzGerald, according to Martin Conway, was that he wouldn't stick to the job. He was a solitary, reserved man, used to getting his own way and petulant when thwarted; he threw up his place at Cambridge when he wasn't made cox of the University boat.[19]

The guide he brought to New Zealand was Mattias Zurbriggen of Macugnaga, who had been with Conway in the Karakoram and who had succeeded Ferdinand Imseng as 'Lord of the East Face' of Monte Rosa. Zurbriggen was destined to be the first man to climb Aconcagua, the highest summit in the western world, and to travel widely as a professional guide, eager to learn and to conquer.[20]

Having pre-empted Mount Cook the local climbers could afford to show no animosity towards FitzGerald – indeed a number of them climbed with him for a few days, anxious as much as anything to have the experience of working with a first-class guide like Zurbriggen, a rare treat for the New Zealanders. Young Jack Clarke, who had been on the Cook escapade, was employed by FitzGerald as a porter. By this time a hotel, called the

Hermitage, had been built near the foot of the Tasman Glacier, and a hut, called Ball's Hut, some six miles up the glacier.[21]

With an English friend called Barrow, who was with him for the first part of the trip, FitzGerald, guided by Zurbriggen and Clarke, made the first ascent of Mount Sealy (8631 ft), which had several times defeated the local climbers and then, when Barrow and the others had left, FitzGerald, Zurbriggen and Clarke climbed Mount Tasman (14,175 ft) and Haidinger (10,059 ft). These were first ascents and the Tasman climb took sixteen hours; already FitzGerald had come to recognise the arduous nature of New Zealand climbing caused by deep soft snow, unpredictable weather which was usually bad, and rotten rock.

Nowhere was this more exemplified than on the first ascent of Mount Sefton (10,359 ft) by FitzGerald and Zurbriggen, which they tried several times before meeting success. The final arête was steep and loose. Tons of rock went crashing down to the glaciers at the merest touch. Near the top a large rock fell and knocked FitzGerald off the ridge. Zurbriggen, badly placed, had all his work cut out to hold him: 'His marvellous sure-footedness was the only thing that saved us from instant death on Sefton,' his companion later wrote. When at last the situation was retrieved it was discovered that two of the three strands of rope had been severed: 'I had been suspended in mid-air by a single strand,' said FitzGerald laconically. On the summit Zurbriggen declared: 'Never, I can truly assert, have I found a mountain so absolutely dangerous ... It was more difficult than Monte Rosa from Macugnaga.'[22]

After an interesting journey across the range to the west and back by a different pass, FitzGerald left for Christchurch, Zurbriggen remaining to tidy up the camp. The guide took the opportunity to make a solo ascent of Mount Cook by the North-East Ridge which he found easy.[23] This was the ridge which Green's original route joined near the top and it is now called the Zurbriggen Ridge.

Another English visitor appeared on the New Zealand scene in 1905 in the shape of Sam Turner,[24] fresh from his Siberian adventures. Turner was intent on traversing Mount Cook and in January 1906, accompanied by Malcolm Ross, a journalist, Tom Fyfe, who had made the first ascent, and the young guide Peter Graham, he succeeded in climbing the Zurbriggen Ridge, then descending to Green's Saddle on the North Ridge and from there down a steep and dangerous couloir to the Hooker Glacier. Turner was struck on the head by a stone flying down the couloir, but managed to keep his footing. Peter Graham cut the steps: 'Young Graham, who was leading, treated us to a splendid example of ice craft and physical endurance as he hacked away with his axe down that 2,000ft of frozen slope ... Hour after hour went by ... and still we could not see the final bergschrund,' Ross wrote.[25] They had started from a bivouac on the Haast Ridge and by the time they returned to the Hermitage they had been on the go for thirty-six hours.

Peter Graham and his brother Alex were to become two of the best known of New Zealand's guides.[26] In 1909 with the English climber L.M. Earle and the guide J.M. Clarke, they climbed Cook from the Hooker Glacier by the long ridge now known as Earle's Ridge and made many other ascents. Amongst the most significant were those with the Australian climber, Freda du Faur. A very determined young woman, she had first visited the Hermitage in 1906, but returned in 1909 when she persuaded Peter Graham to give her some climbing instruction. She turned out to be an apt pupil and tireless. From then until the 1913 season with Peter, Alex and Darby (David) Thomson, she made a remarkable series of first ascents. She was the first woman to climb the three greatest New Zealand peaks, Cook (seventh ascent), Tasman (second ascent) and Sefton (second ascent). The climax to her career was the traverse of the three summits of Mount Cook with Peter Graham and Darby Thomson in 1913, possibly the most difficult first ascent done by a woman at that time.[27] In conservative New Zealand she was considered very forward to climb alone with men, but she seems to have had all the spirit of her Alpine predecessor, Lily Bristow. 'A dauntless lady grappling successfully with the obstacles put in her way by Nature and other members of her sex.'

Of all the places that the pioneers explored after the Alps there was none nearer to their heart's desire than the Russian Caucasus. Here, on the doorstep of Asia, was to be found a range of super-Alps, even bigger and better than the original.

The range is divided into three parts by the natural breaks of the Klukhor and Krestovy Passes in the west and east respectively. Between these two passes lies the Central Caucasus, 160 miles of shapely peaks and fantastically serrated ridges, calculated to lift the heart of any mountaineer. The highest mountain of all, Elbrus (5633 m), is a snowy dome, mirroring Mont Blanc in this respect. It is the highest mountain in Europe and, on average, the Central Caucasian peaks are about 1000 metres higher than their Alpine counterparts. The glaciers tend to be higher and smaller than those of the Alps, but the great valley heads, such as the famous Bezingi Basin, are most impressive. Many of the peaks are quite difficult to climb even by their easiest routes, and apart from Elbrus, the only one which is a simple snow climb is Kasbek (5047 m), which nearly became the first great Caucasian peak to be climbed when the ubiquitous Dr Parrot and his companion Engelhardt almost reached the summit in 1811. There are fourteen 5000-metre peaks in the range, eleven of them in the Bezingi Basin.

Until the middle of the nineteenth century the eastern borders of Russia were ill-defined, touching as they did various feudal states, most of whom

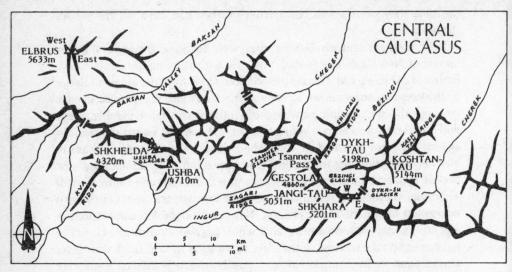

were hostile to strangers. Nevertheless in 1829 a party of savants attempted
to climb Elbrus, assisted by various Cossacks and Circassians, and though
they failed, one of the Circassians, Killar Khasirov, was seen to reach the
top by the expedition's leader, General Emanuel, who was comfortably
ensconced at Base camp with a telescope.

> Killar, as the Circassian was named who had attained the summit
> of Elbrouz, had known how to profit by the morning's frost better
> than we had. He had crossed the limit of eternal snow long before
> us, and when M. Lenz reached his highest point, Killar was already
> on his return from the summit. As the snow did not begin to soften
> till eleven, he found it firm to the very top, and only in the descent
> encountered the same difficulties with us. A bold hunter, and well
> acquainted with the country, he had before ascended to consider-
> able heights, though he had never tried actually to reach the sum-
> mit. He returned to camp a good hour before us, to receive from
> the general the reward due to his courage: but the general waited
> for the arrival of the whole party, in order to render the ceremony
> more solemn. Having spread out on a table the reward which he
> had promised to the man who should first reach the summit, he
> handed it to him in sight of all the camp, adding a piece of cloth
> for a caftan; and we all drank to his health in certain bottles of
> champagne, which our Mussulmen, not to infringe the law of the
> prophet, consumed with great satisfaction under the name of
> sherbet.[28]

The Russians have always claimed this as the first ascent of Elbrus, but it
has never been accepted in the West (even before the Revolution!). It is

difficult to understand why not: if a bunch of sourdoughs can stamp to the top of McKinley and self-taught New Zealanders climb Mount Cook, I fail to see why a bold Circassian shouldn't climb the much easier Elbrus.

This view is reinforced by what happened on the first accredited ascent of Elbrus in 1868 by Freshfield, Moore and Tucker, led by the French guide François Devouassoud. The porters had been left behind in the camp, but had decided to follow the climbers anyway. The day was bitterly cold and the climbers were about to turn back when, to their astonishment, two porters strolled up 'looking fairly comfortable in their sheepskin cloaks'. Somewhat abashed, the 'experts' decided to complete the climb, and the porters accompanied them.[29]

Freshfield's party also climbed Kazbek and explored the range thoroughly, being most impressed by the obvious technical difficulty of the peaks, especially Ushba (4710 m), Koshtan-tau (5144 m) and Shkhara (5201 m).[30]

Before this, in the early 1850s, the Russian army surveyors had produced decent maps of the area and climbed a couple of big peaks, Zilga-Khokh (West Peak, 3854 m) and Bazar-Juzi (4480 m), but it wasn't until Russia finally subjugated the border states in 1864 that the Caucasus became generally accessible. This date coincided with the very height of the Golden Age of alpinism, when most of the big Alpine peaks had been climbed and some mountaineers were fearful that the sport would come to an end. To them – and Freshfield was one such – the opening of the Caucasus could scarcely have come at a better moment.

Moore returned in 1874 with F.C. Grove, H. Walker and F. Gardiner, guided by Peter Knubel when a further exploration of the range was undertaken, including the great Bezingi Basin which almost took their breath away. Of all the soaring peaks above the Bezingi Glacier the only one they reckoned could be climbed with certainty was Gestola! They climbed Elbrus again, this time going to the slightly higher western top (5633 m as against 5621 m) and therefore, technically, making the first ascent of the highest mountain in Europe.

Further exploration was held up by internal troubles and war until Maurice de Déchy, a Hungarian climber, paid the first of his seven visits to the region between 1884 and 1902. Burgener was the chief guide and he was there again in 1886 with C.T. Dent and W.F. Donkin, when the first ascent of Gestola (4860 m) took place. In the following year Freshfield joined de Déchy, with François Devouassoud as chief guide, and climbed Tetnuld (4853 m). Various other peaks and passes were climbed by these expeditions but in 1888 three very strong British parties descended on the Caucasus. Most famous of these was A.F. Mummery and his guide Heinrich Zurfluh who climbed the impressive Dykh-tau (5198 m) from the south-west. A few weeks later H.W. Holder, H. Woolley and J.G. Cockin led by Ulrich Almer and Christian Roth climbed the mountain by the North Ridge, quite unaware that Mummery had preceded them to the top. The same party climbed Katuin-tau (4985 m) by the Bezingi Face and Saluinan-Bashi (4348 m).

These were impressive feats but they paled in comparison with what Cockin achieved alone with the guides. John Garforth Cockin was a Liverpool barrister little known to the Alpine establishment – he only became a member of the Alpine Club after his Caucasian exploits of 1888 – but a very determined and strong climber. Indeed, all these parties were strong in the physical sense: 'A noteworthy feature of the climbs made by these parties is that they were all carried out in a single day from camps high up on or near the main glaciers. It is evident that climbers of that era were strong, fast movers and their guides hard workers and great ice-men. Modern Soviet parties require two to three days for these expeditions, despite their advantage of the use of crampons.'[31]

In the space of three weeks in the middle of September, Cockin climbed Shkhara (5201 m), the East or Second Summit of Jangi-tau (5038 m), and the North or Second Summit of the mighty Ushba (4695 m). He climbed this last peak with Almer as his sole companion since Roth was ill, and they went up to the saddle between the two peaks of Ushba, by a couloir from the Gul Glacier. According to Cockin, Jangi-tau was a 'right pleasant climb' with a superb view but Shkhara was hard and cold ('the coldest climb I ever made') on which he was slightly frostbitten. It involved five or six hours of step-cutting.

Rather surprisingly he dismissed the ascent of Ushba North as nothing more than a long snow grind on which, in descent, he contrived to lose his right boot. He thought that under certain circumstances the climb might be dangerous and put their success down to the exceptionally heavy snow cover of that season. In fact, it is doubtful whether the climb has ever been repeated.[32] Although he returned to the Caucasus on three further occasions, climbing with some very experienced mountaineers, he never again managed to climb Ushba, despite various attempts. He had become by this time a firm devotee of guideless climbing, and was killed whilst leading a party on the Weisshorn in 1900.

The third party of 1888 was led by the President of the Alpine Club himself, C.T. Dent, who had as his companions W.F. Donkin and Harry Fox. Donkin was Secretary of the Club and a noted Alpine photographer;[33] Fox was a very strong climber who had done many of the hardest routes in the Alps without guides. On this occasion they had with them the two guides Kaspar Streich and Johann Fischer.

Dent was forced to return home through illness after a fortnight but Donkin and Fox went on to climb the South-East Peak of Dongus-Orun (4442 m) at the head of the Baksan valley, then turned their attention to Koshtan-tau. Their first attempt, by the North Ridge, failed through lack of time and impending bad weather, but they returned to camp determined to try again. They set out by candlelight from their camp above Bezingi at 3 a.m. on August 30, watched by their porter, Beslau Betaieff, and were never seen again.

Almost four weeks passed before they were reported missing but, although it was already late in the season, a search was made, with no result. Because of the recent tribal troubles in the area there was a suspicion of foul play, but this was disproved the following year when a strong search party comprising Dent, Freshfield, Woolley and Powell,[34] accompanied by the guides Christian Jossi, Andreas Fischer, Kaspar Maurer and Johann Kaufmann, found a bivouac place to which the party had obviously never returned, presumably having met with a fatal accident whilst attempting the mountain by its East Ridge. A few days later Woolley and Jossi, using much the same route on the East Ridge, climbed to the summit of Koshtan-tau (5144 m) where they found no cairn – which seemed to indicate that Donkin and Fox had been overwhelmed before reaching the top. Their bodies have not been recovered.

There were many more expeditions before the end of the century involving many of the best British mountaineers as well as others such as Vittorio Sella, de Déchy, Merzbacher and Purtscheller. By 1896 the exploration of the Central Caucasus was complete and any new climbs demanded a higher degree of technical skill than hitherto.

After 1900 the visitors were mostly German and Swiss but Tom Longstaff and L.W. Rolleston were there in 1903, whilst a Scottish party led by Harold Raeburn visited the Eastern Caucasus in 1913 and 1914; these were, however, the last visits by a British party for many years.

During this period the fame, or notoriety, of Ushba, that 'Matterhorn of the Caucasus', reached a climax. Though Cockin had climbed the North Peak in 1888, nobody had reached the higher South Peak or, indeed, repeated Cockin's climb. In 1903 three groups set out to put this right: a large team of predominantly Austrian climbers from Vienna led by Willi Rickmer Rickmers,[35] a smaller team from Munich, led by Hans Pfann, and 'two semi-attached English freebooters', Longstaff and Rolleston. Between the Austrians and Germans there was intense rivalry for the prize, not unlike that for the other Matterhorn half a century earlier. All the mountaineers were expert guideless climbers, trained in the Eastern Alps. As for Longstaff and Rolleston, they were not above a bit of healthy competition: 'We meant to snatch some of the plums from our Austrian and Bavarian rivals.'[36]

In this they were unsuccessful, as far as Ushba was concerned, so they went off and climbed the West Peak of Shkhara (5057 m) instead. Meanwhile Rickmers, who had visited the Caucasus before, in 1895 and 1900, succeeded in climbing 'about thirty peaks and passes, half of which were new' including the first ascent of Shkhelda (4320 m). The campaign culminated in the dramatic ascent of the South Peak of Ushba (4710 m), achieved after five attempts.

On one such attempt the party had a narrow escape. A lower snowfield on the South Face was separated from an upper snowfield by a very steep wall. After some difficult climbing and a night bivouac the party, made up of Schulze, Rickmers, Ficker, Miss Ficker and the porter Muratbi, tried the ridge at the south-east corner of the wall but could not make it go, so they switched attention to the south-west. Whilst the others remained below, Schulze and Ficker explored the way ahead. Rickmers wrote:

> Suddenly there came a shout; we were to follow. We clambered up three hundred steps or thereabouts in the snow, and then found a rock wall and a cloud, and out of that cloud hung a rope. A voice from above commanded me to attach myself to that rope, and to leave the others behind, as it was getting late (3 p.m.). So the girl and the porter were left in suspense, and up I flew as fast as my comrades' hands could pull. My feelings can only be described as mixed. The scene was weird, and I had curious forebodings, or rather I was suffering from a moral depression and anxiety which I would have forgotten if nothing had happened. I was in that funny or desperate state when a man works away with a will without being conscious about the object of his toil and worry. My situation became uncanny, for I saw nobody, and a thunder cloud, which had gathered around, enveloped the scene in gruesome twilight. After the first thirty feet the rocks became very difficult, and I kept wondering to myself how any man could climb them unaided from above. Now and then, in long intervals, came a muffled shout from above, telling me to follow the tugging rope, and exerting my powers to their highest I gained the next pitch, out of breath and half-strangled by the indispensable help from hands working behind the scenes at a higher level. After each hot and frantic effort came the cold wait at the next stand, and these waits grew longer and longer. I had only two ideas in my mind – that of securing myself firmly and fixing the rope as well as was possible and the question, 'What is this? why am I here?' Now and then a lump of frozen snow, detached from a crevice to free the handholds, came flying past, and I dared not watch its course in the space without. At one place the pause was longer than ever, and I was on the point of shouting to the two above to come back. With hands and feet I clung to the hollow in the rock, where only the edge of a slanting block, two feet square, provided standing room. My arm was stretched up high to grasp the hold, and the water which ran over the whole of the

wall poured into my sleeve. Suddenly I shuddered, for I heard a curious grating noise, and, peering out from my recess, I beheld the soles of two hobnailed boots, toes upturned, facing valleywards. I knew enough to make me sick at heart, for a climber's feet should not tread air. Then came a long and agonising groan, then a short silence which seemed eternity. At last came Ficker's voice, bidding me render assistance, and saying that he was firm. A short scramble brought me to Schulze, the owner of the erratic boots, lying unconscious, but babbling in delirium, his blood painting crimson a little piece of snow near which he lay. Attempting the last and most difficult bit only twenty feet from the upper rim, with success almost in his grasp, he had slipped and fallen the full length of the rope. But Ficker was stout, and Ficker held, and the groan which I had heard was the plaint of him whose vitals are nearly torn out by the thrice-blessed rope; of him who saved three men. To him we owe most, for through him we have been spared to see Ushba from below with living eyes.

I bandaged Schulze's scalp with trembling hands, and then Ficker came down, that we might face the question of 'what now?' A sorry spectacle we should have been to others. Our teeth chattered; we were shivering with excitement, wet and cold; our eyes were full of terror. We had to face the ordeal of taking our helpless friend down the rocks which only he among us knew how to climb. One was prostrate and two had to work in a place which was barely safe for one to stand in. The ropes would have afforded material for the jokes of a humourist had the situation not been highly tragic. There were three ropes – the one between Ficker and me, the one by which we lowered Schulze like a sack, and the one on which we relied to help us down. At each stage they became terribly entangled, stiff and kinked as they were, and our cramped positions made the task of separating them each time an anxious and risky labour. At last, however, after many hours of weary work, when every nerve was strained to neglect no precaution, we reached the snow, and no heartier sigh of relief can I recollect in all my life. One thing had proved a great boon to us, an incentive to be careful and slow, and that was the consciousness that our sister was waiting for us below. She and Muratbi received us silently, for they had seen men fighting for dear life. My companions had spent eight hours on Ushba's final wall; I five.

At the foot Schulze regained semi-consciousness and was able to walk down to camp roped between us. At nine o'clock at night we reached the sleeping-place amid thunder and lightning.[37]

Four days later, head swathed in bandages, Schulze returned to the attack, this time supported by Helbling, Reichert, Schuster and Weber. Using two pitons, he was able to overcome the *mauvais pas*, though it took two hours to climb ten metres and sixteen hours before the party reached the summit at 8 p.m., just as darkness was falling. Before they could make a proper retreat a thunderstorm broke out and they spent a miserable night high on the mountain. Nevertheless, they had conquered the South Peak which was certainly one of the major ascents achieved before the outbreak of the First World War.

The Viennese had won the race to be the first to climb Ushba South and Hans Pfann and his colleagues were very disappointed, but instead of retreating they hit upon the idea of traversing both the Ushba peaks in one expedition. So two weeks after Schulze's success, Georg Leuchs led Pfann and Distel up the Ushba Glacier on the west side of the North Peak to the foot of a great icefall, where the night was spent. Next day, to help lighten their loads, their sleeping-bags were abandoned and they tackled the icefall and the steep, icy, North Ridge. For six or seven hours they fought the ridge until at last they were forced to bivouac some distance below the top.

On the next day they found the traverse of the North Peak followed by the saddle between the two summits of the mountain exceedingly difficult. Leuchs had the misfortune to drop his rucksack, which bounded hundreds of feet to the Ushba Glacier, carrying with it most of his spare clothes and practically all the party's provisions. For the next forty-two hours the climbers had to contain their hunger as best they could. That night they bivouacked at the far end of the saddle, below the South Peak.

On their fourth day the Germans crossed the South Peak. It took four hours to climb from the saddle but their descent was helped by slings and pitons left behind by Schulze. Nevertheless, darkness caught them still on the mountain and it wasn't until 1 p.m. on the fifth day that they staggered into the village of Gul. 'This expedition,' said the *Alpine Journal*, 'must rank as one of the most remarkable displays of skill, determination and endurance in mountaineering annals.'[38]

The traverse of Ushba by Pfann's party marks a distinct step in the Austro-German progress towards Welzenbach and the all-out mountaineering of the 1930s.

Ushba was not climbed again for twenty-six years. Despite the fact that there was an Alpine Club in Imperial Russia, its members were not very ambitious. Some accompanied western climbers, others made a few minor new ascents on their own account, but most simply went up Elbrus and Kazbek. In the inter-war years, when the Soviets began to get their act together, they took as their model the traverse of Ushba by the Germans in 1903, and long hard traverses became the favourite Soviet way of climbing.

CHAPTER TWELVE

The Americas

The earliest ascents of peaks in the New World were made by the Incas at the height of their imperial power. The highest confirmed ascent, from remains found on the summit, was Llullaillaco (6723 m) in the Atacama Desert of Chile, climbed in the late fifteenth or early sixteenth century. Llullaillaco is a volcano without any technical difficulty, but this ascent by the Incas remained the highest ever made until the Schlaginweits climbed Abi Gamin in the Himalaya in 1855, sixty-two metres higher! Altogether the Incas are known to have climbed sixteen peaks of 4800 metres or more. All were volcanoes. There are indications that the Incas may have climbed Aconcagua (6960 m) (in the Inca language, *Quechua*, the name means White Sentinel), but no certain proof.[1]

Popocatepetl in Mexico was climbed by the Spaniards in 1522 in their search for sulphur for gunpowder, Pichincha (4791 m) in Ecuador was possibly climbed by Toribio de Orteguerra in 1582 and a cross was placed on El Misti (5842 m), in Peru, by the Spaniards in 1787, though it had certainly been climbed by Indians previously. These too were volcanoes.

The volcanoes of Ecuador were of particular interest to scientists in the Age of Enlightenment because the Equator ran through them. Cayambe (5786 m) is the highest point on the Equator itself and wasn't climbed until Edward Whymper's great expedition of 1880, but in 1736 a Franco-Spanish expedition to determine the length of a degree of the meridian near the Equator, led by Charles Marie de la Condamine, arrived in Ecuador and climbed Pichincha and Corazon (4791 m) in 1737 and 1738 respectively. They also reached a height of 4745 metres on mighty Chimborazo.

Chimborazo (6267 m) was for many years thought to be the highest mountain in the world.[2] In 1802–3 Alexander von Humboldt reached about 5500 metres on the peak and in 1831 the French geologist Boussingault and his companions reached some 6000 metres, but its final ascent had to await the coming of Whymper.

Second highest of the volcanoes is Cotopaxi (5897 m) which is also the highest active volcano in the world, though it has not erupted since 1877. It was climbed in 1872 by W. Reiss and A.M. Escobar, but whether they reached the actual highest point on the rim – an icy spire – is open to some doubt; it probably wasn't climbed until 1971. The rest of the peak is simple enough. 'Its ascent is not much more difficult than Primrose Hill.'[3] It was climbed several times in the years immediately following the first ascent.

The Ecuadorian volcanoes continued to attract scientists throughout the nineteenth century and to a certain degree they still do. One of the things which interested them was the physiological effects of altitude on the human body. The ascent of Le Buet and then Mont Blanc in the previous century had dispelled earlier fears that even moderate altitudes were fatal, but that there was *some* effect was undeniable. Humboldt's attempt on Chimborazo was only sixteen years after the first ascent of Mont Blanc and so was both daring and innovative. It was made primarily for the purpose of conquest, since Humboldt and his companions thought the ascent of the highest mountain in the world would bring considerable acclaim and in this they were right. It was a basic mountaineering motive. Though they may not have reached the heights they later claimed, Humboldt left a vivid description of altitude sickness:

> One after another we all began to feel indisposed, and experienced a feeling of nausea accompanied by giddiness, which was far more distressing than the difficulty of breathing ... Blood exuded from the lips and gums, and the eyes became bloodshot. There was nothing particularly alarming to us in these symptoms with which we had grown familiar by experience ... All these phenomena vary greatly in different individuals according to age, constitution, tenderness of the skin, and previous exertion of muscular power; yet in the same individual they constitute a kind of gauge for the amount of rarefaction of the atmosphere and for the absolute height that has been attained.[4]

Edward Whymper made the study of altitude sickness the prime scientific target for his expedition of 1880 to the Ecuadorian volcanoes, or as he preferred to call them with his instinctive sense of the dramatic, 'the great Andes of the Equator'. Whymper was a complex man, marked by the dramatic combination of success and tragedy on the Matterhorn. After it, climbing in itself was not enough for him. There had to be some justification and he fell back on the old cloak of scientific respectability. He was not a scientist (he was an engraver), but this did not seem to deter him. He had made largely unsatisfactory trips to Greenland in 1867 and 1872; now he thought that if the polar wastes did not meet his expectations perhaps mountains of prodigious height might. He planned to visit the Himalaya in 1874 but political difficulties prevented this, so he turned his attention to the Andes. Here too there were political problems in Chile, Peru and Bolivia and it seemed the only alternative was Ecuador, then as now, the calmest of the South American states.

He landed in Guayaquil in December 1879. With him he had his old rival Jean-Antoine Carrel and his cousin, Louis Carrel, as guides and they picked up an Englishman called Perring, who was a sort of tourist guide,

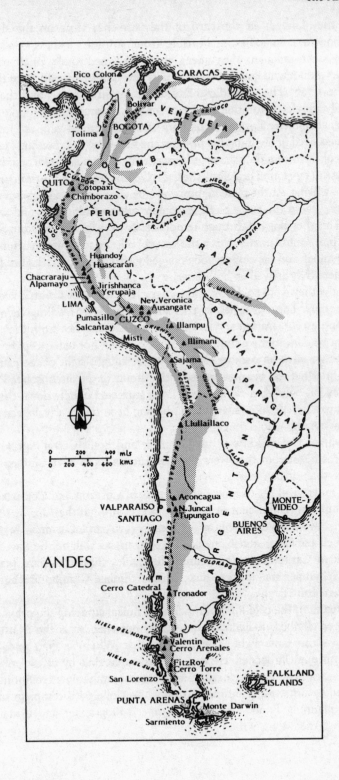

ANDES

when they landed. At the turn of the year they were on the slopes of Chimborazo, and suffering horribly from altitude sickness – all except Perring, who much to Whymper's chagrin seemed totally unaffected. Yet this was a man who could scarcely walk a few hundred yards down the road without a rest! The unpredictability of mountain sickness, and the way it is totally unrelated to fitness, were becoming apparent.

After an abortive attempt on January 3 from their third camp at 17,285 feet, they succeeded in climbing the peak on the following day. Leaving Perring in charge of the camp, they started the ascent at 5.40 a.m. and reached the summit plateau by 11 a.m. in a climb the Carrels compared with the ordinary route up Mont Blanc. At the plateau, however, the wind got up and clouds formed and they found the snow to be extremely soft and fatiguing, and shoulder deep. This they flogged through remorselessly to reach the Western Summit at 3.45 p.m. Unfortunately this is the lesser of the two summits on Chimborazo so Whymper and his companions doggedly struggled to the higher Eastern one where they arrived an hour later.

By now they were cold, wet and hungry. The wind blew with a keen edge and strongly. They struggled to take some barometric readings then began the long descent. Darkness overtook them some distance from their camp: 'A night so dark that we could neither see our feet nor tell, except by touch, whether we were on rock or snow. Then we caught sight of the camp fire, twelve hundred feet below, and heard the shouts of the disconsolate Perring, who was left behind as camp-keeper, and stumbled blindly down the ridge, getting to the tent soon after 9 p.m., having been out nearly sixteen hours, and on foot the whole time.'[5]

Whymper had frostbite in his fingertips and Louis Carrel had both feet badly frostbitten, but they were the first Europeans to have climbed a peak of more than 20,000 feet.

Whymper went on to repeat the ascents of Corazon and Cotopaxi, then in a campaign reminiscent of his great sweep through the Alps in 1864, he climbed Sinocholagua (4901 m), Antisana (5705 m), Cayambe (5789 m), Sara Urco (4676 m) and Cotochachi (4939 m) as well as the lower West Summit of Carihuairazo (5028 m).[6] The guides climbed Illiniza (5263 m) whilst Whymper was ill in Quito. He also climbed Chimborazo again, by a different route.[7]

Looked at in the cold light of modern technical climbing the peaks which Whymper climbed in Ecuador were easy, but then so is the Matterhorn viewed in the same light. The point is that Whymper had once again broken through a barrier. He had demonstrated that by careful planning and management it was possible for a mountaineering expedition to be mounted to distant and difficult parts of the globe with complete success. Of the planning Frank Smythe, Whymper's biographer and a man well versed in expeditions, wrote:

Of Whymper's efficiency in matters of food and equipment there can be no doubt; it was careful attention to food, sleeping bags and tents; in a word comfort as much as was consistent with mobility, that was responsible for the success of his campaigns. Though tremendously tough, and able to withstand hardship and fatigue that would have incapacitated weaker mortals, he had the sense to realize that factors other than mountaineering skill are involved in high ascents; and that the most important of these is health and morale, which can only be maintained over lengthy periods at high altitudes, or in hard conditions, if the body is kept warm and well fed. Unremitting attention to these points was responsible, more than anything else, for the success of his expedition to the Andes, and there is little doubt that had he turned his attention to the Himalayas he would have met with similar success and might have anticipated by many years the pioneers who groped their way up glaciers and peaks far less efficiently and scientifically.[8]

With his usual meticulous care Whymper wrote up the expedition in *Travels amongst the Great Andes of the Equator*, which, though it didn't appear for eleven years, was fundamental in establishing the way such ventures should be run in the future. It was the basis for the Duke of the Abruzzi's great expeditions, those of Martin Conway and ultimately all the great expeditions of the next half-century or more.

This was emphasised by the fate of Güssfeldt's expedition to Aconcagua in 1882. At 6960 metres (22,835 ft) Aconcagua is the highest mountain outside the Himalayan ranges and a suitable ambition for Güssfeldt, a fine mountaineer who had made the first ascent of the Biancograt on Piz Bernina four years earlier. He came to South America with Alexander Burgener, but the great guide was taken ill and Güssfeldt had to climb with the assistance of two local men who proved to be stout-hearted but hardly expert mountaineers.

In February 1883 after climbing the volcano Maipo (5290 m) Güssfeldt arrived at the mountain. He had no tent or shelter but with the two Chileans, Filiberti and Vicente, he proceeded to attack the rocky barrier of Sierra del Penitente which lay between himself and Aconcagua. The wind was bitter and Vicente soon collapsed with frozen feet, but Güssfeldt persuaded Filiberti to carry on. They reached a point some 400 metres below the summit of Aconcagua before a storm sent them scurrying back to base where they arrived exhausted after an absence of thirty-one hours spent without sleep and little food. A second attempt some days later similarly failed and Güssfeldt returned home.

In 1897 Edward FitzGerald arrived on the scene. This was the same man who with the guide Mattias Zurbriggen had done such remarkable work in New Zealand three years earlier.[9]

FitzGerald may have been a rich playboy, but he was very intelligent and he organised his expedition thoroughly and on a lavish scale. Besides himself there was another climber, Stuart Vines, the guide Mattias Zurbriggen, three more guides, a porter, a naturalist, two topographers, a cook and eight tons of equipment![10]

FitzGerald's first camp was at the snout of the Horcones Glacier and his second at 5700 metres at a saddle on the North-West Ridge. Zurbriggen explored higher but the whole party was affected by altitude and so Fitz-Gerald ordered a withdrawal. More attempts were mounted until on the afternoon of January 14, 1897, FitzGerald and Zurbriggen were within 500 metres of the top when FitzGerald was unable to continue. 'The objective of my expedition was to conquer Aconcagua,' he later wrote. 'I therefore sent Zurbriggen to complete the ascent ... It was justice to him that he should have the proud satisfaction of the first climb.'[11]

And so it was. Just as he had done in the case of Mount Cook, three years before, Zurbriggen soloed his way to the top of Aconcagua, reaching it at 5 p.m. 'I saw the whole of South America extended below me,' he wrote, 'with its seas, mountains and plains covered with villages and cities that looked like little specks.'[12]

The ascent caused quite a sensation in the local towns and Zurbriggen was fêted. Philip Gosse, the expedition's naturalist, was with him on one occasion and noticed him handing over bits of rock in return for cash: 'During the evening the enterprising guide had sold at least a dozen "actual summits" of Aconcagua. He disposed of several more before we left Mendoza and afterwards did a brisk trade in them in Chile.'[13] The pieces had actually been collected from the roadside.

FitzGerald made further attempts on the mountain with Vines but was always defeated by altitude, exhaustion or weather.[14] But on February 13, Vines with a porter called Nicola Lanti reached the summit, thus making the second ascent. Vines and Zurbriggen later made the first ascent of Tupungato (6550 m).

Meanwhile, as FitzGerald and Zurbriggen were coming down from the first successful ascent, an ill-equipped party of German and Chilean miners, led by Emil and Robert Conrad, were attempting Güssfeldt's old route without success. They reached 6500 metres and a year later, in another attempt, reached 6300 metres. Such failures could only reinforce the ideal of the big expedition.[15]

In the following year, 1898, Martin Conway arrived in South America with his own expedition. With him were the guides Luigi Pelissier and Jean-Antoine Maquignaz. Their first objective was the splendid peak of Illimani (6462 m) in Bolivia, quite near to the capital, La Paz, which they succeeded in climbing despite the mass defection of their Indian load-bearers. Next they turned to the other end of the Cordillera Real where a mountain mass then under the general name of Sorata contained the great peaks of Illampu (6362 m) and Ancohuma (6388 m). Their attempt on Ancohuma failed by only 150 metres. Fortunately they were not aware that local Indians had seriously considered murdering them for profaning the sacred mountains.

After Bolivia, Conway turned his attention to Aconcagua and with his two guides followed the route made by the FitzGerald expedition the previous year. Pelissier contracted frostbite and was forced to turn back, but Conway and Maquignaz continued with their attempt which ended at 'the top of a peak near, and not many feet lower than, the highest peak'.[16]

Conway estimated he was fifty feet below the top, with no further difficulties. Why then did he turn back? Was it concern for Pelissier, whose frostbite later turned gangrenous? Was it because Stuart Vines already held the altitude record and Conway might be thought to be equalling it out of jealousy?[17] Or was it because his ascent would be harmful to FitzGerald's book if it became known that Conway accomplished in a week what had taken FitzGerald's party some months? Conway put forward each of these reasons at one time or another, but as excuses they are all flawed. Nobody turns back when so near to an important summit without good reason.

After Aconcagua Conway visited Tierra del Fuego where he made an abortive attempt on Sarmiento, a mountain not climbed until 1956.

The two South American expeditions were the last to be made by either FitzGerald or Conway. FitzGerald and his erstwhile companion, Vines, went off to fight in the Boer War and gave up mountaineering, as indeed did Conway a few years later.

Two other explorers – for that is what these early South American climbers were – had a particular influence on Andean climbing before the First World War. Father Alberto De Agostini (1883–1960) was in direct line of spiritual descent from the climber-priests of a century earlier like Spescha or Joseph Imseng. He was born in Italy in 1883, ordained into the Salesian Order in 1909 and the following year went to Patagonia as a missionary, where he soon began exploration of the Martial Mountains of Tierra del Fuego, reaching their highest point, about 1400 metres. In the next two years he explored and surveyed many of the mountains of Tierra del Fuego.

De Agostini's ascent of Monte Olivia (1270 m) was perhaps his greatest achievement. The peak is near Ushuaia, the little town on the Beagle Channel founded by the Bridges family, pioneer settlers of the island. Tried by the Bridges brothers in 1902 without success, its rocky pyramid was considered inaccessible, but in 1913 De Agostini, with his guides Abele and Agostino Pession, set up camp above the tree line to the south-east of the mountain. Next morning they surmounted a tricky icefield to reach the east face of the rock pyramid, which they climbed by a series of chimneys and ledges. This took them on to the exposed North Ridge along which they struggled to a forepeak. Though separated from the real summit by a gap, they were fortunately able to cross this and reach the final summit by 11 a.m. Next day they returned to Ushuaia and considerable acclaim.

In 1913 De Agostini turned his attention to Sarmiento (2404 m), an isolated massif long thought to be the highest in Tierra del Fuego. The peak is a striking one, but often hidden by cloud and storms. Bad weather had turned Conway back in 1898 and now it defeated De Agostini as well.[18] Two years later, with the guides G. Guglieminetti and E. Piani, he reached the top of a subsiduary peak called Monte Conway, which had been the limit of Conway's exploration, then, descending to the glacier, they crossed through deep soft snow, hampered by mists, to a spur descending north from the West Peak of Sarmiento. At first the ascent was steep, but the mists cleared at 1400 metres to show that the ridge had two big steps and the West Summit was guarded by a huge crevasse. Prospects did not look good: the snow was soft and the ridge had the huge cornices so typical of many South American peaks. Agostini struggled on but above the second step (1875 m) they could see that ice blocks were breaking off the summit and sweeping their intended route. It was obviously too dangerous to go on.

There were no more attempts on Sarmiento for forty-one years, but in 1956 De Agostini, then seventy-three, persuaded a strong Italian team to take up the challenge and Carlo Mauri and Clemente Maffei reached the top of the East Summit. The West Summit remains unclimbed.

The other traveller worthy of note at this time in South America was Miss Annie Smith Peck, Professor of Latin at Smith College, Massachusetts, who was not only a tough lady, but an ardent feminist and one of the first people to seek sponsorship for mountain endeavour. Miss Peck was born in 1850 but she did not begin climbing until her thirty-eighth year, when she went up Mount Shasta in the Cascade Range. She does not seem to have done anything further until she was forty-five when she visited Europe and climbed some Alpine peaks, including the Matterhorn. Five years later, in 1900, she was in the Dolomites and also attended as US delegate to the International Congress of Alpinism in Paris. On her return she helped found the American Alpine Club (1902).

Meanwhile, in 1897, with the support of the *New York World* she went to Mexico and climbed Popocatepetl and Citlaltepetl (then called Orizaba). Though these great volcanoes had been climbed by the Conquistadores, they had not been climbed by a woman and Orizaba at 5699 metres (18,700 ft) became the greatest height reached by a woman at that time. It was a world record of which Annie Peck was very proud, especially at the age of forty-seven, and one which was to lead to considerable friction. In the following year she tried in vain to raise funds for an attempt on Illampu (6362 m), in the Bolivian Andes, then unclimbed.[19]

In 1903 she climbed El Misti, another easy volcano, then the following year she reached 5800 metres in the Illampu massif, thereby raising her record, though she did not reach the summit. She also made two attempts on the hitherto unclimbed Huascarán, the great giant of the Cordillera Blanca in Peru, reaching 5800 metres on the east side and 5500 metres on the west. Both Illampu and Huascarán were much more difficult peaks than anything Miss Peck had tried before. She was now fifty-three.

In 1906 she was in Peru again, exploring the upper reaches of the Amazon, climbing in the Raura Range and making her third and fourth attempts on Huascarán, by the west side, though she did not get higher than 5300 metres. In that same year her altitude record fell to her compatriot Mrs Fanny Bullock-Workman who climbed Pinnacle Peak in the Nun Kun massif of the Himalaya. Mrs Workman and her husband measured this as 23,300 feet (7105 m), though later surveyors have corrected it downwards to 22,810 feet (6957 m).[20]

Miss Peck returned to Huascarán two years later with the Swiss guides Rudolf Taugwalder and Gabriel zum Taugwald. On her return she announced that she had climbed the lower North Peak of the mountain which she estimated to be about 7300 metres, although she took no instrumental readings above 5975 metres.[21] She thought the South Peak was probably 100 metres higher and the highest peak in South America.[22] At the age of fifty-eight, Annie had recaptured the altitude record for a woman.

Fanny Bullock-Workman was nine years younger than her rival, but no less determined. Jealous of her reputation, she funded out of her own pocket an expedition to Huascarán by a French surveyor who in 1909 found that Miss Peck was wrong: the North Peak of Huascarán was only 6650 metres and the South Peak 6763 metres. It was not the highest mountain in South America – Aconcagua remained supreme – and moreover, Miss Peck had not broken the women's altitude record.[23]

Miss Peck's ascent by the South-West Face and South Ridge now began to be questioned. It had not gone without incident: Taugwalder was so severely frostbitten he was unable to work again owing to his chivalrous act of giving his gloves to Miss Peck. The two guides now claimed that she had not gone to the summit but only as far as the saddle between the two summits known as the Garganta. The people in Yungay village said the same and so did the doctor who treated the guides.[24] And yet the photographic evidence says otherwise. The pictures used to illustrate her books and articles show the South Peak as it could only be photographed from the North Peak, or as near the top as makes no difference. 'Those who dispute the claim of Miss Peck have not produced, as yet, enough proof to declare her an imposter,' says the distinguished historian of Andean climbing, Evelio Echevarria.[25]

Nevertheless, controversy had not finished with Miss Peck, nor she with it. In 1910 the traveller Adolph Bandelier speculated as to whether the great volcano of Coropuna in the coastal ranges of Peru was not higher than Aconcagua, and therefore the highest peak in South America.[26] Yale University decided to send out an expedition to investigate led by Hiram Bingham,[27] but Annie Peck seized the opportunity to set out earlier and climb the mountain, though it turned out to have several tops and she happened to choose a couple of the lower ones. On the summit of one peak she raised a banner inscribed VOTES FOR WOMEN.

Bingham climbed the highest top and measured its altitude as 6615 metres: 355 metres short of Aconcagua's crown. Annie Peck, now in her sixties, retired from the climbing scene. She died in 1935.[28]

In 1857 Captain John Palliser was sent by the British Government to explore the approaches to the Rocky Mountains in British North America and report on possible routes through the mountains so that a line of communication could be opened between British Columbia and eastern Canada.[29]

The first man to cross Canada in this way was Alexander Mackenzie in 1793 but, apart from a few trappers, not many followed him into the wilderness of the Rockies and even the Indians didn't go there until the 1840s. One of the few who did was David Douglas, the Scottish botanist of fir tree fame, who in 1827 climbed Mount Brown in the central Rockies – an easy ascent of 9157 feet, but the first above the snow line in the Canadian Rockies.

There were four Europeans in Palliser's party, but they split up to explore the mountains. Palliser himself found Kananaskis Pass and Lieutenant Blakison discovered the Kootenay Pass, but the most important discoveries were made by Dr James Hector, who later became Sir James Hector who played an important part in the opening of New Zealand's mountains. Hector was a determined man and very tough. Often on the verge of exhaustion through starvation he still managed to cover incredible distances in the shortest possible time. He crossed the Vermilion Pass and discovered a new river where he suffered the misfortune of being severely kicked in the chest by one of his horses and rendered senseless.

'My recovery might have been much more tedious than it was,' Hector remarks in his report, 'but for the fact that we were starving, and I found it absolutely necessary to push on after two days.'[30] It was five days more before they managed to shoot a moose.

The river became the Kicking Horse River and the pass which Hector discovered near by, the Kicking Horse Pass, was later to become the key to the Canadian Pacific transcontinental railway.

Nothing escaped Hector's eye. 'The most accurate mapper of original country I have ever seen,' enthused his leader. He defined the geology, discovered Glacier Lake, named Mounts Ball, Lefroy, Goodsir, Lyell, Murchison, Balfour and Forbes and measured the last three – albeit incorrectly. He discovered the pass which bears his name and Mount Hector (11,135 ft), near Banff, is also named in his honour.

Hector's wholesale naming of the mountains he discovered was not considered unusual in North America. The Indians rarely named mountains and as a result most North American peaks gained names which were both inappropriate and monumentally boring. This is especially the case in Canada where the majority are named after forgotten politicians and explorers: until recently there was even a Mount Stalin – long after his name had been expunged from any Communist mountain![31] The origins of some names are beyond recall, including that of the highest peak in the Canadian Rockies, Mount Robson, which is believed to be named after some early nineteenth-century fur trader.[32]

It is interesting that two of the men most intimately connected with the early exploration of the New Zealand Alps should also be concerned in the opening of the Canadian Rockies. The Rev. W.S. Green, of Mount Cook fame, made the first specific climbing expedition to the area in 1888, choosing the Selkirk Range in which to operate.

The Selkirks had already attracted attention. The peaks are amongst the most important and accessible of the Canadian Rockies, lying beyond the first crest line, in the big bend of the Columbia River. The range is crossed by the Rogers Pass, the route taken by the Canadian Pacific Railway.[33] In 1886 the area was designated as Glacier National Park. Two years before this the Rev. Henry Swanzy and R.M. Barrington had traversed through it. Swanzy was a relative of Green's and he it was who enthused the climber to give it his attention.

Others were interested, too. A very strong alpinist, H.W. Topham, with one of his brothers, made a reconnaissance of the area a few months before Green got there, and vowed to return at a later date. The rock was an excellent sound quartzite and both parties were able to use the newly completed railroad and base themselves at Glacier House, a huge hotel built by the CPR at the foot of Rogers Pass, with a stunning view of Mount Sir Donald, 'the Matterhorn of the Selkirks'.

Green, accompanied by Swanzy, set about making a map of the area. He also attempted Mount Sir Donald, without success, but he and Swanzy did manage to climb Mount Bonney (10,007 ft) in what was the first technical ascent done in Canada. The crux of the climb was the ascent of a 300-foot tower of shaley snow-covered rock which they tried to avoid on the descent by some steep snow slopes. Green tested these delicately, held on the rope by Swanzy. The whole slope avalanched off with a mighty roar and the two men beat a hasty retreat to the line of their ascent. At the tower they used the rope to lower themselves: 'Taking off the rope and making a bowline hitch on one end, we descended, trusting to the rope for hand-hold, then, jerking it clear of the rock it was fixed to, we hitched it on to one lower down, and thus reached safe footing.'[34] This sounds like a primitive form of abseil.

Two years later Charles Fay, Professor of Modern Languages at Tufts College, and a member of the Appalachian Mountain Club of Boston, visited Glacier National Park and scrambled round the base of the impressive Mount Sir Donald. Despite its name, the Appalachian Mountain Club was more a rambling club than a climbing club at that time, and it was Fay, already forty-four years old, who first directed it towards mountaineering and particularly Canadian mountaineering.

'Only within the last thirteen years – that is to say, since the Canadian-Pacific Railway has been opened – has this country been within the reach of ordinary travellers,' wrote Norman Collie in 1898. 'But the fact remains that Americans from the States were the first who began seriously mountaineering in this district.'[35]

Collie meant specifically the main range of the Rockies, east of the Selkirks, but it was the Selkirks which first inspired Fay after his visit of 1890. A few months after his visit he heard a lecture in Boston by two Swiss climbers, Carl Sulzer and Emil Huber, on the first ascent of Mount Sir Donald (10,818 ft) – the very peak which had first enthralled him.

Also in that year Topham had returned to the Selkirks where he first climbed Mounts Donkin, Fox and Deville (now Selwyn), before being joined by the two Swiss climbers who had meanwhile climbed Sir Donald. Together they ascended Mounts Sugarloaf and Purity.

The railway company was active in promoting Glacier House and in 1899 installed two Swiss guides there, Hasler and Feuz, for the benefit of patrons.[36] Glacier House undoubtedly made the Selkirks a popular climbing area very quickly. The railway also made the Rockies easy to reach from Europe, via New York, the cost being about sixty pounds first-class return.

It did not take the climbers long to realise that in the Rockies they had a virgin wilderness area of mountains not unlike their beloved Swiss peaks, which was readily accessible at a reasonable price. From the 1890s until the First World War, the Rockies were a favourite summer playground for British climbers to meet and climb with their American and Canadian counterparts. The American Alpine Club was formed in 1902 and the Canadian in 1906.

The main chain of the Rockies was less forested than the Selkirks and therefore more accessible by mule and horse. Banff was the chief centre. The peaks were big and brooding, mixed rock and ice climbing, sometimes of dubious quality.

In 1893 two Yale graduates, Samuel Allen and Walter Wilcox, attempted to climb Mount Temple (11,636 ft), near Lake Louise, but were beaten back by bad weather. In the following summer, with L.F. Frissell, they got to the top – it was the first Canadian peak of over 11,000 feet to be climbed, and remained the highest ascent in the Rockies until after the turn of the century. No European guides were involved.

The following year a large party, led by Charles Fay, attempted Mount Lefroy (11,230 ft) but were unsuccessful. Amongst them was a twenty-nine-year-old lawyer called Phillip Stanley Abbot who was a strong climber with Alpine experience.[37] Like Fay himself, Abbot was dissatisfied with the rambling club mentality of the Appalachian Mountain Club and had led two or three trips to the Rockies where he had climbed Mounts Hector, Stephen and others. Chagrined at their defeat on Lefroy, Abbot urged Fay to keep details of their attempt secret. He wanted the mountain for himself and did not want any Britishers coming over to steal it, attracted by reports of its difficulty.

And so, in the following season, 1896, Fay and Abbot returned to Lefroy with Professor Little and Charles Thompson making up the party. Setting out from a chalet on Lake Louise at 6.15 a.m. on August 3, they reached a col on the main ridge just before noon, now called Abbot Pass. Then followed four and half hours' step-cutting up steep ice to the foot of the summit rocks. Charles Fay described what happened next:

> At 5.30 p.m. we drew up under an immense bastion possibly seventy-five feet in height, behind which lay the summit of which as yet, owing to foreshortening, we had had no satisfactory view. This frowning face rose sheer from a narrow margin of tolerably stable scree that lay tilted between its base and the upper edge of the sloping ice that we had just left behind us. Looking past it on the right we saw, a few hundred feet beyond, the tawny southern arête, so shattered as to be utterly impassable. In one place a great aperture, perhaps forty feet high and five or six in width, revealed the blue sky beyond. Evidently our course did not lie in that direction. On the left the dusky northern arête rose with an easy gradient possibly an eighth of a mile away, but across an ice slope similar to that up which we had so long been toiling, and in truth a continuation of the same. To cross it was perfectly feasible, but it would take so long to cut the necessary steps that a descent of the peak before dark would have been out of the question.
>
> But now Mr. Abbot, who had moved forward along the rock-wall to the limit of the rope, cheerfully announced an alternative. His view beyond an angle in the bastion revealed a vertical cleft up which it was possible to climb by such holds as offered themselves.

Bidding Thompson and me to unrope and keep under cover from falling stones, he clambered some thirty feet up the rift, secured a good anchorage, and called upon Professor Little to follow. This the latter proceeded to do, but while standing at the bottom of the cleft preparing to climb, he received a tingling blow from a small stone dislodged by the rope. A moment later a larger one falling upon the rope half severed it, so as to require a knot. As danger from this source seemed likely to continue, our leader had Little also free himself from the rope and come up to where he stood. From here a shelf led around to the left, along which Abbot now proceeded a few yards and discovered a gully leading upward, unseen from the point first attained, and this also he began to ascend. To Mr. Little's question, whether it might not be better to try and turn the bastion on the shelf itself, he replied, 'I think not. I have a good lead here.'

These were the last words he ever uttered. A moment later Little, whose attention was for the moment diverted to another portion of the crag, was conscious that something had fallen swiftly past him, and knew only too well what it must be. Thompson and I, standing at the base of the cliff, saw our dear friend falling backward and head-foremost, saw him strike the upper margin of the ice slope within fifteen feet of us, turn completely over, and instantly begin rolling down its steep incline. After him trailed our two lengths of English rope – all we had brought with us – which we had spliced together in our ascent over the last rock slope, in order to gain time by having less frequent anchorages than were necessitated by the short intervals of one sixty-foot line. As the limp body rolled downward in a line curving slightly towards the left, the rope coiled upon it as on a spool – a happy circumstance amid so much of horror – for not only did this increase of friction sensibly affect the velocity of the descent of nine hundred feet to the narrow plateau of scree above mentioned, but doubtless the rope, by catching in the scree itself, prevented the unconscious form from crossing the narrow level and falling over the low cliff beyond. Had it passed this, nothing, apparently, could have stopped it short of the bottom of the gorge leading up to the pass from the western side of the Divide – a far more fearful fall than that already made.[38]

It took the shocked climbers three hours to descend the steps they had cut and reach their hapless companion. He was still breathing when they reached him but expired shortly after. The body was brought down later – the first climbing victim in America, and predictably perhaps, the subject of all the sort of controversy which had racked Britain after the Matterhorn disaster.

Fay's response was to invite over to Canada those very Alpine Club men that Abbot had feared might steal Lefroy. Professor H.B. Dixon of Manchester had known Abbot – they had shared the same guide, Peter Sarbach of St Niklaus – and he responded to Fay's invitation by bringing both Sarbach and Norman Collie who was one of the best climbers in the world at that time. Sarbach became the first professional guide to climb in Canada. The party was later strengthened further still by the arrival of G.P. Baker, an experienced mountaineer and fine rock climber.[39] To these Europeans were added half a dozen Americans, including C.S. Thompson, who had been on the fatal climb the previous year.[40]

This was by far the strongest team to visit the Rockies and, as Abbot had foretold, Lefroy and other peaks quickly fell to their attacks. Whilst climbing Mount Gordon, Thompson fell into a crevasse where he stuck upside down until rescued by Collie: an episode which formed a lifelong friendship between the two men.

Collie became fascinated by the Rockies and he made no fewer than six expeditions there. The exploration of the unknown seemed to appeal to him as much as the actual climbing, though, as his letters to Thompson show, this vast virgin field of exploration was jealously guarded.

'All this information is private,' he wrote on one occasion, discussing Mount Murchison and some others, 'so don't give me away by telling people of it. It is in fact what I had intended doing had I been able to come out this next summer, but as I am not, you personally are welcome to it, only if you don't do it yourself please don't tell other people and set them on the big peaks. Especially don't give Fay (our mutual friend) any of it.'[41]

In fact, Collie was able to visit the Rockies that year (1898) after all, when with two strong companions, Hermann Woolley and Hugh Stutfield, and their local packers or guides, they struggled into the wilderness north of the railway.[42] Collie had interested himself in the problem of two peaks, reported many years before by Douglas as being of prodigious height, which he had called Mounts Brown and Hooker but which had since 'disappeared'. The Canadian scientist Arthur Coleman had spent three seasons trying to track them down, but had finally come to the conclusion that Douglas had been wrong – that the heights were much less than estimated. The going was hard, not least because of voracious midges, but Collie and Woolley climbed Mount Athabasca, from where they discovered the huge Columbian Icefield – the greatest extent of ice in the Rockies, about 150 square miles.

In 1900 Collie, Stutfield and Sydney Spencer forced their way up Bush River towards the Columbian Icefield, but wretched weather and dense bush frustrated them. In thirty-six days they covered less than a hundred miles, proving that the western approach to the mountains was much more difficult than the eastern.

Nevertheless, the turn of the century had seen considerable progress in

Canadian mountain exploration if not in actual ascents. Of the forty-seven highest peaks in the Rockies (those over 11,000 ft/3355 m) only eight had been climbed by 1900 and only one of those – Mount Temple (11,636 ft), climbed by the unguided American party in 1894 – was in the top ten, at tenth. European guides had scratched the surface but some very good guides were about to arrive with the new century. At the same time, too little recognition has been given to the 'guides', the outfitters or packers, who were native backwoodsmen and who helped the pioneers enormously. They were not experienced mountaineers, of course, but in the tough bush country they were superb. Mention might be made of Bill Peyto, Jimmy Simpson and the incomparable Fred Stephens, the barefooted woodsman with whom Professor Collie kept up a regular correspondence for twenty-five years.

Collie's first three visits had given him a proprietorial concern over the Rockies and when he heard that the great Edward Whymper was to pay them a visit in 1901 he expressed anger and disgust to Thompson: 'All I can say is *damn* the man! . . . Why I am so mad about it is that it is not done for sport at all or because Whymper has any real liking for the hills. From the beginning it is dollars . . .'[43]

In fact, the real reason he was so concerned was that he thought Whymper, aided by four excellent guides, might snatch the prizes he himself had set his heart on. But Collie, like everybody else, mistook the shadow for the man. Whymper was no longer the dynamic force that had whirl-winded through the Alps in 1864 and '65, nor even the determined climber who had ascended the Ecuadorian volcanoes twenty years previously. Racked by rheumatism and insomnia, Whymper was simply enjoying a 'freebie' at the expense of the CPR, who were delighted to reap the publicity his name attracted.

As guides he took with him four of the best available: Christian Klucker, Josef Pollinger, Christian Kaufmann and Joseph Bossonay. Klucker especially was a guide of force and character from the Engadine, and one of the new breed of guides, quite different from those who had dominated the Alps when Whymper first went there. Klucker was an educated man – the school-master of Sils – and he soon realised that the trip to Canada was a wasted opportunity. He and Whymper fell out, and indeed all the guides resented their employer's lack of ambition. About ten minor peaks were climbed, some passes crossed and the valleys near the railway explored.

What Collie did not know was that there was recently resident in Canada a young cleric named James Outram who had all the force of a younger Whymper. Outram had gone out in 1900 to live in Calgary and in that year he made the first ascent of the North Peak of Mount Victoria (11,160 ft), the higher southern peak having been ascended by Collie's party three years earlier.[44]

In 1901 Outram attacked the Ottertail peaks which lie between the Ottertail, Kicking Horse and Beaverfoot rivers, and which had been visited for the first time the previous year by J.H. Scattergood of Philadelphia. Scattergood accompanied Outram, Professor Fay, the Boston climber G.M. Weed and the guide C. Hasler in the ascent of Chancellor Peak (10,761 ft), including part of the jagged South Ridge which extends over ten subsidiary peaks towards the Ice River–Beaverfoot junction. The same party (except for Weed) also climbed Mount Vaux (10,891 ft), but failed on Mount Goodsir (11,686 ft) when dangerous cornices turned them back on the final arête, not 150 feet from the summit. Goodsir is the highest peak in the range and Fay returned with Hasler and others to make the first ascent two years later.

After Ottertail, Outram went to join Whymper's party in the Yoho–Waputik area and took part in several ascents including that of Mount Collie, which must have given him and Whymper much wry amusement, especially as Collie himself had failed on it.

Outram capped a successful season with the ascent of Mount Assiniboine (11,870 ft), a huge triangle of rock and snow rising a mere eighteen miles from Banff (but still two days of hard trekking in those days). The mountain had been named by Dawson of the Geological Survey in 1885 and its foot was first reached in 1893. Attempts had been made to climb it in the two previous seasons and in 1901 yet another attempt failed. No doubt spurred on by tales of this impregnable mountain, Christian Klucker wanted Whymper to make the attempt too, but the old man refused, saying, 'I have no orders to do that.' Klucker was furious. 'We found to our regret that Whymper's ability was not of a high order,' he later wrote, acidly.[45]

Outram had with him the guides Christian Bohren and Christian Hasler. On their first attempt, hampered by thick mist, they reached a mysterious pinnacle which was over 11,000 feet but obviously not the summit. Next day, when the mist had cleared, this was seen to be a point of the South-East Ridge. They returned to camp and the following day not only managed to climb the peak from the south but, despite nervous objections from the guides, descended by the north, thus traversing it. It was a brilliant coup: Outram had climbed the highest peak so far ascended in Canada and according to his own estimation it was 'perhaps the most sensational mountaineering feat then achieved in North America'.

In fact, the Matterhorn of the Rockies, as Assiniboine was called, like its European counterpart, looks more difficult than it actually is.

Outram published details of his ascents in the *Alpine Journal*, and announcing further plans for the next season invited any competent mountaineer to join him. This was too much for Collie, who wrote to Thompson: 'We must try to circumvent that interloper Outram; it is a shame that you, Wilcox etc. should do all the pioneer work and then have the cream skimmed off by a man who has all the hard work done for him . . .'

Nevertheless, Collie realised that Outram was a formidable rival and he thought it wise to adopt the principle that if you can't beat 'em, you should join 'em. Consequently he made arrangements to join Outram for an attempt on Mount Forbes. Collie's party was a strong one: Woolley, Stutfield, Weed and the guide Hans Kaufmann, together with Fred Stephens as chief outfitter and several of his tough cronies. They climbed Mount Murchison (10,936 ft) and then went to meet Outram.[46]

To Collie's undoubted chagrin Outram had upstaged him. With the guide Christian Kaufmann (brother of Hans) he had climbed two prime peaks, Mount Columbia (12,294 ft) and Mount Lyell (11,495 ft), whilst waiting to meet Collie. Columbia is the second highest peak in the Rockies and remained the highest climbed until Robson was ascended in 1913.

The combined parties then attempted Mount Freshfield (10,945 ft), a peak on which Collie had failed in 1897. This time they met success, the only difficulty being the rotten rock which is too often endemic in the Rockies of Canada. The same problem assailed them during the ascent of Mount Forbes (11,902 ft), especially on the ridge which Collie compared with 'a very ill-constructed Scotch dyke' and where Weed caused tons of rock to go crashing into the abyss, thus accidentally clearing the ridge and making it safer for all concerned.[47]

But the climb of Freshfield had already dulled Collie's appreciation of Forbes, for though it enabled Collie to link up the various surveys he had made of the east and west sides of the ranges, it also showed him that Forbes was not quite the giant he thought. It proved to be fifth in height – and it had already been outranked in that respect by Outram's ascent of Columbia.

After climbing Forbes, the two groups went their separate ways again: Collie and his friends to the south where they climbed a number of minor peaks, whilst Outram, with Christian Kaufmann, headed north – his eyes on the difficult giant Mount Bryce (11,507 ft).

Bryce has three summits, connected by a long and complicated ridge. The route is often exposed, with steep ice slopes and large cornices, but the technical difficulty is mainly concentrated in a seventy-foot cliff, climbed by a chimney which has its crux near the top. Owing to the complexity of the climb it took Outram and Kaufmann eleven hours to reach the summit, where Outram planted a Union Jack, 'according to my custom', and they spent half an hour looking at the scenery and resting, before descending into the westering sun.

By the time they reached the top of the seventy-foot cliff it was totally dark. Given the choice by his employer, Kaufmann elected to continue, and Outram began the descent of the steep rocks, held on the rope from above by the guide:

9 Not all the great Alpine ridges were climbed by the pioneers. Some, like these, resisted all efforts until the twentieth century. *Top left*: The Aiguilles du Diable are five pinnacles on the South-East Ridge of Mont Blanc du Tacul, first traversed in 1928 by Miriam O'Brien and Bob Underhill with Armand Charlet and G. Cachat. *Top right*: André Roch and Walter Amstutz on the Mittelegi Ridge of the Eiger, first climbed in 1921 by Yuko Maki with Swiss guides. *Left*: The East Ridge of the Aiguille du Plan follows the prominent left-hand ridge. It is usually called the Ryan-Lochmatter after the first ascent in 1906 by V.J.E. Ryan with Franz and Josef Lochmatter.

10A Mount Cook is the highest peak in the New Zealand Alps, first climbed by local men, G. Graham, T. Fyfe and J. Clarke in 1894, although W.G. Green had almost climbed it twelve years earlier.

10B Huascarán in the Cordillera Blanca is Peru's highest mountain. It has two summits of which the South (left on picture) is slightly higher. It was climbed in 1932. The North Peak was climbed by the indomitable Annie Peck in 1908.

11 ALASKA

Above: the majesty of Denali (Mount McKinley), the highest peak in
North America. The long Karstens Ridge (centre right) was climbed by
the first ascensionists to the upper Harper Glacier, between the two
summits. The sourdoughs (local miners) turned right at this point and
climbed the lower North Summit in 1910. Three years later the higher
South Summit (centre picture) was climbed by Karstens, Stuck, Harper
and Tatum, another local team. *Below*: Mount St Elias on the Alaskan–
Canada border is difficult to approach. It was first climbed by the Duke of
the Abruzzi's expedition of 1897, after he was prevented from attempting
Nanga Parbat in the Himalaya.

12 EVEREST 1922: The first attempt at the world's highest mountain after the reconnaissance of the previous year had opened the North Col route. *Above*: a frostbitten Geoffrey Bruce being helped back to camp. *Left*: The camp on the North Col. The route goes up the ridge above, then slopes away to the right.

13 Jim Birkett climbing on Kern Knotts in the English Lake District. Birkett, a working-class climber and sometime professional guide, was one of the finest rock climbers of the 1940s. *Inset*: Muscroft, Birkett and Wilson (l to r) on top of Castle Rock of Triermain after the first ascent of Overhanging Bastion in 1939, one of the great classic rock climbs.

14 *Top*: C Troop, No 4 Commando in North Wales. When war broke out specialist troops were trained in rock climbing. This has continued ever since. *Left*: Two of Britain's top inter-war climbers, Ivan Waller (right) and Graham Macphee on B Buttress, Dow Crag, Lake District. *Above*: J.E.B. Wright who founded the Mountaineering Association after the war and had a profound influence on the spread of mountaineering in Britain.

15 Jack Durrance was one of the most important American climbers of the inter-war years. Trained in Germany, he knew the methods of the Munich School and brought a hardness of purpose previously lacking in American climbing. The pictures show the first complete ascent of the Exum Ridge on Grand Teton which he did with Kenneth Henderson in 1936, adding 800 feet of more difficult climbing to the base of Glenn Exum's original route of five years earlier.

Summit

IV

III

II

I

Base Camp
(behind shoulder)

16 In 1932 a remarkable American expedition of Burdsall, Emmons, Moore and Young climbed Minya Konka in Szechwan province, the highest peak in mainland China. The summit was reached by Burdsall and Moore by the North-West Ridge (above) using four camps from Base. One of the major features was the 20,000-foot Hump (at III). *Left*: the Hump seen from the foot of the final ridge.

... in a few moments I was working my way slowly and painfully in the numbing wind, down the smooth and treacherous face. It was an eerie sensation, even though knowing that at the slightest suspicion of anything wrong the rope would instantly tighten in the strong grip of my watchful guide. The remembrance is still vivid of the blind feeling for the scanty holds with chilly fingers, the wildly helpless waving of the feet in the dim depths for something on which to rest for the next search, the agonising hopes and fears as to their stability when found, the sickening 'emptiness' that seemed to come with the 'give' of the treasured footing and the sound of its fall reverberating as it leapt into the blackness of 7,000 ft of night.

When about 15 ft from the security of the solid though tiny platform at the base, the rope gave out, and I had to find as firm a set of holds as possible, whilst awaiting in the darkness the tedious descent of Kaufmann, till he bade me move again. Then on once more to the welcome ledge, where I crouched behind a massive rock and hauled in the ever-lengthening slack, prepared for the sudden crash that might at any moment come, however hoped and prayed against. My heart grew lighter as foot by foot the rope came in and Kaufmann's clinging form appeared through the gloom, clearer and closer, until he stood in safety at my side. A nip of cognac was most valuable to our cold, fatigued, and hungry frames, and on we went, deeming it better to keep poking on in the half light than seek a shelter amongst the rocks.[48]

How weary they must have been when they finally reached their camp, twenty and a half hours after setting out.

For Outram, Mount Bryce was a wonderful swan-song to a memorable season and a brief but illustrious climbing career. For some unknown reason he never made another serious ascent and seldom climbed at all, though he retained an interest in the mountain world.

Collie visited the Rockies again on a couple of occasions and even Whymper came back in 1903, though he did less mountaineering than ever, but it was the great Collie–Outram year of 1902 which put the seal on Canadian climbing. The pioneering days were over.

It will not have escaped the reader's notice that all these pioneering climbs in Canada, New Zealand, South America and Africa were done by expatriate Europeans for the most part. The ranges gave nothing back to the sport; even the local climbers made no significant contribution to its development, at least in the early days and in the case of the Rockies, hardly since. This is surprising for such magnificent ranges, but the dominating influences in the years ahead were to be the Alps, the Himalaya and, increasingly, the United States.

CHAPTER THIRTEEN

'Pikes Peak or Bust'

Lieutenant Zebulon Montgomery Pike first saw the mountain which was to bear his name on November 15, 1806. He was near Las Animas in Colorado, when: 'At two o'clock in the afternoon I thought I could distinguish a mountain to our right, which appeared like a small blue cloud.'[1] A little later he and his men climbed a local hill and got a better view of a mountain which Pike instinctively realised must be an outlier of the great Rocky Mountain range.

Pike thought the mountain was in Mexico, which in those days extended to the Arkansas River, but in fact it was in the recently acquired Louisiana Purchase and part of the USA. Such a mistake was not difficult to make: the land was virtually unknown and though Pike was surveying the territory he was more often than not mystified as to his whereabouts – even his biographer dubbed him The Lost Pathfinder.[2] Nevertheless, he was the first American citizen to see and describe some of the magnificent ranges of the Rockies: the Sawatch, Sangre de Cristo, and San Juan mountains particularly, not to mention other great natural phenomena like the Royal George, the Great Sand Dunes and the Rio Grande.

A few days later he made an attempt on what he believed to be his Grand Peak, as he called it, only to find on arrival at the summit that he was on a minor mountain and his goal was still some fifteen or sixteen miles distant.[3] Some years later, when the wagons began to roll west in great numbers, the fact that the peak could be seen over vast distances in the clear atmosphere of the West made it a welcome signpost to thousands of overlanders. The sighting of the mountain meant that the long trail over the plains was over and the promised land was near. Some wagons were even inscribed in paint: PIKES PEAK OR BUST.[4]

Pike didn't climb his peak, nor was he a discoverer in the true sense since the mountain was well known to the Indians and the Spaniards from nearby Santa Fe. It probably got its name from a map drawn by the expedition doctor, John Robinson, who named it Pikes Mountain. When John C. Frémont came this way in 1843 he found the name Pikes Peak in common usage.

The next expedition to Colorado after Pike's was that of Major Stephen H. Long in 1820, who discovered Longs Peak. With the expedition was the twenty-three-year-old Dr Edwin James who, with a wagonmaster called Zachariah Wilson and a Rifleman Verplank (sent along to protect the party against Indians), made the first ascent of Pikes Peak (14,108 ft). It was the first American ascent of one of their high mountains.

After the gold rush of 1858 Pikes Peak became a popular tourist ascent. It was in that year that the bloomers-clad Clara Archibald became the first woman to climb it with a Mr Holmes, to whom she was married 'after the style of their own belief'. In 1876 an observatory was built on the peak and in 1889 a carriage road reached the top and was enlarged into an 'auto-route' in 1916. The subjection of the peak came long before this, however, when a cog railway reached its broad summit in 1890.

In 1833 Captain Benjamin Bonneville on a fur trapping venture tried to cross the Wind River Mountains of Wyoming. Like Zebulon Pike, Bonneville and his companions reached the summit of an unknown peak, which seemed to be the highest in the range – and since the Wind River Mountains were popularly imagined to be the highest in the land, Bonneville immediately claimed to have conquered the highest peak in North America.[5] Similarly, when Frémont came to the Wind River peaks in 1842, he too climbed what he thought was the highest mountain, but wasn't. Frémont climbed either Frémont Peak (13,731 ft) or (more likely) Mount Woodrow Wilson (13,501 ft), but Bonneville's chosen peak remains a mystery. The highest summit in the Wind River Mountains is Gannett Peak (13,793 ft); a rather difficult mountain, not climbed until 1922.

John Charles Frémont was one of those rare individuals upon whom the gods bestowed gifts in plenty. Handsome, dashing, a brilliant mathematical scholar from the aristocratic South, later he was to make (and lose) a fortune and to run for President. His job in 1842 was to survey the Oregon Trail, one of the principal routes to the West, which he did with his usual skill. In the following year he crossed the Sierra Nevada of California in winter. His guide on both occasions was the legendary Kit Carson.[6]

In 1848 Frémont decided on another expedition, this time to prospect a possible railroad to the west coast at or about the Thirty-eighth Parallel. Carson not being available, Frémont hired as guide the equally legendary Bill Williams, known as Old Solitaire from his early days as a lone trapper and explorer. Williams led the way into the high San Juan Mountains of Colorado in mid-winter because Frémont wanted to see what the Rockies were like under the worst possible conditions. He soon found out. Following the Rio Grande into the heart of the mountains, the expedition became trapped by winter on the Continental Divide. 'We were encamped somewhere about 12,000 feet above the sea,' Frémont wrote later. 'Westward, the country was buried in deep snow. It was impossible to advance, and to turn back was equally impracticable.'[7]

It was Christmas and for more than a week the party huddled in snow holes whilst a blizzard raged round them. The mules died and were eaten. Eleven men died and rumour has always persisted that some of them were eaten too. The episode went down in western history as Camp Desolation and it was a bedraggled and chastened party that eventually trailed into Taos when the storm was over.

Williams was sacked but a few weeks later he got a job leading a party of soldiers through the Raton Pass. Out alone one day he was caught and killed by Ute Indians. He was sixty-two.

In 1853 Lieutenant John W. Gunnison with eleven men surveyed a route for the Central Pacific Railroad through the San Juan Mountains by the Cochetopa Pass to the Gunnison River, which was descended to Utah. The Black Canyon of the Gunnison, with its spectacular granite walls and the dramatic Crestone Peaks of the San Juans were mentioned in the subsequent report, prepared by Gunnison's successor. Gunnison himself and most of his party were massacred by Paiute Indians in Utah.[8]

Whilst the scouts and trappers were tentatively exploring the mountains and deserts of the West, further west still stood the great volcanic peaks of the Cascade Range, familiar sights to the well settled territory of Oregon. These were quite different from the Rockies or the Sierras in that they stood out as individual peaks, snow covered, very high and very obvious challenges. That they were dormant rather than extinct was attested to by witnesses who had seen them earlier in the century, when they rumbled and occasionally roared.[9]

Though they stood well inland the mountains were visible from the coast and most of them were named by Captain George Vancouver on his remarkable voyage of discovery 1791–95, during which he first accurately mapped the coast north of San Francisco. For example, Mount Baker was named after his third lieutenant and Mount Rainier after his friend Rear Admiral Peter Rainier.[10] From Puget Sound (named after another of Vancouver's comrades) these mountains impressed the correspondent of the *New York Tribune*: 'Some of the boldest mountains of the continent are here visible – Baker, Adams, St Helens, and, more than any or all others, Mount Rainier, triple-pointed and robed in snow. Shasta is grand; Hood is grander; but, from this stand-point, Rainier is monarch of all – the Mont Blanc of this coast.'[11]

It seems likely that attempts were made on the monarch from a fairly early date. In 1852 a party is said to have reached the crater rim, but it is all very vague and the first well-documented climb in the Cascades is the ascent of Mount St Helens (9,679 ft) by Thomas Dryer and three companions in 1853. Dryer was owner–editor of a local newspaper, and later a judge. The surprising thing was that their equipment seems fairly sophisticated for such an out-of-the-way place, especially as alpinism itself was in its infancy. They had alpenstocks, ropes, crampons and hooks (*vide* Whymper, ten years later).

In the following year Dryer repeated his success by climbing Mount Hood

(11,244 ft). He was accompanied by four companions, though only one, W. Lake, managed to follow his leader to the top of the mountain which is the highest in the state of Oregon. Actually, Dryer's ascent was disputed and it may be that the first complete ascent was not made until 1857 when H. Pittock's party climbed the mountain.[12] However, 1854 was certainly the year for adventure in the Cascades because Mount Adams (12,307 ft) and Mount Jefferson (10,499 ft) were climbed in that year too.

In 1857 an attempt was made on Mount Rainier (14,410 ft), the highest peak in the state of Washington, by Lieutenant August Kautz, stationed at Fort Steilacoom on Puget Sound, together with three companions. Their equipment included alpenstocks, home-made crampons,[13] a fifty-foot rope, a hatchet, a thermometer, hard tack and dried beef. Even to reach the mountain involved 140 miles of tough bush country, but they managed it and spent ten and a half hours attempting to climb the mountain by an ice stream now known as the Kautz Glacier. They almost made it – but the wind was blowing strongly, and urged by companions to descend, Kautz abandoned the attempt. 'Many a long year will pass away before roads are sufficiently good to induce anyone to do what we did in the summer of 1857,' he said later.

Indeed, thirteen years passed before Rainier was climbed. Early on August 17, 1870, General Hazard Stevens, the twenty-eight-year-old surveyor general of Washington State, and Philemon Van Trump, an ex-prospector, set out from their tent armed with 'ice poles, an ice axe, 100 feet of rope, long spikes in their boots, a large canteen of water, a lunch, flag and a brass plate inscribed with their names'[14] – a variety of climbing gear which had been assembled by their erstwhile companion Edmund Thomas Coleman, a forty-seven-year-old artist and alpinist from England. Coleman, who had climbed Mount Baker two years earlier, was intent on climbing Rainier too, but had become separated from his companions before the tree line was reached.[15]

Expecting to reach the summit and return to their camp within the day, the Americans took neither blankets nor coats for protection. Here is Coleman's account of what happened:

> The ascent offered all the difficulties of a Swiss mountain. After five miles over snow-fields, 'they climbed a steep ridge of rocks for 500 yards, along the sides of a 1,000-feet precipice for 200 yards in mid-air upon a narrow ledge filled up with loose débris, then for 200 feet they ascended almost perpendicularly, by the gutter formed by the junction of the rocky precipice and the ice-fields projecting from the crown of the mountain, cutting steps in the ice and clinging to each projecting point of rock. The next 150 feet was made wholly upon the steep ice-fields by cutting steps, and the remainder

of the ascent was made without material difficulty, over perhaps a mile and a half of snow, on ice-fields, across several crevasses, one of which they surmounted by throwing the rope round an overhanging pinnacle of ice and climbing up to the higher side of the crack some 12 feet by that means.' In ten hours and a half they gained the southern peak, a long exceedingly steep narrow ridge striking out from the main dome. They next ascended the middle and highest peak, about a mile distant. 'Climbing over the rock ridge which crowns the summit, they found themselves within a circular crater, 200 yards in diameter, filled with a solid bed of snow, and with a rim of rocks projecting above the snow all round. As they crossed the crater on the snow, Mr. Van Trump detected the odour of sulphur, and the next instant numerous jets of steam, hot air, and thin smoke were observed issuing from the crevices of the rocks forming the rim on the northern side. Never was a discovery more welcome. Hastening forward, they both exclaimed, as they warmed their thoroughly chilled and benumbed extremities over one of old Pluto's fires, that here they would pass the night, secure against freezing to death; for it was now six o'clock, and it would have been impossible to descend the mountain before nightfall.'

'A deep cavern extending under and into the ice, formed by the action of the heat, was found; a short distance within its mouth they built a wall of stones enclosing a space 5 feet by 6 feet around a strong jet of heat and steam. Ensconced within this shelter they discussed their future prospects, while they warmed themselves at their natural register. The heat at the orifice was too great to bear for more than an instant, but the steam wet them, the smell of sulphur nauseated them; and, in short, they passed a most miserable night, freezing on one side and in a hot sulphur steam bath on the other. The wind outside roared and whistled, but secure within their cavern and their wall it did not much affect them except when an occasional gust came down perpendicularly.'[16]

Had they not happened on the ice cave they would surely have suffered terribly and perhaps even have perished. There is a certain irony in realising that in this early ascent Nature offered a means of protection which man hadn't the wit to realise was to his advantage for almost a century. Nowadays, ice caves are dug as camps for high mountain assaults – albeit without the central heating provided by Rainier!

The mountain was climbed again two months later by S.F. Emmons and A.D. Wilson of the US Geological Survey, but then there was a thirteen-year hiatus before it was climbed again. In 1890 a Miss Fuller made the first ascent by a woman and by the turn of the century it had become a popular outing with more than thirty ascents taking place.

Meanwhile, in 1860, influenced by the geologist Josiah Dwight Whitney, the State of California established a Geological Survey and made Professor Whitney its leader. With his principal assistant, William Brewer, Whitney climbed Mount Shasta in 1862 and though this was not a first ascent – E.D. Pearce had climbed it in 1854 – Brewer's description of it to friends at Yale brought the young Clarence King hastening to California where he joined the survey as an unpaid assistant. King worked in the Sierra Nevada range and soon found that there was a peak even higher than Shasta, until then thought to be the highest in the land. This new giant was named Mount Whitney in honour of the chief surveyor (cf. Mount Everest).

King tried on more than one occasion to climb Mount Whitney, but success eluded him. He always ended up on the wrong mountain and when at last he did succeed, in 1873, he discovered to his chagrin that three other parties had preceded him in that same year. The first ascent was probably made by three local men, Charley Begole, Al Johnson and John Lucas. Though Mount Whitney (14,162 ft) is the highest mountain in the United States outside Alaska, its ascent is both easy and popular and there is a road to the top. King's adventures in the high sierra, however, were brilliantly described by him in *Mountaineering in the Sierra Nevada* (1872), the American equivalent of Whymper's *Scrambles*.

In Colorado, Longs Peak and several other high mountains were reputedly climbed by Indians before the coming of the white man. It was officially climbed at last by Major John Wesley Powell[17] and half a dozen companions in 1868 and ten years later Carlyle Lamb and his father, the Rev. Elkanah Lamb, operating from their ranch at the foot of the mountain, were conducting visitors to the summit at five dollars a time – probably the first regular mountain guides in the States.

Elkanah Lamb's acquaintance with Longs Peak had begun shortly after Powell's ascent. In 1871 Lamb had climbed the peak by the usual route (known as the Homestretch Route) and had decided to descend by the sheer East Face, using an easy couloir to reach Broadway, a horizontal ledge which divides the face in half. There were a few tricky 'sloping icy places', but Lamb managed them, confident that he would soon reach the foot of the mountain.

Turning south along Broadway he saw to his horror that the final descent was a steep snowfield. There was no way back, however, so he started his precarious descent. At an icy patch he slipped and began to slide down 'faster than an arrow's rapidity'. Desperately he grabbed at an outcrop of rock, and managed to cling on whilst he took out his pocket-knife, opened it with his teeth and tried to scratch out a toehold in the ice. The knife broke. Saying a prayer, Lamb put his left toe in the small nick he had made and made a lunge for the top of the outcrop. 'If my foot slipped I was a lost lamb,' he quipped some time later. Fortune was with him; he was able to collect his wits and find a somewhat safer way to the bottom. The steep snowfield is now known appropriately as Lamb's Slide. The descent was not repeated for thirty-two years and the route was not climbed until 1919 – and even that is open to doubt.[18]

In 1869 a young shepherd called John Muir was hired to look after a flock in the Yosemite Valley of California. He was at once taken with the spectacular mountains – he called the Sierras 'the Range of Light' – and especially with the Yosemite Valley. Reversing the adversarial role in which mountains were generally regarded (and still are), Muir saw them as friends, as part of the wholeness of nature. He wanted to experience everything about them: 'I will touch naked God,' he wrote enthusiastically. No doubt this is why he climbed high into a tree to experience the full fury of a storm. 'On the giddy cliffs and knife-edges he was not out to test his courage, like the ordinary outdoorsman, but was set upon proving the beneficence of God.'[19] And nothing should mar God's handiwork. 'I never left my name on any mountain, rock or tree,' he claimed.

Unlike his contemporaries Muir became a scientist and writer through his study of the mountain environment. He had no formal training and indeed was derided by some of those who had. Whitney, for example, called Muir 'a mere sheepherder, an ignoramus'. But he went on to found the Sierra Club and become the father of the present-day conservation movement.[20]

Another significant event of 1869, though not directly concerned with mountaineering, nevertheless had a profound effect in opening up the West. The Union Pacific and Central Pacific Railroads linked up at Promontory Point, Utah, on May 10, and so for the first time joined the east and west coasts of the continent. More than that, the railroad opened up the mountain areas of Colorado and other western states to prospectors and farmers as never before, especially as the network of lines began to spread. Some spectacular railroads were built through the mountains, like the Durango to Silverton line through the Animas Valley of Colorado.[21] And since this was the Wild West, some of the mountain railroad companies were tough entrepreneurial outfits. In 1876, for example, there was a gun battle at the Raton Pass between the Atchison, Topeka & Santa Fe Railroad and the Denver & Rio Grande Railroad as to who should have running rights over the Pass, the crucial section of the old Santa Fe Trail. The AT & SF emerged victorious.

The exploration of the western mountains was in full swing throughout the 1870s. Chief amongst these were the surveys done by F.V. Hayden in the twelve years 1868–80. Hayden was a real enthusiast and his influence was profound. He played a large part in establishing the Yellowstone

National Park, the first such in the world. Many peaks were climbed and from time to time the parties were joined by visitors, such as the British alpinist James Eccles and his guide Michel Payot, who made the first ascents of Wind River Peak and Frémont Peak in the Wind River Range of Wyoming.[22]

A feature of these early surveys, and especially Hayden's, was their use of photography in recording the landscape, including, of course, the mountains. These photographers were slightly earlier than their more famous European contemporaries like Donkin, Sella and the Abrahams and so their work is perhaps less refined, but it has a raw vigour that transcends mere recording and the best work represents early photographic art. It has never had the notice it deserves outside the USA.

As early as 1859 Frémont had with him an artist-photographer called Albert Bierstadt, whose photographs, though not matching his paintings in quality, were the first to publicise the spectacular scenery of the western states. Inspired by Bierstadt, the British photographer Eadweard Muybridge (famous for his study showing how a horse gallops) photographed the astonishing scenery of Yosemite between 1868 and 1872. In this he had rivals in Charles L. Weed and especially Carleton E. Watkins. The latter first photographed Yosemite in 1863 and worked for the Whitney survey in 1866. By 1868 his pictures of the valley were internationally famous.

E.O. Beaman was an intrepid photographer who went with Powell down the Grand Canyon and brought back some stark pictures of that epic voyage, but apart from those already mentioned the two outstanding photographers of the period were Timothy O'Sullivan and William Henry Jackson. O'Sullivan was already well known for his daring pictures of the Civil War when he joined the Clarence King surveys of 1867–69 and 1872, and the G.M. Wheeler surveys of 1871–74. His pictures (of the Canyon de Chelly, New Mexico, for example) are landscapes of the finest quality.

William Henry Jackson is better known than O'Sullivan because he had the good fortune to work with Hayden for eight years on the latter's surveys. Both men were enthusiasts and both believed in the colonisation of the West which they saw as an ideal place for the marriage of man and Nature.

Perhaps this is most aptly illustrated by Jackson's best-known photograph, the Mount of the Holy Cross, made in 1873. The peak is in the Sawatch Range of Colorado and gets its name from a great cross of snow, 1200 feet high and 500 feet wide, which Jackson shivered through a long night to photograph. Longfellow wrote a poem inspired by Jackson's photograph, and the photographer's story of the search for the Cross, somewhat touched up for public consumption (as unkind critics have said the photograph was too), appealed to the sentiments of the nation.[23]

Though the Mount of the Holy Cross is Jackson's most famous picture, it by no means represents his best work. Some of his pictures of the Animas

Valley in Colorado are extremely dramatic. The pictures taken by all these photographers were published with the reports of the surveys and also, in some cases, privately. They were very popular and stimulated Congress to provide funds for the surveys and, ultimately, the National Parks.

Colorado figures so largely in the pioneering story of American climbing because that state is 'the roof of the Rockies' with fifty-four peaks over 14,000 feet, though none over 14,500 feet, and no less than 1500 over 10,000 feet. Furthermore, it was the centre of attraction after the opening of the railroad because of rich mineral deposits, especially silver. As the peaks are for the most part easy, many were climbed by prospectors. Nevertheless, in such a plethora of mountains and rocks there has to be some harder climbing and mention might be made of Vestal Peak (14,013 ft), Arrow Peak (13,803 ft) and Lizard Head (13,114 ft) none of which were climbed by the pioneers.

There is probably no other region comparable with the American West where mountain climbing went hand in hand with the everyday activity of the people. There were the survey teams, the railroad engineers, the trappers and the prospectors, all of whom found it necessary from time to time to climb mountains. But sometimes their activities surprise the modern reader. A writer describes winter in the San Juan mountains, where there were many mines: 'The netted shoes are rarely used, the twelve-foot-long boards bent up at the end, known as the Norwegian shoe, being liked better. When a man becomes skillful upon these, he can go down hill safely and with astonishing speed. A sturdy young fellow sent down from some mine away above the usual level of the clouds would reach Silverton in twenty minutes, but thought himself succeeding well if he got back to supper. As for amusement, this sort of snow-shoeing is said to excel coasting, or even tobogganing, and many ladies are expert at the sport.'[24] This is skiing in Colorado in 1882, fourteen years before the first skis appeared in Chamonix!

The activities of adventurers like Eccles and Lamb were however entirely sporting, done for the hell of it or, as Mallory was later to say, 'because it is there'. One such challenge was that offered by the smooth slopes of Half Dome in the Yosemite Valley. This aptly named peak is like an enormous pudding basin chopped in two vertically, so that one face seems impossibly sheer and the rest impossibly smooth. Whitney, in his survey report of 1865 said it was 'perfectly inaccessible, being probably the only one of all the prominent points about the Yosemite which never has been, and never will be, trodden by human foot'.

Attempts to climb the smooth sides were made by the Rev. James Hutchings, who lived in the valley, and others, but it was George G. Anderson, a Scots carpenter and trail-builder, who succeeded in 1875, just ten years after Whitney's pronouncement of inaccessibility.

Finding that he could not keep from sliding with his boots, he tried it in his stocking feet: but as this did not secure a triumph, he tried it barefooted, and still was unsuccessful. Then he tied sacking upon his feet and legs, but as these did not secure the desired object, he covered it with pitch, obtained from pine trees near; and although this enabled him to adhere firmly to the smooth granite, and effectually prevented him from slipping, a new difficulty presented itself in the great effort required to unstick himself; and which came near proving fatal several times.

Mortified by the failure of all his plans hitherto, yet in no way discouraged, he procured drills and a hammer, with some iron eye-bolts, and drilled a hole in the solid rock; into this he drove a wooden pin, and then an eye-bolt; and, after fastening a rope to the bolt, pulled himself up until he could stand upon it; and thence continued the process until he had gained the top – a distance of nine hundred and seventy-five feet.[25]

It was actually the 300-foot crux slab that Anderson bolted. Some writers have drawn attention to the fact that this was the first example of the 'pegging' which was to afflict the valley a hundred years later, but the connection is very tenuous. It was simply the sort of action which was quite common in the Alps, for example, where rocky gorges and even mountain ridges were drilled and pegged, fitted with cables and ladders, and made available to all and sundry. In short, Anderson created a *via ferrata*.

He fitted it with a rope so that others might follow and follow they did. Within weeks Hutchings had been up and so had a sixty-four-year-old lady and thirteen-year-old girl. Thousands have made the ascent since.

The attraction of Half Dome in those early days was undoubtedly its aura of inaccessibility, the very quality that Whitney pronounced on and it was the same sort of challenge which led to the first ascent of an even stranger geological freak of nature, the Devil's Tower in north-east Wyoming. This volcanic plug rises in great basaltic flutings for 865 feet from its flat surroundings, an extraordinary monument like some gigantic decayed tooth.

In 1893 two local ranchers, Willard Ripley and Will Rogers, announced that they would climb the Tower as part of the July 4 celebrations that year, and about a thousand spectators turned up to see them do it.

The technique the two men employed was not all that different from Anderson's on Half Dome, for both created *vie ferrate*. In this case Ripley and Rogers drove dozens of long wooden stakes into a crack to a height of about 300 feet and to their free ends fastened strips of two-by-four to create a ladder. Above this was a steep shoulder and then easier rock to the summit.

On July 4, Will Rogers climbed the Tower, carrying the Stars and Stripes, which he erected on the flat summit, no doubt to the cheers of the multitude!

That evening four small boys (one said to be twelve years old) repeated the ascent, and two years later Mrs Rogers followed her husband to the top.[26]

The Appalachian Mountain Club was founded at Boston's Massachusetts Institute of Technology in 1876 and though it was concerned in the exploration of Canada its members also climbed in Colorado and elsewhere. As its origins might suggest, the club members were generally well-to-do and often had experience of the Alps. From their ranks the American Alpine Club was founded, in 1902. Gradually, other climbing clubs began to appear. For example, in 1896 the Rocky Mountain Club appeared in Denver and in 1906 the Rocky Mountain Climbers Club appeared in Boulder, with the Colorado Mountain Club following in 1912.

It was a member of the Rocky Mountain Club, the Rev. Franklin Spalding, who led the first certain ascent of the Grand Teton (13,767 ft) in 1898. This is the highest point of the spectacular Teton Range of mountains in Wyoming and its ascent had been claimed by Nathaniel Langford and James Stevenson of the Hayden survey back in 1872, but disputed ever since. It seems likely that Langford and Stevenson reached a lesser summit, some 400 feet lower, known as the West Spur, where they discovered a man-made structure called the Enclosure, about six feet in diameter and made of triangular granite slabs of uncertain antiquity. The real difficulties start here and whether Stevenson and Langford overcame them is open to dispute. Spalding's partner, Owen, who had tried the peak several times without success, always maintained that his ascent with Spalding was the first, but Spalding himself saw no reason to disbelieve the pioneers – in his opinion the ascent wasn't all that difficult and anyone who failed to reach the top 'was a mighty poor mountaineer', he said.

When it came to the last few hundred feet of the climb Owen's description was dramatic: the key to the ascent was a horizontal ledge forty feet long and eighteen inches wide.

> There was but one way to pass this point, and that was by lying at full length on the stomach and simply wriggling along like a snake, using one elbow and the abdominal muscles to propel oneself. I recall the fact that my eyes were not for a moment allowed to wander into the depths of that canyon until the shelf had been passed. For a greater portion of the 40 feet the left arm actually overhung and dangled in empty space – a gulf of air 3,000 feet deep ... It is as neat a piece of rock work as one would wish to see, and is certainly not surpassed by anything in North America.[27]

Certainly it was a different sort of climbing from the big volcanoes of the Cascades or the scrambles on the Colorado Fourteens. Owen's reference to 'rock work' shows he was fully aware of what was going on in the Alps and England at that time. Already there were 'thrill seekers' in Boulder – the name given at that time to local rock climbers – who had discovered there was fun to be had on the 1000-foot sandstone slabs near the city. Best of all was the Third Flatiron, climbed by Earl and Floyd Millard in 1906; at that date it was the most technical rock climb in America.

In 1867 the United States purchased Alaska from Russia. Although this far northern territory had mountains of a remoteness and grandeur unmatched elsewhere in the country such a barren place had interest only for the whalers who reaped a rich harvest off its coasts – until 1886, when gold was discovered at Fortymile Creek. From then until 1900, thousands of prospectors trekked over the mountains from the coast to the goldfields.[28]

These coastal mountains are an impressive barrier, especially north of Skagway where they gather themselves into a savage range known as the St Elias Mountains. The principal peak, Mount St Elias (18,008 ft), can be seen for over a hundred miles out to sea and was first observed by Vitus Bering in 1741. He named his anchorage at an adjacent point of land Cape St Elias, because it was made on July 20, which is the saint's day. In 1778 James Cook transferred the name to the mountain. Harold Topham, who led one of the first attempts on the peak, described the seaward approach. 'They rise out of the very waters of the sea, and tower above you to a height of 16,000ft as you sail below. As they approach Yakatat Bay they take a grand curve inland back from the shore, and peak after peak, unknown and unnamed, attracts your attention, and your eye wanders on from one to another till it rests on the final and most beautiful of all – Mount St Elias.'[29]

The first attempt on Mount St Elias was a party sponsored by the *New York Times* in 1886, who declared the summit inaccessible. Two years later the Topham brothers made a more determined attempt but they were turned back. Both parties had approached from the south-west, but the next attempts, by a US Geological Survey party, were from the south-east in 1890 and 1891.

The leader of these expeditions was Professor Israel Russell who discovered the weather was almost always bad. Separated from his companions on one occasion, Russell spent several nights in an improvised snow hole, cooking his meagre rations over a wick dipped in bacon fat.[30] Weather defeated both of his expeditions, but on the second Russell managed to reach a high col between St Elias and Mount Newton and climb to 14,500 feet up the North Ridge of the former peak. He also saw that inland from Mount St Elias, over the Canadian border, 'was a vast snow-covered region, limitless in its expanse, through which hundreds, and perhaps thousands, of barren angular mountain-peaks projected'. One stood out above all others and this he named Mount Logan, after the founder of the Geological Survey of Canada. With an altitude of 19,850 feet (6050 m), Logan proved to be the highest mountain in Canada and the second highest in North America after

McKinley. The high col reached by Russell was named after him and turned out to be the key to the ascent of Mount St Elias.

In 1897 Prince Luigi Amedeo of Savoy, Duke of the Abruzzi, was prevented by an epidemic in India from mounting his planned attack on Nanga Parbat. This was to be the Duke's first expedition. He was influenced by the grandeur of the Himalaya which he had previously visited as a traveller, and by the relative accessibility of Nanga Parbat, one of the easiest Himalayan mountains to reach from the plains. The Duke was a good climber, and had climbed the Zmutt Ridge of the Matterhorn with Mummery and Collie in 1894.

Thwarted of Nanga Parbat, he turned his attention to Mount St Elias and brought to bear immaculate planning, backed up with the best that money could buy. Unlike some that later sought to follow his example his team was carefully chosen and compact – much more like a modern expedition than some of those that came in between. He took Russell's advice (and Russell's map), landed on the huge piedmont glacier called the Malaspina and made his way towards the mountain by the long and tortuous Newton Glacier.

> It is 7 miles long, and rises from an altitude of 3,850ft to one of 8,960, forming three terraces divided by icefalls of gigantic seracs. The sides of the valley are precipitous, heavily laden with snow, and crowned with bold peaks of rock and dizzy pinnacles of ice, whose ridges are fantastically wreathed by huge overhanging snow cornices.
>
> The ascent of this valley took us thirteen days. We made six bivouacs, and our stages averaged about 1 mile 500 yards. We had to contend almost incessantly with heavy snowfall, which went on without interruption for days together. Enveloped in a blinding mist, we toiled laboriously through the powdery snow in which we often sunk to our waists, patiently seeking out routes amidst a labyrinth of ice blocks, over insecure ice bridges, amid the deafening roar of the avalanches and the crash of falling stones that resounded almost incessantly on the edges of the glacier.
>
> Out of thirteen days only three were fine.

Higher up, things were much better and at midnight on July 30, the entire expedition of ten Italians set off from Russell Col and in clear weather stamped their way to the summit of Mount St Elias. The ascent took twelve hours but it was easy. However, that is not the point. The point is it was a superbly planned expedition, a harbinger of the way such things should go. De Filippi, who was the Duke's recording angel, put it thus: 'The ascent of St Elias is easy. In no part of it did we find ourselves confronted by real mountaineering difficulties ... The real difficulty is that of preparing the equipment and organising the expedition. On this preliminary work, more than anything else, success depends. It is necessary to foresee everything in a campaign where we found ourselves completely isolated for a couple of months.'[31]

Much further inland than the St Elias Range lay the great uncharted mountain wilderness rising high into the sky that the Indians called Denali. Vancouver had seen its main peak from Cook Inlet, 200 miles away, in 1794 and the Russians had seen it in the 1830s. A few years later American prospectors had been in the area, too, especially Frank Densmore whose name was at one time attached to the peak. In 1896 another prospector, W.A. Dickey, called it Mount McKinley on hearing that McKinley had been nominated for President. The name stuck, though Denali, the Indian name meaning 'the great one', is used just as frequently today.

It wasn't until 1897 that McKinley (20,320 ft/6194 m) was recognised as the highest mountain in North America and it wasn't properly surveyed until 1902 when the Geological Survey reconnoitred a route from the north. This route was followed a year later by a group led by Judge James Wickersham of Fairbanks, who were forced to retreat by avalanche danger before they had got far. Before this party returned another had set out from New York, led by Dr Frederick Cook, a noted, if not yet notorious, polar explorer.

The party put ashore at Cook Inlet (named after Captain James Cook) and then beat their way through forest and tundra, beset by 'myriads of vicious mosquitoes', for 500 miles towards their objective. It took them nine weeks and they could do little more than make a couple of sporadic attempts at the peak and circumnavigate it on their way home. 'The prospective conqueror of America's culminating peak,' Cook wrote, '... must be prepared to withstand the tortures of the torrids, the discomforts of the North Pole seeker, combined with the hardships of the Matterhorn ascents multiplied many times.'[32]

In 1906 Cook returned to McKinley, leading a strong party including Belmore Browne, who knew Alaska well, and Herschel C. Parker, who had done much climbing in the Canadian Rockies. They spent two and a half months examining the south side of the peak but without much success and by mid-August the party was back at Cook Inlet. Parker went home and Cook and Browne split up to do some exploring. When they joined forces again, some weeks later, Browne was staggered to learn that Cook had returned to McKinley and climbed it! He had photographs showing his single companion, the packer Ed Barrill, standing on the summit.

Browne was mystified. He was convinced that in the time available Cook could not possibly have climbed the mountain. Back in New York, Cook, already President of the prestigious Explorers' Club, was fêted, though in the mountaineering community the doubts expressed by Browne were shared by others, including a reviewer in the *Alpine Journal* who was very sceptical about Cook's book *To the Top of the Continent*, describing it as a 'highly coloured narrative'.

> The following appear to be the main facts recorded by Dr. Cook as to an expedition remarkable in itself, and rendered still more remarkable by the late period of the year at which it was accomplished. The climbing party was composed of Dr. Cook and one companion, Mr. Bareille. They had no porters, but each carried a burden of over 40 lbs., comprising a silk tent, coats capable of being converted into sleeping-bags, provisions, cooking utensils, and certain instruments. They were absent from their base camp (1,000 ft.) 12 days. In the first three of the eight given to the ascent they marched 35 miles up a glacier; the remaining five were occupied in the actual climb, which began at about 8,000 ft. They slept two nights at 12,000 ft. and 16,300 ft. respectively in domed huts formed of snow-blocks (we are not told how the blocks were cut). The intervening night was spent in a hole cut on an ice-slope at an angle of 'nearly 60°,' and another night at 18,400 ft. in a silk tent (temperature 16° below zero). The chief difficulties of the climb were encountered in the middle portion (12,000 to 16,000 ft.), after the northern ridge of the mountain had been gained. Here ridges, cornices, séracs, and ice-slopes were piled up in a bewildering confusion that has communicated itself to the narrative. The final 4,000 ft. took two days to surmount, the rarity of the air proving the chief impediment. The temperature on the top at 10 a.m. was the same as during the previous night in the tent.[33]

With the publication of Cook's book, Browne and Parker were able to show that the photograph claiming to be the summit was not taken on the summit at all, but on a subsidiary spur of no great height. They decided to confront Cook with this evidence but before that could happen news reached America that the indefatigable Dr Cook had reached the North Pole – another first, and an even more outstanding achievement then McKinley! Almost immediately after this another polar explorer, Robert Peary, also claimed to have reached the Pole, and expressed doubts about Cook's claim, but Peary was regarded as a bad loser and Cook was once again fêted on his return to New York. With Cook a public hero, Browne and Parker dared not shout foul too loudly.

Nevertheless, doubts began to grow in official circles. Peary's polar claim gained wider acceptance when it became apparent that Cook's Eskimo companions were not available for questioning, and Cook's log was conveniently lost. The Explorers' club wanted to question him about the faked McKinley photograph, too, but after asking for extra time to gather his defence together Cook quietly disappeared from the scene. The Club sent Browne and Parker back to McKinley to do a bit of detective work.

Dr Cook was a good explorer, praised by no less an authority than Amundsen, whom he served during the latter's 1897 South Pole expedition. Why then did he try to fake an ascent of McKinley and claim to have reached the North Pole? We shall never know for sure, but perhaps Cook saw time slipping by; he was into his forties and had achieved nothing of significance.

Cook's story was never believed in Alaska. Thomas Lloyd was a miner in Fairbanks who was not alone in thinking that local Sourdoughs would have a better chance of climbing McKinley than all the so-called experts put together. Such men were tough, hardened to the bitter conditions, and needed none of the special gear the experts encumbered themselves with. Lloyd determined to try and so he recruited his partner William Taylor and two of their workmen, Pete Anderson and Charles McGonagall, to the cause. To pay for the attempt they got two saloon keepers in Fairbanks, McPhee and Petersen, and a wholesale liquor dealer named Griffin, to put up 500 dollars apiece.[34]

In February 1910 the party set out for McKinley. It was now increased to six by the addition of another miner, Bob Horne, and a surveyor, E.C. Davidson. But Horne and Davidson got no further than the foothills, for after a row with Lloyd, they quit.[35]

Lloyd, Anderson and McGonagall were all intimate with the mountain and realised that the key to a successful ascent was the Muldrow Glacier, a fact which had escaped previous parties. From a base camp in Cache Creek, Anderson and McGonagall scouted the front range to find a way over onto the glacier, and eventually they found a gap at 5700 feet, now called McGonagall Pass. By March 25 the party had traversed the Muldrow Glacier to its head. Steep peaks hemmed in on both sides whilst the end of the glacier was sealed off by a tremendous icefall, which tumbled down McKinley from some upper ice basin. On the left, however, there was a fine steep ridge of snow which seemed to offer a way up. The men camped on the ridge, from where they prospected the upper ice basin, now called the Harper Glacier.

Lloyd, who was a fat man of some sixty years, felt unable to go any further ('Had a kind of nervous breakdown and just keeled over,' said Billy Taylor) but the other three set out to climb McKinley on April 10:

> Taylor, Anderson, and McGonogill set out about two in the morning with great climbing-irons strapped to their moccasins and hooked pike-poles in their hands. Disdaining the rope and cutting no steps, it was 'every man for himself,' with reliance solely upon the *crampons*. They went up the ridge to the Grand Basin, crossed the ice to the North Peak, and proceeded to climb it, carrying the

fourteen-foot flagstaff with them. Within perhaps five hundred feet of the summit, McGonogill, outstripped by Taylor and Anderson, and fearful of the return over the slippery ice-incrusted rocks if he went farther, turned back, but Taylor and Anderson reached the top (about twenty thousand feet above the sea) and firmly planted the flagstaff, which is there yet.[36]

On April 11, Tom Lloyd arrived back in Fairbanks claiming to have climbed both the North and South Peaks of McKinley. His companions had remained behind to do some prospecting and without their corroboration or any photographic evidence, Lloyd's story was not believed; by the time the others returned to Fairbanks, the expedition was wholly discredited, especially as two other climbing parties, also on McKinley later that year, reported seeing no flag.

There is a casualness about the Sourdough Expedition, as it came to be called, that is wholly remarkable. For example, why did they not climb the higher South Peak, as they could easily have done? Well, the North Peak was nearer and it was not until they reached its summit that they realised the South Peak was higher. To climb the South Peak after climbing the North would have meant a night out on the glacier. To them, it wasn't worth it; they had climbed the mountain, planted their flag and that was that. They had rather hoped the flag could be seen from Fairbanks, but it couldn't. And apart from Lloyd, of course, they didn't even bother to report their amazing feat until much later.

The two other groups on the mountain that year were the Parker-Browne expedition on behalf of the Explorers' Club and a party led by Portland lawyer Claude Rusk, of the Mazamas Climbing Club. Both approached from the sea, a back-breaking exercise in which the climbers carried 70 lbs a man, but they didn't know of McGonagall's Pass and in the case of Parker and Browne they had more to do than climb a mountain – they had to find out where Cook faked his picture.

'We knew,' wrote Browne, 'that if we could find one of the peaks shown in his photographs we could trace him peak by peak and snow-field by snow-field, to within a foot of the spot where he exposed his negatives.'

And this is precisely what they did, discovering that the photograph had been taken up a subsidiary glacier. Rusk also discovered the same place independently and solemnly pronounced judgement on Cook: 'As he has sowed, so has he reaped. If he is mentally unbalanced, he is entitled to the pity of mankind. If he is not there is no corner of the earth where he can hide from his past.'[37]

The evidence of Browne, Parker and Rusk certainly destroyed Cook's reputation for good. Yet many believed, and some still believe, that he actually did beat Peary to the Pole. What irony, as historian Chris Jones has pointed out, if the faking of the McKinley photograph ultimately robbed him of his place in history.

Neither the Parker–Browne Expedition, nor that of Rusk, succeeded in reaching the top of McKinley but in 1912 Parker and Browne tried again. They still chose to approach from the seaward side, leaving Resurrection Bay at the end of January along a 400-mile route prepared by Arthur M. Aten and Merl La Voy who were to join them on the venture. They reached the mountain on March 25. Not until June 4 did they begin the ascent however. Leaving Aten in charge of base camp, the other three pushed up the North-East Ridge from where, on June 29, from a camp at 17,000 feet, they made their first attack on the summit. Within 300 feet of the summit they were caught by a sudden blizzard and driven down again. On July 1 they made another attempt but were once more frustrated by the weather. Their supplies and stamina exhausted, the men retired and the expedition ended. Perhaps it was as well: two days after they left the mountain it was struck by a violent earthquake which partly destroyed the summit ridge. Had they still been there they would surely have been killed.

Neither Parker nor Browne claimed to have reached the highest point of the mountain and yet the *Alpine Journal* index lists it as a first ascent and so it was in all but name. The reason for this apparent confusion is explained by Belmore Browne: 'The hummock that formed the highest portion of the ridge was only a short distance away, and reaching it under good weather conditions would have required no more labour than one encounters in walking along a city street. Our danger was the intense cold and the difficulty of correctly retracing our steps through the storm. But the dome on which we stood was the summit of Mt McKinley.'[38]

Yet to the purists, this was not a true first ascent. That came in 1913 when a party, just as curious in their own way as the Sourdoughs, got to the top. The leader was an ex-London University man who had climbed in Britain, Canada and Colorado, Archdeacon Hudson Stuck, Episcopal Missionary for Alaska. With him he had Harry P. Karstens, known as 'The Seventy-Mile Kid', a comrade of Sourdough McGonagall, and a miner-cum-bushwhacker who knew Alaska well. Then there was Robert G. Tatum from Tennessee, a trainee cleric, and a half-breed Indian called Walter Harper, strong, resolute and intelligent. To help them there were two Indian lads who carried loads and looked after base camp.

From the Muldrow Glacier they followed the route pioneered by the Sourdoughs and the Browne–Parker team, up the ridge now called the Karstens Ridge to the upper snow basin, or Harper Glacier. They took a month, carefully building up towards a successful assault.

At 3 a.m. on June 6, after a night of indigestion caused by Karstens' flour dumplings, the four men set off on the final 2500-foot dash for the summit.[39] Walter Harper led throughout, followed by Karstens, Tatum and the

Archdeacon bringing up the rear. The sky was clear and there was nothing to impede them, though it was bitterly cold. At 1.30 p.m. Walter Harper, a native-born Alaskan, stepped onto the summit of McKinley and became the first man to reach the roof of America. The others followed quickly, the fifty-year-old Archdeacon gasping for air.

When they had recovered sufficiently to look around them one of the first things they saw was the Stars and Stripes fluttering from the North Summit, proving that the Sourdoughs really had reached the top.

Then prayers were said, scientific measurements taken and the descent made.

The foundations of American climbing are important because they are the only ones to have developed independently of Alpine influences. The exploration of the Colorado Rockies and the Tetons, the determined ascents of Rainier and other western volcanoes, and the Sourdoughs' attempt on McKinley owed nothing to the Alpine Club or Swiss guides. It was a trend destined to continue for many years, until world travel fused mountaineering into an international whole.

Apart from the work of the founding fathers during the Golden Age of alpinism, this separate American development was the single most important event in the history of mountaineering. Many years later it was to introduce new and vigorous genes into the bloodstock of a somewhat staid, if well-bred, sport.

CHAPTER FOURTEEN

The Abode of Snow

Stretching 1500 miles across the north of the Indian sub-continent from the Indus in the west to the Brahmaputra in the east is the greatest range of mountains in the world, called the Himalaya from the Sanskrit words *hima*, snow, and *alaya*, abode. It rises to its highest point at Everest (29,028 ft/ 8848 m). North of the range lies the bleak Tibetan plateau and at the western end other major ranges include the Karakoram, which contains K2 (28,253 ft/8611 m), the second highest peak in the world. Taken together the Himalaya and Karakoram have all fourteen of the world's 8000-metre peaks and dozens of 7500-metre peaks. Most of the 7000-metre peaks are here, too, and those that are not are in adjacent areas.[1]

To call the Himalaya mountains is like calling the Amazon a river – true, but by no means the whole truth. It is an entire region;[2] a swathe of the earth's crust which is complex and difficult to examine and as such it appealed especially to those geographical climbers whose purpose was as much exploration as ascent. Although satellites can now map the whole lot in the twinkle of a star, there is still something of the old days left even in modern Himalayan climbing and consequently one does not look, nor ever has looked, to the Himalaya to provide the cutting edge of modern mountaineering. The place is unique and because of this makes its own rules, some of which would be considered outrageous elsewhere. Like all rules, they are shaped by the passage of time.

Though the Himalaya was known to the outside world at least since the Middle Ages, through the Silk Road and other ancient ways, and though Jesuit missionaries had penetrated to Tibet in the seventeenth century, the real magnificence of the mountains went unrecognised for a surprisingly long time. It wasn't until the reconnaissance done by Lieutenant W.S. Webb with Captain F.V. Raper and H.Y. Hearsey in 1808, exploring the upper Bhagirathi and Alaknanda, that the world first realised the great height of the Himalaya. Webb took observations and was surprised at the heights he calculated from them. Later he observed the great peak of Dhaulagiri from four survey stations in the plains and calculated its height as 26,862 feet.[3] Until that time it had been confidently assumed that the Andes were the highest mountains in the world.

In 1817 the Gerard brothers explored out of 'the midling sized village' of Simla which they had found nestling in the foothills, crossing various passes and reaching a height of about 19,300 feet on Leo Pargial (22,280 ft) in the

Zaskar range. Dr J.G. Gerard actually climbed an unknown peak calculated to be 20,401 feet, probably the highest peak ascended at that early date. The crossing of the Himalayan axis between Nanda Devi and Nanda Kot, from the Pindari Glacier to the Goriganga Valley, by G.W. Traill in 1830, though only 17,700 feet, was technically as difficult a climb as had been done anywhere at that time and Traill's Pass, as it became known, is not regarded as easy today. Almost a hundred years passed before it was crossed in the opposite direction.[4]

Adolphe and Robert Schlagintweit, as part of a brilliant campaign of exploration (in which they were helped by the third brother, Herman) crossed into Garhwal from Tibet in August 1855 and saw a splendid group of mountains then known collectively as Ibi Gamin. They made an unsuccessful attempt on what they took for the central and highest peak called Kamet (25,447 ft/7756 m), spending ten days on the mountain: 'Every bivouac during this time was above 17,000 ft, the highest being as much as 19,326 ft. They made one determined attempt on the peak, finally reaching a height of 22,239 ft, which for long remained the highest ascent.'[5]

Although the Schlagintweits were on a scientific mission of discovery they were also experienced climbers and this attempt has all the hallmarks of a true climb, where the real purpose was to get to the top just for the satisfaction of the thing. It has a claim to be the first sporting ascent in the Himalaya, but its details are lost in the mass of statistics in six large volumes covering their Indian exploits. C.F. Meade later showed that it wasn't Kamet that they tackled at all, but the adjacent peak now known as Abi Gamin (24,130 ft).[6]

It is hardly surprising that the Schlagintweits made such a mistake. Although the Survey of India was under way, much of the Himalaya was still a blank on the map. Whole areas were virtually unknown, little more than names mentioned by travellers. For example, the German brothers had been the first to point out that the Karakoram and the Kun Lun were separate mountain ranges and not all one as had been thought. If it was so easy to confuse whole ranges, obviously it was easier still to confuse single peaks. Consequently, the first ascents in the Himalaya tend to be full of inconsistencies which later explorers and climbers have sometimes used to denigrate the work of the pioneers. The fact that the Schlagintweits attacked Abi Gamin and not Kamet, as they believed, does not detract from their pioneering effort one bit.

When the Survey of India began its primary triangulation along the foot of the Himalaya in 1846 there could no longer be any doubt that here were the world's highest mountains. The height of Everest was discovered in 1852 and K2 in 1858, setting the seal on the matter once and for all.

Much of the measuring was done from a distance because the small Himalayan kingdoms were fiercely independent and did not allow foreigners within their boundaries except under exceptional circumstances. Naturally, this in itself was a challenge to those indomitable and eccentric Englishmen who forced their way into all sorts of inaccessible places, often just for the hell of it, and who not infrequently suffered torture and death as a result. In addition there were the *pundits*, Indians trained as surveyors and, not to put too fine a point on it, spies, whose job it was to penetrate the forbidden lands, measuring distances and following rivers to see where they went. Between them the surveyors, pundits and explorers built up a picture of the Himalaya, albeit a shadowy one.

Amongst those working for the Survey, William Henry Johnson stands out for his pioneering climbing; he established a survey station at 21,000 feet and climbed another 1300 feet above it. But Johnson was a mere civilian assistant of the Survey and a further handicap was that he was born and educated in India so, even though his parents were English, his colonial upbringing was looked down on. Eventually his frustration at being passed over for promotion led him to leave the service.[7] But before he did so, in 1865 he made a daring journey to the Kun Lun and beyond, which earned him a reprimand from his superiors and a gold watch from the Royal Geographical Society.

During the journey he claimed to have climbed three peaks in the Kun Lun known as E57, E58 and E61. All were high mountains but the last, E61 (later K5 or Muztagh), was then thought to be 23,890 feet, so easily the highest mountain climbed at that time. But did Johnson climb Muztagh? As far as this peak was concerned his report was suppressed by his chief, General Walker, who claimed it contained some inaccuracies, though it seems strange that an experienced surveyor like Johnson would get his figures wrong to such an extent. There is more than a hint that Walker was deliberately snubbing Johnson and Johnson's 'suppressed peak' became a minor geographical *cause célèbre*, never properly cleared up. According to Kenneth Mason, the Himalayan historian, it is likely that the peak Johnson climbed was Zokputaran (22,638 ft). But Mason was himself a Survey man and anxious to defend the department's honour.[8]

Surveyors and their assistants repeatedly went to great heights by European standards: there had been thirty-seven ascents of summits over 20,000 feet (c 6000 m) by 1865, the year the Matterhorn was climbed and the culmination of the Golden Age of alpinism. There had been many more ascents to this height which did not reach summits. Sometimes the ascents were made by Indians, fixing observation poles, as in the case of Shilla in the Zaskar range in what is now Himachal Pradesh. This peak was reckoned to be 23,050 feet (7025 m) and is still marked on some maps as such, but it has since been reduced to 21,000 feet, and the ascent, which would have been a height record for many years, has also been questioned.[9]

In 1879 the Hungarian mountaineer Maurice de Déchy visited Sikkim with the guide Andreas Maurer but was taken ill before any climbing could be done. 'He contracted that malarious fever for which the pestilential valleys of Sikkim are so infamous.'[10] De Déchy forgot the Himalaya and turned instead to the exploration of the Caucasus.

Shortly after this Captain H.J. Harman, who was in charge of the Sikkim survey, attempted Chomiomo, but his men refused to follow him and he had to abandon the attempt. He did however cross the Dongkya La, spending the night on top of the pass, without protection, in order to measure the tremendous peaks all about him. As a result he suffered severe frostbite and was forced to undergo amputations on his feet from which he subsequently died. 'Thus, though he did not actually perish on the field, still he may be considered as the first entry on the roll of casualties which our own Alps have made so long, and of which the Himalaya will no doubt claim their share.'[11]

It was left to William Woodman Graham to make the first visit to the Himalaya for purely climbing purposes, his motives unhindered by any considerations of exploration or science. When he arrived in India in February 1883 he had recently qualified as a barrister, and the previous summer had made the first ascent of the Aiguille du Géant. His Alpine qualifications were extremely good, embracing practically every major summit and many difficult passes and yet, for some unexplained reason, his election to the Alpine Club was thrown out by a heavy majority.[12] After his Himalayan adventures he vanished from the climbing scene, and indeed little more is known of him.

He arrived in Bombay with the guide Josef Imboden of St Niklaus on February 20, 1883, and made his way via Agra to Calcutta and Darjeeling. His plan was to spend spring and autumn in Sikkim and the summer in Garhwal and so on March 23 he set off for the Kangchenjunga massif, reaching the stone hut at Dzongri in six days – a tramp of eighty miles with 23,000 feet of ascent. During the next few days he made an ascent of a minor peak and crossed the Guicha La to the Talung Glacier, but he decided it was too early for climbing; there were too many avalanches and the weather was bitterly cold, besides which the porters were sick. When a porter accidentally burned Graham's boots the time had come to retreat to Darjeeling.

Imboden contracted fever and returned to Switzerland, his place being taken by Ulrich Kaufmann, another notable guide, and the Swiss hotelier-guide Emile Boss. In the previous year Kaufmann and Boss had been with Green in New Zealand, where they took part in the ascent of Mount Cook.[13] At the end of June they set out for Garhwal with the French climber Lionel Dècle who had made a number of minor first ascents in the Alps and who happened to be passing through India on a world tour. Dècle soon succumbed to the rain and the leeches and left the party.[14]

From Josimath they set about the exploration of the Nanda Devi mountains, that impressive ring of peaks around the head of the Rishi Ganga, whose gorge is the only entry to the Sanctuary. They quickly found the gorge was 'a trench of impassable smoothness' and turned their attention to the peak of Dunagiri (23,187 ft). From the head of the glacier at about 18,400 feet Graham had a superb view of the surrounding peaks which he describes with the eyes of a mountaineer, rather than those of a surveyor or sportsman which was usual in the Himalaya of the day:

> I shall never forget that view. Due south, with the awful gorge of the Rishi Ganga between, rose the Trisuli and Nanda Devi; east was Dunagiri, on whose very flanks we were lying; north stood Kamet with his attendant peaks; whilst on the west towered Gangootri, like a wall. Nor was this all, for all these peaks are set with rocky aiguilles, all equally black and all equally impossible. I fear I may be taken to task for using the word 'impossible,' which some aver should not occur in the climber's dictionary. Still, the powers of man are limited, whilst those of nature are hardly so. In Switzerland, even, aiguilles, which rarely give more than 1,000 ft. of hard climbing, long resisted the assaults of the best climbers, and only succumbed after a long day's toil. What shall then be said of these rock-towers, at least equally difficult, and beside which the Matterhorn is a mere dwarf? Many of them show 5,000 to 6,000 ft. of sheer descent; and yet look and are no more than second-class peaks beside their mighty brethren.[15]

The next day they started late for the summit, climbing the West Ridge, but they were surprised at the heat of the sun despite their great altitude. Kaufmann became ill and was left behind, but Graham and Boss pressed on, cutting steps up the steep ridge. Mist came down and with it wind and hail which eventually forced them to turn back. Graham estimated they had reached 22,700 feet. They picked up Kaufmann and returned to their camp where they had a miserable night, wet through and cold and where Boss insisted they all stay awake lest they die in their sleep.

Although the attempt on Dunagiri had been fairly hazardous it convinced Graham that he had nothing to fear from altitude and it is true that neither he nor his companions suffered at all during their several expeditions. He concluded, shrewdly, that altitude might affect different people in different ways, though he thought it might be some function of the heart which differed. His conclusions were to be prophetic: 'Personally I believe that, supposing the actual natural difficulties to be overcome, the air, or want of it, will prove no obstacle to the ascent of the very highest peaks in the world.'

Graham's party then tried to force the Rishi Ganga again, this time along the north bank, but bad weather, sickness amongst the porters and the sheer scale of the gorge defeated him. Nevertheless, when the weather cleared, Graham and his two companions climbed the peak marked on their map as A21, 22,516 feet high and which Graham named Mount Monal. This peak is now called Changabang and is a fairly formidable tower of rock whose ascent by the West Ridge Graham claimed. 'It was a fair climb, but presented no great difficulties,' he said. They then tried the 'third and last peak of the Dunagiri range', A22, which was of lesser height but more formidable appearance, and were defeated by the sheer headwall.

Later observers are agreed that whatever Graham climbed, it wasn't Changabang, whose ascent was not made until 1974 by an Anglo-Indian team. The difficulties would have been too great and especially from the west it presented the climber with a formidable problem which could hardly be knocked off in a day, even from a high camp. He also makes Changabang the highest of the Dunagiri group, whereas the third peak he mentions – if it was the same – is Kalanka, 22,740 feet, or 224 feet higher than Changabang. Kalanka is an easier peak than Changabang and it would make some sort of sense if what Graham climbed was Kalanka and failed on Changabang, except that the topography doesn't seem right. It seems more likely that he was on altogether the wrong ridge, probably the Hunuman ridge of Dunagiri, where he climbed an unnamed peak of rather more than 19,000 feet.[16]

The fact of the matter is that the maps drawn by the Indian Survey were not very accurate. Whilst the major heights and peaks were undoubtedly plotted more or less correctly, the detail was woefully inadequate and a subsidiary ridge with a few 19,000-foot peaks on it could easily be missed off a map. Both Graham and Boss commented on the inadequacies of the mapping. That of the Nanda Devi basin, said Boss, was not a map at all in any scientific sense: 'It was in all its details a work of imagination, with but slender relations to fact.'[17] Both suggested that some of the Survey officers should be trained in mountaineering, possibly by the Swiss army, which, 'happy in having no wars, has, under General Dufour and his successors, made its fame as the producer of the finest cartographic work in the world'. The suggestion was not well received in Dehra Dun.

. It was obvious from the correspondence which ensued, following Graham and Boss's suggestion, that the concept of mountaineering in the Alpine sense was not understood in India at the time. The Survey did not take kindly to criticism of any sort and, like the Indian elephant, never forgot. As with Johnson, one gets the feeling that Graham became *persona non grata* and this undoubtedly influenced opinion on his exploits.

They left the Garhwal, returned to Calcutta, but a few days later set out again for Sikkim. The weather was foul, the leeches worse and the porters little better.[18] Eventually they crossed the Guicha La, intent on climbing

Pandim (22,009 ft) from the north, but found it too formidable and returned instead to Jubonu (19,465 ft). Starting from a camp at about 18,000 feet at 4.30 a.m., with Kaufmann leading all the way over steep ice and rock, they reached the summit at 11 a.m. 'The hardest ascent we had in the Himalaya,' said Graham.

The next few days saw the climax of their campaign: the ascent of Kabru (24,002 ft). Graham's later description of this climb was more than a little vague and, following on the mistakes of the Garhwal trip, it has been questioned. Lying just to the south of the mighty Kangchenjunga and joined to it by a high ridge, Kabru was certainly a lot higher than any-thing else Graham climbed – or anyone else, for that matter. Did he climb it?

He claimed to have made the ascent from the east. They started on September 6, climbing a huge moraine to the foot of the East Face where they camped in a snowstorm. Next day the three climbers pushed ahead of the porters, attempting to reach the Summit Ridge, but when they got there they found themselves on a subsidiary buttress so they descended to meet the porters and turned north along steep snow slopes until they could find a ledge just big enough to take the one Whymper tent. The porters decided not to go down and sat out the night on the ledge. Fortunately the weather was mild. Graham estimated the altitude to be 18,500 feet, or about 5600 metres.

Next day they started at 4.30 a.m. The difficulties commenced at once: an avalanche-prone couloir which had to be crossed, followed by a steep ice slope and then 'nearly 1000ft of delightful rock-work, forming a perfect staircase'. Above they halted for a little food, then climbed a steep and dangerous slope where snow was lying on steep ice. This led them to the first, or lower, summit at 12.15 p.m.

They were met by a stunning view including the distant Mount Everest group and mountains beyond which seemed even higher. But they could not linger; there was the higher summit to climb, a 300-foot steep ice arête topped by a vertical ice pillar of thirty or forty feet. It took them an hour and a half to reach the top, though they wisely omitted the final pillar as being too sheer and time-consuming. The whole ascent was led, as usual, by Kaufmann. They left a bottle with their names in at the top, and a little lower down fixed a large Bhotia flag.[19] After a difficult descent they reached their camp by moonlight at 10 p.m.

They tried a couple of other peaks but in a desultory fashion and nothing more was achieved. The winter was setting in and mountaineering was finished. Kaufmann went home whilst Graham and Boss went shooting in the jungles of the Terai.

It is probably impossible to determine after all this time whether Graham and his companions really did reach the summit of Kabru, or whether, as some suspect, it was an adjacent lesser mountain called Forked Peak (20,340 ft).

We can, I think, discount Changabang, but if Graham did climb Kabru, it was not only the highest summit climbed for many a year to come but a major landmark in mountaineering history, since it marks the successful debut of Himalayan climbing as such. Neither Graham nor Boss had anything further to add after their initial descriptions; they did not join in the controversy which smouldered on for the rest of the century.

Those who opposed Graham's claim included the Survey (still in a huff about Graham and Boss's remarks regarding the Garhwal map), Martin Conway and Dr Bullock-Workman. Conway objected on the grounds that Graham's party seems to have been totally unaffected by altitude, but both he and Dr Workman later did some high-altitude ascents which would have been much less impressive if Graham's Kabru ascent was genuine.[20] In short, all those who damned Graham had an axe to grind, or a motive for proving him wrong.

On the other hand Norman Collie, Tom Longstaff, Douglas Freshfield and E.J. Garwood could see no reason to doubt Graham's ascent. Freshfield and Garwood actually examined Kabru at close quarters, during their circumnavigation of Kangchenjunga in 1899 and could see nothing to prevent the ascent taking place. 'We both of us read Mr Graham's account of his ascent and compared it with the appearance of the mountain on the spot. We agreed that there was no special obstacle to an ascent having been made, and that Mr Graham's account showed that he had not mistaken the mountain for a lower summit,' said Garwood.[21]

Graham was a climbers' climber, not too meticulous in recording his doings and probably not caring overmuch about records and the like. Now that Everest has been climbed in a day and without oxygen, his rapid ascent of Kabru seems less exceptional than it once did and perhaps the man ought now to be given his due.

Tom Longstaff, who followed Graham to Garhwal many years later, was inclined to credit him even with Changabang: 'No one who has not been lucky enough to have been there can realise what he went through, and what a strenuous pioneer and splendid climber he must have been.' Regarding Kabru he wrote:

> One word more before we leave the subject of the greatest Himalayan expedition that has yet been made. Twenty years ago strange ideas were prevalent even in this country on the subject of mountain-sickness, ideas which have not yet entirely disappeared. In India at that time such ideas were probably more exaggerated, and ignorance of mountaineering matters was almost universal. Furthermore, by an unreasonably severe criticism of the G.T.S.,

Graham had set the officials of the Survey Department against him. Thus, mainly from ignorance, most people in India refused to believe in his ascent of Kabru. A well-known Indian official of my acquaintance, who was at Darjeeling at the time of Graham's visit, says now, and said then, that he fully believed in Graham's *bona fides*, but thought he had mistaken Kabur (15,830 ft.) for Kabru (24,005 ft.), an opinion which has since been quoted by others. Now, for anyone who is a mountaineer, and has seen Kabru, it is impossible to believe that Graham, Emil Boss, and Kauffmann could make any mistake as to what peak they were on. They may have been impostors, but they could not have been mistaken; my point is that we have no tittle of evidence to show that they were either. Any climber who will carefully study Graham's paper in its entirety, especially if he knows the country at all, cannot but be struck by the strong internal evidences of truth which it bears. That he did not suffer from mountain-sickness is no proof of bad faith. That he made little pretension to scientific knowledge is no evidence that he was not a very competent mountaineer. I would add that, particularly in India, is it unwise to believe tales and rumours to the discredit of other people. To quote them is distinctly rash.[22]

The next major expedition to the Himalaya was very different from that of Graham. William Martin Conway was an art historian, a gifted writer and a man seeking his own Holy Grail. Intelligent, handsome and popular with a wide range of friends and acquaintances, he was the epitome of the mountain Romantic. He was the compiler of the first real climbing guidebooks (for which he invented names for Alpine peaks previously disregarded, such as Wellenkuppe), and the chief propagandist for the ex-centrist as against the centrist form of Alpine enjoyment, making his famous journey along the Alps 'from end to end' in 1894.

He was active and strong – he once did the Matterhorn from Zermatt and was back for afternoon tea – but he was not another Mummery or Graham, both of whom he admired immensely. 'From the very first,' he wrote, 'my main interest was not in the climbing but in the scenery and the natural phenomena . . .'[23]

He discovered to his dismay that while climbing unlocked many secrets of the hills it was at a price: the mystery which so fired the imagination was gone. The mind of the trained climber reduced sublime mountain walls to tedious scree slopes and superb ridges to so many technical problems. 'I think it was that discovery that drove me from the Alps to the mountain ranges of Asia, Spitsbergen and South America. There at any rate the wonder and the mystery returned in full measure, in spite of all Alpine knowledge and experience.'

Even that couldn't last, of course. On his final expedition, to the Andes in 1898, he suddenly realised his heart wasn't in it any more, despite the fact that he had just made the first ascent of Illimani. Of the mountains he said: 'They had called me as things of beauty and of wonder, things terrible and sublime, and instead of glorying in their splendour here was I spending months in outlining the vagrant plan of them on a piece of paper. That realisation ended my mountain career.'[24]

Perhaps what Conway was really after was fame, and he saw the unknown mountains as a way to achieve this. He started with the Karakoram and came nearest to his ideal with Spitsbergen. All his work in these lands was worthy, but it was a sort of plodding worthiness which does nothing to fire the spirit.

Mummery recognised this and declined to accompany Conway on his trip to the Karakoram in 1892. This western end of the Himalaya was inhabited by particularly warlike tribes and very difficult of access until the 1891 Hunza-Nagir campaign brought peace to the area. Because it was so unknown Conway decided that it would be just right for his journey of exploration and climbing. As a guide he took the great Mattias Zurbriggen and included in the party were Oscar Eckenstein and Charles Bruce.[25] Bruce, a Gurkha officer, brought along some of his men.

July was spent mapping the Hispar and Biafo Glaciers and crossing various passes, including the Hispar Pass which separated the two great glaciers, thus making the longest glacier passage in the world outside Arctic regions: seventy-five miles. The party was not an altogether happy one; it was always unlikely that the arch conservative Conway was going to get along with the socialist and radical Eckenstein, but he also had a disagreement with Bruce over money. The latter difficulty was resolved but Eckenstein left the party after the Biafo exploration.

They then turned to the exploration of the great Baltoro Glacier and named the principal branches at its head as Godwin-Austen Glacier (leading up to K2) and Vigne Glacier, facing it.[26] They climbed a small peak (Crystal Peak, 19,400 ft), then Conway, Bruce, Zurbriggen and two Gurkhas, Harkbir and Karbir, attempted Baltoro Kangri (23,991 ft), which Conway called Golden Throne. They reached a minor summit which they christened Pioneer Peak and estimated at 22,600 feet, but were cut off from the main summit by a deep and unbridgeable gap in the ridge. Two days later the same party, without Conway, tried the mountain again but bad weather stopped them and it became clear that the climbing season was over. They made a leisurely return to India via Leh and Srinagar.

Conway believed he had created a height record on Baltoro Kangri at roughly 22,650 feet, but quite apart from the fact that his measurements were only approximate, based on barometric pressure taken during variable weather, this is doubtful: Johnson had certainly matched this height and possibly climbed to 23,890 feet, Graham claimed to have reached 24,080 feet on Kabru, and an Indian Survey worker might have reached 23,050 feet on Shilla. The common factor to all these claims, however, is the cloud of uncertainty in which each is wrapped.

Conway admitted that he based his expedition on those of Whymper to the Andes. He helped to establish one mainstream tradition in Himalayan climbing, that of the large-scale expedition, followed by Abruzzi, and many others in the twentieth century. However, it should not be overlooked that Graham set a precedent too, the small-scale alpine-style expedition so much more in favour today, and his followers through the years have included the incomparable Tilman and Shipton in the 1930s.

As a voyage of exploration the Conway expedition was important, though in climbing terms little was done. One interesting technical detail is the use of crampons on Baltoro Kangri at a time when they were still frowned on in British Alpine circles. Their use on this occasion is almost certainly due to Eckenstein, who is credited with adapting the age-old peasant crampons to climbing purposes.[27]

There is no doubt that the opening years of Himalayan climbing attracted as rich a variety of characters as ever trod a mountain peak. Besides those already mentioned, before the First World War there were Mummery and Collie, Freshfield, Crowley, Longstaff, Kellas, all of whom were to a considerable degree extraordinary characters. None more so, perhaps, than the American couple, the Workmans or, as they sometimes called themselves, the Bullock-Workmans, since Mrs Workman's maiden name was Bullock and, like her compatriot and arch rival, Annie Peck, she was a great believer in feminist rights.

They came to adventure relatively late in life. Both were wealthy upper-crust New Englanders, he a medical practitioner who had trained in Harvard and Europe, she a daughter of the Governor of Massachusetts. There seems little doubt that Fanny was the driving force.

In 1892 they began a series of intrepid bike rides which took them into remote parts of Asia and the Middle East, Fanny brandishing a whip to fend off importunate dogs and a revolver for importunate men. In 1898 they hit India, cycled up the length of the continent to Kashmir and then, abandoning their bikes, travelled to Ladakh and the Karakoram Pass. Later they tried to climb Kangchenjunga – third highest mountain in the world, and their first attempt at climbing – but were foiled by intransigent porters.[28]

So taken were they by the Karakoram and Himalaya that during the next fourteen years they made six major expeditions to the mountains, he directing operations one year and she the next. They began in 1899 with an expedition to the Biafo Glacier during which they climbed several peaks of about 6000 metres, their first ascents. In 1902–3 they visited the Chogo Lungma Glacier where Dr Workman claimed an altitude record of 23,394 feet. This translates to 7130 metres, or about 230 metres higher than Conway had previously reached, but not as high as Graham. It is hardly surprising that Workman, like Conway, was disinclined to accept Graham's record! At this time Dr Workman was fifty-six years old.

As if not to be outdone by her husband Fanny climbed Pinnacle Peak during a visit to the Nun Kun massif in 1907. Though she measured this at 23,300 feet, later surveyors corrected it to 22,810 feet (6957 m). It was enough to beat off the South American challenge by Annie Peck.

In 1908 they repeated Conway's Hispar-Biafo trek and in 1911 explored the Siachen Glacier, at more than fifty miles the longest in the Himalaya, where they also returned for their final visit in 1912.

Between them the Workmans wrote nine travel books of which five dealt with the Himalaya, handsome volumes, splendidly illustrated with Mrs Workman's fine photographs.[29] But their mapping was faulty and one suspects that for the *pukka sahibs* of the Raj, with their rigid cantonment conventions, Fanny was altogether too ... American. Anyone who, like Fanny, could have her picture taken on the Siachen Glacier carrying a placard declaring Votes for Women, could only meet with stern disapproval, as this from Mason: 'A great deal of ground traversed ... had been visited and described before, though the Workmans often lacked the grace to acknowledge it. When they did refer to the work of their predecessors it was in too carping and controversial a manner. They rarely tried to understand the mentality of their porters and never got the best out of them.'[30]

During the years when the Workmans were beavering away in the Karakoram other groups were taking their first tentative mountaineering steps in the Himalaya, especially in Kashmir, which included most of the Punjab Himalaya and the Karakoram. Young Lieutenant Bruce, who had been with Conway, explored the Nun Kun group, and the Neve brothers, medical missionaries in Kashmir, climbed the peaks of the Pir Panjal, which separate the state from India, and also other spectacular minor peaks like Kolahoi and Haramukh. Dr Arthur Neve, Dr H. Sillem, the Rev. C.E. Barton and, of course, the Workmans also explored the Nun Kun massif and, as we have seen, Mrs Workman climbed Pinnacle Peak. In 1914 Kun (23,253 ft) was climbed by the Italian mountaineer Mario Piacenza, though the highest point of this dramatic little group, Nun (23,408 ft) had to wait until after the Second World War.

In 1902 Oscar Eckenstein returned to the Karakoram with the intention of climbing K2, second highest mountain in the world. Eckenstein, the anti-Establishment rebel, had by this time met the notorious Aleister Crowley, the self-named Great Beast 666, who was something of a climber.[31] Together they determined to climb a higher peak than any yet ascended and formed an expedition with Eckenstein as leader, and containing the noted Austrian climber Heinrich Pfannl, who had made the first ascent of the Géant by the North Ridge and North-West Face two years before, another Austrian called Wesseley, a Swiss doctor called Jacot-Guillarmod and a young engineer friend of Eckenstein, Guy Knowles who, according to Crowley, 'knew practically nothing of mountains'.

Bad weather dogged the expedition but they did valuable work surveying the approaches and Guillarmod and Wesseley reached about 21,430 feet on the North-East Ridge.

The surprising thing is that anything at all was achieved because the expedition was conducted in an atmosphere of comic melodrama. Hardly had they arrived in India than Eckenstein was arrested as a spy and only saved himself from being deported by seeking a personal interview with the Viceroy. The reason for this harassment was never made clear, though some observers detected the hand of Martin Conway in the background: Conway had never forgiven Eckenstein for leaving his own expedition ten years earlier.

However, it was Crowley who added most to the fun and games. When some laden porters refused to cross a steep snow slope which overhung a precipice, Crowley demonstrated its safety by springing down the slope, pulling himself up short a few feet from the edge. His European companions thought him quite mad – but the porters crossed the slope. Later in the expedition he had a violent disagreement with Knowles and chased him off the mountain at pistol point!

Crowley returned to the Himalaya three years later, this time to Kang-chenjunga, and Dr Jacot-Guillarmod, who should have known better, went with him. Crowley remarked that the doctor knew as little of mountaineering as he did of medicine, so it is hardly surprising that things went wrong from the start. The rest of the party consisted of two Swiss climbers called Pache and Reymond and a hotel keeper from Darjeeling called de Righi, whom Crowley seems to have acquired in passing and then had second thoughts about. ('I blame myself for not foreseeing that his pin brain would entirely give way as soon as he got out of the world of waiters.')[32] He does not appear to have had much confidence in any of his team – 'Thanks to the Alpine Club, there was no Englishman of mountaineering ability and experience available' – and was soon exasperated with Jacot-Guillarmod who complained continually at the early starts on which Crowley sensibly insisted, to avoid avalanches.

Crowley, Reymond and Pache established a high camp at 21,000 feet. When the rest of the party arrived there was a violent showdown and in the late afternoon Jacot-Guillarmod, de Righi and Pache decided to descend, despite their leader's warnings of avalanche danger. Crowley later wrote: 'I ought to have broken the doctor's leg with an axe, but I was too young to take such a responsibility. It would have been hard to prove afterwards that I had saved him by so doing.'

The inevitable happened. Two of the porters slipped and in the avalanche this created Pache and all three porters died. De Righi and Jacot-Guillarmod miraculously survived, but despite their cries, Crowley remained sipping tea in his bed. There was nothing he could do, he explained, adding, 'Not that I was over-anxious in the circumstances to render help. A mountain "accident" of this sort is one of the things for which I have no sympathy whatever.'[33]

After this the party broke up with further acrimony over funds.

Not surprisingly Crowley and Eckenstein were both castigated in the *Alpine Journal*, the readers of which were much more comfortable with people like Conway. But in fact, though Crowley may have been an extreme case, disagreements and rows were to be commonplace on future Himalayan expeditions and, like Crowley, several distinguished mountaineers have resorted to fisticuffs!

Throughout this period, exploration still went hand in hand with any possible ascents. There were many blanks on the map, even in the territories which were politically accessible, and whole regions, such as Nepal and Tibet, were largely closed to foreigners. Expeditions which had ambitions on some Himalayan giant back in the comfort of the map room at the Royal Geographical Society often found themselves frustrated by the difficult terrain, the altitude, the native porters, the food, the bugs and the bloodiness of life in general. It was all so different from the dear old Alps.

Nevertheless, the best of these adventurers were incredibly tough and managed quite well with minimal resources. The idea of small 'alpine-style' expeditions, now so fashionable, is nothing new, nor did it begin with Shipton and Tilman: between Graham's expedition and the First World War, small expeditions were the norm. The publicity given to Conway and later to Abruzzi, who attempted K2 in 1909, has perhaps tended to distort the impression.

Amongst those who did sterling work at this time were Freshfield and Longstaff, both of whom combined climbing and exploration. Freshfield's party left Darjeeling on September 5, 1899, intent on climbing Kangchenjunga, though one feels it was more a vague hope than an expressed intention and that exploration was the main thing. The party went up the Tista valley and Zemu Glacier and crossed the Jonsong La (20,080 ft) to the Kangchenjunga Glacier. Heavy snow prevented any attempt on the high peaks but they did manage Kabur (15,830 ft) before finally returning to Darjeeling. It was a brilliant circumnavigation of the massif, and much new country was seen for the first time and photographed by the outstanding mountain photographer of the day, Vittorio Sella.

Freshfield was the first to examine the impressive Western Face of Kangchenjunga, with its unusual great terrace running some 1300 feet below the top and giving access to the summit, although, as Freshfield pointed out, below the terrace stretched a formidable horseshoe of precipices. Freshfield's Horseshoe became the Sickle in later years; he thought it difficult but still the most likely way of climbing the mountain, and half a century later he was proved right.[34]

Tom Longstaff ranged wider during his three expeditions of 1905, 1907 and 1909. 'His pirate beard blazed red against the Himalaya snows,' said L.S. Amery.[35] Longstaff was a qualified medical doctor who was wealthy enough not to need to practise, and who hints in his autobiography, *This My Voyage*, that he qualified simply to prepare himself for his work as an explorer: '. . . In many countries where strangers are unwelcome a doctor's diploma is a good passport.' He was a great believer in preparation and having been inspired as a youngster by Graham's adventures, he concentrated first on the Garhwal.

He took the two Brocherel brothers, Alexis and Henri, from Courmayeur, as guides, and with local porters explored the eastern approach to Nanda Devi. They reached a saddle on the rim of the wall which guards the great peak and made unsuccessful attempts on Nanda Devi East and Nanda Kot.

Longstaff then seized a chance to accompany a British official on a visit to Tibet, a forbidden country full of mystery, changing his plans, as he said, from a mountaineering expedition to 'a walk of some thousand miles across and around the Himalaya'. During this 'walk' he and the Brocherels attempted the remote peak of Gurla Mandhata (25,355 ft), on the border with western Nepal. On their first attempt they chose a subsidiary ridge from which they were unable to reach the main mountain, but as dawn broke they reached a height of about 20,000 feet and looked out over a sea of unknown peaks in forbidden Nepal: 'We were like Cortez seeing the Pacific for the first time; for no other eyes had seen these peaks from such a height spread as a continuous range. I was more elated by this enormous vista of the unknown than by any other discovery or ascent that I have accomplished.'[36]

This sentiment expresses so well the two dynamic forces of the early Himalayan climbers, for Longstaff was trying to make the first ascent of a big peak and at the same time he was also attracted by the vast unknown. The poet James Elroy Flecker summed it up in his famous lines from *Hassan*:

> We are the Pilgrims, master; we shall go
> Always a little further; it may be
> Beyond that last blue mountain barred with snow.

The search for the last blue mountain had its finest flowering in the careers of Shipton and Tilman thirty years later but others like Longstaff had gone before.

They made another attempt on Gurla Mandhata. The first night they camped at over 19,000 feet, from where they made a bid for the top. They were much too low, of course, and found themselves contemplating a forced bivouac, without sleeping-bag or protective clothing, at about 24,000 feet. As they moved off the ridge to find shelter by some rocks, the slope they were on avalanched and in a second they were swept away:

> My mind seemed quite clear, but curious about the end rather than terrified. Thoughts passed at incredible speed, while bodily sensation was blotted out. The glacier two or three thousand feet below seemed to rush towards us, its crevasses widening and widening ... I had no sensation of physical pain, nor even of discomfort, though my hand was deeply cut. I had got turned head downwards, and seeing rocks ahead clawed off my snow spectacles to save my eyes when the smash came![37]

They slid 3000 feet in a couple of minutes, and escaped unharmed. The guides, with admirable sang-froid, climbed back up the avalanche route to locate the ice axes which had been torn from their grip, and returned triumphant three hours later. That night they bivouacked and, not giving up their attempt, were forced to bivouac again next night in a snow hole at 23,000 feet, the highest bivouac attempted at that time and for some time after.

But it was all in vain. Weakened by lack of food and the cold, Longstaff ordered a retreat next day and they embarked on what turned out to be a long and arduous descent of the mountain. Surprisingly the whole six-month trip in India and Tibet, from the railhead, cost less than £100.

In 1907 Longstaff was invited to join the Everest expedition that never was. The idea came about from a suggestion by the Viceroy of India, Lord Curzon, that British mountaineers might like to attempt Kangchenjunga or Everest. A wealthy publisher and member of the Alpine Club called A.L. Mumm decided to take up Curzon's offer by organising an expedition to Everest through Tibet, in celebration of the Club's Golden Jubilee. Mumm guaranteed to meet all the expenses himself. He was to be leader, though he was almost fifty at the time and, as Longstaff described him, 'over refined for the rough work of Himalayan exploration'. As companions he chose Longstaff and Bruce. Moritz Inderbinnen was Mumm's guide, Longstaff had the two Brocherels again and Bruce had nine Gurkhas. Mumm also had the bright idea of taking along some small bottles of oxygen to help with altitude problems, and though it was the first time a mountaineering expedition had carried such an aid, the party regarded it as something of a joke and it had no effect on the outcome.

It was a fairly strong party, though Everest would have been well beyond them at that time, had they but known it. As it was they didn't get the chance to find out. The plan was nipped in the bud by John Morley, Secretary of State for India, who refused to allow them into Tibet.[38]

The expedition was forced to change its target. At Longstaff's suggestion they returned to his earlier area of activity, the Garhwal and Nanda Devi. This beautiful mountain is guarded by a ring of lesser peaks, linked together by an icy curtain. Inside the circle is the Sanctuary, a place where no man had trodden, because the only entrance was the formidable Rishi Ganga gorge. Mumm's party, like Graham's before them, tried to force the Rishi Ganga, but it was an awesome place, quite beyond them or anyone else for the next twenty-seven years. They turned instead to an attempt on Trisul (23,360 ft/7120 m), one of the peaks of the Sanctuary wall.

Even the approach to this mountain was rough and at one stage the porters baulked at a makeshift bridge over the Rishi torrent, until the Gurkha Karbir, laying his hand on his *kukri*, threatened to cut off the head of the first man who refused to cross. There was no further trouble and base camp was established at 11,600 feet in a nullah which led to the northern base of Trisul.[39]

Bruce had left the party because of a damaged knee and after an abortive first attempt, the ascent was finally made by Longstaff, the two Brocherels and Karbir. Alexis led all the way and they reached the summit at 4 p.m. on June 12. It was the highest summit reached at that time and remained so for twenty-one years, except, that is, for Graham's disputed ascent of Kabru.

In that same year, 1907, two Norwegians, C.W. Rübenson and Monrad Aas, made another attempt on Kabru and got to within 100 feet of the summit, but violent winds and intense cold robbed them of ultimate victory. They were lucky to survive the descent when Rubenson slipped and all but one strand of the rope parted! Nevertheless, the relative ease with which they almost got to the top lends support to Graham's claim, which Longstaff fully endorsed, despite his own 'record'.

In 1909 Longstaff, with Arthur Neve, Morris Slingsby and D.G. Oliver, was in the Karakoram where he found and crossed the Saltoro Pass, then discovered the enormous Siachen Glacier and surveyed the Teram Kangri group. This in itself would have established Longstaff as a major figure in Himalayan exploration. There were to be more Himalayan adventures after the War of 1914–18, not to mention the Rockies and Arctic regions.

There were other adventurers too, in the same mould as Longstaff and occupying, like him, the Himalayan scene in the years up to the First World War. One such was C.F. Meade who, for the three years 1910, 1912 and 1913 had a love–hate relationship with the great peak of Kamet (25,447 ft/7756 m) in the Garhwal, about forty miles west of Nanda Devi. Relatively easy of access, the Kamet group had been one of the first Himalayan peaks to be attempted by the Schlagintweit brothers in 1855, and Longstaff had taken a look at it in 1907. Morris Slingsby was there in 1911 and 1913,[40] and A.M. Kellas in 1911 and 1914. Despite all this attention, Kamet was not climbed until 1931.

During his attempts, however, Charles Meade reached Meade's Col in 1913 between Abi Gamin and Kamet and pitched a tent there at 23,420 feet. This was probably a few hundred feet higher than Longstaff's bivouac of eight years before and was the highest camp ever made in the mountains before the Everest expeditions got under way.[41]

Dr A.M. Kellas, who was also on Kamet, taught chemistry to medical students at the Middlesex Hospital and had developed a study of the effects of altitude on the human body. He looked the very model of an absent-minded professor: untidy, stooped, thin and small, his face adorned with pebble glasses because of poor eyesight and, in George Mallory's words, 'beyond description Scotch and uncouth in his speech – altogether uncouth'.[42]

Kellas was a passionate mountaineer: 'Although he was keenly interested in chemistry,' wrote Collie, 'he was also even more interested in mountains.'[43] And in his Himalayan exploits he combined his scientific and mountaineering interests. Besides the Garhwal his main interests were in the Kangchenjunga area, to which he returned time and again between 1907 and 1921, by which time he was fifty-three years old.

On the first trip he took unnamed Swiss guides but found them less than satisfactory and determined in future to use only the native hillmen because 'they seemed more at home in the diminished pressure'. Over the years he found one tribe in particular to be reliable and sturdy; they came from a remote part of Nepal and were called Sherpas.

With only these natives to guide him, Kellas made a remarkable series of ascents in the Kangchenjunga region: Langpo Peak (22,800 ft) in 1909, Chomiomo (22,430 ft) in 1910, Pauhunri (23,180 ft) in 1911 and Kangchenjau (22,700 ft) in 1912. Of these, Pauhunri was only the fourth 7000-metre peak to be climbed at the time and the fourth highest, after Longstaff's Trisal ascent of 1907 and the disputed ascents of Kabru and Muztagh by Graham and Johnson, in 1883 and 1865 respectively.[44]

Kellas is said to have had secret plans to attempt Everest from Tibet, but these were abandoned when the first official expedition became a reality. His name was put forward as leader by Freshfield, but dismissed by Percy Farrar, President of the Alpine Club, in scathing terms: 'Kellas has never climbed a mountain, but has only walked about on steep snow with a lot of coolies.'[45] This was grossly unfair on poor Kellas, of course, but he was simply a victim of the mutual distrust between the Alpine Club, represented by Farrar, and the Royal Geographical Society, represented by Freshfield, the two bodies responsible for organising the Everest venture.

In the event Kellas was to make a less enviable record on Everest: he was the first man to die attempting the world's highest mountain.

*   *   *

The pioneering days of Himalayan climbing, from the time of Graham until the First World War, saw the growth of the dichotomy of outlook we have already noted in high-altitude climbing. On the one hand there was the small affair, a sporting gamble done for the hell of it and, on the other, the ponderous expedition, top heavy with personnel, scientific endeavour and self-importance. Later on the large expedition was to gather to itself another trait, nationalism, which was to colour its thinking to the present day.

The issues are not altogether clear cut: some small expeditions did valuable scientific and exploratory work, whilst some large expeditions risked everything to try and gain a summit. But there was always something of the Cavalier and Roundhead feeling about the two sorts of expedition. One appeals to the heart and the other to the head. Perhaps this is why many climbers felt uneasy throughout the first half of this century as yet another massive juggernaut trundled towards Everest or Kangchenjunga.

In the pioneering days two expeditions illustrated the divergent attitudes better than any others. In 1895 Mummery led an expedition consisting of himself and three friends to Nanga Parbat (26,660 ft/8125 m); it was a purely sporting affair, intent on conquering the great mountain and nothing else.[46] By way of contrast the huge expedition of the Duke of the Abruzzi to K2 in 1909 had thirteen members, including an official geographer and photographer. It also had European guides and porters; Mummery had no guides and relied on Gurkhas for support. The Duke's expedition not only made a spirited attack on the world's second highest mountain but also carried out a survey and took valuable photographs which greatly helped subsequent parties. The fate of these two expeditions was to influence Himalayan thinking for over fifty years.

Mummery's party of 1895, though small, was a strong one. Besides himself there was Professor Norman Collie and Geoffrey Hastings, both of whom were his boon Alpine companions and very good rock climbers on British rock, too, which Mummery was not. Then, for some of the time, there was Charlie Bruce and two of his Gurkhas, Raghobir and Goman Singh. They chose Nanga Parbat because it was big and, being relatively accessible, not too expensive to attempt. At this time the only Himalayan ascents had been those done by Conway, Graham and the various surveyors, none of whose accounts seemed to indicate any special difficulties. Mummery assured his wife that 'the expedition is much less formidable than the first Caucasian' and he wrote from Base Camp, 'I don't think there will be any serious mountaineering difficulties on Nanga ... I fancy the ascent will be mainly a question of endurance.'

Provisional Base Camp was set up at Tarshing in the Rupal valley, on the southern side of Nanga Parbat. Except for the ever present bulk of the huge mountain it might almost have been in England, with lush meadowland echoing to the calls of larks and cuckoos. It seemed an ideal place to get in a bit of training after the long and tedious journey from home, for there were to hand various peaks which, though not as high as Nanga Parbat itself, were quite respectable-looking summits. Bruce and the Gurkhas had not yet arrived so choosing one of the finest looking peaks, Mummery, Collie and Hastings mounted an attack, which promptly failed. Disconcerted, they shifted their attack to a lower peak – and failed again. In the end they climbed an insignificant rocky knoll out of sheer frustration.

They seemed to have learned nothing from these experiments. They put their failure down to their lack of training and the effects of altitude. They seem never to have grasped the scale of the undertaking they were embarked upon; they were still thinking in Alpine terms. In provisions, too, they never got to grips with reality; they were forever running short of supplies and this ultimately affected the climbing.

Meanwhile they had reached the conclusion that the great Rupal Face of Nanga Parbat was too formidable and so they decided to take a look at the western side of the mountain, the Diamir valley. This involved the crossing of a well-known pass called the Mazeno La (17,586 ft), which had been used by traders for centuries. It wasn't a difficult pass in any technical sense but it was a long, painful trudge over an abominable rock-strewn track and the climbers hated it.

The Diamir Face, however, raised their hopes. Mummery described it in another letter to his wife: 'We discovered an absolutely safe way up Nanga. Easy glacier ... and thence onward a broad snow and rock ridge right to the top. I feel fairly confident of getting up and you need feel no anxiety of any sort. I am as fit as I have ever been in my life; you need not feel the least anxiety.'

Mrs Mummery was herself an experienced mountaineer and this insistence of her husband on fitness and safety, repeated over and over in the letters, must have been slightly disturbing. Who was he trying to kid? Perhaps himself.

What they had discovered on the Diamir Face of the mountain was a series of steep rock ribs (later called the Mummery Rib) which seemed to lead to the top without too much trouble, offering what was in fact a gigantic rock climb. Its appeal to Mummery, the ace Alpine rock climber, was instantaneous.

First, however, short of food again, they had to return to base. In order to avoid the hateful Mazeno La Mummery proposed crossing a high col they could see on the southern skyline, which he felt sure would lead back to the Rupal valley. Setting out before midnight with the aid of their glacier lanterns they climbed steep broken ground until dawn showed them a rock rib which proved more satisfactory, though the col itself never seemed to get any nearer. 'These Himalaya are constructed on a scale entirely different from the Alps or any of the ordinary snow mountains,' Collie commented. He was learning.

As they breasted the col after fourteen hours' climbing they realised to their horror that it led not to the Rupal valley as they expected, but merely to the foot of the Mazeno La. They would have to cross it after all!

This so depressed Mummery that he proposed a wild plan of striking from the col across a high intervening peak to reach the top of the Mazeno La, but Collie and Hastings would have none of it. Tired and hungry they descended to the foot of the pass and, realising that the sooner they got it over with the better, decided to press on through the hours of darkness.

This is where the strength of Collie and Hastings carried them through. Mummery, on the other hand, never a good walker in the best conditions, fell further and further behind; his weak sight meant he had hardly any night vision and he was reduced to crawling on hands and knees. They reached the summit of the pass at 8 p.m. and the foot of the other side at 7 a.m. They had been going non-stop for thirty-one hours over the roughest country in the world. By any standards it would remain an extraordinary performance.

When they reached Base Camp Bruce was waiting with the two Gurkhas, Raghobir Thapa and Goman Singh. Bruce was then a young army officer, just married, who could see the value of training his men in what would now be called mountain warfare. Keen on mountaineering himself, he inspired several of his men with enthusiasm akin to his own. He was destined to become a General, and to lead an Everest expedition.[47]

At the end of July the Tarshing camp was struck and sent over the Mazeno La to be erected in the Diamir valley. For their part, the climbers had no wish to walk over the abominable pass yet again and were determined to find an alternative way across the high ridge which separated the two valleys. They realised that this could not be done in a single day and that they would have to bivouac or, at Mummery's suggestion, climb through the night with the aid of moonlight, as he, Hastings and Slingsby had done on the Aiguille du Plan three years earlier. In the event the moon was obscured by banks of mist swirling up from the valley and they were forced into a hasty bivouac at 19,000 feet. As they wore only normal Alpine clothes – tweed suits, pullovers, gloves and balaclavas – it is not surprising that dawn found them in a half-frozen condition and they could do nothing but descend.

They crossed the Mazeno La to Diamir after all. Bruce left the party because he was ill with mumps and Hastings, suffering from a twisted ankle, was sent on a search for food supplies, so there were only four climbers left: Mummery, Collie and the two Gurkhas.

They divided their efforts; Collie and Goman Singh explored the Diama Glacier, the left branch of the Diamir Glacier, whilst Mummery and Raghobir began investigating the Mummery Rib, right up the centre of the face.

A letter to his wife summarised his intentions and again sought to calm her fears:

> Tomorrow I am going to start on an exploration of Nanga itself.
>
> There is a nice little ridge of rock (broken) leading between two glaciers. I think it easy enough for Chilasi porters.
>
> If so I shall fix a camp at the very top, about 18,000 ft.
>
> From that point with the two Gurkhas, one can push a camp to 22,000 ft, at the very foot of the final peak, which on this side is easy rock.
>
> We expect to make our serious attack on Nanga next week (seven days from now); it will require four days ... The air is the very deuce.
>
> I hope you have not been nervous. We have run no risks of any sort (other than sprained ankles) on these infernal moraines.
>
> The peaks are too big and too high for real hard climbing, and as for storms, there are none in these regions, not the symptoms or ghost of one.
>
> No driving snow on the ridges, no thunder-clouds, no fresh snow (other than the merest shatter).
>
> I think we are bound to have the summit, as it is merely a matter of steady training to get our wind in order.

How much of this did Mummery really believe and how much was window-dressing for his wife? In fact, subsequent events indicate that he probably did believe it; supremely confident in his own ability, he was never a one to feel humility in the face of the mountains.

Mummery and Raghobir investigated the rock ribs and found the climbing delightful. After a hiatus due to bad weather, all four climbers united in attacking the ribs and they managed to establish a food dump at about 17,000 feet on the second rib. Collie thought the climbing difficult, comparable with the West Face of the Plan at Chamonix.

After some more bad weather and time out to climb on a minor peak near by, the attack was resumed on August 15. There was Mummery, Collie, and Raghobir, together with a local hunter called Lor Khan who insisted on joining them, and a porter. A camp – what would nowadays be called Camp 1 – was established on the upper glacier below the ribs. At this point Collie was taken ill and retired to Base Camp with the porter whilst Mummery led the other two up the first two ribs, where they spent a miserable night out in a heavy snowfall.

Next day, in thick mist, they pushed on up the third rib for about 1000 feet where they deposited a food store which they hoped would provide a springboard for a summit assault. It was at a height of about 20,000 feet, or 6600 feet below the summit, a long way for a summit dash. They returned to Base content with their efforts.

Next day they set off again, sleeping that night at Camp 1, where Collie was again taken ill and forced to retire whilst Mummery and Raghobir attempted the rib. Again they spent a cold night at Camp 2 then pushed on, picking up the provisions *en route*. A few hundred feet higher, when Mummery was convinced there were no more problems ahead, Raghobir stopped, exhausted,[48] and all Mummery's efforts had to be diverted to getting him down safely. It had been a brave effort, though. Certainly it was the most technically demanding climbing done in the Himalaya at the time and for many years to come.[49]

Time was running out for the expedition. For some reason, despite the good progress made on the first attempt, Mummery declined to try the same route again. Instead he decided to look at the remaining side of the mountain so far unexplored, the Rakhiot Face. His plan was to cross the high ridge which separated the Diamir and Rakhiot Faces by means of an unknown notch which he optimistically called the Diama Pass. Collie thought it foolhardy but Mummery laughed at his fears. 'Don't worry. I'm not going to risk anything for the sake of an ordinary pass,' he assured him.

That evening he wrote to his wife:

> Our chances of bagging the peak look badly enough.
>
> Collie is not keen on it and old Hastings has managed to get a chill, so I am left with the Gurkhas . . .
>
> Well, I shall soon be on my way home; you must not be disappointed about Nanga.
>
> I have had some slap-up climbs, and seen cliffs and séracs such as the Alps and Caucasus cannot touch.
>
> Nanga on this side is 12,000 feet of rock and ice as steep and difficult as a series of Matterhorns and Mont Blancs piled one on the other.
>
> I should have got up, I fancy, if Ragabir (a Gurkha) had not got ill at a critical moment, and I had to see him down . . .
>
> To-morrow I cross a high pass with the Gurkhas to the Rakhiot Nullah. Hastings and Collie go round with the coolies and stores . . .

On the morning of August 24, 1895, Mummery, Raghobir and Goman Singh set out to cross the Diama Pass. They were never seen again.

It was a disastrous end to a sporting expedition much more in tune with modern lightweight expeditions than many which were to follow. The death of Mummery and the Gurkhas, however, blighted it and the Himalayan scene for years to come.

There could hardly have been a greater contrast to the Mummery expedition than that led by the Duke of the Abruzzi to K2 in 1909. The Duke, who was a good climber, had considerable expedition experience by this time, having been to the Ruwenzori, Alaska and the Arctic. His experience had taught him a thing or two about organisation and logistics and since money was no object he was able to set about the task in style. When he landed at Bombay on Good Friday, he was accompanied by eleven compatriots and 262 numbered chests containing 13,280 pounds of baggage. In addition there were 500 pounds of Indian coins with which to pay the porters and for incidentals on the way (large notes being useless in the hills, where change was difficult). Upwards of 500 porters were needed. Looking after all this on the march was a local officer, A.C. Baines, who knew the Karakoram well.[50]

As they threaded their way along the Karakoram trails they must have seemed like an army on the march.

Basing his strategy on the experience of the Workmans and Eckenstein, who had suffered bad weather from mid-June, the Duke aimed to be at the Baltoro by mid-May. He wanted at least a month in the icy wilderness of Concordia and to secure his supply of food, animals were driven up the Baltoro as far as the little alp at Urdukas, where they were grazed under the supervision of Baines, then killed as required, to ensure a supply of fresh meat for the upper camps. Baines also looked after the meteorological station the party set up at Urdukas for the purpose of comparing temperature and pressure at this comparatively low level with those taken at high altitude during the climbing.

With his supply lines secured the Duke could afford to devote his entire attention to reconnoitring K2 for two months. He had scientists, photographers, four good guides and three experienced Alpine porters.

Base Camp was at 5030 metres, below the foot of K2, just north of the stupendous icy crossroads that is Concordia. Huge mountains rose all round. De Filippi described it:

> The scale is so vast that one cannot get an impression of the whole at any one moment; the eye can take in only single portions. And so for a long time we were not fully conscious of the dimensions of the landscape. We had no standard of comparison, and the glaciers, peaks and valleys are so well proportioned that it is hard to judge the size of any one object. This was revealed to us only by detailed observation and by our repeated failures to estimate heights and distances. So it was that our amazement, instead of diminishing, grew greater; and our last day in the Concordia made an even greater impression on us than our first.[51]

A systematic reconnaissance began, commencing with the nearest ridge, the South-East, now called the Abruzzi. With three guides and four porters the

Duke struggled up the increasingly difficult ridge until at last the guides advised retreat on the grounds that it was too difficult for laden porters and too long to be climbed without them. The Duke accepted their advice. He had reached 6710 metres.

He next explored the western side of the mountain, up the Savoia Glacier to the Savoia Pass at its head, but any hope he had of climbing the West Ridge of K2 from the pass was dashed by its formidable appearance. 'The hopes with which the Duke had begun the ascent were annihilated,' said de Filippi.

After this frustration, the Duke moved up the eastern side of the peak, along the Godwin-Austen Glacier, to reach another pass called Windy Gap, from where the North-East Ridge of K2 could be reconnoitred and found to be impractical. However, they did manage to get to about 6600 metres up the South Ridge of Skyang Kangri (7544 m), which was also accessible from the pass.

From the head of the glacier too, they climbed a pass on the eastern rim of mountains, which the Duke called Sella Pass and from which they could see the South-East Ridge of K2. This ridge has a distinct shoulder at 7750 metres (25,427 ft), and it was thought that if the Shoulder could be reached the ridge might be climbed. The Shoulder was to play a tragic part in the story of K2 many years later, but in the meantime the Duke decided it was unattainable. 'The Duke was finally obliged to yield to the conviction that K2 was not to be climbed,' de Filippi concluded.

In fact, the photographs taken by Sella from his eponymous pass were to give later climbers the key to success. The Karakoram expedition provided Vittorio Sella with his last and greatest series of mountain pictures. Fifty years old, his career had spanned some of the earliest winter traverses in the Alps, he had been to the Caucasus with Dent, round Kangchenjunga with Freshfield, to Mount St Elias and the Ruwenzori with the Duke. His photographs of all these places are superb, but most agree that the Karakoram series is best of all; perhaps because the subject could scarcely be improved in nature. One of today's finest mountain photographers has written:

> Sella's work expressed a combination of sensibilities. His panoramas demonstrated his skill as a patient technician; his landscapes showed that he had the romantic eye of an artist. In his mountain portraits he used the trained eye of a climber to single out the essential character of each peak. Many years later an emerging virtuoso in mountain photography, Ansel Adams, wrote an essay in appreciation of Sella. At one point he compared Sella to Edward Weston, noting that both men produced images 'as concise, factual, and miraculously detailed as could be desired, yet they contain that

magical and spiritual potential of vision which transcends analysis.'
Adams was not an aficionado of high-mountain photography for
its own sake. He found most of it dull, merely a factual recording
of the scene. But in Sella's work he saw the qualities of greatness
which, to him, supported the concept 'that intuition is the basic
creative factor rather than a self-conscious awareness of modes and
manners.'[52]

The Duke next turned his attention to Conway's Bride Peak, now called
Chogolisa (7659 m/25,130 ft), which lies across the Concordia basin from
K2. With three guides and forty porters he managed, despite poor weather,
to establish a camp at 6337 metres on the saddle between Bride Peak and
Golden Throne and then a higher one at 6609 metres. From there the Duke,
with the Brocherel brothers and Joseph Petigax made two strong attempts
on the summit.

Their first attempt ended at 7107 metres and was succeeded by six days
of unremitting storm. Their second attempt took place in thick mist: 'They
knew they had to keep midway between a cornice to their right, and a great
crevasse to their left. The snow was soft and two foot deep. The gradient
steep. At each step they could feel no solid ground beneath them; at every
ominous creak of the snow they shied away from the crevasse and toward
the cornice, until the sight of dark fissures and a chill wind warned them
that they were hanging almost literally over the abyss. More than once they
heard, terrifyingly close, the crack of snow detaching itself from the slope
and slithering into the void. They could see no more than a few yards in
any direction, but realized that bottomless gulfs were opening up around
them.'[53]

The snow gave way to rocks which they scaled for two hours, only
to find not the summit ridge they had expected but more mist-shrouded
slopes. They had reached a height of 7503 metres – higher than anyone had
climbed before – and were only 150 metres from the summit, but it was
too risky to continue. If only they could see . . . They waited two hours for
the mists to clear, but in vain, and at 3.30 p.m. the Duke ordered a
retreat.

Meanwhile, other members of the expedition had been photographing
and surveying the region, valuable work which was of immense help to
subsequent expeditions.

There is no doubt that the Abruzzi expedition was the very model of
efficiency. What Whymper and Conway had shaped, the Duke brought to
perfection. He had climbed higher than anyone else, various members of
the party had lived at considerable altitude for long periods without ill-effect,
valuable survey and mapping work was done, the porters had worked har-
moniously even at altitude, and nobody was killed. As a bonus, but an

important one, the expedition was recorded in a very fine book by Filippo de Filippi.[54]

In future years, when the powers that controlled Himalayan endeavour compared Mummery's efforts on Nanga Parbat and the Duke's on K2, there is no doubt which was the favoured role model. Put crudely, the idea became fixed that a big peak needed a big expedition. It was to dominate Himalayan mountaineering for the next half-century or more.

CHAPTER FIFTEEN

No Fun at All

The war which ravaged Europe from 1914 to 1918 scarcely touched the mountains. Only in the Dolomites, where the Italians and Austrians faced one another, was there major fighting. There Alpine troops of both nations performed some incredible feats as they struggled for control of various limestone spires. Tunnels were dug, mines laid and tops blown off peaks in this most bizarre of all campaigns. Austria lost the war and the Dolomites, which became entirely Italian with the result that many of the peaks there have both German and Italian names.

Amongst the casualties were Geoffrey Winthrop Young who lost a leg and Sepp Innerkofler, of the famous guiding family, who was killed attacking an Italian observation post on the Paternkofel. Three-quarters of a century later the tunnels and trenches which still scar the rocks are popular outings for walkers and scramblers who like to combine history with adventure.

'Before 1914 a life lost on the mountains was a black mark against the sport. After the Somme, after Passchendaele, it was difficult to put the same value on human survival,' wrote the historian R.W. Clark, and he went on to attribute the excesses of the Munich School in the thirties to this. Along with other Europeans they were accused of 'giving greater value to success in the accomplishment of new and more difficult routes and less weight to the dangers'. This was undoubtedly true, but it had nothing to do with the late war. After all, those who took part in the most notorious ascents and attempts were still in kindergarten when the war ended.[1]

And why were the British not affected? They too had suffered a terrible war, yet there was no sign of any essential change in their mountaineering values. One must look elsewhere and deeper for the cause of the profound changes which were about to affect the shape of mountaineering.

After the war the majority of alpinists still followed traditional routes done in a traditional manner and progress was measured by overcoming routes which had previously defied all efforts. This meant essentially the great ridges and in the decade following the end of the war all the great ridges fell to strong, if traditional, parties. Curiously enough, at this late stage, they were all led by guides. First to go was the North-East Ridge of the Eiger – the famous Mittelegi – which had been descended as long ago as 1885, but wasn't climbed until the Japanese climber Yuko Maki with the guides Amatter, Steuri and Brawand made the ascent in 1921. This was not the first visit to the Alps by a Japanese climber but it was far and away the most significant and Maki returned home as something of a hero.

In 1927 another old favourite, which had also been descended previously, was climbed: the Hirondelles Ridge of the Grandes Jorasses. This time the party was an Italian one, led by the guide Adolphe Rey.[2] In the following year two great ridges were overcome and women took part in both climbs: Professor and Mrs Richards (Dorothy Pilley) led by Joseph Georges climbed the North-North-West Ridge of Dent Blanche and Miriam O'Brien with Bob Underhill climbed the South-East Ridge of Mont Blanc du Tacul (the formidable-looking Diable Ridge) led by Armand Charlet.

These were rock climbs in the main and in the case of the Hirondelles and the Dent Blanche the difficulties were rather concentrated, making the climb an uneven affair. Why these ridges were so long in being climbed is a bit of a mystery, for despite the thirty-six attempts made on the Hirondelles Ridge, neither it nor any of the others was any harder than similar ridges done in the past, such as the North-West Ridge of Blaitière done by Ryan and the Lochmatters in 1906 and nowhere near as hard as the Gspalten-horn's Rote Zähne Ridge which Young and Herford had done with Knubel and Brantschen in 1914.[3] There were, of course, numerous shorter and harder ridges in many parts of the Alps which continued to be climbed, but of the great ridges it wasn't until 1930, when Brendel and Schaller climbed the South Ridge of the Aiguille Noire de Peuterey, that the standard once again reached that set by Young and Herford.[4]

This great serrated rock ridge marching aggressively down from the Mont Blanc massif towards the Italian Val Veni was a triumph for the Munich School and many of the leading European climbers were eager to repeat it: Gervasutti, Boccalatte, Devies, Grivel and Pietrasanta were amongst those who succeeded. The climb became an Alpine test-piece of the first order and eighteen ascents had been made by the eve of the Second World War. André Roch pointed out that of the first thirty people to climb the ridge more than half were later killed in the mountains, including both Brendel and Schaller.

Meanwhile, Bob Underhill took the skills he had learned from Armand Charlet on the Diable Ridge back to the Tetons. Underhill was a philosophy professor at Harvard who took a rigorous view of climbing: nothing should interrupt the concentration on technique; neither beauty nor nature, he said. In 1929 the Tetons had become a National Park, but little mountaineer-ing had been done there since the first ascent of Grand Teton in 1898. That year Underhill and Kenneth Henderson, both members of the prestigious Appalachian Mountain Club, visited the range and climbed the East Ridge, which Underhill compared with the Zmutt of the Matterhorn. They also made the acquaintance of two park rangers, Phil Smith and Fritiof Fryxell, who were good climbers. In the following season these four climbed Mount Moran, the last unclimbed summit of the Tetons.

In 1931 two parties converged on the Grand Teton simultaneously. One was Underhill, Smith and Frank Truslow, intent on the first ascent of the South-East Ridge – now the Underhill Ridge – and the other a couple of Austrian climbers being guided on the ordinary route by local guide Paul Petzoldt, aided by a teenage student called Glenn Exum. As they climbed up the tedious lower part of their route Petzoldt pointed out a ledge higher up (now known as Wall Street) that led to the middle of the unclimbed South Ridge, up which it might be possible to reach the top. When they arrived at the ledge Exum decided to give it a try and he set off nonchalantly to solo the ridge, armed with very little climbing experience and wearing football boots!

At first the ledge seemed easy going but then, just before the ridge was reached, it broke away in a fearful gap. There did not seem to the youngster any possibility of climbing across, so screwing up his courage, he made a mighty leap . . . and landed safely. The ridge itself gave splendid climbing until a smooth slab blocked the way. Exum inched up this, his football boots scraping desperately for purchase, until at last he was able to grasp good holds and pull himself to safety. Not without reason the slab is now called the Friction Pitch.

The ridge became the Exum Ridge. Five years later Jack Durrance and Kenneth Henderson added the lower, more difficult part of the ridge, to give the direct route.

The year 1931 was an exceptional one in the Tetons, the driest for forty years. There had been little snow cover the previous winter and the rocks were good to the touch. Underhill decided to make use of the conditions to examine the North Ridge and Face, something he had set his mind to. He had done previous reconnaissances and now, aided by Fryxell, determined to have a go.

Fryxell's gear had not arrived at their camp and he was forced to make the attempt in work boots which were not even a pair: one had a rubber sole and the other smooth leather. This does not seem to have worried him.

They were stopped by the fearsome Chockstone Chimney. At first they tried to overcome it by combined tactics, with Fryxell standing on Underhill's head, but that failed and eventually Underhill used a piton which he stood on to overcome the pitch. It was the crux of the route and the route itself was for the time the crux of American climbing. It was not repeated for five years, until Fritz Wiessner made the first unaided ascent of the Chockstone Chimney.

Of these Teton climbers, Underhill, Henderson, Durrance and Wiessner were all European-trained and, though there was a world of difference between the first two and the second two, as we shall see later, they all grafted European techniques and traditions onto native American derring-do as exhibited by Exum. Thirty years later the exchange was to flow the other way!

Further north, in Alaska and Canada, the climbing was still largely in an expeditionary stage. Barely half of the fifty highest peaks in Canada had been climbed by the end of the First World War[5] and even as late as 1923 only two out of the top four peaks had had ascents: Robson and Columbia. Not only were there great ridges to be climbed, but great peaks too awaited their first ascent.

None more so than Mount Alberta. This impressive mountain of 11,870 feet lies between the Lynx and Habel Creeks of the Athabasca River which drains from the Columbia Icefields. On its eastern side it forms a great wedge of dirty-grey limestone, like the upturned blade of a woodman's axe, ribboned across with ice and snow patches, in between which are tiers of steep crags. It is unprepossessing to look at and becomes more so on closer acquaintance: the ledges are covered with detritus, the rock is fractured into millions of loose pieces whose adherence to the mountain is at best uncertain. 'Every grip had a tendency to remain in the hand', as one of the first ascentionists graphically put it.

Alberta can now be reached in a day from the Banff–Jasper highway but earlier this century it required a six-day trek from Jasper towards the headwaters of the Athabasca. In July 1925 Yuko Maki with a party of five other Japanese climbers set out on this trek, led by five packer-guides and supported by thirty-nine horses, carrying enough gear for a month's expedition. In Jasper, Maki had engaged two Swiss guides who were stationed there, Heinrich Fuhrer and Hans Kohler, and had also swept up into the party a Swiss amateur, Jean Weber.[6]

Maki, who four years previously had climbed the Mittelegi Ridge of the Eiger, had been surprised, when studying a recent guidebook to the Rockies, to discover that Mount Alberta was unclimbed. It seemed a reasonable objective for a modest expedition.[7]

On July 20 the party established camp on a meadow at 6800 feet at the head of the Habel Creek and in good weather they reconnoitred possible routes of ascent. They decided that the South-East Flank was the only possibility.

Next day they were up well before first light scrambling up steep slopes of rubble. As dawn emerged on another fine day they started tackling the steep bands of rock which encircle the mountain, finding them even looser than they suspected. Stones rattled down, and Hashimoto was struck on the face. When he touched his cheek the white glove he was wearing was stained crimson. 'First blood!' he declared solemnly. The others laughed in nervous reaction.

They rose higher, gradually approaching the steep headwall which they realised might be the crux. Access was by means of a narrow ledge along which they had to balance largely without benefit of handholds since the rock was so rotten. At the end of this traverse they climbed some pinnacles then came to a fifteen-foot overhang utterly devoid of holds. Fuhrer decided that the only way to overcome it was by a human ladder and so Hayakawa, the expedition doctor, who was the biggest and strongest of the party, unroped and braced himself against the wall, balanced on a tiny ledge. Hans Kohler also unroped and climbed onto Hayakawa's shoulders and finally Fuhrer climbed up the human ladder and after a considerable testing of the dubious holds above, managed to pull himself up. The whole party watched nervously whilst this was going on, conscious that they were only 'anchored to imaginary holds', as Weber put it. Once he was established, Fuhrer pulled each up in turn and they swung free at the overhang like rag dolls.

By four in the afternoon they had reached the summit ridge, long and sharp, armed with cornices, which took them a further three and a half hours to negotiate. But at last, sixteen hours after leaving camp, they stood on the summit of Mount Alberta. They shook hands and Yuko Maki thanked the Swiss for their help. He wrote a note which he concealed in the cairn the party constructed and, topping all, they left a ceremonial ice axe, pointing to the sky.[8]

The tired but exultant party began their descent but were forced to bivouac on the summit ridge at about 11,000 feet. Fortunately the night was fine and they suffered no ill effects. They started again at 5.30 a.m. and though they used four pitons to set up abseils to speed their descent, it was another sixteen hours before they were off the mountain.

'They are to be congratulated upon their good fortune in snatching a victory when this austere peak was off guard,' said the *Alpine Journal* sniffily – but then the man who wrote that, Howard Palmer, had himself failed on Alberta just a short time before. Ironically perhaps, Palmer was the co-author of the very guide which had inspired the Japanese in the first place.

Several attempts were made to repeat the Japanese climb on Mount Alberta but it was twenty-three years before anyone succeeded. In 1948 John Oberlin and Fred Ayres, two strong American climbers, reached the top.

Just as the Americans were influenced by Robert Underhill and others who had trained in the European Alps, so too in Canada was there European influence, not only because climbers like Val Fynn had spent much time there, but also because there was a considerable corpus of European guides in the Canadian climbing centres. This had begun at the end of the last century and continued for many years. Fuhrer and Kohler were two such, and there was Aemmer, the Feuz (father and son), Niederer, Grassi and others, but the undoubted doyen was Conrad Kain.

Like many Canadian guides, Kain came from Austria originally and had travelled widely before he settled in Canada. In 1913 with a railway engineer called William Foster and an ex-captain from the US Navy called Albert MacCarthy he made the first ascent of Mount Robson, the highest peak in the Canadian Rockies. Then, in 1916 he climbed the Howser and Bugaboo Spires in the Purcell Range, first ascents amongst granite needles which rivalled anything at Chamonix.

Kain spent the summers guiding in Canada and the winters guiding in New Zealand. Though undoubtedly a fine climber, there were those who thought him too rash, but this might have been due to his somewhat flamboyant character and liking for telling tall stories. He had the good fortune to have as clients many of the leading American and Canadian climbers of the time, such as MacCarthy and Thorington.[9]

It is reasonable to maintain that by the end of the 1920s the climbing world was an ordered place with strong traditions that had begun in the Alps but had been spread throughout the world. The cult of the guide was still strong, the cult of ridge climbing even stronger. The aim was always to probe the natural weakness of the mountain in the safest possible way. Difficulty was strongly distinguished from foolhardiness.

All this was to change.

The great change that began in mountaineering in the 1930s has been attributed to the struggle for the great north walls and the furore this caused in the bastions of tradition. The walls certainly were involved but only because they were the stage upon which a new philosophy was played out. And even the philosophy wasn't all that new; it was merely an extension of what Lammer and Lorria believed in, which was that the mountain mustn't be allowed to dictate events. *Sturm und Drang* must be conquered, man must become superman, and then he will win through, despite all odds. Earlier attempts on Alpine walls had also suffered from storm, loose rock and the rattle of falling stones, but always they were to be feared and those who risked such dangers often apologised for acting so foolishly. The achievements were often the same; it was the attitude which was to become different. Nor did the men of the 1930s invent wall climbing.

Alpine walls (or faces) had been the subject of attack from pioneering days and, even leaving aside pure rock climbs like Young's East Face of the Grépon (1911), there had been some astonishing attempts and even ascents of great mixed walls long before the Munich School arose.

It is necessary to look at some of these to gain a proper background to the story of the Eigerwand and other famous walls covered in the next chapter. I have already described how Ferdinand Imseng provoked (or inspired) his employers into climbing the huge East Face of Monte Rosa as early as 1872 and the even more remarkable exploit on the West Face of the Matterhorn when Penhall gave chase to Mummery in 1879. Each of these routes has stonefall or avalanche dangers which cannot be avoided and both were the scene of serious accidents when others tried to repeat them. There was, too, Mummery's guideless attempt on the North Face of the Plan in 1892 with its successful retreat, a climb not achieved until 1924. None of these routes was particularly difficult in the technical sense, despite their objective dangers.

The 1890 season of Ludwig Norman-Neruda with his great guide Christian Klucker marks a more distinct starting-point, for amongst the climbs done that year by this talented pair were three north walls of considerable difficulty. The first was the North-East Face of the Piz Bernina, done in poor conditions and finished in the teeth of a storm. This large face had, in fact, been climbed by a similar but more dangerous route as early as 1879 by J.M. Ludwig, with the talented guide Hans Grass and Abraham Arduser. The Klucker route became the accepted climb, though it wasn't repeated until 1911 and after that not until 1931.

A month later, in July 1890, the same pair climbed the North-East Face of Piz Roseg, also in the Bernina group. This large face has since attracted a number of harder variations, but even so the Klucker route was not repeated until 1924.

Then in August came the ascent of the North-East Face of Lyskamm, in the Pennine Alps, when they were accompanied by the Tyrolean Joseph Reinstadler as second guide. Klucker was loath to approach local guides in Zermatt for fear of giving away his plans for the face, which was a much desired prize. It had been attempted unsuccessfully by von Kuffner, a leading Viennese climber, and the great Alexander Burgener. As it was, when they left the Riffelberg Hotel at 1.30 a.m. on August 9, Klucker was annoyed to find that another strong party was heading for the Lyskamm. They were none other than the guides Emile Rey and J.B. Bich, with Katherine Richardson but, as it turned out, they were going for a different route entirely and so the face was left to Klucker.

The North-East Face of Lyskamm is 700 metres high. It is almost entirely composed of snow and ice slopes at sixty degrees or so and guarded by sérac barriers high up, which occasionally break away and sweep down with awesome ferocity. But in the centre of the face, directly below the East, and highest, Summit is an incipient rock rib which offers some protection.

Klucker headed straight for the rib, though Reinstadler, a poor rock climber, objected. He wanted to climb the technically much easier snow on the left but Klucker would have none of it, pointing out the danger of the séracs. Difficulty was preferable to danger, in Klucker's opinion, and this perhaps sets his climb apart from later North Face climbs done by the Munich School: when Welzenbach came to climb the North-East Face of Lyskamm he ignored the rib and chose to risk the séracs.

Even so it was a risky business. They reached the summit at 2.30 p.m.

'It was a grim but satisfying victory,' Klucker commented later, 'if one can so describe an act of folly.' The climb was not repeated for twenty years.[10]

Even closer to the modern north-face climb was the North-East Face of the Finsteraarhorn in the Bernese Oberland. This huge Oberland face is 1070 metres high and has a prominent rib which seems to offer a logical route, but it tempts to deceive. The rib is a series of broken towers, one of which, high on the face, is called the Grey Tower and is very difficult. Climbers are forced to the side of the rib where there is constant stonefall. The rock is consistently rotten. It has all the ingredients of a classic *Nordwand*, yet it was attempted as early as 1892, and by a woman.

Gertrude Bell was no ordinary lady. Later to become a famous Arabist and archaeologist she was, around the turn of the century, an exceptionally daring mountaineer. She made the first systematic exploration of the Engelhorner peaks in 1901 and 1902 (Gertrude's Peak is named after her) and the first traverse of the Lauteraarhorn–Schreckhorn (1902). According to her guide, Ulrich Fuhrer, there were very few climbers who could surpass her in skill and none to equal her coolness, bravery and judgement.

At the end of July 1902, Miss Bell with Ulrich Fuhrer and his brother Heinrich set out from the Dollfuss Hut at 1.35 a.m. In a letter to her father, written immediately after the climb, she describes vividly what happened:

> Crossed the séracs just at dawn and by 6 found ourselves comfortably established on the arête, beyond the reach of the stones which the mountain had fired at us (fortunately with rather a bad aim) for the first half-hour on the rock. We breakfasted, then followed a difficult and dangerous climb. It was difficult because the rocks were exceedingly steep, every now and then we had to creep up and out of the common hard chimney – one in particular about mid-day, I remember, because we subsequently had the very deuce of a time coming down it, or around the face of a tower or cut our way across an ice couloir between two gendarmes and it was dangerous because the whole rock was so treacherous. I found this out very early in the morning by putting my hand into the crack of a rock which looked as if it went into the very foundations of things. About 2 feet square of rock tumbled out upon me and knocked me a little way down the hill till I managed to part company with it on a tiny ledge. I got back on to my feet without being pulled up by the rope, which was as well for a little later I happened to pass the rope through my hands and found that it had been cut half through about a yard from my waist when the rock had fallen on it. This was rather a nuisance as it shortened a rope we often wanted long to allow of our going up difficult chimneys in turn. So on and on we went up the arête and the towers multiplied like

rabbits above and grew steeper and steeper and about 2 o'clock I looked round and saw great black clouds rolling up from the west. But by this time looking up we also saw the topmost tower of the arête far above us still, and the summit of the mountain further still and though we could not yet see what the top of the arête was like we were cheered and pushed on steadily for another hour while the weather signs got worse and worse. At 3 just as the first snow flakes began to fall, we got into full view of the last two gendarmes – and the first one was quite impossible. The ridge had been growing narrow, its sides steeper as we mounted, so that we had been obliged for some time to stick quite to the backbone of it; then it threw itself up into a great tower leaning over to the right and made of slabs set like slates on the top with a steep drop of some 20 feet below them on to the col. We were then 1000 feet below the summit I should guess, perhaps rather less, anyway we could see our way up, not easy but possible, above this tower and once on the top we could get down the other side in any weather. It had to be tried: we sat down to eat a few mouthfuls, the snow falling fast, driven by a strong wind, and a thick mist marching up the valley below, over the Finsteraar joch, then we crept along the knife edge of a col, fastened a rope firmly round a rock and let Ulrich down on to a ledge below the overhang of the tower. He tried it for a few moments and then gave it up. The ledge was very narrow, sloped outwards and was quite rotten. Anything was better than that. So we tried the left side of the tower: there was a very steep iced couloir running up at the foot of the rock on that side for about 50 feet, after which all would be well. Again we let ourselves down on the extra rope to the foot of the tower, again to find that this way also was impossible. A month later in the year I believe this couloir would go; after a warm August there would be no ice in it, and though it is very steep the rocks, so far as one could see under the ice, looked climbable. But even with the alternative before us of the descent down the terrible arête, we decided to turn back; already the snow was blowing down the couloir in a small avalanche, small but blinding, and the wind rushed down upon us carrying the mists with it. If it had been fine weather we should have tried down the arête a little and then a traverse so as to get at the upper rocks by another road. I am not sure that it could be done but we should have tried anything – but by the time we had been going down for half-an-hour we could see nothing of the mountain side to the right or to the left except an occasional glimpse as one cloud rolled off and another rolled over. The snow fell fast and covered the rocks with incredible speed. Difficult as they had been to go up, you may imagine what they were like going down when we could no longer so much as see them. There was one corner in particular where we had to get round the face of a tower.

We came round the corner, down a very steep chimney, got on to a sloping out rock ledge with an inch of new snow on it; there was a crack in which you could stand and with one hand hold in the rock face, from whence you had to drop down about 8 feet on to steep snow. We fixed the extra rope and tumbled down one after the other on to the snow; it was really more or less safe because one had the fixed rope to hold on to, but it felt awful: I shall remember every inch of that rock face for the rest of my life. It was now near 6. Our one idea was to get down to the chimney – the mid-day chimney which was so very difficult – so as to do it while there was still only a little snow on it. We toiled on till 8, by which time a furious thunderstorm was raging. We were standing by a great upright on the top of a tower when suddenly it gave a crack and a blue flame sat on it for a second, just like the one we saw when we were driving, you remember, only nearer. My ice axe jumped in my hand and I thought the steel felt hot through my woollen glove – was that possible? I didn't take my glove off to see! Before we knew where we were the rock flashed again – it was a great sticking out stone and I expect it attracted the lightning, but we didn't stop to consider this theory but tumbled down a chimney as hard as ever we could, one on top of the other, buried our ice axe heads in some shale at the bottom of it and hurriedly retreated from them. It's not nice to carry a private lightning conductor in your hand in the thick of a thunderstorm. It was clear we could go no further that night, the question was to find the best lodging while there was still light enough to see. We hit upon a tiny crack sheltered from the wind, even the snow did not fall into it. There was just room for me to sit in the extreme back of it on a very pointed bit of rock; by doubling up I could even get my head into it. Ulrich sat on my feet to keep them warm and Heinrich just below him. They each of them put their feet into a knapsack which is the golden rule of bivouac. The other golden rule is to take no brandy because you feel the reaction more after. I knew this and insisted on it. It was really not so bad; we shivered all night but our hands and feet were warm and climbers are like Pobbles in the matter of toes. I went to sleep quite often and was wakened up every hour or so by the intolerable discomfort of my position, which I then changed by an inch or two into another which was bearable for an hour more. At first the thunderstorm made things rather exciting. The claps followed the flashes so close that there seemed no interval between them. We tied ourselves firmly on to the rock above lest as Ulrich philosophically said one of us should be struck and fall out. The rocks were all crackling round us and fizzing like damp wood which is just beginning to burn – have you ever heard that? It's a curious exciting sound rather exhilarating – and as there was no further precaution possible I enjoyed the extraordinary magnificence of the storm with a free mind: it was worth seeing. Gradually the night cleared and became beautifully starry. Between 2 and 3 the moon rose, a tiny crescent, and we spoke of the joy it would be when the sun rose full on to us and stopped our shivering. But the sun never rose at all – at least for all practical purposes. The day came wrapped in a blinding mist and heralded by a cutting, snow-laden wind – this day was Friday; we never saw the sun in it. It must have snowed a good deal during the thunderstorm for when we stepped out of our crack in the first grey light about 4 (too stiff to bear it a moment longer) everything was deep in it. I can scarcely describe to you what that day was like. We were from 4 a.m. to 8 p.m. on the arête; during that time we ate for a minute or two 3 times and my fare I know was 5 gingerbread biscuits, 2 sticks of chocolate, a slice of bread, a scrap of cheese and a handful of raisins. We had nothing to drink but about two tablespoonfuls of brandy in the bottom of my flask and a mouthful of wine in the guides' wine skin, but it was too cold to feel thirsty. There was scarcely a yard which we could come down without the extra rope; you can imagine the labour of finding a rock at every 50 feet round which to sling it, then of pulling it down behind us and slinging it again. We had our bit of good luck – it never caught all day. But both the ropes were thoroughly iced and terribly difficult to manage, and the weather was appalling. It snowed all day sometimes softly as decent snow should fall, sometimes driven by a furious bitter wind which enveloped us not only in the falling snow, but lifted all the light powdery snow from the rocks and sent it whirling down the precipices and into the couloirs and on to us indifferently. It was rather interesting to see the way a mountain behaves in a snowstorm and how avalanches are born and all the wonderful and terrible things that happen in high places. The couloirs were all running with snow rivers – we had to cross one and a nasty uncomfortable process it was. As soon as you cut a step it was filled up before you could put your foot into it. But I think that when things are as bad as ever they can be you cease to mind them much. You set your teeth and battle with the fates; we meant to get down whatever happened and it was such an exciting business that we had no time to think of the discomfort. I know I never thought of the danger except once and then quite calmly. I'll tell you about that presently. The first thing we had to tackle was the chimney. We had to fix our rope in it twice, the second time round a very unsafe nail. I stood in this place holding Heinrich, there was an overhang. He climbed a bit of the way and then fell on to soft snow and spun down the couloir till my rope brought him up with a jerk. Then he got up on to a bit of rock on the left about half as high as the overhang. Ulrich came down to me and I repeated Heinrich's process exactly, the iced extra rope slipping through my hands like butter. Then came Ulrich. He was held by Heinrich and me standing a good deal to the left but only half as high up as he. He climbed down to the place we had both fallen from asking our advice at every step, then he called out 'Heinrich, Heinrich, ich bin verloren,' and tumbled off just as we had done and we held him up in the couloir, more dead than alive with anxiety. We gave him some of our precious brandy on a piece of sugar and he soon recovered and went on as boldly as before. We thought the worst was over but there was a more dangerous place to come. It was a place that had been pretty difficult to go up, a steep but short slope of iced rock by which we had turned the base of a tower. The slope was now covered with about 4 inches of avalanche snow and the rocks were quite hidden. It was on the edge of a big couloir down which raced a snow river. We managed badly somehow; at any rate, Ulrich and I found ourselves on a place where there was not room for us both to stand, at the end of the extra rope. He was very insecure and could not hold me, Heinrich was below on the edge of the couloir, also very insecure. And here I had to refix the extra rope on a rock a little below me so that it was practically no good to me. But it was the only possible plan. The rock was too difficult for me, the stretches too big, I couldn't reach them: I handed my axe down to Heinrich and told him I could do nothing but fall, but he couldn't, or at any rate, didn't secure himself and in a second we were both tumbling head over heels down the couloir, which was, you understand, as steep as snow could lie. How Ulrich held us I don't know. He said himself he would not have believed it possible but hearing me say I was going to fall he had stuck the pointed end of the ice axe into a crack above and on this alone we all three held. I got on to my feet in the snow directly I came to the end of my leash of rope and held Heinrich and caught his ice axe and mine and we slowly cut ourselves back up the couloir to the foot of the rock. But it was a near thing and I felt rather ashamed of my part in it. This was the time when I thought it on the cards we should not get down alive. Rather a comforting example, however, of how little can hold a party up. About 2 in the afternoon we all began to feel tired. I had a pain through my shoulder and down my back which was due, I think, to nothing but the exertion of rock climbing and the nervous fatigue of shivering – for we never stopped shivering all day, it was impossible to control one's tired muscles in that bitter cold. And so we went on for six hours more of which only the last hour was easy and at 8 found ourselves at the top of the Finsteraar glacier and in the dark, with a good guess and good luck, happened on the right place in the Bergschrund and let ourselves down over it. It was now quite dark, the snow had turned into pouring rain, and we sank six inches into the soft glacier with every step. Moreover we were wet through: we had to cross several big crevasses and get down the sérac before we could reach the Unteraar glacier and safety. For this we had felt no anxiety having relied upon our lantern but not a single match would light. We had every kind with us in metal match boxes but the boxes were wet and we had not a dry rag of any kind to rub them with. We tried to make a tent out of my skirt and to light a match under it, but our fingers were dripping wet and numb with cold – one could scarcely feel anything smaller than an ice axe – and the match heads dropped off limply into the snow without so much as a spark. Then we tried to go on and after a few steps Heinrich fell into a soft place almost up to his neck and Ulrich and I had to pull him out with the greatest difficulty and the mists swept up over the glacier and hid everything; that was the only moment of despair. We had so looked forward to dry blankets in the Pavillon Dollfuss and here we were with another night out before us. And a much worse one than the first, for we were on the shelterless glacier and in driving drenching rain. We laid our three axes together and sat on them side by side. Ulrich and I put our feet into a sack but Heinrich refused to use the other and gave it to me to lie on. My shoulders ached and ached. I insisted on our all eating something even the smallest scrap, and then I put a wet pocket-handkerchief over my face to keep the rain from beating on it and went to sleep. It sounds incredible but I think we all slept more or less and woke up to the horrible discomfort and went to sleep again. We couldn't see the time but long before we expected it a sort of grey light came over the snow and when at last I could read my watch, behold it was 4. We gathered ourselves up; at first we could scarcely stand but after a few steps we began to walk quite creditably. About 6 we got to where we could unrope – having been forty-eight hours on the rope – and we reached here at 10 on Saturday.''

All three participants in this extraordinary adventure suffered frostbite of the hands and feet and though she soon recovered, Gertrude Bell did little climbing thereafter. Some years later Ulrich Fuhrer in describing the climb had no doubt that the honour belonged to Gertrude Bell. 'Had she not been full of courage and determination we must have perished,' he said.[12]

The North-East Face of the Finsteraarhorn was climbed in 1904 by Gustav Hasler and the guide Fritz Amatter. They started with a bivouac at the foot of the face and reached the summit at 6.30 p.m., following the rib. The Grey Tower was passed on the left by first descending an icy gully with the aid of a fixed rope which they left in place in case they had to retreat,[13] then climbing difficult slabs. They were disconcerted to find that above the tower the climbing was almost as hard. Fortunately the weather was good during their ascent and there was no stonefall, but it was a considerable *tour de force*.

In 1905 the Canadian climber Val Fynn and his companion A. Bruderlin made the first guideless ascent during which they were forced to bivouac twice, the second time sitting in slings, dangling from a chimney – shades of things to come indeed! When the guide Adolf Rübi made the third ascent in 1930, with his brother Fritz and Miss Miriam O'Brien, he said the climbing 'approaches the limits of possibility and for over 100 m. was just flirting with death'. Miriam O'Brien herself, one of the best climbers of the inter-war years, said of it: 'It is the only climb I have ever done which I cannot think about with pleasure. Not that this was the only occasion in the mountains when I have ever been frightened, but it was the occasion when I was most badly frightened, and for the longest period. I may as well admit that I haven't the kind of courage it takes to do such climbs as that. Fun, to my mind, is the only reason for climbing mountains, and the northeast face of the Finsteraarhorn was not fun.'[14]

The direct ascent of the Grey Tower was not achieved until 1967, by two Polish climbers, K. Glazek and K. Zdzitowiecki. The crux was a fifty-metre GrVI crack.

Another early face climb of a standard and character which compares with those of later times, was the South-West Face of the Täschhorn, described in Chapter 8. The face is 900 metres high, ribbed and fluted, with one particularly large central gully which splits into two higher up leaving a diamond-shaped headwall. The rock is friable and in most seasons the stonefall is constant. 'There are more difficult climbs,' said André Roch, who made the third ascent in 1943, 'but none more treacherous or dangerous.' The first ascent was done in 1906 by Ryan, Young, the Lochmatter brothers and Josef Knubel. 'It is the sort of climb one does only once in a lifetime,' said Knubel. It is still TD/TDsup.

CHAPTER SIXTEEN

A Star in the East

In his book *The Making of a Mountaineer*, published in 1924, George Finch
wrote: 'One of the younger generation of mountain climbers once complained bitterly to me that there were no new climbs to be done in the Alps
... To his surprise I replied that ... the fattest and best grains remained
for the man of today who knew where to look.' Finch went on to warn,
'... but the successful climbing of these must be preceded by careful and
patient investigation.'

The previous summer Finch had climbed the North Face of the Dent
d'Hérens, a mountain which hides behind the Matterhorn above Zermatt
and is totally overshadowed by the latter peak's flamboyance. Finch had
followed his own precept, he had studied the Dent d'Hérens carefully for
several years before making his attempt, calculating the dangers, probing
the weaknesses. The main problem is immediately apparent, that the whole
face is an ice wall which has fractured half-way up and that the lower half
has subsequently collapsed into a great sérac barrier. Above the barrier there
is a curious kind of ice ledge, slanting up from right to left and crossing
the entire face.

It was in this ledge that Finch saw the key to the face. He worked out a
plan to get onto the ledge at its lower north-western end, follow it up and
across the face and, by reaching the East Ridge, gain the summit. Aided by
Guy Forster and Raymond Peto this is precisely what he did.

Had Finch climbed the North Face? By his own lights he had: he had
studied the problem and solved it. On the other hand he had let the problem
dictate the solution. The face had shown him clearly that there was no way
straight up it, therefore he had to find an alternative solution. But there
were some to whom this was no solution at all. The face – any face – had
to go from base to summit and the problem was to *make* it go by whatever
means possible. 'The perfect line is that taken by a stone dropped from the
summit' was how the Italian climber Riccardo Cassin defined it.

Two years after Finch climbed the North Face of the Dent d'Hérens a
twenty-five-year-old climber from Munich called Willo Welzenbach, with
his companion Eugen Allwein, climbed the face from bottom to top in
sixteen hours, up ice slopes of sixty and seventy degrees: 'Smooth polished
rocks alternated with bare ice. Belay stances were completely non-existent.
Anyhow, what use would any belay have been in the event of ice avalanches
thundering down?'[1]

The climbing was difficult, the danger considerable, yet the two young Germans judged both to be acceptable and were proved right. Nothing could better illustrate the difference between the traditional way and the Munich School way of tackling a face than Finch and Welzenbach's attempts on the Dent d'Hérens.

The British climbing establishment regarded this sort of thing as outrageous. Commenting on two of Welzenbach's climbs, the editor of the *Alpine Journal*, Colonel E.L. Strutt, said: 'Both the Fiescherhorn and Dent d'Hérens expeditions, as accomplished by Dr Welzenbach, being on faces completely and continuously raked by ice and stones, as opposed to the ribs and ridges traversed in the original climbs, come under the category of foolish variations. We were tempted to employ a harsher term.'[2] Of course, it was the earlier routes which were really the variations in that they avoided the problem, but again we have the two schools of thought plainly laid out. Where there are risks which cannot be avoided, one school said such risks should not be taken, no matter how attractive the potential climb. The other turned the problem round and said the route should be attempted, taking all possible precautions. In the Alps between the wars, it was to become the outstanding moral dilemma.

Though German climbers came in for most of the early *Alpine Journal* criticism, the Groupe de Haute Montagne (GHM) formed by young French climbers was not averse to pushing the limits and tackling north faces. In 1924 J. Lagarde, J. de Lepiney and H. de Ségogne made the first ascent of the North Face of the Plan, by a particularly difficult route, thus solving the problem that Mummery had failed on,[3] and the normally blameless Swiss in the person of E.R. Blanchet made two attempts on the Matterhorn North Face[4] whilst André Roch and R. Gréloz climbed the difficult Triolet North Face and made a sensational descent of the Dru North Face, using hundreds of metres of rope, and incurring the wrath of the *Alpine Journal*. 'This degradation of the peak is undoubtedly the most revolting and unsportsmanlike travesty of mountaineering yet reported in this journal,' thundered Colonel Strutt.

The outstanding traditional climber of this time was the Swiss dentist, Hans Lauper, a man who combined all the qualities of a Victorian mountaineer with the pioneering spirit of the Munich School. Like Welzenbach, Lauper concentrated on the great walls of the Bernese Alps and between 1915 and 1932 he made eighteen difficult first ascents, including the North Faces of Stockhorn, Kamm, Mönch, Jungfrau and Eiger. Each was executed in a single day, which is testimony to the man's strength and ability, and to the meticulous planning which went into every route.

It is said of Lauper that he climbed like an automaton, with never a pause or hitch. Despite the rotten Oberland rock, no hold ever came away in his hands and he never kicked a stone down; even on glaciers his rope was kept away from the snow in textbook fashion. Other climbers found him rather dull company! As for his preparation, this could take years, with the proposed face reconnoitred and photographed from every possible angle. His greatest achievement – the Lauper Route on the Eiger – was conceived in 1923 but not executed until 1932.

The North Face of the Eiger is divided into two parts by a big spur. On the right of this is the Eigerwand – the North Face proper – on the left the North-East Face, steep slopes of rock and ice descending from the Mittelegi Ridge of the mountain. It was this face, and the rib, that Lauper decided to climb. As companions he had Alfred Zurcher and the two guides, Josef Knubel (Young's famous guide) and Alexander Graven. It was a very strong party.

They set off from Kleine Scheidegg at 1.50 a.m. on Saturday, August 20, 1932, and tramped for two hours through the darkness towards the vast, towering wall of the Eiger. At 3.40 a.m. they put on the ropes and began their climb, Graven and Lauper leading, Zurcher and Knubel following. They traversed east, across the little Hoheneiss Glacier until they were immediately below the Mittelegi Hut, perched on the ridge far above. From here they began a diagonal line up the face towards the great rib. Hardly had they started, however, than there was an ominous rattle of stones overhead, probably caused by parties starting the ridge climb. They shouted warnings and the stones ceased – it was the only stonefall they encountered on the whole expedition, and very different from what happened later on the Eigerwand.

By six o'clock they had arrived at a ledge which gave them views of a great rock buttress they had to overcome in order to reach the upper face. Lauper had feared this might be unclimbable, but now they were delighted to discover that the rock was split by a big crack and, though this proved difficult, they were on top of the rock by 8.36 a.m. and taking a well-earned rest of half an hour.

The crack was the key to the upper face. Above lay very steep snow slopes which had to be traversed in order to reach the north rib. There was no protection on this exposed section, no chance of holding a slip. As they gingerly inched across, Knubel was heard to remark, 'We are all of us a bit crazy!'

By noon the traverse was completed. After a little food, they started up the rib, finding it much harder than they expected. In order to expedite matters, when they came to rock barriers Graven would climb first then, leaving Lauper below, would have Knubel and Zurcher join him, so that they could use the stretched rope as extra handholds. The final rocks proved to be the crux, climbed by an ice-filled overhanging crack, horribly loose and rotten. Above it, simple snow slopes led to the summit which they reached at 4 p.m.

It was an astonishing climb, done in a day, by traditional methods. When, a few years later, climbers were dying on the Eigerwand and the Grandes Jorasses, the Lauper Route was held up by the establishment as a shining beacon in a sea of despair.[5]

As for the British, their contribution to the Alpine scene was muted, and the only climbers who did anything remotely comparable to Lauper's efforts were themselves strong-minded individuals who were likely to give the censorious Strutt as good as he gave. One such was R.W. Lloyd, a wealthy industrialist described as having 'often provoked controversy by his hard and unaccommodating outlook', who made the direct ascent of the North Face of the Bionnassay with the guides Josef and Adolf Pollinger. Lloyd was fifty-eight years old at this time and though the route is not to be compared with the great north faces as to difficulty, it was only the last in Lloyd's various adventures. He and the Pollingers had made the first ascent of the Col de Bionnassay by its North Face (just to the left of the peak) in 1919 and had failed in an attempt on the dangerous West Face of the Zermatt Breithorn in 1911.[6]

But the two men who made the greatest British contribution to Alpine climbing between the wars were Graham Brown and Frank Smythe. It was an odd, fortuitous partnership that occurred in 1927 when Brown, forty-five years old and with only three years of Alpine experience, was thrown into the company of Smythe, a dashing twenty-seven-year-old alpinist of the highest class. They could hardly have been more different, except in one thing: both were strong-minded, opinionated characters, quick to take offence.

It was Smythe's first year of mountain freedom. He had thrown up his engineering career to become a writer and photographer specialising in the mountain scene, and a very successful one as events turned out.[7] That season with J.H.B. Bell, a fine Scottish climber, he had made the second ascent of the Ryan–Lochmatter route on the Plan (twenty-one years after the first ascent), followed the gritstone climber George Bower up the Knubel Crack of the Grépon and done the Old Brenva. Brown was not in the same class as an alpinist, but he was strong, and he had come to the Alps with a vision: he wanted to climb the Brenva Face of Mont Blanc.

Though the Brenva Wall is south-facing, it has many of the qualities of a nordwand. It is big, steep and avalanche-prone. It sweeps round in an arc above the Brenva Glacier, from the Brenva Ridge (the Old Brenva) on the right to the Peuterey Ridge on the left, here marked by a huge buttress known as the Eckpfeiler or Grand Pilier d'Angle. It is some 4000 feet high. There is a large central couloir and ribs which are almost lost in the vastness of the face but which offer routes to the top for those determined enough to take them. One such, now called Route Major, is on the left of the couloir and it was this that Brown wanted to try.

It was a bold ambition for an Alpine novice and not one that Smythe agreed with. He simply wanted to make a variation to the Old Brenva climb, but in the event they settled on a compromise which lay between the two: a twisting rib marked at its foot by a big red rock, the Sentinelle Rouge, after which they named the climb. It went without a hitch and by late afternoon they were on the summit of Mont Blanc, having made the first breach in the Brenva Wall.

Any satisfaction which they got out of the climb was soon lost in bickering. Smythe made it plain that the route was his creation and that but for him Brown would not have got up the climb at all. Brown, peeved at not doing the Route Major, objected to Smythe's published descriptions of the climb. Neither man wanted to climb with the other ever again.

Yet the lure of the Route Major drew them together the following year. Brown was as keen on the route as ever and by this time Smythe too could see that it was an important line, but he felt honour bound to invite Brown to join him, distasteful though it might be. He took the precaution of inviting two other climbers to dilute the inevitable friction. But these dropped out and, though both men scoured Chamonix for replacements, it was without success.[8]

The evening of August 6 saw the two men once again at their bivouac below the Sentinelle Rouge. Conditions were much drier than in the previous year and lack of snow had made the steep slopes to the bivouac icy and tricky.

The chief difficulty was an avalanche channel, twelve feet deep with overhanging sides, which they had to cross. With Brown belaying him Smythe lowered himself into the channel, but suddenly the thin lip of ice broke, Smythe jerked back on the rope and in the heat of the moment, dropped his ice axe. It lay tantalisingly out of reach, yet one false flick of the rope and it could go skittering down the face, lost for ever. If that had happened the expedition would have been at an end.

Smythe lowered himself into the bed of the channel where he balanced on his crampon points on the thirty-degree ice slope, still unable to reach his axe. Desperate measures were called for. Brown struck his own axe as firmly as he could into the snow slope and taking a turn of rope round it left the security of his belay to edge delicately towards the groove and the fallen axe. At full stretch he managed to grasp the axe and then tried to pass it to Smythe. Both men now relied on the rope round Brown's implanted axe. Smythe still couldn't reach the outstretched axe so he pulled himself up a few inches on the rope, putting even greater strain on Brown's axe. Fortunately it held. Had it pulled out both men would have slid to their doom.

Once in possession of the axe Smythe was able to climb out of the other side of the channel and take a belay to help Brown across. There was now a climber on each side of the channel with the rope stretched between. The only way Brown could get into the channel was to drop over the edge whilst Smythe held the rope tight. He landed with a sickening jolt and for a moment thought he was all right, then his feet shot from beneath him and he went skidding down the ice channel as if on some mad Cresta Run. The rope came taut, jerking him to a sudden stop. Smythe's belay had held. It was a thankful pair of climbers who bivouacked that night below the Sentinelle Rouge.

At five o'clock next morning they set off up the ridge. At first it was simple scrambling, then there came a succession of snow arêtes, like the famous one on the Old Brenva, alternating with rock buttresses. None of these gave them much trouble until they came to the final buttress which was a two-tiered affair about 400 feet high. On the left there was a chimney, now the usual way up, but rejected by the pioneers as too difficult and it seemed as though the only way was to outflank the buttress to the right.

The crux here was a small corner chimney, full of ice, which quite defeated Smythe's efforts. Brown suggested a shoulder and jamming his own into the crack he bent double whilst Smythe, wearing crampons of course, clambered over him. But the holds were still not there and Smythe, committed, could do nothing but fall off. With a warning cry he landed on Brown, gashing him with his crampon spikes, though fortunately not seriously, and ending up in a tangle of clothes and ropes. How they managed to avoid falling off is impossible to say, but the incredible thing is that they actually *repeated* the manoeuvre, this time with roles reversed. It was still no good: the corner was not climbable.

In the end they had to go much further right, avoiding the buttress entirely, but there were no more problems. By 5.55 p.m. they were above the buttress and by evening had crossed Mont Blanc's summit and were safe in the Vallot Hut.

It was a tremendous climb, but the fruits of victory were lost in mutual antipathy. Brown and Smythe never climbed together again and were scarcely on speaking terms for the rest of their lives.[9]

Five years went by and though the Sentinelle Rouge route had been repeated five times nobody had managed to repeat the Route Major (it even defeated two ace Munich climbers, Heckmair and Kröner), so in 1933 Brown, perhaps to do Smythe one in the eye, himself repeated the climb with the guides Graven and Aufdenblatten. Ten days later, with Graven and Knubel, both of whom had been with Lauper on the Eiger the previous year, Brown managed a third route on the great face: the Via della Pera, so called from the pear-shaped buttress which is its principal feature.[10] Not until 1937 was the Route Major done by anyone else, when the Oberland guide Hermann Steuri led Dr A. Bauer to success. That year, too, Gréloz and Roch managed to repeat the Via della Pera.[11]

Meanwhile, the climbers from Austria and Germany were beginning to break out of their eastern heartland, where they had honed their skills to a remarkable degree, and tackle the larger peaks of the Western Alps. Because Munich was the city at the centre of this activity, and many went to university there, they became collectively known as the Munich School. It was not a fanciful name: they really did represent a new school of thought. It was sad that it coincided with the rise of Fascism – it would have happened anyway, but Fascism latched onto it and besmirched it. There were undoubted links, partly because the hard-up youngsters who were the main protagonists found they could get money out of the Nazi state.[12]

Along with the new mentality they brought new techniques, especially the use of the piton and the karabiner.[13] This alone was enough to rouse the ire of the traditionalists who were still ranting on about the use of crampons on steep ice, a threat to the proper craft of step-cutting which many of the old school regarded as the fundamental art of mountaineering.

The German and Austrian Alpine Clubs had thousands of members whose combined subscriptions provided dozens of superb huts which made access to the mountains easy. Most members were not mountaineers in the technical sense, but the numbers were such that a large corps of dedicated climbers was inevitable, and from these came a series of outstanding leaders like Purtscheller, the Zsigmondy brothers, Preuss, Pfann, Dulfer and others.

Many were students, especially in the early days, but the net was cast wide by the European clubs and people from all walks of life were recruited. Auckenthaler, one of the best rock climbers of the decade following the war, was a chimney sweep and always incredibly poor. Such a rich mixture was bound to produce explosions. The French mountaineer Lucien Devies spelt it out for the Alpine Club. The capital of the mountaineering world, he said, had shifted from London to Munich, 'where youth was ambitious and innovation encouraged'.

Foremost amongst those who helped shape the Munich School was Willo Welzenbach[14] who was born and educated in the city and lived there all his life. He took an engineering degree at the Technical University and joined the Munich Academic Alpine Club where he came under the influence of well-known climbers like Hans Pfann and Wilhelm Paulcke.[15] The club provided many of Welzenbach's climbing companions.

Though Welzenbach was a very good rock climber, it was as an ice climber that he excelled. He brought to ice climbing the precision and techniques of rock climbing and his craft was not superseded until well after the Second World War, when front-pointed crampons and short axes used as daggers eliminated step-cutting and radically altered the whole scene. Welzenbach had no such new equipment; he and his companions relied on the old style of crampon and the long ice axe, but he would cut steps in steep walls and balance up on them as if they were holds on a rock face. By cutting the holds well ahead and placing them judiciously, he could bridge icy chimneys and even tackle ice bulges which tended to throw the climber off balance.

His first great ice climb, in 1924, was the North-West Face of the Grosses Wiesbachhorn which he did with Fritz Rigele. Welzenbach's description of the crux shows the sort of new ice climbing involved:

> Soon we stood at the spot where the angle changed from sloping to vertical, and just to retain our balance we had to press ourselves against the cliff.
>
> The first of several pegs was hammered into the ice. Step after step and hold after hold were carved out of the cliff. Our numb fingers grasped these thin nicks, and slowly we eased our bodies upwards. Metre by metre we were forcing the route and all the details remain clearly imprinted on my mind; directly above me Rigele stood clinging to the ice. Cautiously, so that the swinging action of his ice axe did not unbalance him, he cut one step after another, working his way upwards in the manner of a complete master. I paid the closest attention to every movement of my companion. Uneasily, I watched the rope running out, praying above all that it would reach the next stance. But it was not long enough and just a few metres below a ledge promising deliverance Rigele called upon me to follow. Gingerly, I moved upwards, testing each step deliberately, while it required a supreme effort on Rigele's part to hold out on his tiny stance. Suddenly he yelled frantically: 'Hurry, hurry, I can't stand here any longer.' One thought only flashed through my mind: 'God help us if he falls now.'[16]

Rigele didn't fall and they completed what was certainly the hardest ice climb at that date. It was the first time that ice pegs were used on a major climb; previously Rigele had only tested them on a glacier icefall. For the Wiesbachhorn he had three box section pegs made, though he took along some conventional pegs as reserve. The pitons were for protection, not aid, though Welzenbach admits to grabbing one at the crux described above!

According to Rigele, the idea of the ice piton came about by accident. In 1922 Hermann Angerer[17] had described to him how he had been climbing on the Zillertal peak of Schrammacher when he was caught by nightfall. In order to keep his hand free for step-cutting Angerer had hung his lamp on a piton driven into a crack between the ice and a rock. But Rigele misunderstood the tale and thought Angerer had driven the piton into the ice itself. When he tried out this strange theory he found that it worked. For the first time ever, ice climbing could be protected, which meant greater risks could be taken, steeper ice climbed. Combined with Welzenbach's new methods, the ice piton revolutionised ice climbing technique.

In the following year, when he climbed the North Face of the Dent d'Hérens with Allwein, technique was pushed further still. The rock climbing manoeuvre known as a tension traverse was performed on ice for the first time.

He was also involved with a new guidebook to the Wetterstein range and this made him think about the way climbs were graded, if indeed they were graded at all, for not everyone believed they could, or should be.[18] There were those who thought that grading would bring with it competitive climbing, whilst others argued that in the bigger mountains so much depended on the weather and the fitness of the party that gradings were meaningless. There was a good deal of truth in all this, yet gradings were inevitable and the climbing fraternity, *within its own ranks*, understood perfectly well what grades meant. Amongst British rock climbers a system had evolved based on that of O.G. Jones, whilst in Continental Europe Dulfer introduced a five-point system which he adapted from a rough four-point system in general use: the climbs were classified as *easy, medium difficult, difficult, very difficult and extremely difficult*. In 1926 Welzenbach proposed this be extended to six grades indicated both by a number from I to VI and by an adjectival description – Gr IV, for example, was *sehr schweirig*, very difficult.[19] The grades could be further refined by adding a + or − sign: thus a IV+ is marginally harder than a IV but not quite as hard as a V−, which in turn is not as hard as a straight V. The system was eventually adopted by all the Alpine countries, with modifications. The French idea of applying the adjectival grade to an overall assessment of the route and the numerical to individual rock pitches has found most favour. It now goes beyond the sixth grade, as climbs have become ever harder.

In 1926 Welzenbach mounted a campaign against the steep north faces in the Glockner region of the Austrian Alps. He had by this time developed his own ice hammer, so necessary on the sort of steep faces he was tackling, where a long axe was awkward to wield. In the Glockner area he was completely successful with ascents of the North-West Face of Klockerin, the North Face of Eiskogele and the North Face of Grossglockner. Earlier that summer he had done some interesting climbing in the Western Alps, including an attempt with Allwein on the splendid South Ridge of the Aiguille Noire.[20]

But the year ended on a note of despondency. Welzenbach, a tall, well-built young man, was afflicted by a sudden malady in his right arm which at one stage looked like a permanent paralysis, requiring a couple of operations and some six months in a Swiss clinic.[21] The following summer he was climbing again, though nothing serious, and it was three years before he was able to climb at his old standard.

With Heinz Tillmann in 1929 he climbed the Swiss route made on the North Pillar of the Fiescherhorn by Schumacher and Amstutz in 1926. Welzenbach described the crux:

The rocks were sheathed in ice, steps and holds were filled in by fresh snow. Once again Tillmann tackled this pitch which was blocking off access to a groove continuing above. With the utmost effort he managed to hammer a peg into a thin crack, clip a karabiner on and pull the rope through. Desperate pull ups and lay backs ensued, nailed boots scraping against the smooth wall, then he disappeared from view into the groove. The rope ran out slowly, I could hear nothing but the howling of the storm and the gentle sound of the snow settling. At last, through the raging gale, I heard Tillmann's voice calling me on.

My fingers numb, tensely I worked up the rocks . . . My disabled arm was threatening to fail me. Taxing myself to the limits, I struggled into the groove and jammed myself between its icy walls. The tricouni nails in my boots bit into the thin ice, I dug my fingers into the snow, I moved upwards bit by bit. I negotiated about ten metres in this manner before the groove eased off somewhat. I moved round the corner and joined Tillmann.[22]

Despite this desperate adventure they felt the necessity to return the following year and do the direct route, spurred on by Lammer's description of the Fiescherwand as the finest challenge in the Bernese Alps.[23]

The Fiescherwand was just the first in a series of great north face climbs which Welzenbach executed in the Oberland. In particular he was attracted by the impressive Lauterbrunnen Wall, the southern terminus of the Lauterbrunnen valley, where a ring of icy peaks stretches from the Jungfrau to the Gspaltenhorn. The eastern half of this ring is positively majestic, steep ice walls sweeping down to the valley. In 1932 Welzenbach successfully attacked the wall in three places, climbing the North Faces of Grosshorn, Lauterbrunnen Breithorn and Gletscherhorn. These were all hard climbs, but particularly the last named. On the Gletscherhorn Welzenbach's route is less direct than usual and is today generally superseded by a later, more direct line.

In addition he climbed the North Face of the Gspaltenhorn which, at 1600 metres, almost rivals the Eiger Nordwand in immensity. With Drexel and Schulze as companions he found the rock was steep and rotten and they decided to dispense with the rope:

Ought we to rope up? Ought we to belay rope length by rope length? No, it would have served no purpose. The rock was so friable and devoid of holds, covered with snow, ice and pebbles, running with water and so exceptionally steep besides, that methodical belaying would have been impossible. Looking after the rope would have increased the stone-fall hazard and slowed us down. Moreover, in the event of one of the party falling it would

probably have sealed the fate of us all. We therefore decided to
dispense with the protection of the rope.[24]

They reached the summit at 3 p.m.; the North Face of the Gspaltenhorn
had not simply been climbed, it had been soloed. By any standards it was
a staggering achievement by the three Germans.

The following year, after a frustrating time in the Mont Blanc area due
to the weather, Welzenbach returned to the Oberland where he added the
North Face of the Nesthorn to his tally.

These Oberland walls and his pioneering work on the Austrian walls are
Welzenbach's lasting memorial. He was never to return because the following year he took part in the ill-fated expedition to Nanga Parbat. In the
Oberland, too, he seemed to come nearer to Lauper in the style of his
achievements, and certainly Welzenbach held Lauper in great respect.
Nevertheless, there was a spark about Welzenbach which Lauper never had;
that willingness to push matters just that little bit further, which was the
hallmark of the Munich School, and which so enraged Strutt.

It showed most forcefully in 1931, the year that Welzenbach climbed the
North Face of the Grands Charmoz, the year that the Schmid brothers
climbed the North Face of the Matterhorn, the year that the *Nordwand*
concept became firmly and fatally implanted in the psyche of the Munich
School.

CHAPTER SEVENTEEN

Nordwand

In 1931, the year before Welzenbach made his splendid Oberland north face climbs, he had taken part in a hazardous attempt on the North Face of the Grands Charmoz, above Chamonix. It was an ascent full of death-defying drama, which had the media agog. A month later came a dramatic ascent of the Matterhorn Nordwand by two other young climbers from Munich, the Schmid brothers. Nothing was more calculated than these two events to arouse the interest of the public in the new alpinism. The press had a field day: here was sensationalism, controversy and a 'killer peak' (the Matterhorn has never lived down its fatal first ascent in the perceived wisdom of the popular press). Only sex was missing to make it a perfect story. Popular interest was intense throughout Europe.

Though neither Welzenbach nor the Schmids had any intention of court-ing publicity when they set out on their climbs, the effects were to be far-reaching. It put the wrong ideas into the heads of some young climbers, especially, but not entirely, Germans or Austrians, and it alerted the rising Nazi party to the value of climbing as a means of publicity. Both usurped Nietzsche: the will could overcome anything, even the mountains, they said. It was Lammer's philosophy taken literally – small wonder that the old fire-eater became an ardent Nazi.[1]

The Chamonix Aiguilles are generally regarded as rock climbing peaks but here and there, on the Plan and the Charmoz, for example, there are considerable ice walls. The North Face of the Charmoz looks down on the Mer de Glace and is easily seen from the mountain station at Montenvers, from where it is easily accessible. It is contained within two ridges; on the far side from Montenvers is the North-East Ridge, distinguished by the spear-like Aiguille de la République and on the near side the North-West Ridge which descends from the summit towards another pinnacle, the Doigt de l'Etala, and a col of the same name. The face comprises steep slabs, rising from the small Thendia Glacier, then a 300-metre ice slope and finally a headwall through which a broad central couloir goes to the crest of the ridge. About 750 metres high, it is not one of the biggest nordwands by any means, but it is steep and it does have stonefall dangers.

In 1931 Welzenbach and his friend Willy Merkl started up the face at dawn on June 30. At first they found the climbing delicate and difficult (Welzenbach compared it to some of the modern routes in the Eastern Alps) and so Merkl led, in deference to his partner's weak arm. Stones whizzed down, passing over their heads, and avalanches rumbled down gulleys to the right and left, but by mid-afternoon they had gained the foot of the upper icefield. Here they decided to bivouac because the ice was slushy from the day's heat and they wanted to give it a chance to freeze again overnight.

They were away early next morning and reached the top edge of the ice by 8 a.m. Above them rose the great headwall. The easiest way up this was by means of the large central couloir but the climbers thought this was an obvious stonefall trap and so they avoided it, opting instead to try and find a way up the rocks. Unfortunately, they went too far to the right and ended on the crest of the North-West Ridge.[2] This was a dilemma: either they climbed the ridge, which had never been done at that time, and ended up with an unsatisfactory hybrid route which was part wall, part ridge, or they retreated and tried again. The ridge looked quite fearsome, but the decision was taken out of their hands by gathering storm clouds. They retreated, to spend a miserable storm-lashed bivouac on the Doigt de l'Etala.

When they got back to Montenvers Welzenbach and Merkl were confined by the weather to walking up the glacier to the Leschaux Hut (probably to examine the North Face of Grandes Jorasses) where they met two friends, Anderl Heckmair and Gustl Kröner, who revealed that they too had plans on the North Face of Charmoz.

This news sent Welzenbach and Merkl scurrying back to Montenvers and on July 5 they once again set off for the North Face. They decided on a curious plan and one which was to raise much controversy. Instead of repeating the ascent from the bottom of the face, they decided to traverse in from the North-West Ridge, to a point roughly in line with where they had abandoned the climb last time. They found the climbing difficult and the stonefall intense.

So engrossed were they in the technical difficulties of the route that they had not noticed the gathering storm clouds. When they did they climbed faster, hoping to reach the top before the weather broke, but it was a forlorn hope. As they reached a small ledge, rain and hail struck them in a furious blast, pinning them to the rock for three hours, unable to move. Not until the late afternoon did the storm relent sufficiently for them to continue their ascent. That night they bivouacked on a small ledge below the crest of the North-East Ridge, half-way between the République and the Charmoz summit. They were to spend the next sixty hours trapped there.

Storm followed storm in relentless fashion, lightning flashes illuminating the rocks and thunder reverberating round the peaks. Rain, hail and snow followed each other. Powder snow began to pour down the wall behind the bivouac tent, threatening to force them off the ledge, and a supreme effort had to be made by each man to climb out of his cover and clear the snow away. They had little food, but thirst was their main worry, which no amount of snow seemed to satisfy. They spoke little, each wrapped in his own thoughts and occasionally scribbling in his diary.[3] They hoped their friends had not called out a rescue team.

Towards evening on the fourth day the sky lightened a little but the storm soon came rushing back and they spent another terrible night of shivering and exhaustion. But the dawn came clear, allowing them to make a bid for freedom. It was a desperate bid at that; the rocks were ice-glazed and every ledge was piled with loose fresh snow, which made climbing difficult and dangerous. Inch by inch they crawled towards the crest of the South-East Ridge. It took them four hours to reach it – and just in time, as yet another snowstorm came sweeping in. Both men knew they had to fight on, storm or no storm, for another bivouac could well have been fatal in their weary condition.

The last 100 metres of the ridge took nine hours to climb but, though they had reached the summit, they still could not stop. They had to get off the mountain before dark, or perish.

Stumbling down the ridge they came to the great Charmoz–Grépon couloir which offers a way down to the Nantillons Glacier. But in the storm the wide couloir was confusing and time and again the tired climbers had to retreat from some blind alley. Only as daylight began to fade did they manage to jump the bergschrund onto the Nantillons Glacier. They entered the hotel at Montenvers 110 hours after leaving it, and just in time to prevent rescue attempts.

The world's press were captivated by the dramatic events on the Charmoz, by the 'race' with Heckmair, the desperate fight against all odds, and they made the most of it. Welzenbach does not seem to have resented the publicity, but it was not of great importance to him; he was a relatively well-off professional man, with enough money to indulge his sport as he wished. But there were other climbers in less fortunate circumstances who saw the publicity as a way to attract attention and money.

The Nazis also saw the advantage of such publicity; Aryan gods on the peaks of Valhalla had a ring of Wagner. Nationalism reared its head in climbing, not perhaps for the first time, but more blatantly and persistently than before.[4]

Perhaps for the very first time, climbing entered into the public consciousness. Previously, in Britain at any rate, only events like the Matterhorn disaster of 1865 or the disappearance of Mallory and Irvine on the slopes of Everest in 1924 had made any impact on the general public. This was how climbers wanted it; any sort of publicity was anathema. 'We are very proud of our success at getting the whole party off without interviews,' wrote Hinks, Hon. Secretary of the Everest Committee, to Mallory in 1921.

'Please use a little cunning in making your return. It would be a great pity if we let the reporters in now.'[5] But times were changing and even

Hinks had to reach an agreement with *The Times*. In the 1930s, too, commercial climbing magazines appeared for the first time.[6]

Besides attracting publicity, Welzenbach and Merkl also stirred up controversy about the way they tackled the route. Can it be a genuine first ascent if it is done in two halves at different times? There is no doubt they made a big mistake in route-finding when they first tackled the face. They should have gone straight for the central couloir, which they thought was too dangerous. This is what Heckmair and Kröner did about three weeks later, and reached the summit in seven hours. Heckmair is now credited, rather delicately, with the first *direct* ascent of the face. The tactic of breaking an Alpine climb in the way Welzenbach did has never been fully accepted by the climbing fraternity, though it has been done on occasion since.[7]

The Charmoz North Face was important because of the effect it had on the perception of the sport by the public and the European alpinists. Technically, it was much less important, but later in that same month came a nordwand that was destined to set new standards.

The Matterhorn has always been a rather special mountain because of its unique shape, height and dramatic history. Each of its four magnificent ridges provided excitement for the pioneers (though there are much harder ridges in the Alps) and, overshadowing it all, there is the memory of Whymper's fatal first ascent, itself a watershed in mountaineering history. In between the ridges are the faces. The South, East and West are of little account,[8] but the North Face is different; here is a soaring wall, a thousand metres high from bergschrund to summit, whose rocks are verglassed because they see so little of the sun. With the Eigerwand and North Face of the Grandes Jorasses, it forms the trio of classical nordwands.

The Austrian climbers Alfred Horeschowsky and Franz Piekielko had attempted the face in 1923, but it was a very dry summer and this increased the stonefall which forced them too far left and ultimately onto the Hörnli Ridge near the Solvay Hut. Attempts by Blanchet and others were less determined and came to nothing, but at the end of July 1931, two unknown young brothers from Munich, Franz and Toni Schmid, arrived at Zermatt on their bicycles. It was their first visit to the Western Alps.

They could scarcely have chosen a worse summer for weather and yet, paradoxically, the heavy snows from the storms which had earlier battered Welzenbach were to prove a godsend. As the previous explorers had discovered to their cost, dry conditions are not what is needed on the Matterhorn Nordwand.

At dawn on July 31, the two young Germans set off up the face. They had forty metres of hemp climbing rope apiece, a bivouac bag, some pitons and a little food.

Their first problem was a 300-metre ice slope, which they cramponned up without cutting a single step, urged on by the knowledge that the slope was dangerously exposed to stonefall. They headed towards a large couloir, just left of centre on the face for, although this too looked a dangerous avalanche and stonefall trap, it also seemed the only way up. The Schmids were lucky; though they tried from time to time to escape from the couloir, they were trapped in it all day without incident.

It was towards sunset when a difficult chimney and steep ice wall at last allowed them to break out of the couloir to the right. It was twenty-one hours since they had left camp and they had reached a height of over 4100 metres. They were desperately tired, and as daylight faded they looked for a bivouac site – but where was there to rest on that great face with its inhospitable boiler-plate slabs? Franz, who was leading at that point, suddenly spotted a knob of rock which looked promising, but as he traversed towards it his brother's holds collapsed without warning! Only by a frantic clutch at the rocks did Toni manages to save himself from falling and dragging them both to certain death. Shaken by their experience, they bivouacked for the night, held to the rotten rock by a couple of shaky pitons.

It was seven o'clock before their frozen limbs allowed them to start next morning. At first things looked promising as Toni led off up a spur which took them some way up the cliff, but then, as Franz took the lead, he ran into a band of smooth, impassable rock. There was nothing for it but to traverse horizontally to right or left until they found a new opening. Toni was against going left, because that led to the Hörnli Ridge, safety – and failure. However, the matter was decided for them because watching from the Hörnli was the guide Alexander Pollinger, who shouted across that the way to the ridge was impossible.

So Franz led off to the right along a ledge of rotten snow until he spied a way up a snow-filled crack. At last their luck seemed to be turning. They knew that the summit could not be far off, but even as the angle eased there was a deadly rumble of thunder and a lashing of hail whipped their faces. Hurrying over increasing easy ground the two brothers emerged on the summit of the Matterhorn at 2 p.m. The Nordwand had been climbed.

Their joy was short-lived. Even as they slapped each other on the shoulders in congratulation lightning crackled around them and a furious storm broke. Tired and hungry, they began the descent of the Hörnli Ridge, normally an easy matter for climbers of their calibre, but now treacherous with ice and snow. The fixed ropes which help climbers down the tricky bit were thick with ice and unusable, and fully aware that this was the place where Whymper came to grief on the first ascent, the two men spent hours carefully edging down the shelving rocks. Eventually they reached the Shoulder, and the sanctuary of the Solvay Hut, a tiny bivouac cabin placed there for just such an emergency. Removing their ice-coated clothing, they wrapped themselves in blankets and fell into an exhausted sleep.

The Schmids were trapped for two days in the Solvay hut by the storm and it was two half-starved climbers who eventually staggered down into Zermatt. Here they were given a tremendous reception and accommodated at one of the best hotels. Zermatt had been quick to spot the publicity value that Welzenbach's epic on the Charmoz had had for Chamonix, and now they had heroes of their own! Zermatt never did like Chamonix being one up in anything.

The Schmids took it very calmly. After a few days they mounted their bikes and rode off to Chamonix to try the Grandes Jorasses North Face, though nothing came of their efforts. Toni Schmid was killed in the Austrian Alps the following year.[9]

The ascent of the Matterhorn Nordwand, and the competent way it was achieved, left Strutt without comment, for once.

'Confronted with such a performance, criticism or praise must perforce maintain silence,' he wrote.[10]

Later, as the tide of death washed over the Grandes Jorasses and the Eigerwand, criticism was renewed. Strutt's stridency now looks ridiculous, but it overshadowed more reasoned arguments. Claude Wilson, himself a fine climber of an earlier generation, said there had been 'a vast eruption of irresponsible people and ignorant beginners venturing into areas of which they know nothing ... and the deliberate neglect by more experienced climbers of well recognized rules of reasonable, safe climbing'.[11] This was the traditional view, stated without histrionics. Three years later, in 1934, J.J. Withers in his retiring address to the Alpine Club drew attention to the way the new climbing was being used politically by the Nazis, although he named no party as such:

> At the risk of entering into the zone of other countries' politics, it appears to be my duty to say a few words in strongest condemnation of a cloud that has long threatened and has now materialized as a practice in Alpine Societies – not to say the Governments – of at least one nation ...
>
> It is well known that a large monetary reward has been promised to the first member of a certain country who may achieve the ascent of the northern face of the Grandes Jorasses. The medal for valour has actually been awarded to the conqueror of the Matterhorn's N. face. Young parties of cragsmen who have shown prowess on insignificant boulders are being subsidized to attempt similar feats in the greater Alps.
>
> Such practices I must categorically condemn as nothing less than the most objectionable and fatal form of professionalism ...
>
> I know of a party, hindered by bad weather and, wonderful to relate, hesitating to start on a most dangerous route, of which one

member declared that 'they *must* accomplish the climb, otherwise no more subsidy for next year!'

We cannot blame the young climbers who avail themselves of these payments and rewards, still less can we discourage grants made to assist youth in visiting the Alps. But words are not strong enough to express my opinion of the financiers or inciters of what amounts to nothing else than neck-breaking competitions.

I sincerely trust that a stop will soon be put to the dangerous practice alluded to. Another bad sign is the entry of politics into mountaineering, and Alpine Societies.[12]

Withers was referring particularly to the unseemly scramble which developed for the North Faces of the Grandes Jorasses and the Eiger throughout the thirties. They outclassed even the Matterhorn Nordwand in height and difficulty, for whereas the Matterhorn face is 1035 metres, the Walker Spur on the face of the Grandes Jorasses is 1200 metres and the Eigerwand 1800 metres. Technically, too, the problems of the Walker and the Eigerwand are greater than the Matterhorn, though all three are difficult and dangerous.

The Grandes Jorasses has in many eyes the most attractive of these faces. It is not a single wedge, like the Matterhorn, or pyramid, like the Eiger, but a long high wall with six summits towering over the Leschaux Glacier. The highest of the summits is called Pointe Walker (4208 m), after Horace Walker who made the first ascent in 1868, the second highest is Pointe Whymper (4184 m) and the third is Pointe Croz (4110 m).[13] From Pointe Walker and Pointe Croz, two tremendous spurs of rock, like bastions on some immense castle wall, descend to the glacier and were natural magnets for the nordwand climbers of the thirties.

Geoffrey Winthrop Young had looked at the Walker Spur back in 1907 but dismissed it, then in 1928 Armand Charlet, probably the greatest guide of his generation, with a large party, got some way up it before retreating. Welzenbach, too, fared no better in 1930. Then in 1931, the year of the Matterhorn and Charmoz North Faces, a whole wave of climbers surged at it.

First to arrive, on ancient bikes, were Heckmair and Kröner who tried to climb the large Central Couloir between the two spurs but without success: the route is extremely difficult and dangerous and wasn't climbed until 1972. Undeterred, they repeated Welzenbach's recent route on the Charmoz North Face. Hard on their heels came their rivals Hans Brehm and Leo Rittler, whose projected assault on the Matterhorn Nordwand had just been pre-empted by the Schmid brothers. Now they were afraid that they had been cheated out of the Grandes Jorasses as well, so they rushed at once to the Central Couloir, still regarded as the obvious way up. A week later

Heckmair and Kröner returned to find their mangled bodies: an avalanche had killed them outright.[14]

During the next few years the North Face of the Grandes Jorasses attracted almost every climber of note. The two great spurs were the chief attraction and in 1933 two Italian mountaineers, Gervasutti and Zanetti managed to get a considerable way up the Croz Spur before the weather turned against them. In the following season Charlet and Gréloz got a few metres higher still before they too retreated. Close behind them were Raymond Lambert and Loulou Boulaz, Martin Meier and Ludwig Steinauer. None was successful.

On July 30 there were no fewer than four international ropes on the climb. Two Germans, Rudolf Peters and Rudolf Haringer, had started on the 28th, followed next day by Charlet and a fellow guide, Fernand Belin. That same day Gervasutti and Chabod also started up, as did a team of three unknown Austrians. Charlet soon caught up with the Germans but then decided to retreat, perhaps because the weather looked threatening. The two Italians also caught up with the leaders, Chabod arguing that if they hurried they would make the summit before the storm broke, but Gervasutti thought otherwise, and so they too retreated.[15] The Austrians, seeing the crack French and Italian teams retreat, decided to do likewise. Only Peters and Haringer decided to press on. They were last seen by watchers at the Leschaux Hut about 5 p.m.

Next morning a violent storm swept the Grandes Jorasses, followed by another and yet another. It seemed unlikely that anyone on the mountain could survive such an onslaught and Peters and Haringer were given up for dead. Three days later young Peters staggered into the Leschaux Hut. He had survived five days and four nights on the spur, three of them under the severest weather the mountain had known for years. He had a tragic tale to tell. Caught by the storm, the two had finally been forced to retreat, abseiling for hour after hour until darkness fell. Haringer unroped to look for a bivouac site when, with a sudden cry of 'Ice!' he slipped from the rocks and fell 550 metres to his death. Left alone, Peters fought for three days and nights to descend the spur, an epic of endurance. It was his first visit to the Western Alps.

But Peters was nothing if not determined. That winter he teamed up with Meier to make a difficult training climb in the Eastern Alps in preparation for another attempt on the Grandes Jorasses. When June 1935 arrived, Meier hurried to the Grandes Jorasses to watch for the right conditions. June is early for a serious Alpine climb but on the 24th, Meier hurried to Chamonix Post Office to tell Peters to come at once. The mountain was ready.

The two moved out of Chamonix quietly, telling nobody their plans, but Peters was too well known after his dramatic escape of the previous year and word soon got out that he was back. This pre-emptive strike by the

Germans caught all the other would-be contestants on the hop. The great French climber Edouard Frendo had hopes of climbing the face that summer, but his climbing partner, Maurice Fourastrier, was still at home in Algeria and there was no hope of Fourastrier joining him to catch the Germans. Frendo teamed up with a companion from the military mountaineering school where he was an instructor and hurried to the Leschaux Hut. There he discovered the Swiss team of Lambert and Gréloz from Geneva already ensconced. They too had heard of Peters' arrival and had hurried over immediately.

The French and Swiss decided to join forces, hoping that their combined expertise and knowledge of big mountains would beat the German challenge, but it failed almost before it began. They hadn't gone far when Gréloz had the misfortune to dislocate a shoulder and, though Frendo yanked it back into place without ceremony, it was too painful for Gréloz to continue. All four men decided to retreat.

As it turned out, none of this mattered a jot. The Germans' plan had worked perfectly. Even before the others left the Leschaux Hut, Peters and Meier had reached the summit of the Grandes Jorasses. The Croz Spur was conquered.

They had started on June 28 up a steep slope of bare ice followed by a couloir down which water was spraying, wetting them to the skin. That night they found a comfortable bivouac, more or less out of the line of stonefall, though one stray missile hit their cooking pot, smashing it and the stove. They were now without hot food or drinks. Next morning they soon reached the second great ice slope where Peters demonstrated the techniques of Welzenbach, using the newly developed front-pointed crampons where two special points stick out forwards and can be jabbed into the ice. At every rope's length he cut a platform where he could stand belayed to one of Rigele's long ice pitons. To save time, and thus avoid the worst of the stonefall, Meier hauled himself up the rope hand over hand.

They were still in the middle of the ice slope when a sudden bombardment of rocks caught them unawares, the stones exploding in the ice round them, sending Peters' hat flying and momentarily knocking Meier senseless. Fortunately, Peters was able to hold him on the rope. Bloodied but unbowed, the two Germans continued their climb.

Beyond the ice slope they climbed steep rocks, then another ice slope and even more difficult rock, but nothing could stop them now. At eight o'clock that evening they reached the summit ridge – and suddenly realised they didn't even know the way off! Not until next day did they reach Courmayeur on the Italian side of the mountain.

As the Germans left for home others turned up unaware that the prize had already been snatched. Within a few days the Croz Spur was climbed by three more parties: Gervasutti and Chabod, Raymond Lambert and Loulou Boulaz, Ludwig Steinauer and Toni Messner.

It is interesting to see that a woman took part in these extreme ascents. Louise (Loulou) Boulaz, a twenty-seven-year-old Swiss climber, thus became the first woman to climb one of the major nordwands.[16]

The ascent of the Croz Spur was not the end of the matter as far as the Grandes Jorasses was concerned for there was still the Walker Spur, an even more formidable challenge. The battleground remained the same; only the target changed. 'This is not alpinism,' said Armand Charlet, 'this is war.' Strutt fulminated as always but, a brave man himself, he sometimes showed a sneaking admiration for daring exploits. Of the campaign by Heckmair and Kröner in 1931 he said it was 'surpassing the limits of even modern insanity, yet we cannot in justice refrain from expressing a certain wonder, perhaps admiration, for the remarkable skill, energy and resistance displayed.'[17] Sadly, two years later, Gustl Kröner, one of the best of the Bavarians, was killed by stonefall below the Matterhorn Nordwand.

Later in 1935 another north face was climbed, that of the Petit Dru. The Swiss team of Raymond Lambert, Dupont and Gotch climbed to a point forty-five metres above the prominent Niche and then, three days later, on July 31 and August 1, the ascent was made by the French team of Pierre Allain and Raymond Leininger. The ascent included the Grade VI Fissure Allain, a steep twenty-five-metre crack which is nowadays usually avoided by easier options.

The Munich School were not having things all their own way, as the Dru demonstrates (two of their members had died attempting it in 1930). The Italians in particular were starting to raise eyebrows; already, in 1933 the huge rock wall of the Cima Grande in the Dolomites had been climbed by the three guides Emilio Comici and the Dimai brothers, Angelo and Joseph. The conquest of this wall had long been Comici's dream and he spared nothing in his final effort, knowing that others might snatch the prize from him. The climbers were reported as using 400 metres of rope, 150 metres of line, 90 pitons and 50 karabiners on the 550-metre face. No doubt incensed to see the malaise spreading from its Munich homeland, Strutt thundered, 'Needless to say, conquest was only effected by the means employed by steeple-jacks when dealing with factory chimneys.' He described it as a repulsive farce which could only bring discredit on mountaineering.[18] A month later the route was repeated by the Austrian Aschenbrenner brothers, Paul and Peter. If the Munich School failed to make a first ascent it was always eager to make the second.

In 1937 the Italians scored again in a frightful ascent of the North-East Face of Piz Badile. The leader was a remarkable climber called Riccardo Cassin from Lecco on the shores of Lake Como, where he had learned to climb on the strange limestone pinnacles of the Grigna. He was a member of the New Italy Climbing Club, a group of avant-garde climbers who had learned the use of pitons and other modern aids from the great Comici himself. On July 14, 1937, with his two companions Esposito and Ratti, Cassin started up the steep rock face of this Engadine peak, whilst at the same time two other young men from Como, Molteni and Valsecchi, began to climb the face from a point further to the right. Molteni had tried the face twice before and the previous summer he had taken a bad fall there. Towards evening they all gathered on the same ledge.

Next day it was obvious that the stamina of Molteni and his partner was giving out. They were impecunious young men who had been sleeping rough for a week to save even the miserable hut fees, and had probably been eating not too well. Molteni asked to join Cassin's rope and, though this seriously reduced the chance of success, Cassin felt he could not leave them to their fate. Nevertheless, despite this handicap the rope of five moved well, with Molteni bringing up the rear – the most responsible position after that of leader.

That night they bivouacked below a light-coloured slab. Electric storms flickered fitfully round the peaks, and rainwater poured down the rocks as the five Italians sat and shivered on the narrowest of ledges.

In the morning Ratti took over as last man from the exhausted Molteni. The climbing was extremely difficult and the weather was vile: rain turned to violent hail, lashing in waves across the wall, and finally snow. Visibility was down to a metre and the rocks became dangerous as well as difficult, smeared with verglas and drifted with powder snow. Nevertheless, by superb climbing Cassin led his unwieldy team to the summit. It was 4 p.m. on the third day.

As they began their descent of the easy snow slopes which form the Italian side of Badile the storm blew fiercer than ever and soon they were fighting desperately against raging winds and driving hail. For Molteni it was too much. 'We did everything possible to ward off the death that was stalking us,' wrote Cassin later. 'We poured all our cognac between Molteni's lips; I tried to support him when he no longer had the strength to continue, but in vain. Without so much as a moan he sank to the ground, never to rise again.'[19]

The others struggled on, searching for the Gianetti Hut, but with the storm limiting visibility to a few metres they had no idea where it was. Suddenly young Valsecchi realised for the first time that his friend Molteni was no longer with them. When he heard that Molteni was dead he burst into tears, sank to his knees in the snow and passed away. It was as if the death of his comrade had robbed his poor half-starved body of its last dregs of energy. Cassin, Esposito and Ratti were forced to bivouac for a third night, wet through and frozen, wondering which would be the next to die.

But their luck turned. The storm which had raged unabated for twelve hours stopped in the night and next morning they were able to reach the hut and report their tale of triumph and tragedy.

A year later, frustrated in his plan to make the first ascent of the Eiger Nordwand, Cassin turned his attention to the Walker Spur of the Grandes Jorasses. He had been told that this was a desirable objective, but he had no idea where it was; the whole of the Mont Blanc area was a mystery to him as neither he nor any of his companions had been there. Nevertheless early in August, Cassin, Esposito and Ugo Tizzoni[20] gathered at the Leschaux Hut, unaware that it had just been abandoned by the French aces Pierre Allain and Jean Leininger who had failed in an attempt on the ridge.

Before dawn on the morning of August 4, the three Italians set out on their great adventure. Cassin was in the lead, then came Esposito and finally Tizzoni. They soon reached the great corner which is a prominent feature of the lower part of the route and the climbing became difficult. Slabs above the corner were ice coated and several times Tizzoni slipped whilst trying to recover pitons Cassin had hammered into the ice and rock. Unfortunately, though Tizzoni did a fine job, some were impossible to retrieve and throughout the climb there was a worrying drain on equipment. That night they bivouacked on a good ledge about 450 metres above the start.

Next day the climbing was, if anything, more difficult still, forcing the leader out to the right, away from the crest of the spur. At one place an enormous roof barred the way and, though Cassin traversed below it, he soon ran out of rope and called on Esposito to follow. There was no stance or natural belay, so Esposito sat in a pair of étriers, dangling from a single piton, whilst he payed out the rope to Cassin. Fortunately, he managed to secure another piton for the complicated rope manoeuvres his leader was embarking upon. Cassin was lowered about twelve metres until he was level with a spike of rock he had seen. The spike was out of reach, however, so, letting go of the rock, Cassin pushed himself across the gap in a vigorous pendulum movement, swinging free like an Alpine Tarzan and grabbing for the spike. He missed at first but eventually, after several wild swings, he was able to grab it and pull himself to safety.

Esposito followed his leader. Tizzoni, as last on the rope and carrying the expedition's baggage, had a more tricky job. He had to climb down without assistance from the rope. It was delicate work and, had he slipped, the consequences could have been dire, but Tizzoni climbed superbly and reached his friends without incident. The pitch took five hours.

As they climbed towards a grey tower which they knew was about two-thirds of the way up the spur, snow flakes began to drift down on them. At the foot of the tower they bivouacked a second time and spent the night watching a storm below flash and rumble over Chamonix.

Next morning they continued their climb and were only 150 metres from the top when a violent thunderstorm struck them, forcing them to cower for shelter in their bivouac sacs for half an hour. As it eased off the snow returned, falling persistently for the rest of the day, but at three o'clock on the afternoon of August 6, Cassin and his companions stood on the Pointe Walker. They had conquered the Walker Spur at their first attempt.[21]

Meanwhile, the Munich School had found a new challenge, a wall of such grandeur as to take the breath away, a nordwand which had the ultimate in height, steepness and danger. It was the North-West Face of the Eiger, above Grindelwald in the Bernese Oberland, better known simply as the Eigerwand.

The fanatical struggle for the face from 1935 to 1938 that left behind a string of frozen corpses, and the continuing grim harvest from later and harder struggles for more direct lines, have made the Eigerwand the most notorious of all Alpine walls. The parent mountain, the Eiger, has gained its public reputation from this one face.

'Thanks to this, its name has become better known than that of the Matterhorn or Mont Blanc. It has become familiar to millions of readers of innumerable newspaper reports; it has been mentioned hundreds of times on the radio. It became the epitome of everything tragically sensational that mountaineering had to offer . . .'[22]

The reason for this is not entirely to do with the immensity and difficulty of the face, which is 1800 metres high and bombarded by stonefall. Part of the notoriety stems from the public nature of the climbing. The Grandes Jorasses is a more beautiful mountain and the Walker Spur a more elegant climb, but they are tucked away, reachable only by experienced alpinists. Even the Matterhorn Nordwand is not readily accessible except by some stiff walking, but the Eigerwand can be observed in the minutest detail from the windows of the Kleine Scheidegg hotel. It is like climbing in a goldfish-bowl and though many climbers deplore this some, especially in the early days, made the most of the media opportunities. For the impecunious young Germans, attempting the Eigerwand was a good career move – except of course that you were likely to be killed.

'It has been widely deplored that the very creed of mountaineering should have been debased by the climbs and attempts on this particular Face, in that it has become an arena, a natural stage, on which every movement of the actors can be followed. And the applause accorded to successful climbers on their return is argued as another outward sign of their inward decay . . .'[23]

The Eiger was first climbed in 1858 by Charles Barrington and the guides Bohren and Almer in an effort which for its day was every bit as daring as the later attempts on the wall. Barrington was scarcely any sort of climber and was doing the Eiger more for a dare than anything, pointing out that he couldn't afford the Matterhorn! 'I was surprised to see the families of the guides in a state of distraction at their departure for the ascent, and two elderly ladies came out and abused me for taking them to risk their lives.'[24]

A.W. Moore made the third ascent during his famous tour of 1864 and described the Eigerwand for the first time. He got to a place where he could look straight down the great wall. 'Except in the Dauphiné I have never seen so sheer and smooth a precipice,' he wrote. 'A stone dropped from the edge would have fallen hundreds of feet before encountering any obstacle to its progress.'[25]

Seen from below the Eigerwand resembles the concave side of an inverted shield. The lower third consists of shelving limestone on which the snow lies in ribbons. This offers little difficulty but then it meets a steep First Band, overhanging on the left but less severe on the right where it abuts against a sheer side-wall known as the Rote Fluh. In the First Band are two windows from the Jungfrau Railway which penetrates the mountain as it climbs to the Jungfraujoch. One is the so-called Eigerwand Station, which looks out over the middle of the face and the other is a gallery window, somewhat lower and to the right, below the Rote Fluh.

Above the First Band is the First Icefield, then another steep wall, the Second Band, and then the large, steep, Second Icefield. The top third of the face is very steep and at its heart is a small icefield from which gullies radiate in long arms, and known as the Spider. From above the Spider the mountain spews rocks and ice which bounce down the icefields.

The problem facing the pioneers was threefold: how to escape the bombardment of the lower slopes, how to climb from the Second Icefield to the Spider and how to escape from the Spider to the summit.

The first attempt was made in 1935 by two experienced climbers, Max Sedlmayer and Karl Mehringer of Munich. They studied the wall carefully and then set off, completing the lower part in good time. The steep rock of the First Band took them longer, since they had to sack-haul as well as climb,[26] but by the third day they were moving across the Second Icefield and watchers at Kleine Scheidegg could see them trying to protect their heads against stonefall with their rucksacks. Then the mists closed in and the Eiger began to live up to its reputation as a bad weather mountain – it isn't called Ogre for nothing.

The storm raged all that day and the next. Seasoned climbers gave the men up for dead, but on the very next day there was a small window in the weather which revealed Sedlmayer and Mehringer moving up slowly towards a rock outcrop, the Flatiron, at the top of the icefield.

They were never seen alive again. Though a rescue team was organised the weather never once relented and it wasn't until three weeks later that the ace German pilot Ernst Udet, flying perilously close to the face, with the guide Fritz Steuri as observer, saw a body knee deep in snow frozen to the face at the upper rim of the small Third Icefield, above the Flatiron,

Summit

Summit
Snowfield

Exit
Snowfield

Exit
Cracks

Spider

Ice Bulge
Waterfall
Crack

Traverse
of the Gods

(A) Death Bivouac
Flatiron

Third Icefield

Second
Icefield

First
Icefield

Ice Hose

Swallow's Nest

Hinterstoisser Traverse
(D) (B)

(C)

Difficult
Crack

Shattered
Pillar

First
Pillar

THE EIGER

—— Route of first ascent, 1939

Fatalities before the first ascent:

A - Sedlmayer and Mehringer, 1935

B - Angerer, Rainer, Hinterstoisser, 1936

C - Kurz, 1936

D - Sandri and Menti, 1938

a place since known as Death Bivouac. There was no means of telling which of the Germans it was, but twenty-seven years later two climbers discovered the remains of Mehringer on the Second Icefield; presumably the body had been carried down the face over the years.

The deaths of Sedlmayer and Mehringer drew attention to the Eigerwand and by the start of the following season there were several parties ready to challenge the mountain. The reporters too were out in force, eager to solicit the views of anyone who might be about to dice with death. Two Germans, Herbst and Teufel, had already looked at the face early in the season and sensibly withdrew, only for Teufel to be killed a few days later attempting the Schneehorn's unclimbed North Face. Their place was taken by four eager young climbers: Edi Rainer and Willi Angerer from Austria and Andreas Hinterstoisser and Toni Kurz of Bavaria.

The Austrians were on the scene first. Recognising the difficulty of the First Band, which had taken Mehringer and Sedlmayer so long to overcome in direct assault, they chose a way further right, near the Rote Fluh. Their reconnaissance was successful, but conditions were not good and so they retreated to base. The reporters, whilst rejoicing in their safe return, were also a little disappointed. 'Don't worry,' the Austrians assured them, 'we are going back up!' Asked whether they had retreated because it was too grim they replied no, at present it was just a little too wet.

Meanwhile Kurz and Hinterstoisser, two soldiers on leave from the 100th Jäger Regiment, arrived and made their own reconnaissance, during which Hinterstoisser is said to have fallen thirty-six metres only to land in deep soft snow, uninjured. The reporters, sensing all the drama of a race developing for the face between the two teams, badgered them into making statements. 'We must have the wall, or it must have us!' the Austrians declared. 'If we die, you'll find the photographs in the rucksack,' young Kurz cheerfully assured them.

Remarks like these did nothing to assuage the fears of the climbing establishment who were disgusted by the whole circus; others saw it as typical arrogance from the self-styled Master Race, another aspect of Nazism. And yet a conservative Swiss newspaper described them as 'charming, good-natured lads'. Did they really see themselves as shining examples of the Master Race or were they just innocent youngsters provoked into making wild statements by cynical journalists? Or indeed, were they just winding the journalists up?

At this remove it is impossible to say. They certainly created a furore and when Colonel Konrad, the commanding officer of the 100th Jäger Regiment, heard about it, he at once telephoned Grindelwald, forbidding Kurz and Hinterstoisser to attempt the climb. He was too late.

The four climbers began their attempt on Saturday, July 18, climbing at first as two separate ropes but combining forces at the foot of the Rote

Fluh. They found a way up the First Band by a strenuous pitch now known as the Difficult Crack, which led them to an area of smooth, unclimbable slabs. The only way ahead was to avoid the slabs by making a traverse for forty metres left. Hinterstoisser, as the best rock climber of the four, made the difficult traverse, partly by skilful footwork and partly by the technique of tension traversing, using the rope and pitons to keep him in balance. Once he was across he brought the others over one by one, and then pulled the rope in after them. Little did he know that by pulling in the rope he was sealing their fate.

The pitch is known today as the Hinterstoisser Traverse and *it cannot be reversed unless a rope is left in position.*

But they had no thought of retreat. The weather was fine and they made good progress up the First Icefield. On the Second Band, however, the Austrians seemed to be in trouble. Watchers at Kleine Scheidegg believed that Angerer was struck by a stone and had to be supported by Rainer. The Germans, who were ahead, dropped down a helping rope and pulled the injured man up the difficult rocks. This took so much time that they were forced to bivouac.

There must have been some fateful decisions taken at that bivouac. There is no doubt that had the Germans gone on alone, leaving the Austrians to retreat, they might well have succeeded, but we have no means of knowing just how badly Angerer was injured. Perhaps retreat was not considered necessary. In any event the two ropes could be seen next day climbing the Second Icefield. Time and again the Germans had to wait for the Austrians to catch up. They bivouacked at the Flatiron.

At 7 a.m., Monday, June 20, the Germans started off and reached the Death Bivouac, but the Austrians did not follow. Angerer was obviously feeling bad. The Germans climbed down again and there was a long conference, at the end of which a decision was taken to retreat. They climbed down the Second Icefield and the Second Band, arriving at the upper rim of the First Icefield as darkness fell.

Next day they climbed down the First Icefield only to discover, to their undoubted dismay, that they could not reverse Hinterstoisser's traverse. All day they tried, each in turn, except for the injured Angerer, as the weather started to deteriorate. The climbers were faced with the descent of 200 metres of unknown steep rock.

Meanwhile, a railway worker called Albert von Allmen had been standing on the gallery of the Jungfrau Railway window, listening to the climbers calling to one another. To Albert they seemed to be very near and directly overhead, so he shouted up. The climbers yodelled back and shouted, 'All's well!' Albert expected them to arrive at the window any moment, so he went into his little office and put on the kettle to make them some tea.

But the kettle boiled, the tea was made and two whole hours passed without any sign of the climbers. Albert went outside to investigate. Through the mists came a lone voice desperately crying for help. It was Toni Kurz.

The railwayman dashed into his cabin and telephoned for help. As it happened three guides, Hans Schlunegger, Christian and Adolf Rübi were at Eigergletscher Station and answered the call for help immediately, even though the Chief Guide for Grindelwald had warned all Eigerwand climbers not to expect help in case of an accident. From the gallery they traversed out to a point about 100 metres below young Kurz and in a hurried, shouted conversation they discovered the extent of the tragedy.

It seems that Hinterstoisser had unroped to reconnoitre a way down, but had slipped and fallen to his death. Whether he had been struck by a stone wasn't clear. Rainer had come to grief too, perhaps trying to catch Hinterstoisser, and so had the injured Angerer who had been strangled by the rope and was hanging dead below Kurz. Within seconds, it seems, the Eigerwand had exacted a terrible revenge.

It was evening by this time and there was nothing the guides could do. 'Can you last out the night?' they called. 'No! No!' screamed Kurz. 'Don't leave me!' With his pitiful cries ringing in their ears the guides retreated.

The night was bitterly cold. Kurz hung from his piton. Icicles eight inches long formed on the points of his crampons. He lost his left glove and first his fingers, then his hand and finally his arm gradually froze solid.

Incredibly, Kurz was still alive next morning when the guides returned and his voice sounded as strong as ever. Arnold Glatthard had now joined the other three guides, but still they could not reach the stricken climber. Kurz insisted they could only reach him from above, but the rocks were so ice glazed by this time that it wasn't possible to get above him. Instead they managed to climb to within forty metres of him from the gallery window. They asked him to lower a line so that they could tie on a spare rope he could slide down, but he didn't have any line. Attempts to shoot one up to him by rockets failed miserably.

Despite his terrible ordeal Kurz was not ready to give up the struggle. He managed to climb down the rope to where the dead Angerer was fastened and cut the body free. It refused to fall but remained grotesquely ice gripped to the great face. Nevertheless the manoeuvre had given Kurz a few metres of rope which he began to unravel, using one hand and his teeth. The three strands of rope, tied together, would be sufficient to reach the guides.

As he struggled with the rope an avalanche suddenly came crashing down, pouring over Kurz and the guides and sweeping Angerer's body off the cliff. When the dust settled, Kurz was still there, slowly unpicking the rope . . . it took him five hours.

At last he was able to fasten the strands into one long line and lower it to the guides. They quickly tied on a rope and Kurz hauled it up, and to everyone's dismay, it proved too short. Hurriedly the guides tied a second rope to the first.

With the amazing fortitude and endurance he had shown throughout his ordeal Toni Kurz made ready to abseil. His useless left arm made things difficult, but after an hour he was ready and began to slide down the rope using a karabiner. The guides could almost touch the soles of his boots when suddenly he stopped descending – the knot joining the two ropes had jammed in the karabiner!

He was so close the guides could see what a terrible state he was in. His left arm stuck out at right angles from his body and his face was purple from frostbite and exhaustion. He murmured incoherently as he fiddled unsuccessfully with the jammed knot. The guides exhorted him to keep trying, but for Toni Kurz the trying was over. Few men in the annals of mountaineering have put up such a struggle as he did, but the mountain won in the end. 'I'm finished!' he cried, and swung lifeless on the rope.

The dramatic events of 1935 and 1936 ensured that any attempt on the Eigerwand would be news, especially in the sensational press where *Mordwand* (murder wall) frequently replaced *Nordwand* in the text. The climbers themselves, however, had grown more wary, both of the wall and the reporters. They were helped by a smoke-screen of pseudo-climbers who paraded below the wall, hoping to be noticed by press and public and perhaps get a free meal or a few francs for their 'expert opinion' in the papers.

That year, two Germans died on the Lauper Route, but two more, Matthias Rebitsch and Ludwig Vorg, both extremely good climbers, proved that the Eigerwand was not necessarily a death-trap. Three times they went on the face, on the first occasion to make a supply dump at the Rote Fluh, during which climb they discovered and brought down the mangled body of Andreas Hinterstoisser. Two days later they went higher, climbing the slippery Difficult Crack in bare feet, then crossing the Hinterstoisser Traverse (which they named) and leaving in place the vital rope. They discovered a perfect bivouac site which they called the Swallow's Nest and here they dumped some gear before turning round and retreating to Kleine Scheidegg, all in the course of a single day.

This was competence of a high order, and later in the season they were to exhibit more of it. After weeks of bad weather the face came into condition during the early part of August and Rebitsch and Vörg started up on August 11. By 10.30 a.m. they reached the Rote Fluh and their first supply dump. They carried gear from it to the Swallow's Nest, then returned and took up some more, before bivouacking at the Nest at 5 p.m. Next day they were soon away and by evening had reached Death Bivouac, but instead of bedding down there they decided to carry on a bit further. Unfortunately they were caught by a hailstorm on the Third Icefield and forced into an uncomfortable bivvy on the ice.

Next day the weather looked unpromising so the two Germans once again retreated, reaching the Swallow's Nest by evening and Kleine Scheidegg the day after.

Rebitsch and Vörg had been high on the face and returned. There had been no unnecessary heroics, no traumas. They had conclusively demonstrated that the Eigerwand could be climbed by experienced mountaineers. Observing all this was a man who had been to look at the wall early in the season and had dismissed it as out of condition, the thirty-one-year-old Anderl Heckmair, conqueror of the direct route on the Charmoz.

The 1938 season opened disastrously with the deaths of two Italians, Sandri and Menti, who fell before reaching the Difficult Crack. In Germany Ludwig Vörg had to find a new partner because Hias Rebitsch had been chosen for a Himalayan expedition, and it was perhaps inevitable that the new man should be Anderl Heckmair.[27] They formed a formidable combination: Vörg, known as 'the Bivvy King' because of his ability to make a comfortable bivouac under any conditions, recent conqueror of the tremendous North Face of Ushba in the Caucasus, an ace rock climber, strong and amiable, and the wiry, pinch-faced Heckmair, five years the senior at thirty-two, and already something of a legend after his exploits on the Charmoz and Jorasses. Both men were practically destitute, but by a stroke of good fortune a benefactor came forward who was willing to sponsor them to the best equipment available.

They wished to avoid the reporters and sensation mongers but their problem was that they were so well known, as leading members of the Munich School, that if they had turned up at the camp site below the cliff, word would quickly spread. With their new-found affluence, however, they avoided this by staying at a small hotel and posing as tourists. Whoever heard of Eigerwand climbers with money to spend on hotels? The ruse worked perfectly.

Meanwhile four good Austrian climbers had turned up: Leo Brankowsky, Rudi Fraissl, Heinrich Harrer and Fritz Kasparek. These last two made a cache of gear at the foot of the Rote Fluh and then on July 21 began their attempt proper. Brankowsky and Fraissl followed behind. Picking up the gear they had dumped they made their way, now heavily laden, towards the Difficult Crack, but judge their surprise when, reaching the bivouac cave before the crack, they discovered two climbers just waking up! They recognised at once Vorg and Heckmair.

Six on the face at one time was too many, but who was to go down? Sportingly the two Germans decided to retire, using as an excuse the onset of doubtful weather, though after all their preparation it must have been a bitter blow.

The four Austrians continued their climb, but Kasparek and Harrer were the faster pair and soon out-distanced their companions, who were actually in trouble, Fraissl having been struck by a stone. He shouted up to warn the leaders that he and Brankowski were going down. That night Kasparek and Harrer bivouacked at the foot of the Second Icefield.

Next day the steep ice proved a trial. Kasparek had only old-fashioned ten-point crampons and Harrer had no crampons at all, but relied on his nailed boots. They had to cut careful steps whilst trying to ignore the stones whistling overhead. As they reached the top of the icefield they were surprised to see below them two climbers almost running up the steps they had just cut. It was Heckmair and Vörg come to take the place of Fraissl and Brankowski.

Because of their sponsor's generosity the two Germans were far better equipped than the Austrians, and they were more experienced too, so it was natural that they should take the lead and that Heckmair should occupy pole position throughout. They climbed as separate teams.

The Flatiron and Death Bivouac were passed and, for the first time, the climbers found themselves on a series of icy slabs, sloping across the face, which they called the Ramp. Kasparek slipped here and fell fifteen metres, damaging his hand slightly, but Harrer held him. They all bivouacked for the night at the top of the Ramp.

Next morning they found a large icy chimney soaring up the rock above. Heckmair inched up it but just when it seemed as though he was about to succeed a hold broke away and he came tumbling down, held by a well-placed piton. Uninjured, he set off again, this time reaching the top, and brought up the others to join him.

The next obstacle looked truly formidable: a huge bulge of glistening green ice ten metres high and overhanging. Heckmair placed a piton up-side down in the ice and hung a rope loop from it. Aided by this he moved up but the ice was brittle and his handholds snapped once again, throwing him backwards. Again he was saved by his piton. Uninjured, he again attacked the ice, managing to hammer in a piton on top of the bulge. He passed a rope through this and with his companions tugging at the other end used it as a pulley to lift him just a little bit further. It was enough. He was able to cut holds in the top of the bulge and heave himself up.

It was a fine lead by Heckmair. Vörg soon followed, but it was very doubtful whether Harrer or Kasparek could lead the bulge in their inferior footwear, so the Germans dropped them a rope and pulled them up. The four men remained united for much of the rest of the climb.

They knew that the Ramp and Chimney had taken them too far to the left and that they had to traverse back into the centre of the face where the Spider waited for them. Casting around they came to a remarkable ledge known now as the Traverse of the Gods which took them out onto the small steep glacier of the Spider. Soon they were climbing the steep central rib. Only the headwall remained, with its dark menacing gullies – the 'legs' of the Spider.

But at that moment, just when victory seemed inevitable, one of those sudden storms for which the Eiger is notorious flung itself in fury at the face. Hail and snow lashed the four climbers as they clung on desperately to the steep ice. Then the whole world seemed to fall apart. Torrents of snow poured down from the headwalls, cascading into the natural funnel of the Spider and breaking in waves over the trapped climbers. It seemed certain that they would be swept from the face or suffocated under the enormous press of snow. But when the last avalanche had passed they were still there, hanging on grimly to their ice axes, heads bowed against the storm.

That night they bivouacked at the upper edge of the Spider, thankful to still be alive.

Next day it was still snowing as they set off up the final gullies. These proved far from easy and at one crucial moment Heckmair found himself slipping and cried a warning to Vörg:

> I shouted, 'Look out, Wiggerl!'
> Then I came off.
> Wiggerl was looking out all right. He took in as much rope as he could, but I bore straight down on him – not through thin air, for the gully was inclined, but in a lightning-swift slide. Just as I fell, I turned face outwards so as not to go head over heels.
> Wiggerl let the rope drop and caught me with his hands, and one of the points of my crampons went through his palm. I did turn head over heels, but in a split second I grabbed the rope-piton, which gave me such a jerk that I came up feet first again. I dug all twelve points of my irons into the ice – and found myself standing.
> The force with which I had come down on Wiggerl had knocked him out of his holds but he, too, had been able to save himself and there we were, standing about four feet below our stance on steep ice without any footholds. One stride and we were back on it again. Naturally, the pitons had come out and I immediately knocked new ones in.[28]

It was a close-run thing. Had they both come off they would inevitably have fetched off the Austrians below them and all four would have joined the growing list of Eigerwand victims.

The snow continued throughout the day, but the men climbed quickly, afraid to spend another freezing night on the face. They concentrated intently on what they were doing and what with that and the snow and mist they failed to hear the shouts of would-be rescuers who returned to the valley convinced the party was lost.

At 3.30 p.m., July 24, 1938, Heckmair, Vörg, Kasparek and Harrer stood on the summit of the Eiger having made the first ascent of the Eigerwand. It was a breakthrough as profound as the first ascent of the Matterhorn had been or the Brenva Spur but much more wide-reaching because it became the cornerstone of all modern mountaineering. Even when it was first done, in 1938, it probably wasn't the hardest climb in the Alps, technically, but it certainly was psychologically. The Eigerwand was a mental barrier, as so much of climbing is.

There was an amusing end to the tale. As the four men came down the mountainside there suddenly appeared out of the mist a small boy who gazed at them goggle-eyed. 'Have you come off the face?' he gasped in wonder. They assured him they had, at which he raced off down the hill shouting, 'They're coming! They've done it!'

The reporters had been beaten to the news after all.

CHAPTER EIGHTEEN

To Shoot a Fox

The philosophy of the Munich School quickly spread amongst the young climbers of most Alpine nations, including the Swiss. The cult of the nord-wand was avidly espoused by all who regarded themselves as avant-garde and, interestingly enough, was soon latched onto by the Japanese, a nation later destined to have a huge role to play in world mountaineering. In 1938 Ichiro and Jiro Taguchi with the guides Samuel Brawand and Christian Kaufmann Jnr climbed the North-East Face of the Schreckhorn in the Oberland. Mainly a steep ice wall, it was obviously climbed more in the style of Lauper than Welzenbach, since 300 steps had to be cut; nevertheless it was another sign of Japanese mountaineering advancement which by this time also included the first ascents of the Mittelegi Ridge and Mount Alberta, described earlier.

In the Caucasus where mountaineering had been eliminated by the after-math of the Russian Revolution, the Germans returned in 1928 and several times thereafter, followed in due course by Austrian, Swiss, French parties and even a British one – though the latter 'achieved considerable success in climbing new routes of a character more in line with the best British mountaineering of the day than the climbs made by the German and Aus-trian parties'.[1] It still included the first ascents of the difficult Tetnuld North Face and the South-East Face of Ushba South, a route not repeated for many years, and hardly, one would have thought, in the traditional British mould. Indeed, the Tetnuld climb was suggested by the fine Austrian climber, Schwarzgruber, and as for Ushba – a word which means 'the terrible' – the climbing was quite spectacular. Led by R.A. Hodgkin, with R.L. Beaumont and M.S. Taylor as companions, the crux was a ledge they called the Yellow Gangway:

> Lying on the outward sloping ledge with his back against its upper lip, Hodgkin wriggled along it for 20ft until his progress was barred by a bulge of rock. The only way to reach the continuation a few feet beyond was to tie a rope loop round a jammed stone, and swinging out over space to reach some small holds leading to a foot-wide ledge. The others followed, burdened as they were with rucksacks, and found the traverse even more difficult . . . The cliff opposite was more than sheer, for the great icicles which kept falling off did not touch anything for 2000ft.[2]

In 1936 a Bavarian group of Ludwig Vorg, Ludwig Schmaderer, Herbert Paidar and J. Thurstein climbed the North Face of Shkhelda and the difficult ice climb that is the West Face of Ushba. This last was done by Schmaderer and Vorg, both destined to make their names elsewhere. Schmaderer, who led Paidar on the climb on Shkhelda, was later to climb Tent Peak with him in the Himalaya before meeting his death at the hands of robbers in Spiti. In 1934 he had taken part in the first complete traverse of the Peuterey Ridge which included the Aiguille Noire by its difficult South Ridge and even more difficult descent by its North-West Ridge before continuing over the Aiguille Blanche and Mont Blanc de Courmayeur to Mont Blanc. Such a traverse appealed to the Russian climbers whom Schmaderer came into contact with and probably helped to found the Russian tradition of such long traverses in their own mountains, though the Austrians were also making multi-day traverses in the Causasus at this time.

Before the coming of western climbers to the Caucasus in the inter-war years the Russians had confined themselves to traditional ascents of Elbrus and similar peaks. These were often done in mass group outings. Only nineteen people climbed Elbrus in 1925 but ten years later the ascent was made by 2016. A code of mountaineering grew up in Russia strongly biased towards safety in which parties were graded according to ability and restricted to various routes which had to be done within set times. Where possible observers in the valley kept climbing parties within sight in case of accidents.[3]

That Matterhorn of the Caucasus, Ushba, was not climbed by a Russian party until 1935, yet only two years later fifty-seven climbers reached the top and the mountain had its first Russian traverse by Eugene Abalakov and Vassiliev. The Abalakovs, and especially Eugene's older brother Vitali,[4] played a leading part in establishing Russian mountaineering. In 1938 Eugene's party made the first intégrale traverse of Dykh-tau to Koshtan-tau, the beginnings of the great Russian traverse tradition which reached its pre-war apogee with his traverse of the Bezingi Ridge from Shkhara to Gestola.[5]

Contact between the Russians and the West was reduced during and after the Second World War. Russian climbing grew tremendously in numbers but, starved of western technical knowledge and high-quality equipment[6] and hampered by their restrictive methods, they inevitably fell behind in standards. It was not until the late fifties that Schmaderer's route of Shkhelda was repeated by Vitali Abalakov. Only their multi-day traverses stood them in good stead, enabling them to climb at a high standard for long periods, so that when they eventually came to Everest, in 1982, they were able to put up a new and technically difficult route on the South-West Face, getting eleven men to the top in relays. A multi-day traverse of one of the great Himalayan cirques, notably Nuptse–Lhotse–Everest, could be the ultimate mountaineering goal of all.

In Britain the events on the Continent had no practical effect on the climbing, which was of a smaller, more specialised kind. Most people went along with Strutt's sentiments, even if they did not express them so volubly. The accidents on the Eiger and elsewhere led to a general belief that many of the European climbers were trying to run before they could walk, or as Ken Wilson graphically put it, 'They thought they could walk on water.' The trouble was that Strutt's criticism was so indiscriminate that it included people like Welzenbach, Vorg, Schmaderer and Heckmair who were undoubtedly pushing the standards of mountaineering forward in a manner unparalleled since the time of Mummery.

There is, of course, an anomaly here. Whilst condemning the Munich climbers, the mountaineering Establishment turned a watery eye on Smythe and Brown's daring assaults on the Brenva Face (which, incidentally, some of the German experts were unable to repeat), and Hodgkin's party's ascent of Ushba and Tetnuld.

'We claim no credit for this route,' wrote J.R. Jenkins, one of the party on Tetnuld. 'It was Herr Schwarzgruber, the great Austrian climber, who suggested it to us ... he worked out this magnificent route up the North Face of Tetnuld, which he cherished a great desire to climb. Much to the relief of his wife, circumstances prevented him from carrying out this project ...

'The route appeared to us quite terrifying, and for a modest British party to carry on where an expert Austrian party had left off (and moreover to climb *a north face*) caused us some trepidation and no small degree of amusement.'[7]

It was all of a piece. Daring exploits were permissible done by chaps one knew and trusted. Harold Raeburn's earlier solo traverse of the Meije, in 1919, did no more than raise eyebrows. He was fifty-four at the time: 'a daring exploit justified only by his exceptional powers'.[8]

But by and large British mountaineering between the wars was concerned with two major fields of activity: the advancement of home-based rock climbing and the exploration of the Himalaya, particularly the attempts to climb Everest.

The inter-war years saw the birth of the working-class climber, helped by the youth hostel movement and, regrettably, the leisure which comes from unemployment. The movement did not achieve any real significance until after the Second World War, when things were very different, but the Sheffield lads who explored the gritstone and the Glasgow lads in Glencoe made a solid foundation on which their successors could build. 'Eight years ago,' wrote the chronicler of the Scots, Alastair Borthwick, in 1939, 'fresh air was still the property of moneyed men, a luxury open to few ... Hiking was the hobby of an enthusiastic handful, and climbing was a rich man's sport.'[9] Their leader was Jock Nimlin, who specialised in the crags of the

Cobbler, the rocks nearest to Glasgow. These new climbers were rarely attracted to the existing climbing clubs, most of whose members lived in a different world. Instead they formed their own clubs – the Creag Dhu in Glasgow, for example, the Sheffield Climbing Club on gritstone. 'None of them could afford proper climbing gear. They climbed with all sorts of boots studded with many varieties of nails, and often wore workmen's overalls or cast-off plus-fours purchased for a song in the city's rag-market. A good rope was a rare treasure, and worn-out ropes were passed down and used until the very threads curled up in disdain.'[10]

The doyen of gritstoners was Frank Elliott who was also one of the first to climb on the Peak District limestone, then largely regarded as not sound enough for climbing. Elliott's Unconquerable, a thirty-foot sloping crack in the gritstone outcrop at Cratcliffe, was first climbed in 1933 and remained the hardest route on gritstone until after the Second World War. It is still graded Hard Very Severe.

A new influx of talent came from Cambridge. Fred Pigott, Morley Wood, Ivan Waller, Jack Longland and Alf Bridge were amongst the leaders and if we take one crag only as an example – the Black Rocks of Cromford – they were responsible for the finest and hardest climbs. In 1928 Longland led Birch Tree Wall, seconded by Waller, and in the following year Bridge led Lean Man's Superdirect with Longland and Waller following, a climb thought so difficult and dangerous that for fifteen years they did not record it. This self-censorship and the concept of 'unjustifiable' climbs pointed up the differences between British and European climbing mores.

There is no doubt that the development of gritstone techniques, where friction, delicacy and balance replaced the old grab and pull, helped immeasurably when transferred to the larger cliffs of Wales and the Lakes. The hardest climb in Britain at the outbreak of the First World War was the Central Buttress of Scafell led by Herford, who was a gritstoner. Now it was the turn of the finest Welsh cliff to fall to the gritstone experts: Clogwyn Du'r Arddu, known to all climbers as Cloggy.

This stupendous cliff on the flanks of Snowdon is divided into two halves by a steeply sloping ledge, the Eastern Terrace. On its left is the East Buttress, steep walls leading to a pinnacle, whilst on its right is the West Buttress, a huge bulk of grossly overlapping slabs like a badly shuffled deck of cards. These two contrasting buttresses are supported on either hand by other rocks which were in due course to provide stern sport, but the major challenge is, and always has been, the two main buttresses.

The Abraham brothers, Mallory and others had made tentative probings at the great crag and so had Herbert Carr who wrote in 1926:

> The great defects of the cliff are . . . the extreme steepness and north aspect renders it cold and repellent in any but the best weather, and

even in summer it hardly gets any sun, except late in the day ...
No breach seems either possible or desirable along the whole extent
of the W. Buttress, though there is the faintest of faint hopes for
a human fly rather towards its left side ... The scenery here is not
surpassed on any crag in Wales ... The E. Buttress has never
been climbed. The final wall is quite impossible, but the lower two
hundred feet below a broad green gallery may yet be conquered by
a bold and expert party.[11]

The first real breach in the defences of the crag came in 1927 when a
Rucksack Club party led by A.S. Pigott, after three reconnaissances, climbed
the East Buttress using cracks and corners like a series of gritstone problems
piled one on another. It seemed to the pioneers to be the easiest way
up the cliff, though it was reckoned to be the hardest climb in Britain
after Central Buttress of Scafell. A.B. Hargreaves, who made the third
ascent in 1929 with F.E. Hicks and E.A. Stewardson thought that Pigott's
lead of the final crack, sight unseen, 'must be one of the finest ever
brought off'.[12] It was therefore most appropriate that the route was named
after its originator.

Now the prize became the great sloping slabs of the West Buttress, one
of the most impressive sweeps of rock in Britain. A curious fault below
the slabs makes access difficult, but in 1928 a combined gritstone team of
Cambridge climbers and Rucksack Club men led by Jack Longland succeeded
in breaching the defences near the left edge and climbed a delicate, elegant
line (one pitch was called Faith & Friction) to the top. Longland's Climb,
too, was Very Severe.

Seconding Longland on the climb was Pigott, who therefore had the
distinction of taking part in the first two major ascents of Cloggy. There
was also Frank Smythe, who had been Longland's original partner on an
earlier attempt and even earlier, with the Scots climber J.H.B. Bell, had
poked around the West Buttress and seen the line that Longland eventually
took. But Smythe could never have led the climb; his forte was big bold
expeditions in the Alps and Himalaya, not rock climbing at home. Maybe his
lack of the great rock climbing ability which so many of his contemporaries
possessed was one factor in his inferiority complex. Most of them were also
what he once referred to as 'those horrid northern climbers'. He was not
popular.[13]

There was, however, no dearth of good rock climbers in the inter-war
years. Besides those already mentioned, there were, to select just a few,
F.E. Hicks, C.W. Marshall, Ivan Waller and C.W.F. Noyce in Wales; A.T.
Hargreaves, H.M. Kelly, M. Linnell and R.J. Birkett in the Lake District;
G.G. Macphee, J.H.B. Bell, W.H. Murray and Jock Nimlin in Scotland –
though by this time territorial limits were already disappearing, helped by

motor cars and club huts. Some of these men, like Noyce, climbed in the Alps and Himalaya as well; others remained wedded to British rock, or Scottish snow and ice.

Women, too, took part in the climbing; Mallory's daughters, Clare and Berridge, Ivy Critchley, Mrs E. Kelly, and Mabel Barker, who was the first woman to climb the Central Buttress of Scafell, in 1924. There were several others climbing at a high standard for the time: Nancy Ridyard did six first woman's ascents on Dow Crag and two on Gimmer, whilst Blanche-Eden Smith seconded Kelly on the first ascent of Moss Ghyll Grooves in 1926, one of the most popular climbs on Scafell. In 1921 the Pinnacle Club was formed, largely owing to the effort of Pat (Emily) Kelly. It was the first rock climbing club (as distinct from mountaineering club) founded by women for women: 'It was very splendid for some women to be always able to borrow crutches in the shape of a man's help, and a man's rope, but it is even better to find we have feet of our own and can climb some things as well as a man climber.'[14]

Sadly, Pat Kelly was killed in the following year after a fall on Tryfan.

The spreading popularity of the sport was also signalled by the emergence in the Lake District of the Lakeland Mountain Guides, led by Jerry Wright who after the Second War went on to form the Mountaineering Association. Early in the previous century some of the inns had provided guides for walking the fells and there had been a French climbing guide, Gaspard, at Wasdale Head during the winters round the turn of the century and up to the First World War. The emergence of professional British climbing guides was something new and not altogether welcomed by the clubs. Nevertheless, the guides, all local climbers, seemed to fulfil a need and there were some distinguished clients even amongst the climbing establishment, including Norton, who had led the 1924 Everest expedition. 'They tell me you are to be avoided like the plague,' said Norton, engaging Wright for a climb, 'and that's good enough recommendation for me.'[15]

But as the world spun towards a second war two climbers rose head and shoulders above others on the British rock climbing scene. One was a quiet-mannered youngster called Colin Kirkus and the other a dark-haired strongly built prodigy called Menlove Edwards. Both came from Liverpool and therefore had easy access to the Welsh hills.

The best of Kirkus came between 1929 and 1934 and ended with the terrible accident on a snow-covered Ben Nevis when his great friend and climbing companions, Maurice Linnell, had his head severed by the rope and Kirkus himself was badly injured. Before then, however, he had been the golden boy of climbing in this country with routes still hailed as masterpieces: Lot's Groove, Glyder Fach; Central Route, Tryfan; Direct Route, Dinas Mot; Pinnacle Wall, Craig yr Ysfa and his eponymous route at Cwm Silyn. Above all, though, he is remembered for his routes on Cloggy, a name which he is said to have coined for the great cliff. These were Great Slab, Chimney Route, Pedestal Crack, Birthday Crack and Curving Crack. They were all Very Severe and to them he added three easier routes – the first eight routes to be added to the cliff since Longland's Climb.

Great Slab was the first of these climbs, in 1930, and is now perhaps the easiest of the classic lines. On the first ascent, however, it was littered with loose rock and grass. Kirkus, to whom fear seems an alien concept, made an even bolder climb a year later when he soloed Pinnacle Wall on Craig yr Ysfa. Tragically, Kirkus died during the war when his plane was shot down over Germany.

Kirkus's companion on Chimney Route, done in 1931, was J. Menlove Edwards, who ten years later was to add his own significant contribution to Clogwyn Du'r Arddu in a magnificent route at the side of the Great Slab called Bow-Shaped Slab, after a curious configuration of the rock.[16] But Edwards was not really a Cloggy man; he preferred the more readily accessible cliffs round Cwm Idwal or just above the road in Llanberis Pass.

Edwards was a psychiatrist who was in many ways his own chief patient. He conducted a lifelong test against the limits of fear, climbing sometimes with badly nailed boots or with unknown novices, regardless of the possible consequences, and indulging in madcap adventures like swimming the raging Linn of Dee or trying to row across the storm-tossed Minch. This obsession with mental limits showed in his climbing and just as the Munich School pushed forward the bounds of alpinism, so Edwards pushed forward British rock climbing by refusing to acknowledge the limits already established. Kirkus was a genius, but Edwards was an innovator, and for that reason the more important of the two.

In 1931 he climbed the Flake Crack of Central Buttress in boots instead of the usual rubbers and without any of the complicated rope work at the chockstone then thought essential. Always a man to power his way through problems he simply struggled up the great overhanging flake. In the following year he began his campaign against the repulsive cliffs of Clogwyn y Geifr in Cwm Idwal. The most prominent feature was the great gash of Devil's Kitchen, climbed back in 1898. A few other climbs had been added since, but the place was rotten, grassy and often wet. It always seemed unfriendly. Nevertheless, Edwards began with a solo climb of Devil's Buttress, then between March and September of the following year he added fourteen more routes and a variant. Such thoroughness became typical of the man, though in the case of the Devil's Kitchen cliffs none of the routes became popular.

This acceptance of bad rock and vertical grass was merely a testing of limits again, but sometimes he took it too far. There is a route on the nearby crag of Glyder Fawr called simply Grass Route: 'Whether this strange route will ever gain popularity remains to be seen but it certainly ranks high among Edwards' more futuristic discoveries,' commented a guidebook, forty years later.[17]

In 1936 Edwards produced the guide to Cwm Idwal and he was to produce two more – to Tryfan and Lliwedd – shortly after, in collaboration with Wilfrid Noyce. 'He neither climbed nor wrote easily,' said Noyce later.[18] Everything was a struggle to Edwards, against fear and for perfection. Not for him the sort of guide Kelly was producing in the Lakes, which traces a route up a cliff handhold by handhold with scientific remorselessness. Such a route might be anywhere and Edwards wanted to show his routes in their context; after all, a climb on Clogwyn y Geifr was not like a climb on Clogwyn Du'r Arddu and the guide should indicate that fact. The result was three of the best written guidebooks ever to grace the annals of climbing and certainly the nearest the genre has ever come to literature. Unfortunately as *guidebooks* they were less successful. Climbers standing on a cold ledge, with rain dripping down their necks, were less interested in literary merit than in being told what to grab next.

His fondness for loose rock had led Edwards to the cliffs of the Llanberis Pass as early as 1931. Here he found that the rocks, though relatively short, were extremely steep and technical. On the Three Cliffs – Dinas Cromlech, Carreg Wastad, and Clogwyn y Grochan – his was the first exploratory route and many of the most popular climbs are of his creation and, though many now seem relatively easy, it must be remembered that, like Great Slab, they have been picked clean by generations of climbers. When they were first done they were loose and vegetated. In the final analysis of Edwards it might well be said that his acceptance of 'bad' rock changed the attitude of climbers and had the most profound impact on future route-making in Britain.[19]

If the glamour was with Wales during these years it must not be thought that the Lake District was devoid of action. Some of the Welsh activists also climbed in the Lakes – Linnell and Kirkus, for example, who both did routes on the fierce rocks of Scafell's East Buttress, but there were also some quietly spectacular routes done by locals. Indeed, the area seemed to attract climbers who, for no apparent reason, suddenly put up one or two climbs of outstanding quality and difficulty, often far ahead of their day. As early as 1919 Joe Roper did Great Central Route on Dow Crag, a Hard Very Severe, and a year later the adjacent Black Wall, a grim 100-foot pitch as evil as its name suggests. In 1934 Fred Balcombe, persuaded to help in guidebook work for Great Gable, produced an astonishing series of climbs including Buttonhook on Kern Knotts, HVS, and the classic Engineer's Slabs, VS. Five years later, in 1939, Jim Haggas produced Hangover, the first breach in the formidable main face of Dove Crag above Ullswater. The route was aptly named, for the overhanging nature of the face makes any route seem unlikely to the untrained eye. Haggas showed that he who dares, wins.

Most consistent was A.T. Hargreaves who put up the outstanding Deer Bield Crack, with G.G. Macphee in 1930 and though they thought it only Severe, it was a Hard Very Severe, ahead of its time, and much harder than Longland's or Pigott's on Cloggy, done only a couple of years earlier. In 1936 there was an even more remarkable attempt on this obscure crag when a young South African climber called Dick Barry attempted what was later to become Deer Bield Buttress, a route not climbed until 1951 and still regarded as extreme. Barry actually overcame the first crux before abandoning the climb.

Barry was twenty years old at the time and a mining student at Birmingham University, where he had also been introduced to climbing. He was soon tackling the hardest routes of the day on British rock and with companions like J.R. Jenkins (also a Birmingham mining student) some difficult Alpine climbs. Tragically his promising career was cut short in 1938 whilst attempting an unclimbed South African peak, the Monk's Cowl, in the Drakensberg mountains. Barry's companion had fallen and pulled him from his stance. The two men fell and rolled almost 200 feet before coming to rest, concussed and bruised but otherwise unhurt. Somehow they became separated, darkness approached, and in the morning Barry's body was found in a gully. He had fallen 400 feet.[20]

A group of working-class climbers also arose in the Lake District, similar to those in the Peak, except that they were in work and added their climbing to a week of heavy toil in quarry or mine. The leader was undoubtedly Jim Birkett, a quarryman from Langdale with a passion for collecting birds' eggs, and a teetotal non-smoker who was immensely strong. At first he climbed in his working clogs.

With companions C.W. Hudson and C.R. Wilson in 1938 he made a new breach in the formidable East Buttress of Scafell, the first for five years. May Day Climb was a Hard Very Severe and – much to the disgust of the Establishment – pitons were used for protection. 'The hand that would drive a piton into British rock would shoot a fox or net a salmon,' it thundered, mentioning the two most heinous crimes in the calendar.

It was not the end to controversy. Birkett established a local association of professional guides where members had to be born and brought up in Westmorland or Cumberland and in an unfortunate newspaper interview Hudson took a proprietorial line over Lakeland crags. 'It is time we were recognised as the best guides in our own mountains,' he was reported as saying on the occasion of the first ascent of Birkett's most famous climb, Overhanging Bastion on the Castle Rock of Triermain by Birkett, Wilson and Muscroft in 1939. Other guides, still flourishing, took exception to this and an acrimonious but brief exchange of views took place.

Birkett was to go on to make many more fine climbs through the war years and beyond.

Steady though these advances in British rock climbing were, they were at the same time incestuous: they had little relevance either to what the British themselves were doing in the Himalaya or to new routes in the Alps and elsewhere.[21] In the post-war years this was to change.

For many years American climbing was more or less confined to finding the easiest way to the top. 'You didn't need to find a precipice and push your skills to the limit to find adventure; just to reach Colorado and climb a peak was adventure enough.'[22] The summit was everything and technical climbing, where it existed at all, followed the traditions of Europe rooted in the nineteenth century. Even when climbing began in Yosemite, it was the pinnacles, not the great walls, which first attracted attention. It also explains the early preoccupation climbers had with things like Shiprock, a huge 1700-feet high volcanic plug rising from the desert in New Mexico.

Such textbooks as existed tended to be English-language ones and some of the repugnance felt by the English towards the doings of the Munich School was reflected in America. Kenneth Henderson, one of the best American climbers of the period, thought the men who climbed the Eigerwand were mentally unbalanced. But the American attitude to the use of pitons was not as rigid as the British. For one thing the routes were many times longer and for another there was not the dead hand of tradition weighting them down. Shooting foxes would have seemed entirely logical. Even Henderson used twenty pegs on the first ascent of the Direct Exum Ridge, Grand Teton, with Jack Durrance, though admittedly for belays and not as handholds.

The emerging climbing scene was a fascinating mixture of native adventure, solid old world expertise from leaders like Albert Ellingwood, Kenneth Henderson and Bob Underhill, and immigrants who had been trained in the Eastern Alps like Fritz Wiessner, the Stettner brothers and Jack Durrance.

Ellingwood had been a Rhodes Scholar at Oxford and during the vacations had learned rock climbing in the Lake District. When he returned to Colorado Springs in 1914 he brought with him the techniques of belaying acquired in England and was soon putting up the routes which exceeded anything previously seen in Colorado.

In August 1920 Ellingwood and Barton Hoag climbed the Lizard Head (13,113 ft), last and certainly most difficult of the great Colorado peaks. It had been named by the Hayden survey and it consists of a 350-foot volcanic plug sitting on top of a whaleback covered in detritus. It isn't difficult to see where the scree has come from: the plug is comprised of rotten rock, the like of which most climbers avoid. '. . . The rottenness of its rock tower makes safety too much a matter of luck for comfort,' says the guidebook. 'Take photograph and go away.'[23]

Ellingwood set off up this rotten monolith, raining loose debris onto his unfortunate companion below. Both men wore heavy nailed boots and Ellingwood used three pitons in making the ascent. Four and a half hours after starting they stood on top.

The descent went well until near the base of the tower when their abseil rope jammed and in trying to free it they brought down rocks onto their heads. Stunned, they clung to the rocks for dear life until their senses returned. As they still could not free the rope they simply slid down it as far as they could and then tried, in gathering darkness, to climb down the last few feet of rock. Ellingwood made it but his companion fell and slid until the wall became vertical, fifteen feet from the bottom, where he simply jumped off, fortunately without injury.

The Lizard Head was the hardest climb of its day in the United States but it attracted few others to its shattered walls. It is reputed to be even worse now than it was then.

In 1922 a mathematics professor from Princeton, James Alexander, armed with tennis shoes and an ice axe, climbed the formidable East Face of Longs Peak by a cleft now known as Alexander's Chimney. It was not as difficult as some of Ellingwood's routes but it was the first breach in a major face and was something of a portent in that Alexander began his climbing in Colorado, then went on to climb in the Alps – a reversal of what up to that point had been usual.

Five years later a much more difficult way up the face of Longs was discovered by the two German immigrants, Joe and Paul Stettner. They had climbed and skied in the Kaisergebirge, but when they emigrated to the States they settled in Chicago, a long way from the mountains. In September 1927 they set off for a holiday in Colorado. They had some pitons and they acquired a sisal rope to add to their crampons and long ice axes. Though it was late in the season they insisted against local advice in starting up the face, choosing a line just left of Alexander's Chimney. Climbing in felt-soled *Kletterschuhe*, they romped up the difficult rock, arriving at the top seven hours after starting out. Called Stettners Ledges it was the most difficult climb in the USA and was not repeated for nine years. The brothers went on to make several more exciting climbs including another, the self-explanatory Joe's Solo, on the East Face of Longs Peak in 1936.

Meanwhile Bob Underhill, after his success in the Tetons in 1931, joined some Sierra Club climbers in California, teaching them modern rope techniques, a subject of which they knew nothing. With him they climbed the East Face of Mount Whitney – not particularly hard, but a revelation to the Sierrans. Two years later, with a new influx of talent, the club paid its first visit to Yosemite Valley and twelve months after that made the first ascent of Higher Cathedral Spire by the South-West Face; this was the real beginning in a granite wonderland that was to be the forcing ground of so much present-day climbing.

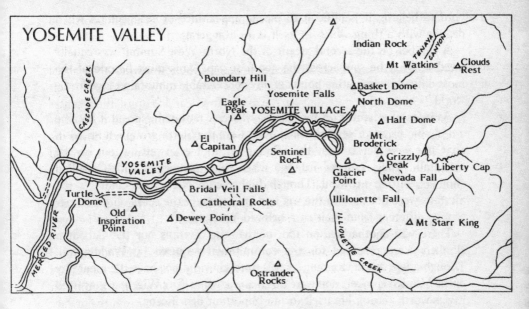

YOSEMITE VALLEY

Indian Rock

Mt Watkins △ Clouds Rest

Boundary Hill

△ Basket Dome

Yosemite Falls

North Dome

Eagle Peak YOSEMITE VILLAGE

△ Half Dome

El Capitan

Mt Broderick △

Sentinel Rock △

△ Grizzly Peak

Liberty Cap

YOSEMITE VALLEY

Glacier Point

Nevada Fall

Turtle Dome

Bridal Veil Falls

Illilouette Fall

Cathedral Rocks

Old Inspiration Point

△ Dewey Point

△ Mt Starr King

Ostrander Rocks

CASCADE CREEK

MERCED RIVER

ILLILOUETTE CREEK

TENAYA CANYON

Techniques were developed to make the most of the pegs: tension climbing, pendulums, double rope techniques in general and, much later, a whole series of specially developed pitons customised for the Yosemite cracks. These began with the hard steel pitons forged by John Salathé, an immigrant Swiss ironworker, in the 1940s and culminated in 1959 with Chouinard and Frost's tiny, plug-like, Rurp (Realised Ultimate Reality Piton) designed specifically for a minuscule crack in Kat Pinnacle.

With techniques sharpened in Yosemite, Colorado and the Tetons, climbers began to look at some of the sensational monoliths which America possesses, especially the Devil's Tower and Shiprock. The former had been climbed in 1893 by some locals who had hammered a series of wooden pegs into the strange fluted columns, creating a ladder soaring into the sky, but by the 1930s this had rotted and was so dangerous that the National Park authorities forbade its use. In 1937 Fritz Wiessner led two companions to the top in the first real ascent.

Wiessner had just returned from a successful ascent of Mount Waddington in British Columbia, the 'mystery mountain' that had first aroused the interest of Don Munday and his wife when they saw it from Vancouver Island in 1925. The Mundays spent several seasons trying to reach their secret and almost inaccessible peak and then trying to climb it. Both were formidable tasks. The peak is one of the most impressive on the American continent and when the Mundays made the first ascent of the subsidiary North-West Summit in 1928 they looked across at the final spire in awe: 'only a few hundred feet distant, the great spire poised in the void, an incredible nightmarish thing that must be seen to be believed, and then is hard to believe; it is difficult to escape appearance of exaggeration when dealing with a thing which in itself is an exaggeration.'[24]

A climber on the second ascent of the North-West Summit was equally awed at what he saw across the 500-foot gap: 'This must be one of the most difficult culminating points of any considerable mountain range in the world.'[25]

As news of attempts on the Mundays' secret mountain spread it became a desirable prize for several teams. First were the Sierra group who tried in 1935 but were defeated by the weather without even setting foot on the mountain. They returned in 1936 when they teamed up with Canadian climbers, but to no avail. Though highly competent rock climbers, the Sierrans were not used to the wet and icy nature of the rocks on Waddington, so different from their own beloved Yosemite.

There was another reason too: neither the Sierrans nor the Canadian climbers were prepared for the commitment required by Waddington. Though adept at aid climbing by this time, they did not have the mentality of the Munich climbers and were taken aback when Fritz Wiessner suggested it was worth risking life itself for an important first ascent.

Wiessner and three companions turned up at the mountain whilst the others were there but held back until failure was certain, allowing the others right of first attempt. Wiessner was trained in the Eastern Alps and had made important ascents there. Indeed, he had been in Europe hoping to take part in the attempts on the Walker Spur of the Grandes Jorasses when a cable had tempted him back to take part in the Waddington expedition.

Wiessner's companion on the climb was Bill House.[26] They stormed up the couloir which led to the final tower – a couloir the Sierrans had avoided because of the danger of stonefall – and though they failed at their first attempt they were back next day, and after climbing the final rock tower in *Kletterschuhe* reached the summit at four in the afternoon. It was so tiny that they could only stand on it one at a time.

The South Face of Mount Waddington was not climbed again for six years, after which there was a gap of thirty-five years before anyone else succeeded.

The Sierrans, fully alive to the use of pitons and double rope techniques, still had moral qualms about the overuse of such aids, perhaps from reading British literature on the subject. In 1939 Bestor Robinson, one of their leading lights, added another weapon to the armoury: expansion bolts, a device which many years later was to divide the climbing world in the same way that pitons had done and before that, crampons. Robinson decided that it was logical to use the bolts for protection where nothing else existed, but not for direct aid.

All this was brought about by the Sierrans' decision to climb the great volcanic plug of Shiprock, which rose out of the desert like some vast ruined cathedral, 1700 feet high. There had been several previous attempts but all had failed. However, the Californians, with their superior aid techniques, climbed the great rock in a two-day push, bivouacking in a shallow cave below the final tower.[27] Four bolts were used: two as belays and two as runners. It was the first use of bolts on American mountains (or possibly anywhere) and opened the floodgates to misuse and misinterpretation. Even the pioneers of Shiprock referred to themselves as 'rock engineers'.

Shiprock wasn't climbed again until 1952. Meanwhile the Californians had continued to perfect their techniques, now developing along unique lines, independent of elsewhere. In later years they were to have a profound influence on the rest of the world.

In 1947 John Salathé and Anton Nelson made the first real ascent of Lost Arrow, the last unclimbed pinnacle of Yosemite Valley. The top had been reached the previous year by some devious rope tricks from the nearby main cliff edge, but now Salathé and Nelson attacked the pinnacle by means of Lost Arrow Chimney, which led to the notch between the pinnacle and main cliff. Salathé had reached this notch before, in a remarkable solo effort when he abseiled down to the notch from above and got some way up the final spire, reaching a ledge which now bears his name. He returned with a companion a week later and got to within fifty feet of the top before retreating. Now he had decided to climb the pinnacle from the bottom and in four days of tough climbing he and Nelson finally reached the summit, using eight bolts on the final blank spire.

It was the hardest climb done in America at that time. Now that all the spires and pinnacles were out of the way, Yosemite climbers could turn their attention to the great blank walls and write a whole new chapter of mountaineering history.

CHAPTER NINETEEN

Blanks on the Map

In the years immediately following the First World War Himalayan climbing was as much about exploration as about ascents. So much was unknown and what was known only served further to whet the appetite of those who wanted to see what lay beyond the last blue mountain. It was not for nothing that the earliest Everest expeditions were joint ventures between the Alpine Club and the Royal Geographical Society.

The effects of altitude needed to be explored as well and, to this purpose, Kellas was persuaded to continue with his physiological experiments interrupted by the war. He tried out some elementary oxygen apparatus on Kamet, helped by Major H.T. Morshead from the Survey of India. Already the Royal Geographical Society had an eye on Everest: talk of climbing the mountain had been around for some years.

A joint committee was set up of the Royal Geographical Society and the Alpine Club to organise an expedition with the specific aim: 'That the principal object of the expedition should be the ascent of Mount Everest, to which all preliminary reconnaissance should be directed.'[1] This seems simple enough, yet such were the characters behind the scenes, each with his own axe to grind, that from the outset the Committee was never unified. For example, J.P. Farrar, President of the Alpine Club and a forceful personality, wanted the great Swiss topographer Marcel Kurz to accompany the expedition as surveyor, but because Kurz wished to be acknowledged as sole author of any map he produced the RGS wouldn't have him. On the other hand, when Freshfield as former President of the RGS proposed that Kellas should lead the expedition, Farrar made his scathing remark about Kellas having 'only walked about on steep snow with a lot of coolies', adding dismissively that 'the only time they got on a very steep place they all tumbled down and ought to have been killed!'[2]

This was hardly fair on poor Kellas, who at the time probably had more Himalayan experience than anybody else, but Farrar wanted George Finch and his brother Max, two Australians who had been educated in Switzerland, to lead the expedition which he wanted to go all-out for the top immediately. In the end it was decided that there should be a two-year plan, with the first expedition reconnoitring all the approaches to the mountain (about which practically nothing was known) and the second to climbing it. The leader was to be General Charles Bruce, who as a young officer had been with Mummery on Nanga Parbat. Unfortunately, the General's duties prevented him from taking over immediately, so in the end the conduct of the first expedition fell to Lieutenant-Colonel Charles Howard-Bury, a wealthy Anglo-Irish traveller and game hunter.[3]

Harold Raeburn was chosen as climbing leader, together with Kellas, George Mallory and Guy Bullock. The Indian Survey seconded a survey team led by two experienced mountaineers, Morshead and Wheeler. The doctor, Wollaston, was also a climber, so the party was a fairly strong one. Unfortunately, Finch was excluded on medical grounds, though there is some reason to think these might have been an excuse used by the Committee to drop the Australian. Finch tended to be outspoken, but he was also a protégé of Farrar who was daggers drawn with the Committee Secretary, Arthur Hinks.[4]

The main party, supported by porters of the Sherpa and Bhotia tribes, as suggested by Kellas, and a hundred mules supplied by the Indian Army, left Darjeeling on May 18 and began the long and arduous journey through Sikkim and onto the bleak Tibetan plateau. The surveyors had gone ahead by a different route, but the two groups met up at Kampa Dzong on June 5.

Already there were serious problems. In the jungles of Sikkim the mules proved totally inadequate and had to be retired. From now on local transport such as yaks and hill mules had to be relied upon and it was sometimes a lengthy process finding sufficient numbers. Then, just before Kampa Dzong, Kellas had a heart attack and died. Wollaston was also worried about Raeburn, who despite being climbing leader, was fifty-six years old, bad tempered and ill. 'Raeburn has become very old and is a great responsibility,' wrote Howard-Bury, 'and like all Scotch, he is very obstinate.'[5] Not wanting another death, Wollaston sent him home. Thus almost at a stroke the party was bereft of its two most experienced Himalayan climbers.

When Raeburn left, Mallory took over as climbing leader. He must have wondered what he was doing there; he had come down from Cambridge with a modest degree, taken up schoolmastering, a job for which he was unsuited, and been persuaded by Winthrop Young that he should do something to get himself noticed, as a launch pad for a writing career. Everest was that something.

He fancied himself as one of the fashionable Bloomsbury intellectual set, but in fact he was only tolerated for his good looks, which were exceptional. 'Mon dieu! – George Mallory! – When that's been written, what more need be said?' wrote the homosexual Lytton Strachey, overwhelmed by Mallory's resemblance to a Greek god.[6] He was a reasonably competent climber, though not in the same class as Finch, and a good writer.

He disliked Tibet, 'a hateful country inhabited by hateful people', and he wrote to a friend: 'I sometimes think of this expedition as a fraud from beginning to end, invented by the enthusiasms of one man, Younghusband;

puffed up by the would-be wisdom of certain pundits in the AC; and imposed upon the youthful ardour of your humble servant.'[7]

He developed a love–hate relationship with the mountain matched only by that of Whymper for the Matterhorn half a century earlier. When asked by a reporter why he wanted to climb Everest, he replied, 'Because it is there.' This enigmatic statement has been argued over ever since, but the explanation might well be that Mallory *didn't know* why he wanted to climb Everest. He was a man trapped between the hammer of uncertainty and the anvil of ambition.

During the reconnaissance his companion was Guy Bullock, an old school friend.[8] Bullock had replaced Finch at the last minute, merely on Mallory's say-so, and this was typical of the *ad hoc* way these early Everest attempts were managed. There was no attempt to find out who were the best climbers in the country; the essential thing was that they should 'fit in'. From this viewpoint, Bullock was certainly an improvement on Finch!

Mallory and Bullock reconnoitred the Rongbuk Glacier which flows below the great North Face of Everest and from the Lho La looked down into Nepal, then a forbidden country to Westerners. They saw the Western Cwm and its tremendous icefall and thought that, even if it were permissible, it would be impractical.

The most obvious way to the summit seemed to be by the North Ridge, a spur of the mountain which ran down from the great North-East Ridge to a dip, the North Col, before rising to the huge subsidiary peak of Changtse. The problem was that to reach the North Col from the Rongbuk Glacier seemed too hazardous and it wasn't until Wheeler discovered the East Rongbuk Glacier, which led to the other side of the col, that the way seemed certain.

The party returned home satisfied with their work and convinced they had found the route to the summit. Based near the Rongbuk Monastery, an expedition would travel up the Rongbuk to the junction with the East Rongbuk, then follow that to below the North Col, where a sort of advanced base (Camp III) would be established. From there by steep slopes to the North Col, then up the North Ridge to its junction with the North-East Ridge and follow that to the summit. This was the route which every pre-war Everest expedition tried to follow.

When the expedition returned in the following year there were fifteen members[9] led by General Bruce and including Finch who, as a scientist, was in charge of the oxygen apparatus. The decision to use oxygen was not taken lightly, partly on ethical grounds – it was regarded by some as cheating – and partly because the apparatus was heavy and clumsy.

Mallory was convinced that the uppermost camp from which the summit attempt should be made could not be lower than 27,000 feet. This meant there needed to be an intermediate camp between there and the North Col

(22,900 ft). In the event it was decided to have four climbers in the assault, rather than two, and because there were not enough Sherpas for the carrying involved in all this, they set off from the col on May 20, hoping to establish the assault camp as high as possible. Already expectation of reaching 26,000 feet had been blighted by five of the nine porters being out of action through mountain sickness. The rest struggled up the ridge against a rising cold wind until at about 25,000 feet Mallory thought enough was enough. Two small tents were pitched on a ledge and the porters were sent down.

At eight next morning the four climbers, Mallory, Somervell, Morshead and Norton, set off up the North Ridge. All but Somervell had some frostbite and Morshead, worst affected, soon turned back. The others struggled on to about 26,800 feet before also retreating. They picked up Morshead at the tents, and because they were all tired and Morshead was in bad shape, they decided to tie onto a single rope with Mallory in the lead. The steps they had made on the ascent had been obliterated by the weather and they found the descent decidedly awkward with interminable step-cutting.[10]

Just as they were crossing a steep couloir, Morshead slipped. Somervell, who was last man, was just moving from one step to the next and was taken completely unawares. He was yanked off the slope and so too was Norton. The three climbers went sliding down the gully, desperately trying to use their axes as brakes. Mallory in the act of cutting a step heard the noise behind him and immediately realised what had happened. Almost by reflex he struck his axe deep into the snow and whipped a coil of the rope round it. The strain came on the axe with a sudden jerk – and both axe and rope held. Mallory had undoubtedly saved all their lives.[11]

Though not injured, they were badly shaken by the incident. Morshead's condition was deteriorating rapidly and it was a slow, painful descent to the col. It took them seven and a half hours to descend 2000 feet. They reached the camp on the North Col exhausted and next morning went down to Camp III from where Wakefield, the doctor, ordered them back to Base.

As they came down a second assault group of Finch, young J.G. Bruce (the General's nephew), John Noel and Gurkha Tejbir moved up, using oxygen. As the General remarked, the gas offensive had begun.

They managed to make their intermediate camp at 25,500 feet. John Noel (the expedition photographer) went down with the porters and the other three settled in. A storm blew up which prevented any action next day but on the following day, May 27, they set off up the ridge. Tejbir had to return but the other two struggled on, leaving the ridge for the North Face where they became the first climbers to discover that this was composed of uncomfortably tilted slabs as if they were the gigantic tiles resting on the roof of the world. They reached a height of about 27,300 feet before turning back, exhausted from a lack of rest and inadequate food. They, too, were returned to Base Camp.

On the morning of June 7 a final assault party began the ascent of the slopes leading to the North Col. On the first rope was Somervell, leading Mallory, a Sherpa and Crawford, whilst thirteen more Sherpas were spread on three ropes below them. Suddenly, from a line about 600 feet below the col, the snow avalanched and all four ropes were swept away. When the slide stopped the front two ropes were able to extricate themselves, but of the nine Sherpas on the other two, only two were saved. Seven Sherpas lost their lives. It was the end of the expedition.

The 1922 expedition set several height records for the time: the highest camps ever occupied, the highest height reached without oxygen and the highest height ever reached by man on earth, when Finch and Bruce reached 27,300 feet (8310 m).[12]

The Tibetan government gave permission for another expedition in 1924. There was a core of experience available: General Bruce as leader, Mallory, Somervell, Norton, J.G. Bruce and John Noel. Added to these were Bentley Beetham, J. de V. Hazard, N.E. Odell and Andrew (Sandy) Irvine.

Mallory was not sure he should go again, although in the public's mind he was by now inexorably identified with the mountain. He felt responsible for the accident on the North Col in 1922, and some influential observers thought so too. His judgement was called into question in private if not publicly, and his forgetfulness was notorious. According to Longstaff he was 'quite unfit to be placed in charge of anything, including himself'.[13] Possibly for these reasons he was not made second in command to Bruce. That job fell to Norton.

The old pal's act was in full swing, of course. Beetham had just spent six weeks in the Alps with Somervell, whilst Odell, another newcomer, had been to Spitsbergen with Longstaff as had the twenty-one-year-old Sandy Irvine. The glaring omission was George Finch. The Committee had never been comfortable with Finch; he was not 'one of us' and his outspokenness rankled. He was also in favour of using oxygen and had demonstrated its effectiveness by putting up a new height record in 1922; but even this counted against him. Furthermore he had given a series of lectures about Everest on the Continent and refused to pay the Committee the fifty per cent of the fees they demanded. The rift was complete and the publication of his autobiography in 1924, with two critical chapters about the 1922 expedition, merely emphasised the fact.

The plan this time was to have three camps along the ridge from the North Col, at 25,500 feet, 26,500 feet, 27,200 feet, all occupied by lead climbers, some with oxygen and some without, so that a series of two-man assaults could be made. Unfortunately the plan was wrecked by a devastating blizzard which hit the porters whilst Camp III was being established below the North Col. After a series of near-disasters only fifteen of the original fifty-five Sherpas were capable of working above Camp III[14] and so the plan was amended to dispense with the middle camp on the ridge.

Eventually on June 3 a tent was established at 26,800 feet and was to be the top camp, Camp VI. Next day Norton and Somervell set out to make the first direct assault on the summit of Everest. Somervell had to give up because of a sore throat which seemed likely to choke him but Norton, crossing the North Face alone and hampered by an increasingly severe bout of double vision, reached the great couloir which fissures the face and which, because of soft snow, he judged impossible to tackle safely.

'The strain of climbing so carefully was beginning to tell and I was getting exhausted. In addition my eye trouble was getting worse and was by now a severe handicap. I had perhaps 200 feet more of this nasty going to surmount before I emerged on the north face of the final pyramid and, I believe, safety and an easy route to the summit. It was now 1 p.m. and a brief calculation showed that I had no chance of climbing the remaining 800 or 900 feet if I was to return in safety.'[15]

Norton had reached a height of 28,126 feet (8573 m) – a new record and one which was not exceeded for nearly thirty years.

The two climbers staggered back down the ridge to the North Col, one half blind, the other choking violently[16] until in the gathering darkness they were met by Mallory and Odell and led back to the camp on the North Col where young Irvine was waiting with soup and tea.

Mallory now decided to make another attempt, this time using oxygen. He decided that his companion should be Sandy Irvine. Why did Mallory choose the young, inexperienced Irvine in preference to the older, more experienced Odell? It is a question which has been endlessly debated. There is no doubt that Mallory was attracted to the good-looking young man, but it was probably a romantic, aesthetic thing without the homosexual overtones sometimes attributed to it. Given that both Odell and Irvine were oxygen experts and very fit, Mallory was likely to choose the better looking.[17]

Norton, temporarily blind and in great pain, queried the choice but Mallory insisted it must be Irvine. 'There is no doubt Mallory knows he is leading a forlorn hope,' Norton told John Noel.[18]

On the evening of June 7 Mallory and Irvine were ensconced in the top camp, Odell was in Camp V alone and Hazard was at Camp IV, the North Col. Early next day Odell set out to make a leisurely ascent to Camp VI. Mist drifted across the face of the mountain but it was obviously sunny above and Odell had no qualms about his two comrades whom he expected to be nearing the summit pyramid. As he neared Camp VI he decided to test his fitness by climbing a little crag. As he reached the top he stepped into one of the great moments of mountaineering history. Here is how he described what happened:

There was scarcely 100 feet of it, and as I reached the top there was a sudden clearing of the atmosphere above me and I saw the whole summit ridge and final peak of Everest unveiled. I noticed far away on a snow slope leading up to what seemed to me to be the last step but one from the base of the final pyramid, a tiny object moving and approaching the rock step. A second object followed, and then the first climbed to the top of the step. As I stood intently watching this dramatic appearance, the scene became enveloped in cloud once more, and I could not actually be certain that I saw the second figure join the first. It was of course none other than Mallory and Irvine, and I was surprised above all to see them so late as this, namely 12.50, at a point which, if the 'second rock step', they should have reached according to Mallory's schedule by 8 a.m. at latest, and if the 'first rock step' proportionately earlier. The 'second rock step' is seen prominently in photographs of the North Face from the Base Camp, where it appears a short distance from the base of the final pyramid down the snowy first part of the crest of the North-east Arete. The lower 'first rock step' is about an equivalent distance again to the left. Owing to the small portion of the summit ridge uncovered I could not be precisely certain at which of these two 'steps' they were, as in profile and from below they are very similar, but at the time I took it for the upper 'second step'. However, I am a little doubtful now whether the latter would not be hidden by the projecting nearer ground from my position below on the face. I could see that they were moving expeditiously as if endeavouring to make up for lost time. True, they were moving one at a time over what was apparently but moderately difficult ground, but one cannot definitely conclude from this that they were roped together – a not unimportant consideration in any estimate of what may have eventually befallen them.[19]

Mallory and Irvine were never seen again, though an ice axe belonging to one or the other was discovered in 1933 lying on some slabs near the ridge, just short of the First Step. Many years later a Chinese climber, Wang Hangbao, claimed that in 1975 he found the body of a European on the ridge at about 8100 metres. It can only have been Mallory or Irvine, but before he could be questioned further, Wang Hangbao was killed by an avalanche. The mysterious body has never been seen since.

If Mallory or Irvine are ever discovered (and it is possible) they may have with them a camera containing film which might solve the fascinating conundrum of whether or not they made it to the top. Given the dry cold air of Everest both the bodies and the film are likely to be preserved. But until such times there can only be speculation: elaborate theories have been advanced as to why or why not the two men reached the summit. My own view, based on an extensive study, is that they did not.[20]

Mallory was so intimately connected with Everest in the public's mind that his disappearance came as an immense shock to the nation. There was a memorial service in memory of both men at St Paul's, attended by representatives of the Royal Family. It was this sense of grief and shock, some said, that prevented there being any more Everest expeditions for nine years. Unfortunately the truth is less dignified. The British agent in charge of negotiations with Tibet, F.M. Bailey, had been looking for an excuse to stop the expeditions, which he disliked, and found the perfect opportunity when John Noel, wishing to boost the attraction of the Everest film he had made, brought over to England several Tibetan monks without the permission of the Dalai Lama. Whilst Bailey remained in office there was never a chance of another Everest expedition.

Even apart from Everest, however, interest in the Himalaya continued to grow in the post-war years. There was continuous activity throughout the range, or at least those parts of it that were open to Europeans. Nepal remained closed and except for the Everest parties, so did Tibet. In 1927 the Himalayan Club was founded.[21] Part of its function was to provide assistance to would-be explorers and mountaineers and to make a register of reliable, experienced Sherpas. Local members of the club often accompanied an expedition as transport or liaison officer, and in some cases this was insisted upon by the Indian Government before permission was granted to an expedition.

The most successful climbing expeditions of the inter-war years were to the Garhwal Himalaya, that stretch of high mountains cradled by the great bend of the Sutlej river and bounded to the east by the Nepalese border. The area had long been under the total control of the Raj who built many famous hill-stations there, including Simla, from where India was governed during the hot season, and Dehra Dun, home of the Indian Survey. Access was therefore relatively easy.

Long before the First War it had been a favourite area too, and Longstaff had climbed Trisul (7120 m) as early as 1907, the first 7000-metre peak to be climbed. Earlier still the Schlaginweits had made a spirited attack on Abi Gamin, and of course there was Graham's famously disputed ascent of Changabang in 1883.

The first major peak to be ascended after the war was Kamet (7756 m) to which there had been no fewer than eight expeditions since 1907, of which four had made serious attempts on the mountain. The obvious route was from a col between Kamet and Abi Gamin where C.F. Meade had camped in 1913 and subsequently known as Meade's Col. He used a light-weight tent (also named after him) and at 7138 metres (23,417 ft) it was the highest camp ever undertaken until the Everest expeditions broke all height records. In 1931 a strong party led by Frank Smythe established a camp just below the col and on June 21, Smythe, Shipton and Holdsworth, with the Sherpas Lewa and Nima Dorje, climbed by the edge of the North Face to within 400 feet of the top where the slope steepened and became icy. Nima Dorje dropped out exhausted but the others struggled on to reach the summit at 4.15 p.m. Eight hours had been spent on the climb, half of it on the final steep bit. At 7756 metres (25,445 ft) it was the highest peak ascended at that date, although, of course, climbers had already been higher on Everest. Two days later Raymond Greene and E. St J. Birnie, with porter Kesar Singh, repeated the ascent.

Two years later Kesar Singh, who was a local Bhotia, not a Sherpa, reached the summit of Trisul with P.R. Oliver, in the first repeat of Long-staff's ascent.

Many of those who took part in these ascents were to figure in the forthcoming Everest expeditions but none were more significant than Bill Tilman and Eric Shipton who together and separately explored and climbed extensively throughout the Himalaya and Karakoram.

The two had met in Kenya in 1930. Shipton, though nine years younger than Tilman, was the more experienced climber and a man of outward-going personality, in stark contrast to Tilman's almost taciturn habits. They had a symbiotic relationship, the one feeding off the other and yet curiously formal. 'It was years before I called him Bill,' Shipton said. Both wrote a series of mountaineering travel books which were immensely popular, almost, if not quite, rivalling the popularity of Smythe.[22]

When they travelled together, self-sufficient except for two or three Sherpas, their food was of the most basic sort, for Tilman believed that most people ate too much, even on expeditions. When he travelled with other companions like Odell or Warren he often had to defend himself over rations:

'The technique of travelling light which Shipton and I employed on our own expeditions does not mean that we deliberately starve ourselves or our porters ... As we once lived perforce for a few days on tree mushrooms and bamboo shoots there is the general impression that this is our normal diet ... Nothing could be further from the truth ... the whole art lies in getting most value for weight.'[23] Even so, he classified soup and porridge as 'luxuries'.

In 1934 they created a sensation in mountaineering circles when they forced entrance to the Nanda Devi Sanctuary in Garhwal. Nanda Devi (7816 m/25,645 ft) is the highest peak in the region. It is named after a legendary princess who fled there to preserve her honour and like the princess the peak was unreachable. It is surrounded by a ring of other high peaks, about twenty of which are well over 6000 metres and some, such as Trisul, Tirsuli, Changabang and Dunagiri, are more than 7000 metres and worthy of

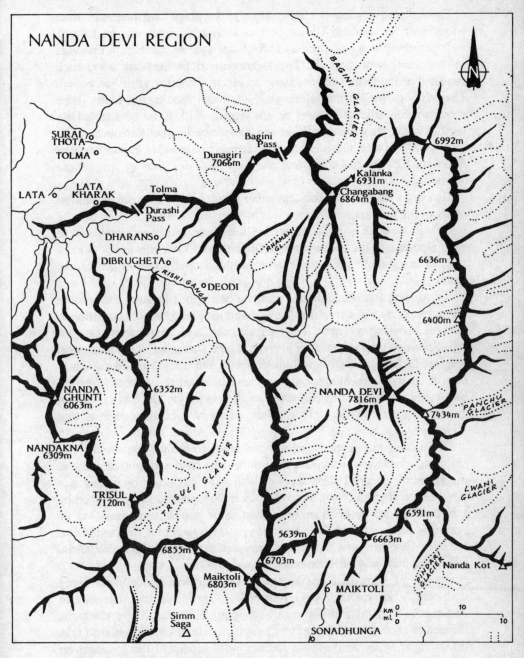

NANDA DEVI REGION

expeditions in themselves. Here and there a desperate pass leads over the wall into the Sanctuary but the only real gap in the defence is where the Rishi Ganga river, draining the Sanctuary, cuts through. In doing so it forms a formidable gorge.

The wall surrounding the Sanctuary and the gorge itself had resisted all efforts until Shipton and Tilman, picking away at the intricacies of the rock walls forming the gorge – some of which are 2500 metres high – managed to find their way through. They reconnoitred in the Sanctuary, then retreated in the face of the monsoon to return when the rains had ceased. They climbed Maiktoli, a minor peak – but still 6800 metres high – then managed to reach 6535 metres on the jagged South Ridge of Nanda Devi itself. Finally, they escaped from the Sanctuary by the difficult Sundardhunga Khal (5820 m), a route they deemed impassable in the opposite direction. The Rishi Ganga was the only real way into or out of the Sanctuary.

Two years later Tilman was a member of an Anglo-American expedition to climb the mountain.[24] Shipton was away trying to climb Everest, but the party was a strong one. By August 28 a bivouac had been established at 7300 metres and the following day Tilman and Odell, starting at 6 a.m., reached the summit nine hours later, finishing up a fine if difficult snow arête.

Nanda Devi was the highest summit to be climbed between the wars. It was achieved by a relatively small expedition with only half a dozen Sherpas and was a striking counter to compare with the large, cumbersome national expeditions by then engaged on Everest, Nanga Parbat and Kangchenjunga. It showed what a modest expedition could do, but it also showed the weakness of such an expedition: only one team reached the summit. Nobody else was fit enough in the final stages of the expedition and had something gone wrong with Tilman or Odell, there would have been no reserves, and no success.

Throughout the thirties Garhwal continued to attract expeditions. The Japanese, who in post-war years were to become such a formidable force in the Himalaya, opened their account with the first ascent of Nanda Kot (6861 m) on the rim of the Sanctuary, as is Dunagiri (7066 m), climbed by a Swiss team led by Roch in 1939. That same year a Polish team led by Karpinski climbed Nanda Devi East (7434 m), the twin peak of Nanda Devi, but later when the same expedition attempted to climb Tirsuli an avalanche killed Karpinski and his team-mate Bernadzikiewicz.

Even in the immediate post-war years, the Garhwal figured prominently in the Himalayan calendar. Roch returned in 1947 with a team that climbed Kedarnath (6940 m) and Satopanth (7075 m). Abi Gamin (7355 m) was climbed in 1950, Mukut Parbat (7242 m) in 1951 and Chaukhamba I (7138 m) in 1952. Many of these expeditions were modest – the Japanese on Nanda Kot, for example, were just a group of four college friends led by the Olympic skier Takebushi[25] – and it could be said that although much of the Himalayan glamour was centred on the great peaks of Nepal and the Karakoram it was Garhwal which was the forcing ground.

Nor were the outer fringes of the Himalaya ignored. In the Pamirs the Soviets had begun to stir. Inspired no doubt by the visit of the German expedition in 1928 (described later), when Pik Lenin (7134 m) was climbed, their climbers set out in 1933 to ascend the highest peak in the Soviet Union, then called Mount Stalin but later renamed Pik Kommunizma.[26] The height seems in dispute; some authorities give it 7482 metres and others 7495 metres.

Leader of the nine climbers was Eugene Abalakov. They tackled the East Ridge which was blocked by six enormous gendarmes between 5600 metres and 6400 metres. The rock proved unreliable and as N. Nikolayev was traversing the second gendarme a handhold broke away, he lost his balance and fell nearly 500 metres to his death. The hardest climbing came between the last two gendarmes, where pitons and rope ladders[27] were employed profusely. Abalakov was roped to Daniil Gushchin on this stretch and the latter was almost brought off when a falling stone cut his hand to the bone. Covered in blood he managed to retain consciousness and hang on until Abalakov could climb back and attend to the wound. There was no turning back for the pair – the final gendarme had to be forced and this they managed to do, pitching the last camp on a patch of névé at 6900 metres. Others joined them but bad weather came howling in with blizzards which sent the temperature tumbling to forty Centigrade below freezing. The season and the food were both running out: already it was September and they were down to their last tin of fish and one chocolate bar.

By September 2 only three men remained at the top camp and two of those, A. Getye and N.P. Gorbunov, were crushed beneath the weight of snow when their tent collapsed. Getye suffered a heart attack and could obviously go no further but on September 3, as the weather cleared, Abalakov and Gorbunov struggled towards the summit through deep, fresh snow which they found utterly exhausting. Gorbunov in particular was feeling the effects, so the two men unroped, each to go his own pace. Abalakov went ahead along a knife-edge ridge. As he neared the summit he fell to his knees in exhaustion and crawled the last couple of metres on all fours.

The descent was a nightmare: Getye still suffering from the effects of his heart attack, Gorbunov frostbitten and Abalakov snow blind! That they managed to get down safely is a tribute to their skill, fitness and, perhaps, luck.

The ascent was repeated in 1937 when, in blizzard conditions, five men reached the top. Unfortunately this too was marred by tragedy when the leader, Oleg Aristov, fell from the final ridge and was killed.[28] The mountain now has numerous routes. The final 7000-metre peak of the Pamirs, Pik E. Korzenevskoi (7105 m) was not climbed until 1953.

Three thousand kilometres east of the Pamirs, where the high Tibetan plateau tips over into the Chinese province of Szechwan, there is a spectacular mountain called Minya Konka (7556 m/24,790 ft). Because it rises 6500 metres above the surrounding countryside, it has tremendous presence; Everest itself rises little more than half that above its surroundings. It was thought by some to be the highest mountain in the world, one of two Chinese mountains which were rumoured from time to time to be 'higher than Everest' (the other, with even less justification, was Amne Machen at 6282 metres.)[29]

In 1932, four Americans, Richard Burdsall, Arthur Emmons, Terris Moore and Jack Young set out to climb Minya Konka. All were in their early twenties except for the thirty-six-year-old Burdsall, but only Moore had high-altitude experience. Emmons had climbed in the Alps and Alaska, but the other two had very limited experience – indeed Young had never really climbed at all although he had been on an expedition near Minya Konka, searching for the giant panda. Young was a Chinese-American and he persuaded the others to learn some Mandarin, which they found useful during the expedition.

The fine American climber Allen Carpe had also been interested in the expedition at an earlier stage, though he later dropped out.[30] He and Moore had climbed in Alaska with the idea of trying out Alaskan tactics to see whether they would work on Minya Konka. Carpe had not been impressed by the lack of success the great expeditions were having on Everest and Kangchenjunga, even though they had regiments of porters and Sherpas to help them establish a series of camps. In Alaska, where porterage had to be done by the climbers themselves by packing things in on their own backs – backpacking, as it came to be called – the idea was to establish just one camp and push it slowly up the mountain, using repeated carries if necessary.[31] However, it was reckoned that loads of fifty pounds would not be feasible at high altitude and that even twenty-five pounds would be a lot, so the plan was adapted whereby tents were left at the four intermediate camps between base and the summit but a single set of sleeping-bags, cooking utensils and Primus stove was carried up and down as required.

They also used a type of boot worn by Alaskan gold prospectors called Barker boots; these were rubber shoes with a chamois leather top above the ankle and fitted inside with felt insoles. They had stiff soles and could only be used with crampons, but they seem to have been a very crude forerunner of the modern plastic double boot. They were warm and seem to have worked admirably.

By the time they were ready to tackle the mountain in October the season was already well advanced. They made the North-West Ridge their route and they advanced up it, using camps at 17,000 feet, 19,000 feet, 20,000 feet and 21,500 feet, from where the summit bid was launched. The chief danger was from avalanches and on October 12 Moore and Emmons had a narrow escape on a feature called The Hump when the entire snow face broke away below their feet and went roaring down into the valley. Young decided to stay behind and look after the base camp when the final attempt started out. Unfortunately Emmons injured his hands with a knife and had to withdraw, so it was left to Moore and Burdsall to crampon up the final ridge, against a strong and biting wind, to reach the top at 2.40 p.m. on October 28. It remained the highest summit reached by Americans until Gasherbrum was climbed in 1958.

Even more remarkable than the American ascent of Minya Konka was the ascent of Chomolhari (7315 m/24,000 ft) by F. Spencer Chapman in 1937. Chomolhari stands on the Tibet–Bhutan border near Phari on the main road from Darjeeling to Lhasa and was a well-known sight to the Everest expeditions of the day. It is however a holy mountain and it is perhaps this which had prevented anyone trying to climb it, as permission was unlikely to be granted by either Tibet or Bhutan. Chapman had the advantage of working in Lhasa and knowing all the right people. Permission was soon obtained.

Permission was about all he had. He had no equipment beyond personal climbing gear, no companions, no Sherpas and precious little money. Yet he seemed to overcome all these obstacles with a determination that a few years later was to make him a formidable guerrilla leader against the Japanese in Malaya.[32] As companion he recruited Charles Crawford from Calcutta, a man whose sole experience of climbing was scrambling in Skye and the Pyrenees. The equipment he borrowed from the Himalayan Club, who also recruited him three Sherpas. It was all remarkably cheap: 'I have great satisfaction in the thought that we reached a height of 24,000 feet at a cost of under £20 each, while the Everest expedition which was being carried on at the same time was unable to get higher than 23,000 feet in spite of the expenditure of several thousand pounds.'[33]

He approached from the south and after a thorough reconnaissance decided to ascend the South-West Ridge. For three days they gradually worked their way through soft snow to establish a camp at 20,013 feet. Here Crawford and two Sherpas retired exhausted but Chapman and a young Sherpa, Pasang Dawa, pushed on next day. Struck by a storm they camped again, but the following day they reached the top about noon.

The descent was difficult. Pasang Dawa slipped out of his steps on a steep slope and pulled Chapman out of his.

'We fell fast, sometimes flying through the air, sometimes bumping and somersaulting over outcrops of ice. Several times I dug my axe point in, but before I could get enough weight on it to stop us I was pulled on by the more rapid acceleration of Pasang ... we were falling faster and faster and further down the slope became so steep that we would not be able to stop before rolling over the edge of the rocks, to drop 3000 feet into Tibet.'[34]

They fell well over 300 feet before coming to a halt on the very lip of the precipice. Two shaken men scrambled down to the camp which they reached at 3 p.m. They tried to take the camp to a more comfortable spot lower down but a storm drove them back, weary. For four nights they camped on the mountain, wet through, with no hot food or drink, as they painfully made their way down through appalling snow conditions. Pasang was a total wreck, frostbitten and exhausted. At one stage Chapman fell through the snow into a crevasse and spent three or four hours climbing out again.

Eventually, however, Chapman brought his companion to safety in the lush meadows of Phari. It was, said General Bruce when he heard of it, the Eighth Wonder of the World.

CHAPTER TWENTY

Reap the Wild Wind

By 1928 the Munich School was ready to test itself abroad, to take the techniques and philosophies cultured in the Eastern Alps beyond the mountains of Western Europe. A party which included two leading personalities of the group – Paul Bauer and Heinz Tillmann – went to the Caucasus, whilst the veteran mountaineer and explorer, Willi Rickmer Rickmers, led a mixed mountaineering and scientific party of twenty-one Russians and Germans to the Pamirs. They climbed a number of peaks at the head of the long Fedchenko Glacier then a group established a base camp below the Saukhdara Glacier. Eugen Allwein, Erwin Schneider and Karl Wien made an arduous fifteen-mile trek up the glacier to a pass on the East Ridge of Pik Lenin (7134 m) from where they managed to climb the mountain, the highest climbed summit in the world at that time.[1] The ascent proved fairly simple, though the three Germans suffered badly from frostbite: inside their tent they recorded thirty-one degrees of frost.

In South America the situation was rather different because many Germans had settled there from the nineteenth century onwards and in Chile, for example, they set up their own climbing club, the Deutscher Ausflugverein, which later became the Chilean Section of the German and Austrian Alpine Club (DOAV). Any expedition from the homeland was sure of a warm welcome and it is not surprising that they came frequently. They dominated Bolivian climbing from 1915 to the 1950s, and included the expedition led by Hans Pfann in 1928 which made the first ascent of Illampu (6362 m).

With Pfann were E. Hein, A. Horeschowski, and H. Hortnagel – all well-known names on the German climbing scene. Hein soloed the difficult North Ridge of Illimani South. A similar high-powered group, led by P. Borchers and including Hein and Schneider, visited the Cordillera Real of Peru in 1932, managing to climb five 6000-metre summits, amongst them Huascarán Sur (6768 m), the highest summit in Peru.[2] In addition, they climbed fourteen more only slightly lower and did some valuable surveying under the direction of Hans Kinzl.

It can be seen from the above that by the early thirties the Germans had a cadre of experienced high-altitude climbers from which to choose teams for the highest mountains of all – the great peaks of the Himalaya. The Nazi state encouraged and financially supported, through the DOAV, such expeditions. No 8000-metre peak had ever been climbed and to achieve such a goal would be a tremendous propaganda coup for National Socialism. It might even break the British stranglehold on Everest – for if the Germans were successful on Nanga Parbat or Kangchenjunga, it would be difficult to deny them a chance at Everest and if they were successful on Everest, the effects would be incalculable for world politics.

The Himalayan historian Mason, regretting the decline of scientific mountaineering in the inter-war years, said: 'A curious brand of nationalism, quite out of place in the Himalaya, caused some to think that the honour of their country was at stake if they did not climb something larger and higher and more difficult than had been achieved by the climbers of some other country ... Possibly the exclusively British expeditions to Everest were partly responsible for this attitude, though climbers in Britain or India never looked on Everest as theirs alone.'[3]

Perhaps the climbers didn't, but the government certainly did. There was not a hope of any other country reaching Everest except by some undeniable right of conquest.

Sir Francis Younghusband wrote: 'The main motive of the German climbers was not to establish a record but to prove that the Germans were men. They were not even moved by love of mountaineering. They did love mountains. But they loved their country more. And it was to show the world that Germany still produced men that they set forth to pit themselves against some of the monarchs of the Himalayas.'[4]

The translator of Paul Bauer's work into English, E.G. Hall, felt constrained to offer some explanation of an attitude to climbing he felt would be alien to his British readers.

'The motive underlying the German Himalaya expeditions is to be sought in the events of 1914–1918 and Germany's re-awakened sense of nationalism which was their result; the members of the fateful Nanga Parbat expedition did not regard themselves as mere sportsmen, but men with a noble mission in life, offering a contribution to Germany's reassertion as a nation to be reckoned with, proving to the world that Germans also are capable of feats of great endurance. It is essential to grasp this fact . . .'[5]

An incident in Bolivia in 1940 made the fact plain, though by then the British were at war and quite aware of Nazi ambitions. Three German nationals, H. Botcher, W. Kuhm and F. Fritz, climbed Illimani South and planted the Nazi flag, surmounting that of Bolivia. The flag was removed a few days later but the incident caused a furore; the surprised Germans hurriedly explained that there should have been a Swiss flag too but their Swiss companion had dropped out at the last minute.[6]

From 1934 the German expeditions to the Himalaya were paid for by the state and so, in addition to their natural desires to climb the mountains, they went armed with motives which were both national and political. They were all fine mountaineers and if some of the individuals subscribed to these

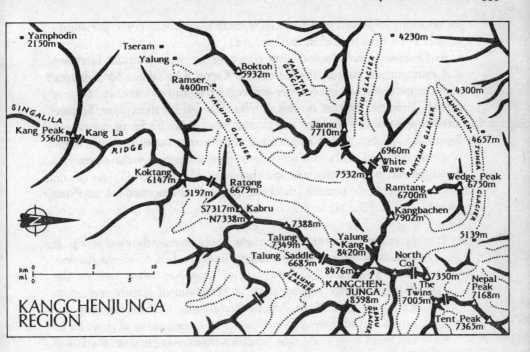

motives, as they undoubtedly did, others were probably less committed. After all, if the alternatives are a bleak future on the dole or an all-expenses paid trip to the greatest mountains in the world, what is easier than to raise an arm and shout 'Heil Hitler!'?

After the experience gained in the Caucasus and Pamirs the Munich School felt ready in 1929 to test themselves and their nationhood against one of the Himalayan giants. 'They want to test themselves against something difficult,' wrote Rickmer Rickmers, 'some mountain that will call out every-thing they've got in them of courage, perseverance, and endurance.'[7] Under the leadership of Paul Bauer a party of nine, including Allwein, conqueror of Pik Lenin, went to Kangchenjunga, at 8586 metres the third highest mountain in the world.[8]

They chose to explore the north-east quadrant of the Kangchenjunga massif from a base camp on the long Zemu Glacier. After some reconnais-sance Bauer decided that the only feasible route lay up a long spur of mountain which ran north-east from the North Ridge of Kangchenjunga, between the summit and a subsidiary peak called the Twins.

With interruptions caused by bad weather, it took three weeks for the Germans to reach the crest of the ridge, including a week to overcome the 200-metre wall of ice with which the ridge began. Once on top, they found their way barred by huge ice pinnacles, each of which had to be circumvented by laborious step-cutting. Camps were established about every 300 metres or so, each a cave hacked in the hard ice.

By October 3, seven weeks after commencing the assault, six Germans and four porters were in the ice cave at Camp X, at about 6900 metres, ready to move ahead, and Allwein and von Kraus had reconnoitred to 7400 metres. Then the weather turned. A blizzard raged for three days. To conserve supplies some climbers and porters went down to lower camps but Bauer and Allwein, with Sherpas Kitar and Pasang, stayed on in the hope of going higher. On the 7th they made their attempt but the storm had deposited too much fresh snow and they too had to retreat.

The retreat almost became a fatal rout. Bauer later described the terrifying ordeal:

> Next day our cave entrance was again completely blocked up. It was snowing fiercely and many times we had to sweep the exit clear. By nightfall at least 7 ft. of snow had fallen and not the slightest change was apparent. A cataclysm of Nature seemed to foreshadow our doom. Any further attempt in the meanwhile was utterly out of the question, and yet with the goal so near we could not begin to retreat. Soon no other choice was possible, the Storm God was still piling snow on us, but, on the following morning, trusting to our powers and experience, we determined to 'wrestle one more fall.' The descent appeared humanly impossible, yet an attempt had to be made. Roped at the fullest possible distance we fought our way down, leaving behind a furrow a man's height in depth. For a slightly *ascending* bit, not 150 ft. long, we took over two hours. Our unfortunate porters, laden each with some 80 lbs., sank so deep in their tracks that we, with our 40 lbs. load, had often to pass them and jerk them loose from below. The steeper slopes mostly peeled off in avalanches as the leader, tightly held from the rear, stepped on to them. The great and most dangerous slope, thank Heaven, had already avalanched: we went down a certain distance in the groove itself and thus saved a good two hours. Another slope, however, parted with Allwein and the two porters on it, but with a final and desperate effort I was just able to hold them. For ten minutes or more we lay motionless and exhausted before we could resume the fight. On our arrival at Camp IX we had to dig for half an hour before we could clear the ice-cave's entrance buried in 7 ft. of snow. Once inside we could lie still during the night, recovering our strength for the ensuing and most difficult portion of the ridge.
>
> Next day things went wrong at the start. The porters were rather nervous and we could not get them down the great step. We led

them back to the cave and, without packs, set out to render possible the traverse of the steepest towers. Next day we jettisoned a good half of our packs, throwing them down the 5000-ft. precipice on to the Twins Glacier; thus relieved, the party could re-attempt the struggle. At last the weather became fine; in spite of the weary labour it would have been pure joy to clamber along that wondrous ridge had we not been torn with anxiety as to our friends' fate, for nowhere on the ridge nor on the Zemu Glacier could we perceive a sign of living beings. At nightfall two days later, however, on entering the 'Alderhorst' we acquired the blessed assurance that all the 'ridge' party were at any rate still alive. Each of the two parties descending before us from Camp X had had a strenuous struggle. The porters kept falling heavily, avalanches poured down continuously. Beigel and Aufschnaiter had fared the worst; on October 7, the most trying day of the entire expedition, they were between Camps IX and VII. Alternately leading, each was swept off his feet in turn by the resistless downward rush of wind-compacted snowy masses. Once when traversing slightly below the crest, the leader slipped and was held only by the second man leaping into space on the reverse slope. This mishap caused the loss of both sacks and all provisions and bivouac material; both climbers had to spend the night on the ridge under a corniche without shelter of any kind. Beigel suffered severe frost-bite in his feet. All his toes and most of the ball of his foot became blue and black. Although Kraus and Thoenes with two porters had rubbed them ceaselessly for two days, his feet could not be saved.[9]

In the following year Oscar Dyhrenfurth, a forty-four-year-old Swiss geologist, organised an expedition to Kangchenjunga which was originally meant to be German but turned out in the end to be, in Mason's words, 'a rather makeshift international party'.[10] It included Frank Smythe.

They decided to tackle the mountain from the north-west, in the belief that this is what Freshfield had advocated after his circumnavigation of Kangchenjunga in 1899. In fact, as Freshfield pointed out in a letter to the *Alpine Journal* he had merely said that the north-west side would bear closer reconnaissance, which is not the same thing at all. About a direct assault he said it 'must be too much exposed to avalanches to offer a reasonable or legitimate route to mountaineers'.[11] In the event Dyhrenfurth mounted a direct attack on the face, which avalanched and killed a Sherpa called Chettan. The expedition retreated and turned to lesser but quite interesting objectives, making first ascents of Jonsong Peak (7420 m), three other 7000-metre peaks, four of 6000 metres and one of 5000 metres.[12]

Minor bickering followed the end of the expedition, with Smythe claiming the expedition boots weighed twelve and a half pounds, and blaming this on Finch, who was a handy whipping-boy for anything at the time. There was criticism of the film made by the expedition and when Dyhrenfurth defended this on the grounds of general interest Colonel Strutt sniffily pointed out that the *Alpine Journal* 'did not have regard for the opinions of the proletariat'.[13]

In 1931 Bauer returned with a hard core of his previous team, five in all: Allwein, Aufschnaiter, Brenner, Fendt and Leupold, to which were added newcomers Hartmann, Pircher, Schaller and Wien, probably the most formidable party yet assembled to lay siege to a great mountain, said the *Alpine Journal*. They used the previous base camp on the Zemu Glacier, helped by Tobin and Shebbeare once again.

Though six weeks earlier than in 1929, this was to no advantage as the monsoon still raged and avalanches reverberated incessantly round the peaks. Nevertheless the Germans pressed on up the North-East Spur. On August 9, some four weeks after the climb had begun, the party were climbing along an exposed part of the ridge, which included a little gully, when disaster struck. Schaller had started up the gully, followed by two Sherpas, Pasang and Tsin Norbu. Suddenly, the snow gave way beneath Pasang and he careered out of control down the gully, pulling Schaller off. The German flew out in an arc from the ridge. Instinctively, the third man whipped the rope round a boulder to hold the fall, but the strain on the rope was so violent, so sudden, that it snapped at the rock's edge and the two climbers fell nearly 550 metres to their deaths.

Though the expedition staggered on for a while many of the climbers were ill, Bauer himself suffered heart trouble and the porters were nervous after the accident. Kangchenjunga remained unclimbed.

Despite the somewhat lavish praise heaped on these expeditions their achievements were quite as modest as those of the British on Everest. In fact, all was not well with the German climbing scene, for it was rent by dissension, back-biting and political placemanship. This manifested itself in the hopes and ambitions of Willo Welzenbach, the most charismatic German climber of the period. Thwarted at every turn in his efforts to mount his own expedition to the Himalaya, in frustration and against advice, he joined another – and it killed him.

Because of illness, Welzenbach had been forced to withdraw from the Pamirs expedition of 1928 and his work kept him from joining Bauer's 1929 Kanchenjunga attempt. Paul Bauer had been a companion of Welzenbach back in 1925 when they were doing new climbs in the Wetterstein and belonged to the same élite club, the Munich Academic Alpine Club, but one senses a growing coolness between the two men. It may have been more than professional commitments which kept Welzenbach away from Bauer's expedition.

Certainly, he started to plan his own expedition about this time. He decided that the best objective would be Nanga Parbat, and for much the same reasons as Mummery – the peak was readily accessible and though one of the desirable 'eight thousanders', it was a fairly modest one. At 8125 metres it is tenth highest in the world. That it had also been Mummery's choice would undoubtedly have influenced Welzenbach in itself because he held the English climber in the highest regard.

Welzenbach made meticulous plans for the expedition to take place in 1930. He obtained the backing of the DOAV, permission from the British authorities and leave from his employers, but at the last moment he was barred from going by the German Foreign Office, who preferred Dyhrenfurth's Kangchenjunga expedition. The Foreign Office had the strange excuse that there could only be one viable German Himalayan expedition a year – though, as we have seen, Dyhrenfurth's expedition was international, with less than half the members German.

In the following year Welzenbach tried again, but this time he was opposed by Bauer, who argued that another Kangchenjunga expedition should take precedence, led by himself. Welzenbach refused to back down and a considerable body of German climbing opinion, who thought he was getting a raw deal, supported him. But the Foreign Office supported Bauer. Privately, Bauer himself thought that an expedition to Nanga Parbat stood a better chance than one to Kangchenjunga.

With three successive failures on Kangchenjunga the German authorities could hardly dare to refuse Welzenbach his chance in 1932. The expedition was formed but Welzenbach himself was denied the opportunity of leading it. This time the blow came from his employers, Munich City Council, who had twice previously granted him leave (not taken up) but now felt unable to do so again. Welzenbach's disappointment was bitter. He nominated Willy Merkl, who had been with him on the Grands Charmoz adventure, as leader.

Was there a deliberate plot to deny Welzenbach his chance of glory? Or was he simply the victim of a set of unfortunate circumstances? There is no way of knowing, but one thing is sure: nobody who went with Bauer in 1929 and 1931 was invited onto Merkl's team.

Beside the leader, the members comprised Peter Aschenbrenner, an Austrian guide, Fritz Bechtold, Hugo Hamberger, Herbert Kunigk, Felix Simon, Fritz Wiessner, Rand Herron and a reporter, Elizabeth Knowlton. The last two were Americans and because of this the expedition was known as the German–American Expedition.[14]

Despite Welzenbach's planning there was a degree of arrogance in the German approach, which reflected on Merkl. Though a first-rate climber, he was not a first-rate leader. He did not appoint a transport officer, made no arrangements about porters with the Himalayan Club, nobody on the team spoke the local languages and none of them had been to the Himalaya before. Bauer does not seem to have been consulted. The result was considerable difficulties right from the start, especially with the porters who were local Hunzas from Kashmir and not the experienced Sherpas.[15] When they reached Base Camp they discovered ten loads – warm clothes for forty porters – had been stolen.

They intended to climb the mountain from the north by the Rakhiot Face, but because of the unsettled nature of Chilas, the district to the north of the mountain, they were forced to approach from the south, keeping fairly high up to avoid villages and crossing not only the Tragbal and Burzil Passes which were still snowbound, but the Lichar, Buldar and Rakhiot Spurs as well to reach the Rakhiot valley. At least here they found one of the most idyllic camping places in the Himalaya, which Merkl named the Marchenwiese, or Fairy Meadow, a lovely alp with the stupendous North-East Face of Nanga Parbat as backdrop.

The Rakhiot Glacier poured down from the mountain to fill the head of the Rakhiot valley. Above it a long ridge ran from Nanga Parbat on the right via the Silbersattel (Silver Saddle) to Rakhiot Peak (7070 m) in the centre and on to Chongra Peak (6820 m) on the left. The Germans decided to attempt to climb via the glacier and this ridge, meeting it to the left of Rakhiot Peak and traversing this and the Silbersattel to the summit.

Despite a scare from an avalanche and more or less continual porter trouble, Camp IV was established just below the ridge on July 8 and used as advance base camp. From it on the 18th Aschenbrenner and Kunigk made the first ascent of Rakhiot Peak.

The fine weather they had enjoyed now broke and it snowed for three days but when it cleared Merkl, Aschenbrenner, Herron and Bechtold traversed below Rakhiot Peak in the soft snow to establish Camp V. Beyond Camp V the route involved a difficult crossing of a huge amphitheatre christened the Mulde (trough) where the ground was broken and ice avalanches seemed likely. Eventually on July 29 a small tent – Camp VII – was established on the ridge at 6955 metres, beyond Rakhiot Peak, by Merkl, Bechtold and Wiessner.

Though they went a little further next day in worsening weather, the expedition had run out of steam. Kunigk had appendicitis and Hamberger (who was a doctor) had taken him to Gilgit. Aschenbrenner was frostbitten and both Herron and Simon had strained hearts. In addition, almost all the porters were sick. 'Too small an expedition run on too modest lines', was the opinion of Kenneth Mason on Merkl's 1932 expedition. But it was inexperience as much as anything which defeated the Germans: they did not appreciate the sheer scale of things and, of course, their disastrous porter problem was also crucial in their defeat. Nevertheless, they had found what looked like a practical route to the top.

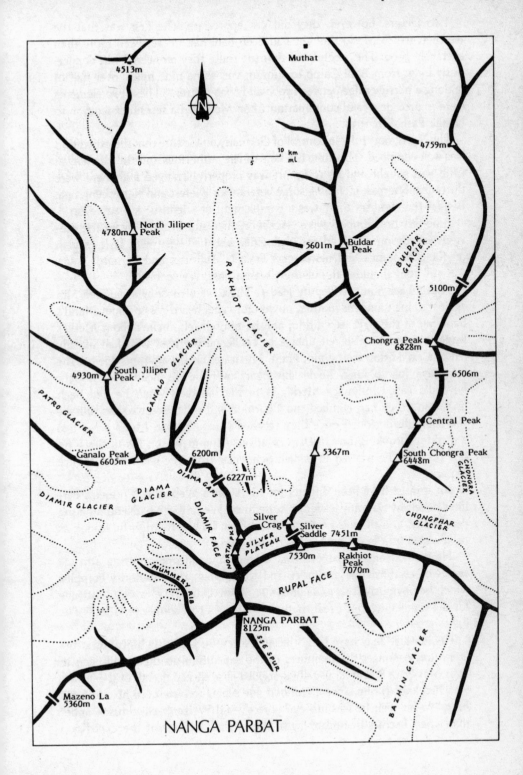

NANGA PARBAT

Two factors, however, they did not appreciate. The first was that the weather, which Merkl thought had been bad, had in fact been more than averagely good. The second was that the route they pioneered was danger-ously long: from Base Camp to summit was some nine miles, over half of it along a narrow ridge between 7000 and 8000 metres.[16] These two elements were to provide a fatal combination when Merkl led a second expedition to Nanga Parbat in 1934.

The Nazis, now fully in control of Germany, made sure that the expedition was well equipped. This time the help of the authorities and the Himalayan Club was sought and so transport was properly arranged and there were thirty-five Sherpas, including some veterans of Everest and Kangchenjunga. Besides the climbers there was a complement of scientists and surveyors.

Amongst the climbers were Aschenbrenner and Bechtold from the pre-vious expedition, Wieland and Schneider who had been with Dyhrenfurth on Kangchenjunga and newcomers Drexel, Mullritter and Bernard. Bauer was still cold-shouldered, but there was, at last, Welzenbach.

Welzenbach went as deputy leader. There were those who advised him against it, including his mother, no doubt having heard gossip about Merkl's handling of the 1932 expedition, and he himself felt qualms about Merkl's leadership but he also felt unable to challenge the man who had already led one expedition to the mountain. Frustrated in his attempts to visit the Himalaya for so long, he let his heart overrule his head. He thought he could easily influence Merkl, as in the old days when he had been leader and they had climbed the Charmoz and other great routes, but he was sadly disillusioned once they reached Nanga Parbat. Merkl acted like a dictator, brooking no criticism or adverse comments on his tactics – on one occasion he wanted to banish Schneider from the team for a chance remark.

But it must have been difficult for Merkl with Welzenbach present. Per-haps he felt he was only leader on sufferance. Welzenbach had a dominating personality, and there is no doubt that he felt he was the rightful leader, as he revealed in a letter home, describing Merkl:

'He really seems to believe that a stern and uncompromising attitude serves to establish his authority and to suppress the inferiority complex which he obviously feels *as an upstart* . . . I am assuming a cautious attitude for the time being, but I fear that we will have a row sooner or later.'[17] The italics are mine.

The 'upstart' may have had other pressures, only vaguely hinted at in the literature. Amongst the members of the expedition, as there had been in 1932, was Fritz Bechtold, usually described as a 'special friend' of the leader, who had known him since childhood. He seems to have been able to bend Merkl to his will; he was 'an evil power', said Welzenbach. Small wonder that when Bechtold came to write the official account of the expedition later, it was a paean of praise for Merkl, 'a born leader of men', and the expedition a glorious defeat against superhuman odds.

By June 6 the first three camps beyond base were established at roughly the same heights as in 1932. The glacier was in a bad condition and siting the camps was no easy matter, with the ice constantly shifting and the threat of avalanches ever present. Drexel complained of a headache and on the night of the 6th became delirious. Next day he was persuaded to go down but got no further than Camp II, where that night he collapsed. Next day Sherpa Pasang climbed up to Camp III to get an additional tent and sleeping-bag but found it empty (the climbers had moved on to Camp IV) so he returned to Camp II then went on down to Camp I and returned to Camp II with the doctor, who declared Drexel had pneumonia and needed oxygen. A blizzard had sprung up but Pasang immediately set off for Camp I yet again, returning at 3 a.m. with Wieland and the oxygen. They had struggled with the crevasses and blizzard through the black night to reach their sick comrade as quickly as possible – but in vain. Drexel was already dead.

Drexel was buried near Base Camp. His death naturally affected the team and seventeen days passed before a start was made again on climbing the peak. Aschenbrenner and Schneider had just established Camp IV before Drexel's death; now it was re-established and used as advance base.

Merkl had intended to follow the route of 1932 to the ridge, crossing the notorious Mulde, that great hollow below Rakhiot Peak, but he found that snow conditions made this impossible. Instead, the route was pushed further up towards Rakhiot Peak itself, where Camp V was established below a steep ice wall. After climbing this and crossing the upper shoulder of the peak, they established Camp VI on the ridge in the same place as in 1932. The crossing of the peak involved steep climbing and fixed ropes for the porters, but the Sherpas coped unflinchingly.

From Camp VI the ridge stretched ahead, first to a snow dome beyond which was a fifteen-metre high black rock they christened the Moor's Head, the traverse beneath which they found extraordinarily attractive, even though it was followed by a disheartening drop of 120 metres. Then in an undulating crest, heavily corniced, the ridge rolled on towards the South-East Summit and a prominent rocky peak to one side, the Silver Crag. Between this and the South-East Summit lay a beautiful curve of snow, from which the sun glinted, the Silbersattel. Beyond lay the summit of Nanga Parbat.

Before the climb up to the Silbersattel, on a billowing snowy formation they called the Schaumrolle (Whipped Cream Roll) the climbers established Camp VII at a little over 7000 metres. They were ten miles from base, four miles from Camp IV, the advance base. It was July 5.

All the Chiefs and a good few of the best Indians were up at Camp

VII that fateful day. There was Merkl, Bechtold, Welzenbach, Wieland, Aschenbrenner and Schneider, together with thirteen Sherpas. Next morning two of the porters were ill and were taken down by Bechtold, who was surprised to discover that at Camp IV the weather had been bad and Mulritter had been unable to climb to Camp VI. On the ridge the weather was perfect. When asked how things were going, Bechtold confidently boasted, 'Tomorrow the peak falls!'[18]

Meanwhile the Austrian climbers Aschenbrenner and Schneider had reached the Silbersattel, breaking the trail for the heavily laden porters who were being shepherded by the rest of the climbers. As they breasted the saddle they saw for the first time the great snow plateau that leads to the summit. Here they waited for two hours until they saw Welzenbach emerge onto the saddle, then they set off again for the summit, crossing the plateau to its far end, where they found a suitable spot for Camp VIII. They waited for the others to arrive, but as time dragged on and nobody appeared, Schneider went back to see what the problem was. As he failed to return, Aschenbrenner also went back to the saddle. There he discovered that because of the lateness of the hour (2 p.m.) when they had reached the saddle, Merkl had decided to camp there. Schneider could not persuade him to cross the plateau. Nevertheless, everyone was in high spirits. They were certain of victory on the morrow.

But that night a storm blew up. The wind became so violent that the tent poles snapped and finely blown snow penetrated to the insides and covered the sleeping-bags. The petrol stoves refused to function so no hot food could be prepared. Despite the wind, a dense fog enveloped the camp and the men found it difficult to breathe.

All next day the storm continued and as darkness fell, the climbers sensed their danger. There was no thought now of the summit, only of survival. Throughout that second dreadful night the storm raged on.

The climbers were caught in a classic trap: because of the good weather they had all pushed on to the top camp and there was nobody holding Camps V, VI or VII. The nearest reserves were in Camp IV, a long way off and below the difficult traverse of Rakhiot Peak. Somebody should have waited in these camps until Mulritter had come up. There should have been no break in the chain. As it was, communications were severed.

On the morning of July 8 the pitiful retreat began. Aschenbrenner and Schneider, with three Sherpas, went ahead breaking the trail. According to Schneider everyone was fit and able to descend though the storm continued unabated.[19] At the Silbersattel, Nima Dorje slipped and was barely held by the two Austrians, but in the accident a sleeping-bag and mattress were lost: 'The storm blew these horizontally and bodily into space – they vanished round a corner,' wrote Schneider later. 'The sleeping bag was ours, the porters still possessed their own.'

Now without their sleeping-bag it was essential that the two Austrians reached Camp V, the first place where there were spares, or they would surely perish. It was probably this fear that led them to unrope from the Sherpas and press ahead. Schneider mentions nothing of the unroping in his account: 'We lost sight of our three porters near the tent of Camp VII,' he wrote blandly. Later, when criticised for unroping, the Austrians defended it on the grounds that it saved the porters all the energy-sapping casting about that had to be done to find the route. The porters were instructed to follow close behind, but of course, they didn't. They were, to all intents and purposes, abandoned. The Austrians were the fittest men on the mountain and simply shot ahead. At 7 p.m. they staggered into Camp IV, completely exhausted. So fierce was the blizzard that they had no idea where their companions were but were confident that they would all make it.[20]

But their three Sherpas got no further than Camp VII that night, whilst the others, led by Wieland, Welzenbach and Merkl, no further than a short distance from the saddle, where they had a terrible open bivouac. The porter Nima Norbu died during the night.

Next morning, July 9, the three climbers and four of the porters descended towards Camp VII, but Ang Tsering, Gaylay and Dakshi stayed at the bivouac because Dakshi felt too ill to move. Welzenbach and Merkl reached Camp VII but Wieland, who had weakened considerably during the night, died just thirty metres above the tent. Welzenbach sent the porters on to try and get help. In its last desperate hours the expedition was his sole responsibility; Merkl, affected by altitude as well as the debilitating storm, was no longer capable of rational decision.

The four porters crawled along the ridge but couldn't reach Camp VI before nightfall and bivouacked on the ridge. Near by were the three porters left behind by the Austrians. They too had been unable to reach Camp VI. Next day the seven porters pushed on, now very much weaker. On the traverse ropes on the Rakhiot Peak, Nima Tashi and Nima Dorje died and Pinju Norbu shortly after.

Meanwhile, three Sherpas were still on the Silbersattel bivvy. On the evening of July 11, Dakshi died and next day his companions Gaylay and Ang Tsering reached Camp VII where they were no doubt surprised to find Welzenbach and Merkl alone. Welzenbach was in great pain, writhing on the tent floor, which was covered in snow. Neither climber had a sleeping-bag. That night, July 12/13, Willo Welzenbach died.

Merkl wanted to wait for help to arrive, but he was persuaded to move down, hobbling with the support of two ice axes. He could not climb the rise of the ridge before Camp VI, however, and so the Sherpas dug a snow cave for shelter. On July 14, Ang Tsering, the only one of the three now in any condition to attempt a move, descended to safety whilst Gaylay and Merkl sat it out on the ridge awaiting certain death.[21]

No rescue was possible; conditions were too bad. Three climbers and seven Sherpas had died in the retreat, the worst mountain disaster since an entire party of eleven had perished in a storm on Mont Blanc in 1870.[22] Of the climbers, only the two Austrians survived; of the Sherpas the survivors were Pasang Norbu, one of those left by the Austrians; Kitar, Pasang Kikuli and Dawa Thondup who had been with Welzenbach and Merkl, and Ang Tsering, the last man to leave the Silbersattel and the last to reach safety.

Irony and tragedy go hand in hand. Because of faulty tactics, men died and yet, had the other members been as fit as Aschenbrenner and Schneider the expedition might have succeeded. They had got within an ace of the summit, but were let down by weaker support groups, who failed to reach the far side of the summit plateau. On the other hand, it is likely the weather would have prevented the final push, and the longer lines of communication might have resulted in an even greater death roll. But it was close – and what a coup it would have been in 1934 to climb the first 8000-metre peak!

There is no denying that the Nanga Parbat disaster was not only a tragedy but also a blow to German pride; a shock to the re-awakening nationalism. The state turned to Paul Bauer, and with its help he founded the Deutsche Himalaja Stiftung (German Himalaya Foundation) whose aim was to co-ordinate and promote German Himalayan mountaineering. With breath-taking insouciance, in view of his earlier attitude, he declared that Nanga Parbat was the logical target for German Himalayan climbers. No doubt his opinions had been changed by events. 'Homage to the dead,' wrote Karl Wien, 'demanded that after 1934 Nanga Parbat should be the goal of the next German expedition to vindicate that tragic blow.'[23] One senses that the Germans had decided to declare war on the mountain.

The mountain certainly declared war on the Germans. Bauer was unable to send a party there in 1936, but went instead to the Kangchenjunga region again, where some useful climbing was done and experience gained by newcomers Adolf Gottner and Gunther Hepp, helped by Karl Wien. Wien had been with Bauer in 1931, and was marked as the next leader for Nanga Parbat.

The expedition took place in 1937. Beside Wien, Gottner and Hepp, there was Hans Hartmann, who had also been on the 1931 Kangchenjunga expedition and had lost the front halves of both feet through frostbite, Peter Mulritter who was a survivor from 1934, Pert Fankhauser, Martin Pfeffer, Uli Luft and Karl Troll. The very best Sherpas were selected to accompany the party.

On June 11 Camp IV was established in a hollow below Rakhiot Peak, nearer the mountain than before. Except for the physiologist Luft, who was working at Base Camp, all the climbers were in Camp IV on the 14th, together with nine Sherpas. Two days later when Luft went to join them he was amazed and shocked to find that there was no sign of either the men or their camp. It was almost unbelievable. 'The Silver Saddle gleamed in the sun high above me, serene and withdrawn,' he said later. 'The team was no more.'

What could have happened, so swiftly, so silently, that those in the lower camps were not aware of it? Judging by watches retrieved later, shortly after midnight on the 14th a massive avalanche had swept down the mountain, filling the hollow where Camp IV was resting and burying everything in its path. Camp IV was obliterated in an instant, like snuffing out a candle, its unfortunate occupants killed as they slept. Sixteen men were dead. It was a worse disaster than 1934; in fact, the worst mountaineering disaster in history.[24]

The world was appalled at news of the tragedy, relayed by a brief message from Reuters, but Germany was stunned. Bauer, who was the instigator of the project, immediately flew out to see what could be done, though nothing could be done but dig out the bodies from their icy burial ground, and reaffirm a determination to climb Nanga Parbat. Nanga Parbat was now recognised as a German mountain,[25] and Bauer had a grim determination to avenge his friends.

Another expedition set out in 1938 but met with bad weather and failed to reach the Silbersattel, though the bodies of Pinju Norbu, Gaylay and Merkl were discovered where they had lain for four years. In 1939, seeking other weaknesses in this seemingly impregnable mountain, a reconnaissance group set out to investigate the Diamir side, which had defeated Mummery in 1895. They discovered technical difficulties of a high order and they were not strong enough to tackle them. Before the party had a chance to leave India, the Second World War broke out and the Germans were interned.[26]

A year after the Germans had begun their struggle with Nanga Parbat, the British resumed the assault on Everest. They had been trying to get permission for the previous two years, fearful of rumours that their exclusive rights to the mountain were under threat from Americans, Germans and Swiss, all of whom had had some considerable Himalayan success. It was this chauvinistic sentiment that finally persuaded the India Office to take action. Under pressure from the British the Dalai Lama gave 'reluctant permission'. And just to make quite sure that no foreigners sneaked in, a codicil was included stating that all members of the expedition must be British, effectively squashing any murmurings about an international party.

Following the advice of General Bruce, the Everest Committee chose Hugh Ruttledge as leader and probably nobody was more surprised than Ruttledge himself. He was an experienced Himalayan traveller, but no mountaineer: forty-nine years old, self-effacing, with a pronounced limp from a pig-sticking accident. 'He felt he had greatness thrust upon him,' said Jack Longland, wryly.[27]

He was in command of a large party of climbers – ten of whom were judged capable of reaching the summit, and all of whom were highly intelligent and strongly opinionated. These in turn were divided into two factions, the military and the non-military,[28] and if Ruttledge remained firmly in command (which he did) the lower pecking order was confused and ultimately contributed to the failure of the expedition.

Amongst them was Colin Crawford from the 1922 expedition; George Wood-Johnson who had been with Dyhrenfurth on Kangchenjunga; Hugh (Hugo) Boustead, a soldier adventurer who had climbed in Sikkim and was commandant of the Sudan Camel Corps; Percy Wyn Harris who had traversed Mount Kenya with Shipton; T.A. Brocklebank, a good alpinist; Jack Longland and Lawrence Wager, friends and fellow alpinists; and Frank Smythe's successful Kamet team: Smythe himself, Shipton, E. St John Birnie and Dr Raymond Greene, who also acted as chief medical officer. Dr W. McLean was assistant medical officer and E.O. Shebbeare – 'old Shebby' – then forty-nine, went along to look after the transport.

Frank Smythe was then thirty-two, with an outstanding record. With Brown he had done the Brenva Face climbs, the best alpine achievement by a British climber between the wars; with Dyhrenfurth's expedition to Kangchenjunga he had climbed Jonsong Peak (7420 m), and in 1931 he had reached the highest summit yet attained with Kamet (7756 m) during an expedition he himself had led.

There was a strong case for Smythe being made leader of any Everest expedition but the Committee in London didn't altogether approve of him. He had what Somervell once called 'an irritating self-sufficiency'. He was bumptious, opinionated, tactless and easily offended – the only man, said Raymond Greene who was a close friend, whose temper improved with altitude. In addition he had been a vocal critic of the Everest Committee and to make matters worse, he earned his living from writing about mountaineering, which smacked of professionalism.

Base Camp was established on April 17 and Camp III at the foot of the North Col by May 6.[29] The weather turned bad, but whenever possible efforts were made to climb the slopes to the Col, slopes which had become materially more difficult since 1924. However, by May 15 Camp IV was established on a ledge below the col and occupied by Smythe, Shipton, Wyn Harris, Longland, Birnie and Boustead.

Equipment was building up nicely, but the severe weather had taken its toll, making tempers short. For some reason best known to himself Bill Birnie had assumed the role of Deputy Leader, and in the absence of Ruttledge and Shebbeare (who was the appointed deputy) took on the role of organising Sherpas and loads. Boustead, a soldier like Birnie, definitely thought the latter was in charge, but the others probably hadn't given it much thought, and just let Birnie get on with it.

On May 20 Wyn Harris, Birnie and Boustead, with eleven Sherpas, struggled up the ridge in an attempt to establish Camp V, earmarked for 25,500 feet. A thousand feet short of this target, however, they dumped their loads and began to descend. Observers on the col were astounded and concerned. They felt something must have gone wrong.

The Sherpas came bounding down the ridge in great fettle, followed by Wyn Harris, his face like thunder, and later Birnie and a tired-looking Boustead. What had apparently happened was that Birnie had decided that because the wind was sharp and cold the Sherpas had had enough, and he had ordered a retreat. Boustead had acquiesced in this but Wyn Harris had objected strongly, only to be overruled. That night a furious row broke out in Camp IV, with accusations flying thick and fast between the soldiers and the others. Next day, Raymond Greene describes the scene in his diary: 'May 21. I spent the morning acting as peace-maker and have I hope settled the B–W row ... At about mid-day Hugh [Ruttledge] arrived. In the afternoon an unpleasant pow-wow took place at which Bill and Hugo were told by Hugh that their effort of the day before was the most disgraceful day in the annals of Everest ... It may be we lost not two days but twenty years.' Boustead apologised, but Birnie stormed out of the tent in a temper. It was indeed twenty years before Everest was climbed.

By next day tempers had cooled and this time the group, now strengthened by the massive frame of Raymond Greene, managed to establish Camp V at 25,700 feet with Longland and Wager in support. But the weather intervened again and it wasn't until the 28th that Camp V was re-established by Wyn Harris, Wager, Birnie and Longland with eight porters. Next day Birnie remained in the camp whilst the other three and the porters set out to establish Camp VI. This they did at 27,400 feet, 600 feet higher than ever before and just short of the junction between the North Ridge and the North-East Ridge. The summit was 1600 feet above.

Wyn Harris and Wager stayed in the tent whilst Longland took the porters down. On the descent they were caught by a blinding snowstorm and Longland had all his work cut out to guide the rapidly demoralised Sherpas to safety. It was one of the finest pieces of pure mountaineering skill ever seen on Everest and averted a disaster of Nanga Parbat proportions.

On the 30th Wyn Harris and Wager made the first summit assault whilst Smythe and Shipton moved into Camp VI. The leaders climbed up below the prow of the second step on the ridge, where they found an ice axe lying on some slabs, an ominous reminder of Mallory and Irvine. Unable to reach the ridge they made for Norton's Couloir where they found the snow loose and treacherous, but they managed to cross it and climb a little further. At 12.30 p.m. they halted. The summit was 1000 feet above and they knew they could not reach it and return in safety. They had equalled the height record set by Norton in 1924.

It was now the turn of Smythe and Shipton. They spent the next day stormbound at Camp VI but the following morning they set out, though neither was in good shape; they had been too high too long. Before long Shipton had to give up but Smythe battled on alone. He too crossed the gully, but like his predecessors came to a halt soon after. Norton in 1924, Wyn Harris, Wager and Smythe in 1933 all reached a height of 28,200 feet (8580 m), the highest point on earth reached by man before the Second World War. It was the end of attempts that year.

Though oxygen apparatus was taken on the expedition it was never used by the climbers, a fact which infuriated George Finch. 'This wretched state of indecision about oxygen must be ended,' he thundered, 'and if the Everest Committee cannot bring itself to decide one way or the other then sack the lot!'[30] Asked for his opinion of Britain's repeated failure to climb Mount Everest he said, savagely, 'We are beginning to look ridiculous!'

If such outright condemnation was only to be expected from Finch, he was by no means alone in his opinions. Amongst many of the younger climbers there was a feeling that the whole business of climbing Everest was being mismanaged. They felt that the leader should be a man capable of leading from the front and when it was announced that Ruttledge was again to be leader in 1936 a furious row broke out behind the secret portals of the Alpine Club. Some members wanted Crawford to be leader, but Smythe, knowing that the leadership would never be given to himself, backed Ruttledge in the certain knowledge that Ruttledge would rely on him at every turn. It was a great opportunity to lead by proxy.

There was a good deal of infighting before the issue was resolved. Crawford, Longland, Wager, Brocklebank and to a certain degree, Greene, all opposed Ruttledge; Smythe, Shipton and Wyn Harris supported him. In the end, after much acrimony[31] the Ruttledge faction won through, though the Everest Committee sought to mollify the Young Turks by organising a preliminary reconnaissance expedition under Eric Shipton during the monsoon period of 1935. This was made possible by the terms of the agreement reached with Tibet.

Shipton's expedition was to be a small one, largely living off the land, and very much on the lines he and Tilman advocated. It consisted of himself, Tilman, Edwin Kempson, Charles Warren, Edmund Wigram, Michael Spender and a New Zealander, L.V. Bryant.[32] Amongst the porters was a Sherpa on his first expedition, Tenzing, destined to be one of the first two men on the roof of the world.

Once Tibet was reached, Shipton, the born explorer, turned aside to climb in the unknown ranges of the Nyonno Ri and Ama Drime, feeling that there was no need to go straight to Everest. Yet they could see from the

Nyonno Ri that Everest was in prime condition and Shipton must have regretted his decision to dally *en route*. What a splendid opportunity it would have been to show what a small team could do on a big mountain. True, a clause in his contract specifically forbade an all-out assault, but if ever there was a time for the Nelson touch, this was it. By the time they did reach Everest, the weather had changed and the opportunity was lost.

Had Shipton gone straight to Everest he might have changed the entire course of Himalayan mountaineering. Success would have put an end to the massive expeditions which were to be the norm for many years, and brought about a more sporting ethic. On the other hand, it might have ended in disaster like the German expedition on Nanga Parbat, which had happened only the previous year. This must certainly have been at the back of his mind and he was always a worrier, always ultra-cautious – a flaw which was to prove his downfall years later.

The fact is that neither the reconnaissance nor the expedition which followed added much to the Everest saga. Nor did the 1938 expedition under Tilman, which embodied all the lightweight concepts he and Shipton had been advocating. Like the 1936 expedition it was beset by bad weather and was a total failure. The only difference was that it failed cheaply.

Whilst the focus of the mountaineering world was on Everest, Kangchenjunga and Nanga Parbat between the wars, speculative eyes were also cast on some of the other great mountains. There are fourteen principal summits over the magic 8000 metres, none of them climbed at that time. Half of them were in Nepal and therefore untouchable since that country barred all foreigners from entering, and Gosainthan (later called Shisha Pangma) was virtually unknown and in Tibet anyway, so equally inaccessible. That left the Karakoram giants: Broad Peak, the two Gasherbrums and K2, the second highest mountain in the world.

Broad Peak, aptly named by Conway in 1892, was long thought to be the fourth highest mountain in the world but when its height was more correctly measured by Mason in 1926 at 8047 metres it dropped to near the bottom of the list.[33] More interest was aroused by the Gasherbrums, I and II, and especially the former. In 1934 Dyhrenfurth organised his second international expedition (following the Kangchenjunga one of 1930) to the mountain, and the German climber Hans Ertl and the Swiss André Roch climbed the South-West Spur to about 6300 metres and reckoned they could have got to the top in three days if they had had experienced porters. Two years later a French party led by Henri de Ségogne and with fine alpinists like Allain, Leininger and Neltner tried the same route and got a little higher, but bad weather and inexperienced porters[34] brought the expedition to an end.

With such a growing interest in the Himalaya it is surprising that since the Duke of the Abruzzi's expedition of 1909, nobody had attempted the second highest mountain in the world, K2. Of all the 8000-metre peaks, K2 is arguably the finest, a mountaineer's mountain, and though the access to it is long it is not too difficult; the surroundings were well known and surveyed at quite an early date.

Perhaps the expense was the chief stumbling-block. The halcyon Edwardian days of the Duke, and similar rich amateurs, had given way to the hungry thirties. The cost of a large expedition – and K2 obviously demanded a large expedition – trekking all that way up the long Baltoro Glacier was perhaps too much to contemplate. The change came in 1938, when an American expedition led by Charles Houston challenged the peak.

Houston had been on Nanda Devi with Tilman and had absorbed some of Tilman's philosophy that small is beautiful. 'Such an expedition is much more interesting,' he said. 'Bigger ones are too hard on the nerves.' Under the auspices of the American Alpine Club he organised an expedition which had six members and six Sherpas.[35] Amongst the climbers were Richard Burdsall, one of the enterprising team that had climbed Minya Konka in 1932, and Captain R.N. Streatfeild, a British climber who had been with the French on Gasherbrum in 1936. Most of the Sherpas were inexperienced but the sirdar was Pasang Kikuli, who had survived the terrible retreat from Camp VIII on Nanga Parbat in 1934.

Basing his campaign on the Duke's previous findings, Houston first of all examined the North-West and North-East Ridges, but finding these unpromising settled for the South-East Ridge, now the Abruzzi Ridge. This wasn't easy either but they made surprisingly good progress. Camp I was placed at the foot of the ridge at the end of June and by July 5, Camp II was placed at 5880 metres. Between Camps IV and V a steep buttress of red rock proved a difficult pitch, but R.H. Bates and W.P. House forced a forty-five-metre chimney (later known as House's Chimney) to place Camp V at 6700 metres on July 16th. The final camp they managed to establish was Camp VII on the 20th, at a height of 7525 metres and from there, next day, Houston and Petzoldt climbed another 500 metres before turning back. They had reached the foot of the final summit slopes and discovered a flat rock which would have made a good site for Camp VIII, but they were afraid the weather might break, and they were short on supplies as well.

Recognising the dangers which had been inherent in the German tactics on Nanga Parbat, Houston ensured that not everyone was on the mountain at the same time, but he was experienced enough to keep climbers in support at Camp VI as he and Petzoldt made their attack. Should they have gambled for the summit? They were near enough and yet, had they done so, they might well have perished, for no sooner had the team returned to Base Camp on the 25th than the mountain was shrouded in storm clouds. Had they stayed on the mountain a moment longer they would have been involved in a desperate descent like the Germans on Nanga Parbat. It was a wise – or lucky – decision. Nevertheless, they had demonstrated what a relatively small expedition could do on the highest mountains.

The outcome might have been different if Fritz Wiessner had joined the Houston team, as he had hoped to do. Wiessner had been on the German Nanga Parbat expedition of 1932, although he had emigrated to America three years before. He was a Saxon from Dresden, trained on the steep sandstone towers of his own district, and a first-rate alpinist of the Munich School. The idea of the K2 expedition had come from Wiessner in the first place and he had hoped to attempt the summit with Bill House (it would have made a strong combination because they climbed together a lot). But Wiessner was unable to go because of other commitments, which was a pity, because it could have been a turning-point in the history of Himalayan climbing. Had the final pair been Wiessner and House, they might have pushed for the summit and hang the consequences.

As it was, Wiessner led his own expedition to K2 the following year, 1939. It seems that none of the previous team members were available for one reason or another, including, in the case of Petzoldt, the fact that the police in India wanted to question him over the death of a man with whom he had had a quarrel on the return across the sub-continent. In any case, Petzoldt, one of the best of American climbers at that time, did not get on well with Jack Durrance, another ace climber, who was on the team. Eventually, however, there were six climbers and a transport officer, Lieutenant Trench, together with nine Sherpas, many of them experienced, once again led by Pasang Kikuli.[36]

One of the team was a forty-something playboy of the western world, Dudley Wolfe, a wealthy East Coast socialite and sportsman. Harvard educated, built like a barn door, and supremely fit, Wolfe's first passion was racing ocean yachts, but he had done three seasons in the Alps with first-class guides and he begged Wiessner to take him to K2. Wolfe was having marital problems and the expedition seemed to him a good way of escaping the mess. He was, of course, prepared to help finance the venture. This, and the man's undoubted fitness, persuaded Wiessner to take him. He warned Wolfe, however, that it was very unlikely he would make the summit.

The route was again the Abruzzi Ridge and at first good progress was made, with camps more or less as before. By July 5, Camp VI at 7100 metres was occupied. But lower down, things were not going so well. Jack Durrance, from whom Wiessner expected much, suffered from altitude sickness and, except for Dudley Wolfe, none of the others was capable of much: Cranmer had developed heart trouble and Sheldon and Cromwell (another wealthy amateur in his forties) were so dispirited they wanted to pull out as soon as they could. They all helped stock the lower camps but by July 11 there were only three climbers and seven Sherpas at work.

Durrance struggled manfully with his altitude problem but he was unable to reach Camp VII and went down with the sirdar Pasang Kikuli.[37] Wiessner, Wolfe and Sherpa Pasang Dawa Lama pushed up to Camp VIII at 7711 metres, but there was then a bout of bad weather and the way to Camp IX (7940 m) was deep in soft snow. Wolfe was too exhausted to make it and retired to Camp VIII. Two days later, on the 19th, Wiessner and Pasang Dawa Lama made a summit bid.

After a breakfast of hot tea they packed enough food for the day and set off for the top. Eventually they reached a rock band where the choice was to climb a steep crumbly wall or traverse round beneath some dangerous-looking ice. Wiessner, one of the greatest rock climbers of the day, naturally chose the rock and the day was so warm and windless that even at 8000 metres he was able to climb without gloves. It was six in the evening before the wall was conquered. Wiessner estimated he was at 8382 metres (27,500 ft)[38] with only 15 metres to go to reach the summit ridge, after which there would be no climbing difficulties!

But to Wiessner's amazement Pasang Dawa Lama refused to follow. It was obvious that the climb would finish in the dark, and though Wiessner reckoned the moonlight would be good enough to see by, the Sherpa was fearful of the mountain's demons, which he said would gather as night fell.

There was nothing for it but to go back to Camp IX and try again on the morrow. As they descended the rocks, the rope caught the crampons which Pasang Dawa Lama was carrying on his rucksack and pulled them off. They went sliding down the mountain and with them went any hope of success. After a day's rest the two men tried again, but without crampons progress was too slow. They reached the rock wall but there turned back.

On the next day they rejoined Wolfe at Camp VIII and were surprised to find that nobody had come up with supplies. For three days Wolfe had only had water to drink, collected from the folds of the tent. He had run out of matches to light the stove and he seemed to have aged considerably in the few days since Wiessner had last seen him. They decided to go down to Camp VII immediately, Wiessner leaving his sleeping-bag because there were plenty more in the lower camps.

On the way down Wolfe tripped on the rope and pulled Wiessner and Pasang Dawa Lama from their steps. All three went sliding down the icy slopes towards the edge of the ridge and a drop into eternity, only saved at the last moment by a patch of exceptionally soft snow where they were able to stop themselves. In the mêlée, Wolfe lost his sleeping-bag.

When they arrived at Camp VII they were devastated to find it totally abandoned, tent flaps open to the elements, stripped of all gear and with the food scattered about in the snow. With only one sleeping-bag between them, which they used as an inadequate coverlet, the three men spent a miserable night. In the morning Wolfe was much weaker and decided to stay where he was whilst the others descended for help.

As Wiessner and the Sherpa descended they were amazed to discover that each camp in turn had been stripped bare. All the reserve air mattresses and sleeping-bags, so laboriously carried up over the preceding days, had gone. That night they rested at Camp II: 'Almost exhausted, mentally and physically, we reached Camp II at nightfall. Here two large tents were standing, but they were unoccupied; one was completely empty, the other half filled with food. The sleeping bags and air mattresses were missing! With our last bit of strength we took down the empty tent and used it as a covering for the night. The cold tentcloth, however, gave no warmth and we shivered miserably; our toes and fingers, frostbitten the previous night, became much worse.'[39]

The following day, July 24, they staggered into Base Camp, emaciated, frostbitten and angry. Wiessner, his throat raw and infected so that he could scarcely speak, demanded to know what the hell was going on.

It had all begun with Durrance going down from Camp VI on the 14th, and taking with him Pasang Kikuli, the sirdar. They left behind the Sherpas Pintso, Tsering, Kitar and Tendrup, with instructions to carry loads up to Camps VII and VIII. Tendrup was in charge of this, but of course Pasang Kikuli should have remained in charge.[40]

On July 17 Tendrup declared, for no apparent reason, that Wiessner, Wolfe and Pasang Lama had been killed by an avalanche and he decided to retreat from Camp VII without going to Camp VIII. He and Kitar went down, but Pintso and Tsering, unconvinced by the avalanche story, remained in Camp VI. In Camp IV, however, Tendrup and Kitar met Pasang Kikuli who was furious with them and ordered them back up. They went back to Camp VII and shouted up to Camp VIII, but receiving no reply – hardly surprising since it was out of earshot – decided to retreat once again. This time Tendrup convinced the others that the summit party was dead and so the camps were stripped and a descent begun.

'Later on, in Base Camp, the Sherpas called Tendrup a devil, who had deceived them with the avalanche story and wanted to wreck the expedition. I myself suspect that the strong but often lazy Tendrup was tired of packing between the high camps and therefore had invented the avalanche story ... At the same time he probably thought the sahibs in Base Camp would praise him for bringing along the valuable sleeping bags from Camps VII and VI.'[41]

By cruel irony, Durrance had already ordered the lower camps to be stripped of sleeping gear because he thought the summit party would bring down their own from the higher camps. Thus, when Wiessner's descent began, there was no sleeping gear at all above Base Camp.

Vague hopes of another attempt were dashed when Durrance, having returned to Camp IV, once again went down with altitude sickness and Wiessner and Pasang Lama failed to recover from their previous ordeal. Meanwhile someone had to reach Wolfe, still in Camp VII. Durrance had told Kitar and Pintso, who had accompanied him to Camp IV, to go on to Camp VII but when Pasang Kikuli and Tsering reached Camp VI later, having climbed from Base in one day, they found them there.

Pasang Kikuli and two Sherpas climbed quickly to Camp VII, intent on bringing Wolfe down. But they found him in a sorry state. He seemed to have given up hope of rescue. His matches had been used up and he had had no hot food for three days. Indeed, he had not even ventured out of his tent and he lay, apathetically, in pools of urine and surrounded by faeces. They could not get him to descend, but he promised he would on the next day if he felt stronger, after the food they fed him. The Sherpas could not stay at Camp VII because they had left their sleeping gear in the camp below, so they had to leave the American yet again.

That night there was a storm which continued the whole of the next day but on the 30th the weather cleared and Pasang Kikuli, Pintso and Kitar began the climb back to Camp VII. From way below Durrance saw them just below the camp, but their companion Tsering waited in vain for their return. 'When they did not return in the evening he thought that evil spirits had killed them . . . Tsering continued to wait in Camp VI through August 1. During the night of August 1 the weather was cold and stormy and Tsering thought the evil spirits were raging around his tent. On the morning of August 2 he fled down the mountain, driven by fear.'[42]

Storms prevented any further attempts at rescue. Wolfe and the three brave Sherpas were left to their fate.

The criticism heaped on Wiessner, particularly by Mason, who spoke of 'inconceivable folly', was undoubtedly prompted by the anti-German feeling building up at the time in Britain and America. It was all a mish-mash of anti-Nazi, anti-Munich School feeling amongst traditional mountaineers, compounded because the facts were never made clear. Mason, in any case, would defend the Sherpas, although Tendrup was certainly chiefly to blame for what happened. Particularly sad, however, was the death of Pasang Kikuli, a brave Sherpa and fine sirdar, who had survived the tragedy of Nanga Parbat, only to die on K2.

CHAPTER TWENTY-ONE

The Last Blue Mountains

At two o'clock on the afternoon of June 3, 1950, two French climbers, Maurice Herzog and Louis Lachenal, stood for the first time on the summit of Annapurna, at 8091 metres the tenth highest mountain in the world.[1] It was a significant event in the mountaineering canon, the first time that a mountain of over 8000 metres had been climbed.

In a world which was still recovering from the effects of the Second World War it is surprising that such a leap forward should be made so soon, and yet, there were cogent reasons why the psychological barrier of 8000 metres should be broken at just this moment. Most important of these was the fact that Nepal opened her frontiers to climbers for the very first time and of the world's fourteen 8000-metre peaks, eight are within Nepal or on its borders, so there was, at a stroke, more than a doubling of possible targets. Secondly, the war had brought about great technological advances in materials – nylon is one example – which were just working their way into civilian life, and thirdly, climbers were avidly repeating the great routes of the Munich School in the Alps; Lachenal himself had made the second ascent of the Eigerwand in 1947, with Lionel Terray, who was also on the Annapurna expedition, as was Gaston Rébuffat, who had, with Edouard Frendo, made the second ascent of the Walker Spur in 1945. Others had followed and the great north faces were becoming the norm by which the best climbers were judged. It was a more assured and confident climber that entered the Himalayan fray after the war.

The Swiss were the first to take advantage of the opening of Nepal. They applied in 1949 for permission to climb Dhaulagiri (8167 m) but for some reason this was refused and instead they explored the area round Kangbachen. Tilman, too, took the opportunity to go exploring and he was back again in 1950 to reconnoitre Manaslu (8156 m) and make an unsuccessful attempt on Annapurna IV (7525 m), with a party of Himalayan novices whom the Himalayan Committee hoped would form a cadre for the future, almost certainly with Everest in mind.[2] Tilman then went on to join a small American party including Charles Houston, the American with whom he had shared the Nanda Devi adventure in 1936, in an exploration of the Khumbu valley, home of the Sherpas and the way to Everest.

Leaving the rest of their small party at Thyangboche Monastery, Tilman and Houston went to the foot of the great icefall tumbling down from the Western Cwm: 'An unpleasant and dangerous place for an advanced base,'

Tilman thought. 'Although we cannot yet dismiss the south side, I think it safe to say that there is no route comparable in ease and safety – at any rate up to 28,000 ft – to that of the north-east.'[3]

But if the British thought in terms of carefully building up a nucleus of Himalayan climbers for the future, the French had no such inhibitions. The British had not caught up with their European contemporaries in alpinism, though a few, like Hamish Nicol and Tom Bourdillon, were sniffing round some of the pre-war lines like the North Face of the Dru: 'We did not know how hard it was, for we had not enough experience of climbs of that nature to interpret the phrases of the Vallot guide,' wrote Bourdillon. 'But we knew it was harder than anything we had done.'[4] But no British climber had done the Eigerwand or Walker Spur, for instance, and so their thinking was two decades behind. Mentally, they were not prepared. The French were.

There had been only one previous French expedition to the Himalaya and that was in 1936 when a strong party under de Ségogne had made a spirited attack on Gasherbrum I, only to be defeated by inexperience and bad weather. In view of this a committee studied the experiences of thirty expeditions and came to the conclusion that failure was often the result of spending too long on the mountain. The high camps should be established and the attempt made as soon as practicable, thus reducing the chance of being caught by bad weather high up, and of course, the physical and moral deterioration which altitude brings about. In other words, get in, get up and get out.

They were fortunate in being given the choice of two prime targets, Dhaulagiri and Annapurna (8091 m) which stand like twin sentinels on either side of the Kali Gandaki Gorge in central Nepal. Very little was known about the area and the peaks had not been reconnoitred. The French, however, were only interested in ascending an 8000-metre peak – 'entirely a climbing venture, a "do-or-die" affair for the "honour of France" '[5] – and so any reconnaissance would have to be swift and to the point.

Maurice Herzog was the leader of a strong but compact team comprising France's best alpinists.[6] They were supported by an equally strong team of Sherpas, led by the redoubtable Ang Tharkay. Their first objective was Dhaulagiri, the higher of the two peaks, but the approach proved difficult and attention soon switched to Annapurna, for the French had only allocated three weeks to the reconnaissance of *both* mountains. On May 18 a base camp was established at the snout of the North Annapurna Glacier but an attempt on the North-West Spur proved abortive and so the camp was moved up the glacier to a height of 4600 metres and a route advanced up the broken North Face towards the distinct wall of the Sickle (so called because of its shape), in reality the edge of the summit icecap.

They had need to hurry because the monsoon had already been reported in Calcutta and would be expected to sweep across the mountain in a matter of days. On June 3, Herzog and Lachenal, having survived a night of storms, started at 6 a.m. for the summit from Camp V at 7300 metres.[7] Plugging steadily upwards through the snow they reached the top at 2 p.m.

It was a brilliant victory, but it almost turned into a tragedy. On the descent Herzog lost his gloves and he and Lachenal became separated in the storm which had blown up. Fortunately for both men, Terray and Rébuffat had moved up from Camp IV to Camp V. They were able to find Lachenal, who had missed the camp entirely in the storm, and give first aid to Herzog who was horribly frostbitten.

Next day the descent was slow and uncertain. Heavy snowfall had obscured the tracks and the mountain lay under a blanket of baffling mist. Not surprisingly, they lost their way and as night descended Lachenal fell into a crevasse. The others crawled in to join him and here they spent the night, huddled together with just one sleeping-bag, which was shared by Terray and Lachenal.

In the morning a snow slide poured into the crevasse, half burying them, but they managed to struggle free. Rébuffat and Terray were snowblind; Lachenal and Herzog so badly frostbitten that they were unable to pull on their boots. Luckily for them they were discovered by Marcel Schatz, who guided them to Camp IV, and from there Schatz, Couzy, Ang Tharkay and the Sherpas Aila, Sarki and Ang Tsering III (known as Pansy) led them down to safety. Even then Annapurna was reluctant to let them go: Herzog and his two supporters, Aila and Pansy, were carried 150 metres down the mountain in an avalanche, but miraculously survived the ordeal. The doctor, Jacques Oudot, worked hard as the team trekked out but several fingers and toes had to be amputated.

The French ascent of Annapurna was one of those intuitive campaigns which are hailed as brilliant because they succeed; had it failed with loss of life it would have been condemned. The French had the good fortune to hit upon the only relatively easy way up the mountain, but one which has since been recognised as very dangerous from avalanches. Mason wrote: 'Herzog quite frankly states he was prepared to reach the summit or die in the attempt. He would have died but for the close support of his friends and the Sherpas.' And, he might have added, an enormous slice of good fortune.

As far as Everest was concerned, time was running out for the British. Tibet was occupied by the Chinese in 1950 and the traditional route to the mountain sealed off more effectively than ever it was by the Dalai Lama in pre-war years. Moreover, with the partitioning of India in 1947 the British Raj came to an end and Britain's influence over the sub-continent was much reduced. No longer was she able to keep out foreigners who might want to attempt the world's highest mountain – and there were plenty who did.

In fact, the French ascent of Annapurna was cause for concern amongst the British climbing Establishment. Here was a nation – admittedly one with good climbers, but with virtually no Himalayan experience – who had walked into Nepal with a fairly small team, and without any previous reconnaissance had climbed the first 8000-metre peak ever ascended at their first attempt. Suppose they did the same to Everest? Not only would the British be robbed of the highest summit in the world, and one they considered their exclusive property, but they would also look extremely foolish in view of all the abortive pre-war effort put into it.

Eric Shipton had wanted to go back to Everest in 1947, but events had ruled that out and it was not until 1951 that a young doctor, Michael Ward, managed to persuade the Himalayan Committee that a full-scale reconnaissance should be made, through the Khumbu in Nepal, following Tilman's preliminary skirmish, to determine whether the great icefall of the Western Cwm could be overcome and a way found to the South Col. Shipton was to be leader.

Because he had a soft spot for New Zealanders Shipton included the strong raw-boned Ed Hillary in the team, but refused to take the Swiss climber René Dittert. The Swiss were quite put out by this and were not to forget when the time came.[8]

After an unpleasant march through the monsoon rains from the Indian railhead at Jogbani the party entered the Sherpa 'capital' of Namche Bazar on September 22 from where they moved up the Dudh Kosi towards Everest. Only Shipton was aware of the contrast between this verdant southern approach and the bleak Tibetan plateau of pre-war years; gone were the knife-like winds that cut to the marrow, gone the dry hacking coughs that debilitated men from the outset: now it was the warm rains, and the black leeches that filled your socks with blood from their bloated bodies.

By the end of the month they had started to explore the great Icefall at the head of the valley, and the key to Everest.

The Icefall is caused by the squeezing together of the open end of a great horseshoe of ridges which sweep round from Nuptse in the south, through Lhotse at the head of the cwm then via the South Col to Everest, whose long West Ridge forms the remaining arm of the horseshoe. Enclosed in this vast amphitheatre is a slightly rising snowfield, the Western Cwm – a Welsh name given it by Mallory, who was the first to see it. As with all glaciers the snows of the cwm are slowly but inexorably sliding down, and where they are compressed they tumble and break into a cascade of crystalline cliffs and pinnacles. It falls 600 metres in a little over a mile and because of the relentless downwards pressure the Icefall is highly unstable – any one of the great ice towers is likely to collapse at any moment. Passing through such a place is the mountain equivalent of Russian roulette. Not only that, but the route is constantly changing: what is viable one season will almost

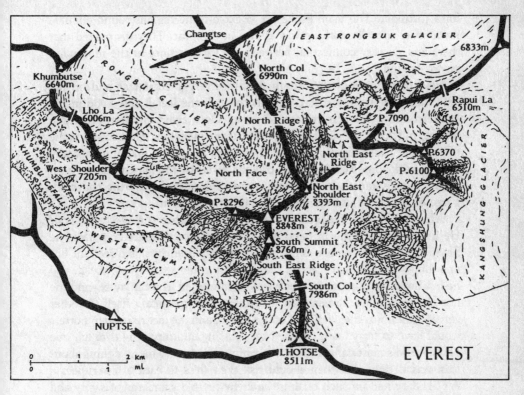

certainly be different the next. Nor is there any escape at the sides; these pour avalanches onto the Icefall from time to time.

The late Dougal Haston described his feelings about it thus: '. . . it was always a mentally exhausting journey. In some places the only possible route was under overhanging shaky seracs. Frequent crossings of this type of passage are more wearing than big wall climbing. You cannot even take the normal safety precaution of going when there is no sun as the sun is on the Icefall for most of the day. One can only go in and hope. On some occasions complete sections of the route were destroyed by movement of ice. When one finally comes out of this icy mess into the Western Cwm it is like being in a newer, brighter land.'[9]

This was the obstacle which Shipton's party were the first to reconnoitre. After some fine preliminary work by Riddiford and Pasang, Hillary, Riddiford and Bourdillon with three Sherpas made a determined attack on the Icefall on October 4. They reached the lip of the Western Cwm just before 4 p.m., but a near-accident with a snowslide persuaded them to retreat without entering the sanctuary. A large crevasse provided a formidable obstacle to entering the cwm. Nevertheless they had demonstrated the feasibility of the route and this satisfied Shipton. He determined not to push any further until the snow had evaporated more: in fact, to leave the mountain alone

for a fortnight. The team broke up to explore the regions round about –
remember, virtually nothing was known at the time. They discovered that
there was no easy connection between the various sides of the mountain,
no way round.

Towards the end of the month they returned to their task and on the
28th the whole team forced their way through the Icefall and stood in the
Western Cwm, the first persons to do so. Once again, Shipton ordered a
retreat, much to the disgust of certain team members. He allowed some
further half-hearted exploration of the Icefall, to try and find an easier way
up, but with some relief he soon ordered a retreat to Namche Bazar from
where various members did some more exploring, discovering the great
gorge of Rowaling and the lovely Menlungtse (7181 m).

Why did Shipton not press on, once he had reached the Western Cwm?
He had plenty of time in hand and could have reconnoitred towards the
South Col, but his nature denied his responsibilities in this direction. For
one thing, once he had reached the cwm, he could *see* the way ahead, and
he lost interest. Shipton was always more interested in what lay beyond the
last blue mountain, rather than in climbing the mountain itself. Another
consideration was the condition of the Icefall, and the fact that laden porters
would have to ferry loads up the cwm, passing and repassing through one
of the world's most dangerous places. Shipton had grave moral doubts about
this: was it right that men should risk their lives to earn a few rupees a
day? Hillary had no such qualms; he knew the old standards of safety and
unjustifiable risk had to be changed: 'The competitive standards of Alpine
mountaineering were coming to the Himalaya, and we might as well com-
pete or pull out.'[10]

This was certainly borne in on the Himalayan Committee when they
sought permission for an expedition in 1952. Much to their surprise they
found the Swiss had got there before them.

Trying to retrieve the situation the Himalayan Committee requested that
the Swiss should make it a joint expedition. There was some merit in this
as far as the Swiss were concerned because the British were the only climbers
to have been through the Icefall and they valued the experience of Shipton.
But when the two sides met, the British, still living in the past, loftily
demanded that Shipton should be leader and that the expedition should be
regarded as British with a Swiss contingent. The Swiss pointed out that
they had been trying to get to Everest since 1926, that they had been
frustrated by the British Imperial policy and that only last year they had
been denied a place on the reconnaissance, although two New Zealanders
were later added to the party. Pigeons were coming home to roost.[11]

In the end the Swiss went to Everest and Shipton took a party to Cho
Oyu (8201 m). Both failed.

The Swiss party had two bites of the cherry, before and after the monsoon. Of the seventeen team members[12] only Chevalley and Lambert were on both attempts, and Lambert, alone with André Roch, who was on the pre-monsoon attempt, were certainly the two best-known climbers internationally. The sirdar, or chief porter, was the dapper little thirty-eight-year-old Sherpa Tenzing Norgay, who had been on the north side of Everest three times with the pre-war expeditions and once with the illegal attempt of Canadian Earl Denman in 1947. Tenzing (he had added the name Norgay – 'the fortunate one' – himself) was intelligent, strong and above all, ambitious. Tenzing had been with Roch and Dittert to the Garhwal in 1947 where the Swiss had come to appreciate and admire the Sherpa's qualities.

The attack on the great Icefall began on April 26, the Swiss finding, as Shipton had, that once within the maze of pinnacles it was difficult to know in which direction to go since all that could be seen was the ice immediately round about. They were forced well to the left, below the avalanche-prone slopes of the West Ridge, into a couloir Roch christened Suicide Passage. At the top, as they entered the cwm, they encountered the giant crevasse which had caused Shipton to turn back, but they managed to erect a rope bridge of sorts by which the Sherpas could be ferried across. They had broken into the Western Cwm. That night after they had all returned safely to camp, an avalanche swept the Suicide Passage.

Camp III at the entrance to the cwm was occupied on May 6, then in the following days Camps IV and V were placed further across the floor of the cwm, ready for an assault on the slopes leading to the South Col. These latter were longer and steeper than they had seemed from afar – Dittert reckoned they were 1060 metres and about the same steepness as the Old Brenva on Mont Blanc.[13] The upper part of these slopes was divided by a rock rib called by the Swiss Eperon des Genevois, or Geneva Spur.

After a reconnaissance it was decided to attack the Spur and on May 25 Lambert, Flory, Aubert, Tenzing and six other Sherpas started up the rocks. Three Sherpas gave up but the rest of the party laboriously dragged themselves and their loads upwards into the unknown. Night fell and still they had not reached the South Col, nor was there anywhere to rest. They could hardly go down but, cold and exhausted, they could not go on for much longer either ... Suddenly, the slope eased off and they found a place to put their two tents. The tents were designed for two men apiece, but now one held three climbers and the other four Sherpas. There was no room for bulky sleeping-bags; the men huddled together for warmth, and listened to the wind howling over the ridge. Nobody slept, though incredibly, Tenzing managed to brew up some soup. Lambert tied himself to his ice axe, convinced he was going to be blown off into the Western Cwm.

The following day, whilst the Sherpas rescued gear which had been abandoned on the ridge the night before, the three Swiss and Tenzing climbed on to reach the South Col for the first time. The wind was a raging fury on the col and there was a hard struggle to establish a camp, the tent cracking and flapping madly, the climbers fighting the canvas like sailors in a Cape Horn hurricane. Tenzing then returned down the ridge to help the other porters and when they arrived at the col, all in, he went down alone twice more to rescue abandoned gear. His, above all, was an astonishing performance.

Next day Lambert and Tenzing, followed by Flory and Aubert, set off for the South-East Ridge. The first obstacle was a large buttress which they overcame by a long steep gully. Once on the ridge they established Camp VII, a lone tent, where Lambert and Tenzing spent the night, whilst the other two withdrew to the South Col to act in support.

Lambert and Tenzing spent a miserable night. They had no sleeping-bags, no stove, very little food. They melted a little ice on an empty can to relieve their raging thirst. Sleep was out of the question. It was hardly an ideal preparation for attempting the highest mountain in the world.

Dawn brought ominous weather signs but the two men started up the ridge, painfully, laboriously. Their oxygen sets were not functioning properly but they didn't like to discard them because nobody knew how long a man could survive above 8000 metres without extra oxygen.

Their progress was funereal, sometimes they were reduced to crawling on all fours, as the mountain mists drifted over them. They reached the main crest. Somewhere miles below on the right lay the Kangshung Glacier. Suddenly, through a rent in the veil, Lambert saw the South Summit. It seemed near enough to touch, but Lambert knew it was beyond their reach. The last 180 metres had taken five hours to climb and it would take at least as long to reach the South Summit. The two climbers turned and went down. They had reached 8600 metres (28,210 ft), higher than anyone had ever climbed before.

Although another group went up to the South Col, the whole expedition had been too high too long. It was time to go down.

The autumn expedition, though largely comprising new personnel and under a new leader, Chevalley, never seemed to get its act together. Illness dogged the party, the leader became less than decisive and morale was low. By the time Lambert, Tenzing (now a climbing member in his own right) and Reiss reached the South Col with seven Sherpas on November 19, the winds were howling at sixty miles an hour and the temperature was down to thirty below zero.

So the Swiss had failed on Everest. But Shipton had failed on neighbouring Cho Oyu too. The British party soon discovered that the most feasible way to climb the mountain lay over the border in Tibet, but Shipton, cautious as ever, was unwilling to risk a possible diplomatic incident by crossing the border although, as Hillary pointed out, even if the Chinese were in that part of Tibet (by no means certain) they were unlikely to be patrolling high on a mountain. A feeble attempt was made from a base camp just on the Nepalese side of the border but it was bound to fail and it did.

One can only imagine it was with some relief that Shipton turned away from Cho Oyu, the expedition breaking up into various parties which ranged far and wide over a countryside still in those days largely unexplored.[14]

It was valuable exploratory work, the sort of thing Shipton was best at, but it was not the reason he had been sent to the Himalaya and in his heart of hearts he knew it. As a preparation for Everest the expedition was practically useless.

Amongst the Himalayan Committee, charged with the 1953 Everest attempt, confidence in Shipton's leadership was wavering. It was not a nettle to be grasped too hastily, however: Shipton was popular both with other climbers and with the public in general and he was easily the most experienced man available for the job. Nevertheless, his hesitancy and diffidence were worrying the Committee who felt, quite rightly, that 1953 was probably the last chance the British would have to reach their goal. In 1954 it was the turn of the French to attempt Everest and the following year the Swiss would be back again: it would be a long time before the British could have another go. There was another reason, too, why success was imperative. In June 1953 the new Queen was due to be crowned in Westminster Abbey, and the ascent of Everest would make a splendid herald to the new Elizabethan Age everyone was talking about.

On July 28, when the Committee met to hear Shipton's report on Cho Oyu his manner confirmed their worst fears: it was hardly the report of a determined leader. In fact, he questioned his own fitness for the job, but in the end they appointed him ... and almost immediately changed their minds. From then until September there was a good deal of name-shuffling and ear-bending. They wanted to be rid of Shipton, but hadn't the guts to say so in public. Then, much to Shipton's surprise, a co-leader was appointed, an unknown army colonel called John Hunt.

'Then, for the first time,' wrote Shipton later, 'it dawned on me that there must have been a good deal of backdoor diplomacy since the last meeting, of which I was totally unaware.'[15]

Hunt was the protégé of Basil Goodfellow, the Committee Secretary, who had met him in Switzerland the previous summer and considered him 'a terrific thruster', and obviously just the man to put a bit of backbone into Shipton's decisions. But Shipton thought otherwise and resigned. The repercussions in the mountain world were considerable.[16] Hunt suddenly found himself sole leader, something he found embarrassing to discuss even a quarter of a century later.[17] With hindsight it is easy to see now that it was the right result obtained in the wrong way.

Hunt brought to the task a positive genius for organisation that Shipton could never have matched. He was, said James Morris, the *Times* correspondent attached to the expedition, 'authority and responsibility incarnate'.[18]

He commanded a team which was founded on the nucleus of Shipton's Cho Oyu party[19] and they were embarking on what Morris perceptively called 'the last innocent adventure'. Indeed, by training, occupations and background they, and the Committee even more so, were made from the same moulds that had turned out the Mummerys and Dents of yesteryear. It was an unbroken succession, but one which was shortly to change for ever. There was no place on the expedition for Joe Brown and Don Whillans, two Manchester plumbers, who happened to be the best climbers in the country at the time.

On March 27 the expedition, which had left Kathmandu in two separate groups, reassembled on the *marg* outside the famous monastery of Thyangboche, a site surrounded by the most magnificent-looking peaks, with the tip of Everest just visible in the background. For the next three weeks parties set off from here on training climbs until on April 9 Hillary, with Mike Westmacott, George Band, George Lowe, Griff Pugh and Tom Stobart moved up-valley to establish Base Camp and attempt the Icefall.

The Icefall provided its usual horrors but these were all overcome and Camp II established about half-way up, as the Swiss had done the year before. From here the upper part consisting of immense séracs and ice cliffs looked impossible but the climbers won through to establish Camp III on the edge of the cwm (April 22).[20] A series of camps was then established across the long bed of the cwm culminating in Camp VI, below the face of Lhotse. It was during this build-up period that Tenzing and Hillary first climbed together and the tall New Zealander, who set a cracking pace, was delighted to see that the little Sherpa had no difficulty keeping up with him. The Sherpa, too, was impressed by Hillary and there is little doubt that they recognised in one another a mutual determination to get to the top.

If any proof was needed that these two were a formidable climbing team it came on May 2 when, ostensibly testing the open-circuit oxygen equipment (which didn't need testing), they climbed the Icefall in about two hours! Two hours later, through deep soft snow, they had ploughed their way to Camp IV. In the late afternoon they set off back, with little daylight to spare and a threatening storm in the offing. Before long they were totally enveloped in a howling blizzard and only Hillary's knowledge of the Icefall enabled them to weave their sightless way through the maze of séracs. Camp III had been abandoned and though there were sleeping-bags and food at Camp II, the two men turned their backs on certain safety and descended the rest of the Icefall in the gathering night. It was pitch dark as they finally stumbled over the moraines of the Khumbu Glacier into Base Camp. 'Well,' thought Hillary, 'we've made it, and I expect we've proved something. But at the moment I've no idea what it is.'[21] Actually, they had proved mutual dependability under the most arduous circumstances. Each now knew that no matter what happened he could depend absolutely on the other.

Work now started on climbing the 4000-foot (1200-metre) slopes from the cwm to the South Col. The Swiss, it will be remembered, had climbed the Geneva Spur, the rib which divided the slopes below the col, but they had found it difficult and had later opted for a route across the Lhotse Face – another struggle with séracs, followed by a long sloping line to the col. Buffeted by cold winds, it seemed as though the attack might falter here; twelve days were spent trying to overcome the slopes before Wilfrid Noyce and the Sherpa Anullu broke through to the South Col.

Meanwhile Hunt had decided that there would be two summit assaults. The first would be Tom Bourdillon and Charles Evans, using closed-circuit oxygen, and the second would be Ed Hillary and Tenzing using open-circuit oxygen.[22]

On May 26 the first two set off from the South Col for the summit, accompanied by Hunt and Sherpa Da Namgyal who carried loads up the introductory couloir to a point a little above the remnants of the Swiss tent occupied by Lambert and Tenzing the year before. This was to support the second attempt. Meanwhile Bourdillon and Evans ploughed on up the ridge, through soft snow, until at 1 p.m. they stood on a distinctive point of the ridge known as the South Summit. It was the highest point (28,740 feet/ 8760 m) that had been attained at that time. But it wasn't the ultimate prize.

The ridge ahead looked difficult and Evans was having trouble with his oxygen set. There was some discussion as to whether Bourdillon should go for the summit solo, but, wrote Evans later, 'at great heights ambitions and frustrations are diminished' and in the end they decided to go down.[23] The descent was a nightmare. Both men were desperately tired, Evans's oxygen set malfunctioning and they slipped continually, only their ingrained mountain sense preventing a major accident. When they stumbled down the final couloir to the South Col, where Hillary and the others came out to meet them, they looked like old bowed figures, encased in ice from head to foot.

Next day the wind was too strong for an attempt. The South Col camp was crowded, however, and it was essential that some should go down. Evans, Bourdillon and Ang Temba started out but before long Bourdillon collapsed and Hunt went down to help him. In doing so he gave up any chance he might have had of attempting the summit. In fact none of the four was really fit and the descent was grim.

The second attempt began at 8.45 a.m. on May 28, when a support team of Lowe, Gregory and Ang Nyima set off with heavy loads to establish a ridge camp. At 10 a.m. Hillary and Tenzing followed, also heavily laden, and caught up with the others at the site of the old Swiss camp. Shortly after this they came to the loads left by Hunt and added these to their own – Hillary was actually carrying sixty-three pounds. At 2.30 p.m. they discovered a sloping ledge which would just about do for a tent, and dumped their sacks. Here, at a record height for a campsite of about 27,900 feet (8500 m), Hillary and Tenzing spent the night, alternately dozing and making brews of sweet lemon tea.

The next morning was fine and the two men set off at 6.30 a.m. for the roof of the world. Below the South Summit they found themselves struggling with powder snow which was dangerously loose. It was the sort of place where if one went they would both go – there was no chance of a firm anchor for the ice axes. Tenzing confessed later that it was the most dangerous place he had ever been on a mountain whilst Hillary said his solar plexus was tight with fear. But to himself he said at the time, 'Ed, my boy, this is Everest – you've got to push it a bit harder.' Which had been his philosophy all along. They reached the South Summit at 9 a.m.

They could now look along the ridge to the final summit. A great cornice of snow curled over to the right, a final cap to the immense East Face which swept thousands of feet to the Kangshung Glacier. On the left fearfully steep snow slopes dropped towards the Western Cwm, but at least they were firm and offered steady progress until a tower suddenly loomed up, blocking the ridge. There was no way of climbing it direct but on the right there was a gap between the rock and the snow which looked as though it might be feasible, though it was a risky climb. What if the snow wasn't firm?

Hillary eased himself into the crack facing the rock and began to climb, jabbing his crampons into the snow behind him. To his great relief the snow was icy enough to be solid and in no time the New Zealander had reached the top of the rock and was bringing up Tenzing. It would be known henceforth as the Hillary Step.

Above the step the going was easier and the two men were able to move together, over an undulating ridge. The ochre brown plains of Tibet appeared below and Hillary saw a snow cone on his right towards which he automatically turned, cutting steps to reach the top, with Tenzing close behind. Suddenly there was only sky. At 11.30 a.m., May 29, 1953, Edmund Hillary and Sherpa Tenzing stepped onto the summit of Everest, the first men ever to reach the ultimate point of the earth's surface.

A few weeks after Hillary and Tenzing had reached the summit of Everest an Austrian, Hermann Buhl, staggered alone to the summit of Nanga Parbat. The expedition was called the Willy Merkl Memorial Expedition, in memory of the man who had led the expeditions of 1932 and 1934 and had perished on the mountain. It was led by Merkl's step-brother, Dr K.M. Herrligkoffer. The climbing leader was Peter Aschenbrenner, the Austrian guide who in 1932 had got higher than anyone else only to be victimised by the Nazis

17 The techniques and equipment used by the Munich School in the 1930s. Note the hemp rope, shoulder belays and very long ice axe.

18 The Swiss climbers André
Roch and Robert Gréloz
were among the leading
alpinists of the 'thirties. Roch
is the upper figure in the
picture above – 'just playing
about', he says. *Left*: One of
the great pre-war climbs;
Gréloz on the first ascent of
the North Face of Triolet in
1931.

19 Some leading American climbers of the inter-war years. *Top*: Henry S. Hall on Mount Buckner. He was on the Logan expedition of 1925 and attempted the unclimbed Waddington in 1934. *Left*: Heinrich Führer, the guide who led the Japanese to victory on Mount Alberta in 1925. *Right*: Kenneth Henderson (standing) who, with Underhill, brought technical standards to the Tetons.

20 The Alpine pioneers soon turned their attention to the Caucasus and
in 1888 J.G. Cockin, with Ulrich Almer as guide, made the first ascent of
the North Summit of Ushba, called the Matterhorn of the Caucasus. The
higher South Summit was climbed by a German party who made a
remarkable traverse of the peak in 1903. *Inset*: R.A. Hodgkin reaching
the summit after the first ascent of the South-East Ridge in 1937.

21 The small British 1937
Caucasus expedition of
Taylor, Hodgkin, Beaumont
and Jenkins made some
remarkable and difficult
ascents, hardly appreciated at
the time. *Top*: Jenkins and
Beaumont climbing Gulba,
Left: Bob Beaumont looking
at the North Face of Tetnuld,
climbed by Jenkins and
Taylor. *Above*: Robin
Hodgkin on the Lizard
Ledge, Ushba East Face.

22 The second highest mountain in the world, K2 (top) was the scene of the American expeditions of 1938 and 1939. *Left*: House's Chimney. *Centre right*: Houston near 26,000 feet in 1938. *Above*: Fritz Wiessner (left) and Paul Petzoldt.

23 The Eigerwand, ultimate battle ground of the Munich School, climbed in 1938 by Heckmair (inset left), Harrer, Kasparek and Vörg. The first serious attempt on the wall was made in 1935 by Sedlmayer (inset right) who died at Death Bivouac with his partner Mehringer.

24 Everest (top), highest mountain in the world. *Above left*: Andy Bakewell, Oscar Houston, Bill Tilman and Charles Houston (l to r), the first western visitors to the Khumbu in 1950. *Above right*: Hillary and Tenzing, the ultimate victors in a long struggle, 1953.

on his return. The expedition followed much the same route as before –
and became as extended as in 1932 – but this time fortune smiled and
though Buhl only reached the summit at 7 p.m. and had to survive a night
in the open standing on a rock without food, sleeping-bag or even a spare
sweater, the mountain was won.

Within five years all the 8000-metre peaks were conquered with the
exception of Dhaulagiri, which wasn't climbed until 1960, and Shisha
Pangma, which the Chinese climbed in 1964.[24]

The ascents of Everest and Nanga Parbat are a good point at which to
draw this survey to a close. The foundations were laid; all the building
blocks were in place.

There were a few who thought that the ascent of Everest was the end of
mountaineering; that all had been done. What remained was simple rep-
etition, and in mountaineering more than most activities, only the first time
counts. Such doubt had been expressed before when all the big Alpine peaks
had been climbed, but mountaineering is infinitely variable. It is the most
chameleon-like of pursuits, adapting itself to the current climate, without
rules or laws, relying on the ethical mores of the time. If it were not it could
not have survived so long, so vigorously, especially after the ascent of Everest.

At the individual level there is a tangible thread running through from
earlier times to the present day; if Mummery were to return today he would
perfectly understand what a modern expert like Messner was trying to
achieve and though he might marvel at the modern gear, he would realise
its advantages at once. Even the nationalism which affects many expeditions
(though to a lessening degree with every passing year) would have been
understood by the pioneers – Carrel was determined the Matterhorn should
be conquered by Italians, for instance, and the local New Zealanders were
certainly intent on beating FitzGerald to the top of Mount Cook in 1894!

Since the Second World War there have been tremendous advances in
gear, techniques and transport which have contributed to some outstanding
mountaineering feats, appreciated by a more knowledgeable public than
ever before. In Britain wartime training in mountaineering – mostly never
used – combined with what was left of the pre-war outdoor movement
to form various sorts of climbing courses from Outward Bound to the
Mountaineering Association, both of which did sterling work in widening
the appeal of climbing. Many famous mountaineers worked for these organisations: for example, Eric Shipton was Warden of Eskdale Outward Bound,
and Doug Scott, Hamish MacInnes, Ian Clough and others worked as
instructors for the Mountaineering Association, a commercial organisation
set up by Jerry Wright. In Britain, every education authority worth its salt
had its own 'outdoor activity centre', in which mountaineering usually
played a significant part, in the somewhat dubious belief that it was 'character building'. The Duke of Edinburgh's Award Scheme, which arose directly

out of the successful Everest ascent and had John Hunt as its first director, also frequently involved mountain activities. Thousands of young people passed through the hands of these various organisations and even if they did not take up mountaineering themselves (many did[25]) at least they had a better appreciation than their parents did of what it was about.

With greater participation it was inevitable that standards would rise dramatically. Before the war the average British rock climber was regarded as competent and experienced if he could lead a Very Difficult grade climb, whereas nowadays Hard Very Severe would have to be regarded as minimum competency.

Better gear helped. Nylon rope, especially of the long fibre kind known as kernmantel, with a braided sheath, proved stronger, more elastic and far easier to handle when wet and frozen than the old Alpine hemp. Duvet jackets keep out the cold and all sorts of breathable and wicking fabrics can now be combined to keep a climber dry and warm. Nailed boots gave way – not without much argument – to the cleated rubber sole invented in Italy just before the war by Vitale Bramani, and called after him, Vibrams.

As far as rock climbing is concerned three pieces of post-war equipment helped to revolutionise the sport. The harness replaced the simple tie-on, making it possible to sustain a free fall in relative comfort, and equally important, to hang there without blacking out as happened with a rope round the waist. It has found universal application, beyond rock climbing to Alpine and Himalayan ascents, and indeed well outside mountaineering altogether. The lightweight rock boot of the Eastern Alps known as the *Kletterschuhe* was refined by the French climber, Pierre Allain, into the PA, a canvas shoe with stiff, smooth rubber soles, that would fit on the smallest holds and gave superb friction. This was the first of the many rock shoes now universally used. Protection, too, advanced: pitons were improved, especially by the American climber Yvon Chouinard, but the most useful accessory was the invention of the artificial chockstone, which dramatically reduced the effects of a fall, improved belaying, and inspired confidence. The first metal chocks were reamed-out nuts with slings attached, but these soon gave way to increasingly sophisticated shapes, with nylon tapes or wires attached, usually obtainable in sets, like spanners, with different sizes for different cracks. The ultimate in this protection came with the invention of a camming device, known as a Friend, by the American climber Ray Jardine in the 1970s.

Belaying was made safer, and certainly more comfortable, when metal descendeurs, originally meant for abseiling, were adapted to belaying, replacing the old waist belay or the even older shoulder belay, still in use long after the war.

The impact of all this on rock climbing has been enormous. In the Alps the West Face of the Dru was climbed by various outstanding routes, in

Yosemite the great faces like those of Half Dome and El Capitan were overcome and the gorges of Verdon in France became a favourite playground. Ethics were adapted to suit. Aid climbing, or artificial climbing as it was first called, was used as necessary and more recently some routes have permanently placed bolts in situ to which a climber can clip short slings, known as quickdraws, for protection. In climbs like this the old ethic, based on the dictum that the leader never falls, gives way to the leader falling repeatedly until he overcomes the problem. Such climbs are known as sports climbs to differentiate them from the older adventure climbs, where the climber is responsible for his own protection.

The sport of rock climbing is set for total divergence along these lines, and this is emphasised by the sport climbing that takes place in indoor stadia, often in competition. There is a World Championship for men and women, won on a points system over several competitions, like the Grand Prix in Formula One motor racing. Exciting to watch, incredibly athletic, it has little to do with mountaineering.

Adventure climbing, though, is in direct line from Mummery and the Zsigmondys, but as far in advance of them as Concorde is to the Wright brothers.

The impact of modern technology on rock climbing has been considerable, but on ice climbing the impact is even more fundamental. Quite simply, ice climbing has been revolutionised. Our resurrected pioneers would recognise modern rock climbing, but modern ice climbing would astonish them. The great step-cutting marathons they described – and one of the reasons they admired their guides so much – diminished under the influence of modern crampons while ice axes have been getting shorter almost from the day they were invented. As steeper ice was climbed the long axe shaft became a positive encumbrance; there simply wasn't room to wield it, so in the 1930s Scottish climbers started using short slaters' picks to cut steps and later this developed into a dagger technique, with an ice dagger (often a sharpened piton) in one hand and a short axe in the other. These were later replaced by 'ice tools' which are in effect two very short axes with specially adapted picks. Climbers such as the Scotsmen John Cunningham and Hamish Mac-Innes, Bill March and the American Yvon Chouinard demonstrated how these could be used on steep ice, in conjunction with the front points of crampons, to effect very rapid ascents. Step-cutting has been eliminated; the axes are simply hooked into the ice in turn, as the climb is front-pointed.

The growth of these various techniques has led to increased level of performance in the Alps and elsewhere. Routes which once took days, such as the Eigerwand, have been done in hours and even Mount Everest has been climbed from Base Camp to summit in twenty-two and a half hours.[26] Large expeditions to the Himalayan giants may not have completely died away but even the largest peaks are being increasingly attempted in a lightweight, alpine style. The great mountains are also going through the phases that all mountains pass through, from simple conquest to the search for more difficult routes, as for example the ascents by Chris Bonington's teams of the South Face of Annapurna in 1970 and the South-West Face of Everest in 1975.

Of course the mountains still fight back and climbers still die. Experiences similar to those suffered by the Germans on Nanga Parbat between the wars still occur, most recently on K2 in 1986 when thirteen died in a fateful season of multiple tragedies.

Climbers sometimes seem to want to demonstrate their mastery over the mountains in ways which reek of arrogance: gimmicks such as hang-gliding from Everest's summit, or skiing down Everest, or attempting (with the aid of a helicopter) all three of the great Alpine faces – Grandes Jorasses, Eiger and Matterhorn – in twenty-four hours. It seems to me that such activities demean great mountains, and perhaps some otherwise great mountaineers. Sometimes these tricks are done for television, a peepshow for the proletariat.

Air travel has opened the world to climbers and more recently many of the restrictive political barriers have gone so that there are few mountain ranges which are not available today. There are even commercial climbs organised to distant ranges. This ease of travel has led to climbers everywhere operating well beyond their parochial boundaries, and not only in the great ranges. British climbers regularly climb in Yosemite or the sun-drenched rock of France and Spain. As a result of this many expeditions to the Himalaya are now genuinely international, formed by groups of climbers from different countries who have got to know one another.

Mountaineering in all its forms is more popular today than it has ever been. The challenge remains the same, of man versus mountain. It is a battle that man can never win. The best he can ever hope for is an honourable draw.

Notes

Chapter One
When Men and Mountains Meet
pp. 19–24

1. The five remarkable medieval manuscripts testifying to this exploit of Antoine de Ville were photographed by W.A.B. Coolidge and reproduced (with transcription) in his book *Josias Simler et les Orgines de l'Alpinisme jusqu'en 1600* (1904). English translations of most of the material appear in *The Early Mountaineers* by Francis Gribble (1899).

Rabelais refers to this ascent in *Pantagruel* (iv.57) but ascribes the ascent to an artillery captain named D'Oyac. It indicates, however, that the event was widely reported and worthy of mention even some forty years after it happened.

2. The extract is from the *Procès-Verbal* of the Ascent of Mont Aiguille, executed in 1834. (Gribble, *op. cit.*)

3. The nine sacred mountains of China are T'ai Shan (Shantung), Heng Shan (Shansi), Sung Shan (Honan), Heng Shan (Hunan), Hua Shan (Shensi), Wu t'ai Shan (Shansi), P'u t'o Shan (Chekiang), Chiu hua Shan (Anhwei) and Omei Shan (Szechuan). The first five are Taoist, the rest Buddhist. See *The Nine Sacred Mountains of China* by M.A. Mullikin and A.M. Hotchkis (1973) and *Hua Shan* by H. Morrison and W. Eberhard (1974).

4. In his best-selling novel, *Lost Horizon*, James Hilton endowed the idea of the isolated community with the goodness and beauty of somewhere spared all contact with a sordid outside world and gave the language the name Shangri La to describe it.

The reality was much less attractive. Isolated communities tended to be inbred, goitre-ridden, impoverished and dirty. They were also frequently sadistic, especially to visitors.

5. Josias Simler, *De Alpibus Commentarius*.

6. Phil. Trans. Royal Society, quoted by R.M. Barrington in 'The Ascent of Stac na Biorrach (the Pointed Stack), St Kilda', *AJ* 27.

7. E. Echevarria, 'The South American Indian as a Pioneer Alpinist', *AJ* 73.

Chapter Two
The Geneva School
pp. 25–36

1. The de Lucs were an influential family and not the 'sons of a poor watchmaker' as some social romantic once put it. The father was author of religious and political writings and Guillaume (1729–1812) author of a few scientific papers. Jean André (1727–1817) began his career as a diplomat and was a member of the Great Council of Geneva – the ruling body. He abandoned politics for science, came to England where he was made a member of the Royal Society and obtained a permanent post as Reader to Queen Charlotte. He died at Windsor, aged ninety.

2. Except for the period of the Napoleonic conquests when it was annexed by France. Part of Savoy (including Chamonix) was ceded to the French in 1860 in return for their help in achieving a united Italy. The transfer was unanimously approved by local plebiscite. The first King of Italy was Victor Emmanuel II of Savoy.

3. Bourrit's map of 1787 is the first cartographical acceptance of Mont Blanc as a name for the mountain.

4. Windham's account *A Letter from an English Gentleman to Mr Arlaud, a celebrated Painter at Geneva, giving an Account of a Journey to the Glacières, or Ice Alps of Savoy, written in the Year 1741* is reproduced in full in the *Annals of Mont Blanc* by C.E. Mathews (1898). The toast to Admiral Vernon didn't do much good: Vernon was beaten by the Spanish and was struck off the flag list in 1745!

5. Dr John Moore was the father of the more famous Sir John Moore who died at Corunna.

6. The two Paccards were cousins of Michel-Gabriel Paccard. Owing largely to the commune system, family names tend to be associated with certain villages, so that you also get several Balmats at Chamonix, and Taugwalders at Zermatt. This is largely true even today. 'The young Couteran' was Jean-Nicolas Couteran, son of the innkeeper at Chamonix.

7. The description of glissading, also mentioned by the de Lucs in their accounts of the Buet, seemed already well known. 1980 toises are actually equal to 12,657 feet. 1 toise = 1.949 metres.

8. Blaikie's plant hunting took him to different parts of the central Alps and Jura. He crossed various passes including the Gemmi. His was the second British ascent of Brévent – it had been climbed by a Colonel A.J. Hervey with Bourrit a few weeks previously. Blaikie's whole 'campaign' was quite outstanding for the period and he has claim to be the founder of British alpinism. He did no more mountain climbing but he did return to France where he served as a court gardener for many years. See his *Diary of a Scotch Gardener at the French Court at the End of the Eighteenth Century*, ed. Francis Birrell, 1931. He was personally acquainted with many leading personalities of the era, from Marie Antoinette to Benjamin Franklin. He lived through the French Revolution and died quietly at his home in Passy in 1834, his eighty-eighth year.

9. C.E. Engel, *Mountaineering in the Alps*, 1971.

10. It is suggested in *AJ* 41 that the hut was about 1000 feet lower than the present CAF hut at Tête Rousse. The ruins were still serviceable over a century later (see Mathews, *The Annals of Mont Blanc*, 1898). The guides had suggested that a hut might be built on the summit of Aiguille du Goûter and this was done many years later (1858). The present large hut is the most popular overnight resting place for the ascent of Mont Blanc.

11. Indicative of the rough state of the art! In crossing glaciers, Alpine peasants often carried two batons (8–9 feet long) horizontally held so that they would prevent the man from falling into a crevasse. Paccard describes exactly the same technique on the first ascent.

12. From an interview recorded by Alexandre Dumas forty-six years later.

13. Judith Balmat was born on July 21. She died on August 8, the day of the ascent.

14. The amount of de Saussure's reward is uncertain. 'Rather considerable' is how the scientist described it. Balmat also received rewards from the King of Sardinia (Savoy) and from Germany, in all about 700 francs, quite a sum for those days. (*AJ* 42, 'Dr Paccard's Lost Narrative'.)

15. Paccard did write to the *Journal de Lausanne* in 1787 and many years later to the *Journal de Savoie* (1823 and 1825) but these newspapers were not widely read.

J.P. Béranger is variously described also as naturalist and historian. The Aiguille de la Bérangère is named after him. There seems no constant spelling of his name – as indeed with several names in this story.

16. From the de Saussure archives come the following assessments of the two men: 'It was solely the lure of a considerable sum ... that in the end brought Balmat to the top of Mont Blanc. If he finally joined Dr Paccard, it was because the latter claimed nothing for his share. In Balmat is found the most pronounced type of Savoyard who thinks of nothing but gain. Balmat the explorer, eager to make discoveries, striving for glory, as some writers have sought to depict him, is a mythical and purely imaginary figure.' And of Paccard: 'This modest and sympathetic character has been very unjustly relegated to the second rank behind the somewhat theatrical figure of his countryman Balmat. Paccard was a mountaineer of great merit.'

In *AJ* 19 Douglas Freshfield says, 'Balmat was a child in the hands of the first of interviewers [Bourrit] and the greatest of storytellers [Dumas].' The chapter by Dumas 'Jacques Balmat, dit Mont Blanc' is from *Impressions de Voyage* (1833). A translation appears in Whymper's Chamonix guidebook.

17. The early history of Mont Blanc and the people involved has been subject to more learned research than almost any other mountaineering event. In particular see C.E. Mathews, *The Annals of Mont Blanc* and G.R. de Beer and T.G. Brown, *The First Ascent of Mont Blanc*. For an ingenious reconstruction of Dr Paccard's lost narrative see E.H. Stevens, *AJ* 41, 42. For a detailed bibliography see H.F. Montagnier, *AJ* 25.

Chapter Three
The Opening of the Alps
pp. 37–52

1. The guidebooks give the ascent as 1784, but in a letter to the *Journal de Lausanne* in 1789, Clément says he climbed the mountain in 1788. The Dents du Midi has several summits and it is uncertain which Clément climbed, his own account being vague.

2. From a Spescha MS printed in the *SAC Yearbook* Vol. 16 and translated in 'Placidus à Spescha and Early Mountaineering in the Bünder Oberland' by D.W. Freshfield, *AJ* 10.

3. They were two chamois-hunters, Placidus Curschallas and Augustin Bisquolm. Spescha's servant, Carli Cogenard, accompanied his master to the col. See D.W. Freshfield, *AJ* 10 and 'The Early Swiss Pioneers of the Alps' by Dr H. Dübi, *AJ* 35. A life of Spescha, together with many of his papers, was published in Bern in 1913, *Pater Placidus à Spescha, sein Leben und sein Schriften*, F. Pieth and P.K. Hager.

4. The highest Tatra peak is Gerlach (2663 m). Some authorities credit Robert Townshead with the first ascent of Lomnica in 1793.

5. The Affair of the Diamond Necklace was a confidence trick played by the Comtesse de La Motte on Rohan. Pretending to act on behalf of the Queen, Marie Antoinette, she persuaded Rohan to acquire a necklace worth 1,600,000 livres from some Paris jewellers. When payment was not forthcoming Rohan was arrested and the plot revealed, by which time, however, the necklace had been broken up and the jewels sold in London. De Carbonnières went to London to try to recover the jewels.

6. When a friend wanted to appeal for de Carbonnières' release, the War Minister, Carnot, counselled against it. 'He is fortunate to have been forgotten,' he observed wryly.

7. During the occupation of Paris in 1814 when all his papers were destroyed by Cossack soldiers (cf. Spescha) he said, 'It was a long way to come to injure an old man.'

8. Possibly the first recorded example of a 'fixed rope', later to become common on some peaks, especially in the Eastern Alps. The Klotz family not only made the first ascent of Gross Glockner, the highest peak in Tyrol, but also the Wildspitze (Leander Klotz, 1848), the second highest. Leander also climbed the Weisskugel (1861) – a family hat trick of the three highest peaks.

9. Reputed to be by J. Zapoth, consistorial secretary, who seems to have been with the party but is vague on details. He does not say who was successful in 1799, apart from the guides. The American Alpine Club possesses an example of the medal in its museum.

10. Including a cook and three servants, guides, porters, grooms and sixteen horses. Their provisions included Malaga, Tokay, melons and pineapples – shades of the early Everest expeditions!

11. Valentin Stanig (1774–1847) later became a cleric. He left 'an ingenious barometer' on the summit of Gross Glockner which endured until 1852 apparently. It is not certain whether he climbed Watzmann in 1799 or 1801.

The quotation is from W.A.B. Coolidge, *The Alps in Nature and History*.

12. The guide, Paul Rohregger, was avalanched, fortunately without fatal result. The peak was eventually climbed in 1841 and Rohregger had the satisfaction of being one of the large summit party. Archduke John of Austria is perhaps best known for losing the battle of Hohenlinden (1800). He seems to have been quite a character – in 1827 he married a local postmaster's daughter. The Emperor at once made her Countess of Meran.

13. They made a relief model of the Alps between Lake Geneva and Lake Constance for Meyer, on a scale of 1:60,000, and Weiss, who was the draughtsman, produced a Swiss Atlas in 16 sheets published between 1796 and 1802, and a general map. 'A rough survey and an insufficient triangulation', was Dübi's judgement. In 1803 Meyer sold the model to Napoleon for 25,000 F.

14. The first ascents of Jungfrau and Finsteraarhorn have been subjected to much research and speculation. For a pro-Meyer view see Dr H. Dübi, 'The Early Swiss Pioneers of the Alps', *AJ* 33. For an anti-Meyer (though very fair) view of the Finsteraarhorn ascent see J.P. Farrar, 'The First Ascent of the Finsteraarhorn: A Re-examination', *AJ* 27.

15. Johann Jakob Friedrich Wilhelm Parrot (1791–1851) was a medical man famous for his exploration of the Caucasus and the first ascent of Ararat in 1829. (He did not ascend the Parrotspitze, named in his honour.)

16. The highest point, Dufourspitze, was named by the Swiss Government in honour of General Guillaume Henri Dufour (1787–1875) who produced the first official Swiss maps, the Carte Dufour.

17. Different authorities give different dates for this attempt: 1813, 1816, 1817.

18. The quotations are from a translation in *AJ* 5 by F.F. Tuckett of Zumstein's narrative in Von Welden's *Der Monte Rosa* (1824). The Zumstein and Vincent families are tricky to sort out. Note, for example, *another* Joseph Zumstein mentioned in the quotation.

Chapter Four
The Coming of the English
pp. 53–65

1. The Wetterhorner consists of four summits: Wetterhorn, or Hasli Jungfrau (3701 m); Mittelhorn (3704 m); Rosenhorn (3689 m);

Berglistock (3656 m). Though not the highest, the Wetterhorn is the most prominent. The Mittelhorn was climbed by Stanhope Templeman Speer in 1845.

2. W.A.B. Coolidge, *The Alps in Nature and History* (1908). The range of Thurwieser's climbs is the only basis for this claim by Coolidge. Valentin Stanig, Paul Rohregger and several others – even Archduke John – were certainly real mountaineers.

3. Frank Walker's Alpine initiation is also quoted as 1826 and 1828 but family records say 1825. The quotation about the Campbells comes from Coolidge, *op. cit.* Though the name Campbell is Scottish, Coolidge used 'English' for anyone who was British – or American. He was American himself, but an ardent Anglophile.

4. H.D. Inglis, quoted in Engel, *Mountaineering in the Alps* (1971).

5. Ruskin's early works were related to art and architecture but mountain forms played a distinctive part in this. He once admitted that his book *The Stones of Venice* (1853) had almost been called *The Stones of Chamouni*.

6. In 1869 he became a member of the Alpine Club, only four years after his condemnation of climbing.

7. Forbes's glacier theory was later disputed by Tyndall and others. John Tyndall was himself a considerable mountaineer and his clash with Forbes became 'the great glacier controversy' of the mid-nineteenth century. Tyndall's theory was based on constant fracture and regelation of the ice. Suffice to say that neither theory is wholly correct and the subject – much more complex than Forbes or Tyndall appreciated – is still imperfectly understood.

Ruskin met Forbes at Simplon in 1844 and became a devoted admirer of the scientist, vigorously defending him against Tyndall. The quotation is from *Fors Clavigera, Letter 34*.

8. The full title of Forbes's book is *Travels through the Alps of Savoy and other parts of the Pennine chain with observations on the phenomena of glaciers*. An abridged version (removing most of the scientific observations) was published in 1855 as *The Tour of Mont Blanc and Monte Rosa*.

9. Dr Hamel's party was overwhelmed by an avalanche and three guides were killed, buried in a crevasse. It was the first fatality on Mont Blanc. *The Peasants of Charmouni* appeared in 1824 and Smith seems to have read it the following year when he was nine. He later came to know Dr Hamel. Another survivor of this tragedy was J.M. Couttet, Ruskin's guide.

10. The Overland Mail was the short route to India by the Isthmus of Suez, which saved several weeks on the alternative voyage round the Cape. It was acquired by the P & O Steamship Company in 1847 and was perhaps a topical peg on which Smith could hang his entertainment. See James Morris, *Heaven's Command* (1973).

11. Though Twain's parody was set in Zermatt the details seem based on Smith's account, which was published in the USA in 1853. For a full list of guides taking part see H.F. Montagnier, 'A Bibliography of the Ascents of Mont Blanc from 1786 to 1853', *AJ* 25.

12. In the first two seasons alone almost 200,000 people saw the show and Smith earned £17,000. He gave two St Bernard dogs to the Prince of Wales, much to the consternation of Queen Victoria!

13. The author had personal experience of this on Mont Blanc when a friend with whom he was climbing exhibited the symptoms described by Smith. He fell asleep at the Vallot Hut, but the ascent was eventually completed and the victim recovered rapidly during the descent. No wine was available on this occasion!

14. The early ascents of the various Wetterhorn peaks have been the subject of dispute among historians (see *AJ* 56, 58 and *Die Alpen*, 1949). The ascent by Wills *may* have been the first *from Grindelwald*, but seems more likely to have been the third from Grindelwald and fifth overall, the other ascents being from Rosenlaui.

Lauener must have known this and Bohren, too. Bohren knew more about the Wetterhorner than any other guide and it seems more than likely that he had already climbed the Hasli Jungfrau twice, once in 1845 and again a few weeks before the present incident.

Because of the historical importance of the Wetterhorner in the establishment of Alpine climbing, a list of first ascents is useful. This was compiled by Carl Egger. (Nos 3, 6, and 7 have been questioned. The actual peak of No. 6 is not known):

1. August 28, 1844. – Desor, Dollfus, Dupasquier and Stengel with the guides Jaun, Bannholzer, Währen and others. First ascent of *Rosenhorn*.

2. August 31, 1844. – Guides Johann Jaun and Melchior Bannholzer. First ascent of the *Wetterhorn*. From Rosenlaui to Hôtel des Neuchâtelois.

3. July 7, 1845. – A. Roth and F. Fankhauser with the guides Peter Bohren, Johann Bohren and Christian Michel.

Second ascent of the *Wetterhorn* and first from Grindelwald.

4. July 9, 1845. – Speer with the guides Johann Jaun and K. Abplanalp. First ascent of the *Mittelhorn*. From Pavillon Dollfus.

5. July 31, 1845. – Agassiz, Vogt and Bovet with the guides Jaun, Bannholzer and Währen. Third ascent of the *Wetterhorn*. From Pavillon Dollfus.

6. Early June 1954. – Eardley J. Blackwell with the guide Christian Bleuler. From Rosenlaui, first ascent by an English tourist.

7. June 13, 1854. – Blackwell with the guides Peter Bohren, Christian Almer and Bleuler. Fourth ascent of the *Wetterhorn* and second from Grindelwald.

8. August 20, 1854. – Pontamine with Peter Bohren, Almer, Bleuler and Thoman. Second ascent of the *Mittelhorn* and first from Grindelwald.

9. September 17, 1854. – Alfred Wills with guides A. Balmat, A. Simond, Ulrich Lauener and Peter Bohren. Fifth ascent of the *Wetterhorn* and third from Grindelwald. Also, same day, Christian Almer and Ulrich Kaufmann. *Wetterhorn* direct from Grindelwald.

Speer intended to make the first ascent of the Wetterhorn but was diverted to the Mittelhorn by Jaun. He published an account in the *Athenaeum* of November 1, 1845, which was widely read and is considered by some to have played a more important role in propagating mountaineering than the subsequent book by Wills.

15. Alfred Wills, *Wandering among the High Alps* (1856). The two interlopers with the fir tree totem were Christian Almer and Ulrich Kaufmann. Almer had been with Bohren on a previous ascent of the Wetterhorn that year. There was certainly a conspiracy of silence in Grindelwald regarding earlier ascents. Perhaps the purpose was to make the expedition more attractive to Wills and so benefit the guides. Almer and Kaufmann obviously had no intention of being left out of a good thing. The success of Wills's book helped all the men to become famous guides, especially Almer.

16. D.W. Freshfield, 'Proceedings of the Alpine Club', *AJ* 26.

Chapter Five
Masters and Men
pp. 66–88

1. Joseph Imseng (1806–69) was a local shepherd who became priest at Saas in 1836. His house was often used as accommodation by climbers (see Wills, *op. cit.*). He was a keen mountain climber with first ascents of several of the Saas peaks to his credit. He died by drowning in the Mattmark Lake in the Saas valley. Foul play was suspected though never proved.

2. J.F. Hardy, 'Ascent of the Finsteraarhorn', *Peaks, Passes and Glaciers* 1.

3. Rev. S.W. King, *The Italian Valleys of the Pennine Alps* (1858).

4. C.E. Mathews, 'In Memoriam: Edward Shirley Kennedy', *AJ* 19.

5. For a detailed history of the foundation of the Alpine Club see W. Longman, 'Modern Mountaineering and the History of the Alpine Club', *AJ* 8 and Dangar/Blakeney, 'The Rise of Modern Mountaineering and the Formation of the Alpine Club 1854–1865', *AJ* 62. The original members in December 1857, were C. Ainslie, E.L. Ames, E. Anderson, J. Birkbeck, J.L. Davies, F.V. Hawkins, T.W. Hinchliff, F.J.A. Hort, E.S. Kennedy, W. Longman, B. St. J. Mathews, E. Mathews, W. Mathews, E.J. Shepherd, A. Smith, I. Taylor, H. Trower, H.W. Watson, A. Wills, G. Yool. To those were added in January 1858: C.J. Blomfield, W.L. Cabell, E.T. Coleman, J.F. Hardy, R.B. Hayward, J.B. Lightfoot, H.B. M'Calmont, R. Walters.

6. The Smyths seem to have climbed only in 1854 and 1855. Edmund Smyth went to India where he was one of the earliest explorers of Kumaun. Stevenson is sometimes recorded as Stephenson.

7. A number of guides' *Führerbücher* are kept at the Alpine Club in London.

8. W.A.B. Coolidge, *The Alps in Nature and History* (1908).

9. C.E. Mathews, *The Annals of Mont Blanc* (1898).

10. The list of chosen guides was: Melchior Anderegg, Johann von Bergen, Johann Jaun, Ulrich Lauener, Christian Lauener, Christian Almer, Johann Baumann, Peter Baumann, Ulrich Almer, Ulrich Kaufmann, Josef Imboden, Aloys Pollinger, Peter Knubel, Alexander Burgener, François Devouassoud, François Couttet, Michel Payot, Alphonse Payot, Edouard Cupelin, Jean Joseph Maquignaz, Jean-Antoine Carrel, Emile Rey, Auguste Balmat,

Michel Croz, Auguste Simond, Laurent Lanier, Franz Andermatten, Ferdinand Imseng, Johann Joseph Bennen, Peter Bohren, Peter Rubi, Christian Michel, Johann Fischer, Andreas Maurer, Jakob Anderegg.

11. Christian Almer (1826–98). His sons were Ulrich, Christian II, Hans, Rudolf and Peter.

12. Lucy Walker (1835–1916). Daughter of Frank Walker (1808–72) and sister of Horace Walker (1838–1908) – all famous pioneer alpinists. Lucy climbed the Balmhorn in 1864, the first time a woman took part in a major first ascent. Melchior was not married when he and Lucy first met in 1859, but they were lifelong friends and companions, long after both had given up climbing.

13. H.B. George, 'The Col de la Tour Noire', *AJ* 1. A dangerous, rather pointless expedition not repeated for twenty-seven years.

14. Miss M.C. Brevoort was the aunt of W.A.B. Coolidge, responsible for his upbringing (his mother being an invalid). She was one of the pioneer women climbers. See R.W. Clark, *An Eccentric in the Alps* (1959).

15. Said by Melchior to Sir Edward Davidson on the Dent Blanche in 1876. Melchior was renowned for his caution.

16. Quoted by F.T. Wethered in *Pioneers of the Alps*.

17. Charles Stuart Parker (1828–1910), Samuel Sandbach Parker (1837–1905) and Alfred Traill Parker (1837–1900) were from a ship-owning family. They were the first to attempt the Matterhorn from Zermatt (1860 and 1861) and probably the first to regard the Zmutt Ridge of that mountain as not impossible. They were pioneer rock climbers in Britain. S.S. Parker and A.T. Parker were elected to the Alpine Club on *guideless* qualifications: rare indeed for those days. In the 1860 season they were accompanied by a cousin, George Parker (d.1915).

18. A.G. Girdlestone (1842–1908) wrote a book, *The High Alps Without Guides* (1870) which was severely criticised by the establishment. In 1865 he accompanied Whymper and Douglas from Breuil to Zermatt and would possibly have taken part in the ill-fated Matterhorn climb had he not been unwell.

19. A.W. Moore, 'The Ascent of Mont Blanc from the Glacier de la Brenva', *AJ* 2.

20. The second route on the Brenva Face was Red Sentinel Route by T.G. Brown and F.S. Smythe, 1927.

21. Whymper's attempts on the Matterhorn with Carrel and the heights reached were:

July 9–10, 1862	12,992 feet
July 23–24, 1862	13,150 feet
Aug. 10–11, 1863	13,280 feet

But climbing *alone* on July 18–19, 1862, he reached 13,400 feet and on July 25–26 with little Luc Meynet ('the hunchback of Breuil') he reached 13,460 feet.

Tyndall's party (July 27–28, 1862) reached 13,970 feet.

22. 1864: Aiguille de la Sausse, South Peak; Barre des Ecrins; Brèche de la Meije; Col de Triolet; Mont Dolent; Aiguille de Trélatête; Aiguille d'Argentière; Moming Pass.

1865: Grand Cornier; Dent Blanche (third ascent); Grandes Jorasses (Pointe Whymper); Col Dolent; Aiguille Verte; Col de Talèfre; Ruinette.

23. Edward Whymper, *Scrambles Amongst the Alps* (1871). The sick man referred to was the Rev. A.G. Girdlestone, a well-known guideless climber of the time. 'The Monday crowd' refers to tourists crossing the Théodule Pass from Zermatt to Breuil.

24. Quoted in Guido Rey, *The Matterhorn* (1907).

25. Michel Croz (1830–65) was the finest Chamonix guide of his generation. He was discovered by Wills in 1859 and took part in many of the famous expeditions of the following five years, including Whymper's campaigns of 1864 and 1865. He was Whymper's favourite guide and only left him in 1865 to fulfil a previous engagement made with Birkbeck. Birkbeck was taken ill, however, and so Croz joined Hudson.

26. The original intention was that both Taugwalder sons should return from the first bivouac, but Young Peter was retained (and promoted to guide) 'because we found it difficult to divide the food', says Whymper. A curious little incident.

Two others might have joined the party. Girdlestone had returned to Zermatt with Whymper, but was presumably not well enough and Hudson should have been joined by the Rev. Joseph M'Cormick who actually arrived in Zermatt on the day of the ascent, having been delayed. If M'Cormick had turned up on time it is likely that Whymper's party would not have been allowed to join Hudson. Another 'if' in the Matterhorn story.

27. He made the first ascent of Monte Rosa (1855), the first guideless ascent of Mont Blanc (1855), the first ascent of the Bosses Ridge of Mont Blanc (1859), and of the Moine Ridge of the Verte (1865).

28. The modern route up the Hörnli from the Shoulder does not follow that taken by Whymper onto the North Face, but goes more or less straight up, aided by a fixed cable. Assuming Whymper started from his bivouac site at 5 a.m., the time of ascent, almost nine hours, was extraordinarily slow.

29. The *Times* editorial is quoted in full in Smythe's *Edward Whymper*. Only three bodies were discovered, all naked. Lord Francis Douglas was never found. The official report of the enquiry (in French) is given in *AJ* 33, together with a commentary by J.P. Farrar. No mountaineering story has gripped the public imagination like that of the first ascent of the Matterhorn. Whole books have been devoted to the subject, not least, of course, Whymper's own *Scrambles Amongst the Alps* (1871). A good modern account is *The Day the Rope Broke* by R.W. Clark (1965). See also F.S. Smythe, *Edward Whymper* (1940) and Guido Rey, *The Matterhorn* (1907).

30. In a letter to *The Times* written shortly after the accident, Whymper never mentioned Carrel's part in precipitating the whole affair. Carrel and J.B. Bich reached the summit on July 17, 1865. The Andean expedition took place 1879–80. On August 20–22, 1874, Whymper, Carrel, J.B. Bich and J.M. Lochmatter climbed the Hörnli Ridge on a photographic expedition. Whymper had become a popular lecturer and needed lantern slides to illustrate his talks.

Chapter Six
Where Angels Fear to Tread
pp. 89–101
The title is a quotation from Middlemore (see Note 11 below).

1. W.A.B. Coolidge, *The Alps in Nature and History* (1908).

2. In 1870, three climbers and eight guides were killed on Mont Blanc. The average annual mortality for climbers between 1866 and 1880 was 3.4. See C.E. Mathews, 'The Alpine Obituary', *AJ* 11, and C. Gos, *Alpine Tragedy* (1948).

3. F.M. Balfour and J. Petrus on the Aiguille Blanche de Peuterey, W. Penhall and A. Maurer on the Wetterhorn, W.E. Gabbett and two Lochmatters on the Dent Blanche. These were all good climbers with good guides.

4. From Sir Henry Ponsonby to Mr William Gladstone.

24th August, 1882.

'Dear Mr. Gladstone, – The Queen commands me to ask you if you think she can say anything to mark her disapproval of the dangerous Alpine excursions which this year have occasioned so much loss of life. – Henry F. Ponsonby.'

From Mr William Gladstone to Sir Henry Ponsonby.

25th August, 1882.

'My dear Sir H. Ponsonby, – I do not wonder that the Queen's sympathetic feelings have again been excited by the accidents, so grave in character, and so accumulated during recent weeks, on the Alps. But I doubt the possibility of any interference, even by Her Majesty, with a prospect of advantage. It may be questionable whether, upon the whole, mountain-climbing (and be it remembered that Snowdon has its victims as well as the Matterhorn) is more destructive than various other pursuits in the way of recreation which perhaps have no justification to plead so respectable as that which may be alleged on behalf of mountain expeditions. The question, however, is not one of wisdom or unwisdom; but viewing it, as you put it, upon its very definite and simple grounds, I see no room for action.' (Signed) W.E. Gladstone.

(Extract from *The Letters of Queen Victoria*, second series, Vol. 3, 1879–95. Edited by G.E. Buckle. Murray, London, 1928.)

Cynics might also say that many of the businessmen who formed the élite of the Alpine Club were Liberals – Gladstone supporters.

5. *Morning Post*, 'The spirit which animated the attacks on Everest is the same as that which . . . led to the formation of the Empire itself.'

6. The Rev. J.M. Elliott of Brighton made the second ascent of the Hörnli Ridge in 1868, guided by J.M. Lochmatter and P. Knubel, and it was repeated a further four times that year. John Tyndall made the first traverse of the Matterhorn, going from Breuil to Zermatt. A few days later O. Hoiler and F. Thioly reversed the traverse. A month later Felice Giordano repeated Tyndall's traverse. Girdlestone also climbed the Hörnli that year (sixth ascent of the ridge). J.J. Maquignaz was probably the first guide to climb both ridges: the Italian in 1867, the Hörnli in 1868. E. Craufurd Grove did the same – the first amateur climber to make two ascents, one by each ridge.

7. Lord Conway of Allington, *The Alps from End to End in 1894* (1895).

8. These changes did not come about

overnight. There was considerable overlap. Many still wandered from valley to valley and some climbers still attempted new and difficult passes – Mummery on the Col du Lion in 1880, for example.

9. Rev. C. Taylor, 'Monte Rosa from Macugnaga', *AJ* 6.

10. A full account by F.T. Wethered appears in the Alpine Accident reports of *AJ* 10. The route is now called the Marinelli Couloir – somewhat unjustly, since it does not follow the couloir and Marinelli's only connection with it is that he was killed there. One feels that if anybody was to be commemorated it should have been Imseng.

11. T. Middlemore, 'The Col des Grandes Jorasses', *AJ* 7. Middlemore (1842–1923) was a leather manufacturer from Birmingham. His Alpine career was short but full of hard routes. Johann Jaun was Middlemore's constant companion in the Alps; a first-rate guide and a pupil of Melchior. The acrimony regarding this climb is sprinkled throughout *AJ* 7 in notes, letters, etc.

12. Freshfield and Conway, 'The Future of the Alpine Club', *AJ* 20.

13. Henri Cordier (1854 or 55–1877) was a fine French climber unfortunately killed in a glissading accident, to which his poor eyesight probably contributed. He was twenty-one years old. The couloir described in the text is now known as the Cordier Couloir and is rarely, if ever, repeated. After this climb Cordier and Middlemore made a fine new climb on Piz Roseg, the North Ridge, or Middlemoregrat.

John Oakley Maund (1846–1902) was a quick-tempered stockbroker who took part in many of the more difficult climbs then being attempted.

14. Ralph Gordon Noel King Milbanke (1839–1906) became Baron Wentworth in 1862 and Earl of Lovelace in 1893. He was Byron's grandson. A daring climber, he made the first ascent of the Aiguille Noire in 1877.

15. J. Oakley Maund, 'The Aiguille Verte from the Argentière Glacier', *AJ* 8.

16. T.G. Bonney, *Outline Sketches in the High Alps of Dauphiné* (1865).

17. It was eventually crossed by L. Purtscheller with Emil and Otto Zsigmondy in 1885 (see Chapter 8). The principal obstacle is a gap now known as the Brèche Zsigmondy.

18. H.E. Boileau de Castelnau, quoted in translation in *Peaks and Pioneers* (1975) by F. Keenlyside. For the epic descent in a storm suf-

fered by this party, see the full account in the book.

19. W.A.B. Coolidge, *Alpine Studies* (1912). The Meije has long since ceased to be the most continuously difficult climb in the Alps. However, as a *voie normale* on a big peak it is probably more difficult than most.

20. J. Stafford Anderson, 'The Dent Blanche from Zinal', *AJ* 11.

Chapter Seven
*'They Have Picked Out the Plums
and Left Us the Stones'*
pp. 102–16

1. C.T. Dent, 'Two Attempts on the Aiguille du Dru', *AJ* 7.

2. Amongst the Tyrolean guides of this time one should mention Joseph Schnell, Peter Dangl, A. Ennemoser, J. Kirschner, J. Praxmerer, J. Huber, the Klotz brothers (who made the first ascent of Wildspitze), the Lechners and Pinggeras. As in the West, the names are repeated in guiding families or dynasties.

3. P. Güssfeldt, *In den Hochalpen* (1885). Güssfeldt was also an explorer, with expeditions to West Africa and the Arabian desert. In 1882–83 he climbed in the Andes, making the first ascent of Maipo (17,717 ft) but failed in two attempts at Aconcagua.

4. Lammer suggested this might happen in the year 2000. He could be right.

5. For Lammer's own account see *Oester-reichischer Alpen Zeitung*, Vol. IX.

6. A high-level walk (*Alta Via*) network has been developed throughout the region, leading from hut to hut. There are also special 'climbing paths', often very airy, protected by cables and joined by metal ladders. Such a path is a *via ferrata* ('iron road').

A large part of the area was transferred from Austria to Italy after the First World War, so most places have two names, e.g. Bozen and Bolzano. This also applies to mountains and is very confusing. I have tried to use the names I think most readers would recognise, but I make no claim for consistency.

7. Douglas Milner, in *The Dolomites* (1951), places the start of the 'rock climbing period' with C.C. Tucker's ascent of Saas Maor in 1875.

8. Popularly, there are only three Vajolet Towers – the southern group of the Winkler, Stabeler and Delago. In fact there is also a northern group of three more, not quite as spectacular: Hauptthurm, Ostthurm and Nordthurm.

The first was climbed by Gottfried Merzbacher with Giorgio Bernard in 1882 and the others by Helversen and Stabeler in 1892, the same season in which they climbed the Stabelerthurm.

9. Stabeler and Darmstaedter tried to climb the mountain via the Daumenscharte in 1888, but failed. A surprising failure for a guide of Stabeler's quality, as Klucker points out (*Adventures of an Alpine Guide*, 1932). The Schmitt Kamin remained the hardest climb on the Fünffingerspitze for many years.

10. Ludwig Norman-Neruda (1864–98) was born in Sweden but lived most of his life in London where he was a member of the Stock Exchange. In 1894 he moved to Asolo, near Venice, in order to be near his beloved Dolomites. His wife, May, often climbed with him and compiled his climbing biography from his notes (*The Climbs of Norman-Neruda*, 1899). Christian Klucker (1853–1928) of the Engadine was one of the greatest of the second generation of Swiss guides.

11. It was a good season for Karl Berger (1880–1915) – he also made the first ascent of the Daumen on the Fünffingerspitze, first traverse of the Sella Towers and first ascent of the Murfreidspitze, all in the Dolomites. An author, he later lived below the Brenta Peaks at Madonna di Campiglio. His companion, Ampferer (1875–1947) became a distinguished geologist.

12. Until the last decade of the nineteenth century, the name Charmoz included the peak now called the Grépon. Early attempts on the 'Charmoz' were really attempts on the Grépon. Just to confuse matters, the Petit Charmoz was then called Aiguille de Grépon!

13. Wentworth invited a couple of Dolomite guides to try their skill on the Devon sea-cliffs near his home at Porlock, but nothing came of it.

14. The huts he built were: Grand Paradis, Col du Géant, Grandes Jorasses, Aiguille Grise.

15. C.D. Cunningham, *Pioneers of the Alps* (1887).

16. 'Fauteuil des Allemands' means 'German armchair' – a French comment on German bottoms. There is also a group of angular rock spires near by known as Les Dames Anglaises!

17. Wentworth called the peak Aiguille de la Yola 'after Madame Caccia Raynaud, an intrepid and accomplished Italian alpinist then staying at Courmayeur'. Such gallantry went unrecognised and the peak remained the Aiguille Noire.

18. Three days before his death Rey was descending a steep ice slope held on a tight rope by his employer. Rey told him to slacken the rope, adding, 'It is not necessary m'sieu. I never slip.'

19. C.D. Cunningham, *Pioneers of the Alps* (1887).

20. It is surprising that the Lenzspitze, being over 4000 metres, had not been climbed sooner. It isn't particularly difficult, and well within the capabilities of the pioneers.

21. C.T. Dent, 'Two Attempts on the Aiguille du Dru', *AJ* 7.

22. George Augustus Passingham (1842–1914) was an acknowledged 'hard man'. He usually climbed peaks direct from the valley, sometimes sending his guides on hours in advance, confident he would catch up with them. He ran a gymnasium for university students at Cambridge for a couple of years, but gave it up when it became a social drawback. He was with Dent on the Zinal Rothorn and later made a difficult climb on the West Face of the Weisshorn.

23. C.T. Dent, 'The History of an Ascent of the Aiguille du Dru', *AJ* 9.

24. *Ibid.*

25. An all-professional ascent was rare in those days. Pitons were used. Jean Charlet married Miss Isabella Straton (or Stratton), a pioneer woman climber, and adopted the family name Charlet-Straton.

26. The Aiguille Blanche de Peuterey, almost 100 metres higher than the Géant, was not climbed until 1885. Pinnacles like the Aiguilles du Diable are also higher and were climbed much later.

27. T.S. Kennedy, 'Excursions from Courmayeur in the Range of Mont Blanc', *AJ* 6. See also E.R. Whitwell, 'Early Attempts on the Aiguilles du Géant and du Dru', *AJ* 30.

28. Letter from J.E. Charlet-Straton to Captain Farrar (March 6, 1916). Farrar found the stick still in position in 1904 and in his opinion if Charlet had had a companion they would have made the first ascent.

29. 'Alpine Notes', *AJ* 9.

30. E.R. Whitwell, 'Early Attempts on the Aiguilles du Dru and du Géant', *AJ* 30. For first-hand accounts of the two first ascents see *AJ* 11, 'The Dent du Géant'.

31. W.W. Graham, 'The Dent du Géant. Part II', *AJ* 11.

32. By T. Maischberger, H. Pfannl and F. Zimmer. There is a certain degree of irony in the fact that the only free climb on the Géant was done by a party from the Eastern Alps!

Chapter Eight
'Too Venturesome to be Imitated'
pp. 117–40

1. C.T. Dent, 'Address to the Alpine Club', *AJ* 15.
2. C.T. Dent, 'Amateurs and Professional Guides of the Present Day', *AJ* 12.
3. *AJ* 11.
4. C.T. Dent, 'Address to the Alpine Club', *AJ* 15.
5. H.G. Willink, 'The Alpine Distress Signal', *AJ* 17.
6. Quoted in H.V.F. Winstone, *Gertrude Bell* (1978).
7. Katherine (Katy) Richardson (1854–1927). The *Morning Post* quoted in Cecily Williams's 'The Feminine Share in Mountain Adventure', Part 1, *AJ* 81. The guidebook is *Guide Vallot: La Chaine du Mont Blanc* Vol. 1. See also her obituary by Mrs Le Blond in *AJ* 40.
8. Margaret Anne Jackson (1843–1906). A.L. Mumm, *The Alpine Club Register 1864–1876* (1925). Mrs Jackson must have been recognised as above average by her contemporaries because Karl Schulz, not a man to tolerate incompetence, usually climbed with Purtscheller and the Zsigmondys.
9. Mrs Le Blond (1861–1934) was the author of a number of climbing books. Her first husband was the dashing Colonel Fred Burnaby of *Ride to Khiva* fame who was killed at Abu Klea, 1885. Mrs Le Blond's obituary is in *AJ* 46.
10. n/a 'The Passage of the Sesia-Joch from Zermatt to Alagna by English Ladies', *AJ* 5.
11. The first woman to traverse the Matterhorn, Zermatt–Breuil, was Meta Brevoort. Jean Martin was forgiven his shortcomings on the Sesiajoch because he took part in the Matterhorn traverse. The other guide was V. Maquignaz. E. Whymper, *Scrambles Amongst the Alps in the Years 1860–69*. Also, Cecily Williams, 'The Feminine Share in Mountain Adventure', Part 1, *AJ* 81.
12. Here is a typical season recorded in the 'Notes and Reviews' of *AJ* 15. The lost summer refers to 1889 when Purtscheller was in Africa making the first ascent of Kilimanjaro:

> Herr L. Purtscheller has been actively engaged in making up for his lost summer. Between May 11 and October 5, 1890, he made no less than 143 ascents in 55 excursions from the Lesser Tauern to the Maritime Alps, and including an ascent of Mont Blanc.

Many of these were what he calls 'ridge walks' ('Gratwanderungen'). On August 18, 19, and 20 he ascended five, four, and six peaks respectively; and on August 22 no less than 10 peaks, three of them being new ascents. On the whole he made 14 new ascents. In 20 of the 55 tours he had a companion. In three he took a guide, probably more to show the way than otherwise, since only one peak, the Kumpfkarspitze (2,394 metres = 7,855 feet), was a first ascent. In five he took a porter. In the others he was alone.

13. Otto Zsigmondy (1860–1918), Emil Zsigmondy (1861–85), were both doctors of medicine from a talented Austrian family. There were two younger brothers – Richard, a scientist who won the Nobel Prize, and Karl, who was a professor of mathematics in Vienna. Richard was a good climber but Karl did little climbing.
14. J. Kugy, *Alpine Pilgrimage* (1934). Julius Kugy (1858–1944) was an Austrian climber who developed the Julian Alps of Yugoslavia (then part of the Austro-Hungarian Empire).
15. E. Zsigmondy, *Die Gefahren der Alpen* (1885). Between 1875 and 1884 the author had fifteen mountain accidents.
16. O. Zsigmondy, 'The Meije from La Grave', *AJ* 12.
17. Modern belaying theory had not developed and the rope was used in some curious ways. Guides would often untie their clients whilst prospecting the route, throwing the end of the rope down when the time came. Some, like Emile Rey, tended to use the rope only on glaciers or where the client was nervous. The Zsigmondys believed steep rock was best climbed without a rope. In general, the rope was regarded as a safety measure to be used *in difficult places*.
18. Accounts by Otto Zsigmondy and Karl Schulz appear in *AJ* 12. Also in C. Gos, *Alpine Tragedy* (1948).
19. Editorial comment by Coolidge, *AJ* 12.
20. Guido Lammer criticised Schulz (violently as usual) for resuming his climbing so quickly after the accident. Forty years later he attacked Schulz again, claiming that his discouraging remarks had probably provoked Emil into rashness.
21. William Penhall (1858–82), like Passingham, was an immensely strong walker. 'I have never been tired in my life,' he once told a friend. A doctor by profession, he was killed

on the Wetterhorn. Of the seven men who took part in the race for the Zmutt, only Zurbriggen and Gentinetta survived to old age.

22. *The Physiology of Industry* (1898). John Atkinson Hobson became a noted economist, strongly socialist in his theories.

23. The Charmoz summit consists of several pinnacles. The one reached by Mummery was not the highest, though he was not aware of this at the time. The true summit was climbed by H. Dunod in 1886. Mummery's party climbed the last part in stockinged feet, a device frequently used later by English climbers on their home crags. The Furggen Ridge of the Matterhorn was climbed in 1911.

24. A.F. Mummery, *My Climbs in the Alps and Caucasus* (1895).

25. J.N. Collie, *Climbing on the Himalaya and Other Mountain Ranges* (1902). Mummery was unfortunate in his one and only Lakeland climb, as he was taken to the Great Gully on Wastwater Screes, notoriously loose and dirty. On the other hand he was completely at home on the dangerous chalk cliffs of Kent and contributed a piece about them to Haskett Smith's *Climbing in the British Isles* (1894).

26. A.F. Mummery, *op. cit.* The phrase 'an easy day for a lady' originated with Leslie Stephen in the first edition of *The Playground of Europe* (1871). The chapter in which it appears was deleted from later editions because Stephen thought it out of date.

27. Blodig lived to be ninety-seven, despite his adventures (1859–1956).

28. Pfannl later went to the Karakoram with Eckenstein.

29. Dr G.F. von Saar, 'In Memoriam: Paul Preuss', *AJ* 28.

30. *Ibid.*

31. Both had been *descended* – the Mittelegi in 1885 and the Hirondelles in 1911.

32. P. Güssfeldt, *Mont Blanc* (1898).

33. They returned to Courmayeur by a long route over the Grand Plateau, Dôme du Goûter and Dôme Glacier. They could have descended much more directly on that side but it seems Güssfeldt wanted to examine the observatory then being built by Dr Jannsen on Mont Blanc. The expedition took eighty-eight hours in all and cost Güssfeldt £60, then a lot of money, reflecting the very up-market guides he had.

34. The two brothers Gugliermina, Giuseppe F. (1872–1960) and Giovanni Batista (1873–1962), made a number of fine climbs on Monte Rosa and Mont Blanc, including the Brouillard Ridge. The Punta Gugliermina, of which they

made the first ascent in 1914, is named after them. They usually climbed without guides.

35. Thomson's books were *The Climbs on Lliwedd* (1909, with A.W. Andrews) and *Climbing in the Ogwen District* (1910).

36. G.W. Young, *A Roof-climber's Guide to Trinity*, 1900.

37. Young did not make the first ascent of his eponymous point – that had been done by Ryan in 1904.

38. H.O. Jones, 'Mont Blanc and the Grépon in 1911', *AJ* 26.

39. G.W. Young, *On High Hills* (1927).

40. M. Kurz, *Guide des Alpes Valaisannes*, Vol. IIIb (1952).

41. Young, *op. cit.*

42. The route was not repeated until August 8, 1943, by André Roch, Georges de Rham, Alfred Tissières and Gabriel Chevalley. Georges de Rham, who led the pitch on the second ascent, later wrote: 'Even with all the resources of modern technique, pitons, clasp-rings and rubber shoes, I thought it was exceptionally severe' (*AJ* 54).

Four pitons were used in 1943 and one was left in place. When told that Young would be furious about this, André Roch replied, 'That may be so – but I'm not going back to remove it!' A variant avoiding the crux was done in 1935 by the guides A. Taugwalder and K. Biner.

43. A body harness made from rope was often used by European climbers before the advent of webbing harnesses after the Second World War. Whether this fashion of tying on was current in 1906 is not clear. Perhaps Young worked it out for himself.

Chapter Nine
Beyond the Alps
pp. 141–51

1. Halford John Mackinder (1861–1947) was Reader in Geography at Oxford. He established the subject as a university study, and was knighted in 1922. The ascent of Batian (17,058 ft), the highest point of Mount Kenya, was made with the guides C. Ollier and J. Brocherel. It was not repeated for thirty years.

2. There was said to be an 'Alpine Club' in Williamstown, USA, as early as 1863, or just six years after the original in London. The various national mountaineering clubs were established as follows:

1862 Austria
1863 Switzerland, Italy

1868 Norway
1869 Germany
1874 France
1878 Spain
1883 Belgium
1885 Sweden
1891 New Zealand, South Africa
1902 Russia, Holland, USA
1906 Canada, Japan

Not all of these survived in their original form but the list does show how the sport had spread world-wide within fifty years.

3. Reports of the Ark's existence on Ararat still recur at frequent intervals. According to eye-witness reports it was examined in 1840 and 1893, and in 1952 Fernand Navarra discovered some ancient timbers. A piece of the Ark used to be kept in a local monastery. The ascent in Persian slippers was made in 1845 by Danby Seymour who had lent his boots to his Armenian guide. See R.A. Redfern, 'The Secret of Ararat', *Climber & Rambler*, December 1972, and D.W. Freshfield, 'Early Ascents of Ararat', *AJ* 8.

4. Miss Lister had done some Alpine walking and in 1830 had made what was probably the first woman's ascent of Monte Perdido in the Pyrenees. The Ossoue Glacier is much altered and is now the usual way up. The Prince de la Moskowa was the son of the famous Napoleonic commander, Marshal Ney. See K. Reynolds, *The Mountains of the Pyrenees* (1982).

5. The guide covered more than mountain ascents. In the Preface Packe wrote that it was 'for mountaineers and botanists', but Mumm (*ACR* 1) says acidly, 'he might have added "fishermen"'. It was expanded and re-issued, 1867.

6. Henry Russell, 'In Memoriam: Charles Packe and the Pyrenees', *AJ* 18.

7. Most mountaineers used blankets, carried by the porter. The idea of sleeping-bags seems to have originated in the Pyrenees, where they were of sheepskin. Francis Dalton, traveller and scientist, picked up the idea in 1860 when he visited Packe and passed it on to others. The early bags were made of wool and mackintosh. For a detailed description see F.F. Tuckett, 'A Night on the Summit of Monte Viso', *AJ* 1.

8. Henri Passet (1845–1919), Célestin Passet (1845–1917). They were invited by Whymper to accompany him on his Andean expedition but declined according to Russell 'for sentimental reasons ... exile will never be popular in France.'

9. Henri Brulle, 'A Pyrenean Centre', *AJ* 20.

10. There is a marvellous pen-portrait of François Salles as an old man in Dorothy Richards' *Climbing Days*, Chapter 10. He once carried an iron stove single handed up to one of Russell's caves – after filling it with wood. 'What use is a stove without wood?' he asked.

11. Henri Brulle, *op. cit.*

12. Patrice de Bellefon, *Les Pyrénées* (1976).

13. The region of the highest mountains was called Jotunfjeldene (Mountains of the Giants) by B.M. Keilau in 1820. This was changed to Jotunheimen (Home of the Giants) by the poet Aasmund Olavsson Vinje (1818–70).

14. U. Boyesen. Report in *Den norske Tilskuer*, 1819. This energetic priest (cf. the Alps at this period also) was the 'discoverer' of the magnificent Vettifossen waterfall. The Norwegians seem to have had a better appreciation of rope technique than the Chamonix guides of the period.

Christen Smith became Professor of Botany at Oslo in 1814 and died two years later on a British expedition to the Congo.

15. C. Wilson, 'Climbing in Norway', *AJ* 13.

16. The ordinary route up the Romsdalhorn today is Grade II/III. It is hard to compare this with, say, the Finsteraarhorn (1812) or with Pillar Rock in the Lake District (1826), each of which were 'difficult' in place and time. And, of course, nobody knows how difficult Mont Aiguille was in 1492!

17. In 1908 a second association, the Norsk Tindekubb (Norwegian Alpine Club), was formed.

18. The first path to have Thelwell cairns was from Bessheim to Memurubu. Records show that in 1883 the paint for the Tyin–Smogret path cost Kr4 – and the Ts can still be seen a century later.

19. W.C. Slingsby, *Norway, The Northern Playground* (1904).

20. Slingsby spells the girl's name slightly differently. There has seldom, if ever, been a gentler, more comprehensive and utterly damning put-down in mountaineering literature.

21. Slingsby gives the dates as one day earlier in each case.

22. W. Scoresby, *Account of the Arctic Regions*, Vol. 1 (1820).

23. J. Bryce, 'Stray Notes on Mountain Climbing in Iceland', *AJ* 7. James Bryce (1838–1922) was a Cabinet Minister in the Gladstone administration. His Report of 1895 laid the foundation for secondary education in England and Wales. In 1884 he tried unsuccessfully to get an Access to Mountains Bill through Parliament.

24. Dr S. Thorarinsson, *Glacier* (1975). Howell was later drowned whilst crossing an Icelandic river (Note in *AJ* 37).

Chapter Ten
'Fine Opportunities for Breaking One's Neck'
pp. 152–69

1. The dead hand of Alpine tradition lay over British rock climbing for decades – certainly until after the Second World War. It was considered proper to finish a climb by walking to the summit of the mountain, a symbolic acknowledgement that rock climbing is only part of the greater game. It was a tradition strongly defended in print – and seldom observed in practice.

2. 'A Rambler' (J. Budworth), *A Fortnight's Ramble in the Lakes in Westmorland, Lancashire and Cumberland* (1792). Reissued with some changes and additions in 1795 and 1810. Budworth changed his name to Palmer in 1811 when he acquired, through his wife, the Palmer estates in Ireland.

3. The small scale of British hills was difficult for Alpine guides to grasp. Even the great Melchior on reaching Crib Goch during a winter ascent of Snowdon, thought it would take five or six hours to reach the summit and was amazed when it only took an hour.

4. C.A.O. Baumgartner (1825–1910) was born in Geneva but educated at Rugby and Oxford. He joined the Australian gold rush, but later returned to London and visited the Lakes again with Haskett Smith. His father believed himself the real Duke of Northumberland!

5. J. Stogdon, 'The English Lakes in Winter', *AJ* 5. The article is one of the best-known pieces in the *AJ*.

6. J. Stogdon, 'Random Memories of Some Early Guideless Climbs', *AJ* 30.

7. Great Gully, Diff (Gr II); Needle Ridge, Diff (Gr II); Napes Needle, Mild Severe (Gr IV-).

8. O.G. Jones, Chapter IX, *Rock Climbing in the English Lake District* (1897). The photograph was in Spooner's window. It was taken by Professor Dixon in 1890 during an attempt by Professor Marshall of Manchester, a biologist who was killed three years later on Scafell. The picture showed Marshall at the Shoulder (just below the top boulder), and Otto Koecher and Miss Koecher on the summit. It was the fifth ascent and the first by a woman.

9. R.W. Clark and E.C. Pyatt, *Mountaineering in Britain* (1957). The reputation of Kern Knotts Crack probably lasted longer than was warranted because of its association with Jones. For many years the grade of the climb was Severe, but polished holds now make it Mild VS.

10. W.M. Conway wrote the *Zermatt Pocketbook* in 1881. It was a climbers' guide to the Alps between Simplon and Arolla. Between 1890 and 1910 this was expanded to 15 volumes covering the Central and Western Alps, known as the *Conway and Coolidge Climbers' Guides*. Haskett Smith's guide appeared in 2 volumes, the first being England (1894) and the second Wales and Ireland (1895). The projected volume on Scotland never appeared.

11. At present the grades are *Easy, Moderate, Difficult, Very Difficult, Severe, Very Severe, Hard Very Severe* and *Extreme*. The Extreme grade is further divided in ascending order of difficulty by numbers – E1, E2, etc. This is open ended. In addition pitches of Severe and above are often numerically graded for technical difficulty.
The adjectival system is uniquely British. It has the advantages of being gloriously imprecise and offering tortuous refinements like Mild Hard Very Severe.

12. The Climbers' Club has traditionally maintained a Welsh bias though the majority of the original Committee were Lakelanders. It owns huts in Wales and publishes its Welsh climbing guidebooks.

13. D.W. Freshfield, *Quips for Cranks* (1923).

14. Quoted in Clark and Pyatt's *Mountaineering in Britain*, Chapter 6.

15. There were five Hopkinson brothers: John (1849–98), Alfred (1851–1939), Charles (1854–1920), Edward (1859–1921), Albert (1863–1949). All achieved distinction in their various careers and all gave up climbing when John was killed in the Alps.

16. John Norman Collie (1859–1942). Professor of Organic Chemistry, University College, London. He was the discoverer of neon gas and the first man to use X-rays medically.

17. *Scottish Mountaineering Club Journal*, 3, 1894. Today the climb is V. Diff.

18. 'In Memoriam', *AJ* 54.

19. G.W. Young, 'Mountain Prophets', *AJ* 54. For a biography of Collie see W.C. Taylor, *The Snows of Yesteryear* (1973).

20. The naming of Faith, Hope and Charity on Idwal Slabs is an early example – possibly the earliest – of the name association game, so prevalent on British crags, where an attempt is made to link the name of a new climb with

existing names. It probably reached its zenith in White Ghyll, Langdale, in the 1950s.

Early climbs were named after a feature or a climber – e.g. North Buttress or Murray's Route. The first climb to be given an imaginative name seems to be Eagle's Nest Ridge on Gable, 1892.

21. *British Mountain Climbs* and *Swiss Mountain Climbs* were published by Mills and Boon, later famous for romantic fiction! Some of the Abrahams' critics would no doubt find this ironic.

Even before its last reprint in 1948, the British book had been long out of date and superseded by club guides.

22. A. Hankinson, *The First Tigers* (1972).

23. G.D. Abraham, *Rock Climbing in North Wales*. Ashley didn't take part: the brothers did not always climb together.

24. Because hard routes can now be so well protected there is a tendency for young climbers to ignore the old classics that once acted as a foundation course. As a result, rock climbing is being perceived as a much more gymnastic sport.

25. The Scottish Mountaineering Club published guides in their journal from 1901, but not in book form until 1919, when *Ben Nevis* appeared. In the Lake District the first Fell and Rock Club guide was *Doe Crag and Coniston* (1922).

26. *Yorkshire Ramblers' Club Journal* (1903).

27. 'Mountain Tragedies in the Lake District' by A Member of the Alpine Club. *Wide World Magazine*, Vol. XXII (1909). Probably written by George Abraham, who illustrated the piece. The climbers killed in the accident were R.W. Broadrick, H. Jupp, S. Ridsdale and A.E.W. Garrett.

28. Early 1904. Spender was the father of the poet Stephen Spender.

29. J. Laycock, Preface to *Recent Developments on Gritstone* (1924).

30. G.S. Sansom, *Climbing at Wasdale Head before the First World War* (1982). Adapted from an account Sansom wrote in the *Journal of the Fell and Rock Climbing Club* of 1914. The book was published posthumously as a memorial to Sansom, who died in 1980 aged ninety-one.

31. C.F. Holland, *Climbs on the Scafell Group* (1926). Some hyperbole here – some climbs in the Eastern Alps were probably as hard. What is too often overlooked is that CB is not only a hard climb but a good one too.

32. H.M. Kelly and J.H. Doughty, 'A Short History of Lakeland Climbing', *FRCC Journal* (1936).

Chapter Eleven
Spreading the Gospel
pp. 170–90

1. This remained the accepted height for Everest until 1955. It is now officially 29,028 feet, although unofficially fresh surveys are always adding to it.

2. William Gowland, a British mining engineer employed by the Osaka Mint, 1872–88, dubbed the Honshu Mountains 'Alps' in his *Japan Guide* (1881).

3. Now called Uhuru Peak (19,340 ft). The three highest tops of Mawenzi are called, appropriately, Hans Meyer Peak (16,890 ft), Purtscheller Peak (16,800 ft) and Klute Peak (16,710 ft).

4. Mawenzi was first climbed by Dr Fritz Klute and Eduard Oehler in 1912. In July 1927, Sheila Macdonald became the first woman to reach the true summit of Kibo, and a week later the first to climb Mawenzi. The first African to climb Kibo was Oforo, a local guide, in 1925.

5. J.W. Gregory, 'Mountaineering in Central Africa, with an Attempt on Mount Kenya', *AJ* 17.

6. Emin Pasha was trapped in Equatoria by the Mahdi's revolt in the Sudan. The Mountains of the Moon had been described by Ptolemy in ancient times.

7. For example, a Mr Moore claimed to have reached 14,000 feet and a German, Dr David, 16,000 feet.

8. The party was Dr A.F.R. Wollaston (1875–1930), R.B. Woosnam and R.E. Dent. Wollaston was a medical man but he was wealthy enough to devote himself to travel and botany. During an expedition to New Guinea in 1912–13 he almost reached the summit ridge of the Carstensz range, not eventually reached until 1936 and the highest point not climbed until 1962. He was on the Everest expedition of 1921. Wollaston was shot by a student at Cambridge in 1930.

The principal groups in the Ruwenzori are named after African explorers.

9. The expedition was the Duke, Commander Cagni, Dr C. Molinelli, Vittorio Sella, A. Roccati, J. Petifax, C. Ollier and J. Brocherel, plus Sella's assistant and an Alpine porter. Luigi Amedeo of Savoia-Aosta, Duke of the Abruzzi (1873–1933) was a good climber and once accompanied Mummery and Collie on the Zmutt Ridge of the Matterhorn. Pic Luigi Amedeo on the Brouillard Ridge is named after him. In the Ruwenzori a whole group, Mount Luigi di Savoia, is called after him, as is Savoia

Peak (16,330 ft), fourth highest of the range.

Vittorio Sella (1859–1943) accompanied Abruzzi on his major mountain expeditions. A member of the influential Sella family, founders of the Italian Alpine Club. He was one of the earliest and greatest of mountain photographers. Sella Peak in the Ruwenzori is named after him.

10. Filippo di Filippi, 'Luigi Amedeo of Savoia-Aosta, Duke of the Abruzzi', *AJ* 45.

11. Quoted by W.S. Green, 'A Journey into the Glacier Regions of New Zealand with an Ascent of Mount Cook', *AJ* 11.

12. Sir James Hector (1834–1907) was a typical Victorian polymath: a Scottish medical man who had assisted Simpson with anaesthetics and who became an ardent geologist and meteorologist. He was on the Palliser Expedition to Canada and discovered Hector's Pass, the key for the Canadian Pacific Railway to cross the Rockies. He became head of the meteorological survey in New Zealand where he remained the rest of his life.

13. John Pascoe in a Foreword to *Peter Graham, Mountain Guide* (autobiography, 1964).

14. Rev. William Spotswood Green, C.B. (1847–1919) later became an official of the Irish Fisheries Board. In 1888 he explored the Selkirk Range in Canada (see Chapter 12).

15. W.S. Green, *op. cit.*

16. The first complete ascent by Green's route was made in 1912 by H.C. Chambers and H.F. Wright with the guides J.P. Murphy and J.M. Clarke.

17. George Edward Mannering (1862–1947) did little mountaineering after 1897 when he moved to North Island. He did, however, climb the Matterhorn at sixty!

18. E.A. FitzGerald, 'Mountaineering in the Southern Alps of New Zealand', *AJ* 17.

19. Martin Conway, 'In Memoriam', *AJ* 43. Edward A. FitzGerald (1871–1931) later went on to attempt Aconcagua (see Chapter 12) and was with Conway on his 'Alps from end to end' venture. 'If he had been obliged to work for a living he would, I am sure, have made a name for himself at any career he might have chosen,' said Conway. A bit much coming from a man who was himself born with a very large silver spoon! Conway was much more determined than FitzGerald, however.

20. Zurbriggen was a self-made man. 'Bold, sturdy and adventurous ... far too exuberant ... passionate, extravagant, lusty and overflowing ... a very hard worker and unrestrained in his relaxations' (Conway). In later years he

took to drink and became a down-and-out; he hanged himself in 1917 – a tragic end for one of the greatest of guides.

21. Both the Hermitage and Ball's Hut still exist. At the time of FitzGerald's visit the Hermitage Hotel had gone bankrupt and was temporarily closed, so they camped near by.

22. Felice Benuzzi, 'Lord of the East Face', *Climber & Rambler*, March 1985.

23. March 14, 1895. Mr Adamson 'of the Hermitage' accompanied him to 10,000 feet. According to Turner in *My Climbing Adventures in Four Continents*, there was some doubt whether Zurbriggen reached the top, having mistaken a subsidiary summit for it. He makes out quite a good case but there is no means of establishing the truth of the matter. Turner was egocentric to a degree and he no doubt felt that Zurbriggen's solo ascent would have detracted from his own accomplishment.

24. Samuel Turner (1869–1929) was a Manchester businessman who was a good climber but who offended the climbing establishment by his brashness. He was, nevertheless, strong and determined. T.E. Donne, Superintendent of the New Zealand Tourist Board, had heard Turner lecture in London and invited him to New Zealand as a guest of the Government. Turner later emigrated to New Zealand.

25. M. Ross, *A Climber in New Zealand* (1914).

26. Peter Graham (1878–1961), Alexander Carter (Alex) Graham (1881–1957). Though other members of the Graham family were guides they were no relation to George Graham who first climbed Mount Cook.

27. Freda du Faur (d.1935) was from Sydney though she lived much of her life in England. She wrote an account of her climbs in a delightful book, *The Conquest of Mount Cook* (1915). It is doubtful whether any New Zealand climbers other than the Grahams had a better list of first ascents. She stopped climbing in 1913, for no apparent reason (but cf. Lily Bristow!). She died in Australia. A tribute on her death by H.E.L. Porter appeared in 'Alpine Notes', *AJ* 48.

28. H.B. George, 'Mount Elbrouz, and the Attempted Ascent of it by a Russian Expedition', *AJ* 2. His account is translated from that of the chief savant, Kupffer. Others attempting the ascent were Meyer, Ménétries, Bernardazzi and Lenz. The latter is said to have got within 200 metres of the summit.

It was not realised that Elbrus had two summits until 1874 when A.W. Moore, F.C. Grove, H. Walker, and F. Gardiner with Peter Knubel as guide climbed the slightly higher western peak (5633 m).

29. D.W. Freshfield, *Travels in the Central Caucasus and Bashan* (1869).

30. Some of the nineteenth-century names for Caucasian peaks were later swapped around, which is confusing. The present names are used in this book, except in direct quotations from old accounts.

Old name	Present name
Dykh-tau	Koshtan-tau
Koshtan-tau	Shkhara
Guluku	Dykh-tau
Koshtan-tau	Dykh-tau (alternative)
Adish-tau (Saddle Peak)	Katuin-tau
Tetnuld	Gestola
Totonal	Tetnuld

31. J. Neill, 'The Mountaineering History of the Caucasus', an appendix to *The Red Snows* by J. Hunt and C. Brasher (1960). This is an excellent summary of Caucasian climbing.

32. J.G. Cockin, 'Shkara, Janga, and Ushba', *AJ* 16. Cockin's route on Ushba has probably never been repeated and, according to Neill (*op. cit.*), Russian climbers doubt that Cockin did it.

33. William Frederick Donkin (1845–88) was a chemistry lecturer at St George's Hospital where Dent was a surgeon. Like so many of these Victorian climbers he was something of a polymath: chemist, electrical engineer, musician and secretary of the Photographic Society (later Royal Photographic Society). His mountain photographs rival those of his great contemporary, Sella.

34. Captain Charles Herbert Powell (1857–1943) spoke Russian, which helped the search considerably. He was more of an explorer than a climber. Later knighted, he became a Major-General.

Hermann Woolley (1846–1920) was a strong climber with several visits to the Caucasus as well as the Lofoten Islands and Canada. Later he was Alpine Club President and continued to climb well into his sixties.

35. W.R. Rickmers, 'Personally Conducted: Saunetia in 1903', *AJ* 22.

Willi Gustav Rickmer Rickmers (1873–1965) came from a well-known Heligoland family. He was awarded the Patron's Gold Medal of the Royal Geographical Society in 1935 for outstanding contributions to exploration in the Caucasus and Pamirs. Fond of practical jokes, he was altogether a bit of a card.

Rickmers' party was A. Schulze, R. Helbling, F. Reichert, O. Schuster, E. Platz, H. Wagner,

F. Scheck, A. Weber, H. von Ficker, Fräulein C. von Ficker (his sister, known as Uschbamädel, meaning Ushba maiden) and the English climber J.H. Wigner. A local porter, Muratbi, accompanied them. Rickmers himself organised the 'meet' for fifty pounds per head for seven weeks, all in.

Pfann's party was L. Distel and Georg Leuchs: they were well known to the others.

36. T.G. Longstaff, *This My Voyage* (1950). Tom George Longstaff (1875–1964) was a wealthy man who climbed in many parts of the world, especially the Himalaya (see Chapter 14).

37. W.R. Rickmers, *op. cit.*

38. Anonymous reviewer, *AJ* 22. Hans Pfann (1863–1958) made similar traverses in the Alps and was one of the leading German climbers at the turn of the century.

Chapter Twelve
The Americas
pp. 191–209

1. In 1950 the frozen carcass of a guanaco, a type of wild llama, was reported discovered on the summit ridge of Aconcagua. Had the animal been driven there by Incas?

2. If measured from the earth's centre then Chimborazo *is* the highest mountain in the world, because the earth is not truly spheroidal, the distance to the Equator being greater than elsewhere.

3. A letter from Baron Max von Thielmann, 1878, *AJ* 8.

4. A. Humboldt and A. Bonpland: *Personal Narrative of Travels to the Equinoctial Regions of America during the Years 1799–1804* (1852–53). Humboldt's companions were Aimé Gaujaud (called Bonpland) and Carlos Montufar.

5. E. Whymper, *Travels amongst the Great Andes of the Equator* (1891–92).

6. The ascent of Carihuairazo was also accomplished by a stray mongrel dog called Penipe, after the village of that name; a canine record at the time but since exceeded: several dogs have climbed Aconcagua. What is it about South American dogs which makes them such dedicated mountaineers?

7. On the second ascent of Chimborazo they were able to watch an eruption on Cotopaxi. Smoke and ash rose 40,000 feet and covered the summit snows of Chimborazo.

8. F.S. Smythe, *Edward Whymper* (1940). Smythe was having a go at the spartan regime of Tilman, with which he profoundly disagreed.

9. One of his climbing companions was Bertrand Russell who adds a gloss to Conway's assessment of FitzGerald quoted in Chapter 11. FitzGerald, he allowed, had remarkable ability in mathematics and a wide knowledge of literature. He was also, said Russell, lazy, lackadaisical and widely acquainted with European brothels.

10. The complete party was FitzGerald, Vines, A.E. Lightbody, A. de Trafford, P. Gosse, M. Zurbriggen, J. and L. Pollinger, A. Lochmatter, N. Lanti and F. Weibel.

11. E.A. FitzGerald, *The Highest Andes* (1899).

12. M. Zurbriggen, *From the Alps to the Andes* (1899).

13. P. Gosse. Letter to *The Times*, 1938, reprinted in *AJ* 50.

14. In his obituary notice of FitzGerald, *AJ* 43, Conway put the blame on FitzGerald's lack of fitness owing to his unwillingness to train. Perhaps all those brothels had something to do with it!

15. Common enough today, it was then unusual (if not unique) for two expeditions to be on the same mountain simultaneously. It may have been locals trying to forestall Fitz-Gerald, as they did on Mount Cook.

16. W.M. Conway, *Aconcagua and Tierra del Fuego* (1902). Mario Fantin in *AJ* 71 reckons Conway was 'scarcely 100 metres below the top', i.e. about 325 feet and not fifty feet as Conway claimed.

17. Conway seems to have ignored Zurbriggen's ascent, possibly because Zurbriggen was a professional guide. Records were for amateurs.

18. His companions were G.B. De Gasperi and 'two guides from Valtournanche'. De Agostini never seems to have wanted for guides. For his work in Tierra del Fuego De Agostini was extensively honoured by both Chile and Argentina, who share control of the island. For further details see Jill Neate, *Mountaineering in the Andes* (1987).

19. 'Food people, manufacturers of shoes and of chocolate, and wealthy private individuals in vain were invited to lend their names and resources to the expedition.' Miss Peck, quoted in *Men, Myths and Mountains* by R.W. Clark. Probably the earliest recorded attempts at commercial sponsorship in climbing.

20. Surveys by the Workmans were not noted for accuracy. See K. Mason, *Abode of Snow* (1955).

21. J.M. Thorington, 'American Alpine Club Annals', *AAJ*, 1946. This agrees broadly with a note by Mrs Workman in *AJ* 25, though E. Echevarria states Miss Peck measured the summit by altimeter. (E. Echevarria, 'Early Moun-

taineers in Peru', in J.F. Ricker's *Yuraq Janka* (1977).)

22. A. Peck, *High Mountain Climbing in Peru and Bolivia* (1911).

23. F.B. Workman, 'The Altitude of Mount Huascaran', *AJ* 25. The surveyor was M. de Larimat, working between August and November 1909.

24. P. Borchers, 'In the Cordillera Blanca; the 1932 D & Oe A-V Expedition', *AJ* 45.

25. E. Echevarria, *op. cit.*

26. A. Bandelier, *The Islands of Titicaca and Coati* (1910). Contenders have never been wanting for Aconcagua's crown. Quite recently Ojos del Salado on the Chile–Argentine border has been a contender, as has Ancohuma in Bolivia. Their present heights are 6885 metres and 6427 metres, compared with Aconcagua's 6960 metres. South American mountain heights are fragile things. (See *Climber & Rambler* May, August 1979.) Everest has been subject to similar rumours of peaks higher than itself, all illusory.

27. 'Hiram Bingham ... had in mind not only to climb Coropuna, but also to search for "the last capital of the Incas"' (E. Echevarria, *op. cit.*). He found Machu Picchu, one of the greatest archaeological discoveries of the century.

28. Miss Peck's party was herself plus the Peruvians C. Volkmar, R. Carpio and four others. Bingham's party was himself, surveyor H. Tucker and two Peruvians, A. Coello and Corporal M. Gamarra (E. Echevarria, *op. cit.*).

29. John Palliser (1807–87) was a member of a noted Anglo-Irish family from Waterford. His qualification for leading the expedition was a season's hunting in the western USA and the subsequent popular book of his experiences, *Adventure of a Hunter in the Prairies* (1853). Palliser continued his exploration of the area in 1858 and 1860.

30. Palliser's reports to the Houses of Parliament published as Blue Books, 1859, 1860, 1863.

31. Mount Stalin is now Mount Peck, named not after Annie, but a local outfitter, Bob Peck. (Personal communication from C. Townsend.)

32. J.M. Thorington, 'A Note on the Naming of Mt Robson', *AJ* 48.

33. The Canadian Pacific Railway crossed the Rogers Pass in 1885 and built Glacier House the following year. In 1916 the rails were taken below the pass by the Connaught Tunnel (at 8.1 km, the longest in Canada). Glacier House no longer exists.

34. W.S. Green, 'Climbing in the Selkirks and Adjacent Rocky Mountains', *AJ* 17.

35. J.N. Collie, 'Climbing in the Canadian Rocky Mountains', *AJ* 19.

36. It is also said they imported Indians into the area to give it a more 'authentic' atmosphere for tourists! The climbers found the Indians not up to scratch as porters: 'They grumble if asked to carry more than 50lbs,' said Topham. ('A Few Notes about the Selkirks', *AJ* 15.)

37. Abbot climbed in the Zermatt area with the guide Peter Sarbach, but whether this was his only Alpine season is not clear. Though Fay is credited with leading the Lefroy expeditions it is evident from accounts that Abbot was the climbing leader.

38. C. Fay, 'Philip Stanley Abbot', *Appalachian* (1897).

39. George Percival Baker (1856–1951) took part in the first ascent of the Viereselgrat of the Dent Blanche (1882) and the first ascent of the Eagle's Nest Ridge Direct on Great Gable in 1892 – both amongst the hardest climbs of their respective kinds at the time. A wealthy man, Baker climbed in many parts of the world.

40. The American contingent was: Fay, A. Michael, H.C. Parker (?), Rev. C.L. Noyes, J.R. Vanderlip, C.S. Thompson.

41. Collie–Thompson correspondence, 1897–1913. Thorington Archives, Princeton University Library.

42. Hermann Woolley (1846–1920) made a number of first ascents in the Caucasus. Hugh Edward Millington Stutfield (1858–1929) was co-author with Collie of *Climbs and Exploration in the Canadian Rockies* (1903). He did no more climbing after 1902.

43. Collie–Thompson correspondence. Letter from Collie, March 21, 1901.

44. James Outram (1864–1925) was grandson of Lieutenant-General Sir James Outram, hero of the Indian Mutiny and first baronet. Outram inherited the title in 1912. He took holy orders at Cambridge in 1889 and was a vicar in Ipswich before emigrating to Canada. At the time of his famous climbs he seems to have been temporarily resident in California. He climbed Mount Victoria with W. Outram, presumably his brother, who does not figure in later ascents.

45. C. Klucker, *Adventures of an Alpine Guide* (1932). Referring to the ascent of a difficult rock peak, Trolltinder, he writes: 'We had to exercise much patience and labour in getting Mr Whymper up the highest pinnacle.'

46. Thompson joined the party but had to leave immediately on the news that his house had burnt down!

47. H.E.M. Stutfield and J.N. Collie, *Climbs and Exploration in the Canadian Rockies* (1903).

48. J. Outram, 'The First Ascent of Mount Bryce', *AJ* 21.

Chapter Thirteen
Pikes Peak or Bust
pp. 210–28

1. D. Jackson, *The Journals of Zebulon Montgomery Pike* (1966).

2. W.E. Hollon, *The Lost Pathfinder, Zebulon Montgomery Pike* (1949).

3. Nobody knows which peak was climbed by Pike in error. His companions were Dr Robinson with Privates Miller and Brown. Suspected of spying (probably true), Pike was arrested by the Spanish authorities, taken to Mexico and later released. He eventually became a Brigadier General and was killed in the attack on York (now Toronto, Canada) in 1813.

4. The slogan has been ascribed to a gold rush of the 1850s. The spelling seems fixed on Pikes Peak and Longs Peak, not Pike's Peak and Long's Peak.

5. The Bonneville expedition was a disgraceful catalogue of massacre and rape amongst the Indians and murderous fights amongst themselves. It was not very successful at fur trapping either. One of the participants was Bill Williams (see later).

6. John Charles Frémont (1813–90) was one of the most important figures in the westwards expansion of the USA, both as explorer and as politician. See A. Nevins, *Frémont, the West's Greatest Adventurer* (1928). Christopher (Kit) Carson (1809–68) was a leading frontiersman, 'soft spoken and likeable'. Both men were rather small in stature, both became generals in the US Army (at least for a time), and both have western towns named after them.

7. L.R. Hafen, ed., *Frémont's Fourth Expedition* (1960). The infamous winter camp was probably on the ridge between the Alder and Wanamaker creeks.

8. Known as the Gunnison Massacre, it took place in Pahvant Valley, Utah, on October 26, 1853. Of the eleven men in Gunnison's party only four escaped.

9. Indians claimed Mount Baker was active about 1830 and Humboldt saw Rainier erupt in 1841 and 1842. St Helens erupted in 1842 (and more disastrously in 1980).

10. George Vancouver (1757–98) rose from the ranks. He was said to be a savage discipli-

narian, but in a difficult four and a half year voyage he lost only one man.

11. A.D. Richardson, *Our New States and Territories* (n.d.).

12. Dryer's party was W. Lake, Captain Travaillot, Major Haller and Judge Olney. The 1857 party was H. Pittock, L. Chittenden, W. Cornell, and T. Wood. Pittock was an employee of Dryer, who was not amused!

13. The crampons used by Kautz were made by driving nails through spare soles and then sewing these onto the boot. It is interesting to note that 1853 when Dryer climbed St Helens coincided with the sensational advent of Albert Smith in London and it is not unlikely that accounts and pictures, such as those in the *Illustrated London News* and Smith's own book, had reached Oregon. Kautz is known to have studied the ascent of Mont Blanc before tackling Rainier.

14. E.T. Coleman, 'Mountaineering on the Pacific', *AJ* 6.

15. Edmund Thomas Coleman (1823–92) was an Original Member of the Alpine Club. An excellent artist but rather a poor climber – 'a clog on the expedition', said Van Trump. Apart from Mount Baker he had climbed Mont Blanc a couple of times and was on the first ascent of the Dôme de Miage. His writings indicate a pedantic and rather petulant nature.

16. Coleman, *op. cit.* Coleman is quoting from General Stevens's account in *Atlantic Monthly*, November 1876.

17. Powell (1834–1902) was a professor of geology and expert on the languages of the American Indians. A year after he climbed Longs Peak, Powell, a one-armed veteran of the Civil War, made an astonishing journey down the Colorado River and through the Grand Canyon, he and his men fighting the rapids all the way. See his *Canyons of the Colorado* (1895).

18. See E.J. Lamb, *Memories of the Past and Thoughts of the Future*, 1906. The ascent was claimed by Werner Zimmerman, a Swiss mountaineer, who undoubtedly climbed the east side of Longs Peak but, judging by his description, not Lamb's Slide.

19. E. Hoagland in his Introduction to Muir's *The Mountains of California* (Penguin edition 1985).

20. John Muir (1838–1914) actually attended Wisconsin University from 1859 to 1863 but took no degree. The Sierra Club is concerned with both climbing and conservation. Founded in 1892 it also has considerable publishing interests in outdoor subjects.

21. The Durango to Silverton line still operates using steam locomotives. Forty-five miles long, it is a popular tourist attraction.

22. For a full account of their climbing see Eccles, 'The Rocky Mountain Region of Wyoming and Idaho', *AJ* 9. Ferdinand Vandeveer Hayden (1829–87) 'laid the foundation for the US geological survey', according to one authority.

23. The original Mount of the Holy Cross was probably Mount Fletcher, also in Colorado, which has a cross of light-coloured strata in its North Ridge. It was mentioned by T.J. Farnham in 1839, but is not readily seen. Jackson's Cross is no longer as well defined as it was – the right arm has withered – which is perhaps why he is sometimes accused of retouching the pictures. Nobody since Jackson has seen it in such perfect shape.

24. E. Ingersoll, 'Silver San Juan', *Harper's New Monthly Magazine* (1882).

25. J.M. Hutchings, *In the Heart of the Sierras* (1886).

26. The flag was flown from a pole 'carried up in pieces', presumably after the flag. In any case it was blown off the top by the wind that afternoon. Rogers retrieved it, cut it up and sold the Stars for fifty cents each and pieces of the Stripes for twenty-five cents (R.W. Clark, *Men, Myths and Mountains*, 1976).

27. W.O. Owen, 'The Ascent of the Grand Teton', *AJ* 19. The party consisted of F.S. Spalding, Thomas Cooper, Hugh McDerment, W.O. Owen, and the packers (guides) John Shive and Frank Petersen. McDerment and Cooper failed to reach the summit. The ascent took place on August 11, 1898, and was repeated two days later by the same party, when Spalding and Shive reached the summit. The route is known as the Owen–Spalding Route; a misnomer since Spalding led throughout.

28. The most famous route was from Scagway (Alaska, USA) to Klondike (Yukon, Canada) over the Chilkoot Pass. After 1900 the journey could be done by train.

29. H.W. Topham, 'An Expedition to Mount St Elias, Alaska', *AJ* 14.

30. Russell's snow hole seems to have been better made than those employed by Frémont at Camp Desolation in 1848 and Stevens on Rainier in 1870, for he claims to have slept soundly.

31. F. de Filippi, 'The Expedition of HRH the Prince Louis of Savoy, Duke of the Abruzzi, to Mount St Elias (Alaska)', *AJ* 19. The Duke's companions were: Lt U. Cagni,

F. Gonella, V. Sella and F. de Filippi with the guides G. Petigax, A. Croux, A. Maquignaz, A. Pelissier and as porter, E. Botta. They all reached the summit together. There were some American outfitters with the party too, but not on the final assault.

Following on the St Elias expedition the Duke organised three others: to the North Pole in 1899 (the Pole was not reached); Ruwenzori in 1906 (see Chapter 11); and Karakoram in 1909 (see Chapter 14). His companions were largely the same throughout: an exclusive little coterie, paralleled by Bonington in the 1970s.

32. Dr Frederick A. Cook MD (1865–1940). Quoted in 'Alpine Notes', *AJ* 22. Cook's party was R. Dunn, R. Shainwald and packer F. Printz.

33. Review, *AJ* 24. Barrill's name has various spellings in different accounts.

34. They were all convinced that a successful expedition would somehow make them a lot of money, but mining prospectors were always professional optimists. McGonagall's name has variations in spelling in different accounts.

35. The departure of Davidson deprived the expedition of its only photographer, a serious loss in view of later events. Davidson later became Surveyor-General of Alaska.

36. H. Stuck, *The Ascent of Denali* (1914).

37. C.E. Rusk, 'On the Trail of Dr Cook', *Pacific Monthly*, October 1910, November 1910, January 1911. See also his *Tales of a Western Mountaineer* (1924). The principals involved in unmasking Dr Cook were Belmore Browne, Dr Herschel Parker and Claude Ewing Rusk.

38. B. Browne, *Outing* magazine, April 1913.

39. The party used crampons, which they called 'creepers'. Ordinary leather boots would have led to frostbite so they wore moccasins with extra soles and six pairs of thick socks. In its crude way, this is the same principle as the modern double boot.

Chapter Fourteen
The Abode of Snow
pp. 229–55

1. The highest mountain outside Central Asia is Aconcagua in Argentina, 6960 metres.

2. Of the three parallel ranges the lowest is the Siwaliks, rising from the Ganges plain in wooded hills of never more than 3000 feet (900 m), the Lesser Himalaya rise to 15,000 feet (4500 m) and the Great Himalaya is seldom less than 18,000 feet (5500 m). K. Mason, in his classic history, *Abode of Snow*, recognises five sections

west to east: Punjab Himalaya, Kumaon Himalaya, Nepal Himalaya, Sikkim Himalaya and Assam Himalaya. Deep river valleys divide the mountains into a series of groups or *himals*, giving them shape and form like gigantic sharks' teeth, and usually named after the highest peak in the group. Dhaulagiri *himal*, for example, is in the Nepal Himalaya. In the Karakoram the equivalent of a *himal* is a *muztagh*.

3. The present figure is 26,795 feet – so Webb was only sixty-seven feet too high. Quite remarkable considering the difficulties attending the measurement of high mountains.

4. By Hugh Ruttledge in 1926.

5. W.W. Graham, 'Travels and Ascents in the Himalaya', *AJ* 12.

6. C.F. Meade, 'The Schlagintweits and Ibi Gamin (Kamet)', *AJ* 33. Meade points out that by approaching from Tibet the brothers would have had to cross Abi Gamin (then called Ibi Gamin) to reach Kamet. Adolphe Schlagintweit was murdered near Yarkand two years later.

Many of the early surveyors and explorers crossed high passes and climbed the occasional small peak but this is not the place to go into their adventures. See the admirable books by John Keay, *When Men and Mountains Meet* and *The Gilgit Game*, as well as Mason.

7. He took service with the ruler of Kashmir and became Governor of Ladakh.

8. Several of the great names of Central Asian exploration such as Godwin-Austen, Stein, and Longstaff commented on Johnson's E61 ascent. Mason's summation in *AJ* 34, 'Johnson's "Suppressed Ascent" of E61', looks at the evidence, though possibly with some bias: 'I hope to refute the charge against the Government of India.' There does not seem to have been any modern analysis, perhaps because the area is still relatively unknown. The peak is now reckoned to be 22,015 feet (6710 m).

9. By Trevor Braham amongst others (see letter *AJ* 65).

10. W.W. Graham, 'Travel and Ascents in the Himalaya', *AJ* 12.

11. *Ibid.*

12. The voting was seven for and forty-nine against – Graham had obviously blotted his social copybook somehow. Yet his controversial Himalayan claims were later supported by some big names. In the early 1890s he was said by Collie to have lost his money and gone to the American West as a cowboy. He was actually British Vice-Consul in Durango, Mexico, from 1910 to 1932 when the post was closed. He would then have been about seventy-three, and

he again slipped from view. (Letter from the Foreign Office to the author, July 4, 1986.)

13. Boss was honoured by the RGS with the Back Grant for 1884 for his pioneering work in New Zealand and the Himalaya.

14. Various authorities have interpreted Dècle's retirement as illness, but I find no evidence of this. Graham says Dècle was 'fairly done up', which is not the same thing at all.

15. Graham, op. cit.

16. See Mason, *Abode of Snow*, Chapter 4, and A.L. Mumm, *Five Months in the Himalaya* (1909).

17. E. Boss and D.W. Freshfield, 'Notes on the Himalaya and Himalayan Survey', *AJ* 12.

18. Two porters confessed to eating 60 lbs of rice in four days! They got an obstruction of the bowels which Graham cleared with castor oil and milk. They were ill for a month.

19. Curious this – not an English or a Swiss flag as one might have expected. The Bhotias are a major ethnic group of Nepal and Sikkim, one branch of whom are the Sherpas.

20. In his otherwise excellent account of Himalayan climbing Kenneth Mason dismisses both Johnson's and Graham's claims. But Mason was himself an ex-Survey officer and he loyally supports the traditional Survey view.

21. E.J. Garwood in a letter to the Editor, *AJ* 22.

22. T.G. Longstaff, 'Six Months' Wandering in the Himalaya', *AJ* 23.

23. W.M. Conway, 'Some Reminiscences and Reflections of an Old Stager', *AJ* 31.

24. *Ibid.* Conway's last climb was the Breithorn in 1901. It had been his first climb twenty-nine years earlier. Born in 1856 he died in 1937 having been created Lord Conway of Allington in 1931.

25. The party was Conway, Bruce, Eckenstein, Zurbriggen, A.D. McCormick (artist), and a friend of Conway, Heywood Roudebush. Lieutenant-Colonel Lloyd Dickin, an ornithologist, joined for part of the time.

26. Captain Henry Haversham Godwin-Austen (1834–1923) was the first to survey the Baltoro and much else in the Karakoram in 1861. It was proposed by General Walker of the Survey that K2 be named Mount Godwin-Austen in his honour but the name was never universally accepted. Godfrey Thomas Vigne (1801–63) was an early explorer of Kashmir.

27. See W. Unsworth, *Because it is There* (1973). Oscar Johannes Ludwig Eckenstein (1859–1921) was a railway engineer and a pioneer of Welsh climbing.

28. The Workmans had a lot of trouble with porters over the years: '(their) instinct for man management was not of the highest order,' wrote R.W. Clark.

29. *In the Ice-World of Himalaya* (1900), *Ice-bound Heights of the Mustagh* (1908), *Peaks and Glaciers of Nun Kun* (1909), *The Call of the Snowy Hispar* (1910), *Two Summers in the Ice Wilds of the Eastern Karakoram* (1917).

30. Quoted in Mason, *Abode of Snow* (1955).

31. Edward Alexander ('Aleister') Crowley (1875–1947) was a diabolist, bad poet, thoroughly rotten egg who betrayed or fell out with just about everyone he knew – except Eckenstein. He was wealthy enough to indulge his absurd fantasies, including his climbing trips abroad. In fact, he was quite a good climber. There is a minor route of his on Napes Needle in the Lake District.

32. Crowley's *Confessions* quoted in R. Campbell, 'The Brief Mountaineering Career of Aleister Crowley, the Great Beast 666', *Mountain* 11, 1970.

33. Letter from Crowley to the Indian newspaper *Pioneer*, September 11, 1905. After the Kangchenjunga affair he gave up active mountaineering, though still retaining an interest.

34. See Douglas Freshfield, *Round Kangchenjunga* (1903).

35. L.S. Amery, 'Valedictory Address', *AJ* 54.

36. T.G. Longstaff, *This My Voyage* (1950).

37. *Ibid.*

38. Morley was opposed to anything Curzon did. His colleagues called him Aunt Priscilla and the Prime Minister referred to him as a 'petulant spinster'.

39. Until well into the present century most of the central Himalayan hill tribes were terrified of the Gurkhas, whose fearsome reputation went back in history.

40. Arthur Morris Slingsby (1885–1916) was one of the Yorkshire Slingsbys and an army officer in India. He was very strong and Collie thought that Slingsby and Mummery would have made the perfect Himalayan team. He died of wounds at Kut, during the Mesopotamian campaign.

41. The *exact* height of Longstaff's bivouac on Gurla Mandhata is not known but he estimated it at 23,000 feet.

42. Letter to Ruth Mallory, 1922. Despite this, Mallory liked Kellas.

43. J.N. Collie, 'In Memoriam', *AJ* 34. Kellas was a very private man and seemed to have few close friends who could speak of his achievements. Collie's obituary of him is an exercise in making bricks without straw.

44. Before the First World War the five probable highest ascents were:

Kabru	24,080ft/7338 m	Graham,	1883
Muztagh	23,888ft/7281 m	Johnson,	1865
Trisul	23,360ft/7120 m	Longstaff,	1907
Kun	23,350ft/7087 m	Piacenza,	1913
Pauhunri	23,178ft/7065 m	Kellas,	1911

No other 7000-metre (23,000-ft) peaks were climbed until 1928. I see no reason to doubt the claims of Johnson and Graham, especially the latter.

45. Alpine Club Archives. Letter from Farrar to Montagnier, May 15, 1919.

46. Mummery was not interested in exploration. This was one of the reasons he had turned down an opportunity to join the Conway expedition of 1892.

47. Stories of Bruce and his Gurkhas are numerous and he became a legendary figure in Nepal, remembered long after his death in 1939. Strangely, there is no biography and his own books tend to be rather dull factual accounts of events.

48. This was the second time Raghobir had collapsed. Collie said he didn't eat enough.

49. The Mummery Rib was descended by Reinhold Messner in 1970.

50. The thirteen European members of the expedition were: The Duke; Filippo de Filippi (naturalist); Federico Negrotto (topographer); Vittorio Sella (photographer); A.C. Baines (supply officer); Erminio Botta (Sella's assistant); the guides Joseph and Laurenzo Petigax, father and son, who had been with the Duke to Ruwenzori and in the Karakoram with the Workmans; the Brocherel brothers, Henri and Alexis, who had been with Longstaff and climbed Trisul; and three porters, Albert Savoie, Emil Brocherel and Ernest Bareux.

51. Filippo de Filippi, *Karakorum and Western Himalaya 1909* (1912).

52. Galen Rowell, *In the Throne Room of the Mountain Gods* (1977).

53. De Filippi, *op. cit.*

54. De Filippi led his own scientific expedition to the Siachen area a few years later.

Chapter Fifteen
No Fun at All
pp. 256–69
The title is Miriam O'Brian's description of the North-East Face of Finsteraarhorn.

1. For example, at the end of the war in 1918, Franz Schmid was thirteen, his brother Tony was nine, Hinterstoisser was four and Toni Kurz, five.

2. There were thirty-six attempts on the Hirondelles before the Italian success. Interestingly, it defeated the great Welzenbach.

3. The Rote Zähne Ridge is TD inf with pitches of V; the others are D/D sup.

4. At the time of the early ascents (eighteen by the outbreak of the Second World War) the route was TD sup, with eight to ten pitons. Overuse of pitons later reduced the standard.

5. Of the forty-six summits over 11,000 feet twenty-four had been climbed by 1918, twenty-two had not. All were climbed by 1930, the last being an unnamed summit on the Columbia Icefield.

6. Weber said the only way he could convince the locals he was really Swiss was to join a climbing expedition, since he couldn't yodel, make chocolate or mend watches!

7. Maki was an official of the Japanese Alpine Club and an aide-de-camp to the Crown Prince Chichibu. His successes gave Japanese climbing a fillip, especially amongst the élite, and laid the foundation for the impressive proliferation of expedition climbing to come out of Japan from the mid-fifties onwards, starting with the first ascent of Manaslu (8156 m) in 1956.

8. A story soon went round the Rockies that the axe was solid silver and had been placed on the summit by the direct orders of the Emperor. In fact it was an ordinary axe which was recovered, together with Maki's note, remarkably preserved, by the second ascent party in 1948. Axe and note are in the museum of the American Alpine Club.

9. Kain's reputation was further enhanced by the posthumous autobiography *Where the Clouds Can Go*, ghosted by J.M. Thorington from Kain's notes.

10. Christian Klucker, *Adventures of an Alpine Guide* (1932). The second known ascent was that of T. Thomas and A. Blanc in 1910, but they claimed only the third ascent.

11. Lady Bell, *The Letters of Gertrude Bell* (1927).

12. Letter from Ulrich Fuhrer to Val Fynn, *AJ* 34.

13. Had Hinterstoisser's party learned this lesson, the Eigerwand tragedy of 1936 would have been averted.

14. Miriam Underhill, *Give Me the Hills* (1956).

Chapter Sixteen
A Star in the East
pp. 270–80

1. Willo Welzenbach, 'Where Shall We Go Tomorrow?' quoted in *Welzenbach's Climbs* by Eric Roberts (1980).

2. Edward Lisle Strutt (1874–1948) edited the *Alpine Journal* from 1927 to 1937 and represented the arch-traditionalist view. Younger Alpine Club members thought him an old fogey but, Dr Charles Warren tells me, they still stood in awe of him. 'He was that sort of person.' Provoked by a foolishly exaggerated article in a German climbing journal, Strutt had written a vituperative piece in *AJ* 46 called 'A Superiority Complex?' about Germans and their Alpine claims. A letter in the next issue from a German reader defending Germany called forth more scathing comments from Strutt, including the one given here.

3. The mountain had changed considerably in the thirty-two years since Mummery's attempt. The ice had shrunk. Lagarde's route is not done today. In 1929 a simpler route was pioneered by Armand Charlet and today the North Face of the Plan is not regarded as difficult.

4. Emile Robert Blanchet with the guide Kaspar Mooser climbed several difficult faces but most of the routes lacked quality: obscure and off-beat, they are seldom, if ever, done today. Blanchet was a professional pianist.

5. There is a certain irony in that the prudent Lauper died comparatively young (aged forty) from the delayed effects of a childhood operation.

6. The face was climbed in 1926 by Blanchet and Mooser, a typical obscure, difficult and dangerous Blanchet route.

7. Smythe was easily the most popular mountain writer of the inter-war years, much more so than his contemporaries, Shipton and Tilman. He was in every respect a professional mountaineer, the Chris Bonington of his day.

8. Personal communication from Ivan Waller, who was approached by both Smythe and Brown, each, he maintains, prepared to steal a march on the other.

9. Both men claimed credit for the Route Major. When Smythe saw a first draft of Brown's book *Brenva* he threatened to take the author to court. The book was substantially redrafted, though it still played down Smythe's role.

10. Brown is possibly the only climber to have inaugurated the three finest routes on a great Alpine face. Note also Graven's record: first ascents of the Lauper and the Pera, second ascent of the Major. Alexander Graven (1898–1977) has never been given the credit due to him by mountain historians.

11. All the Brenva climbs are done frequently these days, and there are many variants. Route Major has been the most popular climb, though recently the Sentinelle, somewhat neglected, has come into fashion.

12. Fascism went deeper in many cases, however. The late J.E.B. Wright, who arranged for a party of thirty Germans to visit North Wales in 1937, told me the climbers who put up the Munich Climb on Tryfan were quite open about how they would soon be marching through London as they applied their new world order.

13. The Munich School was sometimes disparagingly referred to in Britain as 'the dangle and whack school' because they used pitons, in those days despised in Britain.

14. Both Welzenbach and his father were named Wilhelm. As his father was already called Willi, the usual diminutive, he was called Willo.

15. Paulcke was Welzenbach's tutor for a doctorate at Karlsruhe, which he gained in 1930. His thesis was on snow structure: *Investigations into the stratigraphy of snow deposits and the mechanics of snow movements together with conclusions about processes of accumulation.* Fellow students called him 'the avalanche doctor'.

16. Willo Welzenbach, *Birth of a Technique.* Quoted in Roberts, *op. cit.* Rigele remembered the incident differently, claiming he merely stopped whilst Welzenbach passed him some more pitons.

17. This was not the Angerer later killed on the Eiger.

18. Until comparatively recently Swiss guidebooks carried no grades.

19. The Roman numerals were said to be derived from the marking system for Swiss and German school examinations! The adjectival grades were: I *leicht* (easy); II *mittelschwer* (of medium difficulty); III *schweirig* (difficult); IV *sehr schweirig* (very difficult); V *uberaus schweirig*

(extremely difficult); VI *ausserst schweirig* (supremely difficult).

20. A tower on this ridge was later named Pointe Welzenbach.

21. The malady was thought to be tubercular and stemming from a childhood complaint, but was not fully understood.

22. W. Welzenbach, *The Fiescherwand*. Quoted in Roberts, *op. cit.*

23. E.G. Lammer, *Jungborn* (1886).

24. W. Welzenbach, *Bernese Ice Walls*. Quoted in Roberts, *op. cit.*

Chapter Seventeen
Nordwand
pp. 281–303

1. Eugen Guido Lammer, who was Austrian, was born in 1863 and died in 1945 in Vienna, just before the war ended.

2. They discovered a cairn which probably marked the highest point reached on the ridge by other climbers. The ridge was not climbed until 1950.

3. Welzenbach sent a detailed account to the *Alpine Journal*. 'Dr Welzenbach has kindly supplied us with complete details of his route, under the circumstances not perhaps the least remarkable achievement of the week,' wrote Strutt, acidly.

4. Britain's involvement with Everest also had nationalist overtones, of course. No other nation was allowed near the mountain whilst we still ruled India. Minor examples of nationalism – or perhaps patriotism – occurred elsewhere, like the New Zealanders racing to climb Mount Cook before FitzGerald.

5. Royal Geographical Society, Everest Archives, Box 3.

6. *The Mountaineering Journal*, 1932–38. There were many club journals before this, but climbing began to appeal to a wide section of the public who did not belong to any club, except possibly the Youth Hostel Association – which also had its origins in Germany.

7. Notably the West Face of the Dru, climbed in two stages, July 1–5 and July 16–18, 1952, by a French party.

8. The Matterhorn South Face was climbed in 1931 and the East Face in 1932, both climbs led by Enzo Benedetti. The first route subjected the climbers to ten hours of stonefall and the second is described as 'monotonous and dangerous'. The West Face was climbed by Penhall in 1879 (see Chapter 8).

9. Schmid was killed attempting a difficult ice climb on the Gross Wiesbachhorn. He dropped his one remaining piton and in making an impulsive attempt to catch it, fell to his death.

10. *AJ* 43, 'New Expeditions'.

11. *AJ* 47: Claude Wilson quoted in J.J. Withers, 'Valedictory Address'.

12. *Ibid.*

13. Whymper and Michel Croz with Christian Almer and Franz Biner climbed Pointe Whymper in 1865. Strangely enough, Pointe Croz was probably not climbed until 1909 – surely an oversight!

14. One of them had left a diary at their bivouac site in which he had written: 'We are standing at the base of the N. Face. It appears quite harmless. If it wasn't snowing we should try the climb at once. We are expecting hourly Heckmair and Kröner, our strongest competitors.' *AJ* 54, 'Alpine Notes'.

15. Years later Chabod wrote, 'we were too timorous in 1934.' He always maintained they would have reached the summit before the storm broke. (Letter to C.E. Engel, quoted in her *Mountaineering in the Alps*, 1971.)

16. Loulou Boulaz (1908–91) was one of the outstanding women climbers of the century. She made the first woman's ascent of many hard routes, including the South Ridge of the Aiguille Noire (1936); North Face of the Dru (1936); Pear Route on the Brenva Face (1949); Walker Spur (1952); North Face of Cima Grande (1960); North Face of Piz Badile (1964).

17. 'Alpine Notes', *AJ* 44. In 1919 Strutt rescued the Austrian royal family from a revolutionary mob, spiriting them away to Switzerland. Curiously enough, in view of his antipathy to the Munich School, Strutt was educated at Innsbruck University and did a lot of climbing in the Eastern Alps.

18. 'Alpine Notes', *AJ* 45.

19. R. Cassin, *50 Years of Alpinism* (1981).

20. Tizzoni replaced the usual team member, Ratti, who was away on military service.

21. Having completed one of the hardest routes in the Alps, the Italians did not know the way off the mountain and were forced to bivouac again before reaching safety the following day.

22. H. Harrer, *The White Spider* (1959).

23. *Ibid.* Harrer points out that similar applause was meted out to the pioneers in the Golden Age.

24. C. Barrington in a letter published in *AJ* 11.

25. A.W. Moore, *The Alps in 1864* (1902).

26. They took a more direct line than subsequent attempts. Their line was not repeated until 1962 when H. Drachsler and W. Gstrein followed it almost to the Spider before having to retire and follow the normal route.

27. Heckmair was christened Andreas, but often called by the diminutive 'Anderl', a nickname he had shared with Hinterstoisser. This occasionally causes confusion. Similarly Ludwig (Vorg) became 'Wiggerl' and even Brankowski was known as 'Brankerl'.

28. A. Heckmair, *Die drei letzten Probleme der Alpen* (1949). Quoted in Harrer's *The White Spider*.

Chapter Eighteen
To Shoot a Fox
pp. 304–17

1. J. Neill, 'The Mountaineering History of the Caucasus', from *Red Snows* by J. Hunt and C. Brasher (1960).

2. J.R. Jenkins, 'A Light Expedition to the Central Caucasus, 1937', *AJ* 50.

3. Some years ago when the author was in Austria with some Russian climbers he suggested wickedly that the observers were there to prevent the climbers from escaping. The Russians thought this was hilarious. Despite such precautions tragedy still occurred, as in 1974 when eight women climbers died in a storm in the Pamirs.

4. Vitali Mikhailovitch Abalakov (1906–86) is often called the father of Russian mountaineering. His brother Eugene (or Yevgenie) died in unknown circumstances in 1948.

5. Both traverses had been done previously by Austrian climbers, though the Dykh-tau–Koshtan-tau traverse was broken into two halves at the col before Khrumkol.

6. Nevertheless, the Russians the author met in Austria had some titanium pitons, extremely light but very strong. The metal for these, they said, fell off the back of a space programme truck.

7. J.R. Jenkins, 'Tetnuld Nordwand', *Midland Association of Mountaineers Journal*, 1938. His companion on the climb was M.S. Taylor.

8. R.W. Clark and E.C. Pyatt, *Mountaineering in Britain* (1957).

9. A. Borthwick, *Always a Little Further* (1939).

10. E. Byne and G. Sutton, *High Peak* (1966).

11. H.R.C. Carr: *Climbers' Guide to Snowdon and the Beddgelert District* (1926). Herbert Carr was responsible for the post-war revival of the Climbers' Club and the establishment of its hut at Helyg, in Snowdonia. The Climbers' Club and the Rucksack Club of Manchester were responsible for the immediate post-war revival of Welsh climbing.

12. A.B. Hargreaves, '1928–1929 Climbing Notes' in *Helyg* (1985). The second ascent was also led by Pigott, in 1928.

13. Smythe had a reputation for irritability, tactlessness and being easily offended. Somervell disliked him and he had a famous row with Brown (see Chapter 16). He later fell out with Longland, Crawford and others over Everest.

14. E. Kelly, 'The Pinnacle Club', *FRCC Journal*, 1921.

15. Interview with J.E.B. Wright in the early sixties. Probably one of Jerry's apocryphal stories!

16. Modern climbers prefer to start up Great Slab, then continue up Bow from where the routes cross.

17. K. Wilson and Z. Leppert, *Cwm Idwal* (1974).

18. C.W.F. Noyce, 'The Writer in Snowdonia', from *Snowdon Biography* (1957).

19. Unfortunately for Edwards, his professional life became increasingly frustrating. He developed a persecution mania which extended even to close friends and in 1958 he took his own life.

20. Barry's Route on Monk's Cowl was not climbed until 1962.

21. Exceptions prove the rule. There was the quite astonishing trip to the Caucasus by Hodgkin, Jenkins, Beaumont and Taylor in 1937, mentioned earlier, and there was Dick Barry's transfer of his skill to his South African homeland, where he did several climbs of HVS standard – Red Corner at Tunguari Kloof was still regarded as a local test piece in the 1960s.

22. W.M. Bueler, *Roof of the Rockies* (1986).

23. R.M. Ormes, *Guide to the Colorado Mountains* (1952).

24. Quoted in Roper and Steck, *Fifty Classic Climbs in North America* (1979), from Munday's account in the *Canadian Alpine Journal* (1933).

25. H.S. Hall Jnr., 'Climbs in the Coast Range of British Columbia', *AJ* 47.

26. Alanson Willcox and Betty Woolsey remained in a lower camp.

27. The climbers were R. Bedayn, D. Brower, J. Dyer, and B. Robinson. Dyer led most of the climb. Before the final push they spent two days reconnoitring the route.

Chapter Nineteen
Blanks on the Map
pp. 318–32

1. Royal Geographical Society, Everest Archives, Box 1.

2. Alpine Club Archives. Letter from Farrar to Montagnier, May 15, 1919.

3. Charles Kenneth Howard-Bury (1883–1963) was not a mountaineer but had travelled extensively in Central Asia. He had done much of the negotiation in India preparing for a possible Everest expedition, and leadership of the reconnaissance was his reward. He had led a fairly adventurous life and was a capable leader.

4. Arthur Hinks practically ruled the Everest Committee until 1945. He was a mathematician and expert in map projections. He worked for the RGS, was sharp tongued, hopelessly unworldly, and universally disliked.

5. RGS, Everest Archives, Box 12. Harold Raeburn (1865–1926) suffered a complete breakdown on his return home and never recovered.

6. According to the late Duncan Grant (letter to author, 1977) Mallory himself was not homosexual. This is worth keeping in mind in view of later events.

7. Quoted in D. Robertson, *George Mallory* (1968).

8. Both were at Winchester where, with two other boys, Gibson and Tyndale, they formed the Ice Club under the tutelage of a young master, R.L.G. Irving.

9. Leader: Brigadier General C.G. Bruce
   Deputy Leader: Lieutenant-Colonel E.L. Strutt
   G.H. Leigh Mallory, Major E.F. Norton, Major H.T. Morshead, G. Ingle Finch, Dr T.H. Somervell, Dr A.W. Wakefield, Captain J.B.L. Noel, C.G. Crawford, C.J. Morris, Captain J.G. Bruce, Dr T.G. Longstaff
   Interpreter: Karma Paul
   Sirdar: Gyaljen (Gyalzen Kazi of the previous year)

10. Norton occasionally gave Mallory relief in the step-cutting. It seems likely they were off-route for much of the descent.

11. Using an ice axe as a brake on steep snow is a technique practised by climbers on safe slopes for just such an emergency as this. Had they not been braking it is doubtful whether Mallory's axe and the rope could have held them.

12. All the more remarkable because J.G.

Bruce who established the height record with Finch was not a climber. He was included ostensibly because he could speak Nepali, but really because he was the General's nephew! He proved an admirable choice.

13. D. Robertson, *op. cit.*

14. These men became the first 'Tigers', a name later applied to all good porters and for many years to all good rock climbers in Britain.

15. E.F. Norton, *The Fight for Everest, 1924* (1925).

16. Somervell coughed up something which stuck in his throat, choking him. Because they were not roped he was unable to signal to Norton: 'so I just sat down in the snow to die'. Fortunately he managed to clear the blockage.

17. Letter from Duncan Grant to the author, 1977.

18. J.B. Noel, *Through Tibet to Everest* (1927).

19. Quoted in E.F. Norton, *op. cit.*

20. See Chapter 5 of my book *Everest* for a full discussion and Holzell and Salkeld's *The Mystery of Mallory and Irvine* for an alternative argument.

21. Two clubs were founded almost simultaneously: the Mountain Club of India in Calcutta and the Himalayan Club in Simla. They united under the latter name in 1928.

22. The books have recently been collected into omnibus editions as H.W. Tilman, *The Seven Mountain Travel Books* (1983) and Eric Shipton, *The Six Mountain Travel Books* (1985).

23. H.W. Tilman, *Mount Everest, 1938* (1948).

24. The leaders were Graham Brown and the American Charles Houston. Members were (US) W.F. Loomis, Arthur Emmons and H.T. Adams Carter; (GB) N.E. Odell, H.W. Tilman and Peter Lloyd.

25. Takebushi, Hotta, Yamagata, Yuasa, Hamano. All reached the summit with Sherpa Ang Tsering.

26. Pik Kommunizma seems destined for another change of name!

27. It is not certain from the Russian account whether these were real rope ladders or whether the writer means étriers.

28. By strange coincidence, both Nikolayev, killed in 1933, and Aristov were chairmen of the Moscow Alpine Association at the time of their death.

29. Amne Machen's height rise was spectacular. In the 1920s G. Pereira put it at 7600 metres; in 1928 J. Rock estimated it at 8500 metres; and as late as 1949 L. Clark was claiming 9040 metres for it. Rock later revised his figure to 6400

metres. It was climbed by an American party in 1981.

30. A decision which cost Carpe his life. He remained in Alaska and fell into a crevasse on McKinley.

31. Probably the only other occasion this technique was used on a big peak was when W.W. Sayre made his unsanctioned attempt on the North Side of Everest in 1962. See W.W. Sayre, *Four Against Everest* (1964).

32. See F.S. Chapman, *The Jungle is Neutral*.

33. F.S. Chapman, *Helvellyn to Himalaya* (1940).

34. *Ibid.*

Chapter Twenty
Reap the Wild Wind
pp. 333–56

1. In 1930 Schneider beat his own record twice by climbing Nepal Peak I (7145 m) and Jongsong Peak (7473 m).

2. The successful team was Hein, Borchers, Schneider, Hoerlin and Bernard on August 20, 1932.

3. K. Mason, *Abode of Snow* (1955).

4. Foreword to the English-language edition of *Himalayan Quest* by Paul Bauer (1938).

5. *Ibid.*

6. Bolivia was stiff with Germans at the time, many wearing Nazi uniforms.

7. Quoted in K. Mason, *op. cit.*

8. The party was E. Allwein, P. Aufschnaiter, E. Beigel, J. Brenner, W. Fendt, K. von Kraus, J. Leupold, A. Thoenes and P. Bauer. They were assisted logistically by Himalayan Club members H.W. Tobin and E.O. Shebbeare.

9. P. Bauer, 'The Fight for Kangchenjunga, 1929', *AJ* 42.

10. Dyhrenfurth was born German but had adopted Swiss nationality. Curiously enough, his son led an international expedition to Everest some forty years later and that too was an unhappy mix.

11. Letter, 'The Assault on Kangchenjunga, 1930', *AJ* 42.

12. Except for Jonsong these are Dyhrenfurth's estimates for peaks climbed.

13. G.O. Dyhrenfurth, 'The Mountaineer and the Mountain Film', *AJ* 43.

14. Wiessner also became an American citizen later. Rand Herron was an experienced and daring climber. He was killed climbing the Pyramids on the way home from Nanga Parbat.

15. It has been suggested that resources were too meagre to allow Sherpas to be engaged. This seems dubious.

16. This estimate is based on Finsterwalder's map showing the camps in F. Bechtold, *Nanga Parbat Adventure* (1935).

17. Quoted in E. Roberts, *Welzenbach's Climbs* (1980).

18. F. Bechtold, *Nanga Parbat Adventure* (1935).

19. E. Schneider, 'The German Assault on Nanga Parbat, 1934', *AJ* 46, 47. According to the porter Kitar, Wieland was a sick man on the morning of the descent.

20. After the expedition Hitler's Minister for Sport, Von Tschammer und Osten, held a 'court of honour' which accused the two Austrians of abandoning their German comrades, though actually it was the three Sherpas who were abandoned. The Austrians could not possibly know that the others were in trouble. Aschenbrenner and Schneider were declared to be 'without honour'.

21. Merkl and Gaylay must have managed to drag themselves further along the ridge, judging from where the bodies were found in 1938.

22. For details see *AJ* 5. Eight guides or porters plus two Americans, Randall and Beane, and an Englishman, Corkendal, were caught in a storm on the descent. All perished and six of the bodies were never found.

23. Quoted in K.M. Herrligkoffer, *Nanga Parbat* (1954).

24. Thirteen died on Pic Lenin in 1974; thirteen also died on K2 in 1986 – but not from one expedition.

25. 'German mountaineers have a claim to it that all recognize with sympathy,' declared the Calcutta *Statesman* in reporting the tragedy. The British felt the same about Everest because of Mallory and Irvine. There was also a certain bloody-mindedness in both cases.

26. Two members of the team, Aufschnaiter and Harrer, escaped from internment. Harrer later wrote the classic *Seven Years in Tibet* (1953).

27. J.L. Longland, 'In Memoriam', *AJ* 67.

28. Sir Jack Longland in conversation with the author, 1978.

29. Actually Camp IIIa. The initial Camp III, established May 2, was further away from the slopes.

30. *The Listener*, October 10, 1934.

31. For the intricate details of the dispute see my book, *Everest*, Chapter 8.

32. Bryant so impressed Shipton that he henceforth looked on New Zealanders with

favour. This resulted in the inclusion of Hillary and Lowe in the 1953 team.

33. It now ranks twelfth, but is virtually the same height as Shisha Pangma, thirteenth. Gasherbrum II is lowest at 8035 metres.

34. All the experienced Sherpas were on Everest.

35. The members were Houston, R. Burdsall, R.H. Bates, W.P. House, P. Petzoldt and Captain R.N. Streatfeild.

36. The climbers were C. Cranmer, D. Wolfe, O.E. Cromwell, G. Sheldon and J. Durrance.

37. Pasang Kikuli is said to have been afraid that if he lost his toes through frostbite, his wife would leave him. This seems a strange excuse from someone who had survived the Nanga Parbat tragedy. Did Durrance order him to go down? Kikuli's absence at the upper camps was a crucial factor in the tragedy.

38. The height according to Dyhrenfurth. According to L.C. Baume, 8365 metres.

39. F.H. Wiessner, 'The K2 Expedition of 1939', *Appalachia* Vol. 31.

40. Wiessner says Tendrup was put in charge by Pasang Lama, the Sherpa who attempted the summit, but why Pasang Lama had the authority to do this is not clear. Pasang Kikuli was sirdar and it should have been up to him to appoint a deputy.

41. Wiessner, *op. cit.*

42. *Ibid.*

Chapter Twenty-One
The Last Blue Mountains
pp. 357–72

1. A. Bolinder and G.O. Dyhrenfurth, 'Table of all the known Peaks in the World over 7300 Metres', *Mountain World* 1968/69. Annapurna comes tenth only if subsidiary summits of some other giants are ignored.

2. J.O.M. Roberts, R.C. Evans, J.H. Emlyn Jones and New Zealander W.P. Packard. The party was also accompanied by D.G. Lowndes as botanist.

3. H.W. Tilman, 'The Annapurna Himal and South Side of Everest', *AJ* 58.

4. T.D. Bourdillon, 'The North Face of the Dru, 1950', *AJ* 58. They actually made the ascent in eight and a half hours.

5. K. Mason, *Abode of Snow* (1955). Mason, as an ex-Survey of India man, was a dyed-in-the-wool traditionalist to whom the French attitude was anathema.

6. Jean Couzy, Marcel Schatz, Louis Lach-enal, Lionel Terray, Gaston Rébuffat, Marcel Ichac, Jacques Oudot and Francis de Noyelle.

7. Various estimates exist for the height of this camp.

8. The team was E.E. Shipton, M.P. Ward, T. Bourdillon, W.H. Murray, E. Hillary (NZ), H. Riddiford (NZ) and Dr Dutt (Ind).

9. D. Haston. Private note in author's possession.

10. E. Hillary, *High Adventure* (1955).

11. Negotiations continued for some time and the Swiss were eventually prepared to concede Everest to the British in the post-monsoon period, after their own pre-monsoon attempt, but the Nepalese authorities vetoed this.

12. The Swiss teams were, pre-monsoon: E. Wyss-Dunant (leader), G. Chevalley, R. Lambert; R. Dittert, L. Flory, R. Aubert, A. Roch, J.-J. Asper, E. Hofstetter, Tenzing Norgay (sirdar). Scientists Mme Lobsiger, A. Lombard and A. Zimmermann accompanied the team; post-monsoon: G. Chevalley (leader), R. Lambert, E. Reiss, J. Buzio, A. Spohel, G. Gross, N.G. Dyhrenfurth, Tenzing Norgay (sirdar).

13. R. Dittert, G. Chevalley and R. Lambert, *Forerunners to Everest* (1954).

14. Hillary and George Lowe actually crossed into Tibet and explored the pre-war route to Everest up the East Rongbuk Glacier.

15. E.E. Shipton, *That Untravelled World* (1969).

16. For a full discussion of the affair see my book *Everest* and the review of it by Peter Lloyd in *AJ* 87.

17. Letter from Lord Hunt to the author, August 23, 1978.

18. J. Morris, *Coronation Everest* (1958). James Morris later became Jan Morris, the travel writer. *The Times* as usual had exclusive rights and no other official correspondents accompanied the party – though there were several unofficial ones prowling around the Khumbu.

19. The team was: H.C.J. Hunt (leader), R.C. Evans (deputy leader), G. Band, T. Bourdillon, A. Gregory, E.P. Hillary (NZ), W.G. Lowe (NZ), C.W.F. Noyce, M.P. Ward, M. Westmacott, C.G. Wylie, Tenzing Norgay. Attached were L.G.C. Pugh (physiologist), T. Stobart (film cameraman), J. Morris (*Times* correspondent).

20. Base Camp was originally down the Khumbu Glacier at a lake called Gorak Shep and Camp I was much nearer the Icefall. Base was later moved to the Camp I site. Camp I therefore disappeared but the remaining camps were not re-numbered. Thus the first camp after Base was Camp II.

21. E. Hillary, *High Adventure* (1955).

22. In a closed-circuit oxygen system a chemical allows for some recycling of the oxygen. In the open system the gas is expended immediately Due to technical imperfections the closed system never found much favour with climbers.

23. R.C. Evans, letter to the author, January 15, 1979.

24. The 8000-metre peaks were climbed as follows:

1950 Annapurna (French)
1953 Everest (British), Nanga Parbat (Austro-German)
1954 K2 (Italian), Cho Oyu (Austrian)
1955 Kangchenjunga (British), Makalu (French)
1956 Lhotse (Swiss), Manaslu (Japanese), Gasherbrum II (Austrian)
1957 Broad Peak (Austrian)
1958 Gasherbrum (American)
1960 Dhaulagiri (Swiss)
1964 Shisha Pangma (Chinese)

Shisha Pangma would certainly have been climbed sooner had it been accessible to Western mountaineers.

25. A northern education authority did a survey in the 1960s which showed a post-school retention rate for active interest in soccer and cricket was two per cent as against twenty per cent for mountaineering.

26. By the French guide Marc Batard, solo and without oxygen in 1988. As a training climb he ascended Cho Oyu in eighteen hours!

Selected Bibliography

Since men and women first began climbing mountains they have felt the need to record their adventures in books, pamphlets and journals, so the literature is vast. What follows is a selection useful to anyone wishing to follow up the topics dealt with in the present volume.

To make it easier to follow, the list has been divided into areas. Where books, especially biographies, cover more than one area, they have been placed in what seems the most appropriate section for the subject.

JOURNALS

The cornerstone of any historical account of mountaineering in English is the *Alpine Journal*, first published as *Peaks, Passes and Glaciers* in 1859 and 1862, then continuously as the *AJ* from 1863. At the time of writing (1993) there are 97 volumes and it would be impractical to list here all the important articles, though some are given for their special interest.

Other journals and magazines are too numerous to list. Though they vary in quality, they all have something to contribute to the story. Some no longer exist and can be found only on the shelves of specialist libraries. Historians will find the journals of the various Alpine clubs fruitful along with the *Himalayan Journal*, *Appalachia*, *Sierra Club Bulletin*, *Iwa To Yuki*, *Alpinismus* and *Mountain*. British climbing at home and abroad is dealt with in detail in the various club publications, especially the journals of the Climbers' Club, Fell and Rock Club and Scottish Mountaineering Club.

GENERAL

Abraham G.D.
  Modern Mountaineering, London, 1933
Bueler W.M.
  Mountains of the World, Seattle, 1977
Clark R.W.
  Men, Myths and Mountains, London, 1976
Cleare J.
  Mountains, London, 1975

Collins Guide to Mountains and Mountaineering, London, 1979
Dent C.T. (Ed)
  Mountaineering, London, 1892
Franz H. and Mair K.
  Der Mensch am Berg, Munich, 1935
Hiebeler T.
  Lexicon der Alpen, Guterslohe, 1977
Huxley A.
  Standard Encyclopedia of the World's Mountains, London, 1962
Keenlyside F.
  Peaks and Pioneers, London, 1975
Kelsey M.R.
  Guide to the World's Mountains, Springville, 1984
Kurz M. (Ed)
  The Mountain World (10 vols), London, 1953–69
Mumm A.L.
  The Alpine Club Register (3 vols), London, 1923–28
Neate W.R.
  Mountaineering and its Literature, Milnthorpe, 1978
  Mountaineering Literature, Milnthorpe, 1986
Newby E.
  Great Ascents, Newton Abbot, 1977
Noyce C.W.F. and McMorrin I. (Eds)
  World Atlas of Mountaineering, London, 1969
Peters E. (Ed)
  Mountaineering – The Freedom of the Hills, Seattle, 1960
Pyatt E.
  The Guinness Book of Mountains, Mountaineering Facts and Feats, London, 1980
Scott D.K.
  Big Wall Climbing, London, 1974
Spencer S. (Ed)
  Mountaineering, London, 1934
Unsworth W.
  The Encyclopaedia of Mountaineering, London, 1992
Wilson C.
  Mountaineering, 1893
Young G.W.

Mountaincraft, London, 1920

Ziak K.
  Der Mensch und die Berge, Salzburg, 1956

THE ALPS

Manuscript sources, including guides' *Führerbücher*, are not included. There are extensive MS collections at the Alpine Club Library, London, the Bibliothèque Publique et Universitaire, Geneva, and Zentralbibliothek, Zurich, and smaller though important archives elsewhere. Much valuable historical information is contained in the numerous guidebooks to the Alpine regions published by the various Alpine clubs and others and constantly being added to and updated.

Agassiz L.
  Etudes sur les Glaciers, Neuchâtel, 1840

Ball J.
  Ball's Alpine Guides: Western Alps, London, 1863
  ditto: *Central Alps*, London, 1864
  ditto: *Eastern Alps*, London, 1868

de Beer G.R.
  Early Travellers in the Alps, London, 1930
  Travellers in Switzerland, London, 1949
  (with Brown T.G.) *The First Ascent of Mont Blanc*, London, 1957

Blaikie T.
  Diary of a Scotch Gardener at the French Court, London, 1932

Blanchet E.R.
  Hors des Chemins Battus, Paris, 1932

Blodig K.
  Die Viertausander der Alpen, Munich, 1923

le Blond Mrs A.
  Days In, Days Out, London, 1928

Boell J.
  High Heaven, London, 1947

Bourrit M.T.
  Description des glacieres, glaciers et ama de glace du Duche de Savoye, Geneva, 1773

Brockedon W.
  The Passes of the Alps, London, 1828
  Journals of Excursions in the Alps, London, 1833

Brown T.G.
  Brenva, London, 1944

Cassin R.
  Fifty Years of Alpinism, London, 1981

Charlet A.
  Vocation Alpine, Paris, 1949

Clark R.W.
  The Early Alpine Guides, London, 1949
  The Victorian Mountaineers, London, 1953

An Eccentric in the Alps, London, 1959
  The Day the Rope Broke, London, 1965

Cole Mrs H.W.
  A Lady's Tour Round Monte Rosa, London, 1859

Collie J.N.
  'The Ascent of the Dent du Requin', *AJ* 17, 1894

Collomb R.G.
  Mountains of the Alps, Reading, 1971

Conway W.M.
  The Alps from End to End, London, 1895
  The Alps, London, 1904
  'Centrists and Ex-centrists', *AJ* 15, 1890

Coolidge W.A.B.
  Josias Simler et Les Origines de L'Alpinisme jusqu'en 1600, Grenoble, 1904
  The Alps in Nature and History, London, 1908
  Alpine Studies, London, 1912
  'Early Ascents of the Dent Blanche', *AJ* 15, 1890
  'The Early Attempts on Monte Rosa from the Zermatt Side', *AJ* 10, 1890

Cunningham C.D. and Abney W. de W.
  The Pioneers of the Alps, London, 1887

Dent C.T.
  Above the Snowline, London, 1885

Desor E.
  Nouvelles Excursions dans les Alpes, Geneva, 1845

Eccles J.
  'Ascent of Mont Blanc by the Broglia and Fresnay Glaciers', *AJ* 8, 1878

Engel C.E.
  They Came to the Hills, London, 1952
  Mont Blanc, London, 1965
  Mountaineering in the Alps, London, 1971
  'Early Lady Climbers', *AJ* 54, 1943

Finch G.I.
  'The N. Face of the Dent d'Hérens', *AJ* 35, 1928

Fitzsimons R.
  The Baron of Piccadilly, London, 1967

Forbes J.D.
  Travels through the Alps of Savoy etc., Edinburgh, 1845

Frendo E.
  La Face Nord des Grandes Jorasses, Lausanne, 1946

Freshfield D.W.
  Across Country from Thonon to Trent, London, 1865
  Italian Alps, London, 1875
  The Life of Horace-Bénédict de Saussure, London, 1920
  Below the Snowline, London, 1923
  'Paccard v Balmat', *AJ* 19, 1898

Freshfield Mrs H.

Alpine Byways, London, 1861
A Summer Tour in the Grisons and Italian Valleys of the Bernina, London, 1862
George H.B.
The Oberland and its Glaciers, London, 1866
Gervasutti G.
Gervasutti's Climbs, London, 1957
Gilbert J. and Churchill G.C.
The Dolomite Mountains, London, 1864
Girdlestone A.G.
The High Alps without Guides, London, 1870
Gos C.
Tragédies Alpestres, Paris, 1940
Gribble F.
The Early Mountaineers, London, 1899
Güssfeldt P.
In den Hochalpen, Berlin, 1886
Der Montblanc, Berlin, 1894
Harrer H.
The White Spider, London, 1959
Hinchliff T.W.
Summer Months Among the Alps, London, 1857
Hudson C. and Kennedy E.S.
Where There's a Will There's a Way, London, 1856
Irving R.L.G.
'Five Years with Recruits', *AJ* 24, 1909
Javelle J.M.F.E.
Alpine Memories, London, 1899
King H.S.
'First Ascent of the Aiguille Blanche de Peuteret', *AJ* 12, 1885
Klucker C.
Adventures of an Alpine Guide, London, 1932
Kugy J.
Alpine Pilgrimage, London, 1934
de Lepiney J. and T.
Climbs on Mont Blanc, London, 1930
de Luc J.A. and Dentand P.G.
Relation de Differents Voyages dans les Alpes du Faucigny, Maestricht, 1776
Lunn A. (Ed)
The Englishman in the Alps, London, 1913
Magnone G.
West Face, London, 1955
Mathews C.E.
The Annals of Mont Blanc, London, 1898
Meade C.F.
Approach to the Hills, London, 1940
Milner C.D.
The Dolomites, London, 1951
Mont Blanc and the Aiguilles, London, 1955
Montagnier H.F.
'A Bibliography of the Ascents of Mont Blanc from 1786 to 1853', *AJ* 25, 1911 (with additions *AJ* 30, 1916)

'Dr Paccard's Lost Narrative', *AJ* 26, 1912
Moore A.W.
The Alps in 1864, Edinburgh, 1902
'The Ascent of Mont Blanc from the Glacier de la Brenva', *AJ* 2, 1866
Mummery A.F.
My Climbs in the Alps and Caucasus, London, 1895
Neruda Mrs N.
The Climbs of Norman Neruda, London, 1899
Pfann H.
Führerlose Gipfelfahrten, Munich, 1941
Pigeon A. and Abbot E.
Peaks and Passes, London, 1885
Pilley D.
Climbing Days, London, 1935
Purtscheller L.
Uber Fels and Firn, Munich, 1901
Rébuffat G.
Starlight and Storm, London, 1956
Rey G.
The Matterhorn, London, 1907
Peaks and Precipices, London, 1914
Roberts E.B.
Welzenbach's Climbs, Reading, 1981
Roch A.
On Rock and Ice, London, 1947
Climbs of My Youth, London, 1949
de Saussure H.B.
Voyages dans les Alpes, Neuchâtel, 1779–96
Schuster C.
Peaks and Pleasant Pastures, Oxford, 1911
Men, Women and Mountains, London, 1931
Mountaineering, Oxford, 1948
Postscript to Adventure, London, 1950
Smith A.R.
The Story of Mont Blanc, London, 1863
Smythe F.S.
Over Tyrolese Hills, London, 1936
Edward Whymper, London, 1940
Stephen L.
The Playground of Europe, London, 1871
Stevens E.H.
'Dr Paccard's Lost Narrative', *AJ* 41, 1929 (also *AJ* 42)
Strutt E.L.
'A Superiority Complex?', *AJ* 46, 1934
Studer G.
Uber Eis und Schnee, Bern, 1869
Thorington J.M.
Mont Blanc Sideshow, Philadelphia, 1934
A Survey of Early American Ascents in the Alps in the Nineteenth Century, New York, 1946
Tuckett F.F.
A Pioneer of the High Alps, London, 1920
Tyndall J.

Mountaineering in 1861, London, 1862
Hours of Exercise in the Alps, London, 1871

Underhill Mrs M.
Give Me the Hills, London, 1956

Unsworth W.
Matterhorn Man, London, 1965
Tiger in the Snow, London, 1967
Because it is there, London, 1968
North Face, London, 1969
Savage Snows, London, 1986

Welzenbach W.
Ascensions, Paris, 1940

Whymper E.
Scrambles amongst the Alps, London, 1871
Guide to Chamonix and the Range of Mont Blanc, London, 1896
Guide to Zermatt and the Matterhorn, London, 1897

Wills A.
Wanderings among the High Alps, London, 1856

Yeld G.
Scrambles in the Eastern Graians, London, 1900

Young G.W.
Mountain Craft, London, 1920
On High Hills, London, 1927
'Mountain Prophets', *AJ* 54, 1943

Zsigmondy E.
Die Gefahren der Alpen, Leipzig, 1885
Im Hochgebirge, Leipzig, 1889

HIMALAYA, KARAKORAM AND CENTRAL ASIA

An overall map and gazetteer of this area on a scale of 1:3M, *The Mountains of Central Asia*, is published by Macmillan for the Royal Geographical Society and Mount Everest Foundation (London, 1987).

Anderson J.R.L.
High Mountains and Cold Seas, London, 1980

Bauer P.
Himalayan Campaign, Oxford, 1937
Himalayan Quest, London, 1938
The Siege of Nanga Parbat, 1856–1953, London, 1956

Baume L.C.
Sivalaya, Reading, 1978

Bechtold F.
Nanga Parbat Adventure, London, 1935

Borchers P.
Berge und Gletscher im Pamir, Stuttgart, 1931

Braham T.
Himalayan Odyssey, London, 1974

Bruce C.G.
Twenty Years in the Himalaya, London, 1910
Kulu and Lahoul, London, 1914
The Assault on Mount Everest 1922, London, 1923
Himalayan Wanderer, London, 1934

Buhl H.
Nanga Parbat Pilgrimage, London, 1956

Burdsall R.L. and Emmons A.B.
Men Against the Clouds: the Conquest of Minya Konka, London, 1935

Burrard S.G.
Exploration in Tibet and Neighbouring Regions, Dehra Dun, 1915
(with Hayden H.H.) *A Sketch of the Geography and Geology of the Himalaya Mountains and Tibet*, Calcutta, 1907–8

Calvert H.
Smythe's Mountains, London, 1985

Cameron I.
Mountains of the Gods, London, 1984

Campbell R.
'The Brief Mountaineering Career of Aleister Crowley, The Great Beast 666', *Mountain* 11, 1970

Chapman F.S.
Memoirs of a Mountaineer, London, 1945

Collie J.N.
Climbing on the Himalaya and other Mountain Ranges, Edinburgh, 1902

Conway W.M.
Climbing and Exploration in the Karakoram Himalayas, London, 1894
'Some Reminiscences and Reflections of an Old Stager', *AJ* 31, 1918

Desio A.
Ascent of K2, London, 1955

Dittert R., Chevalley G. and Lambert R.
Forerunners to Everest, London, 1954

Dyhrenfurth G.O.
Damon Himalaya, Basle, 1935
To the Third Pole, London, 1955

Eckenstein O.J.L.
The Karakorams and Kashmir, London, 1896

Eggler A.
The Everest–Lhotse Adventure, London, 1957

Fellowes P.F.M. and Blacker L.V.S.
First Over Everest, London, 1933

de Filippi F.
Karakoram and Western Himalaya 1909, London, 1912
The Italian Expedition to the Himalaya, Karakoram and Eastern Turkistan, London, 1932

Finch G.I.
The Making of a Mountaineer (with Memoir by Scott Russell), Bristol, 1988

Freshfield D.W.
Round Kangchenjunga, London, 1903

(with Boss E.) 'Notes on the Himalaya and Himalayan Survey', *AJ* 12, 1886

Graham W.W.
'Travel and Ascents in the Himalaya', *AJ* 12, 1886

Guillarmod J.J.
Six Mois dans l'Himalaya, le Karakorum et l'Hindu Kush, Neuchâtel, 1903?

Herzog M.
Annapurna, London, 1952

Hillary E.
High Adventure, London, 1955

Holzel T. and Salkeld A.
The Mystery of Mallory and Irvine, London, 1986

Houston C. and Bates R.
K2, The Savage Mountain, London, 1955

Howard-Bury C.K.
Mount Everest: The Reconnaissance 1921, London, 1922

Hunt H.J.C.
The Ascent of Everest, London, 1953

Ivanov-Mumjiev G.
Conquering the Celestial Mountains, Moscow, 1958

Kaufman A.J. and Putnam W.
K2 – The 1939 Tragedy, London, 1992

Knight E.F.
Where Three Empires Meet, London, 1893

Kurz M.
Chronique Himalayenne, 1940–1955, Zurich, 1959

Longstaff T.
This My Voyage, London, 1949
'Six Months Wandering in the Himalaya', *AJ* 23, 1907

Markham C.R.
A Memoir on the Indian Survey, London, 1871

Mason K.
Abode of Snow, London, 1955
'Johnson's "Suppressed Ascent" of E61', *AJ* 34, 1923

Meade C.F.
Approach to the Hills, London, 1940
'The Schlagintweits and Abi Gamin', *AJ* 33, 1921

Merzbacher G.
The Central Tian-Shan Mountains, London, 1905

Mullikin M.A. and Hotchkis A.M.
The Nine Sacred Mountains of China, Hong Kong, 1973

Mumm A.L.
Five Months in the Himalaya, London, 1909

Neate J.
High Asia, London, 1989

Neve A.
Thirty Years in Kashmir, London, 1913

Neve E.

Beyond the Pir Panjal, London, 1914

Noel J.B.L.
Through Tibet to Everest, London, 1927

Norton E.F.
The Fight for Everest 1924, London, 1925

Noyce C.W.F.
Mountains and Men, London, 1947
South Col, London, 1954

Phillimore R.H.
Historical Records of the Survey of India (5 vols), Dehra Dun, 1945–62

Pierre B.
A Mountain Called Nun Kun, London, 1955

Pye D.
George Leigh Mallory, London, 1927

Rickers W.R.
Alai! Alai!, Leipzig, 1930

Robertson D.
George Mallory, London, 1969

Romm M.
The Ascent of Mount Stalin, London, 1936

Rowell G.
In the Throne Room of the Mountain Gods, London, 1977
Mountains of the Middle Kingdom, San Francisco, 1983

Ruttledge H.
Everest 1933, London, 1934
Everest: The Unfinished Adventure, London, 1937

von Schlagintweit H.
Reisen in Indien und Hochaisen (4 vols), Jena, 1869–80

Seaver G.
Francis Younghusband, Explorer and Mystic, London, 1952

Shipton E.E.
Nanda Devi, London, 1936
Blank on the Map, London, 1938
Upon That Mountain, London, 1943
Mountains of Tartary, London, 1951
The Mount Everest Reconnaissance Expedition, 1951, London, 1952
That Untravelled World, London, 1969

Smythe F.S.
The Kangchenjunga Adventure, London, 1932
Kamet Conquered, London, 1932
Camp Six, London, 1937
The Valley of Flowers, London, 1938
The Adventures of a Mountaineer, London, 1940

Tilman H.W.
The Ascent of Nanda Devi, Cambridge, 1937
When Men and Mountains Meet, Cambridge, 1946
Mount Everest 1938, Cambridge, 1948
Two Mountains and a River, Cambridge, 1948
China to Chitral, Cambridge, 1951

Nepal Himalaya, Cambridge, 1952
Turner S.
   My Climbing Adventures in Four Continents,
   London, 1911
Unsworth W.
   Everest, Oxford, 1989
Visser-Hooft Mrs J.
   Among the Kara-Korum Glaciers in 1925, London,
   1926
   (with P.C. Visser) *Karakorum* (2 vols), Leipzig,
   1935; Leiden, 1938
Waddell L.A.
   Among the Himalayas, London, 1899
Waller D.
   The Pundits, Lexington, 1990
Waller J.
   The Everlasting Hills, London, 1939
Wiessner F.
   'The K2 Expedition of 1939', *Appalachia XXXI*,
   1956/7
Workman W.H. and Mrs F.B.
   In the Ice World of the Himalaya, London, 1900
   Ice Bound Heights of the Mustagh, London, 1908
   Peaks and Glaciers of Nun Kun, London, 1909
   The Call of the Snowy Hispar, London, 1910
   *Two Summers in the Ice-Wilds of Eastern Karako-
   ram*, London, 1917
Younghusband F.E.
   The Heart of a Continent, London, 1896

THE AMERICAS

Baillie-Grohman W.A.
   Camps in the Rockies, New York, 1882
Bird Mrs I.L.
   A Lady's Life in the Rocky Mountains, London,
   1879
Brooks A.H.
   Mountain Exploration in Alaska, New York, 1914
Browne B.
   The Conquest of Mount McKinley, London, 1913
Bueler W.M.
   Roof of the Rockies, Evergreen, 1986
Chapin F.H.
   Mountaineering in Colorado, Boston, 1889
Chase J.S.
   Yosemite Trails, London, 1912
Coleman A.P.
   The Canadian Rockies, New and Old Trails,
   London, 1911
Conway W.M.
   The Bolivian Andes, London, 1901
de Filippi F.
   The Ascent of Mount St Elias, Alaska, London,
   1900

Fisher M.
   Expedition Yukon, Nelson, 1972
FitzGerald E.A.
   The Highest Andes, London, 1899
Garden J.F.
   The Bugaboos: An Alpine History, Revelstoke,
   1987
Hart J.L.J.
   *Fourteen Thousand Feet: A History of the Naming
   and Early Ascents of the High Colorado Peaks*,
   Denver, 1931
Hutchings J.M.
   In the Heart of the Sierras, Oakland, 1886
Jones C.
   Climbing in North America, Los Angeles, 1976
Kain C.
   Where the Clouds Can Go, New York, 1935
King C.
   Mountaineering in the Sierra Nevada, New York,
   1872
Meany E.S.
   Mount Rainier: A Record of Exploration, New
   York, 1916
Moore T.
   Mount McKinley: The Pioneer Climbs, College,
   1967
Muir J.
   The Mountains of California, New York, 1894
   Steep Trails, Boston, 1918
   The Yosemite, New York, 1912
Munday D.
   The Unknown Mountain, London, 1948
Neate J.
   Mountaineering in the Andes, London, 1987
Palmer H.
   Mountaineering and Exploration in the Selkirks,
   London, 1914
Peck Miss A.
   High Mountain Climbing in Peru and Bolivia,
   London, 1912
Powell J.W.
   Canyons of the Colorado, New York, 1895
Putnam W.L.
   The Great Glacier and its House, New York, 1982
Roper S. and Steck A.
   Fifty Classic Climbs in North America, London,
   1979
Shipton E.E.
   Land of Tempest, London, 1963
Stuck H.
   The Ascent of Denali, New York, 1914
Stutfield H.E.M. and Collie J.N.
   Climbs and Explorations in the Canadian Rockies,
   London, 1903
Tilman H.W.
   'Mischief' in Patagonia, Cambridge, 1957

Washburn B.
  A Tourist's Guide to Mount McKinley, Anchorage, 1971
  (with D. Roberts) *The Conquest of Denali*, New York, 1991
Wheeler A.O.
  The Selkirk Range, Ottawa, 1905
Whymper E.
  Travels amongst the Great Andes of the Equator, London, 1892
Wood R.L.
  Men, Mules and Mountains, Seattle, 1976

EUROPE, AFRICA AND THE NEAR EAST
excluding the Alps and UK
Busk D.
  The Fountain of the Sun, London, 1957
de Filippi F.
  Ruwenzori, London, 1908
Firsoff V.A.
  The Tatra Mountains, London, 1942
Freshfield D.W.
  Travels in the Central Caucasus and Bashan, London, 1869
  Exploration of the Caucasus (2 vols), London, 1896
Grove F.C.
  The Frosty Caucasus, London, 1875
Henrikson V.
  Jotunheimen, Oslo, 1977
Hunt J. and Brasher C.
  The Red Snows, London, 1960
Jackson M.
  The Turkish Time Machine, London, 1966
Jenkins D. (Ed)
  Chronicles of John R. Jenkins, Wittering, 1987
Marlowe C.
  The Harz Mountains, London, 1930
Packe C.
  A Guide to the Pyrenees, London, 1862
Pearse R.O.
  Barrier of Spears, Capetown, 1973
Reynolds K.
  Mountains of the Pyrenees, Milnthorpe, 1982
Shatayev V.
  Degrees of Difficulty, Seattle, 1987
Slingsby W.C.
  Norway, the Northern Playground, London, 1904
Thorarinsson S.
  Glacier, Reykjavik, 1975
Tilman H.W.
  Snow on the Equator, London, 1937
Tuzel O.
  Walks and Climbs in the Ala Dag, Milnthorpe, 1993

Weir T.
  Camps and Climbs in Arctic Norway, London, 1953

NEW ZEALAND AND THE PACIFIC

Chichibu H.I.H. Prince
  'Eight Days in the Japanese Alps', *AJ* 41, 1929
du Faur F.
  The Conquest of Mount Cook and other Climbs, London, 1915
FitzGerald E.A.
  Climbs in the New Zealand Alps, London, 1896
Graham P.
  Peter Graham: Mountain Guide, London, 1965
Green W.S.
  The High Alps of New Zealand, London, 1883
Harper A.P.
  Pioneer Work in the Alps of New Zealand, London, 1896
  Memories of Mountains and Men, Christchurch, 1946
Mannering G.E.
  With Axe and Rope in the New Zealand Alps, London, 1891
Pascoe J.D.
  Unclimbed New Zealand, London, 1939
  Great Days in New Zealand Mountaineering, London, 1958
Powell P.S.
  Men Aspiring, Wellington, 1967
Turner S.
  The Conquest of the New Zealand Alps, London, 1922
Walton W.H.M.
  Scrambles in Japan and Formosa, London, 1934
Weston W.W.
  Mountaineering and Exploration in the Japanese Alps, London, 1896
  The Playground of the Far East, London, 1918
Wilson J.J.
  Aorangi: the Story of Mount Cook, Christchurch, 1968
Wollaston A.F.R.
  Letters and Diaries of A.F.R. Wollaston, Cambridge, 1933

GREAT BRITAIN

Abraham A.P.
  Rock Climbing in Skye, London, 1908
Abraham G.D.
  Rock Climbing in North Wales, Keswick, 1906
  British Mountain Climbs, London, 1909

Borthwick A.
  Always a Little Further, London, 1939
Carr H.R.C. and Lister G.A.
  The Mountains of Snowdonia, London, 1925
Clark R.W. and Pyatt E.C.
  Mountaineering in Britain, London, 1957
Hankinson A.
  The First Tigers, London, 1972
  Camera on the Crags, London, 1975
  The Mountain Men, London, 1977
Haskett Smith W.P.
  Climbing in the British Isles, London, 1894
Jones O.G.
  Rock Climbing in the English Lake District,
    London, 1897
Jones T. and Milburn G.
  Cumbrian Rock, Glossop, 1988
Kirkus C.F.

  Let's Go Climbing, London, 1941
Murray W.H.
  Mountaineering in Scotland, London, 1947
  Undiscovered Scotland, London, 1951
Peascod W.
  Journey After Dawn, Milnthorpe, 1985
Perrin J.
  Menlove, London, 1985
Pyatt E.C. and Noyce W.
  British Crags and Climbers, London, 1952
Sansom G.S.
  Climbing at Wasdale Before the First World War,
    Castle Cary, 1982
Speaker G.R. (Ed)
  Fell and Lake, Manchester, 1937
Young G.W., Sutton G. and Noyce W.
  Snowdon Biography, London, 1957

Index

Aas, Monrad 245
Abalakov, Eugene 305, 329
Abalakov, Vitali 305
Abbot, Phillip Stanley 203–4, 205
Abbühl, Arnold 48
Abi Gamin 191, 230, 325, 328
Abraham, Ashley 156, 161–2, 307
   British Mountain Climbs 156, 161
   Rock-climbing in Skye 161
   Swiss Mountain Climbs 161
Abraham, George 156, 160, 161–2, 307
   Rock-climbing in North Wales 161
Abruzzi, Prince Luigi Amedeo, Duke of
   the 171, 175, 195, 222–3, 247,
   252–5, 352
accidents 117–18, 164–5
Aconcagua 24, 181, 191, 195–6, 197, 199,
   200
Adula Alps 38, 46
Aemmer, R. 260
Agassiz, Louis 53, 56
Aiguille Blanche de Peuterey 99, 103,
   109, 132, 133, 305
Aiguille de Bionnassay 119, 273
Aiguille de Goûter 29, 30, 31
Aiguille du Dru 26, 107, 109, 110–12,
   130, 271, 290, 358, 370
Aiguille du Géant 99, 107, 112–16, 131,
   241
Aiguille du Jardin 131
Aiguille du Midi 42
Aiguille du Plan 130, 138, 273
   North Face 102, 262, 271
Aiguille Noire de Peuterey 107–8, 257,
   278, 305
Aiguille Purtscheller 125
Aiguille Vert 95–6, 110, 128
Aiguilles du Diable 99, 257
Aila, Sherpa 359
Ailefroide 97
Alaska 221–8, 259, 330

Aletschhorn 70
Alexander, James 314
Allain, Pierre 290, 292, 351, 370
Allen, Samuel 203
Allwein, Eugen 270, 278, 333, 335, 336,
   338
Almer, Christian 72–3, 75, 76, 82, 91, 97,
   99, 293
Almer, Ulrich 97, 99, 100, 101, 185, 186
Alpine Club 60, 68–70, 140
   first meeting 68
   Alpine Journal 69
   controversies 94–5
   and accidents 118
   and Mummery 127, 128
   and rock climbing 157
   geographical climbers 170
   and Royal Geographical Society 246,
   318
Alpine distress signal 118
Alpine passes 46
Alpinism
   Silver Age 117
   Golden Age 66–75
   end of Golden Age (1865) 231
Alps
   Hannibal's crossing 21
   1574 account of 22–3
   early ascents 24
   opened up 37–52
   the British and 53–65
   moral dilmma of 271
Alps, Eastern 102, 131
   map 11
altitude 25, 318
altitude sickness 192, 194, 233, 321
Amatter, Fritz 256, 269
American Alpine Club 202, 220, 352
American climbers and Himalaya 330
American climbing 1920s–30s 313–17
Americas, climbs in 191–209

Amery, L.S. 243
Amne Machen 330
Ampferer, Otto 107
Amstutz, Walter 278
Amundsen, Roald 225
Ancohuma 197
Anderegg, Jakob 76–7, 78, 95, 96
Anderegg, Melchior 73, 74, 75, 76–7,
   78
Andermatten, Franz 110, 129
Anderson, George G. 218–19
Anderson, J. Stafford 110–1
Anderson, Peter 225–6
Andes 21, 192–200
   map 193
Andrews, A.W. 160–1
Ang Nyima, Sherpa 367
Ang Temba, Sherpa 367
Ang Tharkay, Sherpa 358, 359
Ang Tsering, Sherpa 345, 346, 355, 356
Ang Tsering III, Sherpa 359
Angerer, Hermann 277
Angerer, Willi 296–8
d'Angeville, Henriette 119
Annapurna
   French first ascent 357–9
Antisana 194
Anullu, Sherpa 367
Appalachian Mountain Club 202, 203,
   220
Archibald, Clara 211
Ardusa, Abraham 262
Aristov, Oleg 329
Arnesen, L. 147
Arrow Peak 218
Aschenbrenner, Paul 290, 368–9
Aschenbrenner, Peter 290, 339, 340, 342,
   343, 344, 346
Aten, Arthur M. 227
Atkinson, John 154
Aubert, René 363, 364
Auckenthaler, Matthias 276
Aufdenblatten, Alfred 275
Aufschnaiter, Peter 337, 338
Austrian Alpine Club 69, 102, 276
Ayres, Fred 260

Bailey, F.M. 325
Baines, A.C. 252

Baker, E.A., *Moors, Crags and Caves of the
   High Peak* 155–6
Baker, G.P. 100, 205
Balcombe, Fred 311
Ball, John 106, 144, 151
   Alpine Guide 143
Balmat, Auguste 61, 62, 63, 64, 74
Balmat, Jacques 24, 27, 33, 34–5, 36
Balmat, Pierre 32, 33
Baltoro Glacier 238
Baltoro Kangri 238
Band, George 366
Bandelier, Adolph 200
Barker, Mabel 309
Barlow, G. 160, 161
Barrau, Pierre 142
Barrill, Ed 223, 224
Barrington, A.J. 176
Barrington, Charles 293–4
Barrington, R.M. 201
Barrow, C.L. 182
Barry, Dick 312
Barth, Hans 106
Barth, Hermann von 104
Barton, Rev. C.E. 240
Barton, Claude 160
Barton, Guy 160
Bates, R.H. 352
Bauer, Paul 333, 334, 335–8, 339, 346
Baumgartner, C.A.O. 154
Bazar-Juzi 185
Bazillac, Jean 145
Beaman, E.O. 217
Beaumont, R.L. 304
Bechtold, Fritz 229, 340, 342–3, 344
Beck, Joseph 50
Beetham, Bentley 322
Begole, Charley 215
Beigel, E. 337
belaying 370
Belin, Fernand 288
Bell, Gertrude 118, 263–9
Bell, J.H.B. 273, 308
Ben Nevis 158
Ben Nuis Chimney, Arran 156
Bennen, J.J. 74, 81
Béranger, J.P. 35
Berger, Karl 107
Bering, Vitus 221

Bernard, Willy 342
Bernardzikiewicz 328
Bernese Alps 46–52
  Oberland guides 71
  map 11
Bertheau, Thérèse 149
Betaieff, Beslau 187
Bettega, L. 131
Bhotia people 319, 326
Biafo Glacier 238, 239
Biancograt (Piz Bernina) 99, 103, 122,
  133, 195
Bich, J.B. 107, 119, 262
Biener, Franz 82
Bierstadt, Albert 217
Bietschhorn 70, 123
Bingley, William 153
Bionnassay Glacier 31, 32–3
Birkbeck, John 70
Birkbeck, John, jr 185
Birkett, R.J. (Jim) 308, 312
Birnie, E.St John 326, 348, 349
Bitihorn 42
Bjermeland, Hans 147
Black Wall 311
Blaikie, Thomas 29–30
Blaitière North-West Ridge 138, 257
Blakison, Lieutenant 200
Blanchet, E.R. 271, 284
Blodig, Karl 131, 135
Boccalatte G.G. 257
Bodmer, Samuel 46
Boeck, Christian Peter Bianco 146
Bohm, A. von 121, 122
Bohr, Gottfried 147
Bohren, Christian 207
Bohren, Peter 61, 63, 74, 293
Boileau de Castelnau, Henri 98–9
Bolivia 196–7, 333, 334
Bonacossa, Count Aldo 132
Bonington, Chris 372
Bonneville, Captain Benjamin 211
boots now used 370
Borchers, P. 333
Borrow, George, *Wild Wales* 152
Borthwick, Alastair 306
Bosniachi, Z. 151
Boss, Emil 176, 179, 232–6
Bossonay, Joseph 206

Bossons Glacier 29
Botcher, H. 334
Botterill, Fred 156, 163–4, 165
Boulaz, Loulou 288, 290
Bourdillon, Tom 358, 361, 367
Bourrit, Isaac 32
Bourrit, Marc Théodore 27, 28, 30, 31–2,
  35, 36
Boussingault, J. 191
Bousted, Hugh (Hugo) 348, 349
Bower, George 273
Bowfell Buttress 163
Bowring, F.H. 155
Boyesen, Pastor Ulrik 146
Bramani, Vitale 370
Brankowsky, Leo 300–1
Brantschen, Hans 257
Brawand, S. 256
Brehm, Hans 287
Breithorn 273, 279
Brenner, J. 338
Brendel, K. 257
Brenta group 106
Brévent 30
Brevoort, Meta 73, 97
Brewer, William 215
Bridge, Alf 307
Bristow, Lily 120, 121, 129, 130
Britain
  as mountain country 152–69
British
  and the Alps 53–65
  and Everest 347–50, 359–62, 365–8
  climbing in 1930s 306–13
British Mountaineering Council 134
Broad Peak 351
Broadrick, R.W. 164–5
Brocherel, Alexis 243–4, 245, 254
Brocherel, Henri 135, 136–7, 243–4, 245,
  254
Brocherel, Joseph 134, 174
Brocklebank, T.A. 348, 350
Broome, Edward 100
Brown, Graham 273–4
Brown, H.E. 161
Brown, Joe 366
Browne, Belmore 223, 224, 226, 227
Bruce, Charles 238, 240, 244, 245, 247–8,
  249, 332, 347

Bruce, Charles – *cont'd.*
　Everest expeditions leader 318–19, 320, 321, 322
Bruce, J.G. 321, 322
Bruderlin, A. 269
Brulle, Henri 145, 146
Bryant, L.V. 351
Bryce, James 150, 170
Buachaille Etive Mor 163
Buckle, H.B. 161
Budworth, Capt. Joseph 153
Buet, Le 25, 192
Buhl, Hermann 104, 368–9
Bullock, Guy 319, 320
Bumiller, Hans 100
Bumillergrat 100
Burdsall, Richard 330, 331, 352
Burgener, Alexander 100, 103, 109, 110, 111–12, 113, 122, 126–7, 128–9, 185, 195, 262
Burgener, Franz 109
Burton, Sir Richard 141

California 216, 314
Cameroon Peak 141
Campbell, Mrs and Miss 54
Canada, mountains in 200–9, 315–16
　map 15
Canadian Alpine Club 202
Canadian Rockies 159–60
Carbonnières, L.-F. Ramond de 42–4, 142
Carihuairazo 194
Carneddau 163
Carpe, Allen 330
Carr, Ellis 121, 129, 130
Carr, Herbert 307–8
Carrel, Jean-Antoine 81–2, 82–4, 86, 87–8, 114, 120, 192, 194
Carrel, Louis 192, 194
Carrier, Joseph 30, 33
Carson, Kit 211
Cascade Range 212
Cassin, Riccardo 270, 290–2
Castle Rock of Triermain 312
Caucasus 125, 126, 129, 183–90, 304, 333
　map 184
Cayambe 191, 194
Cazaux, Henri 142
Chabod, R. 288, 290

Chamonix 25, 26, 33, 34, 36, 58, 59, 107, 140
　guides 71
Chancellor Peak 207
Changabang (Mount Monal) 234, 236, 325
Changtse 320
Chanler, Astor 174
Chapman, F. Spencer 331–2
Charlet, Armand 257, 287, 288, 290
Charlet-Straton, J.E. 112, 113, 119, 120
Charmoz 107, 127, 130
　North Face 140, 280, 281–3, 284
Chaukhamba I 328
Chettan, Sherpa 337
Chevalley, G. 363, 364
Chile 191, 333
Chimborazo 191, 192, 194
China, sacred mountains 21
Cho Oyu 362, 364–5
chockstone, artificial 370
Chockstone Chimney, Tetons 258
Chogo Lungma Glacier 239–40
Chogolisa (Bride Peak) 254
Chomiomo 232, 246
Chomolhari 331
Chouinard, Yvon 370, 371
Chouinard and Frost pitons 315
Cima Grande 103, 290
Cima Piccola di Lavaredo 106
Cima Tosa 106
Cima Trafoi 93
Citlaltepetl (Orizaba) 198
Clark, R.W. 256
Clarke, John M. 181, 182, 183
Clement, Abbé 38
Climbers' Club 157, 165
Climbing
　and danger 94–5, 131
　first guidebooks 134
　guideless 71, 75, 117, 122–3
　Preuss's Six Theorems 132
　route is the essence 90
　solo 104, 118, 122–3
Clogwyn Du'r Arddu 153, 307–8, 309–10, 311
　Eastern Terrace 153
Clogwyn y Geifr 310, 311
Clough, Ian 369

Club Alpin Français (CAF) 144
Clubs, Alpine 68–70
Cobbler, the 306–7
Cockin, John Garforth 185–6, 187
Col d'Hérens 56
Col de la Tour Noire 73
Col de Peuterey 109, 133
Col des Drus 110
Col du Géant 112
Col du Lion 102, 107
Col Passet 144
Coleman, Arthur 205
Coleman, Edmund Thomas 213–14
Coleridge, Samuel Taylor 153
Collie, (John) Norman 121, 129, 130,
        155, 158–9, 236, 246
    and North America 202, 205–6, 207,
        208, 209
    and Himalaya 247–8, 249, 250–1
Collier, Joseph 158, 164
Colorado 211–12, 215–16, 218, 220,
        313–14
Columbian Icefield 205
Comici, Emilio 290
Concordia 252
Condamine, Charles Marie de la 191
Coniston Old Man 153
Conrad, Emil 196
Conrad, Robert 196
Conway, (William) Martin (Lord
        Conway) 95, 109, 150, 171, 175, 195,
        236, 238, 241, 351
    quoted 90–1
    guidebooks to Alps 156, 237
    and Himalaya 237–9
    and South America 196, 238
    Spitsbergen 238
Cook, Dr Frederick 223–5, 226
    To the Top of the Continent 224
Cook, Captain James 221, 223
Cook, Mount (Ao-Rangi) 176, 177–81,
        182–3
Coolidge, W.A.B. 41, 72, 74, 89, 97, 98,
        125
Corazon 191, 194
Cordier, Henri 95, 96, 98
Cordillera Real 333
Cornwall cliffs 160–1
Coroboef, Lt-Col. 142

Corsica 151
Cortez, Hernando 24
Cotochachi 194
Cotopaxi 191, 194
Couloir de Gaube 145
Courtauld, S.L. 134
Les Courtes 95
Couteran, Jean-Nicolas 28
Couttet, Jean Marie 30, 31
Couttet, Marie 31, 33
Couzy, Jean 359
Craig yr Ysfa 309, 310
crampons 22–3, 113, 118, 150, 239, 371
Cranmer, Chappel 353
Cratcliffe 307
Crawford, Charles 331
Crawford, Colin 322, 348, 350
Creag Dhu Mountaineering Club 307
Critchley, Ivy 309
Cromford, Black Rocks 307
Cromwell, O. Eaton 353
Crowley, Aleister (666) 240, 241–2
Croz, J.B. 66, 67, 68, 82
Croz, Michel 84, 85, 86, 87, 89
Crozzon di Brenta 122
Crystal Peak 238
Cuidet, François 31, 32
Cuillin Hills, Skye 158, 163
Cunningham, C.D. 72
Cunningham, John 371
Cupelin, Auguste 115
Curzon, George Nathaniel 244
Cwm Idwal 162, 310–11
Cwm Silyn 309

Da Namgyal, Sherpa 367
Dachstein 131
Dakshi, Sherpa 345
danger 94–5, 131, 154
Dangl, Peter 94
Daniell, E.H. 161
Dauphiné Alps 96–9
Davidson, Sir William 126, 127
Davies, J.Ll. 70
Dawa Thondup, Sherpa 346
De Agostini, Fr Alberto 197–8
Déchy, Maurice de 93–4, 185, 187, 231–2
Dècle, Lionel 232
Deer Bield Buttress and Crack 312

Dehra Dun 325
Delago, Hermann 106
Delfico, Orazio 42
Denali *see* Mount McKinley
Denman, Earl 363
Densmore, Frank 223
Dent, Clinton Thomas 102, 109, 117,
    118, 185, 186, 187
    and the Drus 110–12
Dent Blanche 70, 100–1, 119, 122, 257
Dent d'Hérens 70, 270–1, 277–8
Dent du Requin 130, 159
Dents du Midi 38
Desor, Edouard 53
Davies, Lucien 257, 276
Devil's Tower, Wyoming 219–20, 315
Dévouassoud, François 103, 185
Dhaulagiri 229, 357, 358, 369
Dibona, Angelo 131
Dickey, W.A. 223
Dimai family 106
Dimai, Angelo 290
Dimai, Antonio 107, 131
Dimai, Joseph 290
Dinas Mot 309
Distel, L. 190
Dittert, René 360, 363
Dixon, Prof. H.B. 205
Dixon, M.J. 181
Dolomites 103, 105–7, 122
    guides 106
    map 14
Dôme du Goûter 33, 119
Dongus-Orun 186
Donkin, W.F. 185, 186–7
Doughty, A.H. 161
Douglas, David 200
Douglas, Lord Francis 84, 86–7, 89
Douglas, W. 157
Dove Crag 311
Dow Crag 311
Drexel, Alfred, 279, 342, 343
Les Droites 96
Drus 26, 107, 109, 110–12, 130, 271, 290,
    358, 370
Dryer, Thomas 212–13
Dufourspitze 70
Duhamel, Henri 98
Duke of Edinburgh's Award Scheme 369–70

Dülfer, Hans 276, 278
Dumas, Alexandre 36
Dunagiri 233, 328
Dundas, Captain 174
Dupont 290
Durrance, Jack 258, 313, 353–4, 355–6
Dyhrenfurth, Oscar 337, 338, 339, 342,
    351
Dykh-tau 185, 305

Earle, L.M. 183
Eastern Alps 102, 131
    map 11
Eberstein, Leutnant von 171
Eccles, James 98, 100, 128
    in America 217, 218
Echevarria, Evelio 200
Eckenstein, Oscar 118, 160, 238, 240,
    242
Ecrins 70, 97
Ecuador 191–2
Edwards, J. Menlove 309, 310–11
Egypt, pyramids 21
Eiger 54, 70, 100, 133, 271, 272, 294
    diagram 295
    Eigerwand 272, 292, 294–300, 358
    Eigerwand first ascent 300–3
    Lauper Route 271–2, 299
    Mittelegi (North-East) Ridge 100, 133,
        256, 272, 304
Eiskogele 278
El Capitan 371
Elbrus 183–5, 305
Elferkogel 106
Ellingwood, Albert 313–14
Elliott, Frank 307
Ellis, J.C.W. 66
Emanuel, General 184
Emmons, Arthur 330–1
Emmons, S.F. 214
Engelhörner peaks 263
Engineer's Slabs 311
Eotvos, Ilona and Rolanda 131
Ertl, Hans 351
Escobar, A.M. 191
Esposito, L. 291–2
Estats 142
ethics of mountaineering 371
Evans, Charles 367

Everest 170, 229, 230
  abortive 1907 attempt 244
  approach routes 320
  Alpine Club/Royal Geographical
    Society talks 318–19
  British 1921 reconnaissance 319–20
  British 1922 expedition 320–2
  British 1924 expedition 322–5
  British 1933 expedition 347–51
  British 1951 reconnaissance 360–2
  British 1953 first ascent 365–8
  Icefall 360, 366
  map 361
  North Col 320
  Russians' 1982 South-West Face route
    305
  South Col 363–4
  South Summit 364
  South-West Face 305, 372
  Swiss 1952 expedition 362–4, 367
  Western Cwm 360–1, 362, 363
Ewigschneehorn 56
expansion bolts 316, 317
Exum, Glenn 258

Falkenaebbe 146
Fankhauser, Pert 346
Farrar, Percy (J.P.) 246, 318, 319
Fascism *see* Nazism
du Faur, Freda 183
Fay, Charles 202, 203–5, 207
Feldkopf 122
Fendt, W. 338
Feuz family (guides) 260
Ficker, Mr and Miss 188, 189
Field, A.E. 160
Fiescherhorn 278–9
Fiescherwand 279
de Filippi, F. 222–3, 252, 253, 255
de Filippi, G. 113
Finch, George 270–1, 318, 319, 320, 321,
    322, 338, 350
  The Making of a Mountaineer 270
Finch, Max 318
Finsteraarhorn 48–9, 53, 66–8, 71
  Grey Tower 269
  North-East Face 263–9
Firndreieck 122
Fischer, Andreas 187

Fischer, Johann 186
Fitzgerald, Edward A. 181, 182, 195–6,
    197
Flecker, James Elroy, quoted 243
Flory, L. 363, 364
Flotten, S. 147
Folliguet, F. 112
Fontaine, E. 131
footpath marking 147
Forbes, Prof. James David 53, 55–6, 65,
    154
  Travel Through the Alps 56–7, 60
Forked Peak 236
Forster, Guy 270
Foster, William 261
Fourastrier, Maurice 289
Fox, Harry 186–7
Fox, J.H. 103
Fraissl, Rudi 300–1
de Franqueville, Count Albert 142
Frémont, John Charles 211–12,
    217
Frémont Peak 211
French climbers, postwar 358–9
Frendo, Edouard 289, 357
Freshfield, D.W. 94, 95, 103, 113, 141,
    157, 175, 185, 186, 236, 242–3, 246,
    318, 337
Frisak, H. 151
Frissell, L.F. 203
Fritz, F. 334
Fryxell, Fritiof 257–8
Fuchs, P. 103
Führer, Heinrich 259, 260, 263
Führer, Ulrich 263–9
Fuller, Miss 214–15
Fünffingerspitze 106
Fussstein 104, 121
Fyfe, Tom 181, 182
Fynn, Val 260, 269

Gabari, Carlo 107
Galdhopiggen 146, 147
Gannett Peak 211
Gardiner, Frederick 185
Garrett, A.E.W. 165
Garhwal 243, 245, 325, 328
Garwood, E.J. 236
Gasherbrum I 331, 351, 352, 358

Gasherbrum II 351
Gaspard (guide) 309
Gaspard, Pierre I and II 98–9
Gaylay, Sherpa 345, 347
Gebhard, Dr M. 45, 46
Geneva 37
Geneva School 25–36
Gentinetta, Augustin 127
George, Rev. H.B. 73, 94
Georges, Antoine 100
Georges, Joseph 100, 257
Gerard brothers 229–30
Gerard, Dr J.G. 230
Gerlach 151
German Alpine Club 102, 276
German and Austrian Alpine Club
    (DOAV) 333
German climbers in the Alps 103–4, 131
    see also Munich School
German Himalaya Foundation (DHS)
    346
Germany and Himalaya 333–47
Gertsch, Christian 97
Gervasutti, Giusto 257, 288, 290
Gestola 185
Getye, A. 329
Gibson, H.B. 166, 167–8
Gibson, J.H. 157
Giordani, Pietro 49
Giordano, Felice 82, 83, 84, 86
Girdlestone, Rev. A.G. 75
Gjende 147
glaciers 24, 56
Gladstone, W.E. 89
Glasgow rock climbers 306–7
Glatthard, Arnold 298
Glazek, K. 269
Glencoe 158, 306
Gletscherhorn 279
Glittertind 147
Glockner region, Austrian Alps 278
Glockturm 103
Glyder Fach 309
Gnifetti, Giovanni 49
Godwin-Austen Glacier 238
Goman Singh 247, 249, 251
Goodfellow, Basil 365
Gorbunov, N.P. 329
Gosainthan (Shisha Pangma) 351, 369

Gosaukamm area 132
Gosse, Henri-Albert 29
Gosse, Philip 196
Gotch 290
Gottner, Adolf 346
gradings of climbs 278
Graham, Alex 183
Graham, George 181
Graham, Peter 182, 183
Graham, William Woodman 115–16,
    232–7, 239, 325
Grand Teton 220, 258, 313
Grande Rocheuse 131
Grandes Jorasses 90, 100, 130, 133, 286,
    287–8
    Croz Spur 288–90
    Hirondelles Ridge 100, 130, 133, 135,
        257
    Walker Spur 287, 290, 292–3, 357
Grands Charmoz 281
grappling irons 23
Grass, Hans 103, 262
Grassi (guide) 260
Graven, Alexander 272, 275
Great Gable 156, 311
Green, Miss 149
Green, J.R. 58
Green, Rev. W.S. 176–80
    in North America 201–2
Greene, Dr Raymond 326, 348, 349, 350
Greenland 151
Gregory, Alfred 367
Gregory, Dr J.W. 174
Gréloz, R. 271, 288, 289
Grenzsattel 92
Gressoney 49
Grigna 290
Grindelwald 61
gritstone climbs 306–7
Grivel, L. 257
Grohmann, Paul 103, 106
Grohmannspitze 106
Gross Venediger 46
Grosser Moseler 122
Grossglockner 44–5, 278
Grosshorn 279
Groupe de Haute Montagne 271
Grove, F.C. 70, 185
Grüber, G. 109

Grzegorzek, W. 151
Gspaltenhorn 100, 134, 257, 279–80
Guglia di Brenta 107
Guglieminetti, G. 198
Gugliermina, G.B. 134
guidebooks, British 161, 163
guides
  Alps 71–5, 117
  Corporation des Guides 71
  Dolomites 106
  United States 215
  Wales 311
Guillembet, Bernard 142
Gunnison, Lt John W. 212
Gurla Mandhata 243–4
Gushchin, Daniil 329
Güssfeldt, Paul 99, 103, 109, 122, 133
  South America 195

von Haast, Dr Julius 176
Hadow, Douglas 84, 85, 86–7
Haggas, Jim 311
Half Dome 218–19, 371
Halkett, Mr 142
Hall, Carl Christian 147, 149
Hall, E.G. 334
Hamberger, Dr Hugo 339, 340
Hamilton, Mr and Mrs 119
Hampshire, chalk cliffs 154
handhooks *see* grappling irons
Hangendgletscherhorn 46
Hangover, Dove Crag 311
Hannibal crosses the Alp 21
Haramukh 240
Hardy, Rev. J.F. 66–8
Hargreaves, A.B. 308
Hargreaves, A.T. 308, 312
Haringer, Rudolf 288
Harland, H. 163
Harman, Capt. H.J. 232
harnesses 370
Harper, A.P. 181
Harper, Walter 227–8
Harpprecht, T. 94
Harrer, Heinrich 300–3
Harris, Percy Wyn 174, 348, 349, 350
Hartley, J.W. 110
Harmann, Hans 338, 346
Hasler, Christian 207

Hasler, Gustav 269
Hastings, Geoffrey 121, 129, 130, 158,
  159, 247–8, 249, 250
Haston, Dougal 361
Hausberg, C.B. 174
Hawaian Islands 170
Hawkins, Vaughan 80
Hayakawa, Dr 260
Hayden, F.V. 216–17, 220
Hayward, J.W. 70
Hazard, J. de V. 322, 323
Headland, E. 70
Hearsey, H.Y. 229
Heckmair, Anderl 275, 282, 283, 284,
  287, 290, 300–3
Hector, Sir James 176, 200–1
Heftye, Johannes 149
Heftye, Thomas J. 147
height, as factor in climbing 27
Hein, E. 333
Hekla 170
Helbling, Robert 190
Helvellyn 153
Helversen, Dr Hans 106
Henderson, Kenneth 257, 258, 313
Henderson R.B. 161
Hepp, Gunther 346
Herbst, Albert 296
Herford, Siegfried Wedgwood 134,
  165–8, 169, 257, 307
Herligkoffer, Dr K.M. 368
Herron, Rand 339, 340
Herzog, Maurice 357, 358–9
Hess, H. 121
Hicks, F.E. 308
Higher Cathedral Spire, Yosemite 314
Hillary, Sir Edmund 360, 361, 362, 364,
  366, 367–8
Himalaya 126, 229–55, 325
  holy mountains 21
  map 12
  Peak XV (Everest) 170
  see also Everest
Himalayan Club 325, 331, 342
Hinchliff, Thomas 74, 144
Hindu Kush 22
Hinks, Arthur 283–4, 319
Hinter Brochkogel 105
Hinterstoisser, Andreas 296–8, 299

Hispar Glacier 238
Hoag, Barton 313–14
Hochfeiler 103
Hochvernagtspitze 121–2
Hodgkin, R.A. 304, 306
Hodgkinson, Rev. G.C. 70
Hoel, Christen 147
von Hohnel, Leutnant 174
Holder, H.W. 185
Holdsworth, R. 326
Holland, C.F. 166–8
Holland, E.T. 150
Hopkinson family 155
Hopkinson, Bernard 158
Hopkinson, Charles 158
Hopkinson, Edward 158, 164–5
Hopkinson, John 117, 158
Horasch, Fr 45
Horeschowsky, Alfred 284, 333
Hort, Rev. F.J.A. 68
Hortnagel, H. 333
Hossard, M. 142
House, Bill (W.P.) 316, 352, 353
Houston, Charles 352, 357–8
Howard-Bury, Lt-Col. Charles 319
Howell, F.W. 150–1
Hua Shan 21
Huascarán 199, 333
Huber, Emil 202
Huber, J. 103
Hudson, Rev. Charles 60–1, 70, 70–1, 84, 85, 86–7, 89, 154
Hudson, C.W. 312
Hugi, F.J. 53–4
Humboldt, Alexander von 191, 192
Hunt, Colonel John (Lord Hunt) 365–7, 370
Hunza people 340
Hutchings, Rev. James 218, 219
huts, North Wales 163
Hvannadalshnuker 151

ice axes and daggers 371
ice climbing now 371
ice pegs 277
Iceland 150–1
Ilam Rock, Peak District 170
Illampu 197, 199, 333
Illimani 196, 238, 334

Illiniza 194
Imboden, Josef 149, 232
Immink, Jeanne 107
Imseng, Ferdinand 91–2, 93, 110, 126, 181, 261
Imseng, Joseph 66
Incas 21, 24, 191
Inderbinner, Moritz 175, 244
Innerkofler, Michael 106
Innerkofler, Sepp 256
Irvine, Andrew 'Sandy' 283, 322, 323, 324–5
Irving, R.L.G. 140
Italian Alpine Club 82
Italian climbers 1930s 290–1

Jackson, Mrs E.P. 118, 119, 122
Jackson, William Henry 217
Jacot-Guillarmod, Dr J. 241, 242
James, Dr Edwin 210–11
Jangi-tau 186
Japan 21
Japanese Alpine Club 170
Japanese Alps 170
Japanese climbers 304, 328
Jardine, Ray 370
Jaun, Johann 66, 94, 95–6, 108
Jeffcoat, S.F. 165, 169
Jeffrey, May 149
Jenkins, J.R. 306, 312
Joad, G.C. 70
John, Archduke of Austria 45–6
Johnson, Al 215
Johnson, William Henry 231, 238–9
Jones, H.O. and Mrs 132, 135, 136
Jones, Owen Glynne 119, 155, 156–7, 160, 164
Rock Climbing in the English Lake District 156
grading system 278
Jonsong La 242
Jonsong Peak 348
Jossi, Christian 187
Jotunheimen 42, 146, 147
Jubonu 235
Jungfrau 46–7, 53, 271

K2 229, 230, 240, 247, 351, 372
American 1938 expedition 352–6

Duke of the Abruzzi 1909 expedition
252–5, 352
Kabru 235–7, 239, 245
Kabur 242
Kain, Conrad 260–1
Kalanka 234
Kalkalpen 102, 104
Kamet 230, 245–6, 318, 325–6, 348
Kamm 271
Kangchenjau 246
Kangchenjunga 180, 232, 239, 241–2,
242–3, 246, 346
Bauer expeditions 335–7, 338
map 335
karabiner 276
Karakoram 22, 229, 230, 238, 245, 253,
351
map 13
Karbir, Gurkha 245
Karpinski, Adam 328
Karstens, Harry P. 227–8
Kasbek 184, 185
Kashmir 240
Kasparkek, Fritz 300–3
Katuin-tau 186
Kaufmann, Christian 206, 208–9
Kaufmann, Christian, jr 304
Kaufmann, Johann 187
Kaufmann, Ulrich 176, 179, 232–5
Kautz, Lt August 213
Kedarnath 328
Keilau, Baltazar Mathias 146, 150
Kellas, Dr Alexander M. 239, 246, 318,
319
Kelly, H.M. 308, 311
Kelly, Mrs Pat (Emily) 309
Kempson, Edwin 350
Kennedy, E.S. 60–1, 66, 67, 68,
70–1
Kennedy, Thomas Stuart 70, 110, 113
Kenya, Mount 174
map 172
Kern Knotts 311
Khasirov, Killar 184
Khumbu Valley 357
Kicking Horse Pass 200
Kilimanjaro 125, 171–4
Kibo 171–2
map 173

Mawenzi 171, 172
King, Clarence 215, 217
Mountaineering in the Sierra Nevada
215
King, Sir Henry Seymour 109
King, Rev. S.W. 66
Kinzl, Hans 333
Kirkus, Colin, 309–11
Kitar, Sherpa 336, 346, 355, 356
Klausner, J. 45
Kletterschuhe 370
Klingenberg, Jens 149
Klockerin 278
Klotz, Martin 44, 45
Klucker, Christian 103, 107, 109, 133,
206, 207, 262–3
Knowles, Guy 241
Knowlton, Elizabeth 339
Knubel, Josef 131, 134, 135–7, 138, 139,
257, 269, 272, 275
Knubel, Peter 176, 185
Knutsholstind 149
Kohler, Hans 259
Kojima, Usi 170
Kolahoi 240
Koldewey, Captain 151
Koshtan-tau 185, 186–7
Kraus, von 336, 337
Kröner, Gustl 275, 282, 284, 287, 290
Kuffner, Moriz von 262
Kugy, Julius 122
Kuhm, W. 334
Kun 240
Kun Lun 230, 231
Kunigk, Herbert 339, 340
Kurz, Marcel 318
Kurz, Toni 296–9

La Voy, Merl 227
Lachenal, Louis 357, 359
Ladies' Alpine Club 119
Lagarde, Jacques 131, 271
Lake, W. 213
Lakeland climbing 126, 129–30
origins 152–4, 155–6, 163–9
1920s 309, 311–12
Lakeland Mountain Guides 309
Lamb, Carlyle 215
Lamb, Rev. Elkanah 215–16, 218

Lambert, Raymond 289, 290, 363, 364
Lammer, Eugen Guido 104–5, 118, 121, 122, 281
Langdale 163
Langford, Nathaniel 220
Langpo Peak 246
Langtauferer Spitze 103
Lanti, Nicola 196
Laudals Kaupe 146
Lauener, Christian 112
Lauener, Ulrich 61, 62, 63, 64, 112
Lauper, Hans 271–2, 280
Lauteraarhorn-Schreckhorn Traverse 263
Lauterbrunnen Breithorn 279
Lauterbrunnen Wall 279
Laycock, J., *Some Gritstone Climbs* 165–6
Le Blond, Mrs Aubrey 119–20, 149
Leininger, Jean 292, 351
Leininger, Raymond 290
Leitner, J. 45
Lenzspitze 109
Leo Pargial 229–30
de Lepiney, J. 271
Lester, W.R. 157
Leuchs, Georg 190
Leupold, J. 338
Leutholt, Jakob 53
Lewa Dorje, Sherpa 326
Linnell, Maurice 308, 309, 311
Liotard, Jean 20
Lister, Anne 142
Little, Professor 203–4
Lizard Head, Colorado 218, 313–14
Llanberis Pass 310, 311
Lliwedd 160–1, 163
Lloyd, Thomas 225–6
Llullaillaco 24, 191
Lochmatter, Franz 134, 136, 138–40, 257, 269
Lochmatter, Josef 134, 138–40, 257, 269
Lodowy 151
Lofoten Island 160
Lomnica 42, 151
Long, Major Stephen H. 210
Longland, Sir Jack 307, 308, 348, 349, 350
Longman, William 68, 79
Longs Peak 215, 314

Longstaff, Tom 187, 236–7, 242, 243–5, 322, 325
This My Voyage 243
Lor Khan 250
Lorria, August 104–5
Lost Arrow, Yosemite 317
Lowe, George 366, 367
de Luc, Jean André and Guillaume Antoine 25
Lucas, John 215
Ludwig, J.M. 262
Luft, Uli 346–7
Lunn, Sir Arnold 97
Lykken, Knut 147, 148, 159
Lyskamm 262–3

MacCarthy, Albert 261
Macdonald R.J.S. 81
McDonnell, Lady Evelyn 120
McGonagall, Charles 225–6, 227
MacInnes, Hamish 369, 371
Macintyre, Duncan 154
Mackenzie, Alexander 200
Mackenzie, John 158
Mackinder, Sir Halford 141, 174
Mackinnon, Quintin 176
McLean, Dr W. 348
Macphee, G.G. 308, 312
Macugnaga 91–2
Maffei, Clemente 198
Maiktoli 328
Main, Mrs *see* Le Blond, Mrs Aubrey
Maipo 195
Maischberger, Thomas 131
Maki, Yuko 100, 256–7, 259–60
Maladetta 142
Malczewski, Antoni 42
Mallory, Berridge 309
Mallory, Clare 309
Mallory, George Leigh 134, 140, 246, 283, 307
'because it is there' 218, 320
Everest 319–22, 323, 324–5
Malte Brun 181
Manaslu 357
Mandlwand 132
Mannering, G.E. 180, 181
Maquignaz, Battiste 114–15
Maquignaz, Daniel 114–15

Maquignaz, Jean-Antoine 196, 197
Maquignaz, Joseph J. 114–15
March, Bill (W.J.) 371
Marinelli, Damiano 93, 122
Marmolata 131
  Marmolata Di Rocca 106
  Marmolata Glacier 105
Marshall, Prof. Arthur Milnes 164
Marshall, C.W. 308
Marshall, Garth 110
Martial Mountains, Tierra del Fuego 197
Martin, Jean 120
Mason, Kenneth 231, 240, 334, 337, 340,
  356, 359
Mathews, Benjamin St John 66
Mathews, C.E. 72, 118, 157
Mathews, George 76
Mathews, William 66–7, 68
Matterhorn
  and Whymper 79–88, 285
  accidents 89
  drawing of 57–8, 80
  Furggen Ridge 126, 127
  guideless ascents 123
  Hörnli Ridge 285
  North Face 271, 280, 281, 284–6, 293
  Penhall and Mummery 126–7, 261
  first photograph 55
  Tiefenmatten Face 105
  Zmutt Ridge 100, 126, 130
Mauna Loa 170
Maund, Oakley 95–6, 98
Maurer, Andreas 95, 96, 232
Maurer, Kasper 110, 111, 187
Mauri, Carlo 198
Maya temples 21
Mayer, G. 131
Mazeno La 248, 249
Meade, Charles F. 230, 245, 246, 325
Mehringer, Karl 294, 296
Meier, Martin 288, 289
Meije 97, 98–9, 123, 306
  Grand Pic 97, 124–5
Melheim, Peder 149
Menti, M. 300
Menlungtse 362
Merkl, Willy 281–3, 284, 347, 368
  Nanga Parbat expeditions 339–40,
    342–6

Meryon, L.F. 160
Merzbacher, Gottfried 122, 187
Messner, Reinhold 133
Messner, Toni 290
Meunier, Lombard 'Grand Joras' 30, 31
Mexico 24, 191, 198
Meyer, Gottlieb 46, 47–8
Meyer, Hans 171–4
Meyer, Hieronymus 46–8
Meyer, Johann Rudolf 46
Meyer, Johann Rudolf II 46–8
Meyer, Johann Rudolf III 46, 47–8
Michel, P. 103
Middlemore, Thomas 94, 95, 96, 98, 99,
  102
Millard, Earl 221
Millard, Floyd 221
Minya Konka 330–1, 352
Mischabel peaks 138
El Misti 191, 199
Mohn, Emanuel 148
Molinatti, engineer 50, 51
Molteni, M. 291
Mönch 271
Monk's Cowl 312
Mont Aiguille, Grenoble 19–20
Mont Blanc 24, 70, 192
  Bosses Ridge 33
  Brenva Face 75–91, 133, 273, 306
  Brenva Glacier 75–9
  Brenva Spur 130, 159
  Brouillard Ridge 134, 135
  description 25–6, 26–7, 27–8
  Diable Ridge 257
  early attempts 28–32
  first ascent by Paccard and Balmat 34–5
  Géant Glacier approach 31
  Gite à Balmat 34
  first woman climber 119
  first winter ascent 119
  Innominata Ridge 134
  map 10
  Old Brenva Ridge 273–4
  panorama of 58
  Peuterey Ridge 100, 103, 108–9, 133,
    305
  Route Major 273–4
  Albert Smith's ascent 55, 58–60
  Via della Pera 275

Mont Blanc de Courmayeur 109, 133, 305
Mont Blanc du Tacul 257
Mont Maudit 26
Mont Rouge de Peuterey 132
Montagne de la Côte 29
Montcalm 142
Monte Conway 198
Monte Corno 42
Monte Olivia 197
Monte Pelmo 106
Monte Perdido 42–4
Monte Rosa 49–52, 70, 122, 131
    East Face 91–2, 261
    Marinelli Couloir 122, 123
    Santa Caterina Ridge 138
Monte Viso 70
Montenvers 26, 140, 281–2, 283
de Monts, Count Roger 145
Monts Maudits 143
Moore, A.W. 75–9, 82, 94, 97, 120, 185, 294
Moore, Dr John 26
Moore, Terris 330–1
Moray, Sir Robert 23
Morley, John 244
Morris, James 366
Morshead, Major H.T. 318, 319, 321
Morten, John 152
Moskowa, Prince de la 142
Mount Adams 213
Mount Alberta 259–61, 304
Mount Ararat 141–2, 170
Mount Assiniboine 207
Mount Athabasca 205
Mount Baker 212, 213
Mount Bonney 201
Mount Brown 200
Mount Bryce 208–9
Mount Collie 207
Mount Columbia 209, 259
Mount Cook (Ao-Rangi) 176, 177–81, 182–3
Mount Donkin 202
Mount Forbes 208
Mount Fox 202
Mount Freshfield 208
Mount Fuji 21

Mount Goodsir 207
Mount Gordon 205
Mount Haidinger 182
Mount Hector 201, 203
Mount Hood 212–13
Mount Ida, Crete 21
Mount Jefferson 213
Mount Kenya 141, 174
    Batian 174
    map 172
    Point Lenana 174
Mount Lefroy 203–4, 205
Mount Logan 221
Mount Lyell 208
Mount Murchison 205, 208
Mount McKinley (Denali) 223–8
Mount Moran 258
Mount Newton 221
Mount Purity 202
Mount Rainier 212, 213–15
Mount Robson 201, 209, 259, 261
Mount St Elias 175, 221, 222
Mount St Helens 212
Mount Sefton 182, 183
Mount Selwyn (Deville) 202
Mount Shasta 215
Mount Sinai 21
Mount Sir Donald 201, 202
Mount Stalin (Pik Kommunizma) 329
Mount Stephen 203
Mount Sugarloaf 202
Mount Tasman 182, 183
Mount Temple 203, 206
Mount Vaux 207
Mount Victoria 206
Mount Waddington 315–16
Mount Whitney 215, 314
Mount Woodrow Wilson 211
mountain sickness *see* altitude sickness
mountaineering
    condemned 55
    ethics 371
    after the conquest of Everest 369–72
    expeditions 170–1
    publicity 283–4
    see also climbing
Mountaineering Association 309, 369
mountains
    as barrier 21–2

as sacred objects 21
Muir, John 216
Mukut Parbat 328
Muldrow Glacier 225, 227
Muller, J.E. 46
Mulritter, Peter 342, 344, 346
Mumm, A.L. 175, 244, 245
Mummery, Albert Frederick 100, 102,
    112, 113, 120, 121, 125–31, 137, 141,
    159, 160, 185, 186, 238, 262, 263,
    339
  on Matterhorn Zmutt Ridge 126–7
  on Nanga Parbat 247–51
  My Climbs in the Alps and Caucasus
    130–1
Mummery, Mary 118, 120, 129, 130, 248
Munday, Don, and Mrs 315–16
Munich Academic Alpine Club 276,
    338
Munich School 138, 256, 257, 261, 271,
    276, 280, 304
  Caucasus and Pamirs 333
  Himalaya 335
Muratbi 188, 189
Murith, Abbé Laurent-Joseph 37–8
Murray, W.H. 308
Muscroft, L. 312
Muybridge, Eadweard 217
Muztagh 231

Naismith, W.W. 147
Nanda Devi 233, 243, 245, 326–7, 328,
    352
  map 327
Nanda Kot 243, 328
Nanga Parbat 130, 160, 222, 280, 268
  Diamir Face 248
  map 341
  Mazeno La 248
  Mummery 1895 expedition 247–51
  Rupal Face 248
  Merkl expeditions 339–40, 342–6
  Rakhiot Face 251
  Silbersattel 343, 344, 345, 347
  Wien expedition 346–7
Nantillons Glacier 283
Napes Needle 155
nationalism, and Everest 247, 334
Naumann, C.F. 147

Nazis and climbing 105, 276, 281, 283,
    286, 333–4
  and Himalaya 333–5, 342
Nelson, Anton 317
Neltner, L. 351
Nepal 243, 325, 351
  reopened 357
Nesthorn 280
Neve, Dr Arthur 240, 245
New Italy Climbing Club 291
New Zealand 141, 175–83
New Zealand Alpine Club 181
New Zealand Alps (Southern Alps)
    176–82
  map 177
Newtontoppen 150
Nicol, Hamish 358
Nicolussi, Bonifacio 106
Niederer (guide) 260
Nietzsche, F.W. 104, 105, 281
Nikolayev, N. 329
Nima Dorje, Sherpa 326, 344, 345
Nima Norbu, Sherpa 345
Nima Tashi, Sherpa 345
Nimlin, Jock 306–7, 308
Noel, John 321, 322, 323, 325
Nordre Dyrhaugstind 147
Nordre Skagastölstind 146
Nordwand concept 280
Norman-Neruda, Ludwig 106, 262–3
Den Norske Touristforening (DNT) 147
North America, climbing in 200–9,
    257–9
  map 15
Norton, Edward Felix 309, 321, 322, 323,
    350
Norway 141, 146–50
Noyce, Wilfrid (C.W.F.) 308, 309, 311,
    367
Nun 240
Nun Kun massif 240
Nuptse-Lhotse-Everest traverse 305

Oberalpstock 39, 40
Oberland *see* Bernese Alps
Oberlin, John 260
Oberto, Giovanni 92
O'Brien, Miriam 257, 269
Odell, N.E. 322, 323, 324, 328

Ogwen district 163
Oliver, D.G. 245
Oliver, E.G. 134
Oliver, P.R. 326
Ollier, César 109, 133, 174
Olperer 103, 121
Olperer-Fussstein Traverse 104
Oppenheimer, L.J. 156, 163, 165, 169
Oregon 212–13
Orteguerra, Toribio de 191
O'Sullivan, Timothy 217
Ottertail peaks 206–7
Otztal range 103, 121
Oudot, Dr Jacques 359
Outram, Sir James 206–7, 208–9
Outward Bound 369
Owen, William 220
oxygen
    first carriage of 244
    experiments 318
    and Everest 310, 321, 350, 366, 367

Paccard, François 28, 33–6
Paccard, Joseph 29
Paccard, Michel 24, 28
Paccard, Michel-Gabriel 27, 29, 30–1, 32
Pache, A.A. 241
Packe, Charles 142–5, 154
    Guide to the Pyrenees 143
Paidar, Herbert 305
Palliser, Captain John 200–1
Palmer, Howard 260
Pamirs 329–30, 333
Pandim 235
Paradis, Maria 36, 119
Parker brothers 75, 80
Parker, A.G. 158
Parker, Herschel, C. 223, 224, 226, 227
Parrot, Dr 49, 141–2, 183
Partridge, Robin 152, 153
Pasang, Sherpa 336, 338, 343, 361
Pasang Dawa, Sherpa 331–2
Pasang Dawa Lama, Sherpa 354–5, 356
Pasang Kikuli, Sherpa 346, 352, 354, 355, 356
Pasang Norbu, Sherpa 331–2
Passet, Célestin 144, 145–6
Passet, Henri 144, 145
Passet, Hipplyte 144

Passet, Laurent 144
Passingham, George 110, 119, 126
Pasteur, C.H. 129
Pasteur, Miss 130
Pauhunri 246
Paulcke, Wilhelm 276
Paulsen, Fanny 149
Payer, Julius 151
Payot family 100
Payot, Alphonse 115–16
Payot, Michel 140, 217
Payot, P. 112
Peak District 165, 170, 307
Pearce, E.D. 215
Peary, Robert 224, 226
Peck, Annie Smith 198–200, 240
Pedranzini, Battista 93
Pellissier, Luigi 196, 197
Pelvoux 97
Pendlebury, Richard 92, 93, 98, 110
Pendlebury, William 92, 98, 110
Penhall, William 105, 126–7
Pennine Alps 46
    map 10
Perren, Clemens 75, 122
Perring 192, 194
Peru 191, 333
Pession, Abele and Agostino 197
Peters, Rudolf 288–9
Petersen, Harald 148–9
Petersen, Theodor 103
Petersenspitze 122
Petherick, W.J. 129
Petigax, Joseph 254
Peto, Raymond 270
Petrus, Johann 110, 127
Petzoldt, Paul 258, 352, 353
Peytier, M. 142
Peyto, Bill 206
Pfann, Hans 187, 190, 276, 333
Pfannl, Heinrich 131, 240–1
Pfeffer, Martin 346
photography 156
    United States 217–18
    see also Abrahams; Donkin; Noel; Sella
Piacenza, Mario 240
Piano, E. 198
Pic du Midi 24
Pichincha 191

Pichl, Eduard 106
Pichler, Josef 45
Pico de Aneto 142
Pico des Posets 142
Pidgeon, Anna and Ellen 118, 120–1
Piekielko, Franz 284
Pietrasanta, Nina 257
Pigott, A.S. 305
Pigott, Fred 307
Pik E. Korzenevskoi 329
Pik Kommunizma 329
Pik Lenin 329, 333
Pike, Lt Zebulon Montgomery 210–11
Pikes Peak 210, 211
Pilkington family 155
Pilkington, Charles 158
Pillar Rock, Ennerdale 153–4, 156, 160,
    161, 163
Pilley, Dorothy (Mrs Richards) 257
Pinggera, A. and J. 93
Pinju Norbu, Sherpa 345, 347
Pinnacle Club 309
Pinnacle Peak (Nun Kun) 199, 240
Pintso, Sherpa 355, 356
Pir Panjal 240
Pircher, H. 338
pitons 23, 113, 276, 277, 312, 313, 315,
    370
Piz Aul 38–9
Piz Badile 100, 290–2
Piz Bernina 99, 103, 122, 133, 195, 262
Piz Cristallina 39
Piz Palu 90, 100, 120
Piz Roseg 99, 262
Piz Urlaun 39
Plantade, M. 24
Pococke, Richard 26
Pointe Louis Amédée 135
Polish climbers 151, 328
Pollinger, Adolf 273
Pollinger, Alexander 285
Pollinger, Aloys 100, 101, 119
Pollinger, Josef 206, 273
Poltinger, Lt-Col 103
Pontresina guides 71
Popocatepetl 24, 291, 198
Portjengrat 109
Powell, Sir Charles Herbert 187
Powell, Major John Wesley 215

Pralong (guide) 56–7
Preuss, Paul 131–2, 276
    Six Theorems 132–3
Prochownick, Carl 132
Pugh, Griffith 366
pundits 231
Purcell Range 261
Purtscheller, Ludwig 121–5, 141, 171–2,
    187, 276
Puttrell, J.W. 155, 156, 165
Pyramids as mountains 21
Pyrenees 42, 142–6
    map 143

Raeburn, Harold 187, 306, 319
Raghobir Thapa 247, 249, 250–1
Rainer, Edi 296–8
Rakhiot Peak 340, 343, 346
Ramond de Carbonnières, Baron
    Louis-François 42–4, 142
Raper, Capt. F.V. 229
Ratti, Achille 291–2
Ravanel, Joseph 131
Rebitsch, Matthias 299–300
Rébuffat, Gaston 357, 359
Redonnet, P. 142
Reichert, F. 190
Reilly, Adams 73, 82
Reinstadler, Joseph 262
Reiss, W. 191, 364
Rey, Adolphe 257
Rey, Emile 107–8, 109, 119, 130, 133, 262
Rey, Joseph 94, 103
Reymond, C.A. 241
Reynolds E.S. 161
Rheinwaldhorn 39–40
Richards, Prof. and Mrs I.A. 100, 161,
    257
Richardson, Katherine 119, 262
Rickmers, Willi Rickmer 187–9, 333, 335
Riddiford, Earle 361
Ridyard, Nancy 309
Riffelhorn 55
Rigele, Fritz 277–8
de Righi, R. 242
Ripley, Willard 219
Rishi Ganga 245
Rittler, Leo 287
Robinson, Bestor 316

Robinson, J.W. 155, 159
Roch, André 257, 269, 271, 328, 351, 363
Rochmelon 71
rock climbing 102, 117, 152, 370–1
Rocky Mountains 200–9, 259–61
    in America 210–21
Rocky Mountain Club 220
Rodier, J.-B. 98
Rogers, Will 219–20
Rolland, Martine 75
Rolleston, L.W. 187
Romsdalhorn 147, 149
rope
    early use 23–4
    nylon 370
Roper, Joe 311
Ross, Malcolm 182
Rote Zähne Ridge, Gspaltenhorn 100, 134
Roth, Christian 185
Roxburgh, T. 161
Royal Georgraphical Society 141, 151,
        231
    and the Alpine Club 246, 318
Rübenson, C.W. 245
Rübi, Adolf 269, 298
Rübi, Christian 298
Rübi, Fritz 269
Rucksack Club 163, 308
Rusk, Claude 225, 227
Ruskin, John 55, 56, 57, 60
Russell, Count Henri 143–4
Russell, Prof. Israel 221–2
Russian climbers 305
    and Himalaya 329
Ruttledge, Hugh 347–50
Ruwenzori 170, 174–5
    map 173
Ryan, V.J.E. 131, 134, 138–40, 257, 269

Saas guides 109–10
St Elias mountains 221
St Gervais 33
St Kilda 23–4
Salathe, John 315, 317
Saltoro Pass 245
Salles, François Bernard 145
von Salm-Reifferscheid, Count Franz
        Xaver 44–5, 103
Saluinan-Bashi 186

Samer, G. 103
San Juan mountains, Colorado 211–12,
    218
Sandri, Bartolo 300
Sansom, G.S. 166–9
Santner, Johann 107
Sara Urco 194
Sarbach, Peter 205
Sarki, Sherpa 359
Sarmiento 197, 198
Sassolungo 103
Satopanth 328
Saussure, Horace Bénédict de 27, 28, 29,
        30, 31–3, 35, 37, 49
    ascent of Mont Blanc 36
Scafell 156, 164–5, 166–9
    Botterill's Slab 163–4
    Central Buttress 134, 166–9, 307, 309,
        310
    East Buttress 311, 312
    Moss Ghyll 159
Scattergood, J.H. 207
Scerscen Eisnase 103, 133
Schaller, Hermann 257, 338
Schalligrat 100
Schatz, Marcel 359
Schlaginweit family 191, 245
Schlaginweit, Adolphe 230, 325
Schlaginweit, Herman 230, 325
Schlaginweit, Robert 230, 325
Schlunegger, Hans 298
Schmaderer, Ludwig 305
Schmid, Franz and Toni 280, 281, 284–6
Schmitt, Robert Hans 107
Schneider, Erwin 333, 342, 343, 344, 345,
    346
Schrammacher 103, 277
Schreckhorn 304
Schreckjoch 129
Schultz, Dr Karl 119, 122, 124, 125
Schulze, A. 188–90
Schulze, E. 279
von Schumacher, Pierre 278
Schuster, Claud (Lord Schuster) 190
Schwarzgruber, Rudolf 304, 306
scientific interests 24, 25, 30, 291
    decline 54
Scoresby, William 150
Scotland, and climbing 157–8

Scott, Doug 369
Scottish Mountaineering Club 157
Sedlmayer, Max 294
Ségogne, Henri de 271, 351, 358
Selkirk Range 201, 202
Sella, Alessandro 113, 114, 115
Sella, Alphonso 114
Sella, Corradino 114
Sella, Gaudenzio 114
Sella, Quintino 82, 83, 86, 113
Sella, Vittorio 114, 187, 242, 253-4
Senn, Franz 103
Sennoner, Joseph 40
Sgurr Coire an Lochain 158
Sgurr nan Gillean 154
Shebbeare, E.O. 338, 348
Sheffield Climbing Club 307
Sheldon, George 353
Shepherd, C.W. 150
Sherpa people 319, 321, 322, 323, 325,
    342, 344-5, 349, 358
Shilla 231, 239
Shiprock 313, 315, 316-17
Shipton, Eric 174, 239, 326, 328, 348,
    350-1, 360, 361, 362, 364-5, 369
Shisha Pangma 351, 369
Shkhara 185, 186, 187
Shkhelda 188, 305
Siachen Glacier 240, 245
Sierra Club 216, 316-17
Sillem, Dr H. 240
Simla 229-30
Simler, Josias 22
Simon, Felix 339, 340
Simond, Auguste 'Sampson' 61, 62, 64,
    66, 67
Simond, Pierre 28, 31
Simpson, Jimmy 206
Singh, Kesar 326
Sinocholagua 194
Siorpaes, Santo 106
Siorpes, G. 131
Sixt 25
Skagastöltind 148-9
skiing 140, 218
Skyang Kangri 253
Skye 158, 161
Slater, E.V. 168
Sletten, H. 147

Slingsby, Miss 149
Slingsby, (William) Cecil 121, 129, 130,
    135, 155, 158
    in Norway 147-9
    Norway: The Northern Playground 149-50
Slingsby, Morris 245
Smith, Albert Richard 55, 58
    The Ascent of Mont Blanc 60
    The Overland Mail 58-9
    The Story of Mont Blanc 60
Smith, Blanche-Eden 309
Smith, Christen 42, 146
Smith, Phil 257-8
Smith, W.P. Haskett 144, 154, 155, 156
Smyth, Christopher 70
Smyth, Edmund 70
Smyth, James Grenville 70
Smythe, Frank S. 194-5, 273-4, 308, 326,
    337-8, 348, 349, 350
Snowdon 153
Snowdonia 157, 162
Société Ramond 144
Society of Welsh Rabbits 157
Solly, Godfrey A. 129, 155, 158
Somervell, T.H. 321, 322, 323
Sorata 197
Sourdough expedition (Mount
    McKinley) 225-6, 228
South America 191-200, 333
Spain 151
Spalding, Rev. Franklin 220
Spechtenhauser, Gabriel 92, 93, 103
Spencer, Sydney 205
Spender, Harold 165
Spender, Michael 350
Spescha, Placidus a 38-41
Spitsbergen 150, 238, 322
sport climbing, World Championship 371
Stabeler, Hans 106
Stac-na-Biorrach 23
Stanig, Valentin 45, 103
Stanley, H.M. 174
Starr, Russell 121
Staszic, Stanislas 42
Steeple, E.W. 160, 161
Steinauer, Ludwig 288, 290
stemples (pitons) 23
Stephen, Sir Leslie 70, 74, 94, 106
    The Playground of Europe 90

Stephens, Fred 206, 208
Stettner, Joe and Paul 313
Steuri, Fritz 294, 296
Steuri, Hermann 252, 275
Stevens, General Hazard 213
Stevenson, E.J. 70
Stevenson, James 220
Stewardson, E.A. 308
Stob Maol 157–8
Stobart, Tom 366
Stocker, A.H. 158
Stockgron 39
Stockhorn 271
Stogdon, John 154
Strahlhorn 70
Straton, Isabelle 118, 119, 120
Streatfeild, Capt. R.N. 352
Stretch, Kasper 186
Strutt, Col. E.L. 119, 271, 286, 290, 306, 338
Stuck, Archdeacon Hudson 227–8
Studer, Prof. Bernard 56
Studer, Gottlieb 53, 66
Stutfield, Hugh 205, 208
Suilven, Grey Castle 158
Sulheim, Steinar 147
Sulzer, Carl 202
Sundardhunga Khal 328
Supersax, A. 109
Survey of India 230–1, 234, 236, 237, 239
Swan, F.E.L. 145
Swanzy, Rev. Henry 201–2
Swiss climbers 304
    and Everest 362–4
Sylfestdotter, Oliner Marie 149

Taguchi, Ichiro and Jiro 304
Tairraz, Victor 56, 57
Takebushi, S. 328
Taoist worship of mountains 21
Täschhorn 70, 100, 138–40, 269
Tatra mountains 42, 151
Tatum, Robert G. 227–8
Taugwald, Gabriel zum 199
Taugwalder, Joseph 84, 85
Taugwalder, Peter 84, 86, 87
Taugwalder, Peter II 84, 85, 86
Taugwalder, Rudolf 199
Taylor, Rev. Charles 92–3, 98, 110

Taylor, M.S. 304
Taylor, William 225–6
de Tchihatcheff, Platon 142
Tejbir, Gurkha 321
Teleki, Count 174
Tendrup, Sherpa 355
Tenzing Norgay, Sherpa 350, 363–4, 366, 367–8
Teram Kangri group 245
Terray, Lionel 357, 359
Testu 142
Tetnuld 185
    North Face 304, 306
Teton range, Wyoming 220, 257–8, 314, 315
Teufel, Hans 296
Teufelsgrat 100, 130
Thelwell, W.R. 147
Thilo, Dr 47
Third Flatiron 221
Thoenes 337
Thompson, Charles S. 203–4, 205, 206, 207
Thomson, Darby (David) 183
Thomson, Gilbert 157, 158, 160–1
Thomson, J.M. Archer 134, 157, 163
Thomson, Joseph 174
Thorington, J.M. 261
Thurstein, J. 305
Thurweiser, Prof. Peter Carl 54, 103
Tibet 243
    mountaints as security 21
    relations with outside world 325, 331, 347
    now Chinese 359
Tierra del Fuego 197–8
Tillman, Heinz 278–9, 333
Tilman, Bill (H.W.) 174, 239, 326, 328, 350, 351, 352, 357–8, 360
Tirsuli 326, 328
Tissay, Victor 28
Tista valley 342
Titlis 46
Tizzoni, Ugo 292
Tobin, H.W. 338
Todhunter, Ralph 135–6
Tödi Alps 38, 41
Tofana 131
Tomasson, Beatrice 131

Topham, Harold, W. 201, 221
Tournier, Jean Michel 33
Townsend, Robert 15
Trafoierwand 94
Traill, G.W. 230
traverses, by Russians and Austrians 305
Trench, Lieutenant 353
Triolet 271
Trisul 245, 325
Troll, Karl 346
Troltind 149
Truffer, J.J. 119, 132
Truslow, Frank 258
Tryfan 161, 162, 309
Tsin Norbu, Sherpa 338
Tucker, C.C. 185
Tuckett, Francis Fox 70, 103, 106
Tupungato 196
Turner, Sam 170, 182
Twain, Mark, *A Tramp Abroad* 59
Tyndall, Prof. John 70, 74, 80, 81, 114, 154
Tyrol 102-3
    guides 103

Udet, Ernst 294, 296
Ulrich, Melchior 66
Underhill, Bob (R.C.M.) 257, 258, 260, 313, 314
United States of America 210-28, 257-9
Urden, Ola 146
Ushba 185, 186, 187, 188-90, 300, 305
    South 304
    West Face 305

Vajolet Turmer 106
Valsecchi, G. 291
Valsorey Glacier 38
Van Trump, Philemon 213, 214
Vancouver, Captain George 212
Vassilev, A. 150
Vassiliev 305
Vatnajokull 150
Vélan 38
Venetz, Benedict 110, 127-9
Verdon gorges 371
Verzi, A. 131
Vestal Peak 218
vibrams (boot soles) 370

Viereselgrat 101
Vigdal, Johannes 147, 149
Vigne Glacier 238
Vignemale 142, 144, 145-6
de Villamont, Segnar 71
de Ville, Antoine 19-20
Vincent, Joseph Niklaus 49, 50, 51
Vincent, Niklaus 49, 51
Vines, Stuart 196, 197
Vole, Knut 147
Vörg, Ludwig 299-300, 301-3, 305

Wager, Lawrence 348, 349, 350
Währen, Johannes 53
Wales 157, 160-3, 309-11
Walker, General 231
Walker, Frank 54, 76
Walker, Horace 76, 82, 155, 158, 185, 287
Walker, Lucy 73, 97, 120
wall climbing 261
Waller, Ivan 307, 308
Walter, Anton 81
Wang Hangbao 324
Ward, Dr Michael 360
Warren, Charles 350
Watkins, Carleton E. 217
Watson, Evelyn Spence 149
Watts, W.L. 150
Watzmann 122
Webb, Lt W.S. 229
Weber, A. 190
Weber, Jean 259, 260
Weed, Charles L. 217
Weed, G.M. 207, 208
Weiss, J.H. 46
Weisshorn 70, 80, 100, 123
    West Face 104
Welden, Baron Ludwig von 49
Welzenbach, Willo 140, 190, 262, 270-1, 276, 278-9, 287
    Grands Charmoz 281-3, 284
    Nanga Parbat 338-9, 342-5
    death 345
Wentworth, Lord 95, 98, 107-8, 113
Wergeland, H.N. 147
Wesseley, V. 241
Westmacott, Mike H. 366
Weston, Rev. Walter 170
Wetterhorn 53, 61-5

Wetterstein range 278
Wharncliffe Rocks 155
Wheeler, Sir Edward Oliver 319
Wheeler, G.M. 217
Wherry, George 74
Whillans, Don 366
Whitney, Prof. Josiah Dwight 215, 218
Whitwell, E.R. 112–13
Whymper, Edward 23, 36, 73, 79, 126
  and the Matterhorn 79–88
  Scrambles Amongst the Alps 89–90
  need for unclimbed summits 90
  Greenland 151
  South America 191, 192–5
  *Travels Amongst the Great Andes of the
    Equator* 195
  and North America 206, 207, 209
Wickersham, Judge James 223
Wieland, U. 342, 344, 345
Wien, Karl 333, 338, 346
Wiesbachhorn 277
Wiessner, Fritz 258, 313, 315–16, 339,
    340, 353, 354–5, 356
Wigram, Edmund 350
Wigram, W. 70
Wilcox, Walter 203
Williams, Rev. Peter 153
Williams, William (Bill) 211–12
Wills, Sir Alfred 61, 72–3
  account of Wetterhorn 61–5
Wilson, A.D. 214
Wilson, C.R. 312
Wilson, Claude 286
Wilson, Ken 306
Windham, William 26
Winkler, Georg 104, 117
Withers, J.J. 286–7
Wolfe, Dudley 353, 354–5, 356
Wollaston, Dr A.F.R. 175, 319
women climbers 118–21, 131
  first known 54
  admitted to Alpine Club 69, 118
  first up the Matterhorn 73
  first up Mont Blanc 119
  first Alpine guide 75

Norway 149
South America 198–200
British in 1930s 309
Wood, Morley 307
Wood-Johnson, George 348
Woodhouse, A.G. 161
Woolley, Hermann 185, 187, 205, 208
Worafka, E. 122
Workman, Fanny Bullock 199, 239, 240
Workman, Dr W.H. 236, 239–40
Wright, Jerry 309, 369

Yosemite valley 216, 217, 218–19, 313,
    314, 317, 371
  map 315
  pegging in 219
Young, Geoffrey Winthrop 100, 131,
    134–40, 160, 257, 269, 287
  quoted 3, 160
  On High Hill 134
  Mountain Craft 135
  on the Täschhorn 138–40
Young, Jack 330
Younghusband, Sir Francis 319–20, 334

Zagonel, B. 131
Zanetti, P. 288
Zecchini, Giuseppe 107
Zemu Glacier 242, 338
Zermatt 49, 56, 58, 70, 109, 286
Zilga-Khokh 185
Zillertal 103, 121, 122
Zimmer, F. 131
Zinal Rothorn 70, 109, 123, 130
Zokputaran 231
Zozitowiecki, K. 269
Zsigmondy, Emil 122, 123, 124–5
Zsigmondy, Otto 122, 123–4, 125
Zumstein, Joseph 49, 50–2
Zumstein Spitze 52
Zurbriggen, Louis 126
Zurbriggen, Mattias 181–2, 196, 238
Zurcher, Alfred 100, 272
Zurfluh, Heinrich 185
Zwolferkogel 106